CONTENTS

Preface x
Acknowledgements xi
Real-world examples at a glance xii

CHAPTER 1 Introduction to tourism management   1

Introduction 2
The phenomenon of tourism 2
Definition of tourism 2
    The importance of tourism   3
Tourism as an academic field of study 3
    Obstacles to development   4
    Indications of development   7
    A sequence of tourism platforms   10
    Universities and community colleges   12
Characteristics, outline and structure 13
    Chapter outline   14
    Chapter structure   14
Chapter review 16
    Summary of key terms   16
    Questions   17
    Exercises   18
    Further reading   18

CHAPTER 2 The tourism system   19

Introduction 20
A systems approach to tourism 20
    The basic whole tourism system   20
The tourist 22
    Spatial component   22
    Temporal component   24
    Travel purpose   26
    Major tourist categories   30
    Data problems   32
Origin region 33
    Origin community   33
    Origin government   34
Transit region 36
    Management implications of transit regions   36
    Effects of technology   37
Destination region 38
    Destination communities   39
    Destination governments   39
The tourism industry 40
Chapter review 42
    Summary of key terms   42
    Questions   43

Exercises   44
Further reading   44
Case study 45

CHAPTER 3 The evolution and growth of tourism   47

Introduction 48
Premodern tourism..48
    Mesopotamia, Egypt and the Indus Valley   48
    Ancient Greece and Rome   49
    The Dark Ages and Middle Ages   50
Early modern tourism (1500–1950)....................................52
    The Grand Tour   52
    Spa resorts   53
    Seaside resorts   54
    Thomas Cook   55
    The post-Cook period (1880–1950)   57
Contemporary tourism (1950 onwards) 57
    The world's biggest industry?   59
Factors associated with increased tourism demand 59
    Economic factors   59
    Social factors   61
    Demographic factors   63
    Technological factors   68
    Political factors   70
Australian tourism participation 71
Future growth prospects 72
Chapter review 73
    Summary of key terms   73
    Questions   76
    Exercises   76
    Further reading   77
Case study 77

CHAPTER 4 Destinations   80

Introduction 81
Global destination patterns: MDCs and LDCs 81
    Tourism market share and growth   81
    Reasons for the emergence of the LDCs as destinations   82
Pull factors influencing a destination...............................86
    Geographical proximity to markets   87
    Accessibility to markets   88
    Availability of attractions   89
    Cultural links   90
    Availability of services   91
    Affordability   91
    Peace, stability and safety   91
    Pro-tourism policies   95
Regional destination patterns.......................................95
    Europe   96
    Asia–Pacific   98

W I L   R I E S

DAVID WEAVER | LAURA LAWTON

Australia, Ltd

Fourth edition published 2010 by
John Wiley & Sons Australia, Ltd
42 McDougall Street, Milton Qld 4064

First edition published 2000
Second edition published 2002
Third edition published 2006

Typeset in Berkeley LT Book 10/12

National Library of Australia
Cataloguing-in-Publication entry

Author:	Weaver, David B. (David Bruce)
Title:	Tourism management / David Weaver, Laura Lawton.
Edition:	4th ed.
ISBN:	978 0 470 82022 3 (pbk.)
Notes:	Includes index. Bibliography.
Subjects:	Tourism — Australia — Marketing. Tourism — Australia — Management. Ecotourism — Australia.
Other Authors/Contributors:	Lawton, Laura.
Dewey Number:	338.4/91

Cover and internal design images: © Corbis Royalty Free/Copyright 1999
Corbis Corporation.

Typeset in India by diacriTech

Printed in China by
1010 Printing International Limited

10 9 8 7 6 5 4 3 2 1

The Americas   99
The Middle East   100
Africa   102
Australia   102
Internal destination patterns   104
The Australian pattern   106
Chapter review   108
Summary of key terms   108
Questions   109
Exercises   110
Further reading   110
Case study   111

CHAPTER 5 The tourism product   114

Introduction   115
Tourist attractions   115
Natural sites   115
Natural events   122
Cultural sites   123
Attraction attributes   132
The tourism industry   136
Travel agencies   136
Transportation   137
Accommodation   140
Tour operators   141
Merchandise   143
Industry structure   143
Chapter review   146
Summary of key terms   146
Questions   148
Exercises   148
Further reading   149
Case study   149

CHAPTER 6 Tourist markets   152

Introduction   153
Tourist market trends   153
The democratisation of travel   153
The emergence of simple market segmentation and multilevel segmentation   153
Niche markets and 'markets of one'   154
The destination selection process   155
Multiple decision makers   156
Tourist market segmentation   157
Geographic segmentation   158
Sociodemographic segmentation   160
Psychographic segmentation   167
Behavioural segmentation   170
Chapter review   175
Summary of key terms   175
Questions   176

Exercises   177
Further reading   177
Case study 178

CHAPTER 7 Tourism marketing   181

Introduction 182
The nature of marketing.. 182
Definition of marketing   182
Services marketing... 182
Intangibility   183
Inseparability   184
Variability   184
Perishability   185
Managing supply and demand 185
Daily variations in demand   187
Weekly variations in demand   187
Seasonal variations in demand   187
Long-term variations in demand   187
Supply/demand matching strategies   188
Market failure 192
Destination tourism organisations   192
Strategic tourism marketing... 194
SWOT analysis and objectives   194
Objectives   195
Control/evaluation   196
Marketing mix 197
Place   197
Product   197
People   198
Price   199
Packaging   200
Programming   201
Promotion   201
Partnerships   205
Chapter review 206
Summary of key terms   206
Questions   208
Exercises   208
Further reading   208
Case study 209

CHAPTER 8 Economic impacts of tourism   212

Introduction 213
Economic benefits 213
Direct revenue   213
Indirect revenue   218
Economic integration and diversification   220
Employment (direct and indirect)   220
Regional development   220

Formal and informal sectors   222
Economic costs   223
Direct financial costs   224
Indirect financial costs   225
Fluctuations in intake   226
Competition with other sectors   230
Employment problems   230
Chapter review 232
Summary of key terms   232
Questions   233
Exercises   234
Further reading   234
Case study 235

CHAPTER 9 Sociocultural and environmental
            impacts of tourism   238

Introduction 239
Sociocultural benefits 239
Promotion of cross-cultural understanding   239
Incentive to preserve culture and heritage   240
Promoting social wellbeing and stability   242
Sociocultural costs..242
Commodification   242
The demonstration effect revisited   244
The relationship between tourism and crime   245
Factors contributing to the increased likelihood of sociocultural costs   247
Resident reactions   251
Environmental benefits...252
Environmental costs 252
Environmental impact sequence   253
'Permanent' environmental restructuring   253
Generation of waste residuals   256
Climate change   256
Tourist activities   257
Indirect and induced activities   257
Ecological footprinting   258
Management implications of sociocultural and environmental impacts   259
Chapter review 260
Summary of key terms   260
Questions   261
Exercises   262
Further reading   262
Case study 263

CHAPTER 10 Destination development   266

Introduction 267
Destination cycle 267
The Butler Sequence   268
Critique of the Butler sequence   276

Factors that change the destination cycle 282
    Internal-intentional actions   283
    External-unintentional actions   283
    Internal-unintentional actions   283
    External-intentional actions   283
National tourism development 284
    Spatial diffusion   284
    Effects of hierarchical diffusion   285
    Effects of contagious diffusion   285
    Model of national tourism development   287
Chapter review 289
    Summary of key terms   289
    Questions   290
    Exercises   291
    Further reading   291
Case study 292

CHAPTER 11 Sustainable tourism   294

Introduction 295
A paradigm shift 295
    Dominant Western environmental paradigm   295
    Contradictions in the dominant Western environmental paradigm   296
    Towards a green paradigm   297
Sustainable tourism 299
    Indicators   300
Sustainability and mass tourism 302
    Reasons for adoption   302
    Practices   306
    Quality control   307
Sustainability and small-scale tourism 310
    Alternative tourism   310
    Manifestations   312
    Critique of alternative tourism   312
Ecotourism 314
    Soft and hard ecotourism   316
    Magnitude   317
    Location   317
Destination sustainability 319
    Extending the Butler sequence   319
Chapter review 322
    Summary of key terms   323
    Questions   324
    Exercises   325
    Further reading   325
Case study 326

CHAPTER 12 Tourism research   330

Introduction 331
Types of research...331
   Basic research   331
   Applied research   334
   Cross-sectional research   335
   Longitudinal research   336
   Qualitative research   336
   Quantitative research   337
   Primary research   338
   Secondary research   343
The research process 345
   Problem recognition   345
   Question formulation   346
   Identification of research methodology or methods   348
   Data collection   349
   Data analysis   350
   Data presentation   350
   Data interpretation   350
Chapter review 352
   Summary of key terms   352
   Questions   353
   Exercises   354
   Further reading   354
Case study 355

Appendix 1..357
Appendix 2..359
Appendix 3..363
References...370
Glossary..391
Index 407

■ PREFACE

As this book came to press, the authors were informed by a newly released UNWTO bulletin that the number of international stayover tourists in 2008 was estimated to have increased by 2 per cent over 2007, from 908 to 924 million. This would appear, at first blush, to affirm international tourism's status as a juggernaut soon to approach the one billion stayover mark. The remainder of the bulletin, however, made for more sobering reading. The 2 per cent rate, for example, is the summary of robust growth during the first half of 2008 followed by a decline during the second half. Consumers around the world know that 2008 was an exceptionally turbulent year on multiple fronts, including the global financial crisis and credit crunch, and the soaring cost of oil. That cost fell considerably near the end of 2008 and during early 2009, but few expect those decreases to last. At the same time, the financial situation around the world continued to deteriorate in early 2009, with one sensing a snowball effect as the growing legions of the unemployed, underemployed and debt-ridden help to pull the economy further into recession (or even into depression). The societal anxiety that was generated by the terrorist attacks of 2001 and its aftermath now appears very far away indeed, while the 2004 Indian Ocean tsunami that killed an estimated 180 000 people and devastated the tourism industry in much of South-East and South Asia now feels like a distant memory. Of course, incidents of similar magnitude are possible at any time, and one can only speculate on the impact they would have on an already reeling industry. UNWTO prognosticators speculated in their bulletin that tourism numbers in 2009 would be flat 'at best' and 'a few per cent down at worst', but we wonder if they are being overly optimistic.

Tourism may well be in for its 'roughest ride' since the first global tourism statistics were released in 1950, and a good argument can therefore be made that the time has never been better for the management, planning and marketing of the tourism industry to be informed by concerted scientific investigations and a solid understanding of global tourism systems. As consumers cut back their discretionary travel or alter their travel patterns, it is the most knowledgeable, adaptive and innovative destination and business managers that will be best positioned to weather the storm, and perhaps even benefit from the opportunities that are inherent in any threat. This fourth edition of *Tourism Management* was written with such assumptions in mind, and serves as a platform from which qualities of innovation, flexibility, adaptability, broad thinking and research rigour can flourish, so that destinations and businesses can prosper in bad as well as good times. The authors are grateful to the numerous colleagues who volunteered suggestions and feedback for improvement. We especially appreciate the input of Dr Justine Digance of Griffith University, whose 'coalface' efforts in the classroom and finely tuned radar to tourism developments in Australia and beyond have yielded particularly insightful comments. The anonymous feedback of numerous textbook adopters has also proven extremely valuable. We also thank Carolyn Gibson, communication manager at Qualmark (New Zealand) for her careful read of the Qualmark case study and helpful suggestions for improvement. With regard to the publisher, John Wiley & Sons Australia, the authors continue to be privileged to work with a team that exemplifies the qualities reflected in this textbook. We especially thank Dan Logovik, the content editor, and Nina Sharpe, associate publishing editor (Higher Education), for their professionalism, encouragement, and friendship which have greatly facilitated the timely production of this new edition.

Dr Dave Weaver
Dr Laura Lawton
June 2009

■ ACKNOWLEDGEMENTS

The authors and publisher would like to thank the following copyright holders, organisations and individuals for their permission to reproduce copyright material in this book.

Images

• © Neil Leiper: **21** (top)/Adapted from Tourism Management, by Neil Leiper, RMIT, 1995 included with permission of Neil Leiper; **22** (top)/From Tourism Management, RMIT, 1995 © Neil Leiper included with permission of Neil Leiper • © John Wiley & Sons UK: **56** (middle)/ From: 'An Historical Geography of Recreation and Tourism in the Western World 1540–1940' by John Towner © John Wiley & Sons Limited. Reproduced with permission • © Australian Bureau of Statistics: **67** (bottom)/ABS data used with permission from the Australian Bureau of Statistics • © Digital Vision: **67** (top) • © Gold Coast Tourism Bureau: **94** (middle), **94** (top)/ Gold Coast Tourism www.verygc.com • © AAP Image: **101** (bottom)/AFP/AAP; **202** (bottom)/ AAP Image/Tim Cole • © Viewfinder Australia Photo Lib: **118** (middle)/© Viewfinder Australia Photo Library • © Colonial Willamsburg Foundation: **126** (top)/The Colonial Willamsburg Foundation • © iStockphoto: **165** (top)/ © iStockphoto.com/Simon Gurney; **223** (middle)/ iStockphoto.com/Nuno Silva; **274** (bottom)/iStockphoto.com/Jaime Roset • © Copyright Clearance Center: **172** (top)/From: Martin Opperman, *Journal of Travel Research* 33 (4) pp 57–61 fig. 1. Reprinted by permission of Copyright Clearance Center; **351** (middle)/'Visa-free Travel Privileges: An Exploratory Geographical Analysis' Brendan Whyte, *Tourism Geographies*, Vol. 10, 5 Jan., 2008, Taylor & Francis Group. Reprinted with permission of Taylor & Francis Group, www.informaworld.com • © Pacific Yurts Inc: **191** (bottom), **191** (top)/© 2009 Pacific Yurts Inc., Cottage Grove, Oregon USA • © Araluen Cultural Precinct: **241** (bottom)/Courtesy of Araluen Cultural Precinct. Photo by Claire Ashard • © Canadian Association of Geographers: **268** (middle)/Reprinted from The Canadian Geographer, Vol 24, Issue 1, 1980 article by RW Butler included with permission • © PATA: **308** (top)/© Asia Pacific Economic Corporation/ Pacific Asia Travel Association • © Dept of Environment & Conservation: **316** (top)/Department of Environment and Conservation • © Elsevier: **320** (top)/Reprinted from *Tourism Management Journal*, Vol. 21, Weaver, A Broad Context Model of Destination development scenarios, pp. 217–24 © 2000 with permission from Elsevier.

Text

• © Commonwealth Copyright Administration: **35**/© Commonwealth of Australia reproduced by permission • © Tourism Australia: **116**/Tourism Research Australia, 'International Visitor Survey' 2008 Tourism Australia reproduced by permission • © Hotels Magazine: **141**/*Hotels Magazine* • © David Weaver: **149–51**/ 'Not just surviving, but thriving: Perceived strengths of successful US-based travel agencies', by D. Weaver & L. Lawton, *International Journal of Tourism Research*, Vol. 10, pp. 41–53. Reproduced with permission from the authors • © Copyright Clearance Center: **164**/From: Lawson, *Journal of Travel Research*, 1991, 30 (20) p. 14 reprinted with permission of Copyright Clearance Center • © John Wiley & Sons, Inc.: **169**/*Leisure Travel: Making it a Growth Market Again!* by Stanley C Plog 1991, with permission of John Wiley & Sons, Inc. • © Elsevier: **170**/Reprinted from *Global Tourism,* 3rd edition, Theobald (ed), p. 281 © 2005 with permission from Elsevier • © World Tourism Organization: **300–1**/'Indicators of Sustainable Development for Tourism Destinations: A Guidebook', 2004 © UNWTO, 9284402109. • © Pearson Education US: **337**/Adapted from: 'Social Research Methods: Qualitative and Quantitative Approaches 4e' by W. Lawrence Neuman, 2000, Allyn and Bacon, Boston, MA © Pearson Education.

Every effort has been made to trace the ownership of copyright material. Information that will enable the publisher to rectify any error or omission in subsequent editions will be welcome. In such cases, please contact the Permissions Section of John Wiley & Sons Australia, Ltd who will arrange for the payment of the usual fee.

■ REAL-WORLD EXAMPLES AT A GLANCE

Chapter	Managing tourism	Breakthrough tourism	Technology and tourism	Contemporary issue	Case study
2	Cruise ship excursionists in the South Pacific	Cultivating smart Australian travellers through smartraveller.gov.au	A clearer picture of domestic tourism in Australia	Health concerns about medical tourism in India	A perfect storm in Australian tourism
3	Spa experiences in modern hotels	Waiting for the train in the Alpine Pearls	War as an innovation stimulant	Backpacking: the modern Grand Tour?	Behold the boomer
4	3S tourism development in Hainan province, China	Exceeding expectations In Dubai	Australia's National Visitor Safety Handbook	America's war on tourists?	Attracting Chinese tourists to Australia
5	Declining attendance at Colonial Williamsburg	In the lap of luxury at the destination club	Getting to know 'the hood'	Fighting for water in Spain and Australia	US travel agencies that are not just surviving but thriving
6	Gay and lesbian tourists in the Cayman Islands	The influence of face and harmony on loyalty in Chinese customers	Differences between females and males in online travel information search	Tourism websites and persons with disabilities	Identifying the green consumer
7	Intangibility in the hotel sector	Spreading the word digitally through eWOM	The case for object-oriented database marketing	Reducing demand by demarketing	What the bloody hell is happening to Australia's destination brand?
8	Seasonality through VFR tourism	Garden path to rural development in north-eastern England?	An Encore performance for festivals and events	International tourism students and part-time employment	Government give and take in Australia
9	The sand on Australia's Gold Coast	Celebrating Aboriginal art at Desert Mob	The real cost of admission	Deportation and crime in the Caribbean	Pushing the boundaries of indigenous tourism
10	The tourist area life cycle in a Chinese protected area	From setting to sightseeing in Iowa, USA	Seeing Norway through the tunnels	Indigenous people and 'pre-exploration dynamics'	Bali on the brink?
11	Volunteer tourism	A collective approach to corporate sustainability	Above the tree tops and beneath the waves	Morally obligated Australian tourists	Towards quality tourism in New Zealand
12	Web-based survey responses	Accessing tourism data in New Zealand	Using GPS to track tourists in Germany	An inductive model of indigenous tourism development	Pursuing research on climate change and tourism in Australia

CHAPTER 1

INTRODUCTION TO TOURISM MANAGEMENT

LEARNING OBJECTIVES

After studying this chapter, you should be able to:

1. define tourism and appreciate its status as one of the world's most important economic sectors

2. critique the factors that have hindered the development of tourism studies as an academic field

3. explain why theory is important in the development of an academic discipline

4. identify the contributions of each the four 'platforms' to the evolution and maturation of tourism studies

5. outline the growth of tourism as a university-based field of study

6. explain why the growing number of refereed tourism journals is a core indicator of development in the field of tourism studies, but also a potential danger

7. compare and contrast the distinctive and mutually reinforcing roles of universities and community colleges in the provision of tourism education and training.

INTRODUCTION

Tourism is increasingly widespread and complex, and sophisticated management is therefore required to realise its full potential as a positive and sustainable economic, ecological, social and cultural force. Complicating this task is its particular vulnerability to uncertainty, which is dramatically demonstrated by contemporary concerns about dramatically fluctuating energy costs and the role of tourism in both affecting and being affected by climate change. This textbook, informed by the two 'mega-themes' of complexity and uncertainty, gives students an introductory exposure to tourism that provides a foundation for further informed engagement with the sector, first in the remainder of their tertiary studies and then in their capacity as managers.

This opening chapter introduces the text. The following section defines tourism and emphasises its global and national economic importance. The section 'Tourism as an academic field of study' traces the development of tourism studies as an academic focus and considers the factors that have hindered its evolution as such. Finally, we consider the themes, outline and structure of the book.

THE PHENOMENON OF TOURISM

This book is about tourism management, and it is therefore important to establish what is meant by the term **tourism**. Most people have an intuitive and simplistic perception of tourism focused around an image of people travelling for recreational purposes. But how far from home do they have to travel before they are considered to be tourists, and for how long? And what types of travel qualify as tourism? Most people would agree that a family vacation trip qualifies a form of tourism while the arrival of an invading army or the daily commute to work does not. But what about attendees at a business convention, Muslims embarking on the pilgrimage to Mecca, a group of international students, or participants at the Olympic Games? All qualify as tourists, but challenge our sense of what it means to be a tourist. We therefore need to establish definitional boundaries. The questions posed here are complex ones beyond the scope of this introductory chapter, but it should be apparent that the definition of tourism depends largely on how we define the **tourist** (see chapter 2).

DEFINITION OF TOURISM

There is no single definition of tourism to which everyone adheres. Many definitions have been used over the years, some of which are universal and can be applied to any situation, while others fulfil a specific purpose. Local tourism organisations, for example, often devise definitions that satisfy their own specific requirements and circumstances. The more universal definition that informs this text builds on Goeldner and Ritchie (2006), who place tourism in a broad stakeholder context. Additions to the original are indicated by italics:

> Tourism may be defined as the *sum of the* processes, activities, and outcomes arising from the relationships and the interactions among tourists, tourism suppliers, host governments, host communities, and surrounding environments that are involved in the attracting, *transporting,* hosting *and management of tourists* and *other* visitors.

'Surrounding environments' include origin governments, tertiary educational institutions and nongovernmental organisations (NGOs), all of which play an increasingly important role in tourism. Figure 1.1 depicts these stakeholders as members of an interconnected network, in which possibilities exist for interaction among any two or more components within the system. Also notable in the expanded definition is the extension of the tourism dynamic to include transportation from origin to destination as well as the management process, which is the core theme of this text.

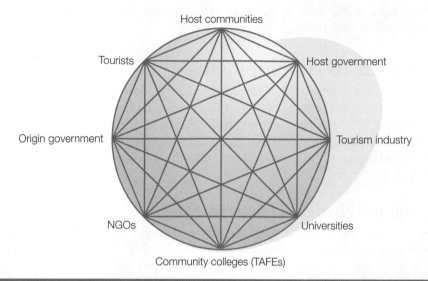

FIGURE 1.1   The tourism stakeholder system

The importance of tourism

Although the importance of tourism as an economic, environmental and sociocultural force will be detailed in later chapters, it is useful at the outset to convey a sense of tourism's economic significance. Essentially, tourism evolved during the latter half of the twentieth century from a marginal and locally significant activity to a widely dispersed economic giant, which in 2008 directly and indirectly accounted for more than 10 per cent of the global GDP, or approximately $6.0 trillion. This places tourism on the same global order of magnitude as agriculture or mining. According to the World Travel and Tourism Council (WTTC) (www.wttc.org), the major organisation representing the global tourism industry, 231 million jobs were dependent on the 'tourism economy' in 2007. During that year, more than 900 million international tourist trips of at least one night were undertaken (UNWTO 2008). Many tourism experts, moreover, believe that the incidence of domestic tourist travel is about ten times this volume. Such figures attest to the massive economic impact of tourism and its status as a primary agent of globalisation that involves billions of host/guest contacts and the incorporation of most places into an integrated global tourism network.

■ TOURISM AS AN ACADEMIC FIELD OF STUDY

The previous section suggests that tourism can exercise an enormous impact on host destinations as well as transit and origin regions. How much this impact is positive or negative, however, depends on whether tourism is appropriately managed by host governments, communities and businesses in particular. For a destination, management implies some deliberate effort to control the development of tourism to help fulfill the economic, social, cultural and environmental aspirations and strategic goals of the people living in that destination. If, in contrast, tourism is allowed to develop without any kind of formal management, experience tells us that the likelihood of negative outcomes is greatly increased, as later chapters will illustrate. The tertiary educational sector has much to contribute to the evolving science of tourism management, and the ongoing evolution of tourism studies is an interesting and promising development that has accompanied the expansion of tourism itself.

Obstacles to development

The emergence of tourism as a legitimate area of investigation within the university sector is a recent development, and one that has encountered many obstacles. It can be argued that this field, like other non-traditional areas such as development studies and leisure studies, is still not given the respect and level of support that are provided to the more traditional disciplines. Several factors that help to account for this situation are outlined here.

Tourism perceived as a trivial activity

Many academics and others in positions of authority have regarded tourism over the years as a nonessential and even frivolous activity involving pleasure-based motivations and activities. Hence it was and still often is seldom given the same attention, in terms of institutional commitment or financial support, as agriculture, manufacturing, mining or other more 'serious' and 'essential' pursuits (Davidson 2005). Most tourism researchers, like their leisure studies counterparts, can relate to tales of repeated grant application rejections, isolation within 'mainstream' discipline departments and ribbing by colleagues who believe that a research trip to the Caribbean or some other tourist destination is little more than a publicly subsidised holiday. These problems still occur, but there is now a much greater awareness of the significant and complex role played by tourism in contemporary society, and the profound impacts that it can have on host communities as well as the natural environment. This growing awareness is contributing to a 'legitimisation' of tourism that is gradually giving tourism studies more credibility within the university system in Australia and elsewhere.

Large-scale tourism as a recent activity

Residual tendencies to downplay tourism are understandable given that large-scale tourism is a relatively recent phenomenon. In the 1950s, global tourism was a marginal economic activity that did not seem to deserve focused attention from the university community. By the 1970s, its significance was much more difficult to deny, but specialised bodies such as the World Tourism Organization (UNWTO) were not yet large or well known enough to effectively spread awareness about the size and importance of the sector. The sophistication of these organisations has now improved greatly, but most people even today are still not aware that tourism is as large or economically influential as it is.

Bureaucratic inertia and echo effects

Even where there is respect for tourism and appreciation for its magnitude, the administrative structures of tertiary institutions often make it difficult for new programs and curricula to be introduced. Universities, like other bureaucratic institutions, are characterised by a high degree of inertia and are reluctant to change entrenched (and protected) structures. When significant change does occur, it is as likely to be as much the consequence of government or legal pressure, interest from large donors, or the arrival of a new vice-chancellor wishing to make their own mark on the institution, as any well-considered examination of societal trends. This results in an 'echo effect' whereby universities only started to accommodate specialised tourism programs in the 1980s, and are still in many cases trying to determine where and how such programs should be housed.

Tourism perceived as a vocational field of study

To the degree that tourism in the past was accepted as a legitimate area of tertiary study, it was widely assumed to belong within the community college or TAFE system. This reflected the simplistic view that tourism-related learning is only about applied vocational and technical skills training, and that relevant job opportunities are confined to customer service-oriented sectors such as hotels, travel agencies and restaurants. It has historically been easier therefore to incorporate emerging elements of tourism-related learning (such as managerial training) into existing and receptive TAFE structures than to 'sell' them to resistant or sceptical university administrators. Fortunately, TAFEs and universities are now both widely recognised as important tertiary stakeholders in the tourism sector, each making distinctive but complementary contributions to its operation and management.

Lack of clear definitions and reliable data

The development of tourism studies has been impeded by the lack of clear terms of reference. Aside from the lack of consensus on the definition of tourism, the term is often used in conjunction or interchangeably with related concepts such as 'travel', 'leisure', 'recreation', 'visitation' and 'hospitality'. The focus of tourism and its place within a broader system of academic inquiry is therefore not very clear. A similar lack of precision is evident within tourism itself. It is only since the 1980s that the UNWTO has succeeded in aligning most countries to a standard set of international tourist definitions. Yet, serious inconsistencies persist in the international tourism data that are being reported by member states. Attempts to achieve standardisation and reliability among UNWTO member states with regard to domestic tourism are even more embryonic, making comparison extremely difficult.

Tourism-related industrial classification codes are also confusing. Any attempt to find data on the tourism industry in Australia and New Zealand, for example, is impeded by the lack of a single 'tourism' category within the **Standard Industrial Classification (SIC)** code used by these two countries (ABS 2006). Instead, tourism-related activities are subsumed under at least 15 industrial classes, many of which also include a significant amount of nontourism activity (see figure 1.2). This system, in turn, bears little resemblance to the North American Industry Classification System (NAICS) used by the United States, Canada and Mexico, which subsumes tourism under more than 30 individual codes. The tourism 'industry', then, loses respect and influence because of official classification protocols that disguise the sector and divide its massive overall economic contribution into a variety of relatively small affiliated industries such as 'accommodation', 'travel agency services' and 'recreational parks and gardens'.

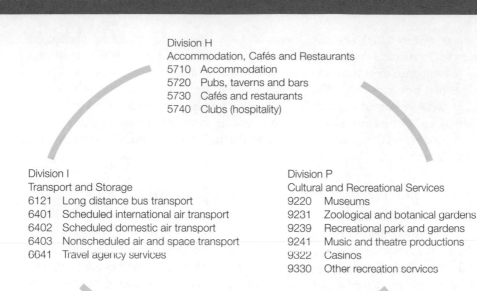

Division H
Accommodation, Cafés and Restaurants
5710   Accommodation
5720   Pubs, taverns and bars
5730   Cafés and restaurants
5740   Clubs (hospitality)

Division I
Transport and Storage
6121   Long distance bus transport
6401   Scheduled international air transport
6402   Scheduled domestic air transport
6403   Nonscheduled air and space transport
6641   Travel agency services

Division P
Cultural and Recreational Services
9220   Museums
9231   Zoological and botanical gardens
9239   Recreational park and gardens
9241   Music and theatre productions
9322   Casinos
9330   Other recreation services

FIGURE 1.2 Australian and New Zealand SIC classes related to tourism

Lack of indigenous theory or a strong academic tradition

Tourism-related data that are unreliable, inconsistent or dispersed do not facilitate the generation and testing of relevant **theory**. This discourages those who hope to develop the field into a fully fledged **academic discipline**, with its own **indigenous theories** and methodologies. Theory is essential to the development of an academic field because it provides coherent and unifying tentative explanations for diverse phenomena and processes that may otherwise appear disconnected or unrelated. In other words, theory provides a basis for understanding and organising certain aspects of the real world and is therefore central to the revelation and advancement of knowledge in any field. Students often find theory to be boring, abstract or difficult to understand, but a grasp of theory is essential for those who intend to pursue tourism, or any other field of study, at the university level.

The lack of indigenous tourism theory can also be associated with the absence of a strong academic tradition in the field of tourism studies. Before the creation of specialised schools and departments, tourism researchers were dispersed among a variety of traditional disciplines, and most notably in social sciences such as geography, anthropology, economics and sociology. Isolated from their tourism colleagues in other departments, tourism researchers could not easily collaborate and generate the synergy and critical mass necessary to stimulate academic progress. Even where tourism researchers have been brought together in tourism studies schools or departments, they still often pursue their research from the perspective of the mainstream disciplines in which they received their education, rather than from a 'tourism studies' perspective. Tourism geographers, for example, emphasise spatial theories involving core/periphery, regional or gravitational models, while tourism economists utilise input/output models, income multiplier effects and other econometric theories.

This **multidisciplinary approach** undoubtedly contributes to the advancement of knowledge as tourism researchers come together in tourism departments, but inhibits the development of indigenous tourism theory.

Figure 1.3 suggests that the multidisciplinary approach is gradually giving way to an **interdisciplinary approach** in which the perspectives of various disciplines are combined and synthesised into distinctive new 'tourism' perspectives. This dynamic is more likely to generate the indigenous theories and methodologies that will eventually warrant the description of tourism studies as an academic discipline in its own right. The following subsections consider the contention in figure 1.3 that the area of tourism studies is currently moving from a multidisciplinary to an interdisciplinary perspective.

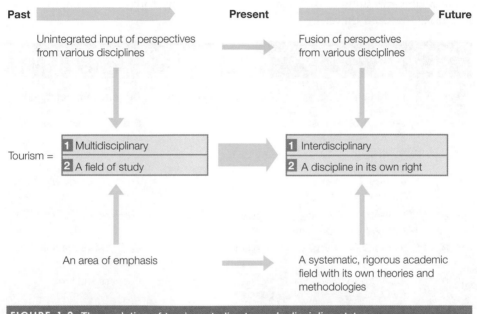

FIGURE 1.3 The evolution of tourism studies towards discipline status

Indications of development

The maturation of tourism studies is indicated by its increased visibility within university-level education and research in Australia and beyond. This is apparent in the large number of specialised departments and programs as well as the increase in the number of tourism-related refereed journals and other academic publications.

Expansion within the university sector

Many tourism academics are still based in traditional disciplines such as geography and economics, but an increasing proportion are located within more recently established tourism-related units. This is extremely significant, given its impact on the field's visibility and its effect of transforming tourism into a formally recognised and structured area of investigation. This process has also played an important role in creating the critical mass of tourism specialists necessary to progress towards discipline status. Notably, it has been the newer universities (e.g. Griffith University, La Trobe University), the satellite campuses of older universities (e.g. Gatton Agricultural College of the University of Queensland) and former polytechnic institutions (e.g. RMIT University, Curtin University of Technology), that have played a leadership role in the development of such units, less constrained as they are by the elitist pretensions and greater structural rigour of some of the more established institutions (see table 1.1).

Table 1.1 lists the 26 Australian universities that offered or announced domestic tourism-related programs in 2009. Most were based within business faculties (reflecting the widespread perception of tourism as a primarily economic phenomenon), and frequently in units that combine tourism with related fields, such as hospitality or leisure. Note that almost all of these units or programs were established during the 1980s and 1990s. That a consolidation level has been reached is evidenced by the decline in the number of such universities from 29 in 2001, with programs or units closing during the 2000s at the Queensland University of Technology (QUT), Royal Melbourne Institute of Technology (RMIT), University of New England, and Central Queensland University.

TABLE 1.1 Australian universities offering or announcing tourism programs, domestically, 2009

Year	Institution	Current name of unit	Current name of faculty
1974	University of Queensland (Gatton Agricultural College)	Tourism	Business, Economics and Law
	Victoria University (Footscray Institute of Technology)	Hospitality, Tourism and Marketing	Business and Law
1985	University of Technology, Sydney (Kuring-gai CAE)[1]	Leisure, Sport and Tourism	Business
1988	James Cook University[1]	Business (tourism management program)	Law, Business and the Creative Arts
1989	Edith Cowan University (WA CAE)	Marketing, Tourism and Leisure	Business and Law
	Griffith University (Gold Coast CAE)	Tourism, Leisure, Hotel and Sport Management	Griffith Business School
	Southern Cross University (Northern Rivers CAE)	Tourism and Hospitality Management	Business and Law
	University of Newcastle (Newcastle CAE)	Economics, Politics and Tourism	Business and Law
	University of NSW	Marketing (tourism and hospitality program)	Australian School of Business
1990	University of Canberra (Canberra CAE)	Tourism Management	Business and Government
	Charles Darwin University	Tourism and Hospitality	Law, Business and Arts
	Charles Sturt University (Mitchell CAE — Albury Campus)	Business and Information Technology (tourism management program)	Business
	Monash University	Undergraduate and postgraduate tourism programs	Business and Economics; Arts
	University of Western Sydney	Tourism Management program	Social Sciences

Year	Institution	Current name of unit	Current name of faculty
1991	University of Ballarat (Ballarat CAE)	Business (tourism program)	Higher Education Portfolio
1993	La Trobe University	Sport, Tourism and Hospitality Management	Law and Management
	University of South Australia	Management (Tourism and Hospitality Group)	Business Division
1995	Flinders University	Integrated (ecotourism) Cultural Tourism, Legal Studies and Professional Studies	Science and Engineering Humanities
1996	University of the Sunshine Coast (Sunshine Coast University College)	(Tourism program)	Business
1997	Murdoch University	(Tourism program)	Social Sciences and Humanities
	Swinburne University of Technology	(Bachelor of Tourism and Management)	Business and Enterprise
1998	Curtin University of Technology (Western Australian Institute of Technology)	(tourism management program) Built Environment, Art and Design (Sustainable Tourism Development program)	Curtin Business School Humanities
	The International College of Tourism and Hotel Management in association with Macquarie University	(Business, Hospitality and Tourism program)	n/a
2000	University of Tasmania	Management (Tourism management program)	Business
	University of Southern Queensland	(Tourism management program)	Business
2009	Bond University	Hotel, Resort and Tourism Management	Business, Technology & Sustainable Development

Note:
1 CAE = College of Advanced Education
Inaugurating institution listed in parentheses

Growth in the number of refereed journals

The growing maturity of tourism studies can also be gauged by the increase in the number of tourism-related **refereed academic journals**, which consolidate tourism research into a single location and sometimes encourage multidisciplinary or interdisciplinary discourse, depending on the scope of the publication. Because the articles they publish are subject to a normally rigorous procedure of **double-blind peer review**, refereed academic journals are widely considered to be the major showcase of a discipline and the best indicator of its intellectual development (Van Doren, Koh & McCahill 1994). A 'double-blind' process means that the author does not know who the editor has approached to assess the submitted manuscript, while the reviewers (two or three are usually employed) do not know the identity of the author.

Disadvantages of refereed journals include:

- the large interval (often several years) between the time the research is submitted to the journal and the time of publication (by which time it may no longer be relevant)
- the likelihood that experts who are asked to referee a submission can identify the author(s) because of their familiarity with research activity in the field, thereby compromising the objectivity of the double-blind review process
- the use of 'academic' terminology, vocabulary and methods that are not readily understood by the practitioners and residents who are most likely to benefit from an understanding of the material
- their location within (increasingly electronic) university library collections that cannot easily be accessed by practitioners and residents.

Appendix 2 lists the English-language refereed tourism journals that existed in 2008. Only four 'pioneer' journals existed prior to 1990, three of which (*Annals of Tourism Research, Journal of Travel Research and Tourism Management*) are interdisciplinary outlets widely regarded as the most prestigious in the field. The proliferation of journals since 1990, which roughly parallels the proliferation of university programs in Australia and elsewhere, has produced a number of additional interdisciplinary publications, but also ones that focus on the perspective of particular fields (e.g. geography, economics, anthropology, marketing, sport), regions (e.g. Asia–Pacific, China) or types of tourism (e.g. ecotourism, sustainable tourism, marine tourism).

Driving this trend towards more specialised outlets is the generation of tourism-related research output sufficient to warrant their establishment. Moreover, once they have been established, a research momentum is fostered as their very existence encourages even more output by providing outlets for those interested in conducting research in the focus area. This specialisation, however, may also have negative effects. Faulkner (1998) has speculated that the topical specialisation of journals may unintentionally inhibit the integration of the field by further encouraging the generation of theory based on particular disciplines. The existence of so many journals may also dilute the quality of research output if editors and publishers become desperate to publish in order to survive, and high quality manuscript reviewers become more difficult to recruit. Surprisingly, only one peer-reviewed journal (*Journal of Tourism Studies*, established in 1990 at James Cook University) has thus far ceased production, though it is difficult to see how many of the newer and more marginal or hyper-specialised outlets will survive the university consolidation process that was noted earlier.

A sequence of tourism platforms

As tourism has become increasingly visible within the university sector, the perspectives through which academics in the field of tourism studies view the world have also evolved. Jafari (2001) has identified four **tourism platforms** that have sequentially and incrementally influenced and enriched the development of the field.

Advocacy platform

The early tourism literature of the 1950s and 1960s was characterised by a positive and uncritical attitude towards the sector, which was almost universally regarded as an economic saviour for a wide variety of communities. Although this **advocacy platform** can be seen in retrospect as strongly biased and naïve, it must be interpreted in the context of the era in which it emerged. Europe and Asia were recovering from the devastation of World War II, and the issue of global economic development was focused on the emergence of an impoverished 'Third World'. As a potential economic stimulant, tourism offered hope to these regions, especially as there were then few examples of unsustainable, large-scale tourism development to serve as a counterpoint.

The prevalent attitude, therefore, was that communities should do all they can to attract and promote tourism activity within a minimally constrained free market environment. The primary role of government, accordingly, is to facilitate tourism growth through pro-tourism legislation and by maintaining law and order. Notwithstanding such 'anti-regulation' or 'anti-management' sentiments, the advocacy platform has made a valuable contribution to the tourism management field by raising awareness of the possibilities of tourism to serve as an agent of economic development, especially for poverty-stricken regions.

Cautionary platform

The **cautionary platform** emerged in the late 1960s as an ideological challenge to the advocacy platform by the political left. Where the former advocates free markets and is suspicious of 'big government', supporters of the cautionary platform endorse a high degree of public sector intervention and are suspicious of 'big business'. Tourism's rapid expansion into new environments, and the Third World in particular, produced numerous tangible examples of negative impact by the late 1960s and early 1970s that called into question the logic of unrestrained 'mass tourism' development. The contribution of the cautionary platform to tourism management, therefore, has been to emphasise the need for restraint and regulation. Classic and highly politicised works representing this platform include Finney and Watson (1975), who edited a book (*A New Kind of Sugar: Tourism in the Pacific*) which views tourism as an activity that perpetuates the inequalities of the colonial plantation era. Another is *The Golden Hordes: International Tourism and the Pleasure Periphery* by Turner and Ash (1975), who compare the spread of tourism with a barbarian invasion (see chapter 4 for more discussion of the pleasure periphery).

The destination lifecycle model of Butler (1980), which argues that unrestricted tourism development eventually leads to product degradation as the place's environmental, social and economic carrying capacities are exceeded (see chapter 10), can be regarded as the culmination of this platform.

Adaptancy platform

Supporters of the **adaptancy platform** are aligned with the cautionary platform; what sets them apart is their proposal of various modes of tourism that they allege to be better 'adapted' to the needs of local communities. Specifically, they introduced 'alternative tourism' in the early 1980s as a catchphrase to describe small-scale, locally controlled and highly regulated modes of tourism that provide a preferable alternative to mass tourism (see chapter 11). Holden's examination of alternative tourism options for Asia is a classic application of the adaptancy platform (Holden 1984). 'Ecotourism', notably, first appeared in the mid-1980s as a specialised, nature-based form of alternative tourism.

Knowledge-based platform

According to Jafari's model, the academic study of tourism has moved towards a knowledge-based platform since the late 1980s, in response to at least three factors:
• earlier perspectives are limited by their adherence to ideologies of the right or left, which provide only a narrow perspective on a complex issue such as tourism

- they are further limited in their emphasis on impacts (advocacy and cautionary) or solutions (adaptancy)
- the alternative tourism proposed by the adaptancy platform is a limited solution that is not feasible for the great number of destinations already embedded in mass tourism.

The **knowledge-based platform** addresses these limitations by shifting from the emotive and ideologically driven perspectives of previous platforms to one that is more objective and aware that tourism of any type results in positive as well as negative impacts. It also adopts a holistic view of tourism as an integrated and interdependent system in which large scale and small scale are *both* appropriate and potentially sustainable, depending on the circumstances of each particular destination. Effective management decisions about this complex system are based not on emotion or ideology, but on sound knowledge obtained through the application of the scientific method (see chapter 12) and informed by relevant models and theory. It is through the adherence of tourism academics to the knowledge-based platform, which is strongly associated with the emergence of 'sustainable development' and 'sustainable tourism' in the early 1990s (see chapter 11), that the field of tourism studies is most likely to achieve the status of a discipline. Leiper's (2004) textbook, *Tourism Management*, is an example of the knowledge-based approach.

Universities and community colleges

The emphasis in this chapter on the evolution of tourism studies within the university sector is in no way intended to imply an inferior role or status for the TAFE system. Rather, it is worth reiterating that both play a necessary and complementary role within the broader tertiary network of educational and training institutions. In this framework, TAFEs and similar institutions have had, and will likely continue to have, a dominant role in the provision of practical, high-quality training opportunities across a growing array of tourism-related occupations. These will increasingly involve not just entry-level training, but also staff development and enhancement.

Universities often provide or at least require similar training credentials (e.g. it is becoming increasingly common for students to earn an advanced diploma in tourism at a TAFE then transfer to a university to complete a bachelor's degree in tourism), but their primary responsibilities are in the areas of education and research. Specific roles coherent with the knowledge-based platform include the following (no order of priority is intended):

- provide relevant and high-quality undergraduate and postgraduate education, directed especially at producing effective managers, planners, researchers, analysts and marketers for both the public and private sectors
- conduct rigorous and objective scientific research into all aspects of tourism
- accumulate and disseminate a tourism-related knowledge base, especially through refereed journals, but also through reports and other avenues that are accessible to practitioners
- apply and formulate theory, both indigenous and imported, to describe, explain and predict tourism-related phenomena
- critically analyse all tourism-related phenomena
- position this analysis within a broad context of other sectors and processes, and within a framework of complexity and uncertainty
- contribute to policy formulation and improved planning and management within both the public and private sectors.

■ CHARACTERISTICS, OUTLINE AND STRUCTURE

This fourth edition, like previous editions, provides university students with an accessible but academically rigorous introduction to topics relevant to tourism management in the Australasian region. It is not, strictly speaking, a guidebook on how to manage tourism; those skills will evolve through the course of the undergraduate program, especially if the tourism component is taken in conjunction with one or more generic management courses or as part of a management degree. No prior knowledge of the tourism sector is assumed or necessary.

Characteristics

In concert with the knowledge-based platform, this book maintains a strong academic focus and emphasises methodological rigour, objective research outcomes, theory, critical analysis and healthy scepticism. This is evident in the use of scientific notation throughout the text to reference material obtained in large part from refereed journals and other academic sources such as edited books. The inclusion of a chapter on research (chapter 12) further supports this focus. At the same time, however, this book is meant to have practical application to the management and resolution of real-world problems, which the authors believe should be the ultimate goal of any academic discourse.

FIGURE 1.4 Multidisciplinary linkages within tourism studies

Second, this book provides a 'state-of-the-art' introduction to a coherent field of tourism studies that is gradually moving towards formulation as a discipline. An inter-disciplinary approach is required to realise the outcome envisaged in figure 1.3, recognising that an integrative and comprehensive understanding of tourism requires exposure to the theory and perspectives of other disciplines. The emergence of indigenous theory in tourism studies is likely to involve the combination and synthesis of theory from these other areas. Prominent among the disciplines that inform tourism studies are geography, business, economics, sociology, anthropology, law, psychology, history, political science, environmental science, leisure sciences, and marketing. Figure 1.4 demonstrates how some of these more traditional disciplines are affiliated with selected tourism themes (see Holden 2005).

Third, the book is national in scope in that the primary geographical focus is on Australia, yet it is also international in the sense that the Australian situation is both influenced and informed by developments in other parts of the world, and especially the Asia–Pacific region.

Chapter outline

The 12 chapters in this book have been carefully arranged so that together they constitute a logical and sequential introductory tourism management subject that can be delivered over the course of a normal university semester. Chapter 2 builds on the introductory chapter by providing further relevant definitions and presenting tourism within a systems framework. Chapter 3 considers the historical evolution of tourism and the 'push' factors that have contributed to its post–World War II emergence as one of the world's largest industries. Tourist destinations are examined in chapter 4 with regard to the 'pull' factors that attract visitors. Global destination patterns are also described. Chapter 5 concentrates on the tourism product, including attractions and sectors within the broader tourism industry such as travel agencies, carriers and accommodations. The emphasis shifts from the product (or supply) to the market (or demand) in the next two chapters. Chapter 6 considers the tourist market, examining the tourist's decision-making process as well as the division of this market into distinct segments. Chapter 7 extends this theme by focusing on tourism marketing, which includes the attempt to draw tourists to particular destinations and products. Subsequent chapters represent another major shift in focus toward the impacts of tourism. Chapters 8 and 9, respectively, consider the potential economic and sociocultural/environmental consequences of tourism, while chapter 10 examines the broader context of destination development. The focus here is on Butler's (1980) destination life cycle model. The concept of sustainable tourism, which is widely touted as the desired objective of management, is engaged in chapter 11. Chapter 12 concludes by focusing on the role of research in tourism studies, thereby preparing the reader for further university-level pursuit of the topic.

Chapter structure

Chapters 2 to 12 are all structured in a similar manner (see figure 1.5). Each begins with a set of learning objectives that students should achieve at the completion of the chapter. This is followed by an introduction and subsequent text that is arranged by topic area into major sections, major subsections, secondary subsections and minor subsections, as per figure 1.5. Four features that support the text are dispersed throughout these sections, as appropriate:

- the 'Managing ...' feature focuses on situations related to the chapter theme that have important implications for the management of the tourism sector
- the 'Contemporary issue' feature examines a broader current theme or trend relevant to the chapter that has significant management implications
- the 'Breakthrough tourism' feature identifies new developments that could have an important influence on tourism management
- the 'Technology ...' feature considers the actual or potential role of technological innovations in shaping the tourism sector and its management.

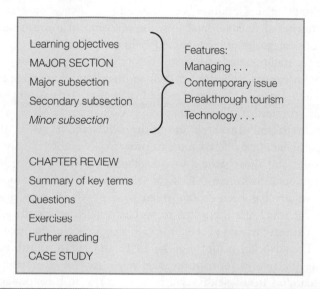

FIGURE 1.5 Chapter structure

Following a review of the content, each chapter concludes with a sequence of additional features. The 'Summary of key terms' summarises important concepts and terms in bold type within the chapter. These are listed in the order that they appear and grouped to show the links between the key concepts and their subconcepts. Relevant questions and exercises follow which allow the student to engage and discuss chapter content beyond the level of simple reiteration. An annotated 'Further reading' section suggests additional sources that allow the pursuit of specific topics in greater depth. Finally, each chapter ends with an expanded case study that incorporates multiple themes relevant to the chapter.

CHAPTER REVIEW

This chapter defines tourism and provides a preliminary indication of its rapid development as a major global economic activity. The evolution of tourism studies as an emerging field of academic inquiry within the university system is also considered. It is seen that this development has long been hindered by the widespread perception of tourism as a trivial subject and the recent nature of large-scale tourism. Also important are the echo effects produced by the bureaucratic inertia of university administrative structures, the traditional association between tourism and vocational training, the lack of clear definitions and reliable databases, the diffusion of tourism-related activities among numerous categories of the Standard Industrial Classification code, the lack of a strong academic tradition and indigenous theory, and the persistence of disciplinary and multidisciplinary approaches rather than an interdisciplinary perspective.

However, these obstacles have been eroded since the 1980s as tourism studies has moved towards an interdisciplinary perspective. Concurrently, there was a proliferation within Australia and elsewhere during the 1980s and 1990s in the number of university departments that offered tourism programs. Notably, this mostly involved newer universities and those with a CAE background, rather than the more established and traditional institutions. This consolidation of tourism studies as a legitimate area of inquiry has been accompanied by a proliferation of refereed tourism journals, many of which are according to specific topicsspecialised. Philosophically, the field of tourism studies has evolved through a sequence of dominant perspectives or 'platforms'. The advocacy platform of the 1950s and 1960s contributed to the field by emphasising the role of tourism as an effective tool of economic development. Regarded by many as insufficiently critical, it gave rise to a cautionary platform in the 1970s that identified the potential negative impacts of uncontrolled mass tourism and argued for a high level of regulation. The adaptancy platform that followed in the 1980s proposed small-scale alternative tourism activities that are supposedly better adapted to local circumstances. The current knowledge-based platform arose from the sustainable tourism discourse that began in the early 1990s. It is alleged to be more scientific and objective than earlier perspectives, regarding tourism as an integrated system in which both large- and small-scale tourism can be accommodated through management based on sound knowledge. This book provides an academically oriented introduction to tourism management that adheres to these aspirations of the knowledge-based platform.

■ SUMMARY OF KEY TERMS

Academic discipline a systematic field of study that is informed by a particular set of theories and methodologies in its attempt to reveal and expand relevant knowledge; e.g. psychology examines individual behaviour, while geography examines spatial patterns and relationships

Adaptancy platform a follow-up on the cautionary platform that argues for alternative forms of tourism deemed to be better adapted to local communities than mass tourism

Advocacy platform the view that tourism is an inherent benefit to communities that should be developed under free market principles

Cautionary platform a reaction to the advocacy platform that stresses the negative impacts of tourism and the consequent need for strict regulation

Double-blind peer review a procedure that attempts to maintain objectivity in the manuscript refereeing process by ensuring that the author and reviewers do not know each other's identity

Indigenous theories theories that arise out of a particular field of study or discipline

Interdisciplinary approach involves the input of a variety of disciplines, with fusion and synthesis occurring among these different perspectives

Knowledge-based platform the most recent dominant perspective in tourism studies, arising from the sustainability discourse and emphasising ideological neutrality and the application of rigorous scientific methods to generate knowledge so that communities can decide whether large-or small-scale tourism is most appropriate

Multidisciplinary approach involves the input of a variety of disciplines, but without any significant interaction or synthesis of these different perspectives

Refereed academic journals publications that are considered to showcase a discipline by merit of the fact that they are subject to a rigorous process of double-blind peer review

Standard Industrial Classification (SIC) a system that uses standard alphanumeric codes to classify all types of economic activity. Tourism-related activities are distributed among at least 15 codes

Theory a model or statement that describes, explains or predicts some phenomenon

Tourism the sum of the processes, activities, and outcomes arising from the relationships and the interactions among tourists, tourism suppliers, host governments, host communities, and surrounding environments that are involved in the attracting, transporting, hosting and management of tourists and other visitors

Tourism platforms perspectives that have dominated the emerging field of tourism studies at various stages of its evolution

Tourist a person who travels temporarily outside of his or her usual environment (usually defined by some distance threshold) for certain qualifying purposes

■ QUESTIONS

1. Lack of respect for tourism, or appreciation of its magnitude, are among the factors which have hindered the acceptance of tourism as a legitimate topic of academic inquiry.

    (a) What is the best way of changing these perceptions of tourism?

    (b) How could the improvement of these perceptions help to overcome the remaining three obstacles discussed in the 'Obstacles to development' section?

2. What are the advantages and disadvantages, respectively, of a multidisciplinary and interdisciplinary approach toward tourism studies?

3. (a) Why is theory so important to the development of an academic discipline?

    (b) How can theory be made more interesting for students and practitioners?

4. (a) Why are refereed journals considered to be the main source of tourism-related research results?

    (b) What are the weaknesses of refereed journals?

5. (a) What kinds of universities, faculties and units are associated with tourism-related programs in Australia?

    (b) What factors account for these particular patterns?

6. What is the most appropriate 'division of labour' between universities and TAFEs in terms of the provision of tourism education and training?

■ EXERCISES

1. (a) Randomly select any three stakeholder groups as depicted in figure 1.1.
   (b) Describe a tourism management scenario in which these three stakeholder groups would be required to work closely together.
2. Prepare a 1000-word report in which you:
   (a) Provide an example from your place of residence (country, province, town, etc.) of tourism-related activity (e.g. projects) or discourse (e.g. legislation, reports, letters to editor) that represents each of the four tourism platforms this chapter describes. Clearly show how each example represents its respective platform.
   (b) Describe the strengths and weaknesses of each project or discourse with respect to their potential impact on your place of residence.
   (c) Identify the stakeholders (e.g. developers, residents, interest groups, administrators) responsible for each of the identified projects or discourses, and speculate why they hold these views.

■ FURTHER READING

Davidson, T. 2005. 'What are Travel and Tourism: Are They Really an Industry?' In Theobald, W. (Ed.) *Global Tourism*. Third Edition. Sydney: Elsevier, pp. 25–31. Davidson argues that not only is tourism not a single industry, but it is counterproductive to treat it as such when attempting to gain respect for the field.

Holden, A. (Ed.) 2005. *Tourism Studies and the Social Sciences*. Abingdon, UK: Routledge. This collection of authored chapters demonstrates the multidisciplinary approach to tourism by applying theories from various disciplines within the social sciences to the study and management of tourism.

Jafari, J. 2001. 'The Scientification of Tourism'. In Smith, V. L. & Brent, M. (Eds) *Hosts and Guest Revisited: Tourism Issues of the 21st Century*. New York: Cognizant, pp. 28–41. This article updates Jafari's analysis of tourism as having experienced four distinct philosophies or 'platforms' in the post-World War II period.

Jamal, T., Smith, B. & Watson, E. 2008. 'Ranking, Rating and Scoring of Tourism Journals: Interdisciplinary Challenges and Innovations'. *Tourism Management* 29: 66–78. Tourism journal proliferation has led to attempts to rank these outlets, as critiqued by the authors who propose a more innovative way of judging journal merit.

Leiper, N. 2000. 'An Emerging Discipline'. *Annals of Tourism Research* 27: 805–09. Leiper provides a well-written discussion of issues associated with the evolution of tourism as a field of study.

Meyer-Arendt, K. & Justice, C. 2002. 'Tourism as the Subject of North American Dissertations, 1987–2000'. *Annals of Tourism Research* 29: 1171–4. The exponential increase in the production of tourism dissertations is the focus of this analysis, along with a discussion of the disciplines within which they were produced.

CHAPTER 2

THE TOURISM SYSTEM

LEARNING OBJECTIVES

After studying this chapter, you should be able to:

1. describe the fundamental structure of a tourism system

2. assess the external forces that influence and are influenced by tourism systems

3. outline the three criteria that together define tourists

4. explain the various purposes for tourism-related travel, and the relative importance of each

5. identify the four major types of tourist and the definition criteria that apply to each

6. evaluate the importance of origin and transit regions within the tourism system

7. explain the role of destination regions and the tourism industry within the tourism system.

INTRODUCTION

The introductory chapter defined tourism and described the development of tourism as a widespread area of focus within the university system in Australia and elsewhere, despite lingering prejudices. This is indicated by the growth of tourism-related programs and refereed journals as well as the movement towards a more objective knowledge-based philosophy that recognises tourism as a complex system requiring rigorous scientific investigation.

Chapter 2 discusses the concept of the tourism system and introduces its key components, thereby establishing the basis for further analysis of tourism system dynamics in subsequent chapters. The following section outlines the systems-based approach and presents tourism within this context. The 'The tourist' section defines the various types of tourist, considers the travel purposes that qualify as tourism and discusses problems associated with these definitions and the associated data. The origin regions of tourists are considered in the 'Origin region' section, while transit and destination regions are discussed in 'Transit region' and 'Destination region' sections, respectively. The industry component of the tourism system is introduced in the final section.

A SYSTEMS APPROACH TO TOURISM

A **system** is a group of interrelated, interdependent and interacting elements that together form a single functional structure. Systems theory emerged in the 1930s to clarify and organise complex phenomena that are otherwise too difficult to describe or analyse (Leiper 2004). Systems tend to be hierarchical, in that they consist of subsystems and are themselves part of larger structures. For example, a human body comprises digestive, reproductive and other subsystems, while human beings themselves are members of broader social systems (e.g. families, clans, nations). Systems also involve flows and exchanges of energy which almost always involve interaction with external systems (e.g. a human fishing or hunting for food). Implicit in the definition of a system is the idea of interdependence, that is, that a change in a given component will affect other components of that system. To examine a phenomenon as a system, therefore, is to adopt an integrated or holistic approach to the subject matter that transcends any particular discipline — in essence, an interdisciplinary approach that complements the knowledge-based platform (see chapter 1).

The basic whole tourism system

Attempts have been made since the 1960s to analyse tourism from a systems approach, based on the realisation that tourism is a complex phenomenon that involves interdependencies, energy flows and interactions with other systems. Leiper's **basic whole tourism system** (Leiper 2004) places tourism within a framework that minimally requires five interdependent core elements:

1. at least one tourist
2. at least one tourist-generating region
3. at least one transit route region
4. at least one tourist destination
5. a travel and tourism industry that facilitates movement within the system (see figure 2.1).

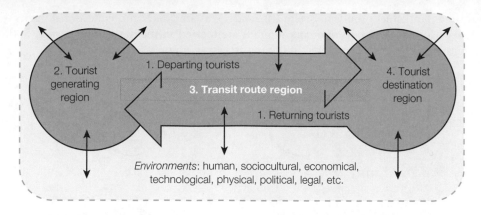

Note: The travel and tourism industry (5) is located throughout the system

FIGURE 2.1 A basic whole tourism system

Source: Adapted from Leiper (2004)

The movement of tourists between residence and a destination, by way of a transit region, and within the destination, comprise the primary flow of energy within this system. Other flows of energy involve exchanges of goods (e.g. imported food to feed tourists) and information (e.g. tourism-related blogs) that involve an array of interdependent external environments and systems in which the tourism system is embedded. The experience of the tourist, for example, is facilitated (or impeded) by the energy and political systems which, respectively, provide or do not provide sufficient fuel and accessibility to make the experience possible. Natural and cultural external factors can have dramatic and unpredictable effects on tourism systems, as illustrated by the Indian Ocean tsunami of 26 December 2004. This event killed an estimated 200 000 local residents and tourists, and devastated destinations throughout the Indian Ocean basin, including the popular Thai seaside resort of Phuket (Main and Dearden 2007). In the first decade of the 2000s, a variety of external factors have combined to seriously harm the Australian domestic and inbound tourism systems (see Case study: A perfect storm in Australian tourism).

Tourism systems in turn influence these external environments, for example by stimulating a destination's economy (see chapter 8) or helping to improve relations between countries (see chapter 9). Following the 2004 tsunami, a high priority was placed by affected destination governments and international relief agencies on restoring international tourist intakes, on the premise that this was the most effective way of bringing about a broader and more rapid economic and psychological recovery (Henderson 2007). Despite such critical two-way influences, there is a tendency in some tourism system configurations to ignore or gloss over the external environment, as if tourism were somehow a self-contained or closed system.

The internal structure of the tourism system is also far more complex than implied by figure 2.1, thereby presenting more challenges to the effective management of tourism. Many tourist flows are actually hierarchical in nature, in that they involve multiple, nested and overlapping destinations and transit regions (see figure 2.2). Cumulatively, the global tourism system encompasses an immense number of individual experiences and bilateral or multilateral flows involving thousands of destinations at the international and domestic level. Regarding the stakeholders depicted in figure 1.1, the tourists and the tourism businesses (or tourism industry) are present throughout Leiper's tourism system (figure 2.1), as are NGOs and educational institutions. Host governments and communities are located in the destination region, and origin governments are situated in the tourist-generating region.

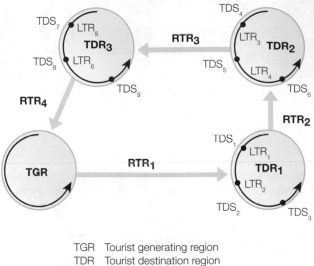

TGR	Tourist generating region
TDR	Tourist destination region
TDS	Tourist destination site
RTR	Regional transit route
LTR	Local transit route

FIGURE 2.2 Tourism system with multiple transit and destination components

Source: Adapted from Leiper (2004)

Finally, the overall tourism system is a hyperdynamic structure that is in a constant state of flux. This is apparent not only in the constant travel of millions of tourists, but also in the continuous opening and closing of accommodation facilities and transportation routes across the globe. This instability represents yet another challenge faced by tourism managers, who must realise that even the most current profile of the sector soon becomes obsolete.

■ THE TOURIST

As suggested in chapter 1, the definition of tourism is dependent on the definition of the tourist. It is therefore critical to address this issue in a satisfactory way before any further discussion of management-related issues can take place. Every tourist must simultaneously meet certain spatial, temporal and purposive criteria, as discussed below.

Spatial component

To become a tourist, a person must travel away from home. However, not all such travel qualifies as tourism. The UNWTO and most national and subnational tourism bodies hold that the travel must occur beyond the individual's 'usual environment'. Since this is a highly subjective term that is open to interpretation, these bodies normally stipulate minimum distance thresholds, or other criteria such as state or municipal residency, which distinguish the 'usual environment' from a tourist destination (see the 'Data problems' section). The designation and use of such thresholds may appear arbitrary, but they serve the useful purpose of differentiating those who bring outside revenue into the local area (and thereby increase the potential for the generation of additional wealth) from those who circulate revenue internally and thereby do not induce such an effect.

Domestic and international tourism

If qualifying travel occurs beyond a person's usual environment but within his or her usual country of residence, then that individual would be classified as a **domestic tourist**. If the experience occurs outside of the usual country of residence, then that person would be classified as an **international tourist**. The concept of 'usual environment' does not normally apply in international tourism. Residents of a border town, for example, become international tourists as soon as they cross the nearby international border (providing that the necessary temporal and purposive criteria are also met). An aspect of international tourism that is seldom recognised is the fact that such travel always involves at least some movement within the international tourist's own country — for example, the trip from home to the airport or international border. Although neglected as a subject of research, this component is nonetheless important, because of the infrastructure and services that are used and the economic activity that is generated. Vehicles queued for a kilometre or more waiting to cross the United States – Canada border at Detroit attest to this influence.

International tourism differs from domestic tourism in other crucial respects. First, domestic tourists far outnumber international tourists at a global scale and within most countries. In Australia, for example, Australian residents aged 15 or older accounted for 288.1 million visitor-nights within Australia between 1 April 2007 and 31 March 2008 (TRA 2008a), compared with 160.5 million visitor-nights by international tourists (TRA 2008b). This ratio is in line with the UNWTO estimate that domestic tourists account for about 70 per cent of the total world demand for commercial accommodation. In terms of overall global participation and revenue, it is widely accepted that domestic tourism is in the order of ten times larger than international tourism, although the ratio varies dramatically between countries (Goeldner & Ritchie 2006).

Second, relatively little is known about domestic tourists compared with their international counterparts, despite their numbers and economic importance. One reason is that most national governments do not consider domestic tourists to be as worthy of scrutiny, since they do not bring much-valued foreign exchange into the country but 'merely' redistribute wealth from one part of the country to another. It is often only when international tourist numbers are declining, for example in the aftermath of the Indian Ocean tsunami of 2004, that governments are prompted to support local tourism businesses by promoting their domestic tourism sector. Another reason for the relative neglect is that domestic tourists are usually more difficult to count than international tourists, since they are not subject, in democratic countries at least, to the border formalities faced by most international tourists. However, where countries are moving towards political and economic integration, and hence more open borders, international tourist flows are becoming just as difficult to monitor as domestic flows. This is well illustrated at present by the 27 countries of the ever-enlarging European Union (see chapter 4).

Finally, there are some cases where the distinction between domestic and international tourism is not entirely clear. This occurs when the tourism system incorporates geopolitical entities that are not part of a fully fledged country. For example, should a resident of the Israeli-controlled West Bank (Jewish or Arab) be considered an international or domestic tourist when he or she travels to Israel? Travel between the Hong

Kong Special Administrative Region and China is another ambiguous situation, as is travel between Taiwan and mainland China.

Outbound and inbound tourists

When referring specifically to international tourism, a distinction is made between **outbound tourists** (those leaving their usual country of residence) and **inbound tourists** (those arriving in a country different from their usual country of residence). Any international tourism trip has both outbound and inbound components, with the distinction being based on whether the classification is being made from the perspective of the country of origin or destination. Take, for example, an Australian who spends two weeks on vacation in Thailand. This person would be considered outbound from an Australian perspective but inbound from the Thai perspective.

During any year, the cumulative number of inbound trips will always exceed the total number of outbound trips at a global scale, since one outbound trip must translate into at least, but possibly more than, one inbound trip. This is demonstrated by the hypothetical example of an Australian tourist who visits five countries during a trip to South-East Asia. From Australia's perspective, this trip equates with one outbound tourist experience. However, each of the Asian countries will record that traveller as one inbound tourist, resulting in five separate instances of inbound tourism. Some origin governments require returning outbound tourists to report all visited destination countries, while others do not.

Long-haul and short-haul travel

A distinction can be made between **long-haul tourists** and **short-haul tourists**. There are no universal definitions for these terms, which are often defined according to the needs and purposes of different organisations, sectors or destinations. The United Nations regards long-haul travel as trips outside the multi-country UNWTO region in which the traveller lives (Lockwood & Medlik 2001). Thus, a United Kingdom resident travelling to Germany (i.e. within Europe, the same region) is a short-haul tourist, while the same resident travelling to South Africa or Australia is a long-haul tourist. Airlines usually base the distinction on distance or time thresholds, 3000 miles (6600 kilometres) or five hours commonly being used as a basis for differentiation (Lo & Lam 2004). One implication is that long-haul routes require different types of aircraft and passenger management strategies. Diabetics travelling on long-haul flights, for example, are more likely than those on short-haul flights to experience diabetes-related problems while in flight, though the actual number of those having problems is small (Burnett 2006). From a destination perspective, long-haul tourists are often distinguished from short-haul tourists by expenditure patterns, length of stay and other critical parameters. They may as a result also warrant separate marketing and management strategies.

Temporal component

The length of time involved in the trip experience is the second basic factor that determines whether someone is a tourist and what type of tourist. Theoretically, there is no minimum time that must be expended, although most trips that meet domestic tourism distance thresholds will require at least a few hours. At the other end of the time spectrum, most countries adhere to a UNWTO threshold of one year as the maximum amount of time that an inbound tourist can remain in the visited country and still be considered a tourist. For domestic tourists such thresholds are less commonly applied or monitored. Once these upper thresholds are exceeded, the visitor is no longer classified as a tourist, and should be reassigned to a more appropriate category such as 'temporary resident' or 'migrant'.

Stayovers and excursionists

Within these time limits, the experience of an overnight stay is critical in defining the type of tourist. If the tourist (domestic or international) remains in the destination for at least one night, then that person is commonly classified as a **stayover**. If the trip does not incorporate at least one overnight stay, then the term **excursionist** is often used. The definition of an 'overnight stay' may pose a problem, as in the case of someone arriving in a destination at 2.00 am and departing at 4.00 am. However, ambiguous examples such as this one are rare, and the use of an overnight stay criterion is a significant improvement over the former standard of a minimum 24-hour stay, which proved both arbitrary and extremely difficult to apply, given that it would require monitoring of exact times of arrival and departure.

Excursion-based tourism is dominated by two main types of activity. Cruise ship excursionists are among the fastest growing segments of the tourist market, numbering 12.5 million in 2007 (CLIA 2008) but many more if quantified as inbound tourists from the cumulative perspective of each cruise ship destination country. Certain geographically suitable regions, such as the Caribbean and Mediterranean basins, are especially impacted by the cruise ship sector. Cross-border shoppers are the other major type of excursionist. This form of tourism is also spatially concentrated, with major flows being associated with adjacent and accessible countries with large concentrations of population along the border. Examples include Canada/United States, United States/Mexico, Singapore/Malaysia, Argentina/Uruguay and Western Europe.

As with domestic tourists and other domestic travellers, the distinction between stayovers and excursionists is more than a bureaucratic indulgence. Significant differences in the management of tourism systems are likely depending on whether the tourism sector is dominated by one or the other group. An important difference, for example, is the excursionists' lack of need for overnight accommodation in a destination (see Managing tourism: Cruise ship excursionists in the South Pacific).

managing tourism

CRUISE SHIP EXCURSIONISTS IN THE SOUTH PACIFIC

The islands of the South Pacific recorded 2 million cruise ship 'bed days' in 2008, an almost 100 per cent increase over 2000 and over 2 per cent of the global total (CLIA 2008). As cruising becomes an ever more important component of the regional tourism product, it is essential that South Pacific tourism managers become aware of and responsive to the unique challenges posed by this sector. Dominant among these are exceptionally high levels of localised visitor congestion associated with the arrival of cruise ships into ports-of-call. Queues of waiting taxis and buses, for example, cause traffic bottlenecks in already busy downtowns of ports, while local roads and drivers are stressed by van and bus excursions travelling to a small number of 'must-see' natural and cultural attractions in the hinterland (Dowling 2006). In addition, a 'drought-deluge' cycle distorts the economy as businesses catering to cruise ships are either closed during off-visit periods, or must find large numbers of temporary employees during cruise ship visits (Lück 2007a).

It is unclear whether the economic benefits of cruise ship tourism sufficiently compensate for the resulting congestion, imbalanced employment patterns and stress on infrastructure. This is because of low per person expenditures in port by cruise ship excursionists since they do not need to purchase overnight accommodations on land, and most meals are provided on ship. Many shore excursions are purchased on the ship, while money that is spent in port tends to benefit luxury retail chains providing duty free goods. Additional considerations include the 'footloose' nature of the industry, whereby cruise lines unhappy with a destination policy such as increased berthing taxes can shift to other ports-of-call with relative ease. The trend toward ever larger mega-ships also means that economically less developed islands must invest large sums in port expansion, or be content to accommodate smaller, older vessels that are not as attractive to high-spending passengers and are more likely to cause environmental damage such as oil spills and air pollution from smoke stacks.

Travel purpose

The third basic tourist criterion concerns the **travel purpose**. Not all purposes for travelling qualify as tourism. According to the UNWTO, major exclusions include travel by active military personnel, daily routine trips, commuter traffic, migrant and guest worker flows, nomadic movements, refugee arrivals and travel by diplomats and consular representatives. The latter exclusion is related to the fact that embassies and consulates are technically considered to be part of the sovereign territory of the country they represent. The purposes that do qualify as tourism are dominated by three major categories:

1. leisure and recreation
2. visiting friends and relatives
3. business.

Leisure and recreation

Leisure and recreation are just two components within a constellation of related purposes that also includes terms such as 'vacation', 'rest and relaxation', 'pleasure' and 'holiday'. This is the category that usually comes to mind when the stereotypical tourism experience is imagined. Leisure and recreation account for the largest single share of tourist activity at a global level. As depicted in table 2.1, this also pertains to Australia, where 'holiday' (the Australian version of the category) constitutes the main single purpose of visits for both domestic and inbound tourists.

Visiting friends and relatives (VFR)

The intent to visit friends and relatives (i.e. VFR tourism) is the second most important purpose for domestic tourism in Australia, and third most important for inbound visitors after 'education' (table 2.1). An important management implication is that, unlike pleasure travel, the destination decision is normally predetermined by the place of residence of the person who is to be visited. Thus, while the tourism literature emphasises destination choice and the various factors that influence that choice (see chapter 6), the reality is that genuinely 'free' choice only exists for pleasure-oriented tourists. Another interesting observation is the affiliation of VFR-dominated tourism systems with migration systems. About one-half of all inbound visitors to Australia from the United Kingdom, for example, list VFR as their primary purpose (as opposed to about one-fifth of inbound tourists in total), and this over-representation is due mainly to the continuing importance of the United Kingdom as a source of migrants.

TABLE 2.1 Main reason for trip by inbound and domestic visitor nights, Australia, 2007/08[1]

Purpose of trip	Domestic tourists		Inbound tourists	
	Number[2]	%	Number[2]	%
Holiday	142 700	50	60 000	38
Visiting friends and relatives	86 200	30	27 000	17
Business-related	43 400	15	10 000	6
Other purposes[3]	13 300	5	62 000	39
Total[4]	288 100	100	160 000	100

Notes:
1 All visitors 15 years of age and older
2 In thousands
3 Other inbound purposes = education, employment
4 Includes visitor-nights where purpose was not stated
Source: TRA (2008a, 2008b)

Business

Business is roughly equal to VFR as a reason for tourism-related travel at a global level. Even more so than with the VFR category, business tourists are constrained in their travel decisions by the nature of the business that they are required to undertake. Assuming that the appropriate spatial and temporal criteria are met, business travel is a form of tourism only if the traveller is not paid by a source based in the destination. For example, a consultant who travels from Sydney to Perth, and is paid by a company based in Perth, would not be considered a tourist. However, if payment is made by a Sydney-based company, then the consultant is classified as a tourist. This stipulation prevents longer commutes to work from being incorporated into tourism statistics, and once again reflects the principle that tourism involves the input of new money from external sources.

There are numerous subcategories associated with business tourism, including consulting, sales, operations, management and maintenance. However, the largest category involves meetings, incentive travel, conventions and exhibitions, all of which are combined in the acronym **MICE**. Most, but not all, of MICE tourism is related to business. Many meetings and conventions, for example, involve such non-business social activities as school and military reunions. Similarly, exhibitions can be divided into trade and consumer subtypes, with the latter involving participants who attend such events for pleasure/leisure purposes. Incentive tourists are travellers whose trips are paid for all or in part by their employer as a way of rewarding excellent employee performance. In the period from 1 June 2007 to 31 May 2008, 186 100 inbound visitors arrived in Australia to attend conferences or conventions, or about 4 per cent of the total intake (Business Events Australia 2008). Weber and Ladkin (2003) note the impetus for the international component of this sector that was created by the 2000 Sydney Olympics but cite competition from ultra-efficient regional competitors such as Singapore and Hong Kong as a major contemporary challenge.

Sport

Several additional purposes that qualify a traveller as a tourist are less numerically important than the three largest categories outlined above, though potentially more important in certain destinations or regions. Sport-related tourism involves the travel and activities of athletes, trainers and others associated with competitions and training, as well as the tourist spectators attending sporting events and other sport-related venues. High-profile sporting mega-events such as the Olympic Games and the World Cup of football not only confer a large amount of visibility on the host destination and participating teams, but also involve many participants and generate substantial tourist expenditure and other 'spin-off' effects. For example, the 2003 America's Cup yachting competition hosted by Auckland generated about $500 million in net additional expenditure within New Zealand and a similar value-added effect within the national economy. These Cup-related revenues sustained the equivalent of 9360 years of full-time employment (Market Economics Ltd. 2003). Sporting competitions in some cases have also been used to promote cross-cultural understanding and peaceful relations between countries and cultures (see chapter 9).

Spirituality

Spiritual motivation includes travel for religious purposes. Pilgrimage activity constitutes by far the largest form of tourism travel in Saudi Arabia due to the annual pilgrimage or Hajj to Mecca by several million Muslims from around the world. Religious travel is also extremely important in India's domestic tourism sector (Singh 2004). One festival alone, the six-week Maha Kumbh Mela, drew an estimated 70 million Hindu pilgrims to the city of Allahabad in 2001. It is commonly regarded as the world's biggest event of any type.

More ambiguous is the **secular pilgrimage**, which blurs the boundary between the sacred and the profane (Digance 2003). The term has been applied to diverse tourist experiences, including commemorative ANZAC events at the Gallipoli battle site in Turkey (Hall 2002), as well as visits to Graceland (Elvis Presley's mansion in Memphis, Tennessee) (Rigby 2001) and sporting halls of fame (Gammon 2004). Secular pilgrimage is often associated with the New Age movement, which is variably described as a legitimate or pseudoreligious phenomenon. Digance (2003) describes how the central Australian Uluru monolith has become a contested sacred site, in part because of conflicts between Aboriginal and New Age pilgrims seeking privileged access to the site.

Health

Tourism for health purposes includes visits to spas, although such travel is often merged with pleasure/leisure motivations. More explicitly health related is travel undertaken to receive medical treatment that is unavailable or too expensive in the participant's home country or region. Such travel is often described as **medical tourism** (Chambers & McIntosh 2008). Cuba, for example, has developed a specialty in providing low-cost surgery for foreign clients. In Australia, the Gold Coast of Queensland is building a reputation as a centre for cosmetic surgery and other elective medical procedures. Many Americans travel to Mexico to gain access to unconventional treatments that are unavailable in the United States. While often perceived as a lucrative opportunity to capitalise on aging populations in the major tourist-generating regions, the potentially destabilising effects of such activity on some destination health systems have also been emphasised (see Contemporary issue: Health concerns about medical tourism in India).

contemporary issue

HEALTH CONCERNS ABOUT MEDICAL TOURISM IN INDIA

A growing number of international tourists are travelling to India in order to access an array of medical services that are technologically sophisticated, relatively inexpensive, and available almost on demand. Advocates of this sector, including the Indian government, enthuse over the expectation that it will stimulate the inbound tourism industry and generate more than $1 billion by 2012. National pride and incentives to further develop the country's medical technology and infrastructure are additional factors cited in its support. Critics, however, point out that the related activity and benefits are almost entirely confined to the private health care system. The public health system, in contrast, is characterised by declining standards, overcrowding, and poor working conditions. Although chronic underfunding is a major underlying factor, with India ranking among the lowest in the world in terms of public health spending, medical tourism is also implicated in the growing disparity between the public and private health care systems. For example, many physicians and technicians trained at public expense in India's universities are diverted to profit-seeking private institutions where wages and working conditions are superior due to the expenditures of wealthy foreign patients. Private institutions are also subsidised by a supportive government through concessions to physicians establishing private clinics and nursing homes, the provision of land at low rates, and tax exemptions on imported drugs and equipment from taxes, all of which further support medical tourism (Sengupta & Nundy 2005).

A further negative consequence of medical tourism is the incentive it provides to potential organ donors. It has been claimed, for example, that kidneys for 'transplant tourists' in the city of Chennai were supplied by victims of the 2004 tsunami, and that more than 2000 kidney transplants involving foreign recipients had been performed in neighbouring Pakistan by 2007 (Budiani-Saberi & Delmonico 2008). While the ethical merits of a 'willing buyer/willing provider' arrangement in such situations can be argued, it is often the case that the 'willing provider' is financially desperate due to poverty or indebtedness and thus is forced to sell a kidney. More disturbing is the possibility of a black market in which valuable body organs are harvested from unwilling victims.

Study

Study, and formal education more broadly, is a category that most people do not intuitively associate with tourism, even though it is a qualifying UNWTO criterion. Australia, New Zealand, Canada, the United States and the United Kingdom are especially active in attracting foreign students. Although participant numbers may not appear large in relation to the three main categories of purpose, students have a substantial relative impact on host countries because of the prolonged nature of their stay and the large expenditures (including tuition) that they make during these periods of study. For example, international students accounted for about 7 per cent of all inbound arrivals to Australia in 2007–08 but 32 per cent of all visitor-nights. Accordingly, the average expenditure in Australia by international students was $13 800, compared with $2350 for inbound 'holiday' tourists (TRA 2008b). Foreign students also benefit Australia by attracting visitors from their home country during their period of study, and by spending money in regional cities such as Ballarat and Albury that otherwise attract few international tourists.

Multipurpose tourism

If every tourist had only a single reason for travelling, the classification of tourists by purpose would be a simple task. However, many if not most tourist trips involve **multipurpose travel**, which can be confusing for data classification and analysis. The current Australian situation illustrates the problem. Departing visitors are asked to state their subsidiary travel purposes as well as their primary purpose for travelling to Australia. It is on the basis of the primary purpose alone that table 2.1 is derived, and policy and management decisions subsequently made. These data, however, may not accurately reflect the actual experiences of the tourists.

Take, for example, a hypothetical inbound tourist who, at the conclusion of a two-week visit, states 'business' as the primary trip purpose, and pleasure/holiday and VFR as other purposes. The actual trip of that business tourist may have consisted of con-ference attendance in Sydney over a three-day period, a three-day visit with friends in the nearby town of Bathurst and the remaining eight days at a resort in Port Douglas. While the primary purpose was business, this is clearly not reflected in the amount of time (and probably expenditure) that the tourist spent on each category of purpose. Yet without the conference, the tourist might not have visited Australia at all. On the other hand, if the delegate had no friends in Australia, the country might not have been as attractive as a destination, and the tourist might have decided not to attend the conference in the first place. Thus, there is an interplay among the various travel purposes, and it is difficult to establish a meaningful 'main' purpose.

A further complication is that people in the same travel group may have different purposes for their trip. Our hypothetical conference delegate, for example, may be accompanied by a spouse who engages solely in pleasure/holiday activities. However, most surveys do not facilitate such multipurpose responses from different members of the same party. Rather, they assume that a single main purpose applies to all members of that group.

Major tourist categories

This chapter has earlier demonstrated that tourists can be either international or domestic, and also be either stayovers or excursionists. The combination of these spa-tial and temporal dimensions produces **four major types of tourist** (see figure 2.3) and these categories account for all tourist possibilities, assuming that the appropriate purposive criteria are also met:

1. **International stayovers** are tourists who remain in a destination outside their usual country of residence for at least one night (e.g. a Brisbane resident who spends a two-week adventure tour in New Zealand).
2. **International excursionists** stay in this destination without experiencing at least one overnight stay (e.g. a Brisbane resident on a cruise who spends six hours in Wellington).
3. **Domestic stayovers** stay for at least one night in a destination that is within their own usual country of residence, but outside of a 'usual environment' that is often defined by specific distance thresholds from the home site (e.g. a Brisbane resident who spends one week on holidays in Melbourne, travels to Perth for an overnight business trip or travels to the Gold Coast to spend a day at the beach).
4. **Domestic excursionists** undertake a similar trip, but without staying overnight (e.g. a Brisbane resident who flies to and from Melbourne on the same day).

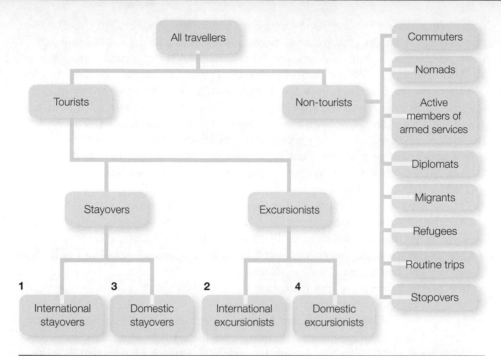

FIGURE 2.3 Four types of tourist within a broad travel context

UNWTO terminology

The above tourist terms, while commonly used in the literature, do not match the terms that are used by the UNWTO. As indicated in figure 2.4, the UNWTO refers to all tourists as 'visitors' and reserves the word 'tourist' for the specific category of stayovers. In addition, those who are described as excursionists in this text are classified as 'same-day visitors' by the UNWTO. We reject this terminology as being counterintuitive. If interpreted literally, cruise ship excursionists and cross-border shoppers are excluded in any reference to the 'tourist'. They fall instead under the visitor subcategory of 'same-day visitor'. Nevertheless, students should be aware of the UNWTO terms, since they will be encountered in the many essential publications released by that organisation, and by governments who adhere to their terminology.

Tourist terms used in this textbook		Tourist terms used by the WTO
■ Tourists	=	Visitors
■ Stayovers	=	Tourists
■ Excursionists	=	Same-day visitors

FIGURE 2.4 Textbook and UNWTO tourist terminology

Stopovers

Stopovers are tourists or other travellers temporarily staying in a location while in transit to or from a destination region. The main criterion in international tourism that distinguishes a stopover from an inbound stayover or excursionist is that they normally do not clear customs or undergo any other border formalities that signify their 'official' presence in that location. To illustrate the point, a person travelling by air from Sydney to Toronto normally changes flights in Honolulu or Los Angeles. Most passengers disembark from the aeroplane in these transit nodes late at night, and wait in the transit lobby of the airport for three or four hours until it is time to board the aircraft for the second and final leg of this long-haul journey. These transit passengers are all stopovers. If, however, someone chooses to clear customs and spend a few hours shopping in Honolulu or Los Angeles, they would be classified as an international excursionist or stayover to the United States, depending on whether an 'overnight stay' was included.

The paradox in this situation is that most stopovers are indeed outbound tourists (unlike the other nontravelling categories), but are not classified as such from the perspective of the transit location. Several factors underlie this exclusion:

- there is the previously mentioned fact that such travellers do not clear border formalities and hence are not official visitors
- stopovers are not in the transit location by choice, although many may appreciate the opportunity to stretch their legs
- the economic impact of stopovers is usually negligible, with expenditures being restricted to the purchase of a few drinks, some food or a local newspaper.

Most stopover traffic occurs in the international airports of transportation hubs such as Honolulu, Singapore, Bangkok, Dubai and Frankfurt. In contrast, Australia's location and size result in limited stopover traffic. Singapore, whose Changi Airport provides diverse services to stopovers including city tours (which converts them to excursionists and future stayovers), illustrates an innovative management approach toward deriving maximum economic benefit from transit passengers.

Data problems

Inbound tourist arrival statistics should be treated with caution, especially if they are being used to identify temporal trends. This is in part because of the high margin of error that characterises older data in particular. For example, the UNWTO figure of 25 million international stayovers for 1950 (see table 3.1) is nothing more than a rough estimate, given the primitive data-collecting techniques of that era. Yet it is used as a baseline for calculating the relative growth in global tourist arrivals since then. At the scale of any individual country, this margin of error is amplified. More recent statistics have a smaller margin of error as a result of UNWTO initiatives to standardise definitions and data collection protocols. However, error still results from such things as inconsistencies from country to country in the collection and reporting of arrivals, expenditures and other tourism-related statistics. This is why UNWTO often adjusts country-level and aggregate arrival data from year to year and why only the statistics that are around five years old are stable.

Data-related problems are even more pronounced in domestic tourism statistics, owing in part to domestic tourist movements being difficult to monitor in most countries. Such statistics are often derived from the responses to surveys distributed at points of departure or solicited from a sample of households, from which broader national or state patterns are extrapolated. These surveys do not always employ appropriate survey design or sampling techniques (see chapter 12), though increasingly sophisticated computer-assisted techniques are being implemented by countries such as Australia and Canada that are committed to the effective development and management of their tourism industries (see Technology and tourism: A clearer picture of domestic tourism in Australia). At the subnational level, authorities sometimes rely on extremely unreliable information sources such as sign-in books provided at welcome centres, visitor bureaus or attractions. Attempts to compare domestic tourism in different domestic jurisdictions are impeded by the proliferation of idiosyncratic definitions.

——— technology and tourism

A CLEARER PICTURE OF DOMESTIC TOURISM IN AUSTRALIA

In 1998, the Domestic Tourism Monitor was replaced by the National Visitor Survey (NVS) as the primary source for obtaining information about Australian domestic travel. Since this time, the rapidly growing sophistication of computer-assisted technologies has allowed Tourism Research Australia (the research arm of Tourism Australia) to greatly enhance and expand its knowledge of such activity. Adhering to UNWTO definitions, the NVS uses random digit dialing to obtain an annual sample of 120 000 Australian resident adults who answer more than 70 questions related to overnight and day trips within Australia as well as outbound travel (TRA 2008a). An ever-improving Computer Assisted Telephone Interviewing system (or CATI) allows interviewers to read out by telephone the mostly multiple-choice questions that appear on the computer screen, efficiently key in responses which are then automatically coded into a database, and then rely on the computer to branch out to the next applicable question depending on what responses are given. The computer also assists with data verification and re-scheduling uncompleted interviews if required.

Aside from advantages of not having to canvas respondents door-to-door or by mail (which both tend to yield low response and high error and fabrication rates), CATI respondents are usually not aware of or put off by the involvement of computers, and are not frustrated by delays in the questioning, as long as trained interviewers are used. Standardised interviewing structures, moreover, minimise interviewer bias and allow for consistent and stipulated data outcomes which can be analysed immediately. Quota cells, for example, can be closed by CATI automatically, once the surveying has produced the desired number of female or foreign-born respondents. Alternatively, once the gender of the respondent is entered, the computer can automatically display all future questions using gender-sensitive wording. Disadvantages include the costs of providing effective training and adequate supervision as well as a central facility from which surveying is conducted. Computer system malfunctions, power failures and the incidence of households without a home phone are additional prohibiting factors.

■ ORIGIN REGION

The **origin region**, as a component of the tourism system, has been neglected by researchers and managers. No tourism system could evolve but for the generation of demand within the origin region, and more tourism-related activity occurs there than is usually recognised. For discussion purposes, it is useful to distinguish between the origin community and the origin government.

Origin community

Research into origin regions has concentrated on market segmentation and marketing (see chapters 6 and 7). Almost no attention, in contrast, has been paid to the impacts of tourism on the **origin community** even though there are numerous ways in which these impacts can occur. For example, some major origin cities can resemble ghost towns during long weekends or summer vacation periods, when a substantial number of residents travel to nearby beaches or mountains for recreational purposes. Local businesses may suffer as a result, while the broader local economy may be adversely affected over a longer period by the associated outflow of revenue. Conversely, local suppliers of travel-related goods and services, such as travel agencies, may thrive as a result of this tourist activity.

Significant effects can also be felt at the sociocultural level, wherein returning tourists are influenced by the fashions, food and music of various destinations. Such external cultural influences, of course, may be equally or more attributable to immigration and mass media, so the identification of tourism's specific role in disseminating these influences needs to be investigated. Other tangible impacts include the unintended introduction of diseases such as malaria and STDs (sexually transmitted diseases)(see Abdullah et al. 2004), or pathogens that can devastate the local farming sector. The role of the expanding global tourism system as a disseminator of such influences should not be underestimated. For example, of 209 cases of *Plasmodium vivax* malaria infection reported to the Royal Melbourne Hospital between early 1997 and mid-2001, 128 (61 per cent) were associated with Australian travellers who had visited high-risk regions such as the South Pacific, sub-Saharan Africa and Latin America (Elliott et al. 2004).

The formation of relationships between tourists and local residents also has potential consequences for origin communities. It is, for example, a common practice for male sex workers (i.e. 'beach boys') in Caribbean destinations such as the Dominican Republic to initiate romantic liaisons with inbound female tourists in the hope of migrating to a prosperous origin country like Canada or Italy (Herold, Garcia & DeMoya 2001). These examples demonstrate that at least some tourism management attention to origin regions is warranted, although another complicating variable is the extent to which the origin region also functions as a destination region, and is thus impacted by both returning and incoming tourists.

Origin government

The impacts of the **origin government** on the tourism system have also been largely ignored, in part because it is taken for granted in the more developed countries that citizens are free to travel wherever they wish (within reason). Yet this freedom is ultimately dependent on the willingness of origin national governments to tolerate a mobile citizenry. Even in democratic countries, some individuals have their passports seized to prevent them from travelling abroad. At a larger scale, prohibitions on the travel of US citizens to Cuba, imposed by successive US governments hostile to the regime of Fidel Castro, have effectively prevented the development of a major bilateral tourism system incorporating the two countries. In countries, such as North Korea, governed by totalitarian regimes, such restrictions are more normative. An extremely important development in this regard has been the liberalisation of outbound tourist flows by the government of China, which in recent years has dramatically increased the number of countries with approved destination status (ADS).

In effect, the role of origin governments can be likened to a safety valve that ultimately determines the energy (i.e. tourist flow) that is allowed into the system (see chapter 3). Outbound flows are also influenced by the various services that origin governments offer to residents travelling or intending to travel abroad. In addition to consular services for citizens who have experienced trouble, these services largely involve advice to potential travellers about risk factors that are present in other countries (see Breakthrough tourism: Cultivating smart Australian travellers through smartraveller.gov.au).

breakthrough tourism

CULTIVATING SMART AUSTRALIAN TRAVELLERS THROUGH SMARTRAVELLER.GOV.AU

The Australian government has long enjoyed a reputation for providing relevant and timely information to residents wishing to travel abroad, especially through the website of its foreign affairs department. In early 2007, the federal government sought to further improve its services with the launch of a four-year, $13 million campaign to publicise its new smartraveller.gov.au internet site. Aimed in particular at adventure tourists visiting high risk destinations, the site facilitates foreign travel by providing a gateway to all relevant services. The Travel Advisory section, for example, offers information about security and other risks for every foreign country, and rates each along a five-point security scale. (Figure 2.5 depicts the Summary of this information for Papua New Guinea as of August 2008.) Periodic Travel Bulletins supplement this with information about specific events such as the 2008 Beijing Summer Olympic Games and issues such as international scams and avian influenza. A particularly important function of smartraveller.gov. au is the online registration option, which advises the government of the registrant's presence in a particular country at a particular time. This allows the government to locate the tourist in the event of a family emergency at home or a crisis within the country visited, or to contact family if the traveller experiences problems. The site also emphasises the importance of travel insurance and allows the user to access guides advising how to purchase this. Various audio and video pieces on television and radio try to ensure that as many outbound Australians as possible will benefit from the available services.

SUMMARY

- We advise you to exercise a high degree of caution in Papua New Guinea because of the high levels of serious crime.
- Pay close attention to your personal security at all times and monitor the media for information about possible new safety or security risks.
- Crime rates are high in the capital Port Moresby and in other areas of Papua New Guinea, especially in Lae, Mt Hagen and other parts of the Highland provinces.
- Local land and compensation disputes occasionally lead to threats by landowners to close the Kokoda Track. When walking the Kokoda Track, Australians are advised to travel only with guides from reputable trekking companies. See the Local Travel section for more advice and information.
- Be a smart traveller. Before heading overseas:
  - organise comprehensive travel insurance and check what circumstances and activities are not covered by your policy
  - register your travel and contact details, so we can contact you in an emergency
  - subscribe to this travel advice to receive free email updates each time it's reissued.

FIGURE 2.5 Summary of security information for travellers to Papua New Guinea, as of 8 August 2008

Source: Commonwealth of Australia

Evidence of a broader attempt to educate Australians about responsible and sustainable travel is evident in the Children's Issues section, which includes information about child sex crime and other relevant concerns. The availability of additional sustainability information such as carbon footprint calculators and cultural sensitivity would further enhance Australia's image as an innovator in traveller awareness and education. Also meriting consideration is a monitored blogging option that would allow travellers to share their personal experiences with potential travellers and government, and for the questions of potential travellers to be posed to a broad audience for public response. Links to relevant media clips would also be useful for providing users with more detailed information about problems and crises that are occurring in a particular destination.

TRANSIT REGION

As with origin regions, few studies have explicitly recognised the importance of the **transit region** component of the tourism system. This neglect is due in part to its status as a space that the tourist must cross to reach the location that he or she really wants to visit. Reinforcing this negative connotation is the sense, common among tourists, that time spent on the journey to a destination is vacation time wasted. Transit passages, moreover, are often uncomfortable, as economy-class passengers on a long-haul flight will attest. Under more positive circumstances, however, the transit region can itself be a destination of sorts as illustrated by the Changi airport example in Singapore, which illustrates what McKercher and Tang (2004) describe as 'transit tourism'. This may also be the case, for example, if the journey involves a drive through spectacular scenery, or if the trip affords a level of comfort, novelty and/or activity that makes the transit experience comparable to that which is sought in a final destination.

As these examples illustrate, the distinction between transit and destination regions is not always clear (as in the use of the term 'touring'), given also that the tourist's itinerary within a destination region will probably include multiple transit experiences (see figure 2.2). An inbound tourist staying in Sydney, for example, may opt to visit a nearby National Park, which requires a one- or two-hour transit journey. In many instances a location can be important both as a transit and destination region. The Queensland city of Townsville, for instance, is an important transit stop on the road from Brisbane to Cairns, but it is also in itself an important emerging destination. The transit/destination distinction is even more ambiguous in cruise ship tourism, where the actual cruise is a major component of the travel experience and a 'destination' in its own right.

Management implications of transit regions

Once the status of a place as a transit node or region is determined, specific management implications become more apparent, such as the need to identify associated impacts. For airports, this frequently involves increased congestion that impedes the arrival and departure of stayovers. In highway transit situations, a major impact is the development of extensive motel (*mo*tor ho*tel*) strips along primary roads on the outskirts of even relatively small urban centres. A related management consideration is the extent to which the transit region can and wishes to evolve as a destination in its own right, a scenario that can be assisted by the presence of transit motels or airports.

Managers of destination regions also need to take into consideration the transit component of tourism systems when managing their own tourism sector. Pertinent issues include whether the destination is accessible through multiple or single transit routes and which modes of transportation provide access. Destinations that are accessible by only one route and mode (e.g. an isolated island served by a single airport and a single airline) are disadvantaged by being dependent on a single tourism 'lifeline'. However, this may be offset by the advantage of having all processing of visitors consolidated at a single location. A further consideration is the extent to which a transit link is fixed (as with a highway) and can be disrupted if associated infrastructure, such as a bridge, is put out of commission. In contrast to road-based travel, air journeys do not depend on infrastructure during the actual flight, and have greater scope for rerouting if a troublesome situation is encountered (e.g. a war breaking out in a fly-over country or adverse weather conditions).

Destination managers also need to consider the possibility that one or more locations along a transit route could become destinations themselves, and thus serve as **intervening opportunities** that divert visitors from the original destination. Cuba, for example, is currently little more than an incidental transit location in the United States-to-Jamaica tourism system due to the above-mentioned hostility of the US government towards the Castro regime. However, if the 2008 election of a Democratic president led to the re-opening of Cuba to US mass tourism, then the impact upon the Jamaican tourism sector could be devastating.

Effects of technology

Technological change has dramatically affected the character of transit regions. Faster aeroplanes and cars have reduced the amount of time required in the transit phase, thereby increasing the size of transit regions by making long-haul travel more feasible and comfortable. New aircraft models such as the Airbus A380 promise to radically re-shape the transit experience for travellers as well as airports, although its introduction has not been problem-free. Deliveries for the first aircraft were delayed for two years due to wiring and other problems, while not all major airports have strong or long enough runways, or properly configured gates, to accommodate these giants. The option of lounges and extra personal space in all classes (necessitated by competition with its rival Boeing), moreover, means that fuel savings from increased efficiency may be largely offset by lower passenger capacity.

Such aircraft also no longer require as many refuelling stops on long-haul flights, resulting in further reconfigurations to transit hubs and regions. Figure 2.6 shows that a flight from Sydney or Auckland to a North American port of entry prior to the 1980s required transit stops in Fiji (Nadi airport) and Hawaii (Honolulu). By the 1980s only one stopover landing was required — Hawaii on the flight to North America and Fiji on the return journey. By the mid-1990s such flights could be undertaken without any stopovers. The old routes were retained, but the overall effect has been the marginalisation of many former stopover points, a process that in some cases has had negative implications for their development as final destinations.

A similar marginalisation effect has resulted from the construction of limited access expressways in countries such as the United States, Canada and Australia. By diverting traffic from the old main highways, these expressways have forced the closure of many roadside motels that depended on travellers in transit. In the place of the traditional motel strip, clusters of large motels, usually dominated by major chains (such as Holiday Inn, Motel 6 and Comfort Inn) have emerged at strategic intersections readily accessible to the expressway. These clusters contribute to suburban sprawl by attracting affiliated services such as petrol stations and fast-food outlets. Another implication of technology is the exploitation of otherwise inaccessible areas as transit regions — for example, aeroplanes on the Sydney-to-Buenos Aires route fly over Antarctica (which may itself increase the attractiveness of the journey and thereby increase the volume of traffic).

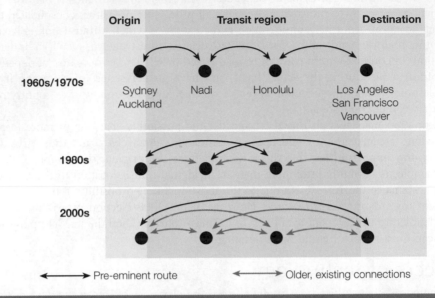

FIGURE 2.6 The evolution of the trans-Pacific travel system

In broad terms, the latter half of the twentieth century was the era in which the car and the aeroplane became pre-eminent, at the expense of the passenger ship and the passenger train (see chapter 3). Places that relied on the ship and the train, accordingly, have declined in importance as transit and destination regions (e.g. train stations and some ports), if they were unwilling or unable to compensate by developing their road or air access, or by catering to niche nostalgia-motivated markets.

■ DESTINATION REGION

The **destination region** is the geographical component of the tourism system that has received by far the greatest scrutiny. During the era of the advocacy platform, this attention focused on the destination-based tourism industry. Researchers were then concerned largely with determining how the industry could effectively attract and satisfy a profit-generating clientele. During the period of the cautionary and adaptancy platforms, the research emphasis shifted towards the identification of host community impacts and strategies for ensuring that these were more positive than negative. More of a balance between industry and community is apparent in the present knowledge-based platform, based on a growing realisation that the interests of the two components are not mutually exclusive.

The distribution of destination regions changed dramatically during the latter half of the twentieth century, and is constantly being reconfigured, vertically as well as horizontally, through technological change and consumer interest. In the vertical reconfiguration, **space tourism** is now a reality since the American multimillionaire Dennis Tito went into space aboard a Russian Soyuz capsule in 2001 as a tourist (Duval 2007). Relatively large numbers of space tourists have already signed up for or taken much less expensive 'parabolic flights' in which zero-gravity conditions are maintained briefly prior to descent. At the other end of the vertical spectrum, several underwater hotels were under construction as of late 2008, the best known being the Hydropolis facility in Dubai.

Change in the configuration of destination regions is the result of internal factors such as active promotional efforts and decisions to upgrade infrastructure, but also external factors associated with the broader tourism system or external environments. An example is the emergence of consumer demand for 3S (i.e. sea, sand, sun) tourism after World War II, which led to the large-scale tourism development of hitherto isolated tropical islands in the Caribbean, South Pacific and Indian Ocean (see chapter 4). Concurrently, the opening of these islands to mass tourism could not have taken place without radical developments in aircraft technology. One implication of this external dependency, and of systems theory in general, is that destinations can effectively manage and control only a very small proportion of the forces and variables that affect their tourism sectors. Even the most effectively managed destinations can be destroyed by the negative intervention of forces over which they have no control (see the case study at the end of this chapter).

Destination communities

Even under the advocacy platform, destination residents were recognised as an important component of the tourism system because of the labour they provide, and in some situations because of their status as cultural tourism attractions in their own right. However, only in rare situations when that platform was dominant was the **destination community** recognised as an influential stakeholder in its own right, on par with industry or government. The increasing recognition of host communities as such has arisen from increased awareness of at least three factors:

* local residents have the most to lose or gain from tourism of any stakeholder group in the tourism system
* discontented local residents can negatively affect the tourism industry by fostering a hostile destination image among tourists (see chapter 9)
* local residents possess knowledge about their area that can assist the planning management and marketing of tourism, as through interpretation of local historical and cultural attractions that benefits from their deep knowledge.

For all these reasons, host communities are now often included as equal partners (at least in rhetoric) in the management of tourist destinations, and not seen as just a convenient source of labour or local colour, or a group whose interests are already represented by government.

Destination governments

If origin governments can be compared with a safety valve that releases energy into the tourism system, then the **destination government** can be likened to a safety valve that controls the amount of energy absorbed by the destination components of that system. This analogy is especially relevant at the international level, where national governments dictate the conditions under which inbound tourists are allowed entry (see chapter 4). To a greater or lesser extent, countries exert control over the number of tourist arrivals by requiring visas or passports from potential visitors, and by restricting the locations through which access to the country can be gained. Most countries, in principle and practice, encourage tourist arrivals because of the foreign exchange that they generate. However, the governments of a few countries (Bhutan and North Korea are the most notable examples) have made conscious decisions to drastically limit entries because of the perception that tourists are a cultural threat (as in the case of Bhutan) or political threat (as in the case of North Korea).

In addition to this entry control function, destination governments also explicitly influence the development and management of their tourism products through support for tourism-related agencies. These include tourism ministries (either tourism by itself or as part of a multisectoral portfolio) that are concerned with overall policy and direction, and tourism boards, which focus on destination marketing. Less prevalent are agencies that focus on research, such as Tourism Research Australia. Many high-profile tourist destinations, such as the United States and Germany, have no federal-level portfolio emphasising tourism. This reflects to some extent the residual negative perceptions of tourism discussed in chapter 1, but also political systems that devolve responsibilities such as tourism to the state level. Thus, while tourism promotion in the US at the federal level is negligible, states such as Florida and Hawaii operate enormous tourism marketing entities. In Australia, well articulated federal structures are complemented by similarly sophisticated state bodies such as Tourism Queensland.

■ THE TOURISM INDUSTRY

The **tourism industry** may be defined as the sum of the industrial and commercial activities that produce goods and services wholly or mainly for tourist consumption. Broad categories commonly associated with the tourism industry include accommodation, transportation, food and beverage, tour operations, travel agencies, commercial attractions and merchandising of souvenirs and other goods purchased mainly by tourists. These activities are discussed in chapter 5, but several preliminary observations are in order. First, the tourism industry permeates the tourism system more than any other component other than the tourists themselves. However, as depicted in figure 2.7, segments of the industry vary considerably in their distribution within the tourism system. Not all spatial components of the system, moreover, accommodate an equal share of the industry. Destination regions account for most of the tourism industry, whereas origin regions are represented in significant terms only by travel agencies and some aspects of transportation and merchandising. The inclusion of industry into tourism management considerations is therefore imperative at the destination level, but less so in origin regions.

Categories	Origin regions	Transit regions	Destination regions
Travel agencies	■	◆	◆
Transportation	●	■	■
Accommodation	◆	■	■
Food and beverages	◆	■	■
Tour operators	●	●	■
Attractions	◆	◆	■
Merchandisers	●	◆	■

■ Major   ● Minor   ◆ Negligible

FIGURE 2.7 Status of major tourism industry sectors within the tourism system

A confounding element in the above definition of the tourism industry is the extent to which various commercial goods and services are affiliated with tourism. At one extreme almost all activity associated with travel agencies and tour operators is tourism-related. Far more ambiguous is the transportation industry, much of which involves the movement of goods (some related to tourism) or commuters, migrants and other travellers who are not tourists. Great difficulties in particular are encountered when attempting to isolate the tourism component in automobile-related transportation. Similar problems face the accommodation sector despite its clearer link to tourism, since many local residents purchase space at nearby hotels for wedding receptions, meetings and other functions. It is largely because of these complications that no Standard Industrial Classification (SIC) code has ever been allocated to tourism (see figure 1.2).

CHAPTER REVIEW

The complexities of tourism can be organised for analytical and management purposes by applying a systems perspective to the topic. A basic whole systems approach to tourism incorporates a number of interdependent components, including origin, transit and destination regions, the tourists themselves and the tourism industry. This system, in turn, is influenced by and influences various physical, political, social and other external environments. The challenge of managing a destination is compounded by this complexity. The tourist component of the system is defined by spatial, temporal and purposive parameters, and these lead to the identification of four major tourist types: international and domestic stayovers, and international and domestic excursionists. Recreation and leisure are the single most important purposes for tourism travel, followed more or less equally by visits to friends and relatives, and business. There are also many qualifying minor purposes including education, sport, health and pilgrimage. Despite such definitional clarifications, serious problems are still encountered when defining tourists and collecting tourist-related data, especially at the domestic level. In terms of the geography of tourism systems, origin and transit regions are vital but neglected components of the tourism system in terms of the research that has been conducted. Much greater attention has been focused on the destination region and the tourism industry. Important preliminary observations with regard to the latter include its concentration within the destination region, and the difficulty in isolating the tourism component in many related industries such as transportation.

■ SUMMARY OF KEY TERMS

Basic whole tourism system an application of a systems approach to tourism, wherein tourism is seen as consisting of three geographical components (origin, transit and destination regions), tourists and a tourism industry, embedded within a modifying external environment that includes parallel political, social, physical and other systems

Destination community the residents of the destination region

Destination government the government of the destination region

Destination region the places to which the tourist is travelling

Domestic excursionists tourists who stay within their own country for less than one night

Domestic stayovers tourists who stay within their own country for at least one night

Domestic tourist a tourist whose itinerary is confined to their usual country of residence

Excursionist a tourist who spends less than one night in a destination region

Four major types of tourist an inclusive group of tourist categories that combines the spatial and temporal components, and assumes adherence to the qualifying purposes of travel

Inbound tourists international tourists arriving from another country

International excursionists tourists who stay less than one night in another country

International stayovers tourists who stay at least one night in another country

International tourist a tourist who travels beyond their usual country of residence

Intervening opportunities places, often within transit regions, that develop as tourist destinations in their own right and subsequently have the potential to divert tourists from previously patronised destinations

Long-haul tourists variably defined as tourists taking trips outside of the world region where they reside, or beyond a given number of flying time hours

Medical tourism travel for the purpose of obtaining medical treatment that is unavailable or too expensive in the participant's region of origin

MICE an acronym combining meetings, incentives, conventions and exhibitions; a form of tourism largely associated with business purposes

Multipurpose travel travel undertaken for more than a single purpose

Origin community the residents of the origin region

Origin government the government of the origin region

Origin region the region (e.g. country, state, city) from which the tourist originates, also referred to as the market or generating region

Outbound tourists international tourists departing from their usual country of residence

Secular pilgrimage travel for spiritual purposes that are not linked to conventional religions

Short-haul tourists variably defined as tourists taking trips within the world region where they reside, or within a given number of flying time hours

Space tourism an emerging form of tourism that involves travel by and confinement within aircraft or spacecraft to high altitude locations where sub-orbital effects such as zero-gravity or earth curvature viewing can be experienced

Stayover a tourist who spends at least one night in a destination region

Stopovers travellers who stop in a location in transit to another destination; they normally do not clear customs and are not considered tourists from the transit location's perspective

System a group of interrelated, interdependent and interacting elements that together form a single functional structure

Tourism industry the sum of the industrial and commercial activities that produce goods and services wholly or mainly for tourist consumption

Transit region the places and regions that tourists pass through as they travel from origin to destination region

Travel purpose the reason why people travel; in tourism, these involve recreation and leisure, visits to friends and relatives (VFR), business, and less dominant purposes such as study, sport, religion and health

■ QUESTIONS

1. (a) Why and how in practical terms is a systems approach useful in managing the tourism sector?
   (b) How does this approach complement the knowledge-based platform?
2. (a) What are the main external natural and cultural environments that interact with the tourism system?
   (b) What can destination managers do to minimise the negative impacts of these systems?
3. What management strategies could a small South Pacific island implement in order to derive maximum economic benefits from the presence of cruise ship excursionists?
4. (a) Why is it important to make formal distinctions between the 'tourist' and other types of traveller?
   (b) What associated problems may be encountered when attempting to determine whether a particular traveller is a tourist or not?

5. (a) Why are domestic tourists relatively neglected by researchers and government in comparison to international tourists?
   (b) What can be done to reverse this neglect?
6. (a) To what extent are the various travel purposes discretionary in nature?
   (b) What implications does this have for the management and marketing of the main types of tourism?
7. (a) What are the advantages and disadvantages of adding a blogging feature to the smartraveller.gov.au website that is used by the Australian government to inform and educate Australian outbound tourists?
   (b) How could such a blogging feature be designed to ensure that the advantages are maximised?
8. (a) How are origin regions influenced by returning outbound tourists?
   (b) How can origin regions reduce the negative impacts of returning outbound tourists?
9. What management issues will need to be addressed as space tourism becomes increasingly popular?

▪ EXERCISES

1. Write a 1000-word report in which you:
   (a) describe the positive and negative impacts that four external systems (e.g. agriculture, mining, banking) have had on the tourism system in your home country or city, and
   (b) describe and critically assess the reaction (or non-reaction) of the applicable national or local tourism organisation in that time.
2. (a) Have each class member define their most recent experience as a tourist, in terms of which of the four categories in figure 2.3 it falls under, and also which purpose or purposes as outlined in 'Travel purpose' section.
   (b) Describe the overall patterns that emerge from this exercise.
   (c) Identify any difficulties that emerged in defining each of these tourist experiences.

▪ FURTHER READING

Digance, J. 2003. 'Pilgrimage at Contested Sites'. *Annals of Tourism Research* **30: 143–59.** A useful perspective of this article is the interplay at Uluru between the interests of secular pilgrims and traditional Aboriginal pilgrims, both of whom believe that they should have privileged access. Relevant management considerations are discussed.

Dowling, R. (Ed.) 2006. *Cruise Ship Tourism.* **Wallingford, UK: CABI.** This compilation of 38 chapters provides the most thorough academic investigation of the cruise ship industry to date, with sections devoted to demand and marketing, destinations and products, industry issues, and impacts.

Glaesser, D. 2003. *Crisis Management in the Tourism Industry.* **Sydney: Butterworth-Heinemann.** This is one of the first textbooks to focus systematically on the management of crises within the tourism sector. The sphere of 'crisis' is defined, methods of analysis are discussed and crisis management instruments are identified and evaluated.

Raj, R. & Morpeth, N. (Eds) 2007. *Religious Tourism and Pilgrimage Festivals Management.* **Wallingford, UK: CABI.** International case studies representing major world religions are featured in this compilation, which considers the management implications and issues associated with pilgrimages and other forms of religion-based tourism.

Ritchie, B. & Adair, D. (Eds) 2004. *Sport Tourism: Interrelationships, Impacts and Issues.* **Clevedon, UK: Channel View.** Fourteen chapters in this edited book cover diverse sport topics related to winter activity, policy, museums, event leverage, secular pilgrimage, host community reactions and urban renewal.

— case study

A PERFECT STORM IN AUSTRALIAN TOURISM

During mid-2008, the Australian tourism industry faced crisis conditions caused by an unprecedented combination of factors both internal and external to the sector. Inbound tourists, for example, increased just 1 per cent in the period from 1 April 2007 to 31 March 2008 (TRA 2008b), well below the 6 per cent increase experienced globally during the same period (UNWTO 2008). Notable were 13 per cent and 7 per cent declines, respectively, in the crucial Japanese and UK markets (TRA 2008b). In domestic tourism, the number of overnight trips by Australians within Australia increased by 2 per cent, but there was no change in the number of total visitor-nights (TRA 2008a). Adding insult to injury, Australians continued to travel abroad in ever-larger numbers, with 4.9 million taking an overseas trip in 2007 — a 9 per cent increase over 2006 and an 18 per cent increase in related expenditures (TRA 2008a).

Various factors internal to the tourism industry partly explain this poor performance, including international and domestic flight curtailments by QANTAS, and the generally poor assessment given to the controversial 'Where the Bloody Hell Are You?' international marketing campaign. Most of the blame, however, has been directed toward factors external to tourism. Prominent among these is the strong performance of the Australian dollar against international currencies, and the US dollar in particular. From 77 cents in December 2006, the Australian dollar rose to 85 cents against the latter in September 2007 and 98 cents in July 2008, making overseas travel relatively more affordable to at least some overseas destinations. The strong dollar, in turn, has been associated with a vibrant primary sector (especially mining) stimulated by trade with the rapidly expanding Chinese economy.

A second major factor is escalating oil prices, which have dramatically increased the price of petrol while stimulating concurrent inflationary and recessionary effects within the economy as a whole. The Future Fuels Forum (CSIRO 2008) suggests that the 'real' (i.e. adjusted for inflation) price of petrol in Australia could rise by 300 per cent between 2007 and 2018 if alternative energy sources are not mobilised to replace declining oil supplies. A third factor is declining consumer confidence caused in part by the inflation/recession effect but also high interest rates that make mortgage and other loan payments increasingly expensive (although this did not yet seem to have a dampening effect on overseas travel by Australians as of 2008). By the end of July 2008, Australian cumulative household debt was 177 per cent of GDP, almost a world record, and indicative according to some analysts that Australia was facing a worse financial crisis than that experienced by the US (Evans-Pritchard 2008).

While the strong Australian dollar has contributed to the weak inbound performance by making Australia more expensive for some foreign markets, concerns about climate change may also be emerging as an increasingly influential factor. In early 2008, the director of the Tourism and Transport Forum, a lobby group for those sectors, suggested that the industry needed to move rapidly to change growing perceptions in major market regions that long-haul travel is contributing significantly to the greenhouse gas emissions that are exacerbating global warming and thus threatening the global environment (Ketchell 2008). It was hoped as well that positive publicity for Australia would be generated by the 2008 release of the epic movie 'Australia', which features iconic actors such as Nicole Kidman and has been adapted for use in a major international marketing campaign (Semuels 2008). Less dramatic are suggestions by the Australian Tourism Export Council (a lobby group for the inbound tourism sector) that tax break incentives be offered on domestic tourism travel expenses, a strategy that had positive effects when it was used in Australia during 2001 after the terrorist attacks in the US (Hoffman 2008). The Council also supported a formal accreditation process to ensure quality control within the tourism industry, and was critical of government moves to increase tourism-related fees in a time of crisis. These included an increase in the departure tax from $38 to $47 in early 2008 and increases in visa processing fees, which are alleged to continue a federal government tradition of 'milking' the inbound tourism sector while giving preferential treatment to the mining and farming sectors which, unlike tourism, have had their exports exempted from the GST (Goods & Services Tax) (ATEC 2008).

QUESTIONS

1. Write a 1000-word report in which you:
   (a) compare the inbound arrival statistics for Australia and New Zealand over the 2006-2008 period, and
   (b) list and assess the factors that might help to account for the discrepancies
2. (a) Describe in class discussion the extent to which current petrol prices have affected your own tourist travel behaviour.
   (b) What cumulative patterns emerge from the class?
   (c) What measures could be taken personally and by the government to stimulate your tourism-related travel?
3. In class, list and critique the measures that could be pursued by the Australian tourism industry to:
   (a) increase the number and visitor-nights of inbound tourism
   (b) increase the number and visitor-nights of Australian domestic tourists
   (c) decrease the number of outbound Australian tourists.

CHAPTER 3

THE EVOLUTION AND GROWTH OF TOURISM

LEARNING OBJECTIVES

After studying this chapter, you should be able to:

1. describe the main characteristics and types of premodern tourism in the 'Western' tradition

2. explain the basic distinctions and similarities between premodern and modern tourism

3. identify the role of Thomas Cook and the Industrial Revolution in bringing about the modern era of tourism

4. outline the growth trend of international tourism arrivals since 1950

5. discuss the primary factors that have stimulated the demand for tourism during this period of time, and especially since 1950

6. describe global stages of economic development and associate these stages with evolving patterns of tourism demand and behaviour

7. identify the additional social, demographic, technological and political forces that are positively and negatively associated with increased tourism demand.

■ INTRODUCTION

The previous chapter considered tourism from a systems approach and described the spatial, temporal and purposive criteria that distinguish international and domestic tourists from other travellers and from each other. Management-related observations were also made about the origin, transit and destination components of the tourism system. Chapter 3 focuses on the historical development of tourism in the 'Western' or Eurocentric tradition and describes the 'push' factors that have stimulated the demand for tourism especially since the mid-twentieth century.

The following section outlines **premodern tourism**, which is defined for the purposes of this textbook as the period prior to approximately AD 1500 (figure 3.1). Its purpose is to show that while premodern tourism had its own distinctive character, there are also many similarities with modern tourism. Recognition of these timeless impulses and characteristics is valuable to the tourism manager, as they are factors that must be taken into consideration in any contemporary or future situation involving tourism. Moreover, modern tourism would not have been possible without the precedents of Mesopotamia, the Nile and Indus valleys, ancient Greece and Rome, the Dark Ages and the Middle Ages. The 'Early modern tourism (1500–1950)' section considers the early modern era, which links the premodern to the contemporary period through the influence of the Renaissance and the Industrial Revolution. The 'Contemporary tourism (1950 onwards)' section introduces contemporary mass tourism, while the section that follows describes the major economic, social, demographic, technological and political factors that have stimulated the demand for tourism during this era. Australian tourism participation trends are then considered briefly, as well as the future growth prospects of global tourism based on the factors discussed in this chapter.

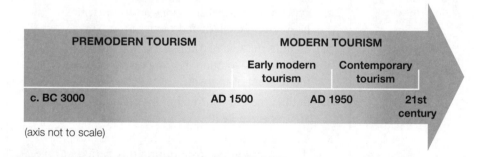

FIGURE 3.1 Tourism timelines

■ PREMODERN TOURISM

Mesopotamia, Egypt and the Indus Valley

Mesopotamia, or the 'land between the rivers' (situated approximately in modern-day Iraq), is known as the 'Cradle of Civilisation' and the first place to experience tourism. The factors that gave rise to civilisation, and hence to emergent tourism systems, include the availability of a permanent water supply (the Tigris and Euphrates rivers), rich alluvial soils (deposited during the annual flooding of these waterways), a warm climate and a central location between Asia, Africa and Europe, all of which contributed to the development of agriculture. For the first time in human history, hunting and gathering societies were replaced by permanent settlements cultivating the same plots of land year after year. Surplus food production was a critical outcome of this process, as it fostered the formation of wealth and the emergence of a small **leisure class** of priests, warriors and others that did not have to worry continually about its day-to-day survival.

The availability of sufficient **discretionary time** and **discretionary income** was the most important factor that enabled members of this leisured elite to engage in tourism. Moreover, Mesopotamia was the birthplace of many fundamental inventions and innovations that heralded both the demand and ability to travel for tourism-related purposes. These included the wheel, the wagon, money, the alphabet, domesticated animals such as the horse, and roads. Early cities (another Mesopotamian invention) such as Ur and Nippur were apparently overcrowded and uncomfortable at the best of times, and these inventions allowed the elite to escape them whenever possible. Also critical was the imposition of government structure and civil order over the surrounding countryside, that provided a foundation for the development of destination and transit regions (Casson 1994).

Egypt

Civilisation gradually spread from Mesopotamia westward to the Nile Valley (in modern-day Egypt) and eastward to the Indus Valley (in modern-day Pakistan), where similar physical environments and factors enabled additional tourism travel. Ancient Egypt provides some of the earliest explicit evidence of pleasure tourism. An inscription, carved into the side of one of the lesser known pyramids and dated 1244 BC, is among the earliest examples of tourist graffiti (Casson 1994). This and other monuments of the Nile Valley attracted religious and ceremonial tourists as well as the simply curious. Numerous inscriptions from ancient Egypt also describe the acquisition of souvenirs, suggesting that this, along with the urge to leave behind some physical indication of one's presence through graffiti, is an ancient human impulse that long predates the modern era.

Ancient Greece and Rome

Tourism in ancient Greece is most associated with national festivals such as the **Olympic Games**, where residents of the Greek city–states gathered every four years to hold religious ceremonies and compete in athletic events and artistic performances. The participants and spectators at this festival, estimated to number in the tens of thousands, would have had little difficulty in meeting the modern criteria for international stayovers. Accordingly, the game site at Olympia can be considered as one of the oldest specialised, though periodic, tourist **resorts**. The Games themselves are one of the first recorded examples of sport and event tourism and the precursor to the modern Olympics (Toohey & Veal 2007).

The transit process in ancient Greece was not pleasant or easy. Although a sacred truce was called during the major festivals, tourists were targeted by either highway robbers or pirates, depending on their mode of travel. Roads were primitive and accommodation, if available, was rudimentary, unsanitary and often dangerous. It is useful to point out that the word 'travel' is derived from the French noun *travail*, which translates into English as 'hard work'. As with the Mesopotamians and Egyptians, the proportion of ancient Greeks who could and did travel as tourists was effectively restricted to a small elite. However, the propensity to engage in tourism was socially sanctioned by the prevalent philosophy of the culture (applicable at least to the elite), who valued leisure time for its own sake as an opportunity to engage in artistic, intellectual and athletic pursuits (Veal & Lynch 2006).

Rome

With its impressive technological, economic and political achievements, ancient Rome (which peaked between 200 BC and AD 200) was able to achieve unprecedented levels of tourism activity that would not be reached again for another 1500 years. An underlying factor was the large population of the Roman Empire. While the elite class was only a fraction of the 200 million-strong population, it constituted a large absolute number of potential tourists. These travellers had a large selection of destination choices, given the size of the Empire, the high level of stability and safety achieved during the *Pax Romana* (Roman Peace) of its peak period, and the remarkably sophisticated network of Roman military roads (many of which are still used today) and associated rest stops. By AD 100 the Roman road network extended over 80 000 kilometres.

The Roman tourism experience is surprisingly modern in its resonance. Fuelled by ample discretionary time and wealth, the propensity of the Roman elite to travel on pleasure holidays (an innovation introduced by Rome) gave rise to an 'industry' of sorts that supplied souvenirs, guidebooks, transport, guides and accommodation. The number of specialised tourism sites and destinations also increased substantially. Famous Roman resorts included the town of Pompeii (destroyed by the eruption of Mount Vesuvius in ad 79), the spas of the appropriately named town of Bath (in Britain), and the beach resort of Tiberius, on the Sea of Galilee. These three sites of ancient tourism are now popular tourist attractions in the contemporary era, and ones that can be authentically presented through modern virtual reality technology (Vlahakis et al. 2002).

Second homes, or *villas*, were an important mode of retreat in the rural hinterlands of Rome and other major cities. Wealthy Romans often owned villas in a seaside location as well as the interior, to escape the winter cold and summer heat, respectively, of the cities. Villas were clustered so thickly around the Bay of Naples during the first century ad that this area can legitimately be described as one of the earliest resort regions. For Romans wealthy enough to travel a long distance, the historical sites of earlier cultures, especially those of the Greeks, Trojans and Egyptians, held the most interest. This is partly because of cultural connections, but also because sites such as the Pyramids were already ancient during the time of the Roman Empire. In addition, Casson (1994) maintains that the ancient ruins were popular due to the opportunities for acquiring souvenirs, including pieces of the structures themselves. It is apparent then that issues of ecological and cultural sustainability resonate even in ancient times.

The Dark Ages and Middle Ages

The decline and collapse of the Roman Empire during the fifth century AD severely eroded the factors that facilitated the development of tourism during the Roman era. Travel infrastructure deteriorated, the size of the elite classes and urban areas declined dramatically, and the relatively safe and open Europe of the Romans was replaced by a proliferation of warring semi-states and lawless frontiers as barbarian tribes occupied what was left of the Roman Empire. Justifiably, this period (c. 500–1100) is commonly referred to as the **Dark Ages**. The insularity to which Europe descended during this period is evident in contemporary world maps that feature wildly distorted cartographic images dominated by theological themes (e.g. Jerusalem at the centre of the map), grotesque characters and oversized town views. These busy and cluttered maps reveal no practical information to the traveller.

The social, economic and political situation in Europe recovered sufficiently by the end of the eleventh century that historians distinguish the emergence of the **Middle Ages** around this time (c. 1100–1500). Associated tourism phenomena include the Christian **pilgrimage**, stimulated by the construction of the great cathedrals and the consolidation of the Roman Catholic Church as a dominant power base and social influence in Europe (see figure 3.2). The pilgrimages of the Middle Ages (popularised in the writings of English author Geoffrey Chaucer) are interesting to tourism researchers for several reasons:

- Even the poorest people were participants, motivated as they were by the perceived spiritual benefits of the experience.
- Because of these perceived spiritual benefits, many pilgrims were willing to accept (and even welcomed) a high level of risk and suffering.
- At the same time, the opportunity to go on a pilgrimage was welcomed by many because of the break it provided from the drudgery of daily life.

FIGURE 3.2 A scene from one of Chaucer's pilgrimages

Another major form of travel, the **Crusades** (1095–1291), also contributed to the development of the premodern travel industry, even though the Crusaders themselves were not tourists, but invaders who attempted to free the Holy Land from Muslim control. Religiously inspired like the pilgrims, the Crusaders unwittingly exposed Europe once again to the outside world, while occasionally engaging in tourist-like behaviour (e.g. souvenir collecting, sightseeing) during their journeys.

■ EARLY MODERN TOURISM (1500–1950)

Europe began to emerge from the Middle Ages in the late 1300s, assisted by the experience of the Crusades and later by the impact of the great explorations. By 1500 the **Renaissance** (literally, the 'rebirth') of Europe was well under way, and the world balance of power was beginning to shift to that continent, marking the modern era and the period of **early modern tourism**.

The Grand Tour

The **Grand Tour** is a major link between the Middle Ages and contemporary tourism. The term describes the extended travel of young men from the aristocratic classes of the United Kingdom and other parts of northern Europe to continental Europe for educational and cultural purposes (Towner 1996). A prevailing 'culture of travel' encouraged such journeys and spawned a distinctive literature as the literate young participants usually kept diaries of their experiences (Towner 2002). It is therefore possible to reconstruct this era in detail. We know, for example, that the classical Grand Tours first became popular during the mid-sixteenth century, and persisted (with modification) until the mid-nineteenth century (Withey 1997).

While there was no single circuit or timeframe that defined the Grand Tour, certain destinations feature prominently in the diaries and other written accounts. Paris was usually the first major destination of the *Tourists* (authors' italics), followed by a year or more of visits to the major cities of Italy, and especially Florence, Rome, Naples and Venice (Towner 1996). Though the political and economic power of Italy was in decline by the early 1600s, these centres were still admired for their Renaissance and Roman attractions, which continued to set the cultural standards for Europe. A visit to these cultural centres was vital for anyone aspiring to join the ranks of the elite. The following quote from 1776, attributed to Samuel Johnson, the eminent English author, captures this status motive:

> A man who has not been in Italy, is always conscious of an inferiority, from his not having seen what it is expected a man should see. The grand object of travelling is to see the shores of the Mediterranean ... All our religion, almost all our law, almost all our arts, almost all that sets us above savages, has come to us from the shores of the Mediterranean (in Burkart & Medlik 1981, p. 4).

The journey back to northern Europe usually took the traveller across the Swiss Alps, through Germany and into the Low Countries (Flanders, The Netherlands) where the Renaissance flowered during the mid-1600s.

According to Towner (1996) about 15 000–20 000 members of the British elite were abroad on the Grand Tour at any time during the mid-1700s. Wealthier participants might be accompanied by an entourage of servants, guides, tutors and other retainers. Towards the end of the era, the emphasis in the Grand Tour shifted from the aristocracy to the more affluent middle classes, resulting in a shorter stay within fewer destinations. Other destinations, such as Germany and the Alps, also became more popular (Withey 1997). The classes from which the Grand Tour participants were drawn accounted for between 7 and 9 per cent of the United Kingdom's population in the eighteenth century.

Motives also shifted throughout this era. The initial emphasis on education, designed to confer the traveller with full membership into the aristocratic power structure and to make important social connections on the continent, gradually gave way to more stress on simple sightseeing, suggesting a continuity between the classical Grand Tour and the backpacker of the modern era (see Contemporary issue: Backpacking: the modern Grand Tour?). Whether as an educational or sight-seeing phenomenon, however, the Grand Tour had a profound impact on the United Kingdom, as cultural and social trends there were largely shaped by the ideas and goods brought back by the Grand Tourists. These impacts were also felt at least economically in the destination regions through the appearance of the souvenir trade and tour guiding within major destination cities. Further indication of tourism's timeless tendency to foster business opportunity was the first appearance in the 1820s of the practical travel guide, directed toward would-be Grand Tourists (Withey 1997).

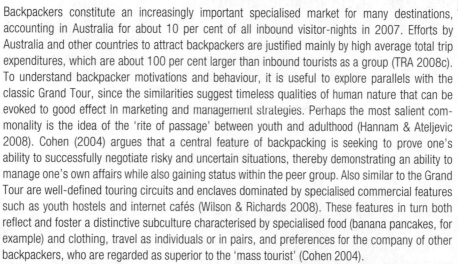

contemporary issue

BACKPACKING: THE MODERN GRAND TOUR?

Backpackers constitute an increasingly important specialised market for many destinations, accounting in Australia for about 10 per cent of all inbound visitor-nights in 2007. Efforts by Australia and other countries to attract backpackers are justified mainly by high average total trip expenditures, which are about 100 per cent larger than inbound tourists as a group (TRA 2008c). To understand backpacker motivations and behaviour, it is useful to explore parallels with the classic Grand Tour, since the similarities suggest timeless qualities of human nature that can be evoked to good effect in marketing and management strategies. Perhaps the most salient commonality is the idea of the 'rite of passage' between youth and adulthood (Hannam & Ateljevic 2008). Cohen (2004) argues that a central feature of backpacking is seeking to prove one's ability to successfully negotiate risky and uncertain situations, thereby demonstrating an ability to manage one's own affairs while also gaining status within the peer group. Also similar to the Grand Tour are well-defined touring circuits and enclaves dominated by specialised commercial features such as youth hostels and internet cafés (Wilson & Richards 2008). These features in turn both reflect and foster a distinctive subculture characterised by specialised food (banana pancakes, for example) and clothing, travel as individuals or in pairs, and preferences for the company of other backpackers, who are regarded as superior to the 'mass tourist' (Cohen 2004).

The similarities, however, should not be exaggerated. Grand Tourists, for example, emerged from a tiny elite in their home society, whereas the modern backpacker typically represents the middle class. Backpackers, moreover, claim to be less materialistic and more open-minded and self-reflexive than conventional members of their class (Binder 2004), whereas the Grand Tour perpetuated narrow and well-established ideas of cultural desirability and social hierarchy. A much higher rate of female participation has additionally been noted (Maoz 2008) along with a higher level of spontaneity and informality with regard to travel and activity patterns. Backpackers also appear to be ageing, with those in the 40 to 49 year age cohort in 2007 accounting for 12 per cent of inbound backpackers in Australia, compared with 8 per cent in 2000 (TRA 2008c). This might suggest modern society's greater emphasis on individuality and flexibility in the life stage progression, and/or a desire of people already established in society to 'find themselves' or seek out a deeper authenticity.

Spa resorts

The use of hot water springs for therapeutic purposes dates back at least to the ancient Greeks and Romans (e.g. the spas at Bath in the United Kingdom) (Casson 1994). Established in the Middle Ages by the Ottoman Empire within its European possessions, several hundred inland **spas** served wealthy visitors in continental Europe and the United Kingdom by the middle of the nineteenth century. Many, however, were small and did not survive as tourist destinations. Others, such as Karlsbad (in the modern-day Czech Republic), Vichy (in France) and Baden–Baden (in Germany), were extensive and are still functioning as spas (Towner 1996). The availability of accessible and suitable water resources was the most important factor in influencing the establishment, character and size of spas, though proximity to transportation, urban areas and related amenities and services were also influential. In contemporary times, larger hotels are increasingly likely to offer spa-type facilities as a form of product diversification that provides a lucrative revenue stream (see Managing tourism: Spa experiences in modern hotels).

managing tourism

SPA EXPERIENCES IN MODERN HOTELS

Consumers are placing an increasingly high priority on their health and personal well-being, prompting hotels and other accommodations to add services and facilities which address these needs. Once regarded as a novelty side attraction or a focus of specialised destinations, spa-type facilities are now emerging as a 'must have' add-on to existing hotels and a basic component of new construction. According to a study of spa departments in US-based hotels conducted in 2006 (Mandelbaum & Lerner 2008), such facilities in urban hotels yielded a 12.6 per cent increase in net profit over 2005, with 73 per cent of revenues obtained from the purchase of massages, body wraps and facials. Hair and nail treatments produced just 7.4 per cent of revenue due to the tendency of people to patronise regular providers of such services within their own communities. Almost as important at 6.6 per cent is the rapidly growing clothing and merchandise component, apparently reflecting a desire of clients to incorporate spa-related experiences into their day-to-day living. Other important revenue streams included membership fees (5.6 per cent) and club use (2.9 per cent), which indicates a high level of local (i.e. non-tourist) patronage and a potential for cultivating repeat, high-loyalty customers. Finally, personal training, fitness lessons and other unspecified health/wellness services collectively accounted for 1 per cent of services but are regarded as areas of very strong growth potential due to the long-term personal benefits that they are perceived to provide.

A major challenge for hotels is the high labour cost (about 75 per cent of all relevant costs) associated with the labour-intensive services that dominate revenue intakes. High-cost therapy specialists often sit idle due to the inefficient nature of scheduling, wherein clients often book or cancel treatments at the last minute, or demand the services of particular providers. Strategies to address the labour issue include clustering appointments under one therapist, imposing penalties for last minute cancellations, and maintaining a database of potential local customers who could be alerted to openings caused by no-shows and offered discount rates on last-minute bookings.

Seaside resorts

By the early 1800s tourism opportunities were becoming more accessible to the lower classes of the United Kingdom and parts of western Europe. This was a result of the **Industrial Revolution**, which transformed the region (beginning in England during the mid-1700s) from a rural, agricultural society to one that was urban and

industrial. Crowded cities and harsh working conditions created a demand for recreational opportunities that would take the workers, at least temporarily, into more
pleasant and relaxing environments. Domestic **seaside resorts** emerged in England
to fulfil this demand, facilitated by none of the large population centres being more
than 160 kilometres from the English coast. Interestingly, many seaside resorts began
as small and exclusive communities that catered like the inland spas only to the upper
classes.

A stimulus for travelling to the coast was the belief, gaining in popularity by the mid-
eighteenth century, that sea bathing, combined with the drinking of sea water, was an
effective treatment for certain illnesses. The early seaside resorts therefore demonstrate
continuity between the classic spa era described above and the modern phenomenon
of hedonistic mass tourism at beach locations. Seaside resorts such as Brighton and
Scarborough soon rivalled inland spa towns such as Bath as tourist attractions, with
the added advantage that the target resource (sea water) was virtually unlimited, and
the opportunities for spatial expansion along the coast were numerous.

A primary factor that made the seaside resorts accessible to the working classes was
the construction of railways connecting these settlements to nearby large industrial
cities. During the 1830s and 1840s, this had the effect of transforming small English
coastal towns into sizeable urban areas, illustrating how changes in a transit region
can produce fundamental change in a destination region. As the Industrial Revolution spread to the European mainland and overseas to North America and Australia,
the same demands were created and the same processes repeated. The well-known
American seaside resort of Atlantic City traces its origins as a working-class seaside
resort to the construction of a rail link with Philadelphia in the 1850s, and subsequent
expansion to the novelty effect of impressively large and comfortable hotel facilities
(Stansfield 2005). In Australia, seaside resorts such as Manly, Glenelg and St Kilda
were established in the late nineteenth century to serve, respectively, the growing
urban areas of Sydney, Adelaide and Melbourne.

The progression of the Industrial Revolution in England and Wales coincided with
the diffusion of seaside resorts to meet the growing demand for coastal holidays.
Figure 3.3 depicts their expansion from seven in 1750 to about 145 by 1911, at which
time few sections of the coastline lacked at least one resort (Towner 1996). This pattern of diffusion, like the growth of individual resorts, was largely a haphazard process
unassisted by any formal management or planning considerations. Many British seaside resorts today, in large part because of this poorly regulated pattern of expansion,
are stagnant or declining destinations that need to innovate in order to revitalise their
tourism product (see chapter 10).

Thomas Cook

Along with several contemporaries from the mainland of Europe, **Thomas Cook** is
associated with the emergence of tourism as a modern, large-scale industry, even
though it would take another 150 years for mass tourism to be realised on a global
scale. A Baptist preacher who was concerned with the 'declining morals' of the
English working class, Cook conceived the idea of chartering trains at reduced fares
to take the workers to temperance (i.e. anti-alcohol) meetings and bible camps in the
countryside. The first of these excursions, provided as a day trip from Leicester to
Loughborough on 5 July 1841, is sometimes described as the symbolic beginning of
the contemporary era of tourism. Gradually, these excursions expanded in the number
of participants and the variety of destinations offered. At the same time, the reasons for

taking excursions shifted rapidly from spiritual purposes to sightseeing and pleasure. By 1845 Cook (who had by then formed the famous travel business Thomas Cook & Son) was offering regular tours between Leicester and London. In 1863 the first international excursion was undertaken (to the Swiss Alps), and in 1872 the first round-the-world excursion was organised with an itinerary that included Australia and New Zealand. The Cook excursions can be considered the beginning of international tourism in the latter two countries, although such trips remained the prerogative of the wealthy. By the late 1870s, Thomas Cook & Son operated 60 offices throughout the world (Withey 1997).

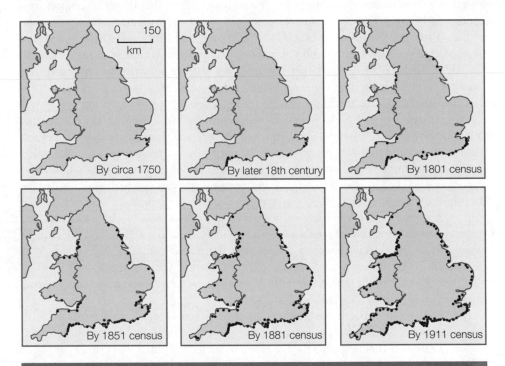

FIGURE 3.3 Pattern of seaside resort diffusion in England and Wales, 1750–1911

Source: Towner (1996, p. 179)

Arrangements for the Great Exhibition of 1851, held in London, illustrate the innovations that Thomas Cook & Son introduced into the tourism sector. The 160 000 clients who purchased his company's services (accounting for 3 per cent of all visitors to the Exhibition) were provided with:

- an inclusive, prepaid, one-fee structure that covered transportation, accommodation, guides, food and other goods and services
- organised itineraries based on rigid time schedules
- uniform products of high quality
- affordable prices, made possible by the economies of scale created through large customer volumes.

The genius of Thomas Cook & Son, essentially, was to apply the production principles and techniques of the Industrial Revolution to tourism. Standardised, precisely timed, commercialised and high-volume tour packages heralded the 'industrialisation' of the sector. Thus, while the development of the seaside resorts was a mainly unplanned phenomenon, Thomas Cook can be described as an effective entrepreneurial pioneer of the industry who fostered and accommodated the *demand* for these and other tourism products. The actual connection between supply and demand, however, was only made possible by communication and transportation innovations of the Industrial Revolution such as the railway, the steamship and the telegraph, which the entrepreneur Cook used to his advantage. As a result of such innovative applications, Thomas Cook & Son exposed an unprecedented pool of potential travellers (i.e. an increased *demand*) to an unprecedented number of destinations (i.e. an increased *supply*). Today, the **package tour** is one of the fundamental, taken-for-granted symbols of the contemporary tourism industry.

The post-Cook period (1880–1950)

Largely as a result of Thomas Cook & Son and its adaptation of Industrial Revolution technologies and principles to the travel industry, tourism expanded significantly from the 1870s onwards. Much of this growth was initially concentrated in the domestic sector of the more industrialised regions such as the United States, western Europe and Australia. The American west, for example, experienced a period of rapid tourism growth associated first with the closing of the frontier in the 1890s and then with the increase in car ownership (Gunn 2004). Domestic tourism also flourished in the United Kingdom, and by 1911 it is estimated that 55 per cent of the English population were making day excursions to the seaside, while 20 per cent travelled as stayovers to the coastal resorts (Burton 1997).

International tourism growth in the **post-Cook period** of the early modern era was less robust than in the domestic tourism sector. This was due in part to the feasibility of outbound travel for the middle and working classes only where countries shared an accessible common border, as between Canada and the United States, and between France and Belgium. Switzerland, for example, which shared frontiers with several major countries, received about one million tourists annually by 1880 (Withey 1997). In addition, the period between 1880 and 1950 was characterised by four events that drastically curtailed international tourism. The first of these was the global depression of the 1890s, and this was followed two decades later by World War I (1914–18). Resumed tourism growth in the 1920s was subsequently cancelled out by the Great Depression of the 1930s and World War II (1939–45). No wars or economic downturns of comparable magnitude, however, have thus far interrupted the expansion of the tourism industry since the end of World War II.

CONTEMPORARY TOURISM (1950 ONWARDS)

The rapid growth of tourism during the contemporary era of **modern mass tourism** is reflected in the global trend of inbound tourist arrival and associated revenue estimates (see table 3.1). The statistics from the 1950s and 1960s are speculative due to the irregular nature of data collection at that time (see chapter 1). But even allowing for a substantial margin of error, an exponential pattern of growth is readily evident, with inbound stayovers increasing more than 36 times between 1950 and 2007, from an estimated 25 million to over 900 million. International tourism receipts have grown even more dramatically over the same period, from US$2 billion to over US$850 billion. An aspect of table 3.1 that is worth noting is the consistent pattern of growth, interrupted only by the economic recession of the early 1980s, the terrorist attacks of 2001, and the combined effects of the Iraq War and the SARS epidemic in 2003.

TABLE 3.1 International stayover arrivals, 1950–2007

Year	Arrivals of tourists from abroad (excursionists excluded)		Receipts from international tourism (international transport excluded)	
	Total (Million)	Per cent change over previous year	Total (US$ billion)	Per cent change over previous year
1950	25	—	2	—
1960	69	—	7	—
1961	75	8.7	7	6.1
1962	81	8.0	8	10.2
1963	90	10.7	9	10.7
1964	105	16.1	10	13.4
1965	113	7.9	12	15.2
1966	120	6.3	13	15.0
1967	130	8.2	14	8.4
1968	131	1.1	15	3.7
1969	144	9.4	17	12.1
1970	166	15.5	18	6.6
1971	179	7.9	21	16.5
1972	189	5.8	25	18.1
1973	199	5.2	31	26.1
1974	206	3.4	34	8.9
1975	222	8.1	41	20.3
1976	229	3.0	44	9.2
1977	249	8.9	56	25.2
1978	267	7.2	69	23.7
1979	283	6.0	83	21.1
1980	286	1.0	105	26.4
1981	287	0.4	107	2.0
1982	286	−0.4	101	−6.1
1983	290	1.2	102	1.6
1984	316	9.2	113	10.0
1985	327	3.4	118	4.8
1986	339	3.6	143	21.5
1987	364	7.4	177	23.2
1988	395	8.5	204	15.6
1989	426	8.0	221	8.3
1990	458	7.5	268	21.0
1991	464	1.3	278	3.7
1992	503	8.3	314	13.0
1993	518	3.1	323	23.0
1994	553	6.8	353	9.1
1995	568	2.7	403	14.3
1996	600	5.5	438	8.6
1997	620	3.3	438	0.1
1998	636	2.7	442	0.8
1999	664	4.5	466	5.5
2000	680	3.2	475	1.9
2001	684	−0.3	463	1.7
2002	703	2.8	480	3.7
2003	691	−1.7	523	9.0
2004	760	10.0	635	21.4
2005	803	5.7	680	7.1
2006	847	5.5	742	9.1
2007	903	6.2	856	15.4

Source: UNWTO (2008), WTO (1998), WTO (1999) and WTO (2004)

The world's biggest industry?

Interest groups such as the World Travel and Tourism Council (WTTC) maintain that tourism is the world's single largest industry, accounting directly and indirectly in 2007 for approximately one of every ten jobs and 10 per cent of all economic activity as noted in chapter 1. Whether this does indeed constitute the world's biggest industry, however, depends on how it is quantified and what it is compared against. For example, tourism is larger than either the oil or grain industry taken individually, but probably does not exceed the broader global mining or agricultural sectors as a whole.

■ FACTORS ASSOCIATED WITH INCREASED TOURISM DEMAND

Many of the generic factors that influence the growth of tourism have been introduced briefly in the earlier sections on the evolution of tourism. This section focuses specifically on those factors that have stimulated the demand for tourism (or **push factors**) since World War II. However, to maintain historical continuity, the trends are considered in the context of the entire twentieth century. Although outlined under five separate headings, the factors are interdependent and should not be considered in isolation.

Economic factors

Affluence is the most important economic factor associated with increased tourism demand. Normally, the distribution and volume of tourism increases as a society becomes more economically developed and greater discretionary household income subsequently becomes available. Discretionary household income is the money available to a household after 'basic needs' such as food, clothing, transportation, education and housing have been met. Such funds might be saved, invested or used to purchase luxury goods and services (such as a foreign holiday or expensive restaurant meal), at the 'discretion' of the household decision makers. Average economic wealth is commonly measured by per capita gross national product (GNP), or the total value of all goods and services produced by a country in a given year, divided by the total resident population. It is also important, however, to consider how equitably this wealth is distributed. A per capita GNP of $10 000 could indicate that everyone basically makes $10 000 or that a small elite makes much more than this while most remain in poverty. The latter scenario greatly constrains the number of potential tourists, and is essentially the structure that prevailed before the modern era.

In the early stages of the development process, regular tourism participation (and pleasure tourism in particular) is feasible only for the elite, as demonstrated by the history of tourism in Europe prior to Thomas Cook. As of the early 2000s, there were only a few societies that demonstrate a level of economic development comparable to Europe before the Industrial Revolution. In her **tourism participation sequence**, Burton (1995) refers to these pre-industrial, mainly agricultural and subsistence-based situations as *Phase One* (table 3.2).

In *Phase Two,* the generation of wealth increases and spreads to a wider segment of the population as a consequence of industrialisation and related processes such as urbanisation. This happened first in the United Kingdom, and then elsewhere, during the Industrial Revolution. At present, India and China are roughly at the same stage of development as that which England passed through during the early 1900s and are similarly experiencing an explosion in demand for domestic tourism that is fuelling the development of seaside resorts and other tourism facilities. From being almost non-existent in the early 1970s, domestic tourism in China expanded to an estimated 639 million domestic tourist arrivals in 1996 to 870 million in 2003 and 1.61 billion in 2007 (Chinatour.com 2008). Concurrently, an ever-increasing number of *nouveau riche,* or newly rich individuals, are visiting an expanding array of foreign destinations.

TABLE 3.2 Burton's four phases of tourism participation		
Phase	**Economic developments**	**Tourism participation**
One	• Mainly subsistence-based and pre-industrial • Rural, agrarian • Large gap between poor masses and small elite	• No mass participation in tourism • Elite travel to domestic and international destinations
Two	• Industrialising • Rapid growth of urban areas • Growing middle class	• Widespread participation in domestic tourism • Increased scope of international tourism by elite
Three	• Almost industrialised • Population mostly urban • Middle class becoming dominant	• Mass participation in domestic tourism, and increase in short-haul international tourism • Elite turn towards long-haul international tourism
Four	• Fully industrialised, 'high tech' orientation • Mostly urban • High levels of affluence throughout the population	• Mass participation in domestic and international (long-haul and short-haul) tourism

By *Phase Three,* the bulk of the population is relatively affluent, leading to further increases in mass domestic travel as well as mass international tourism to nearby countries. The elite, meanwhile, engage in greater long-haul travel. This began to occur in the United Kingdom not long after World War II, and will characterise China within the next 15–20 years. In 2007, 41 million Chinese travelled abroad (an 18.6% increase over 2006), an impressive figure suggesting Phase Three dynamics until one realises that this represents only about 3% of the population and overwhelmingly involved travel to the adjacent Chinese-controlled territories of Hong Kong and Macau (Chinadaily.com 2008).

Finally, *Phase Four* represents a fully developed country with widespread affluence, and a subsequent pattern of mass international tourism to a diverse array of short- and long-haul destinations. Almost all residents, in addition, engage in a comprehensive variety of domestic tourism experiences that differ greatly from those in the earlier phase societies. The major regions and countries included in this category are western Europe (including the United Kingdom), the United States and Canada, Japan, Taiwan, South Korea, Singapore, Australia and New Zealand. These origin regions have a combined population of approximately 850 million, or 13 per cent of the world's population, but account for roughly 80 per cent of all outbound tourist traffic. With the **BRIC countries** (Brazil, Russia, India and China) expected to attain Phase Four dynamics within the next two or three decades, the environmental impacts of several billion outbound travellers will probably emerge as a major focus of management in the global tourism system, depending on the extent to which measures are taken to minimise these impacts (see chapter 11).

Increasing income and expenditure in Australia

The emergence of a prosperous Australian population during the past century mirrors Australia's transition from Phase Two to Phase Four status. Consumption expenditures are a good if partial indicator of living standards, as they show to what extent individuals are able to meet their material needs and desires through the purchase of goods and services. As depicted in figure 3.4, per capita consumption expenditures in Australia were stable or declined slightly until the late 1930s, due in part to the effects of World War I and the Great Depression. Large increases occurred after World War II, and by 2003–04, these expenditures were about three times higher than the 1938–39 levels in 'real' terms — that is, after controlling for inflation by calibrating the figure 3.4 data in 1938–39 pounds (Australia's currency at that time). Not evident in this figure, however, are the increased levels of personal debt required to sustain these levels of expenditure, and the influence in the early 2000s of the exceptionally high demand for Australian raw materials from the burgeoning Asian economies. Significantly from a tourism perspective, expenditures on 'travel' increased from 3.6% of the total in 1900 to 11.6% in 2003–04 (Haig & Anderssen 2007).

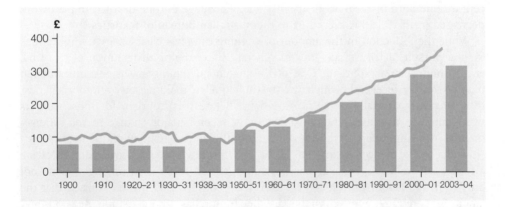

FIGURE 3.4 Per capita real consumption expenditure in 1938–39 pounds, Australia 1900–01 to 2003–04

Source: Haig and Anderssen 2007

Social factors

The major social trends that have influenced participation in tourism are the increase in discretionary time, its changing distribution, and shifts in the way that society perceives this use of time. During Phase One, the rhythm of life is largely dictated by necessity, the seasons and the weather. Formal clock time or 'periods of life' have little or no meaning as nature imposes its own discipline on human activity. According to Thompson (1967), people in this phase are 'task oriented' rather than 'time oriented', and no fine lines are drawn between notions of 'work', 'rest' or 'play'.

The effect of industrialisation is to introduce a formalised rigour into this equation. Phase Two societies are characterised by a deliberately orchestrated system wherein discrete notions of work, leisure and rest are structured into rigorous segments of clock time, and the life rhythm is regulated by the factory whistle and the alarm clock rather than the rising or setting of the sun. Young (usually male at first) adults are expected to enter the labour force after a short period of rote education, and then to retire after a specified period of workplace participation. The structure that most symbolises this industrial regime is the division of the day into roughly equal portions of work, rest and leisure activity, with the latter constituting the discretionary time component (Lynch & Veal 2006). Leisure and rest time are not generally seen as important in their own right, but as a necessary interruption to the work schedule to maintain the labourer's efficiency. The Phase Two industrial era can therefore be said to be dominated by a **'play in order to work' philosophy**.

Ironically, the early stages of industrialisation are often accompanied by a substantial increase in the amount of time spent at work. For example, the average European industrial labourer by the mid-1800s worked a 70-hour week (or 4000 hours per year), with the weekly work routine interrupted only by the Sunday day of rest. Since then, the situation has improved dramatically in conjunction with the transition to Phases Three and Four. The average working week for the European labour force declined to 46 hours by 1965 and 39 hours by the 1980s. Australia, however, was the first country to institute a standard eight-hour working day (Lynch & Veal 2006). The difference in available discretionary time in Australia between the beginning and end of the twentieth century is illustrated by the observation that 44 per cent of time for an average Australian male adult born in 1988 is discretionary, compared with 33 per cent for one born in 1888. Concurrently, the percentage of time devoted to paid work decreased from 20 to 11, according to the Australian Bureau of Statistics.

While the reduction in the amount of working time has clear positive implications for the pursuit of leisure activities in general, the changing distribution of this time is also important to tourism. One of the first major changes was the introduction of the two-day weekend, which was instrumental in making stayover tourism possible to nearby (usually domestic) locations. Before this, tourism for most workers was limited to daytime Sunday excursions. A second major change in the arrangement of working time was the introduction of the annual holiday entitlement. Again, Australia was a pioneer, being one of the first countries to enact legislation to create a four-week holiday standard. The pressure for such reform, surprisingly, came not only from the labour movement, but also from corporations, which realised that the labour force required more discretionary time to purchase and consume the goods and services that they were producing (Lynch & Veal 2006). It can be said therefore that the transition to the more mature phases of economic development is accompanied by the increasing importance of consumption over production. In any event, the holiday portion of the reduced working year makes longer domestic and international holidays accessible to most of the population.

Flexitime and earned time

More recently, the movement of the highly developed Phase Four countries into an information-oriented **postindustrial era** has resulted in innovative work options that are eroding the rigid nine-to-five type work schedules and uniform itineraries of the industrial society. The best known of these options is **flexitime**, which allows workers, within reason, to distribute their working hours in a manner that best suits their individual lifestyles. Common flexitime possibilities include three 12-hour days per week followed by a four-day weekend, or a series of 40-hour working weeks followed by a two-month vacation.

Earned time options are production rather than time-based. They usually involve the right to go on vacation leave once a given production quota is met. If, for example, a worker meets an annual personal production target of 1000 units by 10 August, then the remainder of the year is vacation time, unless the individual decides (and is given the option) to work overtime to earn additional income. Such time management innovations have important implications for tourism, in that lengthy vacation time blocks are conducive to extended long-haul trips and increased tourism participation in general. Evidence of the prevalence of flexible working arrangements in a Phase Four setting is provided by the United Kingdom, where 17.9% of male and 26.7% of female employees participated in such schemes during 2003 (Office for National Statistics 2003) .

Changing attitudes

Social attitudes towards leisure time are also changing in the late industrial, early postindustrial period. As in ancient Greece, leisure is generally seen not just as a time to rest between work shifts, but as an end in itself and a time to undertake activities such as foreign travel, which are highly meaningful to some individuals. This change in perception is consistent with the increasing emphasis on consumption over production. In contrast to the industrial era, a **'work in order to play' philosophy** (i.e. working to obtain the necessary funds to undertake worthwhile leisure pursuits) is emerging to provide a powerful social sanctioning of most types of tourism activity.

Beyond sanctioning, tourism is also increasingly perceived as a basic human right. Article 7 of the 1999 WTO Global Code of Ethics for Tourism, for example, affirms the right to tourism and emphasises that 'obstacles should not be placed in its way', since 'the prospect of direct and personal access to the discovery and enjoyment of the planet's resources constitutes a right equally open to all the world's inhabitants'. A related issue, however, is the tendency of many individuals to spend a growing portion of their discretionary time in additional work activity to maintain a particular lifestyle or pay debts, thereby constraining their opportunities for engaging in tourism or other leisure activities. In 2001, over one-half of the Australian labour force worked more than 40 hours per week while one-third exceeded 50 hours. About 60 per cent of all overtime work, moreover, was unpaid (Phillips 2001).

Demographic factors

The later stages of the development process (i.e. Phases Three and Four) are associated with distinctive demographic transformations, at least four of which appear to increase the propensity of the population to engage in tourism-related activities.

Reduced family size

Because of the costs of raising children, small family size is equated with increased discretionary time and household income. If the per capita GNP and fertility rates of the world's countries are examined, a strong inverse relationship between the two can be readily identified. That is, total fertility rates (TFR = the average number of children that a woman can expect to bear in her lifetime) tend to decline as the affluence of society increases. This was the case for Australia during most of the twentieth century (table 3.3), the post–World War II period of increased fertility (i.e. the 'baby boom') being the primary exception. The overall trend of declining fertility is reflected in the size of the average Australian household, which declined from 4.5 persons in 1911 to 2.6 persons in 2001. It is expected to decline further to between 2.2 and 2.3 persons per household by 2026 (ABS 2008a).

One factor that accounts for this trend is the decline in infant mortality rates. As the vast majority of children in a Phase Four society will survive into adulthood, there is no practical need for couples to produce a large number of children so that at least one or two will survive into adulthood. Also critical is the entry of women into the workforce, the elimination of children as a significant source of labour and the desire of households to attain a high level of material wellbeing (which is more difficult when resources have to be allocated to the raising of children).

However, rather than culminating in a stable situation where couples basically replace themselves with two children, these and other factors have combined in many Phase Four countries to yield a total fertility rate well below the replacement level of 2.1 (it is slightly higher than 2.0 to take into account child mortality and adults who do not have children). While the resulting 'baby bust' may in the short term further enable adults to travel, the long-term effects on tourism if this pattern of low fertility persists are more uncertain. One consideration is the reduction in the tourist market as the population ages and eventually declines, if the natural population decrease is not compensated for by appropriate increases in immigration (see the following pages). Another is the shrinkage of the labour force, which could reduce the amount of pension income that can be used for discretionary purposes such as travel, while forcing longer working hours and a higher retirement age to fund future pension disbursements.

TABLE 3.3 Australian demographic trends, 1901–2008

Year	Population (000s)	Per cent urban	Total fertility rate	Life expectancy (m/f)	Per cent population over 64
1901	3 826	n/a	n/a	55/59	4.0
1911	4 574	57.8	n/a	n/a	4.3
1921	5 511	62.1	3.0	58/62	4.4
1931	6 553	63.5	2.2	63/67	6.5
1941	7 144	65.0	2.5	n/a	7.2
1947	7 579	68.7	3.0	66/71	8.0
1954	8 987	78.7	3.2	67/73	8.3
1961	10 508	81.7	3.3	68/74	8.5
1966	11 551	82.9	2.9	68/74	8.5
1971	12 937	85.6	2.7	68/75	8.4
1976	14 033	86.0	2.0	70/76	8.9
1981	14 923	85.7	1.9	71/78	9.8
1986	16 018	85.4	1.9	73/79	10.5
1991	17 336	85.3	1.9	74/80	11.3
1996	18 311	n/a	1.8	75/81	12.0
2002	19 641	n/a	1.7	77/82	12.8
2008	21 390	n/a	1.9	79/83	13.1

Source: ABS (1998a, 2001 and 2003), Lattimore & Pobke (2008)

Population increase

All things being equal, a larger population base equates with a larger overall incidence of tourism activity. Because of a process described by the **demographic transition model (DTM)** (see figure 3.5), Burton's Phase Four societies tend to have relatively large and stable populations. During Stage One (which more or less corresponds to Burton's Phase One), populations are maintained at a stable but low level over the long term due to the balance between high crude birth and death rates. In Stage Two (corresponding to Burton's Phase Two), dramatic declines in mortality are brought about by the introduction of basic health care. However, couples continue to have large families for cultural reasons and for the contributions that offspring make to the household labour force. Rapid population growth is the usual consequence of the resulting gap between the birth and death rates.

As the population becomes more educated and urbanised, the labour advantage from large families is gradually lost. Subsequently, the economic and social factors described in the previous subsections begin to take effect, resulting in a rapidly declining birth rate and a slowing in the rate of net population growth during Stage Three (roughly corresponding to Burton's Phase Three). This is occurring currently in heavily populated countries such as India, Brazil, Indonesia and China and is accompanied by the stabilisation of mortality rates. The conventional demographic transition is completed by Stage Four (Burton's Phase Four), wherein a balance between low birth rates and death rates is attained.

The confounding factor not taken into account in the traditional demographic transition model, however, is the pattern of collapsing fertility and eventual population decline described above. If this persists and becomes more prevalent, it may indicate a new, fifth stage of the model (see figure 3.5). The experience of Australia does not yet indicate whether very low fertility is an aberration or not, since total fertility rates have been increasing since 2002 but remain below the replacement level of 2.1 (see table 3.3).

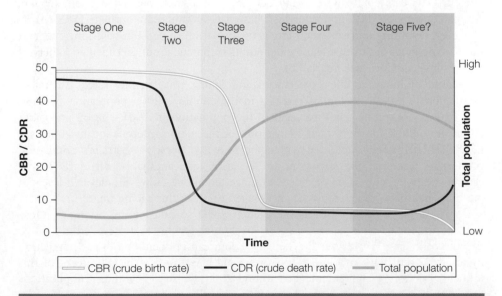

FIGURE 3.5 The demographic transition model

The demographic transition model basically describes the natural growth of the Australian population during the past 150 years, although the overall pattern of population increase was also critically influenced by high immigration levels as in the United States, Canada, New Zealand and western Europe. From a population of less than four million at the time of Federation, Australia's population increased more than fivefold by 2008 (see table 3.3). Similar patterns have been experienced in all of the other Phase Four countries, culminating in the 850 million Phase Four consumers mentioned earlier.

Urbanisation

As happened in Ur and Rome, the concentration of population within large urban areas increases the desire and tendency to engage in certain types of escapist tourism. In part, this is because of urban congestion and crowding, but cities are also associated with higher levels of discretionary income and education, and lower family size. Australia differs from most other Phase Four countries in its exceptionally high level of urban population, and in its concentration within a small number of major metropolitan areas. By 2003, 61 per cent of Australians lived in the five largest metropolitan areas (Sydney, Melbourne, Brisbane, Perth and Adelaide). The 'urban' population in total peaked at about 85 per cent in the early 1970s and has remained at this level.

Increased life expectancy

Increased life expectancies have resulted from the technological advances of the industrial and postindustrial eras. In 1901, Australian men and women could expect a lifespan of just 55 and 59 years, respectively (see table 3.3). This meant that the average male worker survived for only approximately five years after retirement. By 2008 the respective life expectancies had increased to 79 and 83 years, indicating 15 to 20 years of survival after leaving the workforce. This higher life expectancy, combined with reduced working time means that the Phase Four Australian male born in 1988 can look forward to 298 000 hours of discretionary time during his life, compared with 153 000 hours for his Phase Two counterpart born in 1888 (ABS). However, favouring tourism even more is the provision of pension-based income, and improvements in health that allow older adults to pursue an unprecedented variety of leisure-time activities (see figure 3.6).

Because of increased life expectancies and falling total fertility rates, Australia's population is rapidly ageing, as revealed in the country's 2003 population pyramid (see figure 3.7). From just 4 per cent of the population in 1901, the 65 and older cohort accounted for more than 13 per cent of the nation's population in 2008 (see table 3.3). It is conceivable that within the next two decades Australia's population profile will resemble that of present-day Germany or Scandinavia, where 18–20 per cent of the population is 65 or older. As suggested above, however, elevated levels of international in-migration could be encouraged to offset this ageing trend.

Contributing to this process is the ageing of the so-called **baby boomers**, those born during the aforementioned era of relatively high fertility that prevailed in the two decades following World War II. The baby boom can be identified in the population pyramid by the bulge in the 40- to 59-year-old age groups. The retirement of this influential cohort, which commenced around 2008, will have significant implications for Australia's economy and social structure, as well as its tourism industry (see the case study at the end of this chapter).

FIGURE 3.6 Tourists making the most of retirement

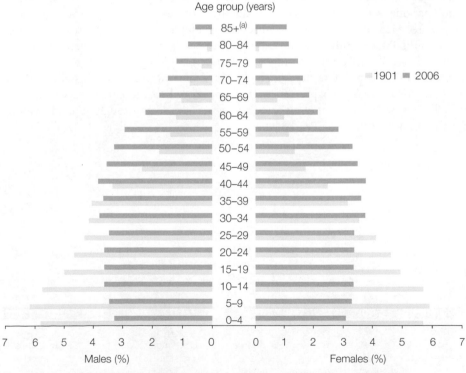

(a)   The 85+ age group includes all ages 85 years and over and therefore is not strictly
        comparable with the five-year age groups in the rest of this graph.

FIGURE 3.7 Australia's population pyramid, 1901 and 2006, by five-year age cohort

Source: ABS 2004, 2008b

Technological factors

The crucial role of transportation in the diffusion of tourism is demonstrated by the influence of the railway on the development of seaside resorts and by the steamship on incipient long-haul tourism during the late 1800s. However, these pale in comparison to the impact of aircraft and the automobile. Figure 3.8 illustrates the twentieth-century evolution of the aviation industry. An interesting characteristic of this evolution is the absence of milestone developments in aircraft technology between the 1976 debut of the Concorde (which has now been decommissioned) and the introduction of new long-haul aircraft such as the A380 in the early 2000s. Nevertheless, the world's airline industry now accounts for more than 1.6 billion passengers per year (Goeldner & Ritchie 2006), and is a primary factor underlying the spatial diffusion of tourist destinations.

The development of the automotive industry during the twentieth century paralleled aviation in its rapid technical evolution and growth (see Technology and tourism: War as an innovation stimulant). The United Kingdom is typical of the Phase Four countries, with private car ownership increasing from 132 000 in 1914 to two million in 1938, eleven million in 1969 (Burkart & Medlik 1981) and 23 million in 2004 (Eurofound 2007). The effect has been profound in both the domestic and international tourism sectors. Road transport (including buses, etc.) accounted for about 77 per cent of all international arrivals and an even higher portion of domestic travel during the mid-1990s (Burton 1995). Unable to compete against the dual impact of the aeroplane and the car, passenger trains and ships have been increasingly marginalised, in many cases functioning more as a nostalgic attraction than a mass passenger carrier. A notable Australian example of a 'heritage' railway-related attraction is Puffing Billy, a steam train from the early 1900s that transports tourists along a 24.5 kilometre route through the Dandenong Ranges of Victoria, which was originally built to facilitate the settlement of the area. Recent concerns about global warming, however (see chapters 9 and 11), appear to be stimulating renewed interest in rail as a sustainable form of mass tourist transit (see Breakthrough tourism: Waiting for the train in the Alpine Pearls).

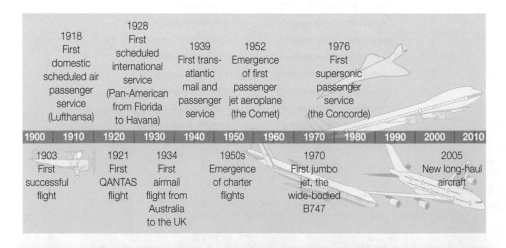

FIGURE 3.8 Milestones in air travel

technology and tourism

WAR AS AN INNOVATION STIMULANT

War, or the anticipation of war, has played a major role in the twentieth century diffusion of car-based tourism. In the USA, construction of the much-vaunted dual carriage interstate highway system began in 1956 to expedite the movement of military vehicles and troops in anticipation of and to deter armed conflict with the Soviet Union, and to effectively evacuate civilians in the event of such a conflict (McNichol 2005). The Americans, in turn, were influenced by the experience of Germany's *autobahn* highway network, which was initiated in 1932 partly to facilitate the movement of troops and military hardware. Frontier roads in Alaska and the Amazon basin were also constructed primarily because of war-related considerations. Military influences are evident as well in contemporary automotive technology. The jeep and 'hummer' are perhaps the most obvious example of this influence, both having contributed substantially to the recent penetration of tourists into remote areas. In aviation, the innovative impact of armed conflict is best demonstrated by the rapid technological development of jet aircraft during World War II by the Germans, who started mass production of the first operational jet fighter, the Messerschmitt Me 262 in 1944. Without this brief period of accelerated innovation, it is highly unlikely that the commercial Comet jet aeroplane would have been introduced as early as 1952.

Limited access highway networks, jet aircraft and some types of recreational vehicles are just three technology-related examples of the **war dividend** that continues to benefit tourism long after the war in which the innovation was spawned has ended (Weaver 2000a). Battlefield attractions, military cemeteries and the provision of millions of people with travel experience are non-technological aspects of this dividend effect. Of considerable current interest to the tourism sector is the expanding influence of global positioning systems (GPS), which were developed by the United States Department of Defense during the Cold War with the Soviet Union but were designated a common good by President Ronald Reagan in 1983. Recent tourism-related applications of GPS include voice and display-assisted vehicle and pedestrian navigation, and the generation of maps that reflect 'real-time' road conditions and configurations.

breakthrough tourism

WAITING FOR THE TRAIN IN THE ALPINE PEARLS

In early 2006, 17 tourism resorts in the European Alps banded together to form the Alpine Pearls, a network dedicated to reducing the members' dependency on cars as a mode of tourist transportation. Expanding to 22 destinations in Germany, France, Italy, Austria, Switzerland and Slovenia, the European Union-funded network has a dual goal of (a) providing tourists with a fully satisfying holiday experience without having to use their personal vehicle, and (b) facilitating convenient travel to each member destination by mass public transit (Alpine Pearls 2008). Both objectives are carried out under the banner of 'soft mobility', which means in principle that arrivals can easily access all local attractions by bicycle, foot, ski, horseback or electric vehicle. Increasingly large areas of each community are being designated as 'vehicle-free' during at least some time periods to accommodate these alternative modes of transport, and a 'comfortable and relaxed' trip by bus or train to every member destination is 'guaranteed'. By uniting under a single umbrella organisation, the members hope to benefit from collective marketing and management efforts that will strengthen the Alpine Pearl brand and its public recognition. Economies of scale, in addition, allow the network to negotiate concessions from travel providers, including the Alpine Pearl Ticket, a discount rate rail pass issued by Railtours Austria. Integration of the members as a collective tourism product is being encouraged by the construction of long-distance hiking trails that connect the Pearls.

Among the problems that continue to impede the attainment of the soft mobility ideal is the continued parallel use of private vehicles both in transit and within the member communities, which endangers non-vehicular travellers and continues to cause congestion in areas where they are still allowed. It is also apparent from the experience of visitors that a successful soft mobility holiday must be planned well in advance to avoid fully-booked transportation, accommodation and tours. Nevertheless, progress is evident in the Alpine Pearl of Werfenweng (Austria), where the share of visitors arriving by train has increased from seven per cent in 1999 to 25 per cent in 2005 while the number of local accommodation businesses supporting the concept has concurrently grown from 14 to 40. The permanent population of the once-dying Alpine village has also increased by 25 per cent since the late 1990s, at least in part due to interest in the commitment to soft mobility.

Information technology

Information technologies have also played a vital role in the diffusion of tourism. Computerised reservation systems (CRS), for example, expedite travel by providing travel agencies and carriers with greater flexibility (and thus even further departure from the standardisation and rigidity of industrial era modes of service), integration with other components of the industry and improved cost-effectiveness (Kurtzman & Zauhar 2003). In addition, **virtual reality (VR)** technologies that present and interpret destinations such as ancient Pompeii and Tiberius have an enormous potential to redefine the tourism industry as well as the demand for tourism products. A relevant consideration is whether VR will provide a surrogate or stimulant for actual travel.

Political factors

Tourism is dependent on the freedom of people to travel both internationally and domestically (see chapter 2). Often restricted for political and economic reasons in the earlier development stages, freedom of mobility is seldom an issue in Phase Four countries, where restrictions are usually limited to sensitive domestic military sites and certain prohibited countries (e.g. Cuba relative to the United States). The collapse of the Soviet Union and its socialist orbit in the early 1990s has meant that an additional 400 million people now have greater freedom — and, increasingly, the money — to travel. More deliberate has been the Chinese government's incremental moves to allow its 1.3 billion people increased access to foreign travel. Chinese leisure travel groups can only visit a foreign country that has successfully negotiated Approved Destination Status (ADS) with the Chinese government. In theory this assures that Chinese tourists receive a well-regulated, quality visitor experience. As of 2008, at least 130 countries (including Australia and New Zealand) were ADS-conferred (DRET 2008). A critical factor influencing whether this high level of global mobility is maintained will be concerns over the movement of terrorists and illegal migrants.

AUSTRALIAN TOURISM PARTICIPATION

The economic, social, demographic, technological and political factors described above have all contributed to increased tourism activity by residents of Phase Four countries in the post-World War II era. Australia is no exception, although trends since 2000 indicate both a dramatic growth in inbound travel (see table 3.4) and a concomitant stagnation in domestic tourism trips (see table 3.5), as described more fully in the case study at the end of chapter 2.

TABLE 3.4 Outbound resident departures from Australia, 1965–2006

Year	Number of departures	Growth (%)	Year	Number of departures	Growth (%)
1965	161 700	—	1986	1 539 600	1.8
1966	183 200	13.3	1987	1 622 300	5.4
1967	217 700	18.8	1988	1 697 600	4.6
1968	251 900	13.6	1989	1 989 800	17.2
1969	288 800	14.6	1990	2 169 900	9.0
1970	352 500	22.0	1991	2 099 400	−3.2
1971	413 900	17.4	1992	2 276 260	8.4
1972	504 500	21.9	1993	2 267 080	−0.4
1973	638 100	26.5	1994	2 354 310	3.8
1974	769 700	20.6	1995	2 518 620	7.0
1975	911 800	18.5	1996	2 731 970	8.5
1976	973 800	6.8	1997	2 932 760	7.3
1977	971 300	−0.3	1998	3 161 060	7.8
1978	1 061 200	9.2	1999	3 209 990	1.5
1979	1 175 800	10.8	2000	3 498 200	9.0
1980	1 203 600	2.4	2001	3 442 600	−1.6
1981	1 217 300	1.1	2002	3 461 000	0.5
1982	1 286 900	5.7	2003	3 388 000	−2.1
1983	1 253 000	−2.6	2004	4 369 000	28.9
1984	1 418 500	13.2	2005	4 754 000	8.8
1985	1 512 000	6.6	2006	4 941 000	3.9

Source: ABS (1996, 2001 and 2004), TRA (2007b)

TABLE 3.5 Domestic tourism trips in Australia, 1998 to 2007

Year	Number (000s)	Growth (%)
1998[1]	73 811	n/a
1999	72 981	−1.1
2000	73 771	1.1
2001	74 585	1.1

(continued)

TABLE 3.5 *(continued)*		
Year	Number (000s)	Growth (%)
2002	75 339	1.0
2003	73 621	−2.3
2004	74 301	0.9
2005	69 924	−5.9
2006	73 564	5.2
2007	73 800	0.3

Note:
[1]Results from this and subsequent reporting periods are not comparable to previous periods due to a change in sampling procedure.
Source: Data derived from TRA (2007a, 2007b)

■ FUTURE GROWTH PROSPECTS

Given the incredibly rapid pace of change that is affecting all facets of contemporary life, any attempt to make medium- or long-term predictions about the tourism sector is very risky. It can be confidently predicted that technology will continue to revolutionise the tourism industry, pose new challenges to tourism managers and restructure tourism systems at all levels. However, the nature and timing of radical future innovations, or their implications, cannot be identified with any precision. In terms of demand, the number of persons living in Phase Four (and Phase Five?) countries is likely to increase dramatically over the next two or three decades as a consequence of the **condensed development sequence** and the nature of the countries currently in Phases Two and Three. The former term refers to the fact that societies today are undergoing the transition towards full economic development (i.e. a Phase Four state) in a reduced amount of time compared to their counterparts in the past. The timeframe for the United Kingdom, for example, was about 200 years (roughly 1750–1950). Japan, however, was able to make the transition within about 80 years (1860–1940) while the timeframe for South Korea was only about 40 years (1950–90).

One reason for this acceleration is the ability of the transitional societies to use technologies introduced during earlier stages of the industrialisation process. Therefore, although England had the great advantage of access to the resources and markets of its colonies, it also had to invent the technology of industrialisation. Today, less developed countries such as India can facilitate their economic and social development through already available technologies. It is possible that China, in particular, with its extremely rapid pace of economic growth, will emerge as a Phase Four society by the year 2020. If this is achieved, then tourism managers will have to allow for 1 billion or more additions to the global market for international tourism. However, there are also the countervailing risks of a major economic depression, further spectacular acts of terrorism, health epidemics, or regional or global war involving nuclear, chemical or biological weapons.

CHAPTER REVIEW

Tourism is an ancient phenomenon that was evident in classical Egypt, Greece and Rome, as well as in the Middle Ages. Distinctive characteristics of tourism in this pre-modern stage include its limited accessibility, the importance of religious as well as educational and health motivations, and the lack of a well-defined tourism 'industry'. Other features include the risky, uncomfortable and time-consuming nature of travel, its restriction to relatively few well-defined land and sea routes, and the limited, local-ised and unplanned spatial impact of tourism upon the landscape. Premodern tourism is similar to modern tourism in the essential role of discretionary time and income in facilitating travel, and the desire to escape congested urban conditions. Other commo-nalities include curiosity about the past and other cultures, the desire to avoid risk and the proclivity to purchase souvenirs and to leave behind graffiti as a reminder of one's presence in a destination region.

The emergence of Europe from the Middle Ages marked the transition towards the early modern era of tourism, during which spas, seaside resorts and the Grand Tour were important elements. The transition towards modern mass tourism was closely associated with the Industrial Revolution, and especially with Thomas Cook & Son's application of its principles and innovations to the travel sector by way of the package tour and related innovations. Mass tourism emerged as a result of a conver-gence between the reduced costs of such travel and the rising wages of the middle and working classes.

The post-Cook era was characterised by the rapid expansion of domestic tourism within the newly industrialised countries. However, large-scale international tourism was delayed by primitive long-haul transportation technology, and by the appearance of two major economic recessions and two world wars between 1880 and 1945. It was not until the 1950s that international tourism began to display an exponential pattern of growth, stimulated by five interrelated 'push' factors that increased the demand for tourism in the economically developed Phase Three and Four countries. Economic growth provided more discretionary income and time for the masses. Concurrently, society perceived leisure time in a more positive way, moving towards a 'work in order to play' philosophy. Demographic changes such as population growth, urbanisation, smaller family size and rising life expectancies increased the propensity of the popula-tion to engage in tourism-related activities. Technological developments such as the aeroplane and car provided relatively cheap means of transport, while overall political stability facilitated travel between countries. The experience of Australia is typical, with large-scale increases in outbound and domestic tourism being in the post-World War II period. The global pattern of growth is likely to continue largely on the strength of a condensed development sequence that is rapidly propelling countries such as China and India into the ranks of the Phase Three and Four societies.

■ SUMMARY OF KEY TERMS

Baby boomers people born during the post–World War II period of high TFRs (roughly 1946 to 1964), who constitute a noticeable bulge within the population pyramid of Australia and other Phase Four countries

BRIC countries Brazil, Russia, India and China, which had a collective population of about 2.7 billion in 2008 and are expected to achieve Burton's Phase Four status within two decades

Condensed development sequence the process whereby societies undergo the transition to a Phase Four state within an increasingly reduced period of time

Crusades a series of campaigns to 'liberate' Jerusalem and the Holy Land from Muslim control. While not a form of tourism as such, the Crusades helped to re-open Europe to the outside world and spawn an incipient travel industry

Dark Ages the period from about AD 500 to 1100, characterised by a serious deterioration in social, economic and political conditions within Europe

Demographic transition model (DTM) an idealised depiction of the process whereby societies evolve from a high fertility/high mortality structure to a low fertility/low mortality structure. This evolution usually parallels the development of a society from a Phase One to a Phase Four profile, as occurred during the Industrial Revolution. A fifth stage may now be emerging, characterised by extremely low birth rates and resultant net population loss

Discretionary income the amount of income that remains after household necessities such as food, housing, clothing, education and transportation have been purchased

Discretionary time normally defined as time not spent at work, or in normal rest and bodily maintenance

Early modern tourism the transitional era between premodern tourism (about AD 1500) and modern mass tourism (since 1950)

Earned time a time management option in which an individual is no longer obligated to work once a particular quota is attained over a defined period of time (often monthly or annual)

Flexitime a time management option in which workers have some flexibility in distributing a required number of working hours (usually weekly) in a manner that suits the lifestyle and productivity of the individual worker

Grand Tour a form of early modern tourism that involved a lengthy trip to the major cities of France and Italy by young adults of the leisure class, for purposes of education and culture

Industrial Revolution a process that occurred in England from the mid-1700s to the mid-1900s (and spread outwards to other countries), in which society was transformed from an agrarian to an industrial base, thereby spawning conditions that were conducive to the growth of tourism-related activity

Leisure class in premodern tourism, that small portion of the population that had sufficient discretionary time and income to engage in leisure pursuits such as tourism

Mesopotamia the region approximately occupied by present-day Iraq, where the earliest impulses of civilisation first emerged, presumably along with the first tourism activity

Middle Ages the period from about AD 1100 to the Renaissance (about AD 1500), characterised by an improvement in the social, economic and political situation, in comparison with the Dark Ages

Modern mass tourism (Contemporary tourism) the period from 1950 to the present day, characterised by the rapid expansion of international and domestic tourism

Olympic Games the most important of the ancient Greek art and athletics festivals, held every four years at Olympia. The ancient Olympic Games are one of the most important examples of premodern tourism

Package tour a pre-paid travel package that usually includes transportation, accommodation, food and other services

Pilgrimage generic term for travel undertaken for religious purpose. Pilgrimages have declined in importance during the modern era compared with recreational, business and social tourism

'Play in order to work' philosophy an industrial-era ethic, which holds that leisure time and activities are necessary in order to make workers more productive, thereby reinforcing the work-focused nature of society

Post-Cook period the time from about 1880 to 1950, characterised by the rapid growth of domestic tourism within the wealthier countries, but less rapid expansion in international tourism

Postindustrial era a later Phase Four stage in which hi-tech services and information replace manufacturing and lower-order services as the mainstay of an economy

Premodern tourism describes the era of tourism activity from the beginning of civilisation to the end of the Middle Ages

Push factors economic, social, demographic, technological and political forces that stimulate a demand for tourism activity by 'pushing' consumers away from their usual place of residence

Renaissance the 'rebirth' of Europe following the Dark Ages, commencing in Italy during the mid-1400s and spreading to Germany and the 'low countries' by the early 1600s

Resorts facilities or urban areas that are specialised in the provision of recreational tourism opportunities

Seaside resorts a type of resort located on coastlines to take advantage of sea bathing for health and, later, recreational purposes; many of these were established during the Industrial Revolution for both the leisure and working classes

Spas a type of resort centred on the use of geothermal waters for health purposes

Thomas Cook the entrepreneur whose company Thomas Cook & Son applied the principles of the Industrial Revolution to the tourism sector through such innovations as the package tour

Tourism participation sequence according to Burton, the tendency for a society to participate in tourism increases through a set of four phases that relate to the concurrent process of increased economic development

Phase One: pre-industrial, mainly agricultural and subsistence-based economies where tourism participation is restricted to a small leisure class

Phase Two: the generation of wealth increases and tends to spread to a wider segment of the population as a consequence of industrialisation and related processes such as urbanisation. This leads to increases in the demand for domestic tourism among the middle classes

Phase Three: the bulk of the population becomes increasingly affluent, leading to the emergence of mass domestic travel, as well as extensive international tourism to nearby countries. The elite, meanwhile, engage in greater long-haul travel

Phase Four: represents a fully developed country with almost universal affluence, and a subsequent pattern of mass international tourism to an increasingly diverse array of short- and long-haul destinations. Almost all residents engage in a comprehensive variety of domestic tourism experiences

Virtual reality (VR) the wide-field presentation of computer-generated, multisensory information that allows the user to experience a virtual world

War dividend the long-term benefits for tourism that derive from large conflicts, including war-related attractions, image creation, and the emergence of new travel markets

'Work in order to play' philosophy a postindustrial ethic derived from ancient Greek philosophy that holds that leisure and leisure-time activities such as tourism are important in their own right and that we work to be able to afford to engage in leisure pursuits

■ QUESTIONS

1. Why is it useful to understand the major forms and types of tourism that occurred in the premodern era?
2. (a) Why is Thomas Cook referred to as the father of modern mass tourism?
   (b) Why did it take more than a century for Cook's innovations to translate into a pattern of mass global tourism activity?
3. (a) Why have international tourism receipts grown at a much greater rate than international tourist arrivals since 1950 (see table 3.1)?
   (b) Why do international tourism receipts display much greater levels of annual fluctuation than international tourist arrivals?
4. (a) Is your household more or less time-stressed than it was ten years ago?
   (b) How has this affected the tourism activity of your household?
5. (a) Do you believe that people have a basic human right to travel?
   (b) If so, how far should these rights extend?
   (c) What are the implications for destinations?
6. In the long term, is a major war a net benefit or liability for the tourism industry?
7. To what extent are virtual reality technologies likely to help or hinder participation in tourism?
8. To what degree should your home country be focusing on the emerging BRIC countries (Brazil, Russia, India, China) as a tourist market?

■ EXERCISES

1. Write a 1000-word report in which you describe:
   (a) the pattern of participation in domestic and outbound tourism by the people of China between 1970 and 2010
   (b) the push factors that help to account for these patterns
   (c) your analysis of how these push factors will change during the next five years and what effects these changes will have on tourism participation.
2. Write a 1000-word report in which you describe:
   (a) how a typical Australian household in 2001 (i.e. Phase Four) differs from its 1901 counterpart (i.e. Phase Two)
   (b) the patterns of tourism activity that might be expected from each household over a one-year period
   (c) what a future Phase Five Australian household and its tourism-related patterns might look like.

■ FURTHER READING

Gunn, C. 2004. *Western Tourism: Can Paradise be Reclaimed?* Elmsford, USA: **Cognizant.** Gunn's analysis of tourism in the western United States focuses around a trip that the author made to the region in the late 1920s.

Hannam, K. & Ateljevic, I. (Eds) 2008. *Backpacker Tourism: Concepts and Profiles.* **Clevedon, UK: Channel View.** The chapters in this book provide a diverse examination of backpacker attitudes, behaviour and motivations informed by various social science perspectives.

Lynch, R. & Veal, A. 2006. *Australian Leisure.* **Third Edition. Sydney: Longman.** This book provides an Australia-specific account of historical and modern leisure trends, and effectively places these in the broad global context.

Toohey, K. & Veal, A. 2007. 'The Ancient Olympics and Their Relevance to the Modern Games.' In Toohey, K. & Veal, A. (Eds.). *The Olympic Games: A Social Science Perspective.* **Wallingford, UK: CABI, pp. 9–25.** The authors describe the characteristics of the ancient Olympic Games, emphasising factors that have influenced and are relevant to the modern Olympic Games.

Towner, J. 1996. *An Historical Geography of Recreation and Tourism in the Western World 1540–1940.* **Chichester, UK: Wiley.** Major topic areas within this well-researched, academically oriented text include the Grand Tour and spas and seaside resorts, within both Europe and North America.

Withey, L. 1997. *Grand Tours and Cook's Tours.* **New York: William Morrow & Company, Inc.** Two critical eras in the historical development of tourism are covered in a thorough and well-written manner by Withey.

case study

BEHOLD THE BOOMER

Baby boomers, individuals born between 1946 and 1964 in the USA, Canada, Australia and New Zealand, are both a demographic anomaly and an enormously influential group within their respective societies. The anomaly aspect relates to the relatively high fertility rate that characterised the period, caused in large measure by great numbers of young returning soldiers from World War II who started families in an era of growing economic prosperity and confidence in the future. In Australia, this phenomenon is reflected in a total fertility rate which increased from 2.2 in 1931 to 3.2 in 1954 and 3.3 in 1961 (see table 3.3). About 4 million Australians were born during the baby boom and now account for about 20 per cent of the population. However, their position in the peak earning stages of their working lives means that they account for a much high proportion of Australia's wages and overall personal savings and wealth. With the oldest boomers celebrating their sixtieth birthdays in 2006, providers of all types of goods and services are now competing vigorously with each other to attract the attention of retiring boomers.

Market knowledge is the first step in capturing the boomer dollar. Being the first generation to have no personal experience with deep poverty, a major war or economic catastrophe, it is not surprising that baby boomers are substantively different from either their parents or children with respect to values, attitudes, and behaviour. Regarding travel and tourism specifically, research indicates that boomers are *experienced travellers* who *regard leisure travel as a necessity rather than a luxury* (Ross 2000). They were the first to take regular family vacations as children, travelled as backpackers in their early adulthood, took their own children on holidays, and see this as an entitlement they will continue to pursue throughout their lives. Boomers are highly experienced and well-educated tourists who will not be satisfied with standard package tours to well-known destinations. Ecotourism, adventure tourism, and wine tours are instead the type of exotic niche products which are poised to attract boomers, especially since they *perceive themselves to be forever young* and will pursue physically and mentally taxing activities that their parents would have avoided. Even conventional hotels, however, should provide workout facilities so that boomers can maintain a high level of physical conditioning.

Having been raised in an era of affluence during which few of their needs or wants went unmet, boomers tend to *believe that they are special*, and are prone to *demanding instant gratification*. Thus, they seek out luxury goods and experiences, and often purchase these spontaneously on their credit cards; not for them their parents' frugal holiday savings fund or desire to leave an estate to their children. The need for instant gratification also means that boomers are impatient with long transit journeys or waits in queue. Long-haul destinations must therefore be able to provide experiences that are worth the wait (but don't include queuing), while airlines and other transportation providers must pay more attention to the provision of passenger diversions and the *desire for creature comforts*. The need for diversions and comforts, and conveniences in general, in turn relates to the fact that most boomers feel *time deprived* due to hectic working, social and personal schedules. All aspects of the tourism experience must therefore be 'worthwhile'. For some, this is achieved in a hectic schedule of vigorous physical activity; for others, an 'authentic' encounter with a new culture. Others still prefer a relaxing spa or 'wellness' experience as the best way to restore physical and mental wellbeing. Many seek a combination of all these impulses. Segmentation studies in Australia's Lamington National Park, for example, reveal a desire by a majority of ecolodge customers (who average over 50 years in age) to offset a daytime of vigorous hiking and environmental learning in semi-wilderness settings with an evening of gourmet food, warm mineral baths, expert lectures and comfortable bedding. Nighttime pampering apparently makes daytime challenging all the easier (Weaver & Lawton 2002).

Raised to challenge authority, boomers tend to be *skeptical of institutions* and are not easily swayed in their travel decisions by slick marketing techniques. Similarly, they do not join clubs or other organisations to the degree that their parents did, and thus prefer to travel as pairs or in small groups, especially with other baby boomers since they *prefer to associate with people like themselves.* Word of mouth information from fellow boomers therefore has a very important influence in travel decisions.

Marketers and other tourism stakeholders, however, must avoid thinking that baby boomers are a homogenous market. 'Classic' tendencies are more evident among older boomers who protested the Vietnam War, participated in the hippie movement, toured Asia to 'find themselves', experimented copiously with drugs and sex and women's liberation, and cheered the resignation of US President Richard Nixon in the early 1970s. Those born after 1955, in contrast, faced recession and high unemployment in the 1980s. Because they were not protesting against authority figures such as their parents, younger boomers are more likely to look back nostalgically to the past and to place more emphasis on family than their own individuality (Ross 2000). The second generation of boomer retirees, therefore, is likely to behave very differently than their older boomer counterparts.

QUESTIONS

1. Prepare a 1000-word report that describes a tourism product (resort, attraction, destination etc.) which would appeal to an older (i.e. born between 1946 and 1955) baby boom market. Design, activities, price, and services are aspects of the product that should be taken into account. Explain why the hypothetical project would appeal to boomers.

2. (a) Describe how individuals born after 1980 (i.e. children of baby boomers) are different from baby boomers in terms of the characteristics italicised in the case study. Do this by asking your peers to agree or disagree with these characteristics and explain the reasons for their stance.

   (b) Discuss how the tourism behaviour and preferences of those born after 1980 contrast accordingly with those of the baby boomers.

CHAPTER 4

DESTINATIONS

LEARNING OBJECTIVES

After studying this chapter, you should be able to:

1. describe and explain the relative status of the more developed and less developed world as tourist destination regions

2. identify the major generic factors that attract or 'pull' visitors to tourist destinations

3. discuss how much destinations and various tourism stakeholders can influence these pull factors

4. describe and explain the status of tourism in each of the world's major regions, and assess the pull factors that have contributed to these patterns

5. account for the tendency of tourism at all scales to develop in a spatially uneven pattern and discuss the implications of this tendency

6. identify and assess the basic pattern of inbound and domestic tourism within australia.

INTRODUCTION

Chapter 3 described the remarkable growth of contemporary international and domestic tourism from a demand perspective, without reference to the specific destinations that are the focus of this growth. Chapter 4 addresses the supply perspective by considering the spatial variations in the growth and distribution of tourism among and within the world's major regions, and the factors that underlie these patterns. The following section examines these variations at the most basic level by describing the **global inequality in tourism** that exists between the economically 'more developed' and 'less developed' worlds. The major factors that have stimulated or hindered the development of tourism in each of these two 'macro-regions' are also discussed in this section, but the 'Pull factors influencing a destination' section considers the generic 'pull' factors that draw tourists to destinations in general. The 'Regional destination patterns' section describes the tourism situation in each of the world's major geographical regions and examines the pull factors (or lack thereof) that apply in each case. The spatial characteristics of tourism within individual countries are outlined in the final section.

GLOBAL DESTINATION PATTERNS: MDCS AND LDCS

The world is roughly divided into two 'macro-regions' based on relative levels of economic development and associated sociodemographic characteristics such as social structure and fertility rates. The **more developed countries (MDCs)** (collectively constituting the 'more developed world') correspond with Burton's Phase Three and Phase Four countries (see chapter 3). They include Australia, New Zealand, the United States, Canada, Europe, Japan, South Korea, Hong Kong, Taiwan and Singapore. Relatively poor European countries such as Russia, Ukraine, Yugoslavia, Albania and Bulgaria are included essentially by default because of their cultural affinities with that otherwise prosperous continent.

The **less developed countries (LDCs)** (or cumulatively the 'less developed world') are synonymous with those still situated in Burton's Phase Two. The major less developed regions are Latin America and the Caribbean, most of Asia, Africa and the islands of the Pacific and Indian oceans. Wealthy Middle Eastern oil-producing states, including Libya, Kuwait and Saudi Arabia, are included in this category despite their high per capita incomes. This is because of cultural affiliations with other regional countries and social indicators (such as higher fertility and infant mortality rates) that suggest Phase Two dynamics. The designation of countries into either the MDC or LDC category, by convention and perception, remained remarkably stable during the latter half of the twentieth century, though it must not be assumed that all MDCs are more economically developed than all LDCs. Moreover, many countries have MDC-like and LDC-like spaces within their own boundaries (e.g. large cities and Aboriginal reserves).

Tourism market share and growth

Table 4.1 depicts the status of the more developed and less developed worlds as recipients of inbound tourism for selected years in the period between 1950 and 2007. The continuing dominance of the more developed world is evident, but so too is the gradual erosion of this status. MDC destinations accounted for about 65 per cent of all international stayovers in 2007, compared with more than 90 per cent before 1970. This reduction, moreover, occurred despite the acquisition of MDC status by Singapore, Hong Kong, South Korea and Taiwan, which together accounted for 5 per cent of all inbound tourism in 2007. The LDCs cumulatively have experienced a 160-fold increase in their stayover arrivals (i.e. from 2 million to 316 million) between 1950 and 2007, while the MDCs have experienced a 'mere' 25-fold increase (i.e. from 23 million to 587 million).

TABLE 4.1 International stayover arrivals by LDCs and MDCs, 1950–2007

Year	MDCs[1] (million)	Share (%)	LDCs (million)	Share (%)	Global total (million)
1950	23.2	91.7	2.1	8.3	25.2
1960	64.8	93.5	4.5	6.5	69.3
1970	142.0	88.9	17.7	11.1	159.7
1980	226.0	79.0	60.1	21.0	286.1
1990	352.7	77.4	103.2	22.6	455.9
1994	419.3	76.8	126.6	23.2	545.9
1998	467.4	73.5	168.6	26.5	636.0
2002	504.5	71.8	198.2	28.2	702.7
2007	587.3	65.0	315.9	35.0	903.2

Note:
1 Includes South Korea, Singapore, Hong Kong and Taiwan since 1990
Source: UNWTO (2008), WTO (1998, 2005)

Reasons for the emergence of the LDCs as destinations

Many factors have combined to elevate the less developed world into the position of an increasingly prominent destination macro-region. However, particularly important are changing consumer preferences in the major international tourist markets, and economic growth within the less developed world itself.

Demand for 3S tourism: the emergence of the pleasure periphery

Seaside resorts were already established as tourist destinations in the era of the Roman Empire, but became especially important within Europe, North America and Australia in conjunction with the Industrial Revolution (see chapter 3). Nineteenth-century limitations in technology as well as discretionary income and time restricted the development of these resorts to domestic coastal locations close to expanding urban markets. However, dramatic twentieth-century advances in air transportation technology combined with the overall development process and changing social perceptions to greatly extend the distribution, scale, and market range of seaside and beach resorts. This modern phase of expansion in **3S tourism** (i.e. sea, sand and sun) initially affected the warmer coastal regions of the more developed countries. Among the destination regions spawned by this trend were the French, Italian and Spanish Rivieras, the east coast of Florida (and the American **sunbelt** in general), Australia's Gold Coast and Japan's Okinawa Island. Tourism development subsequently spread into adjacent parts of the Mediterranean, Caribbean, South Pacific and Indian Ocean basins within the less developed world.

The expansion of 3S tourism occurred at such a rate and extent that it was possible by the mid-1970s to discern the emergence of a pan-global **pleasure periphery** (Turner & Ash 1975). 'Pleasure' refers to the hedonistic nature of the 3S product, while 'periphery' alludes to the marginal geographic and economic status of its constituent subregions, which straddle both the more developed and less developed world (figure 4.1). The Mediterranean basin is the oldest and largest (in terms of visitation) subcomponent, followed by the Caribbean basin. Less geographically coherent is a band of more recently developed 3S destinations extending from the South Pacific through South-East Asia, coastal Australia and the Indian Ocean basin. Notable among these are the southern Chinese island-province of Hainan and the south-western Indian state of Kerala, where 3S tourism development is progressing rapidly but primarily in response to the explosive growth in the domestic rather than inbound tourism market (see Managing tourism: 3S tourism development in Hainan province, China).

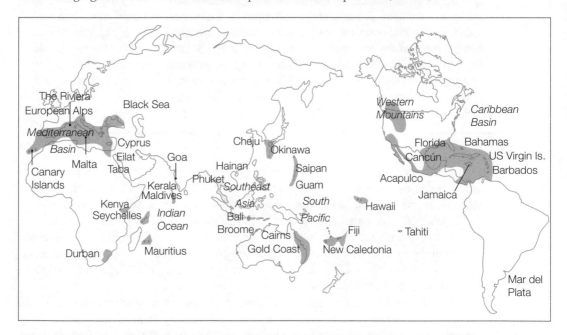

FIGURE 4.1 The pleasure periphery

managing tourism

3S TOURISM DEVELOPMENT IN HAINAN PROVINCE, CHINA

In 1986, the Central Government of China designated the island of Hainan as a priority area for tourism development along with six other key cities and provinces. Six years later, the provincial government of Hainan identified Yalong Bay, in the resort city of Sanya, as a priority site for a major beach resort project. This and subsequent developments exemplify a 'top-down' model of planning in which government regards itself as the most appropriate entity for making decisions about future tourism expansion, having both the necessary expertise as well as concern and responsibility for the wellbeing of the population (Wang & Wall 2007). Population displacement is an accepted aspect of this planning model, justified by the greater good gained from resulting tourism revenues, and the positive 'modernisation' effects of development on 'backward' local people.

In the early 2000s, two villages on Yalong Bay occupied by members of the local Li minority — a 'backward' group — were relocated to make room for golf courses and other tourism-related facilities. Beyond the issue of whether it was ethical to displace long-established local communities to accommodate tourism, the resettlement effort was widely regarded as unsatisfactory from several perspectives (Wang & Wall 2007). First, the entrenched top-down nature of the decision-making process meant that local input was minimal despite the provision of formal channels for obtaining such feedback. In addition, administrative arrangements were not well integrated or coordinated, with representatives from participating agencies focusing only on their own sphere of concern rather than the overall process or the wellbeing of the communities involved. Displaced villagers regarded their new settlement area as more crowded and confined than their original village. One time payments for the confiscation of the villagers' farmland, moreover, were seen as insufficient compensation for the permanent loss of future crop revenue from that land. Promised new jobs were criticised as menial and low-paying, offering less freedom and flexibility than their old farming work. It may be unreasonable in the foreseeable future to expect China to implement the decentralised and participatory planning models that are now normative in Western countries, but it is clear that processes of administrative structure and compensation associated with population displacement need to be reformed if the country is to avoid widespread public dissatisfaction as it continues to expand its tourism capacity.

The growth of tourism in most pleasure periphery destinations has been dramatic, as illustrated by a selection of relevant countries (see figure 4.2). This growth has been especially apparent in **small island states or dependencies (SISODs)**, such as Fiji and the Seychelles, which are concentrated in the pleasure periphery and are for the most part endowed with suitable 3S resources. As a result, they are greatly overrepresented as inbound tourist destinations in proportion to their resident populations. Specifically, the world's 63 SISODs account for only 0.3 per cent of the global population, but around 5 per cent of total international stayover arrivals.

Although best known for its 3S opportunities, the pleasure periphery has expanded to incorporate other types of tourism product. Skiing and other alpine-based winter sporting activities are now widespread in the North American Rockies and the European Alps, while wildlife-based activities are becoming increasingly important in destinations such as Kenya, Australia, New Zealand, Thailand and Costa Rica (see chapter 11).

Economic growth of LDCs

Inbound tourist traffic into the less developed world, and into the pleasure periphery in particular, has traditionally occurred as a **north–south flow** involving North American, European and Japanese travellers. For Australians and New Zealanders the direction of flow is reversed, although the labels are still valid to the extent that developed countries are sometimes referred to collectively as the 'North'. This pattern, however, is now eroding due to accelerated economic growth within the less developed world, which is generating a significant outbound tourist market among its emergent middle and upper classes, and creating greater complexity in the global tourism system. As noted in chapter 3, the middle classes in Phase Three societies tend to visit nearby countries, while the rich extend their visits to more prestigious long-haul destinations, often within the more developed world. The net result is that much of the growth in LDC inbound tourism is accounted for by arrivals from other (usually nearby) LDCs. In effect, the stereotype of the Australian tourist in Bali, or the Japanese tourist in Thailand is being challenged by the image of the Brazilian tourist in Argentina, the Indian tourist in Dubai, the Chinese tourist in Malaysia and the Kenyan tourist in Tanzania.

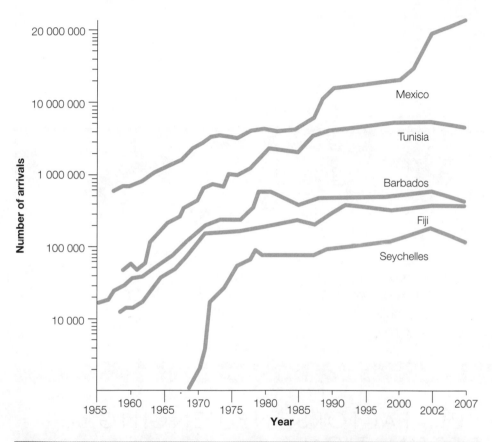

FIGURE 4.2 Performance of selected pleasure periphery destinations: international stayover arrivals

Source: UNWTO

This movement of international tourists within the less developed world may be characterised as the third geographical stage of international tourism in the contemporary era. The stages are as follows:

- The first stage, involving the movement of international tourists within the more developed world, emerged in the post–World War II period and still accounts for perhaps 63 per cent of all traffic (i.e. the 65 per cent share indicated in table 4.1 minus the approximately 2 per cent who are LDC residents travelling to MDCs — see figure 4.3).
- The second stage, largely associated with the emergence of the pleasure periphery after the late 1960s, involves the movement of MDC residents to LDC destinations. Approximately 20 per cent of international stayover traffic presently falls into this category.

- The third stage, involving LDC-to-LDC traffic, accounts for 5 to 8 per cent of all tourism but has the greatest growth potential. The realisation of this potential, however, will mean that many of these countries will have been reclassified as MDCs.
- An emergent fourth stage, accounting for about 2 per cent of international tourism flows, involves LCD residents visiting the MDCs. Examples include the rapidly increasing growth in Chinese visitors to Australia and New Zealand (see the case study at the end of this chapter).

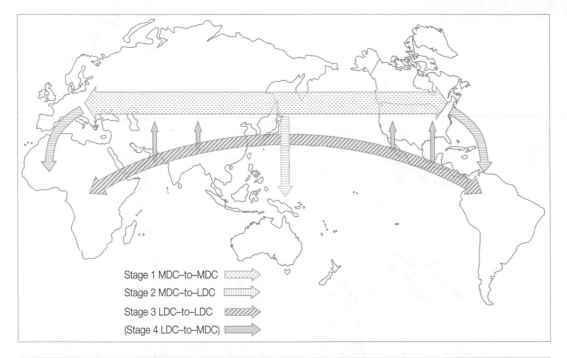

Stage 1 MDC–to–MDC
Stage 2 MDC–to–LDC
Stage 3 LDC–to–LDC
(Stage 4 LDC–to–MDC)

FIGURE 4.3 Four stages of contemporary international tourist flows

■ PULL FACTORS INFLUENCING A DESTINATION

Two of the major forces (i.e. the fashionability of 3S tourism, and internal economic development) that have stimulated growth in the less developed world's share of the inbound tourist market have been examined above. Consideration will now be given to the general factors that can potentially encourage or discourage tourist traffic to any particular destination. These pull factors differ from the push factors outlined in chapter 3 in being focused on the supply side of tourism (i.e. product or destination-based forces) rather than on tourist demand (i.e. market or origin-based forces). As with the *push factors*, the use of the term 'pull' is metaphorical rather than literal.

One important implication of this geographical differentiation between supply and demand is that destinations are better positioned to exert influence over the pull factors than they are over the push factors. For example, a destination does not normally influence whether another country evolves into a significant tourist-generating market, but it can take tangible measures to develop its supply of attractions and create a welcoming environment to attract potential visitors from that market. This issue of control will be considered in the discussion of each individual factor. No priority is intended in the order that these factors are presented, since the combination and relative importance of individual factors will vary from one destination to another.

Geographical proximity to markets

Controlling for all other factors, an inverse relationship is likely to exist between the volume of traffic flowing from an origin region to a destination region and the distance separating the two. That is, the number of visitors from origin X to destination Y will decrease as distance increases between X and Y, owing to higher transportation costs and longer travel times. This is known as a **distance-decay** effect (McKercher & Lew 2003). The volume of traffic will also be proportional to the size and prosperity of the origin region market, with large and wealthy markets generating larger flows.

These basic relationships are discernible throughout the world. The Caribbean, Mediterranean and South-East Asian subregions of the pleasure periphery, for example, are dominated respectively by American, European and Japanese outbound tourists. A distance–decay relationship is evident as well in the pattern of Australian outbound travel, with eight of the top ten destinations being located in Oceania or Asia (figure 4.4). Although not apparent in figure 4.4, the effect also influences Australian outbound travel to the United States, where most visits are concentrated in the Pacific and western states of Hawaii, California and Nevada (the state where Las Vegas is located). Destination managers cannot alter the location of their city or country relative to the market, but distance can serve as an incentive (or disincentive if the distance is short) to pursue strategies such as more aggressive marketing that will help to compensate for this effect. These strategies may include attempts to reduce the psychological distance between the destination and target origin regions. Geographical proximity, however, is likely to become an increasingly important pull factor as energy costs continue to increase.

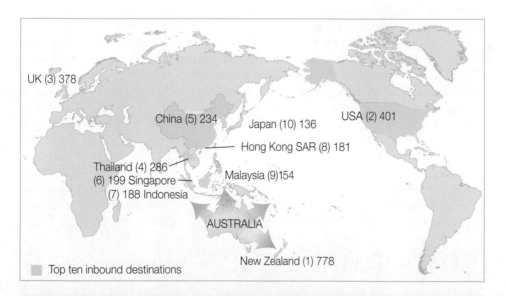

FIGURE 4.4 Main destinations for Australian outbound tourists, 2007 (year ending March)

Notes:
Rank of countries in parentheses.
Number beside country equals number of Australian outbound tourists received
(in thousands).
Source: Data derived from TRA 2007c

Accessibility to markets

The effects of distance can also be reduced by developments that make destinations more accessible to origin regions. **Infrastructural accessibility** refers to the availability and quality of transportation linkages such as air routes, highways and ferry links within transit regions, and of gateway facilities such as seaports and airports within the destination and origin regions. The level of infrastructural accessibility in a destination depends on many factors, including the availability of funds, physical barriers (including distance itself) and cooperation with other destinations as well as intervening jurisdictions in the transit region to establish effective air, land and/or water linkages.

Political accessibility refers to the conditions under which visitors are allowed entry into a destination. Except in authoritarian states such as North Korea, where restrictions on internal travel are imposed, political access is not a significant issue in domestic tourism. However, it is critical in international tourism. The right to allow or deny entry to potential arrivals from other countries is a basic sovereign prerogative of all states, as discussed in chapter 2. In some cases this right has been eroded or conceded altogether through bilateral or multilateral treaties. Citizens and permanent residents of Australia and New Zealand, for example, share a reciprocal right to reside in each other's country for an indefinite period of time. On a larger scale, the 1993 opening of boundaries between the countries of the European Union has meant that travel between Germany and Denmark or the United Kingdom and France is no longer mediated by any border formalities, and is therefore equivalent in effect to domestic tourism. Such initiatives in border liberalisation, however, became subject to new scrutiny and criticism following the terrorist attacks of 11 September 2001, given their effect of expediting the movements of individuals involved with terrorism. There is now a greater possibility, for example, that a 'Fortress Europe' will emerge wherein internal border liberalisation will be accompanied by the tightening of borders with adjacent countries in Eastern Europe and North Africa. Political access is one of the pull factors over which destination countries (though not subnational destinations) can exercise a high level of control.

Government and the tourism industry often differ in their perceptions of the degree to which borders should be opened to inbound tourism. The immigration and security arms of national governments tend to favour less open borders (especially since September 2001), on the assumption that some international visitors may attempt to gain illegal entry or constitute a potential threat to the state in terrorism-related or other ways (see Contemporary issue: America's war on tourists?). In contrast, the business sector views tourists as potential customers, and is therefore supportive of more open borders and an internationally recognised right to travel. This view is usually shared by government departments responsible for the development and promotion of the tourism sector, if such bodies exist within that state. Most destination countries compromise between completely closed and completely open borders by requiring visitors to produce passports or visas and, in some cases, evidence of a local address and return fare.

contemporary issue

AMERICA'S WAR ON TOURISTS?

Believing that it is contending with a never-ending war on terrorism, USA government officials in the early 2000s launched a parallel but unintended war on tourism (Huck 2007). Fixated on denying entry to potential terrorists, immigration and security forces since 2001 have introduced increasingly draconian measures that counter the broader international trend toward open borders and invite growing levels of visitor dissatisfaction and anxiety. Los Angeles International Airport (LAX) has come to symbolise the cold US welcome with its extremely long queues for non-resident alien visitors, unfriendly immigration and customs officials, and excessive security screening procedures. A recent poll of international tourists by the Discover America Partnership (a coalition of tourism organisations) found that 70 per cent of respondents feared US immigration and security officials more than terrorists or criminals, while 66 per cent were concerned that they could be detained for a minor error or mistaken identity. US government officials insist that only a very small proportion of visitors are seriously inconvenienced by these procedures, but fail to appreciate that anecdotal horror stories of strip searches and summary deportations are spread broadly and rapidly through the media and word of mouth communication, seriously damaging the image of the US as a welcoming destination.

Despite evidence of longer term damage to inbound tourist flows and international public opinion, US government officials unapologetically defend the Fortress America approach as a necessary measure to protect the American people. As of late 2007, officials were continuing to pursue a proposal which would require all visitors from Europe (most of whom previously had their travel to the USA expedited by a visa waiver program) to register online and provide personal information to a US government website two days prior to arrival. The move is strongly opposed by the Europeans, who are threatening to retaliate in kind if the measure is adopted (Spiegel Online 2007). Since 1 June 2009, the Western Hemisphere Travel Initiative (WHTI) requires inbound Canadians and returning US citizens to present a valid passport or Trusted Traveler Card for entry into the US, a move that overrides previous acceptance of an oral declaration of citizenship at the border (Homeland Security 2008). Although criticised strongly by the US tourism industry, such initiatives may be quietly welcomed by competing destination-countries who stand to gain additional visits from disgruntled former or would-be visitors to the USA. Notably, the election of Obama to the US presidency in 2008 has not yet resulted in a more open border policy.

Availability of attractions

A detailed discussion of tourist attractions is provided in chapter 5, but several introductory comments are appropriate here in relation to their pull effect and the question of control. There is widespread agreement among tourism researchers that attractions, because of their crucial role in drawing tourists, are the most important component of the tourism system, and a major factor around which the development of a destination will depend (Goeldner & Ritchie 2006; Richardson & Fluker 2008). Attractions include specific features such as theme parks and battlefields, and generic or nonspecific features such as scenery and climate. The presence of friends and relatives as well as business opportunities, which foster VFR (visits to friends and relatives) and non-event business-related tourist flows respectively, are not normally included in the scope of 'attractions' although in a literal sense they do attract certain types of tourist. The ability of attractions to draw visitors depends among other factors on their quality, quantity, diversity, uniqueness, carrying capacity, market image and accessibility (see chapter 5).

Pre-existing and created attractions

With regard to the issue of the control that a destination has over its tourism assets, attractions range from those that are 'pre-existing' to those that are entirely 'created'. Examples of the former include climate and spectacular topographical or hydrological features (e.g. the Himalaya or Niagara Falls), or significant historical sites (e.g. the Hastings or Waterloo battlefields). Such features already exist independent of any tourism context, and it is really only a question of the extent to which tourism managers and planners exploit the available opportunities that they present. On the other hand, destinations usually possess a great deal of latitude for creating attractions to induce a tourist flow or augment the pre-existing attractions. Examples of augmentation can be found on the Gold Coast, where outstanding inherent natural attractions are supplemented by theme parks, shopping opportunities and other 'built' attractions that contribute to product diversity. In some cases a locality with no significant inherent attractions may emerge as a major destination through the effective introduction of such 'built' opportunities. High profile examples from the United States include Disney World, established in the midst of a scrub pine and pasture landscape outside Orlando, and Las Vegas, the well-known gambling venue. On a much smaller scale, certain Australian towns and cities have become known among tourists for their larger-than-life models of local symbols, including the Big Banana at Coffs Harbour, Nambour's Big Pineapple and Ballina's Big Prawn. Communities also have considerable scope for establishing events and festivals, usually on an annual basis, that may or may not focus on the local culture, economy or climate.

A final point to be made here about attractions is their susceptibility to fashion and social change, suggesting again that the ability of a destination to attract tourists is always subject to demand-side factors beyond its control. For instance, the emergence of the pleasure periphery was in large part a consequence of the high value assigned to sun exposure by Western societies during the latter half of the twentieth century, which converted beaches and warm climates into tourism resources. Throughout most of human history, the idea of lying on a beach to gain a suntan would have been considered ludicrous. Should sun exposure once again become unpopular due to concerns over its relationship to skin cancer and accelerated skin ageing, then the implications for 3S destinations such as the Gold Coast, and Australia in general, could be ominous as tourism managers are forced to reinvent or abandon their product base. This might, for example, require 3S destinations to place more emphasis on contrived cultural attractions or wildlife-based tourism (see chapter 11).

Cultural links

A desire to seek out exotic and unfamiliar venues has been an important motivating force for tourism throughout history. However, similarities in culture, language and religion are also a powerful 'pull' factor in some types of tourism. This is partly because of the increased likelihood that people will migrate to culturally familiar countries (e.g. Finnish people to Sweden, British people to Australia) and subsequently foster VFR tourist flows between their old and new countries. Close cultural links are the main factor underlying the status of the distant United Kingdom as the second most important destination for outbound Australian tourists (figure 4.4).

Immigration aside, religious links have generated significant spiritually motivated tourist flows, as illustrated by strong movements of American Jews to Israel, Muslim pilgrims to Saudi Arabia, and Roman Catholics to Italy and Vatican City. In addition, the tendency of destinations to attract culturally similar markets attests to the importance of the convenience and risk-minimisation factors in tourism. Simply put, many tourists feel insecure or inconvenienced by having to cope with unfamiliar languages and social norms, and therefore prefer destinations similar to their own origin areas (see chapter 6).

Availability of services

Most tourists will avoid attractions if affiliated services are unavailable or of poor quality. The importance of transportation access has been discussed earlier, and to this must be added the presence of adequate accommodation, toilets and dining facilities. Visitor bureaus are also an important facilitating service. At a broader destination level, the presence of basic services nonspecific to tourism, such as policing and medical facilities, is essential. The private sector usually provides the tourism-related elements (except for visitor bureaus), while local governments tend to provide the general services. In general, the MDCs are able to offer a superior level of general service provision because of their greater wealth and higher level of physical development.

Affordability

All other factors being equal, reductions in cost generate increased tourist traffic to a destination, as demonstrated by the effect of distance on transportation costs (see page 88). The cost of living in a destination region relative to an origin area is one important component, since a high proportion of total trip costs are normally incurred within the destination through food and accommodation expenditures. Many travellers from the more affluent countries are attracted to LDCs such as Indonesia or Costa Rica because of the low relative costs of locally denominated goods and services. However, this advantage may be lost in situations where accommodation and other tourist-related goods and services are priced in American dollars or other nonlocal currencies. Tourist flows, nevertheless, are usually sensitive to significant exchange rate fluctuations, as demonstrated by dramatic increases in the number of outbound Australians during the mid-2000s and concomitant stagnation in international tourist arrivals associated with the strong Australian dollar (see the case study at the end of chapter 2).

Destination managers can do little to influence cost of living differentials, given that these result from macrolevel forces such as the development process and global or regional economic dynamics, including the rapid economic growth of China and India. The situation is somewhat different with respect to exchange rates, as national governments can and do intervene in the money markets, or announce radical currency revaluations, when such actions are deemed to be in the national interest. Destinations within a currency bloc (such as most of the European Union), or within a country, however, have no such power. When a high national or bloc currency places the industry at a disadvantage, managers at the provincial or local level can attempt to offset its potentially negative effects through the implementation of price reductions and other incentives. Alternatively, they may restructure their marketing campaigns to attract higher-end markets that are less sensitive to price.

Peace, stability and safety

The tourist market is sensitive to any suggestion of social or political instability within a destination, given the in situ or 'on site' nature of consumption inherent to tourism — that is, consumers must travel to the product in order to engage in its 'consumption'. Accordingly, and not surprisingly, significant declines in tourist arrivals occur during periods of warfare or other conflicts. In Israel, inbound arrivals during the first six months of 2001 were 53 per cent lower than during the comparable period one year earlier, due to the escalation in violence between the Israelis and Palestinians. One consequence was that the proportion of domestic guests in Israeli hotels increased from 53 per cent in September 2000 to 86 per cent in March 2002 (Israeli & Reichel

2003). Inbound arrivals in Lebanon, similarly, have fluctuated in concert with out-breaks of internal sectarian conflict (Issa & Altinay 2006).

The negative effect of war on tourism, moreover, is not necessarily confined to the actual war zone or period of conflict. The unusual decline in cumulative international stayover arrivals during 2003 (see table 3.1), for example, was due in large part to global uncertainty associated with both the prelude and aftermath of the invasion of Iraq by the United States.

Tourism-directed terrorism

The deliberate targeting of tourists and tourism facilities by terrorists is an increasingly disturbing trend that has resulted from several factors (Nielsen 2001; Smith, V. 2004). Among these is the knowledge that the disruption of tourist flows can have severe econ-omic and sociopolitical repercussions in countries where this sector makes a signifi-cant contribution to GNP. This was the main intent of the radical Islamic groups that launched a series of attacks on foreign tourists in Egypt during the 1990s. Similarly, the bombings of two nightclubs in Bali by Muslim radicals in 2002, which killed 200 people and injured another 300, had the desired effect of reducing hotel occupancy rates from 75 to 10 per cent in some parts of the island (Henderson 2003). Such attacks on foreigners (and wealthy, white foreigners in particular) are guaranteed to generate the publicity and media coverage sought by terrorist groups, while tourists and tourism facilities make easy and 'cost-effective' targets compared with military and political sites that are now better secured against terrorist attacks. An extremely important factor is the expansion of tourism into remote areas of the pleasure periphery (e.g. rainforests and isolated beaches) where insurgent and terrorist groups are already established and where it is difficult to ensure the security of visitors. In some of these destinations, tourists have become attractive targets for kidnappers because of the ransom payments they generate. The kidnapping and subsequent release of 9 foreign tourists in Colom-bia's Tayrona National Park by leftist guerillas in 2003 is illustrative (Ospina 2006).

Other personal safety issues

Beyond the macrolevel forces of war, unrest and terrorism, destination viability is affected by the extent to which tourists perceive a place to offer a high level of per-sonal safety in terms of everyday health and wellbeing. Dissuasive factors include high crime levels (see chapter 9), susceptibility to natural disasters such as earthquakes and hurricanes, unsafe drinking water and food, and the prevalence of diseases such as malaria and AIDS. Tourist deaths and injuries associated with traffic-related and other accidents can also generate negative market perceptions, prompting some destinations to pursue strategies that attempt to minimise their occurrence (see Technology and tourism: Australia's National Visitor Safety Handbook).

technology and tourism

AUSTRALIA'S NATIONAL VISITOR SAFETY HANDBOOK

In 2008, the Commonwealth Government and all Australian State Tourism Organisations released a National Visitor Safety Handbook to minimise the incidence of personal injury among inbound tourists. Readily accessible as an online resource through multiple government websites (National

Visitor Safety Program 2008), the handbook provides 'a glossary of tourism safety messages' that are freely available to tourism businesses and the media for use in their own marketing efforts. At the time of writing, an HTML application was being developed that would allow these other entities to position the safety material within their own websites. The opening section on water safety illustrates the comprehensive coverage of the handbook, incorporating subsections on beaches (surf lifesavers; flags for safety; waves, rips and water dangers; sun safety; sun stroke; sharks; marine stingers; crocodiles; smoking on beaches), water holes and lagoons (submerged dangers; crocodiles) and dive safety (check dive conditions first; know your limitations; shipwreck diving; cave diving). Other sections cover transport safety, rural areas safety, weather safety, fire safety, enjoying nature, safety in urban areas, health, and terrorism. Where appropriate, hot links are provided to access the websites of relevant outside organisations such as Surf Live Saving Australia, the Office of Road Safety Queensland, and the Environmental Health Directorate of Western Australia.

The handbook is one major element of the National Visitor Safety Program launched in 2002. Related initiatives include a safety video featured on inbound international flights, and mini-booklets on safety in multiple languages available for distribution at major tourist information centres (Prideaux 2003). While the effectiveness of the program has not yet been empirically tested, it is an important indication of Australia's desire to exercise appropriate duty of care with respect to international visitors — a rapidly emerging component of emerging international travel and tourism law (Atherton & Atherton 2003). Technological advances related to the internet increase the likelihood that the program will yield significant benefits as the handbook continues to evolve in an ever more integrated way in relation to other safety-related sources of information.

Positive market image

Image is the sum of beliefs, attitudes and impressions held by a person or group of people towards some phenomenon (Baloglu & Brinberg 1997). Generally speaking, images can be either descriptive (e.g. the objective perception that the Gold Coast is a seaside resort) or evaluative (the subjective perception that the Gold Coast is tacky and overdeveloped) (Walmsley & Jenkins 1993). Destination images are often an amalgam of assessments related to previously described pull factors such as accessibility, attractions, cultural links, affordability, stability and safety. Such images are immensely important in discretionary forms of tourism such as recreational vacations where the destination is not predetermined by business or social considerations. This is because the product, at least for first-time visitors, is an intangible one that cannot be directly experienced prior to its consumption (i.e. prior to the actual visit) — see page 183. In such cases, potential visitors rely on their images in deciding to patronise one destination over another. Accordingly, image research within tourism studies has traditionally focused on the market awareness and evaluation of destinations and their products as a means of informing the marketing effort. The outcomes of this research often lead destination managers to manipulate their public symbols and promotion in order to improve their market image. This is illustrated by the VeryGC campaign of Australia's Gold Coast, in effect during the early 2000s. This initiative initially conveyed a sophisticated and upmarket image to recruit new markets, and later a more family-oriented set of images to reinforce traditional markets. Note that the 'GC' appellation in the latter images has been amended to feature the more recognisable 'Gold Coast' name in full (see figure 4.5).

FIGURE 4.5 Very GC destination branding campaign — old and new imagery

To eventuate in an actual visit, the potential tourist must first be aware that a destination exists. This is seldom a problem for high-profile destination countries such as the United States, France, China or Australia, but a major problem for more obscure countries such as Namibia, Suriname or Qatar, or for less known places within individual countries. Next, it is vital that the awareness of the potential destination is positive. The continuing unrest in Iraq, for example, has made this formerly obscure country familiar to potential tourists in Australia and other MDCs. However, the negative nature of this awareness ensures that most travellers will avoid it. As described earlier, it is often a question of 'guilt by association', as the tourist market extends what is happening in Iraq to the entire Middle East. Similarly, the unsophisticated would-be tourist may apply a national stereotype to all destinations within a particular country, perceiving for example all Swiss localities in tired alpine/lederhosen terms, or all Californian cities as 'free-fire' zones dominated by street gangs. These stereotypes complicate the ability of tourist destination managers and marketers to disseminate a positive image to the tourism market. A discussion of tourism marketing, which includes the attempt to manipulate destination image within particular tourist markets, is provided in chapter 7.

Pro-tourism policies

The pull effect of a destination can be positively influenced by the introduction and reinforcement of pro-tourism policies that make a destination more accessible. Governments, for example, can and often do employ awareness campaigns among the resident population to promote a welcoming attitude towards visitors, in order to foster a positive market image. However, because such campaigns depend on widespread social engineering, and because their effects can be counteracted by random acts of violence, positive outcomes cannot be guaranteed. Furthermore, it is the behaviour of some tourists, and the structure and development of tourism itself, that often generate negative attitudes within the host community (see chapter 9). This implies that major structural changes to tourism itself, rather than awareness campaigns, may be required to foster a welcoming attitude.

In contrast, more control is possible at the microlevel, as when employers encourage and reward the pro-tourist behaviour of individual hotel employees, travel guides and customs officials. Other pro-tourism measures available to governments include the easing of entry requirements (as within the European Union) and the creation of trans-boundary parks that encourage the cross-border flow of tourists. The reduction or elimination of tourism-related taxes and duties, and the introduction of technologies that expedite security checks, are additional options. In Canada, the government-sponsored Katimavik program supports nation-building by encouraging Canadians from English-speaking areas to participate in community enhancement projects in French-speaking areas (and vice versa). The willingness of government to initiate financial incentives, however, is usually limited by its concurrent desire to maximise the revenues obtained from the tourism sector (see chapter 8). As demonstrated by the recent experience of the USA, efforts by tourism-related agencies and interest groups to increase the volume of international tourist arrivals are often offset by the efforts of the interior and security apparatus to strictly screen all visitors (see pages 88–9).

■ REGIONAL DESTINATION PATTERNS

The uneven distribution and growth of the global tourism sector is evident in the changing balance of tourism between the more developed and less developed worlds. International tourist destination patterns will now be examined from a regional perspective, along with the combinations of factors that have given rise to these patterns. The regions are outlined below in their order of importance as recipients of tourist arrivals. Table 4.2 provides stayover and population data (actual numbers and percentage shares) by major global regions and subregions, as defined by the World Tourism Organization (UNWTO). Data for the individual countries that comprise each region and subregion are provided in appendix 3. It must be emphasised that these and all other stayover statistics in this book are impeded (as a basis for comparing the level of tourist activity between destinations) by their failure to take into account average length of stay. For example, a destination receiving 100 000 stayovers per year with an average stay of ten nights (one million visitor nights) probably has a greater level of tourism intensity than a destination that receives 200 000 stayovers per year with an average stay of three nights (600 000 visitor nights).

TABLE 4.2 International stayover arrivals by region and subregion, 2007

Region/Subregion	Arrivals (million)	Percentage of all arrivals	Population[1] (000s)	Percentage of world population
Europe	**484.4**	**53.6**	**860 744**	**13.3**
Northern Europe	57.6	6.4	89 280	1.4
Western Europe	154.9	17.1	188 302	2.9
Central/Eastern Europe	95.6	10.6	358 594	5.5
Southern/Mediterranean Europe	176.2	19.5	224 568	3.5
Asia and the Pacific	**184.3**	**20.4**	**3 721 084**	**57.4**
North-East Asia	104.2	11.5	1 546 659	23.9
South-East Asia	59.6	6.6	581 909	9.0
Australia/South Pacific	10.7	1.2	33 102	0.5
South Asia	09.8	1.1	1 559 414	24.0
The Americas	**142.5**	**15.8**	**892 343**	**13.8**
North America	95.3	10.6	438 993	6.8
Caribbean	19.5	2.2	38 344	0.6
Central America	07.7	0.9	39 566	0.6
South America	19.9	2.2	375 440	5.8
Middle East	**47.6**	**5.3**	**198 376**	**3.0**
Africa	**44.4**	**4.9**	**812 261**	**12.5**
North Africa	16.3	1.8	117 582	1.8
Sub-Saharan Africa	28.2	3.1	694 679	10.7
World	**903.2**	**100.0**	**6 484 808**	**100.0**

Note:
1 Includes only those countries reporting data to the WTO
Source: Data derived from CIA (2007), UNWTO (2008)

Europe

Europe is by far the most overrepresented destination region relative to its population, accommodating 13 per cent of the world's population but 54 per cent of its stayovers in 2007. This dominant position is further indicated by the fact that seven of the top ten destination countries, and 14 of the top 25 (including Turkey), were located within Europe as of 2007 (see table 4.3). In accounting for this status, an examination of Europe reads as a showcase of the push and pull factors discussed in chapter 3 and earlier this chapter, respectively.

Densely populated and prosperous states share several common land borders (9 in the case of Germany), making international travel convenient and affordable. Excellent land and air infrastructure facilitates traffic through increasingly open borders, while the widespread adoption of the euro as a common regional currency eliminates the need to obtain foreign notes or allow for exchange rate differentials in trip budgeting. Tourist and nontourist services are generally excellent, and attractions range from outstanding and diverse historical and cultural opportunities to the natural attributes of the Mediterranean coast, the boreal forests of Scandinavia and the Alps. Since World War II the western half of Europe has experienced a high level of political and economic stability, while the disintegration of the former Soviet Union has eliminated most of the political uncertainty fostered by the Cold War. All these factors have contributed to a market image of 'Europe' as a safe and rewarding destination brand that has not yet been seriously undermined by recent terrorist attacks in Madrid (in 2004) and London (in 2005), or by residual ethnic conflict in the Balkans.

TABLE 4.3 Top 25 destination countries, 2007

Rank	Country	Inbound stayovers (Million)	Increase 2002–07 (%)
1	France	81.9	6.3
2	Spain	59.2	14.5
3	USA	56.0	33.7
4	China	54.7	48.6
5	Italy	43.7	9.8
6	United Kingdom	30.7	26.9
7	Germany	24.4	35.6
8	Ukraine	23.1	266.7
9	Turkey	22.2	79.7
10	Mexico	21.4	8.6
11	Malaysia	21.0	57.9
12	Austria	20.8	11.8
13	Russia	20.2[1]	155.7[2]
14	Canada	17.9	−10.9
15	Hong Kong SAR	17.2	3.6
16	Greece	16.0[1]	12.7[2]
17	Poland	15.0	7.1
18	Thailand	14.5	33.0
19	Macau	12.9	95.5
20	Portugal	12.3	5.1
21	Saudi Arabia	11.5	53.3
22	The Netherlands	11.0	14.6
23	Egypt	10.6	116.3
24	Croatia	9.3	34.8
25	South Africa	9.1	37.9

Notes:
1 2006 statistic
2 change from 2002–2006
Source: Data derived from UNWTO (2008)

Geographically, the above qualities, and hence intensity of tourism activity, are most evident in western Europe. Eastern Europe is more complex, with former Soviet bloc states such as Poland, the Czech Republic and Hungary already tourism-intensive because of their proximity to western Europe and their systematic incorporation into the European Union (Hall, Marciszweska & Smith 2006). This saturation effect, and the accompanying erosion of the novelty factor, together help to account for Poland's poor performance in attracting tourist arrivals between 2002 and 2007 (see table 4.3). Concurrently exceptional growth rates for Russia and Ukraine may indicate that Western Europeans are seeking out more novel tourist experiences in the eastern periphery of Europe. These more easterly countries, however, continue to experience problems with accessibility and services, while a Cold War atmosphere was reintroduced in 2008 by Russian's invasion of Georgia and NATO's efforts to construct a missile defence shield in Poland and the Czech Republic.

Asia–Pacific

The Asia–Pacific region represents the reverse situation to Europe with respect to relative share of population and stayover totals. However, its size and diversity warrant analysis at the subregional level.

North-East Asia

North-East Asia has a large subregional tourism sector in absolute numbers, but this pales in comparison with its one-quarter share of the global population. With almost three-quarters of the intake, China and Hong Kong together dominate the market. To place China's current status as the world's number four destination in perspective, it is interesting to note that only 303 foreign visitors were allowed to enter the country in 1968 (Zhang, Pine & Zhang 2000). Since the 1970s, the Chinese government has expanded inbound tourism through a policy of **incremental access** that has seen the number of cities open to inbound tourists increase from 60 in 1979 to 1068 by 1994 (Bailey 1995). Most of China is now accessible to foreign tourists, except for some areas near international borders and military sites, as well as parts of Tibet and Xinjiang where ethnic tensions have increased in recent years. Nevertheless, inbound tourism remains concentrated in eastern cities such as Shanghai, Beijing and Shenzen (CNTA, nd). China is unique in that a high proportion of inbound tourists are 'compatriots', that is ethnic Chinese residents of Taiwan, Hong Kong SAR and Macau.

South-East Asia

Next in relative importance on a subregional basis is South-East Asia, where the proportional share of population does not as dramatically exceed its share of stayovers as in North-East Asia. The internal subregional pattern is diverse, with Malaysia, Singapore and Thailand displaying the most developed tourism sectors, while Cambodia and Laos remain in an incipient phase. The former three countries have benefited from the presence of major transit hubs, good infrastructure, prolonged political and social stability, a diverse array of high-quality attractions, favourable exchange rates relative to major tourist markets, a mostly positive market image and the pursuit of pro-tourism policies by government. Large and prosperous ethnic Chinese populations also engage in extensive travel between these countries. The emergence of Indonesia as an important destination country has been curtailed since the late 1990s by political and social instability, which culminated in the Bali bombings of 2002.

Australia/South Pacific (Oceania)

International tourism in Oceania is impeded by the relative remoteness of this region from major market sources. However, it is facilitated by high-profile natural attractions and a favourable exchange rate against the world's major currencies. The regional image, however, has been harmed by instability in Fiji (Rao 2002) and the Solomon Islands. As is the Caribbean, the South Pacific islands are overrepresented as a tourist destination, accounting for about 0.5 per cent of the global population, but 1.2 per cent of stayovers. To an even higher degree than in the Caribbean, tourism in the region is unevenly distributed, with just two of 22 destination states or dependencies (Guam and the Northern Mariana Islands, both US dependencies) accounting for almost two-thirds of all stayovers. Also similarly to the Caribbean, Oceania is a subregion of the pleasure periphery where historic and contemporary political and economic linkages largely dictate the nature of local tourism systems. Guam, for example, is dominated by Japanese and American tourists, New Caledonia by French visitors, and the Cook Islands by New Zealanders. Australia, influential in the tourism systems of several Oceanic destinations, including Papua New Guinea, Fiji and Vanuatu, is considered as a specific destination country under a separate subsection later in this chapter.

South Asia

South Asia is the most underrepresented inbound tourism region relative to population, with almost one-quarter of the world's people but just over one per cent of its inbound tourists. A negative regional destination image, a rudimentary network of services and facilities, widespread poverty and distance from major markets are all factors that have contributed to this deficit. Recent events and issues that have exacerbated the negative image of the region include the United States-led invasion of Afghanistan in 2001 and its aftermath, the acquisition of nuclear technology by Pakistan and ongoing sectarian violence in that country, the Maoist insurgency in Nepal and the massacre of its royal family in 2001, the rogue status of Iran and rising tensions with the United States, and the Indian Ocean tsunami of 2004. Nevertheless, pleasure periphery enclaves flourish in the Maldives as well as in the Indian states of Goa and Kerala.

The Americas

The Americas are overrepresented as a regional tourist destination relative to their population, although only marginally. However, as in Asia, this status disguises significant variations in the relative importance of tourism at the subregional level.

North America

North America accounts for about 7 per cent of the global population, but 11 per cent of all stayovers. Consisting of only three countries (the United States, Mexico and Canada), North America accommodates two of the world's largest bilateral tourist flows: United States/Canada and United States/Mexico. Some 80 per cent of all inbound tourists to Canada are from the United States, while Canadians account for at least one-third of all arrivals to the United States. Proximity is the primary factor accounting for these flows, given that more than 90 per cent of Canadians reside within a one-day drive to the United States. Other factors include strong cultural affinities, the complementarity of attractions (i.e. Americans seeking the open spaces of Canada, and Canadians travelling to the American Sunbelt during winter), good two-way infrastructural and political accessibility (i.e. through NAFTA), and a highly stable political and social situation in both countries.

While most crossborder travellers between the two countries apparently do not perceive the international boundary as a significant obstacle (Timothy & Tosun 2003), a somewhat changed climate has been evident as a result of the 2001 terrorist attacks and the invasion of Iraq by the United States. In the first case, elevated security concerns in the United States, often voiced as criticism of the relatively porous Canadian border, have made the crossing a slower and more stressful process for many travellers. In the second case, Canada's decision not to join the so-called 'coalition of the willing' or the continental 'Star Wars' missile defence program has continued to strain bilateral relations, contributing to a growing sense of psychological separation as well as other impediments to crossborder traffic. Similar issues are impeding the travel of Mexicans to the United States, as are concerns about the influx of illegal migrants from that country and Central America, and the escalating drug war along the US border.

The Caribbean

Owing to its endowment of 3S resources and its accessibility and proximity to the United States, the Caribbean has emerged as one of the world's most tourism-intensive subregions, with 0.6 per cent of the world's population but 2.2 per cent of its stayovers. The Caribbean is also the single most important region for the cruise ship industry and the region in which the cruise ship industry has the greatest presence relative to tourism as a whole (Dowling 2006). This general level of overrepresentation, however, disguises major internal variations. Haiti and the Republic of Trinidad & Tobago both have relatively weak tourism sectors, which belie the region's image as the personification of the pleasure periphery. In the former case this is due to decades of instability and extreme poverty, and in the latter case due to an economy sustained by oil wealth and industralisation. Cuba's potential, as described in chapter 2, has been hindered by the imposition of restrictions by the US government. In contrast, Caribbean SISODs such as the Bahamas, Antigua and Saint Lucia are among the world's most tourism-dependent countries. Jamaica is also a tourism-intensive destination but has a destination image that is suffering due to rising levels of serious crime (Altinay et al. 2007).

South and Central America

South and Central America, unlike North America, are underrepresented as tourist destinations. Spatially, the highest levels of international tourist traffic occur in the southern destinations of Argentina, Uruguay, Brazil and Chile, which each had at least 1.7 million tourist arrivals during 2007. Most of this traffic is from other subregional countries, given isolation from major international markets. Factors that account for the overall underrepresentation of South America include isolation from the major origin regions of North America and Europe, poor accessibility and a general lack of international standard tourism services. Residual market negativity also persists as a consequence of historical experiences with political instability, hyperinflation and economic uncertainty.

The Middle East

The Middle East is overrepresented as a destination region. However, as we have seen with all the other regions, this fact obscures a pattern of internal variability. For example, Egypt and Jordan have relatively strong tourism industries, while Saudi Arabia's robust tourism sector consists almost entirely of Muslim pilgrims visiting Mecca and other holy sites associated with Islam. In contrast, international tourism is embryonic in Yemen and Libya, and still almost non-existent in Iraq. The Middle East, as a Muslim-dominated region, has been disproportionately harmed by the terrorism of September 2001 and the subsequent 'war on terrorism', although this has not negatively affected the growth of innovative destinations such as the United Arab Emirates (see Breakthrough tourism: Exceeding expectations in Dubai).

breakthrough tourism

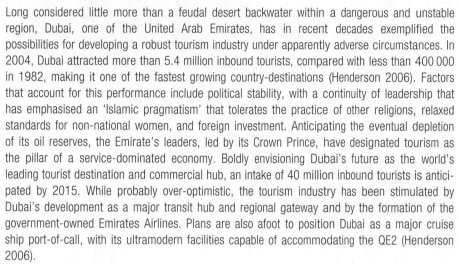

EXCEEDING EXPECTATIONS IN DUBAI

Long considered little more than a feudal desert backwater within a dangerous and unstable region, Dubai, one of the United Arab Emirates, has in recent decades exemplified the possibilities for developing a robust tourism industry under apparently adverse circumstances. In 2004, Dubai attracted more than 5.4 million inbound tourists, compared with less than 400 000 in 1982, making it one of the fastest growing country-destinations (Henderson 2006). Factors that account for this performance include political stability, with a continuity of leadership that has emphasised an 'Islamic pragmatism' that tolerates the practice of other religions, relaxed standards for non-national women, and foreign investment. Anticipating the eventual depletion of its oil reserves, the Emirate's leaders, led by its Crown Prince, have designated tourism as the pillar of a service-dominated economy. Boldly envisioning Dubai's future as the world's leading tourist destination and commercial hub, an intake of 40 million inbound tourists is anticipated by 2015. While probably over-optimistic, the tourism industry has been stimulated by Dubai's development as a major transit hub and regional gateway and by the formation of the government-owned Emirates Airlines. Plans are also afoot to position Dubai as a major cruise ship port-of-call, with its ultramodern facilities capable of accommodating the QE2 (Henderson 2006).

The developing amenities and attractions of Dubai are no less impressive than its infrastructure. The 'seven star' Burj al-Arab luxury hotel has already emerged as a regional icon, while two high profile residential developments — The Palm and The World — will help to attract ultra-wealthy seasonal tourists from around the world (see figure 4.6). Natural attractions are focused on Dubai's unspoiled coastline, although ecotourism is also being promoted as a product

FIGURE 4.6 Burj al-Arab hotel, Dubai

for Dubai's new wildlife sanctuary. A proposed $5 billion Dubailand theme park will augment the Mall of the Emirates (with its indoor ski facilities) as pillars of a strategy to become the 'playground' of the Middle East, while a series of festivals (including one focused on shopping) and sporting events will help to diversify the tourism product and reduce the effects of seasonality associated with intensely hot summers. Threats to Dubai's tourism development include external instability, especially in respect to Iran and to ongoing concerns over religious fundamentalism and terrorism. Other considerations include the growing competition from regional destinations such as Oman, and possible over-capacity induced by the red-hot pace of hotel and housing construction. The novelty effect of the Burj and the ski slope may also quickly erode as other destinations open newer and even more innovative attractions and facilities. Nevertheless, Dubai appears destined to attract more than its fair share of the international tourist market.

Africa

Africa as a region displays a high discrepancy between population share and stayover share. This underrepresentation can be accounted for by the persistently negative image of Africa in the tourist market, foreign exchange constraints, chronic political instability, a lack of skilled labour to develop the industry, and weak institutional frameworks that inhibit effective tourism planning and management. Other factors include widespread corruption, distance from the major markets, competition from more stable intervening opportunities, poor infrastructural developments and concerns over personal safety due to high crime rates and widespread infectious diseases such as AIDS.

Africa, similarly to South and Central America, is characterised by a skewed pattern of spatial distribution that favours the extreme north (e.g. Tunisia and Morocco) and the extreme south (e.g. South Africa and Botswana), although political instability and hyperinflation in Zimbabwe threatened the relatively positive market image of southern Africa during 2008. Tourism in the north is fuelled by 3S-motivated tourists from Europe, while intra-regional sources dominate the south. In contrast, Middle and West Africa are minor destinations for international tourist arrivals that embody the dissuasive factors outlined earlier. The largest African state in terms of inbound stayovers, South Africa, managed a global ranking of only twenty-fifth place in 2007, based on 9.1 million arrivals.

Australia

Australia's share of the global inbound market steadily increased from 0.15 per cent in 1965 to 0.70 in 1997 before declining slightly since that time (see table 4.4). It ranked in the fortieth position among country destinations in 2007, down from the thirty-fourth position in 2002. High growth from 1986 to 1988 represented not only good conditions in major market economies, but also the staging of high-profile events such as the 1988 bicentennial of European settlement and the international exposition in Brisbane that same year. The 1989 decline, accordingly, should be interpreted at least in part as a correction or normalisation of visitor intakes following these major events. The same effect occurred in the wake of the 2000 Sydney Olympics, while subsequent declines reflected the sensitivity of Australia to incidents of financial and political instability within the broader region, and its vulnerability as a long-haul destination (see the case study at the end of chapter 2).

TABLE 4.4 International stayover arrivals in Australia, 1965–2007

Year	Number of Arrivals	Growth (%)	Percentage of global stay over arrivals	Year	Number of Arrivals	Growth (%)	Percentage of global stay over arrivals
1965	173 300	–	0.15	1987	1 784 900	24.9	0.49
1966	187 300	8.1	0.16	1988	2 249 300	26.0	0.57
1967	215 100	14.8	0.17	1989	2 080 300	–7.5	0.49
1968	236 700	10.0	0.18	1990	2 214 900	6.5	0.48
1969	275 800	16.5	0.19	1991	2 370 400	7.0	0.51
1970	338 400	22.7	0.20	1992	2 603 300	9.8	0.52
1971	388 700	14.9	0.22	1993	2 996 200	15.1	0.58
1972	426 400	9.7	0.23	1994	3 361 700	12.2	0.61
1973	472 100	10.7	0.24	1995	3 725 800	10.8	0.66
1974	532 700	12.8	0.26	1996	4 164 800	11.8	0.69
1975	516 000	–3.1	0.23	1997	4 317 900	3.7	0.70
1976	531 900	3.1	0.23	1998	4 167 200	–3.5	0.65
1977	563 300	5.9	0.23	1999	4 459 500	7.0	0.67
1978	630 600	11.9	0.24	2000	4 931 400	10.6	0.72
1979	793 300	25.8	0.28	2001	4 855 700	–1.5	0.71
1980	904 600	14.0	0.32	2002	4 841 200	–0.3	0.69
1981	936 700	3.5	0.33	2003	4 745 900	–2.0	0.69
1982	954 700	1.9	0.33	2004	5 215 000	9.9	0.69
1983	943 900	–1.1	0.33	2005	5 499 500	5.5	0.68
1984	1 015 100	7.5	0.32	2006	5 532 500	0.6	0.65
1985	1 142 600	12.6	0.35	2007	5 644 000	2.0	0.63
1986	1 429 400	25.1	0.42				

Source: ABS (1996, 2001, 2005 and 2008c); ONT (1998); WTO (1998a)

TABLE 4.5 Australian inbound market regions and major countries, 1995–2007

Market region Selected country	1995 (000s)	Share (%)	1999– 2000 (000s)	Share (%)	2003 (000s)	Share (%)	2007 (000s)	Share (%)
Asia	**1872**	**50.2**	**1932**	**41.4**	**1917**	**40.4**	**2198**	**38.9**
Japan	783	21.0	706	15.2	628	13.2	573	10.2
China	43	1.1	120	2.6	176	3.7	357	6.3
Singapore	202	5.4	277	6.0	253	5.3	264	4.7
South Korea	168	4.5	139	3.0	207	4.4	253	4.5
Malaysia	108	2.9	147	3.2	156	3.3	160	2.8
Hong Kong	132	3.5	149	3.2	129	2.7	147	2.6
India	17	0.5	–	–	46	1.0	95	1.6
Taiwan	152	4.1	141	3.0	87	1.8	93	1.6
Indonesia	135	3.6	85	1.8	90	1.9	89	1.6
Europe	**752**	**20.2**	**1132**	**24.4**	**1212**	**25.5**	**1334**	**23.6**
United Kingdom	365	9.8	598	12.9	673	14.2	689	12.2
Germany	124	3.3	147	3.2	138	2.9	152	2.7

(continued)

TABLE 4.5 *(continued)*

Market region Selected country	1995 (000s)	Share (%)	1999– 2000 (000s)	Share (%)	2003 (000s)	Share (%)	2007 (000s)	Share (%)
Oceania	647	17.4	909	19.5	957	20.2	1278	22.6
New Zealand	538	14.5	773	16.6	839	17.7	1138	20.2
Americas	382	10.5	551	11.8	538	11.3	624	11.1
United States	305	8.2	437	9.4	422	8.9	460	8.2
Canada	58	1.6	85	1.8	88	1.9	115	2.0
Sub-Saharan Africa	42	1.0	72	1.5	69	1.5	122	2.2
Middle East and North Africa	29	0.8	53	1.1	53	1.1	88	1.6
Total[1]	3726	100.0	4652	100.0	4746	100.0	5644	100.0

Note:
1 Includes 'not stated'
Source: Data derived from ABS (1996, 1998b, 2001, 2003, 2008c)

Australia's inbound traffic is diverse, and this is a characteristic deliberately cultivated by the federal and state governments in order to avoid dependency on one or two primary markets. As shown in table 4.5, East Asian sources are dominant, but have displayed an inconsistent pattern of growth through the 1990s and 2000s. Strong growth in the first half of the decade, attributable to robust domestic economic growth, was followed by decline, especially in South Korea and Indonesia, as a consequence of economic crises. More recently, South Korea has recovered well, while the Chinese inbound market has demonstrated consistent and dramatic growth. This has helped to compensate for a pattern of steady decline in the maturing Japanese market. Traditional markets in New Zealand have performed well, while Europe and the Americas have increased in absolute terms but decreased in relative terms (percentages).

INTERNAL DESTINATION PATTERNS

The consideration of destinations has thus far been directed towards the global and regional levels, with individual countries, for the sake of simplicity, being treated as uniform entities. In reality, the spatial distribution of tourism within countries also tends to be uneven. This **subnational inequality** is evident even in small pleasure periphery destinations such as Zanzibar (Tanzania), where tourism accommodations are concentrated at seaside locations or in the capital city (figure 4.7). In general, waterfocused resources such as coastlines, lakes, rivers and waterfalls are considered potentially attractive as tourist venues in most destinations, and therefore help to promote a spatially uneven pattern of tourism development.

Large urban concentrations also tend to harbour a significant portion of a country's tourism sector. This is because of their status as international gateways, the high level of accommodation and other tourism-related services that they provide, the availability of important urban tourist attractions, and their status as prominent venues for business and VFR tourism. Within these cities the pattern of tourism distribution is also uneven, being highly concentrated in downtown districts where accommodation, restaurants and attractions are usually clustered (see page 140). The management implications of spatial concentration are compounded in many destinations by the concurrent presence of temporal concentrations, or the tendency of tourism activity to be focused on particular times of the year. The issue of seasonality is addressed more thoroughly in chapter 8.

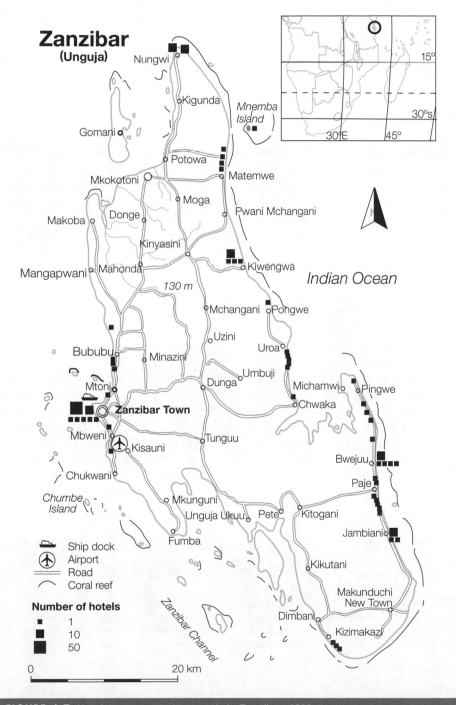

FIGURE 4.7 Hotel accommodation supply in Zanzibar, 2003

Urban-rural fringe

Adding to the complexity of internal distribution patterns is the increasing concentration of tourism activity in the transitional **urban–rural fringe (or 'exurbs')** that combines urban and rural characteristics and benefits from proximity to each. There is increasing evidence that tourism in such areas have at least three distinctive characteristics that require special management considerations (Weaver 2005):

• It has a distinct combination of products that may include theme and amusement parks, **tourist shopping villages** (small towns such as Tamborine Mountain and Maleny (Queensland) where the downtown is dominated by tourist-oriented businesses), factory outlet malls and golf courses.

• Distinct market characteristics are evident in the preponderance of excursionists who use overnight accommodation in nearby urban areas, and in the presence of **hyperdestinations** where tourist arrivals dramatically outnumber local residents. In the case of Tamborine Mountain, 7000 residents host each year approximately 500 000 visitors. A high proportion of these visitors, moreover, are residents of the nearby urban area who may or may not meet the travel distance thresholds associated with domestic tourism. This all suggests that revenues derived largely from the use of overnight accommodation are minimal and do not compensate for the congestion and utility use generated by large numbers of visitors.

• Management of exurban tourism is complicated by the fact this zone is inherently unstable, in transition and characterised by conflict among the diverse users of this exceptionally complex space.

The Australian pattern

The basic pattern shown in figure 4.8 pertains to Australia, where New South Wales and Queensland together account for almost 60 per cent of visitor nights in both the inbound and domestic tourism sectors (table 4.6). However, it should also be noted that this figure is similar to the proportion of Australia's total population that resides in these two states. Further analysis at the substate level shows that inbound tourism, as in Zanzibar, is highly concentrated along the coastline, and especially in the portion of coast extending from the Sunshine Coast to Sydney (figure 4.8). In the remainder of the country inbound tourism is largely a phenomenon of the state or territorial capitals, with the interior represented in the top 16 tourism regions only by Canberra. Domestic tourism, in contrast to inbound tourism, is more evenly distributed in comparison with state populations, due largely to the high incidence of geographically non-discretionary VFR travel within that sector.

TABLE 4.6 Distribution of domestic and inbound visitor-nights in Australia by destination state or territory, 2007

State/ territory	No. of inbound visitor nights (000s)	Percentage of all inbound visitor nights	No. of domestic visitor nights[1] (000s)	Percentage of all domestic visitor nights	Percentage of national population
NSW	57 267	36	83 176	29	33
Qld	36 115	23	77 069	27	20
Vic.	30 953	20	53 244	18	25

State/ territory	No. of inbound visitor nights (000s)	Percentage of all inbound visitor nights	No. of domestic visitor nights[1] (000s)	Percentage of all domestic visitor nights	Percentage of national population
WA	17 908	11	32 684	11	10
SA	6 855	4	19 107	7	7
Tas.	3 084	2	10 219	4	2
NT	3 024	2	7 159	2	1
ACT	2 596	2	5 844	2	2
Total	157 806	100	288 502	100	100

Note:
1 Refers to Australians 15 years of age and older.
Source: TRA 2007b, 2008b

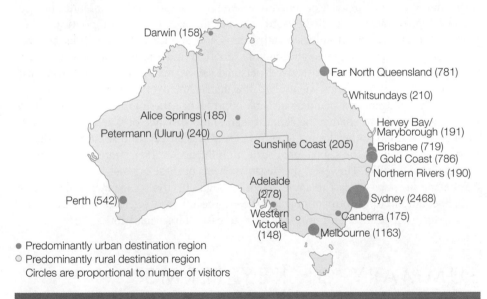

● Predominantly urban destination region
○ Predominantly rural destination region
   Circles are proportional to number of visitors

FIGURE 4.8 Top 16 destination regions in Australia by percentage of all inbound visitor-nights, 2007

Note:
Applies to visitors 15 years of age and older only. Totals exceed visitor numbers reported in table 4.4 because of visits to more than one region.
Source: Data derived from TRA (2008b)

CHAPTER REVIEW

Most inbound tourism occurs in the more developed world. However, the less developed world's share is steadily increasing due to the emergence of 3S tourism as a major form of activity after World War II. Furthermore, economic growth and the appearance of a substantial middle class within the LDCs are promoting increased inbound travel between the LDCs as well as from LDCs to MDCs. The formation of a pleasure periphery at the interface of the more and less developed worlds is indicative of tourism's increasing status as a global economic activity and agent of landscape change. Europe, North America, Oceania, the Middle East and the Caribbean are all overrepresented as destination regions relative to their resident populations. In contrast, South America, Africa and Asia are all underrepresented. The pattern of uneven distribution is also apparent within each of these regions and within individual countries such as Australia, where coastal areas and metropolitan area cores and exurbs account for most inbound and domestic tourism activity.

Tourism's uneven pattern of distribution reflects differences in the influence of the 'pull' factors that encourage tourism in particular locations, and hence help to determine the global pattern of tourism systems. These pull factors include the geographical proximity of destinations to markets, infrastructural and political accessibility, the availability of sufficient attractions and services, cultural links between origin and destination regions, affordability, political and social stability at the local, national and regional levels, perceived personal safety, market image, and the existence of pro tourism policies. Central to the management of tourism destinations is how much managers and planners are able to influence these forces. Nothing can be done, for example, to change the actual geographical distance of a destination from a market, or to modify the destination's primary physical features. Similarly, little can be done, especially at the subnational scale, to influence exchange rates or the level of sociopolitical stability. However, the negative effects of these factors, where they exist, can be counteracted at least to some extent through effective image manipulation, the implementation of pro-tourism policies, the establishment of 'created' attractions, and the provision of political and infrastructural access to target markets.

■ SUMMARY OF KEY TERMS

3S tourism a tourism product based on the provision of sea, sand and sun; that is, focusing on beach resorts

Distance-decay in tourism, the tendency of inbound flows to decline as origin regions become more distant from the destination

Global inequality in tourism a fundamental distinction pertaining to the relative spatial distribution of tourism at a global level

Hyperdestinations destinations where the annual intake of visitors dramatically outnumbers the permanent resident population; often characteristic of tourist shopping villages

Image in tourism, the sum of the beliefs, attitudes and impressions that individuals or groups hold towards tourist destinations or aspects of destinations. Destination image is a critical factor in attracting or repelling visitors

Incremental access a policy, practised most notably in China, whereby new destinations within a country are gradually opened up to international (and possibly domestic) tourists

Infrastructural accessibility the extent to which a destination is physically accessible to markets by air routes, highways, ferry links, etc., and through entry/exit facilities such as seaports and airports

Less developed countries (LDCs) countries characterised by a relatively low level of economic development. Until recently, the less developed world has not been very important as a recipient or generator of global tourist flows

More developed countries (MDCs) countries characterised by a relatively high level of economic development. Collectively, the more developed world remains dominant as a recipient and generator of global tourist flows

North–south flow a common term used to describe the dominant pattern of international tourist traffic from the MDCs (located mainly in the northern latitudes, except for Australia and New Zealand) to the LDCs (located mainly to the south of the MDCs)

Pleasure periphery those less economically developed regions of the globe that are being increasingly mobilised to provide 3S and alpine tourism products

Political accessibility the extent to which visitors are allowed entry into a destination by a governing authority

Pull factors forces that help to stimulate a tourism product by 'pulling' consumers towards particular destinations

Small island states or dependencies (SISODs) geopolitical entities with a population of less than three million permanent residents and a land mass of less than 28 000 km^2. SISODs are overrepresented as tourist destinations because of their ample 3S tourism resources

Subnational inequality the tendency of tourism within countries, states and individual cities to be spatially concentrated

Sunbelt the name frequently applied to the 3S-oriented American portion of the pleasure periphery. Well-known destinations within the sunbelt include Hawaii, southern California, Las Vegas (Nevada), Arizona, Texas and Florida

Tourist shopping villages small towns where the downtown is dominated by tourism-related businesses such as boutiques, antique shops and cafés

Urban–rural fringe (or 'exurbs') a transitional zone surrounding larger urban areas that combines urban and rural characteristics and benefits from proximity to each

■ QUESTIONS

1. (a) How much is spatial inequality evident in tourism at the international, national, subnational and local level?
   (b) Why does this inequality occur?
   (c) What are the managerial implications of this inequality at all four levels cited in (a)?
2. (a) To what extent are destinations able to influence or manage each of 'pull' factors discussed in this chapter?
   (b) How does this influence vary between the local, state and national scale?
3. (a) Is the US government justified in implementing security procedures for visitors that cause significant inconvenience and aggravation?
   (b) How could the USA and other countries attain a better compromise between open borders and adequate security?
4. (a) Why are tourists being increasingly targeted by terrorist groups?
   (b) What can destination managers do to combat this phenomenon?

5. (a) Why is Europe, in general, far more developed as a tourist destination region than Africa?
   (b) What strategies could African countries implement to improve their status as destinations?
6. What strategies could be implemented in order to increase Australia's share of global stayover tourism to 1 per cent of the total? Take into account the data provided in table 4.5.
7. What lessons for other peripheral tourist destinations can be learned from the experience of Dubai?
8. (a) How does tourism in the urban–rural fringe depend upon tourists and local residents in nearby large urban areas?
   (b) What challenges does this pose to managers of destinations in the urban–rural fringe?

■ EXERCISES

1. (a) Rank the following ten destination countries beginning with the one that you would most like to visit for a one-month vacation, and ending with the one that you would be least interested in visiting for a one-month vacation.

Zimbabwe	Fiji	Mexico	China
United States	France	Dubai	India
United Kingdom		Russia	

   (b) Indicate the reasons for your rankings, referring in each case to each of the pull factors discussed in this chapter.
   (c) Assigning a value of '5' for each first choice, '4' for each second choice, and so on, add up the class responses for each of the five destinations.
   (d) Identify the overall class rankings.
   (e) Do any consistent patterns emerge as to the reasons given for these rankings?
2. (a) Using appendix 3, identify the top 25 destination countries for 2002 in terms of the number of international stayover arrivals.
   (b) How does this list of countries compare with table 4.3, which provides the 2007 rankings?
   (c) What factors help to account for these patterns?

■ FURTHER READING

Aramberri, J. & Butler, R. (Eds) 2004 *Tourism Development: Issues for a Vulnerable Industry.* **Clevedon, UK: Channel View.** Several chapters in this edited book discuss the links between tourism and terrorism as well as sociopolitical instability more generally.

Duval, T. (Ed.) 2004. *Tourism in the Caribbean: Trends, Development, Prospects.* **London: Routledge.** The Caribbean is arguably the most tourism-intensive of the world's regions, and this edited volume considers relevant issues such as the role of hedonism in developing the product, cruise ships, ecotourism, postcolonialism, and community and small business perspectives.

Gössling, S. (Ed.) 2003. *Tourism and Development in Tropical Islands: Political Ecology Perspectives.* **Cheltenham, UK: Edward Elgar.** Ten case studies of SISODs and other tropical island destinations are provided in this book, which focuses on the political and ecological factors that have influenced the growth of this sector.

Hall, D., Marciszweska, B. & Smith, M. 2006. *Tourism in the New Europe: The Challenges and Opportunities of EU Enlargement.* **Wallingford: CABI.** A feature of this book is a country-by-country analysis of new European Union members in terms of implications for tourism policies and flows as well as attendant economic, cultural, social and environmental implications.

Wilks, J. & Page, S. Eds. 2003. *Managing Tourist Health and Safety in the New Millennium.* **London: Pergamon.** This is the first edited text to comprehensively examine emerging issues of high risk tourist activities, international travel and tourism law, and tourist epidemiology.

case study

ATTRACTING CHINESE TOURISTS TO AUSTRALIA

Australia was the first non-Asian country to achieve ADS, and has since aggressively pursued the rapidly growing Chinese outbound market. Such a proactive approach is necessary given the Chinese preference for European destinations, which offer a desirable combination of cultural and historical attractions, low crime rates, brand name purchases, status, and business links. The attainment of ADS by the USA is another consideration, with the latter offering an impressive combination of iconic attractions not far from the Los Angeles gateway (e.g. Disneyland, Hollywood, Grand Canyon, Las Vegas), family connections, and a favourable exchange rate (Tourism Australia 2008a). To obtain their 'fair share' of the Chinese outbound market, Australia must compete with a growing number of ADS rivals by understanding the Chinese outbound market, promoting itself within China, and improving air links.

Understanding the Chinese market

In 2005, Tourism Australia conducted research which revealed five distinct Chinese outbound segments, each requiring its own marketing strategy (Tourism Australia 2008a). About 22 per cent of the market consisted of 'self-challengers', relatively well educated and wealthy individuals who like to travel and immerse themselves in the places they visit. Self-challengers have a very positive attitude toward Australia and are likely to be repeat visitors. Another 13 per cent are 'family connections' who are influenced mainly by the presence of family members who can host and guide them through an alien destination culture. 'Sightseers', accounting for 18 per cent, stick close to their own group and visit iconic sites such as Sydney's Opera House that confer status. The 25 per cent who are 'ready to leave' are eager to visit destinations outside of Asia, and are similar to the self-challengers in their quest for the exotic and authentic. Finally, the 22 per cent who are 'close to home' do not wish to stray too far from familiar Asian destinations and therefore are the least likely to visit Australia. Tourism Australia subsequently identified self-challengers and sightseers are the two core markets that they would target.

An earlier study conducted in 2003 was the first to solicit the attitudes of Chinese inbound tourists travelling under the ADS agreement (Tourism Australia 2003). Most expected to experience natural landscapes (70 per cent) and beaches/water (61 per cent), and wanted free time to explore (55 per cent). They were enthusiastic about their Australian experience and were likely to return (54 per cent saying that they would 'definitely' return within the next five years), but were less satisfied with their group holiday tour in Australia (53 per cent satisfied) compared with tours in other Western destinations (73 per cent). Issues to be addressed in this respect include provision of in-depth experiences that are perceived to be authentically Australian, highly trained and Mandarin-speaking tour guides, and more freedom to shop and explore on their own and at their own pace rather than in regimented groups on frenzied schedules.

Promoting Australia within China

Given its massive size and population, Australia's promotional efforts in China have initially been focused on the three major market regions of Guangdong Province (adjacent to Hong Kong, with a population of 93 million), Beijing (16 million) and Shanghai (18 million). However, trade shows are currently being undertaken experimentally in 'second tier' urban areas such as Nanjing, Tianjin, Dalian, Qingdao and Chengdu (each with more than 3 million residents) as a prelude to a more permanent presence in these emerging city-regions. Major tourism-related promotional events range from the Australia Travel Mission to China (ATMC), held annually in late October or early November, to the China International Travel Mart (CITM), which is the largest professional travel show in Asia and widely regarded as a 'must' place to see and be seen. It is recommended that visits to China by interested Australian travel professionals should take place from March to late May, or mid-October to early December, when national holidays are less likely to interfere. The services of an interpreter must also be sought if fluency in Mandarin is not possessed. Among the more innovative recent initiatives was a network and training seminar in China, co-sponsored in July 2008 by Tourism Australia, five Australian state tourism organisations and four airlines, for Chinese travel agencies specialising in Australia. Such events have helped Australia to build a 'family' of almost 2000 specialised travel agencies within China. Also in 2008, Tourism Australia supported the opening of an Australian-themed retail store in Guangzhou (the capital of Guangdong Province), a one-stop shop for purchasing any kind of Australian travel product (Tourism Australia 2008a).

Improving air links

Direct non-stop air capacity between China and Australia increased eight-fold between 1998 and 2008, although future growth is hindered by the restriction of direct flights to and from just two Australian gateways — Sydney and Melbourne. Other Australian cities such as Brisbane and Perth require an extra leg from those gateways, or a stopover in Asian transit hubs such as Hong Kong, Singapore or Kuala Lumpur (Tourism Australia 2008b). Lower cost carriers based in both Australia and Asia are likely to result in further strong increases in capacity, although Sydney and Melbourne will continue to be the main beneficiaries until direct flights are introduced to other major cities.

Assisting promotional efforts in China is positive publicity associated with the Mandarin fluency of the Australian Prime Minister, Kevin Rudd. However, consumer perceptions of Australia as a desirable holiday destination are damaged by frequent Chinese media reports of unethical business practices such as shopping subsidies and questionable surcharges on members of tour groups. Also disruptive have been unanticipated events such as the Sichuan Province earthquake of May 2008, which resulted in the almost total cancellation of official and business bookings to Australia over the following month as funds were diverted from travel to earthquake relief (Tourism Australia 2008c).

QUESTIONS

1. (a) Consult the Tourism Research Australia website to identify the size and growth of the Chinese student market in Australia.
   (b) Describe how this student market could be mobilised to support further increases and distribution of inbound Chinese leisure tourists.

2. (a) Identify all articles about Australia in the People's Daily Online (http://english.peopledaily.com.cn/) during the past 12-month period.
   (b) Classify these articles as either 'positive' or 'negative', and sort the articles in each category into sub-categories that reflect their dominant themes.
   (c) Write a 1000-word report that summarises this coverage and describes the implications for the emerging image in China of Australia as an overseas tourist destination.

CHAPTER 5

THE TOURISM PRODUCT

LEARNING OBJECTIVES

After studying this chapter, you should be able to:

1. divide tourist attractions into four major types and their attendant subtypes

2. appreciate the diversity of these attractions

3. discuss the management implications that pertain to each attraction type and subtype

4. identify the various attraction attributes that can be assessed in order to make informed management and planning decisions

5. explain the basic characteristics of the tourism industry's main sectors

6. critically assess the major contemporary trends affecting these sectors

7. describe the growing diversification and specialisation of products provided by the tourism industry

8. discuss the implications of the concepts of integration and globalisation as they apply to the tourism industry.

■ INTRODUCTION

The previous chapter outlined the 'pull' factors that stimulate the development of particular places as tourist destinations, and described the tourism status of the world's major regions in the context of these forces. Chapter 5 continues to examine the supply side of the tourism system by focusing on the **tourism product**, which can be defined as the combination of **tourist attractions** and the **tourism industry**. While commercial attractions such as theme parks, casinos and museums are elements of the tourist industry, others, such as generic noncommercial scenery, local people and climate, are not. For this reason, and because they are an essential and diverse component of tourism systems, attractions are examined separately from the industry in the following section. We then follow with a discussion of the other major components of the tourism industry, including travel agencies, transportation, accommodation, tour operators and merchandise. The chapter concludes by considering structural changes within the contemporary tourism industry.

■ TOURIST ATTRACTIONS

The availability of tourist attractions is an essential 'pull' factor (see chapter 4), and destinations should therefore benefit from having a diversity of such resources. The compilation of an **attraction inventory** incorporating actual and potential sites and events, is a fundamental step towards ensuring that a destination realises its full tourism potential in this regard. There is at present no classification system of attractions that is universally followed among tourism stakeholders. However, a distinction between mainly 'natural' and mainly 'cultural' phenomena is commonly made. The classification scheme proposed in figure 5.1 adheres to the natural/cultural distinction for discussion purposes, and makes a further distinction between sites and events. Four categories of attraction are thereby generated: natural sites, natural events, cultural sites and cultural events. The use of dotted lines in figure 5.1 to separate these categories recognises that distinctions between 'natural' and 'cultural', and between 'site' and 'event', are not always clear. The use of these categories in the following subsections therefore should not obscure the fact that many if not most attractions are category hybrids. A national park, for example, may combine topographical, cultural, floral and faunal elements of the site.

The following material is not an exhaustive treatment of this immense and complex topic, but rather it is meant to illustrate the diversity of attractions as well as management issues associated with various types and subtypes. One underlying theme is the likelihood that most places are not adequately utilising their potential range of attractions. A related theme is the role of imagination and creativity in transforming apparent destination liabilities into **tourism resources**, reflecting the subjective nature of the latter concept.

Natural sites

Natural attractions, as the name implies, are associated more closely with the natural environment rather than the cultural environment. **Natural site** attractions can be subdivided into topography, climate, water, wildlife, vegetation and location. Inbound tourists are strongly influenced to visit Australia by natural sites such as beaches, botanical gardens, zoos and national parks (see table 5.1). Destinations have little scope for changing their natural assets — that is, they either possess high mountains and a tropical climate, or they do not. A challenge, therefore, is to manipulate market image so that 'unattractive' natural phenomena are converted into tourism resources.

Category	Site		Event
Natural	TOPOGRAPHY e.g. mountains, canyons, beaches, volcanoes, caves, fossil sites	protected areas, hiking trails	volcanic eruptions
	CLIMATE e.g. temperature, sunshine, precipitation, sky		sunsets, sunrises
	HYDROLOGY e.g. lakes, rivers, waterfalls, hot springs	scenic highways, scenic lookouts, spas	tides, geyser eruptions
	WILDLIFE e.g. mammals, birds, insects, fish, reptiles	wildlife parks, botanical gardens	animal migrations (e.g. caribou and geese)
	VEGETATION e.g. forests, wildflowers		autumn leaf colour and spring bloom displays
	LOCATION e.g. centrality, extremity		
Cultural	PRE-HISTORICAL e.g. Aboriginal sites		
	HISTORICAL e.g. battlefields, old buildings, museums, ancient monuments, graveyards, statues		battle re-enactments, commemorations
	CONTEMPORARY CULTURE e.g. architecture, ethnic neighbourhoods, modern technology, arts		festivals, world fairs, concerts, art oxhibitions, fashion shows
	ECONOMIC e.g. farms, mines, factories		
	RECREATIONAL e.g. integrated resorts, golf courses, ski hills, theme parks, casinos		sporting events, Olympics
	RETAIL e.g. mega-malls, shopping districts		markets

FIGURE 5.1 Generic inventory of tourist attractions

TABLE 5.1 Leisure activities undertaken by international visitors to Australia, 2008

Rank	Activity	Number of participants	% of total visitors
1	Eat out/dine at a restaurant and/or café	4 474 967	87
2	Go shopping for pleasure	3 952 062	76
3	Go to the beach (including swimming, surfing, diving)	3 695 938	72
4	Go to the markets	3 142 864	61
5	Visit national parks/state parks	2 320 620	45
6	Attend Pubs, clubs, discos etc.	2 202 848	43
7	Visit wildlife parks/zoos/aquariums	2 153 645	42
8	Visit botanical or other public gardens	1 952 457	38
9	Charter boat/cruise/ferry	1 882 212	36
10	Visit history/heritage buildings, sites or monuments	1 641 260	32

Source: Tourism Australia (2008)

Topography

Topography refers to geological features in the physical landscape such as mountains, valleys, plateaus, islands, canyons, deltas, dunes, cliffs, beaches, volcanoes and caves. Gemstones and fossils are a special type of topographical feature, locally important in Australian locations such as Coober Pedy in South Australia (opals), O'Briens Creek in Queensland (topaz) and the New England region of New South Wales. The potential for dinosaur fossils to foster a tourism industry in remote parts of Queensland has also been considered (Laws & Scott 2003).

Mountains

Mountains illustrate the subjective and changing nature of tourism resources. Long feared and despised as hazardous wastelands harbouring bandits and dangerous animals, the image of alpine environments was rehabilitated during the European Romanticist period of the early 1800s, and in a more induced way by the efforts of trans-continental railway companies in North America to increase revenue through the construction and promotion of luxury alpine resorts (Hart 1983). As a result, scenically dramatic alpine regions such as the European Alps and the North American Rockies emerged as highly desirable venues for tourist activity, and were gradually incorporated into the global pleasure periphery. Beedie and Hudson (2003) describe how remoteness fostered an elitist 'mountaineer' form of tourism until the latter half of the twentieth century, when improved access (a pull factor) and increased discretionary time and money (push factors) led to the 'democratisation' of alpine landscapes through skiing and mass adventure tourism. Lower and less dramatic mountain ranges, such as the American Appalachian Mountains, the Russian Urals and the coastal ranges of Australia, are also highly valued for tourism purposes although arguably they did not undergo the elite-to-mass transition to the same extent (Godde, Price & Zimmermann 2000). Previously inaccessible ranges, such as the Himalayan mountains of Asia, the South American Andes, the Southern Alps of New Zealand and the Atlas Mountains of Africa, are now also being incorporated into the pleasure periphery.

Certain individual mountains, by merit of exceptional height, aesthetics or religious significance, possess a symbolic value as an iconic attraction that tourists readily associate with particular destinations. Uluru (formerly Ayers Rock) is the best Australian example, while other well-known examples include Mt Everest (Sagarmatha), the Matterhorn, Kilimanjaro (Tanzania) and Japan's Mt Fuji, which is notable as an almost perfect composite volcano.

Beaches

As with mountains, beaches were not always perceived positively as tourist attractions. Their popularity is associated with the Industrial Revolution and particularly with the emergence of the pleasure periphery after World War II (see chapters 3 and 4). Currently, beaches are perhaps the most stereotypical symbol of mass tourism (see figure 5.2). Not all types of beaches, however, are equally favoured by tourists. Dark-hued beaches derived from the erosion of volcanic rock are not as popular as the fine white sandy beaches created from limestone or coral, as the former generate very hot sand and the illusion of murky water while the latter produce the turquoise water effect highly valued by tourists and destination marketers. This in large part accounts for the higher level of 3S resort development in 'coral' Caribbean destinations such as Antigua and the Bahamas, as opposed to 'volcanic' islands such as Dominica and St. Vincent.

The centrality of the beach to the Australian tourism experience is reflected in table 5.1, which shows that 72 per cent of inbound visitors spent at least some time at the beach during 2007. Going to the beach is also, by far, the most popular outdoor holiday activity among Australians, with one-quarter of domestic stayovers reporting participation in 2007 for a total of 19 million trips (TRA 2008d).

FIGURE 5.2 The iconic beaches of Australia's Gold Coast

Climate

Before the era of modern mass tourism, a climate change was the prevalent attraction. There was a search for cooler and drier weather relative to the uncomfortable summer heat and humidity of urban areas. Thus, escape to coastal resorts in the United Kingdom and the United States during the summer was and still is a quest for cooler rather than warmer temperatures. The British and Dutch established highland resorts in their Asian colonies for similar purposes, and many of these are still used for tourism purposes by the postcolonial indigenous elite and middle class. Examples include Simla and Darjeeling in India (Jutla 2000), and the Cameron Highlands of Malaysia. This impulse is also evident among the increasing number of Middle Eastern visitors to Australia during the torrid summer of the Arabian Peninsula.

With the emergence of the pleasure periphery, temperature and seasonal patterns were reversed as great numbers of 'snowbirds' travelled to Florida, the Caribbean, the Mediterranean, Hawaii and other warm weather destinations to escape cold winter conditions in their home regions. A snowbird-type migration is also apparent on a smaller scale from Australian states such as Victoria and South Australia to the coast of Queensland. Thus, warm and sunny conditions complement the white-sand beach and the turquoise water effect to define the dominant stereotypical 3S destination image of the early twenty-first century.

Some areas, however, can be too hot for most tourists, as reflected in the low demand for equatorial and hot desert tourism. Essentially, a subtropical range of approximately 20–30 °C is considered optimal for 3S tourism, and this is a good climatic indicator of the potential for large-scale tourism development in a particular beach-based destination, provided that other basic 'pull' criteria are also present (Boniface & Cooper 2005). The one major exception to the cool-to-hot trend is the growing popularity of winter sports such as downhill skiing, snowboarding and snowmobiling, which involve a cool-to-cool migration or, less frequently, a warm-to-cool migration. Whatever the specific dynamic, cyclic changes in weather within both the origin and destination regions lead to significant seasonal fluctuations in tourist flows, presenting tourism managers with additional management challenges (see chapter 8).

Water

Water is a significant tourism resource only under certain conditions. For swimming, prerequisites include good water quality, a comfortable water temperature and calm and safe water conditions. For surfing, however, calm waters are a liability — which accounts for the emergence of only certain parts of the Australian east coast, Hawaii and California as surfing 'hotspots'. Oceans and seas, where they interface subtropical beaches, are probably the most desirable and lucrative venue for nature-based tourism development. Freshwater lakes are also significant for outdoor recreational activities such as boating, and for the establishment of second homes and cottages. Extensive recreational hinterlands, dominated by lake-based cottage or second home developments, are common in parts of Europe and North America. The Muskoka region of Canada is an excellent example, its development having been facilitated by the presence of several thousand highly indented glacial lakes (i.e. the destination region), its proximity to Toronto (i.e. the origin region) and the existence of connecting railways and roads (i.e. the transit region) (Svenson 2004).

Rivers and waterfalls

Waterfalls in particular hold a strong inherent aesthetic appeal for many people, and often constitute a core iconic attraction around which secondary attractions, and sometimes entire resort communities, are established. Niagara Falls (on the United States/Canada border) is a prime example of a waterfall-based tourism agglomeration. Other examples include Victoria Falls (on the Zimbabwe/Zambia border) and Iguaçú Falls (on the Brazil/Paraguay border). Small waterfalls, in contrast, are an integral part of the tourism product in the hinterland of Australia's Gold Coast (Hudson 2004).

An important management dimension of freshwater-based tourism is competing demand from politically and economically powerful sectors such as agriculture (irrigation), manufacturing (as a water source and an outlet for effluents) and transportation (bulk transport). Such competition, which implicates the importance of water as an attraction in itself as well as a facilitator of other attractions such as golf courses, is likely to accelerate as freshwater resources are further degraded and depleted by the combined effects of mismanagement and climate change (see Contemporary issue: Fighting for water in Spain and Australia).

contemporary issue

FIGHTING FOR WATER IN SPAIN AND AUSTRALIA

'Unusual' weather circumstances along the Spanish Mediterranean coast during the early 2000s produced exceptional drought conditions that called into question the wisdom of policies encouraging the expansion of the region's water-hungry farming and tourism sectors (Vidal 2005). Abetted historically by the wholesale transfer of water from more humid parts of Spain, the semi-arid Riviera is rapidly being converted into a vast conurbation of tourism resorts and high-rises as well as areas of intensively irrigated croplands. The tourism and agriculture sectors have both called for further regional transfers, desalinisation plants and borehole drilling to increase the available water supply, but persistent shortages have forced some farmland to be abandoned. Farmers and local residents are increasingly resentful of tourism, which does not seem to be facing similar restrictions on either construction or water use, much of it devoted to 'unimportant' purposes such as swimming pools and golf course irrigation. Increased pressure from the agricultural lobby may combine in future with further depletions in the water supply to force a basic re-thinking of the region's tourism development policy and water use guidelines.

The problems of Spain are being played out in many other destinations, including southeastern Australia, where the economically and ecologically vital Murray–Darling basin is similarly threatened by chronic drought and mismanagement. Conflict between competing sectors is looming as basin farmers vigorously oppose plans to divert river water to threatened lakes, wetlands and estuaries near the mouth of the Murray River in South Australia. One report asserts that these diversions would destroy $1 billion worth of agricultural production. Tourism operators near the mouth, however, cite a 25 to 40 per cent decline in boat, fishing and wildlife-based tourism business due to the loss of the fresh water that sustains their industry (Wiseman 2008). Their resultant strong support for the diversions promises to ignite a prolonged conflict with the agriculture lobby, while federal and state agencies concurrently struggle to implement policies that will prevent the 'death' of the basin.

Geothermal waters

As discussed in chapter 3, spas were an historically important form of tourism that receded in significance during the ascendancy of seaside tourism. The greatest present-day concentration of spas is associated with geologically active areas of the Earth's surface such as Iceland and New Zealand, where geothermal waters with purported therapeutic qualities are readily accessible. Spas are also found along the Czech–German border and in the Appalachian Mountains of the eastern United States. European spas alone are estimated to attract 20 million visitors per year (Smith & Jenner 2000). Australia, however, is characterised by an underdeveloped spa industry (Bennett, King & Milner 2004) despite the trend of incorporating spa-type services within hotels.

Wildlife

As a tourism resource, wildlife can be classified in several ways for managerial purposes. First, a distinction can be made between captive and noncaptive wildlife. The clearest example of the former is a zoo, which is a hybrid natural/cultural attraction (Tribe 2004). At the opposite end of the continuum are wilderness areas where the movement of animals is unrestricted. Trade-offs are implicit in the tourist experience associated with each scenario. For example, a visitor is virtually guaranteed of seeing the animal in a zoo, but there is minimal habitat context and no thrill of discovery. In a wilderness or semi-wilderness situation, the opposite holds true. Many zoos are now being reconstructed and reinvented as 'wildlife parks' or 'zoological parks' that provide a viewing experience within a quasi-natural and more humane environment, thereby compromising between these two extremes (Mazur 2001). As indicated in table 5.1, 38 per cent of inbound tourists in Australia in 2007 visited a wildlife park, aquarium or zoo.

Consumptive and nonconsumptive dimensions

Wildlife is also commonly classified along a consumptive/nonconsumptive spectrum. The former usually refers to hunting and fishing, which are long established as a mainly domestic form of tourism in North America, Australia, New Zealand and Europe (Lovelock 2008). Related activities that have more of an international dimension include big-game hunting (important in parts of Africa and Canada) and deep-sea fishing, which is significant in many coastal destinations of Australia (Bauer & Herr 2004). Because of the consumptive nature of these activities, managers must always be alert to their effect on wildlife population levels. In destinations such as Australia, hunting is valued as a management tool for keeping wildlife populations, including exotic pest species, in balance with environmental carrying capacities (Craig-Smith & Dryden 2008).

In many areas 'nonconsumptive' wildlife-based pursuits such as ecotourism are overtaking hunting and fishing in importance (Valentine & Birtles 2004) (see chapter 11). This is creating a dilemma for some hunting-oriented businesses and destinations, which must decide whether to remain focused on hunting, switch to ecotourism or attempt to accommodate both of these potentially incompatible activities. One criticism of the 'consumptive/nonconsumptive' mode of classification is that both dimensions are inherent in all forms of wildlife-based tourism. The 'nonconsumptive' experience of being outdoors for its own sake, for example, is usually an intrinsic part of hunting and fishing, while ecotourists consume many different products (e.g. petrol, food, souvenirs) as part of the wildlife-viewing experience. Maintaining an inventory of observed wildlife, moreover, can also be regarded as a symbolic form of 'consumption' (Tremblay 2001).

Vegetation

Vegetation exists interdependently with wildlife and, therefore, cannot be divorced from the ecotourism equation. However, there are also situations where trees, flowers or shrubs are a primary rather than a supportive attraction. Examples include the giant redwood trees of northern California, the wildflower meadows of Western Australia and the endemic Mediterranean plants of southern Cape Province, South Africa (Turpie & Joubert 2004). The captive/noncaptive continuum is only partially useful in classifying flora resources, since vegetation is essentially immobile. For managers this means that inventories are relatively stable, and tourists can be virtually guaranteed of seeing the attraction (although this may not pertain to weather-dependent attractions such as autumn colour and spring flower displays). However, these same qualities may imply a greater vulnerability to damage and overexploitation. The carving of initials into tree trunks and the removal of limbs for firewood are common examples of vegetation abuse associated with tourism. The 'captive' flora equivalent of a zoo is a botanical garden. These are usually located in larger urban areas, and as a result often draw in a particularly large visitor base (see table 5.1).

Protected natural areas

Protected natural areas such as national parks are an amalgam of topographical, hydrological, zoological, vegetation and cultural resources, and hence constitute a composite attraction. As natural attractions, high-order protected areas stand out for at least four reasons:

- Their protected status ensures, at least theoretically, that the integrity and attractiveness of their constituent natural resources is safeguarded.
- The amount of land available in a relatively undisturbed state is rapidly declining due to habitat destruction, thereby ensuring the status of high-order protected areas as scarce and desirable tourism resources.
- Such areas were usually protected because of exceptional natural qualities that are attractive to some tourists, such as scenic mountain ranges or rare species of animals and plants.
- An area having been designated as a national park or World Heritage Site confers status on that space as an attraction, since most people assume that it must be special to warrant such designation.

For all these reasons, protected natural areas are now among the most popular international and domestic tourism attractions (Butler & Boyd 2000). Some national parks, such as Yellowstone, Grand Canyon and Yosemite (all in the United States), Banff (Canada) and Kakadu and Uluru (Australia) are major and even iconic attractions in their respective countries. This is ironic given that many protected areas were originally established for preservation purposes, without any consideration being given to the possibility that they might be alluring to large numbers of tourists and other visitors. However, as funding cutbacks and external systems such as agriculture and logging pose an increased threat to these areas, their managers are now more open to tourism as a potentially compatible revenue-generating activity that may serve to pre-empt the intrusion of more destructive activities (see chapter 11).

Location

Extreme or centralised locations fascinate many people and thus have the potential to be exploited as tourist attractions. For example, the town of Rugby (in the US state of North Dakota) has erected a large cairn on its outskirts to publicise its status as 'the geographical centre of North America'. Many tourists stop at this site each year to have their photograph taken and to purchase basic services in transit to other destinations. Other cases where geographical extremity has evolved into a tourism product include Land's End (the most westerly spot on the mainland of England) and the Byron Bay lighthouse in New South Wales, which is close to the most easterly point of land in Australia.

Natural events

Natural events are often independent of particular locations and unpredictable in their occurrence and magnitude. Bird migrations are a good illustration. The Canadian province of Saskatchewan is becoming popular for the spring and autumn migrations of massive numbers of waterfowl, but the probability of arriving at the right place at the right time to see the spectacular flocks is dictated by various factors, including local weather and larger-scale climate shifts.

Solar eclipses and comets are rarer but more predictable events that attract large numbers of tourists to locations where good viewing conditions are anticipated. Volcanic eruptions (which appeal to many tourists because of their beauty and danger) are generally associated with known locations (thus they are sites as well as events), but are often less certain with respect to occurrence. However, lodgings have been established in the vicinity of Costa Rica's Arenal volcano specifically to accommodate the viewing of its nightly eruptions, while the predictable volcanic activity of Mt Yasur is the primary attraction on the island of Tanna in the Pacific archipelagic state of Vanuatu. The eruption of Italy's Mount Etna in 2001 had the interesting effect of attracting curious tourists while at the same time destroying ski facilities, a local tourist attraction.

A natural event associated with oceans and seas is tidal action. To become a tourism resource, tidal activity must have a dramatic or superlative component. One area that has taken advantage of its exceptional tidal action is Canada's Bay of Fundy (between the provinces of Nova Scotia and New Brunswick), where ideal geographical conditions produce tidal fluctuations of 12 to 15 metres, the highest in the world. Extreme weather conditions can produce natural events, for example when abundant rainfall replenishes the usually dry Lake Eyre basin in South Australia, creating a brief oceanic effect in the desert. This is a good example of an **ephemeral attraction**.

Cultural sites

Cultural sites, also known as 'built', 'constructed' or 'human-made' sites, are as or more diverse than their natural counterparts. Categories of convenience include prehistorical, historical, contemporary, economic activity, specialised recreational and retail. As with natural sites, these distinctions are often blurred when considering specific attractions.

Prehistorical

Prehistorical attractions, including rock paintings, rock etchings, middens, mounds and other sites associated with indigenous people, occur in many parts of Australia, New Zealand, Canada and the United States. Many of these attractions are affiliated with existing indigenous groups, and issues of control, appropriation, proper interpretation and effective management against excessive visitation therefore all have contemporary relevance (see the case study at the end of chapter 9). A distinct category of prehistorical sites is the megalithic sites associated with 'lost' cultures, which are attractive because of their mysterious origins as well as their impressive appearance. The New Age pilgrimage site of Stonehenge (United Kingdom) is a primary example. Others include the giant carved heads of Easter Island and the Nazca lines of Peru.

Historical

Historical sites are distinguished from prehistorical sites by their more definite associations with specific civilisations that fall under the scope of 'recorded history'. There is no single or universal criterion that determines when a contemporary artefact becomes 'historical'. Usually this is a matter of consensus within a local community or among scholars, or simply a promotional tactic. Historical sites can be divided into many subcategories, and only a few of the more prominent of these are outlined below.

Monuments and structures

Ancient monuments and structures that have attained prominence as attractions within their respective countries include the pyramids of Egypt, the Colosseum in Rome and the Parthenon in Athens. More recent examples include Angkor Wat (Cambodia), the Eiffel Tower, the Statue of Liberty, the Taj Mahal (Agra, India), the Kremlin (Moscow), Mount Rushmore (South Dakota, USA) and the Tower of London. Sydney's Harbour Bridge and Opera House also fall in this category. Beyond these marquee attractions, generic structures that have evolved into attractions include the numerous castles of Europe, the Hindu temples of India and the colonial-era sugar mills of the Caribbean.

Battlefields

Battlefields are among the most popular of all tourist attractions, which again demonstrates that the long-term impacts of war on tourism are often positive. Battle sites such as Thermopylae (fought in 480 BC between the Spartans and Persians), Hastings (fought in 1066 between the Anglo-Saxons and Normans) and Waterloo (1815) are still extremely popular centuries after their occurrence. The emergence of more recent battlefields (such as Gallipoli and the American Civil War site at Gettysburg) as even higher profile attractions is due to several factors, including:

- the accurate identification and marking of specific sites and events throughout the battlefields, which is possible because of the degree to which modern battles are documented
- sophisticated levels of interpretation made available to visitors
- attractive park-like settings
- the stature of certain battlefields as 'sacred' sites or events that changed history (e.g. Gettysburg as the 'turning point of the American Civil War' and Gallipoli as a catalyst in the forging of an Australian national identity)
- personal connections — many current visitors have great-grandparents or other ancestors who fought in these battles.

Other war- or military-related sites that frequently evolve into tourist attractions include military cemeteries, fortresses and barracks (e.g. the Hyde Park Barracks in Sydney), and defensive walls (e.g. the Great Wall of China and Hadrian's Wall in England). Battlefields and other military sites are an example of a particularly fascinating phenomenon known as **dark tourism**, which encompasses sites and events that become attractive to some tourists because of their association with death or suffering (Lennon & Foley 2000). Other examples include assassination sites (e.g. for John F. Kennedy and Martin Luther King), locales of mass killings (e.g. Port Arthur (Tasmania), the World Trade Center site, and Holocaust concentration camps) and places associated with the supernatural (e.g. Dracula's castle in Transylvania, and 'haunted houses').

Heritage districts and landscapes

In many cities, historical districts are preserved and managed as tourism-related areas that combine attractions (e.g. restored historical buildings, shopping) and services (e.g. accommodation, restaurants). Preserved walled cities such as Rothenburg (Germany), York (England), the Forbidden City (Beijing) and the Old Town district of Prague (Czech Republic) fall into this category, as does the French Quarter of New Orleans, USA. The Millers Point precinct of downtown Sydney is one of the best Australian examples, with its mixture of maritime-related historical buildings, small hotels, public open space, theatres and residential areas. Rural heritage landscapes are not as well known or protected. An Australian example is the German cultural landscape of the Barossa Valley in South Australia.

Museums

Unlike battlefields, museums are not site specific, and almost any community can augment their tourism resource inventory by assembling and presenting collections of locally significant artefacts. Museums can range in scale from high-profile, internationally known institutions such as the British Museum in London, to lesser known city sites such as the National Wool Museum in Geelong, Victoria, and small community museums in regional towns such as Gympie in Queensland. That museums differ widely in the way that items are selected, displayed and interpreted is an aspect of these attractions that has important implications for their market segmentation and marketing. Recent trends include the movement towards 'hands-on' interactive interpretation as a way of accommodating a new and more demanding generation of leisure visitors (see Managing tourism: Declining attendance at Colonial Williamsburg).

managing tourism

DECLINING ATTENDANCE AT COLONIAL WILLIAMSBURG

Colonial Willamsburg, in the US state of Virginia, is one of America's most celebrated outdoor 'living museums'. Yet, while regarded as an exemplar of historical preservation and interpretation, attendance has steadily declined from 1.2 million in 1988 to 710 000 in 2005 (Barisic 2008). Managers attribute this in part to increased competition from more newly established historical attractions, but also to the site's failure to meet the demands of a new generation of consumers variably described as impatient, demanding, 'hands-on', and tech savvy. These consumers are no longer content to patiently and passively observe a period blacksmith at work, or tour the governor's mansion, and the managers of Colonial Williamsburg are therefore turning to highly successful theme parks such as Disney World for inspiration on how to increase visitation levels (Morrison 2004).

A core feature of the 'new' Williamsburg is a high level of visitor involvement, so that tourists can now help the blacksmith to make a horseshoe, or participate in a political discussion in the governor's mansion. Key to such experiences is augmenting the core learning experience with entertainment and emotional connections that will long be remembered. A second main element is diversification of experience, so that a visitor would need to return four times in a year to witness events associated respectively with the formative years of 1773 to 1776. Diversity will also be evident in a higher number of 'spontaneous' events such as a fire brigade responding to a blaze or the mustering of militia for training, and in ongoing eighteenth-century 'soap operas' that would require a visit of several days to be fully appreciated (see figure 5.3). Technological innovations will be used increasingly to make all facets of interpretation more realistic. Assessing the outcome, one visitor described the new Williamsburg as 'Disney World for the mind' (Barisic 2008). Finally, managers recognise that younger consumers place a high value on comfort and convenience, and therefore plans are being made to augment the core historical area with a resort spa, golf courses and gourmet restaurants to attract longer stays and higher expenditures (Morrison 2004). An early indication of success is the increase in visitation to 785 000 in 2007 (Colonial Williamsburg 2008).

FIGURE 5.3 Re-enactment event at Colonial Williamsburg

Source: The Colonial Williamsburg Foundation

Contemporary

Ethnic neighbourhoods and sites providing distinctive food and drink are examples of contemporary cultural attractions.

Ethnic neighbourhoods

Large cities in Australia, Canada, the United States and western Europe are becoming increasingly diverse as a result of contemporary international migration patterns. This has led to the emergence of neighbourhoods associated with particular ethnic groups. For many years such areas were effectively alienated from the broader urban community, but now the Chinatowns of San Francisco, Sydney, Vancouver, New York and Toronto, for example, have evolved into high-profile tourist attractions. This trend has been assisted by the placement of Chinese language street signs and the approval of Asian-style outdoor markets and other culturally specific features. The effect is to provide the tourist (as well as local residents) with an experience of the exotic, without having to travel far afield. A surprising development has been the transformation of certain New York neighbourhoods (e.g. parts of Harlem) from what were perceived to be dangerous and hostile ghettos into vibrant centres of African-American music, food and theatre that attract many white visitors. In recent years, the appeal of urban neighbourhoods has been enhanced through the adoption of digital touring technologies that offer a personalised experience of place (see Technology and tourism: Getting to know 'the hood').

Food and drink

While taken for granted as a necessary consumable in any tourism experience, food is increasingly becoming an attraction in its own right, as illustrated by the experience of all the ethnic urban neighbourhoods mentioned above and numerous other destinations (Hall et al. 2003). In places such as Singapore, **culinary tourism** is encouraged not just to compensate for the lack of iconic attractions but also to reinforce the country's desired image of harmonious multiculturalism (Henderson 2004). For any place, food and drink are means by which the tourist can literally consume the destination, and if the experience is memorable, it can be exceptionally effective at inducing the highly desired outcomes of repeat visitation and favourable word-of-mouth promotion.

technology and tourism

GETTING TO KNOW 'THE HOOD'

As with conventionally presented historical sites, standard guided tours of urban neighbourhoods are not popular with younger travellers seeking stimulation, involvement and instant gratification. To attract these demanding tourists, some companies and destination organisations are offering fully guided tours that can be loaded onto an iPod or MP3 player. A US-based company, Audissey Guides (audisseyguides.com), offers iPod travel guides (or PodGuides) of Boston, Chicago, Miami Beach, New Orleans and Seattle that are not only free, but allow the tourist to begin and conclude the tour wherever they want, and to simply use the pause/resume sequence if they want to interrupt the tour at any time. The typical PodGuide includes a map of the covered area with numbered features that match an individual track of the digital tour; accompanying images ensure that you are interacting with the correct site.

Described by the company's founder as the 'anti-tour' because of its focus on areas that are off the beaten track, the iPod travel guide uses long-time local residents as well as expert commentators to provide personalised exposure of featured neighbourhoods, including 'inside' advice about the best local restaurants and coolest nightclubs (Gaylord 2006). An important benefit for self-conscious visitors not wanting to look like tourists is that they can easily pass as local iPod-tuned residents, thereby allowing them to feel even more immersed in the experience while never having to divert their eyes to an actual tour guide or tour book. The Belgium-based company PodGuides.net is now taking the PodGuide concept to a new level by allowing anyone to make and post their own creations on their website. This means ordinary members of the public will have the opportunity to influence the tourism system by creating innovative PodGuides that may attract more tourists to obscure destinations (these can also be rural or suburban) not currently featured on conventional tours.

A particularly well-articulated form of culinary tourism in some destinations is wine tourism (Getz 2000). Scenic **winescapes** are the focus of tourism activity in well-established locations such as the Napa Valley of California, the Hunter Valley of New South Wales, and the Clare and Barossa Valleys of South Australia (Macionis & Cambourne 2000) and in emerging locations such as Canada's Niagara Peninsula (Stewart, Bramble & Ziraldo 2008). The more established regions have all benefited from a pattern of producing reliably high quality wines, a strong and positive market image, well-managed cellar door operations, and exurban locations. However, while tourism has been described as a 'perfect partner' for the wine industry (Dowling & Carlsen 1998), attendant challenges include:

• internal competition among producers that impedes collective marketing and management

- increasing competition from new regions that diverts visitors and dissuades repeat visitation
- difficulties in co-managing the tourism and production aspects of business
- increased urbanisation that reduces the winescape's aesthetic appeal and relaxed lifestyle.

Economic activity

'Living' economic activities such as mining, agriculture and manufacturing are often taken for granted by the local community, and particularly by the labour force engaged in those livelihoods. However, these activities can also provide a fascinating and unusual experience for those who use the associated products but are divorced from their actual production. At a deeper level, the widespread separation of modern society from the processes of primary production in the 'postindustrial' era, and the subsequent desire to participate at least indirectly in such activities, may help to explain the growing popularity of factory, mine and farm tours (Jansen–Verbeke 1999).

Canals and railways

Recreational canals and railways provide excellent examples of **functional adaptation** (the use of a structure for a purpose other than its original intent). As with factory, mine and farm tours, such adaptations are associated with the movement from an industrial to a postindustrial society, in which some canals and railways are now more valuable as sites for recreation and tourism than as a means of bulk transportation for industrial goods — their original intent. England is an area where pleasure-boating on canals is especially important, as the Industrial Revolution left behind a legacy of thousands of kilometres of now defunct canals, which have proven ideal for accommodating small pleasure craft. A similar phenomenon is apparent in North American locations such as the Trent and Rideau Canals (Ontario, Canada) and the Erie Canal in New York State.

Specialised recreational attractions (SRAs)

Of all categories of tourist attraction, specialised recreational attractions (SRAs) are unique because they are constructed specifically to meet the demands of the tourism and recreation markets. With the exception of ski lifts and several other products that require specific environments, SRAs are also among the attractions least constrained by context and location. Their establishment, in other words, does not depend on particular circumstances such as the location of certain cultures or physical conditions. SRAs are in addition the attraction type most clearly related to the tourism industry, since they mostly consist of privately owned businesses (the linear SRAs discussed below are one exception).

Golf courses

Golf courses are an important SRA subcategory for several reasons, including:
- the recent proliferation of golf facilities worldwide (more than 30 000 by the early 2000s)
- the relatively large amount of space that they occupy both individually and collectively
- their association with residential housing developments and integrated resorts
- their controversial environmental impacts.

In addition, high concentrations of golf activity, in areas such as Palm Springs, California, and Orlando, Florida, have led to the appearance of **golfscapes**, or landscapes where golf courses and affiliated developments are a dominant land use. The Gold Coast is the best Australian example of a golfscape, with some 40 courses available within council boundaries, and a similar number under construction or approved.

Casinos

For many years, casinos were synonymous with Monte Carlo, Las Vegas and few other locations. However, casinos have proliferated well beyond these traditional strong-holds as governments have become more aware of, and dependent on gaming-based revenues. Casinos are now a common sight on North American Indian Reserves, in central cities (e.g. Melbourne's Crown Casino and Brisbane's Treasury Casino), and as Mississippi River-style gambling boats in the American South and Midwest. An interesting development is the transformation of Macau, China into the 'Las Vegas of the East' (Hsu 2006). Increasing competition has prompted the Las Vegas tourism industry to erect ever larger and more fantastic themed casino hotels (e.g. Excalibur, Luxor and MGM Grand), which increasingly blur the distinction between accommo-dation and attraction. Though ideally intended to attract external revenue, casinos such as Jupiters Casino on the Gold Coast are also attractive to local residents, and their presence is often therefore controversial due to the possibility of negative social impacts (see chapter 9).

Theme parks

Theme parks are large-scale, topical and mostly exurban SRAs that contain numerous subattractions (e.g. rides, shows, exhibits, events) intended to provide family groups with an all-inclusive, all-day recreational experience. The Disney-related sites (e.g. Disneyland at Anaheim, California; DisneyWorld at Orlando, Florida; and Eurodisney in Paris) are the best known international examples, while the Gold Coast theme parks (Dreamworld, Sea World and Warner Bros. Movie World) are the best known Aus-tralian examples. Theme parks provide a good illustration of social engineering in that they purport to offer thrilling and spontaneous experiences, yet in reality are hyper-regulated and orchestrated environments that maximise opportunities for retail expen-diture by visitors (Rojek 1993).

Scenic highways, bikeways and hiking trails

Linear recreational attractions are sometimes the result of functional adaptation, as for example canals (see above) and bicycle and walking trails that are constructed on the foundations of abandoned railway lines. The Rails to Trails Conservancy is a US-based organisation that specialises in such conversions. In other cases linear SRAs are custom built to meet specific recreational and tourism needs. The Blue Ridge Parkway and Natchez Trace are US examples of custom-built scenic roadways, while the Appala-chian Trail is a well-known example of a specialised long-distance walking track. A variation of the road theme is the multipurpose highway that is designated as a scenic route. Australian examples include Victoria's Great Ocean Road and the Birdsville Track from Marree (SA) to Birdsville (Qld).

Ski resorts

More than most SRAs, ski resort viability is dependent on the availability of specific climatic and topographical conditions, although the invention of affordable snow-making technology greatly facilitated the spread of the industry into regions otherwise unsuitable. A process of consolidation, however, is now evident, with the number of ski areas in the United States declining from 745 to 509 between 1975 and 2000 (Clifford 2002). Concurrently, the average size of resorts has increased and corporate ownership has become prevalent. As with golf courses, the profitability of the contemporary ski megaresort is increasingly dependent on revenues from affiliated housing developments, in which case the actual ski facilities serve primarily as a 'hook' to attract real-estate investors.

Retail

Under certain conditions, retail goods and services, similarly to food, are major tourist attractions in their own right, and not only an associated service activity. Singapore and Hong Kong are South-East Asian examples of destinations that offer shopping opportunities as a core component of their tourism product (Heung & Cheng 2000). In cities such as Kuala Lumpur (Malaysia), shopping malls are built into large hotels to create an integrated accommodation–shopping complex. The attraction of retail shopping is also evident in Australia, where 76 per cent of main-market inbound tourists reported participation in shopping for pleasure during 2008 (see table 5.1).

Mega-malls

The 'mega-mall' phenomenon has historically been associated with North America, where the West Edmonton Mall (Canada), the Mall of the Americas (Minneapolis) and other complexes vied to be recognised as the world's largest shopping centre. In recent years, East Asian malls have competed exclusively for this title, with the three largest by gross leasable area (GLA) all located in that region in 2006 (South China Mall in Dongguan, Golden Resources Shopping Mall in Beijing, and SM Mall of Asia in Pasay City, The Philippines) (Pocock 2008). As with theme parks and large casinos, mega-malls are composite attractions that contain numerous individual subattractions, all designed to maximise the amount of time that visitors remain within the facility and the amount of money that they spend. Similarly, they are usually contrived in character, incorporating fake Italian townscapes, ski slopes (as in Dubai) or exotic South Pacific themes.

Markets and bazaars

'Colourful' Caribbean markets and 'exotic' Asian bazaars are generic tourism icons of their respective destination regions. The ability to compromise between authenticity (which may repel some tourists) and a comfortable and safe environment for the conventional tourist is a major challenge to the manager of market and bazaar attractions. Within Australia, country or 'farmers' markets in communities such as Mount Tamborine and Eumundi (Queensland) are major local attractions, especially for domestic tourists.

Cultural events

Cultural events can be categorised in several ways, including the extent to which they are regular or irregular in occurrence (e.g. the Summer Olympics every four years versus one-time-only special commemorations) or location (the British Open tennis tournament held at Wimbledon versus the changing Olympics site). Cultural events can range in size from a small local arts festival to international mega-events such as the football World Cup. In addition, events may be 'single destination' (e.g. Wimbledon) or 'multiple destination' in space or time (e.g. the Olympics sites spread over a region or the circuit-based Tour de France bicycle race). Finally, thematic classification assigns events to topical categories such as history, sport, religion, music and arts. For tourism sites such as theme parks and historical destinations, periodic events are an important supplementary attraction that add to product diversity and offer a distraction from routine. They may also serve as a management device that redistributes visitors in a more desirable way both in time and space. As with museums, communities have the ability to initiate cultural events by creatively capitalising on available local resources.

Historical re-enactments and commemorations

The re-creation of historical events can serve many purposes in addition to its superficial value as a tourist attraction. Participants may be primarily motivated by a deep-seated desire to connect with significant events of the past, while governments often encourage and sponsor such performances to perpetuate the propaganda or mythological value of the original event, especially if the recreations or commemorations occur at the original sites. Re-enactments associated with the landings of Captain Cook featured prominently in the 1988 Bicentenary commemorations in Australia, although their association with the post-1788 Aboriginal dispossession injected an element of controversy. Less contentious are the periodic re-enactments of American Civil War battles such as Gettysburg and Napoleonic War battles such as Waterloo, which attracts thousands of re-enactors and much higher numbers of spectators.

Sporting events

The modern Olympic games are the most prestigious of all sporting events, although the football World Cup is emerging as a legitimate contender for the title in the wake of the highly successful 1998 and 2002 events. That the World Cup and the Olympics do take place in the same year is a deliberate attempt to avoid competing mega-event hype and coverage. Major sporting events are exceptional in the degree to which they attract extensive media attention, and the number of television viewers far outweighs the on-site audience. These events are therefore additionally important for their potential to induce some of the television audience (which may number several billion consumers) to visit the host city, thereby creating a post-event ripple effect.

The fierce competition that accompanies the selection of host Olympic cities or World Cup nations is therefore as much about long-term image enhancement and induced visitation as it is about the actual event. The 2000 Sydney Games were highly symbolic because of their occurrence at the turn of the millennium and their role in positioning the host city as a globalised 'world city' (Waitt 2004), while the 2008 Beijing Games were unofficially seen as heralding China's emergence as a world sporting (and economic) power. Other sporting events of note are associated with golf and tennis tournaments, while the regular season itineraries of professional sports teams (e.g. baseball, basketball, ice hockey, rugby league) are significant generators of mostly domestic tourist activity.

World fairs

While less prestigious than the Olympics, world fairs (designated as such by an official organisation similar to the International Olympic Committee, or IOC) also confer a significant amount of status and visibility to host cities. The 1988 World Fair in Brisbane, for example, was similar to the 2000 Sydney Games in that it is often associated with that city's 'coming-of-age' as a more open and cosmopolitan place.

Festivals and performances

Most countries, including Australia, host an extremely large and diverse number of festivals and performances. Attendance in Australia (not all of which is accounted for by tourists) is for the most part related to the 'arts' (see table 5.2). As mentioned above, destinations have considerable ability to establish festival- and performance-type events, since these can capitalise on anything from a particular local culture or industry to themes completely unrelated to the area. For example, the highly popular Woodford Folk Festival, held annually in the Sunshine Coast hinterland of Queensland, could just as easily be located on any one of a thousand similar sites within an easy drive from Brisbane. In other cases, festivals are more associated with particular destination qualities. The Barossa Vintage Festival in South Australia is a well-known Australian example that capitalises on the local wine industry.

TABLE 5.2 Attendance by age group at selected cultural events in Australia, 2005–06

Event	Total attendance (000s)	Total	Percentage by age group						
			18–24	25–34	35–44	45–54	55–64	65–74	75+
Popular music concerts	4036	25	40	31	25	27	19	13	7
Art galleries	3631	23	18	23	23	27	26	22	16
Museums	3612	23	16	24	27	25	25	19	11
Theatre	2723	17	16	15	16	20	20	17	8
Musicals/opera	2614	16	14	14	17	19	20	16	12
Dance	1625	10	8	9	12	13	9	7	4
Classical music concerts	1508	9	6	7	8	12	13	12	10

Source: Data derived from ABS (2007)

Attraction attributes

Destination managers, as stated earlier, should compile an inventory of their tourism attractions as a prerequisite for the effective management of their tourism sector. It is not sufficient, however, just to list and categorise the attractions. Managers must also periodically assess their status across an array of relevant **attraction attributes** to inform appropriate planning and management decisions (see figure 5.4). A spectrum is used in each case to reflect the continuous nature of these variables. Each of the attraction attributes will now be considered, with no order of importance implied by the sequence of presentation. Image is not discussed below, as this attribute is addressed elsewhere in the text in some detail (see chapters 4 and 7).

Ownership

The ownership of an attraction significantly affects the planning and management process. For example, the public ownership of Lamington National Park, in the Gold Coast hinterland, implies the injection of public rather than private funding, a high level of government decision-making discretion and the assignment of a higher priority to environmental and social impacts over profit generation. Public ownership also suggests an extensive regulatory environment and long-term, as opposed to shorter-term, planning horizons.

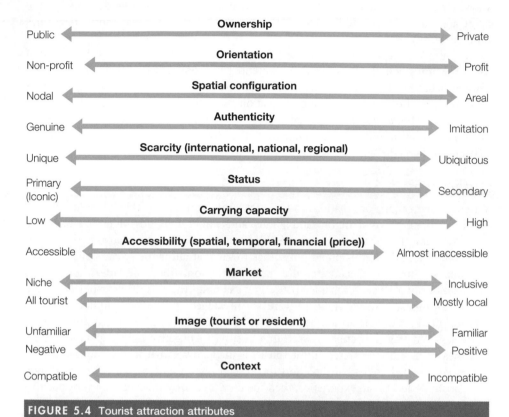

FIGURE 5.4 Tourist attraction attributes

Orientation

An emphasis on profitability is affiliated to, but not identical with, private sector ownership. Revenue-starved governments may place more stress on profit generation, which in turn modifies many management assumptions and actions with respect to the attractions that they control. Among the possible implications of a profit reorientation in a national park is the introduction of user fees, an easing of visitor quotas, greater emphasis on visitor satisfaction and increased latitude for the operation of private concessions. The national park, in essence, becomes a 'business' and its visitors 'customers' who must be satisfied.

Spatial configuration

Geographical shape and size have important managerial implications. Spatially extensive linear SRAs, for example, may cross a large number of political jurisdictions, each of them having some influence therefore over the viability of the resource. In addition, long-distance walking trails in particular pass through privately owned land for much of their length, which renders them susceptible to relocation if some landowners decide that they no longer want the trail to pass through their property because of security, liability or vandalism concerns. In the United Kingdom, the status of public walking trails on private property has become a highly contentious and politically charged issue. Linear SRAs are also likely to share extensive borders with adjacent land uses that may not be compatible with tourism or recreation. There is potential for conflict and dissatisfaction from the fact that these trails, roads and bike-ways rely to a large extent on the scenic resources of these adjacent landscapes, yet the latter are vulnerable to modification by forces over which the attraction manager has no control.

In contrast, a circular or square site (e.g. some national parks) reduces the length of the attraction's boundary and thus the potential for conflict with adjacent land uses. This also has practical implications in matters such as the length of boundary that must be fenced or patrolled. The classification of a site often depends on the scale of investigation. For example, a regional strategy for south-east Queensland would regard Dreamworld as an internally undifferentiated 'node' or 'point', whereas a site-specific master plan would regard the same attraction as an internally differentiated 'area'.

Authenticity

Whereas ownership, orientation and spatial configuration are relatively straightfor-ward, 'authenticity' is a highly ambiguous and contentious attribute that has long been the subject of academic attention (MacCannell 1976). An exhaustive discussion is beyond the scope of this book, but suffice to say that authenticity can consider how 'genuine' an attraction is as opposed to imitative or contrived. The latter, however, is not necessarily a negative characteristic. For example, the 40 000-year-old Neolithic cave paintings at Lascaux (France) were so threatened by the perspiration and res-piration of tourists that an almost exact replica was constructed nearby for viewing purposes. Whether the replica is seen in a positive or negative light depends on how it is presented and interpreted; if the tourist is made aware that it is an imitation, and that it is provided as part of the effort to preserve the original while still providing a high quality educational experience, then the copy may be perceived in a very positive light. Similarly, the mega-casinos of Las Vegas offer a contrived experience, but this is not necessarily problematic as long as patrons recognise that contrivance is a central element of the tourist experience (see chapter 9).

The issue of authenticity is associated with **sense of place**, an increasingly popular management concept defined as the mix of natural and cultural characteristics that distinguishes a particular destination from all other destinations, and hence positions it as 'unique' along the scarcity spectrum (see below).

Scarcity

An important management implication of scarcity is that a very rare or unique attrac-tion is likely to be both highly vulnerable and highly attractive to tourists as a conse-quence of its scarcity. At the other end of the spectrum are ubiquitous resources such as golf courses or theme parks; that is, those that are found or can be established almost anywhere. Scarcity or uniqueness is most valuable at the global scale, as the ability of a destination to boast the world's deepest lake, for example, will generate far more tourist interest than claiming the deepest lake in South Australia or Tasmania.

Status

A useful distinction can be made between primary or **iconic attractions** and sec-ondary attractions, which tourists are likely to visit once they have already been drawn to a destination by the primary attraction. A destination may have more than one primary attraction, as with the Eiffel Tower and Louvre in Paris, or the Opera House and harbour in Sydney. One potential disadvantage of iconic attractions is their power to stereotype entire destinations (e.g. the Royal Canadian Mounted Police, Swiss Alp villages or the Pyramids of Egypt). Another potential disadvantage is the negative publicity and loss of visitation that may occur if an iconic attraction is lost due to fire, natural forces or other factors, prompting managers in some cases to try to resurrect such sites as 'residual attractions' (Weaver & Lawton 2007).

Carrying capacity

Carrying capacity is difficult to measure since it is not a fixed quality. A national park may have a low visitor carrying capacity in the absence of tourism-related services, but a high visitor carrying capacity once a dirt trail has been covered in cobblestones and biological toilets installed to centralise and treat tourist wastes. In such instances of **site hardening**, managers must be careful to ensure that the remedial actions themselves do not pose a threat to the site or to the carrying capacity of affiliated resources such as wildlife (see chapters 9 and 11). It is crucial that managers have an idea of an attraction's carrying capacity at all times, so that, depending on the circumstances, appropriate measures can be taken to either increase this capacity or reduce the stress so that the existing carrying capacity is not exceeded.

Accessibility

Accessibility can be measured in terms of space, time and affordability. As considered on page 37, spatial access only by a single road will have the positive effect of facilitating entry control, but the negative effects of creating potential bottlenecks and isolating the site in the event of a flood or earthquake. Another dimension of spatial accessibility is how well an attraction is identified on roadmaps and in road signage. Temporal accessibility can be seasonal (e.g. an area closed by winter snowfalls) or assessed on a daily or weekly basis (hours and days of operation). Affordability is important in determining likely markets and visitation levels. All three dimensions should be assessed continually as aspects of an attraction that can be manipulated as part of an effective management strategy.

Market

Destination and attraction markets often vary depending on the season, time of day, cost and other factors. One relevant dimension is whether the attraction appeals to the broad tourism market, as with a theme park, or to a particular segment of the market, as with battle re-enactments or hunting (see chapter 6). This dictates the type of marketing approach that would be most appropriate (see chapter 7). A second dimension identifies sites and events that are almost exclusively tourist-oriented, as opposed to those that attract mostly local residents. Because of the tendency of clientele to be mixed to a greater or lesser extent, the all-encompassing term 'visitor attraction' is often used in preference to the term 'tourist attraction'. Positive and negative impacts can be associated with both tourist-dominant and resident-dominant attractions. For instance, an exclusively tourist-oriented site may generate local resentment, but the mixing of tourists and locals in some circumstances can increase the probability of cultural conflict (chapter 9).

Context

Context describes the characteristics of the space and time that surround the relevant site or event and, as such, is an attribute that considers the actual and potential impacts of external systems. An example of a compatible external influence is a designated state forest that serves as a buffer zone surrounding a more environmentally sensitive national park. In contrast, an adjacent strip mine is likely to be incompatible with that park. The influence of temporal context is demonstrated by a large sporting event that is held shortly after a similar event in another city, which could either stimulate or depress public interest depending on the circumstances.

◾ THE TOURISM INDUSTRY

The **tourism industry**, as described in chapter 2, includes the businesses that provide goods and services wholly or mainly for tourist consumption. Some but not all attractions belong to the tourism industry. It is worth reiterating that some aspects of the tourism industry are straightforward (e.g. accommodation and travel agencies), but others (e.g. transportation and restaurants) are more difficult to differentiate into their tourism and nontourism components. In addition, commercial activities such as cruise ships and integrated resorts do not readily allow for the isolation of accommodation, transportation, food and beverages, and shopping as distinct components.

Travel agencies

More than any other tourism industry sector, **travel agencies** are associated with origin regions (see chapter 2). Their primary function is to provide retail travel services to customers on a commission basis from cruise lines and other tourism sectors or on a fee basis from customers directly. Travel agents in addition normally offer ancillary services such as travel insurance and passport/visa services. As such, they are an important interface or intermediary between consumers and other tourism businesses. Often overlooked, however, is the critical role of travel agents in shaping tourism systems by providing undecided consumers with information and advice about prospective destinations. Furthermore, travel agents provide invaluable feedback to destination managers because of their sensitivity to market trends and post-trip tourist attitudes about particular destinations and services.

Disintermediation and decommissioning

All these traditional assumptions about the role and importance of travel agents within tourism systems have been challenged by the ongoing phenomenon of **disintermediation**, which is the removal of intermediaries such as travel agents from the distribution networks that connect consumers (i.e. the tourist market) with products (e.g. accommodations and destinations). This is associated with the rise of the internet, which allows hotels, carriers and other businesses to offer their products through ecommerce directly to consumers in a more convenient and less expensive package (cheaper because it eliminates the agent's commission). The internet, in addition, has spawned the creation of specialised 'e-travel agencies' such as Travelocity and Expedia. By 2002, an estimated 15 per cent of all leisure travel in the United States was booked online (Tse 2003).

An added challenge has been the process of **decommissioning,** which began in the mid-1990s, wherein airlines no longer pay a standard commission (usually 10 per cent) to travel agents in exchange for airfare bookings. Disintermediation and decommissioning have combined with the market uncertainty that followed the 2001 terrorist attacks to create an era of unprecedented challenge for conventional travel agencies in certain countries, although some businesses have performed exceptionally well despite these adverse circumstances (see the case study at the end of this chapter).

Transportation

The overriding trend in **transportation** over the past century (see chapters 2 and 3) is the ascendancy of the car and the aeroplane at the expense of water- and rail-based transport. The technological and historical aspects of these trends have already been outlined in earlier chapters, and the sections that follow focus instead on contemporary business considerations.

Air

As a commercial activity, air transportation is differentiated between scheduled airlines, charter airlines and private jets. The last category is by far the smallest and most individualised. The major difference between the first two is the flexibility of charter schedules and the ability of charters to accommodate specific requests from organisations or tour operators. Many of the larger airlines have established charter subsidiaries to attain wider market coverage. For example, Air New Zealand controls Freedom Air, while Singapore Airlines owns the charter carrier airline Silk Air.

Airline alliances

Another major development in the airline industry is the trend towards airline alliances such as the *Star Alliance*, *OneWorld* and *SkyTeam*. Purportedly established on the premise that individual airlines can no longer provide the comprehensive array of services demanded by the contemporary traveller, these alliances offer:
* expanded route networks
* ease of transfer between airlines
* integrated services
* greater reciprocity in frequent flier programs and lounge privileges (Fyall & Garrod 2005).

However, more frequent code-sharing (i.e. two airlines sharing the same flight) also means fewer flight options, higher prices (because of reduced competition) and more crowded flights for consumers.

Deregulation

Deregulation (the removal or relaxation of regulations) is intended to introduce or increase competition within the air transportation sector. Associated with deregulation is the increased application of the so-called seventh and eighth **freedoms of the air**, which respectively allow a carrier based, for example, in Australia to carry passengers between two other countries and to carry passengers on domestic routes within another country (see figure 5.5). Although not aimed at this level yet, the open skies aviation agreement signed in February 2008 between Australia and the USA effectively breaks the trans-Pacific monopoly of United Airlines and Qantas by allowing the market rather than government to dictate the most efficient structure of the air transit network that connects the two countries (MarketWatch 2008). Greater competition from new entries such as V Australia (the long-haul arm of Virgin Blue), in theory, should give consumers added convenience and cheaper fares.

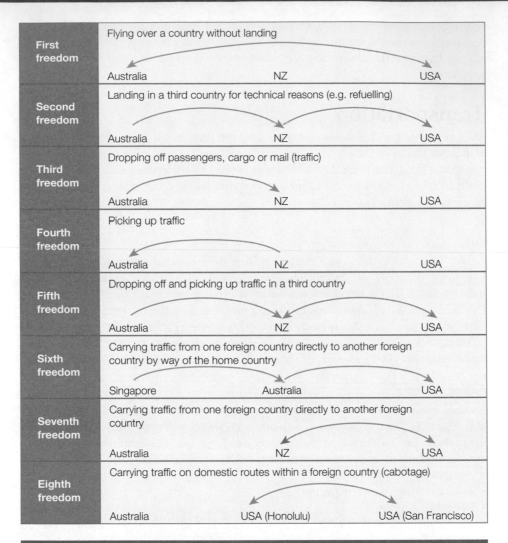

FIGURE 5.5 Freedoms of the air

Privatisation

Privatisation, or the transfer of publicly owned airlines to the private sector, is a trend closely related to deregulation. This can be undertaken (a) as a wholesale transformation, (b) as a partial measure achieved through the sale of a certain portion of shares, or (c) through the subcontracting of work. The main rationale for privatisation, as with open skies agreements, is the belief that the private sector is more efficient at providing commercial services such as air passenger transportation. One potential concern in such developments is the increased likelihood that privatised airlines will eliminate unprofitable routes vital to regional or rural destinations. In contrast, national carriers are usually mandated in the broader 'national interest' to operate such marginal routes despite their unprofitable returns.

Security

A trend that is affecting the airline industry perhaps more than other forms of transportation since September 2001 is concern over security. Drastic measures are being adopted to address consumer sensitivities about the vulnerability of aircraft passengers to hijackings and onboard bombings. These include the presence of air marshals on some flights and security clearance procedures that require substantially more lead-in time before flight departure.

Escalating fuel costs

Finally, airlines are increasingly vulnerable to the effects of rapidly rising fuel costs. According to Qantas CEO Geoff Dixon, a 'new world order' loomed in 2008 in which the sector would eventually be dominated by (a) a small number of ultra-efficient and integrated giants such as KLM and Singapore Airlines, (b) specialised airlines serving niche markets and destinations, and (c) national carriers such as Emirates that are generously subsidised by oil-rich countries (Hatch 2008).

Road

Only certain elements of the road-based transportation industry, including coaches, caravans and rental cars, are directly affiliated with the tourism industry. Coaches remain a potent symbol of the package tour both in their capacity as tour facilitators and as transportation from airport to hotel. Caravans remain popular because of their dual accommodation and transportation function. The car and the aeroplane in many contexts are seen as competing modes of transportation. However, the rental car industry (e.g. Hertz, National, Avis, Budget) has benefited from the expansion of air transportation, as many passengers appreciate the flexibility of having access to their own vehicle once they arrive at a destination.

Railway

The rail industry as a whole now plays a marginal role in tourism, but there are two areas where this involvement is more substantial. The first concerns regions, such as western Europe, where concentrated and well-used rail networks facilitate tourism travel. Rail pass options that allow unlimited access over a given period of time are a popular product among free and independent travellers (FITs). Australia, among many such nationwide and state-specific options, offers the Austrailpass, which provides unlimited economy travel over the entire network over consecutive days, and the Sunshine Rail Pass, which allows 14-, 21- or 30-day unlimited travel over the Queensland Rail network on either a first-class or economy basis. In future, and as demonstrated by the Alpine Pearls initiative in Europe (see page 69), trains could once again play a more important transit role as escalating fuel costs and environmental concerns curtail travel by air or road.

The second perspective pertains to train tours as attractions. As with cruise ships, the trip itself is as much part of the 'destination' as the points of origin and terminus. Train tours also attract the higher end of the market in terms of income. Well-known examples include the Orient Express between London and Istanbul and the Eastern Orient Express between Bangkok and Singapore. A notable Australian example is The Ghan, which connects Adelaide and Darwin (Winter 2007).

Water

The great ocean liners that once dominated the trans-Atlantic trade are now in a situation comparable to the great rail journeys — a high-end but residual niche product. Yet the resilience of this sector is indicated by the launching in 2004 of the *Queen Mary II*, which is the first major liner to be launched on the trans-Atlantic route since the *Queen Elizabeth II* in 1969. The regional cruise market in areas such as the Caribbean and Mediterranean has been more robust, expanding continuously since the 1980s (Dowling 2006). Cruising has become increasingly popular in Australia as well, with P&O permanently basing ships in major ports, and lines from other countries basing vessels in Australia for three-to-four-month seasons. Important trends include the proliferation of mega cruise liners of 140 000 tonnes or more which are capable of accommodating in excess of 3000 passengers, and the acquisition of private islands (e.g. Royal Caribbean International's CocoaCay in the Bahamas), which help the cruise lines to retain passengers' off-ship expenditures.

Accommodation

Notwithstanding the local importance of cruise ships and caravans, the vast majority of stayovers who do not stay in the homes of friends or relatives use commercial tourist accommodation. Once restricted to a narrow range of conventional hotels and motels, the **accommodation** industry is now characterised by a high level of diversity and specialisation.

Hotels

Traditionally, **hotels** were established in central cities, often near major railway stations, to meet the needs of business travellers. Such hotels are usually no longer dependent on rail access and have often been reinvented as exclusive 'boutique hotels' that feature intimacy and often quirky urban design. Another inner city facility is the 'convention hotel', which emerged during the 1960s to provide specialised meeting, conference and convention services and, increasingly, diversions such as gaming facilities. As such, they are closely affiliated with MICE tourism (see chapter 2). 'Airport hotels' are a more recent innovation. Usually clustering along distinctive hotel strips, their proximity to major airports attracts aeroplane crews and transit passengers. Event organisers use them with increasing frequency because they are convenient for tourists arriving by air. Airport hotels may also benefit as passengers are forced to allow more lead-in time to clear security for morning flights. 'Motels' (*motor hotels*) in a sense are the opposite of airport hotels, as they offer independent access to units for tourists travelling mainly by car.

'Resort hotels' are a 3S tourism symbol. These can range from specialised providers of accommodation such as spas or ecolodges to fully integrated resorts that offer comprehensive recreational, retail and other opportunities. Other specialised facilities include the 'apartment hotel' and 'extended stay hotel', which provide cooking facilities and other services appropriate for a stay of at least one week, and **timesharing**, which involves the purchase of 'intervals' (usually measured in weeks) at a resort over a given period of years. In some cases these are consumed during the same week each year, and in others on a more flexible basis. The ability to exchange intervals so that a holiday can be spent at a different resort is a major attraction of timesharing, which is facing increasing competition from **destination clubs** (see Breakthrough tourism: In the lap of luxury at the destination club).

As with cruise ships, hotel guest capacities are constantly being increased. Las Vegas hotel structures such as the MGM Grand and Luxor each offer more than 5000 rooms, or an amount equivalent to all the hotel rooms in Bermuda. From a corporate perspective, the hotel sector is controlled by a relatively small number of large chains (see table 5.3). United States-based corporations are dominant, reflecting not just the strong global US corporate presence, but also the enormous size of the US domestic tourism sector. Notable, however, is the appearance of a China-based chain in the top 25 for the first time in 2007, as well as two 'Las Vegas' corporations (MGM and Harrah's) that feature a small number of extremely large casino-type facilities.

Rank	Chain	Country	Number of rooms	Number of hotels
	TABLE 5.3 The 25 largest hotel chains worldwide, 2007			
1	InterContinental (II IG)	United Kingdom	585 094	3949
2	Wyndham Worldwide	United States	550 576	6544
3	Marriott International	United States	537 249	2999
4	Hilton Hotels	United States	502 116	3000
5	Accor	France	461 698	3871
6	Choice Hotels	United States	452 027	5570
7	Best Western International	United States	308 636	4035
8	Starwood	United States	274 535	897
9	Carlson	United States	146 600	969
10	Global Hyatt Corp.	United States	135 001	721
11	Westmont Hospitality	United States	108 503	703
12	Golden Tulip	The Netherlands	86 585	944
13	TUI AG/TUI	Germany	83 192	288
14	Extended Stay Hotels	United States	76 384	686
15	Sol Melia	Spain	75 022	301
16	LQ Management	United States	69 089	633
17	Jin Jiang International	China	68 797	380
18	Rezidor Hotel Group	Belgium	67 000	329
19	Group du Louvre	France	60 807	848
20	Vantage Hospitality	United States	55 167	798
21	NH Hoteles SA	Spain	49 677	341
22	MGM Mirage	United States	42 802	17
23	Interstate	United States	42 620	191
24	Barcelo Hotels & Resorts	Spain	42 173	162
25	Harrah's Entertainment	United States	38 130	35

Source: Hotels, www.hotelsmag.com

Tour operators

Tour operators are intermediaries or facilitating businesses within the tourism distribution system that can be differentiated between an outbound (or wholesaler) component and an inbound component. **Outbound tour operators** are based in origin regions and generally are large companies that organise volume-driven package tours and the travel groups that purchase these. This involves the negotiation of contracts with carriers, travel agencies, hotels and other suppliers of goods and services, including the **inbound tour operators** that 'take over' the tour groups once they arrive in the destination. Revenue is usually generated on a commission basis. The inbound component, often based in major gateway cities, arranges (also on a commission basis) destination itineraries and local services such as transportation, access to attractions, local tour-guiding services and, in some cases, accommodation. By the destinations and services that they choose to assemble, both types of tour operators exercise an important influence over the development of tourism systems.

breakthrough tourism

IN THE LAP OF LUXURY AT THE DESTINATION CLUB

Sometimes described as a high-end form of timesharing, destination clubs offer their clients exclusive access to a selection of fully serviced luxurious mansions, apartments and yachts, in exchange for a one-time membership fee and annual dues (Desmarest & Monroe 2008). Stays normally last for two weeks and include access to concierges, chefs, travel advisors and other personal vacation facilitators. The high-end nature of destination clubs is illustrated by Exclusive Resorts (based in Denver, USA), which controls over one-half of the market and provided more than 300 properties by the end of 2005, each valued on average at US$3 million. The more than 1600 members each pay an initial membership fee of US$395 000 and subsequent annual dues ranging from US$20 000–30 000 depending on the level of use desired (Frank 2005).

Destination clubs appear to be testing the limits as to what the ultra-wealthy are willing to pay for exclusive experiences that in their most common form offer no actual ownership of facilities. The Montana-based Yellowstone Club, for example, charges membership fees ranging from US$4–10 million and annual dues of US$100 000, but justifies this price by providing access to an allegedly unparalleled global network of ultra-exclusive beach and ski resorts in the most desirable locations (Frank 2005). Ultimately, however, such clubs are gambling on the willingness of the ultra-rich to pay extravagant amounts in order to be differentiated from the mere 'very rich'. The more 'average' facilities currently attract families, baby boomer couples, and corporations seeking to reward high performing executives (Desmarest & Monroe 2008), and some clubs are hoping to increase business from these and other markets by offering more affordable membership options. Colorado-based Private Escapes is one such 'economy' provider, allowing access to US$500 000–600 000 homes in Las Vegas, California's Napa Valley and Colorado for a 'mere' US$95 000 membership fee and US$7200 in annual dues (Frank 2005).

Like travel agencies, contemporary tour operators are challenged by rapidly changing developments in technology and markets and must respond by being innovative. The uniform package tour was suitable for the industrial mode of production that dominated the era of Thomas Cook, but is increasingly less suited for postindustrial society. It is necessary now to provide specialised products for a more diverse and discriminating market that likes to use the internet to assemble its own customised itineraries.

One means of achieving product diversification is to treat each unit of the tourism experience as a separate 'mini-package', thereby allowing consumers to assemble units into a customised package tour that fits their particular needs. One consumer may choose a two-week beach resort holiday with full services, followed by one week in the outback on a coach tour, while another can select from the same operator a two-week stay at an outback lodge, followed by a one-week, limited-service stay at a beach resort.

Merchandise

Tourism-related **merchandise** can be divided into items purchased in the origin region or the destination region. Origin region merchandise includes camping equipment, cameras and film, luggage and travel guidebooks. The last two items are most clearly related to tourism, whereas it is difficult to measure the tourism component of the first two items in terms of total sales. However, unlike items bought in the destination region, the purchase of a guidebook or luggage does not necessarily eventuate in a tourism experience.

Travel guidebooks influence destination selection and tourist behaviour once in the destination. Established travel guide publishers such as Fodor, Fielding and Frommer have widespread brand recognition within the tourist market and are therefore highly influential in shaping travel patterns and tourism systems. Since the 1980s there has been a proliferation of new travel guides and travel guide publishers, many of which occupy a highly specialised market niche. Perhaps the most bizarre is Fielding's *Guide to the World's Most Dangerous Places*, which informs the reader how to survive in high risk destinations such as Iraq, Afghanistan and Somalia. The Lonely Planet series, started in 1973, has evolved from a similarly offbeat, peripheral publication into a mainstream source of information accessed by millions of consumers.

All hard copy travel guidebooks are handicapped by the transitory nature of tourism systems. Highly recommended hotels and restaurants may cease to operate even before the guide is released. Some publishers cope with such uncertainty by maintaining interactive websites in which updated information is provided, often by tourists who are invited to send in new information to special email addresses provided in the guidebooks. The Lonely Planet website (www.lonelyplanet.com), for example, includes employee-written travel blogs and a 'Thorn Tree Forum' in which site visitors are invited to share their travel experiences and product recommendations.

Souvenirs are the dominant form of merchandise purchased by tourists within destinations. These can range from jewellery trinkets and T-shirts to expensive, highly ornate crafts, artworks and clothing. Ironically, many of these items may be imported, calling into question their validity as 'souvenirs' of a particular destination. In contrast, duty-free shopping is based not on the desire to acquire souvenirs, but to obtain luxury items at a discount. Accordingly, whether such items are imported into the destination or not is irrelevant to most tourists. Duty-free shopping is dominated by larger corporations and chains, whereas souvenirs are often more associated with cottage industries. In Australia, the souvenir sector is dominated by Aboriginal-themed artefacts, leading to issues of authenticity, proprietary rights, and the formation of 'consumer' images and expectations about the Australian tourism product.

Industry structure

Frequent corporate changes and re-alignments are taking place within the tourism industry and illustrate a process known as integration. **Horizontal integration** occurs when firms attain a higher level of consolidation or control within their own sector. This can be achieved through mergers and alliances with competitors, outright takeovers or through the acquisition of shares in other companies within the sector. Wyndham Worldwide, the second largest hotel chain as of 2007 (see table 5.3) illustrates this phenomenon, incorporating the Wyndham, Ramada, Super 8, Wingate Inn, and Days Inn brands. Horizontal integration also results from the independent establishment of subsidiaries, which diversify the firm's basic product line and thereby cushion the impact of any shifts in consumer demand, for example from first-class to budget accommodation preferences. Figure 5.6 illustrates these options in the context of a hypothetical tour operator.

In contrast, **vertical integration** occurs when a firm obtains greater control over elements of the product chain outside its own sector. If this integration moves further away from the actual consumer (e.g. a large tour operator gains control over a company that manufactures small tour buses), then vertical 'backward' integration is evident. If this integration moves closer to the consumer (e.g. the tour operator acquires a chain of travel agents), then vertical 'forward' integration is occurring. Both forms of integration imply that a firm is gaining control over more components of the tourism system as a way of becoming more competitive and ultimately maximising its profits. An excellent example is the Germany-based corporation TUI (www.tui-group. com/en/), which branched out from its core outbound tour operations to acquire or establish various subsidiary airlines, travel agencies, hotel chains and cruise lines.

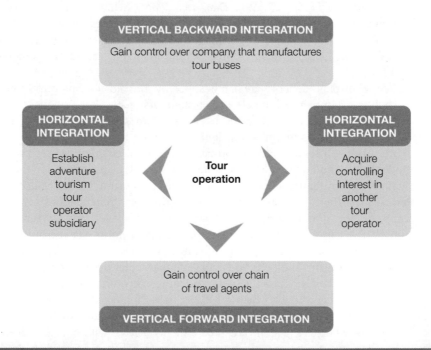

FIGURE 5.6 Horizontal and vertical integration

Vertical and horizontal integration are common and longstanding phenomena within the business world, as evidenced by the flurry of acquisitions and mergers that occurred in the car industry during the first half of the twentieth century. What distinguishes integration since the 1980s, however, is its global character. As the world moves towards a single global capitalist system (a process aided by advances in communications technology), firms are less constrained than ever by the presence of national boundaries and regulations in their attempt to maximise profit. This trend is commonly regarded as indicative of **globalisation**, although no precise definition actually exists for the term. The original five freedoms of the air are an early example of globalisation, while the formation of airline alliances is a more recent example.

Within the context of globalisation, it is likely that the hypothetical tour operation in figure 5.6 will expand from its Sydney base to acquire a rival in Auckland, and then set up its specialised subsidiaries in North America and western Europe, while negotiating to acquire a chain of Japanese travel agencies. The re-aligned tour operator, under the imperatives of globalisation, emerges as a powerful, globally integrated force rather than one that is only nationally influential, and benefits from an increasingly deregulated, privatised global business environment. The private sector tourism manager of the future is a highly mobile individual who expects to reside in several countries during his or her working career.

CHAPTER REVIEW

Tourist attractions are a central element of the tourism product that may or may not be part of the tourism industry, depending on their level of commercialisation and other factors. For organisation and discussion purposes, attractions (excepting VFR and business-related 'attractions') can be categorised into natural sites, natural events, cultural sites and cultural events, recognising that the distinctions between these categories are often blurred. The potential range of attractions is extremely diverse, and destinations benefit from having a broad array, since this increases potential market draw. However, destinations are limited in how much they can influence their attraction inventory — there is considerable flexibility in establishing museums, theme parks and cultural events, for example, but little or no scope for changing a location's history, topography or climate. Whatever a destination's inventory of attractions, it is important to assess and monitor their critical attributes in order to make informed planning and management decisions that will maximise the positive impacts of tourism for operators as well as residents. These attributes include ownership structure, spatial configuration, authenticity, scarcity, carrying capacity, accessibility, market and context. Some variables, such as carrying capacity and image, are difficult to measure and monitor, while others, such as context, are difficult to change or control.

The tourism product also includes the broader tourism industry, which, in addition to some attractions, can be divided into travel agencies, transportation, accommodation, tour operators and merchandise retailers. The available consumer options within all these sectors are becoming more specialised and diverse, but the industry itself, ironically, is growing more consolidated and concentrated within the hands of a few horizontally and vertically integrated corporations. Because of globalisation, this integration is occurring as an increasingly deregulated and transnational phenomenon, suggesting that the large global corporations are gaining more control over international tourism systems.

■ SUMMARY OF KEY TERMS

Accommodation within the context of the tourism industry, commercial facilities primarily intended to host stayover tourists for overnight stays

Attraction attributes characteristics of an attraction that are relevant to the management of an area as a tourist destination and thus should be periodically measured and monitored; includes ownership, orientation, spatial configuration, authenticity, scarcity, status, carrying capacity, accessibility, market and image

Attraction inventory a systematic list of the tourist attractions found in a particular destination

Culinary tourism tourism that involves the consumption of usually locally produced food and drink

Cultural events attractions that occur over a fixed period of time in one or more locations, and are more constructed than natural; these include historical commemorations and re-creations, world fairs, sporting events and festivals

Cultural sites geographically fixed attractions that are more constructed than natural; these can be classified into prehistorical, historical, contemporary, economic, specialised recreational and retail subcategories

Dark tourism tourism involving sites or events associated with death or suffering, including battlefields and sites of mass killings or assassinations

Decommissioning the process whereby vendors of travel products (e.g. airlines, cruise lines) no longer provide a monetary or other commission to an intermediary such as a travel agency in exchange for the sale of their products to consumers

Destination clubs an accommodation option that offers exclusive access to luxury facilities, usually for two weeks, in exchange for a membership fee and annual dues

Disintermediation the removal of intermediaries such as travel agents from the product/consumer connection

Ephemeral attraction an attraction, such as a wildflower display or rarely filled lakebed, that occurs over a brief period of time or on rare occasions only

Freedoms of the air eight privileges, put in place through bilateral agreements, that govern the global airline industry

Functional adaptation the use of a structure for a purpose other than its original intent, represented in tourism by canals used by pleasure boaters and old homes converted into bed and breakfasts

Globalisation the process whereby the operation of businesses and the movement of capital is increasingly less impeded by national boundaries, and is reflected in a general trend towards industry consolidation, deregulation and privatisation

Golfscapes cultural landscapes that are dominated by golf courses and affiliated developments

Horizontal integration occurs when firms attain a higher level of consolidation or control within their own sector

Hotels the most conventional type of tourist accommodation; can be subcategorised into city, convention, airport, resort and apartment hotels, and motels

Iconic attraction an attraction that is well-known and closely associated with a particular destination, such as Mt Fuji (Japan) or the Statue of Liberty (United States)

Inbound tour operators tour operators that coordinate and manage the component of the package tour within the destination, in cooperation with a partner outbound tour operator

Merchandise goods purchased as part of the anticipated or actual tourism experience; includes tour guidebooks and luggage in the origin region, and souvenirs and duty-free goods in the destination region

Natural events attractions that occur over a fixed period of time in one or more locations, and are more natural than constructed

Natural sites geographically fixed attractions that are more natural than constructed; these can be subdivided into topography (physical features), climate, hydrology (water resources), wildlife, vegetation and location

Outbound tour operators tour operators based in origin regions that organise and market volume-driven package tours that include transportation, accommodation, visits to attractions and other items of interest to tourists

Sense of place the combination of natural and cultural characteristics that makes a destination unique in comparison to any other destination, and thus potentially provides it with a competitive advantage

Site hardening increasing the visitor carrying capacity of a site through structural and other changes that allow more visitors to be accommodated

Timesharing an accommodation option in which a user purchases one or more intervals (or weeks) per year in a resort, usually over a long period of time

Tour operators businesses providing a package of tourism-related services for the consumer, including some combination of accommodation, transportation, restaurants and attraction visits

Tourism industry the businesses providing goods and services wholly or mainly for tourist consumption

Tourism product consists of tourist attractions and the tourism industry

Tourism resources features of a destination that are valued as attractions by tourists at some particular point in time; a feature that was a tourism resource 100 years ago may not be perceived as such now

Tourist attractions specific and generic features of a destination that attract tourists; some, but not all, attractions are part of the tourism industry

Transportation businesses involved in conveying tourists by air, road, rail or water

Travel agencies businesses providing retail travel services to customers for commission on behalf of other tourism industry sectors

Vertical integration occurs when a corporation obtains greater control over elements of the product chain outside its own sector

Winescapes a cultural landscape significantly influenced by the presence of vineyards, wineries and other features associated with viticulture and wine production; an essential element of wine-focused culinary tourism

■ QUESTIONS

1. Where do each of the 10 activities listed in table 5.1 fit into the inventory provided in figure 5.1?
2. What is the effect of climate on 3S and urban tourism respectively?
3. Why are linear attractions often more difficult to manage than those which are compact?
4. (a) What is meant by 'functional adaptation' with respect to tourist attractions?
   (b) What are some examples of functional adaptation?
5. How do sites differ from events in terms of their management implications?
6. How can the manager of an attraction deal with the attribute of 'context' (see figure 5.3), which is difficult to control because it involves the external environment?
7. (a) In what ways do PodGuides radically differ from traditional guided tours?
   (b) How might the PodGuide revolutionise the future development of tourist systems?
8. (a) What indications of structural adjustment are evident in the airline industry?
   (b) What are the positive and negative implications of these indicators for destinations and consumers?
9. (a) What effect does horizontal and vertical integration have on the structure of tourism systems?
   (b) How is this effect influenced by globalisation?

■ EXERCISES

1. (a) Access the website www.PodGuides.net and construct a PodGuide to your home city or neighbourhood consisting of ten specific attractions.
   (b) Prepare a 500-word report in which you describe how your PodGuide effectively captures your destination's sense of place.

2. (a) Contact five travel agencies in your local community to find out:
   (i) how much their business is being affected by the phenomenon of disinter-mediation, and
   (ii) the strategies that they are adopting in response.
   (b) Prepare a 500-word report that offers an optimal strategic response, based on a comparative assessment of these responses.

■ FURTHER READING

Hall, C.M., Sharples, L., Mitchell, R., Macionis, N. & Cambourne, B. (Eds) 2003. *Food Tourism Around the World: Development, Management and Markets.* **Sydney: Butterworth-Heinemann.** Eighteen authored chapters consider a range of related topics, including marketing, product development and inculcating a sense of local place through food and drink. A global case study approach is adopted.

Higginbottom, K. (Ed.) 2004. *Wildlife Tourism: Impacts, Management and Planning.* **Altona, Vic.: Common Ground Publishing.** A comprehensive and up-to-date analysis of wildlife-based tourism, this edited book is divided into three parts: the phenomenon of wildlife tourism, its impacts and appropriate management. The contributors and case studies are mainly Australian, and focused mainly on non-consumptive wildlife tourism.

Higham, J. (Ed.) 2005. *Sport Tourism Destinations: Issues, Opportunities and Analysis.* **Sydney: Elsevier.** Sporting events are featured in this edited book in terms of specialised destinations, policy and planning, marketing and management and economic as well as environmental impacts. International case studies illustrate the analysis.

Hsu, C. (Ed.) 2006. *Casino Industry in Asia Pacific: Development, Operation, Impact.* **Binghampton, USA: Haworth Press.** A combination of academic and practitioner perspectives characterises this book, which examines impacts and operational considerations in various Asia Pacific destinations, including Australia and Macao.

Lovelock, B. (Ed.) 2008. *Tourism and the Consumption of Wildlife: Hunting, Shooting and Sport Fishing.* **London: Routledge.** This first edited volume on the phenomenon of consumptive wildlife tourism features historical perspectives, impacts, and current issues and trends, including ethical implications of such activity.

case study

US TRAVEL AGENCIES THAT ARE NOT JUST SURVIVING BUT THRIVING

Despite strong growth in travel demand, conventional travel agencies in the United States declined from 33 775 ARC-accredited (Airlines Reporting Corporation) retail locations in September 1997 to 21 552 in May 2004 (Goeldner & Ritchie, 2006) as a result of the triple challenge from disintermediation, decommissioning and chronic economic/geopolitical uncertainty. Yet, some conventional agencies are thriving, and understanding the basis for their success may assist the travel agency sector more broadly to improve its performance. To identify a sample of successful agencies, Weaver and Lawton (2008) emailed a web-based survey to all US-based travel gency sector more broadly to improve its performance. To identify a sample of successful agencies, Weaver and Lawton (2008) emailed a web-based survey to all US-based travel agencies accredited under IATAN (International Airlines Travel Agent Network), requesting basic financial performance information. This survey ultimately yielded a convenience sample of 19 extremely successful agency owners who were willing to be interviewed in depth. These interviews were conducted during late 2005 and early 2006 using a grounded theory approach in which the underlying theories arose from the actual data rather than the biases of the researchers. The interviews lasted on average for one hour and were conducted face-to-face in the offices of each sampled agency.

Perceived personal agency strengths

The interviews ultimately revealed that highly successful travel agency owners were excellent relationship builders. This was evident for example in the emphasis on *customer service*, wherein agents engaged in effective interactive counselling that allow agents to learn about their clients and distinguish their needs from their wants. Effective agents were also able to garner respect through their professionalism, and foster mutual trust and respect through their honesty and willingness to 'invest' in potential clients who might not actually give their business to the agency. Finally, customer service was evident in the practice of follow-up marketing, where customers returning from trips are greeted by the agency and asked their opinions of their experiences. All these customer-focused practices meant that the sampled agencies all received most of their business from repeat customers and their referrals to others.

Relationship building also involved continual *employee enrichment* through empowerment that included allocating employees their own niche areas (e.g. cruises or destination weddings) and a high level of autonomy in their decision-making. High morale was achieved through employee recognition and incentive schemes, while managers emphasised their practice of hiring agents who displayed strong 'people' skills and an optimistic personality. *Networking* is another essential element of relationship building which embedded the agencies in a complex network of facilitating organisations, vendors and other travel agencies. In addition, a positive public image and sense of confidence was attained through the active involvement of owners within their local communities as volunteers and leaders.

In addition to the cultivation of strong ties with customers, employees and wider networks within the business and community, relationship building was facilitated by three other practices. First, the agencies excelled at *customer selection*, attracting high income clients and customers who were most likely to purchase travel products rather than seek free advice. Second, the agencies fostered a *climate of learning* that favoured higher education degrees for employees, encouraged continual environmental scanning of social and travel trends, and facilitated product exposure so that agents would have first-hand and up-to-date experiences of the products they were selling. Third, all the agencies were governed by a philosophy of *adaptability*. When airlines initiated decommissioning in the mid-1990s, several immediately took the daring move of charging their clients a service fee. More common was the attitude that the internet is far more of a friend than a foe. The interviewees actually encouraged their customers to use Travelocity and similar sites to book simple airfares (for which they received no commission in any case), while convincing them that conventional agencies were better qualified to research and arrange complex travel products and to provide ongoing advice and service as required. All the agents actively used the internet to facilitate customer communication through well designed websites and chat forums. Adaptability also entailed a willingness to realign their products and markets as required. Many, for example, were cruise specialists while others focused on church groups, destination weddings and baby boomers.

Sector threats and opportunities

The sampled owners were also asked to comment on the threats and opportunities that faced the travel agency sector as a whole (Lawton & Weaver 2009). Surprisingly, neither disintermediation, decommissioning nor terrorism-related uncertainty were cited as major threats. Instead, the owners were most concerned with what they perceived to be an unfavourable public image of conventional travel agencies. This was attributed in part to excessive consumer enthusiasm with internet agencies. In addition, their public reputation was harmed by unqualified travel agents who obtain questionable credentials through 'card mills' that provide misleading identification cards and give the false impression that they are certified agents entitled to discounts, airline upgrades and vendor commissions. Mass media was also criticised for providing bad publicity about conventional travel agencies and anomalous travel-related tragedies such as passengers who disappear from cruise ships. One serious consequence of the negative public image was the failure of the sector to attract sufficient numbers of bright and enthusiastic young people to consider travel agencies as a viable career option.

The major perceived opportunity was a direct response to the image problem and involved a concerted public outreach campaign by the sector to foster a more positive perception. Although the sector's lack of financial resources was cited as an impediment, owners alluded to the real estate sector as an example of a group similarly affected by disintermediation that has successfully protected its market share through innovative media publicity and political lobbying. Also, it was felt strongly that the outreach campaign needed to focus on broader themes of enhancing geographic literacy and a love for travel as a basic human need and right. In keeping with their innate optimism, many owners cited the decline in the number of conventional agencies as a significant opportunity that weeded out the weaker businesses and left behind a leaner and more efficient sector better able to cope with the challenges of the new century.

QUESTIONS

1. (a) To what extent have conventional Australian and New Zealand travel agencies been negatively affected by the triple effect of disintermediation, decommissioning and post-2001 uncertainty?
   (b) Account for the differences and similarities with the US experience.
2. Prepare a 1000-word media release that supports conventional (that is, non-electronic) travel agencies as the best place for the public to purchase travel experiences.

CHAPTER 6

TOURIST MARKETS

LEARNING OBJECTIVES

After studying this chapter, you should be able to:

1. outline and summarise the pattern of the major tourist market trends since World War II

2. describe the process that culminates in a decision to visit a particular destination

3. explain the need for, and the evaluative criteria involved in, the practice of market segmentation

4. discuss the strengths and limitations of major segmentation criteria, including country of origin and family lifecycle

5. differentiate between allocentric, midcentric and psychocentric forms of psychographic segmentation

6. analyse the various dimensions of motivation as a form of psychographic segmentation

7. discuss the types and importance of travel-related behavioural segmentation.

INTRODUCTION

The previous chapter considered the variety and characteristics of attractions within the tourism system and also examined other supply-side components of the tourism industry, including travel agencies, transportation, tour operators, merchandisers and the hospitality sector. Chapter 6 returns to the demand side of the tourism equation by refocusing on the tourist. The next section reviews the major market trends in the tourism sector since World War II, and this is followed by a discussion of the destination selection process. The final section considers the importance of tourist market segmentation and examines the geographical, sociodemographical, psychographical and behavioural criteria that are used in segmentation exercises.

TOURIST MARKET TRENDS

The **tourist market** is the overall group of consumers that engages in tourism-related travel. Since World War II there have been several major trends in the evolution of this market and these are discussed below. Essentially, the overall tendency has been towards a gradually increasing level of **market segmentation**, or the division of the tourist market into distinctive **market segments** that are presumed to be relatively consistent in terms of their behaviour.

The democratisation of travel

The first trend was considered thoroughly in chapters 3 and 4 and can be described as the democratisation of travel. This emerged as increased discretionary time and income, among other factors, made domestic and then international travel accessible to the middle and working classes. Involvement in international travel grew rapidly in the 'Western' world during the 1960s and 1970s, while a similar development occurred in certain Asian societies during the 1980s and 1990s. This was the classic era of 'mass tourism', during which the tourism industry perceived tourists as a more or less homogeneous market that demanded and consumed a very similar array of 'cookie-cutter' goods and services (see figure 6.1). Such an approach did not differ essentially from that adopted by Thomas Cook during the mid-1800s (see chapter 3).

The emergence of simple market segmentation and multilevel segmentation

The second major trend emerged during the mid-1970s, as a large increase in oil prices made marketers and planners come to appreciate that a continuous growth scenario was not practical for every destination, and that some portions of the tourist market were more resistant to crisis conditions than others. This resulted in the practice of **simple market segmentation**, or the division of the tourist market into a minimal number of more or less homogenous subgroups based on certain common characteristics and/or behavioural patterns. Initially, marketers tried to isolate the smallest possible number of market segments in their desire to simplify marketing and product development efforts. Hence, broad market segments were treated as uniform entities (e.g. 'women' versus 'men', 'old' versus 'young', 'Americans' versus 'Europeans' and 'Asians').

By the 1980s the concept of market differentiation was refined through the practice of **multilevel segmentation**, which subdivided the basic market segments into more specific subgroups. For example, 'Americans' were divided into 'East Coast', 'West Coast', 'African–Americans' and other relevant categories that recognised the diverse characteristics and behaviour otherwise disguised by simple market segmentation.

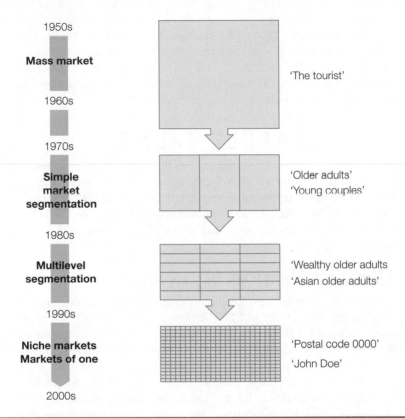

FIGURE 6.1 Tourist market trends since World War II

Niche markets and 'markets of one'

By the 1990s the tourist market in Phase Four societies was more sophisticated and knowledgeable, having had three decades of mass travel experience. Consumers were aware of what the tourism experience could and should be, and thus demanded higher quality and more specialised products that cater to individual needs and tastes. The tourism industry has been able to fulfil these demands because of the internet, flexible production techniques and other technological innovations that made catering to specialised tastes more feasible.

At the same time, the rapid expansion of the tourist market has meant that traditionally invisible market segments (e.g. older gay couples, railway enthusiasts, stargazing ecotourists) were now much larger and thus constituted a potentially lucrative market for the tourism industry. This has led to the identification of **niche markets** encompassing relatively small groups of consumers with specialised characteristics and tastes, and to the targeting of these tourists through an appropriately specialised array of products within the tourism industry (see chapter 5). Extreme segmentation, based on **markets of one**, or segments consisting of just one individual, has also become a normal part of product development and marketing strategies at the beginning of the twenty-first century. This does not mean that mass marketing will disappear, especially given that attractions such as theme parks continue to emphasise their universal appeal, but simply that it will be technologically and financially feasible to tailor a product to just one consumer, in recognition of the fact that each individual is a unique market segment.

■ THE DESTINATION SELECTION PROCESS

Further insight is gained into the importance of market segments and the methods that can be used to target these segments for marketing and management purposes by understanding the process whereby tourists arrive at a decision to visit one or more destinations. Destination marketers need to identify and understand the elements of this process that they can influence to achieve their visitation goals. They may, for example, have considerable influence over pull factors, such as the design and distribution of brochures and maps, but no influence over push factors (see chapter 3) that induce people to travel. This is especially relevant to travel that is undertaken for leisure/recreation purposes, since the destination is usually predetermined in business and VFR tourism (see chapter 2). There are many destination selection models in the tourism literature (e.g. Um & Crompton 1990; Goodall 1991), and figure 6.2 represents just one simplified way in which this process can be depicted. Figure 6.2 begins with the decision to travel (1), which is driven by a combination of the 'push' factors discussed in chapter 3 and the potential tourist's personality, motivations, culture, prior life experience, gender, health and education (box A in figure 6.2).

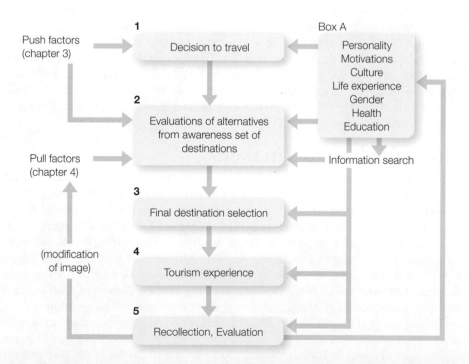

FIGURE 6.2 The destination selection process

The next stage (2) involves the evaluation of potential destinations from an 'awareness set' of all places known to the decision maker. This awareness set includes places that are known from prior direct or indirect experiences (that is, places known through past visits or through reading, media or word-of-mouth exchanges), as well as new places that emerge from subsequent information search. The latter search, as with the broader process of destination evaluation, is filtered by the personal characteristics listed in box A as well as push factors such as income, available time and family size. An open-minded, wealthy and well-educated person with no children, for example, is likely to undertake a very different information search and evaluation process than an inhibited person from an insular and proscriptive culture who also has a large family. The latter individual is likely to begin with a small awareness set and to rule out many destinations straight away because of the limitations just described (i.e. destinations that are too expensive, risky or child-intolerant). This requires assessment of the pull factors described in chapter 4, so that the final selection (3) will likely focus on an affordable, politically stable and accessible destination with many interesting attractions and a culture similar to that of the decision maker. It is widely believed that most consumers reach a final decision after the serious consideration of just three to five options (Crompton 1992), though the original awareness set might contain hundreds of potential destinations. The actual complexity of the evaluation process is also evident in the fact that this often involves 'final' decisions that are subsequently revoked or altered by changing push and pull factors — such as being denied an expected pay increase, or news of a coup d'état in the destination to be visited. Similarly, a decision could be made as to which specific country to visit (e.g. New Zealand), but uncertainty may continue as to which destinations to visit within that country (North Island or South Island).

Feedback loops, such as occur when a tentative destination decision is rejected and the evaluation process is revisited, are found elsewhere in the model. This commonly occurs through the refinement of the destination image 'pull' factor as a result of direct experience (4) (e.g. the traveller had a wonderful vacation and thus carries a strongly positive destination image into the next evaluation process). The influence can also be indirect, as when the travel experience leads to modifications in the individual's personality or culture (e.g. the traveller becomes more open to further travel to exotic destinations). Post-trip recollection and evaluation (5) also usually influences subsequent travel decisions.

Multiple decision makers

The destination selection process is further complicated by the fact that more than one person is often involved in the decision-making process. In such cases, purchase decisions both before and during the trip tend to require more time, as they often represent a compromise among group members. Wang et al. (2004), with regard to the purchase of group package tours by South Koreans, found that husbands and wives were equally influential in making the decision to travel and selecting a destination, as well as in budgeting, determining length of stay, and selecting airlines and restaurants. However, wives played a dominant role in the information search and in selecting accommodation, travel agents and shopping venues. Young children are an interesting factor in the decision-making process, since they do not usually have much of an actual say, but exercise a strong influence over their parents' decisions because of their special needs and wants (Nanda, Hu & Bai 2006). In the South Korean study cited, children were found to have a major influence, particularly over the activities undertaken during the trip.

TOURIST MARKET SEGMENTATION

Market segmentation, as stated, divides the total tourist population into smaller, relatively homogeneous subgroups that can be catered to or managed as separate market segments. There are at least eight factors that should be considered concurrently when evaluating the utility of market segmentation in any given situation, including:

- *Measurability*. Can the target characteristics be measured in a meaningful way? Psychological criteria, for example, are more difficult to quantify than age or education level.
- *Size*. Is the market segment large enough to warrant attention? Very small groups, such as female war veterans over 85 years of age, may be insufficiently large to warrant attention by smaller companies or destinations that lack the capacity to engage in niche marketing.
- *Homogeneity*. Is the segmented group sufficiently distinct from other market segments? It may be, for example, that the 45–49 age group of adult males is not significantly different from the 50–54 age group, thereby eliminating any rationale for designating them as separate segments. A related consideration is whether the segmented group is internally homogeneous; if not then it may need to be divided into separate segments.
- *Compatibility*. Are the values, needs and wants of the segment compatible with the destination or company's own values, corporate strategies, and so on? The experience of gay and lesbian tourists in some Caribbean destinations illustrates the problem of incompatibility (see Managing tourism: Gay and lesbian tourists in the Cayman Islands).
- *Accessibility*. How difficult is it to reach the target market? Sex tourists are relatively inaccessible because they are less likely to admit participation in a socially unsanctioned activity. A more frequently encountered illustration is a small business in an English-speaking country that lacks the capacity to market its products overseas in languages other than English.
- *Actionability*. Is the company or destination able to serve the needs of the market segment? For example, a wilderness lodge is usually not an appropriate venue for catering to gamblers or those with severe physical disabilities.
- *Durability*. Will the segment exist for a long enough period of time to justify the pursuit of specialised marketing or management strategies? For example, the population of World War II veterans is now experiencing a high rate of attrition, and will be negligible in size by 2020. In contrast, baby boomers will constitute a lucrative market probably until the 2040s.
- *Relevance*. Is there some underlying logic for targeting a particular segment? Segmentation on the basis of eye colour meets all the previous criteria, but there is no rational basis for thinking that eye colour influences consumer behaviour in any significant way.

The following sections discuss the major market segmentation criteria that are commonly used in the contemporary tourism sector, as well as those that are not widely employed, but could be of potential value to tourism destinations and the tourism industry. These criteria include the box A characteristics in figure 6.2, which also influence the behaviour of individuals during and after the actual tourism experience. Ultimately, the appropriateness of particular segmentation criteria to a destination or business will depend on the conclusions reached in the evaluation of the eight factors outlined above (see the case study at the end of this chapter).

managing tourism

GAY AND LESBIAN TOURISTS IN THE CAYMAN ISLANDS

In early 1998, the cruise liner *Leeward* with its 900 gay male passengers was denied berthing facilities at the popular Caribbean port of George Town, Cayman Islands. Citing local laws that criminalised sexual acts between persons of the same sex, the then-Minister of Tourism stated that there was no guarantee the passengers 'would uphold appropriate standards of behaviour expected of visitors', based on alleged past experience of locals who were offended by public displays of same-sex affection from some cruise ship passengers (Waitt & Markwell 2006). Subsequent lobbying by international gay and lesbian rights organisations persuaded the British government to pressure the Cayman Islands, a dependency, to rescind anti-homosexual legislation. However, anti-gay sentiments have remained very high in the destination, with opposition led by government and some prominent churches.

Several important issues emerged from this incident and subsequent developments. First, with regard to reciprocal due diligence, to what extent were the parent cruise line and the Cayman Island authorities aware of each others' intentions regarding the impending arrival of a cruise ship carrying a large group of gay men? Whether the response of island authorities was justifiable or not, appropriate knowledge would have compelled the parent cruise line to avoid the Cayman Islands and save its passengers considerable inconvenience and humiliation. The deeper issue exposed by this incident, however, is the compatibility between the Cayman Islands tourism sector and the gay/lesbian market segment. An unofficial 'don't ask/don't tell' policy was apparently followed by Cayman authorities and people wherein gay visitors were not confronted as long as they did not act in an overtly gay manner. The shortcomings of this approach were revealed by the 1998 incident, one almost immediate repercussion being extensive negative publicity and the designation of the Cayman Islands as a 'no go' zone by some gay and lesbian activists. While the repeal of anti-gay legislation now makes arrests and other formal confrontations unlikely, overtly gay visitors (perhaps encouraged by the repeal) will undoubtedly continue to attract hostility from some residents, and authorities will need to ensure that all visitors are kept safe, regardless of their sexual orientation.

Geographic segmentation

Geographic segmentation, the oldest and most popular basis for segmentation, takes into account spatial criteria such as country of birth, nationality or current residence of the consumer. Geographic segmentation declined during the 1980s as other segmentation criteria emerged, but it is now reasserting its former dominance through cost-effective **GIS (geographic information systems)** that facilitate the spatial analysis of tourism-related phenomena. GIS encompasses a variety of sophisticated computer software programs that assemble, store, manipulate, analyse and display spatially referenced information (Feng & Morrison 2002). In a GIS package, the exact location of a person's residence can be specified and related to other criteria relevant to that same location (e.g. income level, age structure, education levels, rainfall, road network). It is therefore possible to compile detailed combinations of market characteristics at a very high level of geographic resolution (e.g. individual households), making feasible the 'markets of one' described on page 154. Before GIS, the best level of resolution that could be hoped for was the equivalent of the postal code or census subdistrict.

Region and country of residence

The least sophisticated type of geographical analysis, but the simplest to compile, is regional residence, which has often been used as a surrogate for culture. Traditionally, tourism managers were content to differentiate their markets as 'Asian', 'North American' or 'European', because of low numbers and on the assumption that these regional markets exhibited relatively uniform patterns of behaviour. Most destinations and businesses now realise that such generalisations are simplistic and misleading, and prefer to differentiate at least by country of origin. In the case of Australia, for example, useful distinctions can be made between the mature Japanese and emerging Chinese inbound tourist markets (see table 6.1).

TABLE 6.1 Characteristics of Japanese and Chinese tourists visiting Australia, 2007

Criterion	Japanese inbound	Chinese inbound
Holiday visitors (%)	78	48
VFR visitors (%)	6	12
Repeat visitors (%)	38	42
Unaccompanied visitors (%)	29	49
Female (%)	54	54
Visiting New South Wales (%)	39	79
Visiting Queensland (%)	66	45
Visiting botanical or other public gardens (%)	19	50
Visiting history/heritage sites (%)	17	38
Visiting museums/art galleries (%)	14	40
Average length of stay (nights)	21	44
First-time visitors consulting travel guides (%)	51	10
First-time visitors consulting travel agents (%)	33	35
First-time visitors consulting the internet (%)	46	44
First-time visitors consulting friends who have visited Australia previously (%)	8	11
Average total trip expenditure ($)	3691	5860
Average expenditure per day ($)	176	133
Percentage of expenditure on shopping for souvenirs and gifts	333	514
Percentage of expenditure on food/drink/accommodation	754	1390

Source: Data derived from TRA (2008e, 2008f)

Subnational segmentation

It is appropriate to pursue geographical segmentation at a subnational level under two circumstances. First, larger countries tend to display important differences in behaviour from one internal region to another. Reduced cost and travel time, for example, position the California market as a stronger per capita source of tourists for Australia than New York or Florida.

The second factor is the number of people that travel to a destination from a particular country. A large number justifies the further division of that market into geographical subcomponents. For example, when the number of Chinese inbound tourists to Australia involved only a few thousand visitors, there was no compelling reason to make any further distinction by province of origin. However, as this number approaches 400 000, it makes more sense to consider subnational criteria as a basis for market segmentation. As described in chapter 2, Australian tourism authorities are currently focusing their promotional efforts on the three large coastal 'gateway' markets of Beijing, Shanghai and Guangdong Province.

Urban and rural origins

Useful insights may be gained by subdividing the tourist market on the basis of community size. Residents of large metropolitan areas have better access to media and the internet than other citizens, and more options to choose from at all stages of the destination buying process. Yet, within those same communities, the residents of gentrified inner-city neighbourhoods (e.g. North Sydney) are quite distinct from the residents of working-class outer suburbs (e.g. Parramatta) or the exurbs. Rural residents also have distinctive socioeconomic characteristics and behaviour. The urban–rural dichotomy is particularly important in less developed countries, where large metropolitan areas are likely to accommodate Phase Three or Four societies, while the countryside may reflect Phase Two characteristics (see chapter 3).

Sociodemographic segmentation

Sociodemographic segmentation variables include gender, age, family life cycle, household education, occupation and income. Such variables are popular as segmentation criteria because they are easily collected (though respondents often withhold or misrepresent their income) and often associated with distinct types of behaviour.

Gender and gender orientation

Gender segmentation can be biological or sociocultural. If construed in strictly biological terms, gender is a readily observable and measurable criterion in most instances. Some activities, and notably hunting, are an almost exclusively male domain (Lovelock 2008), while it is alleged that ecotourists are disproportionately female (Weaver 2008). Females are also overrepresented as patrons of cultural events. During 2005–06, 21 per cent of Australian females 15 or older attended at least one theatre performance, compared with 13 per cent of males. Similar discrepancies were found in dance performances (13 and 7 per cent respectively) and musicals and operas (21 and 12 per cent) (ABS 2007). According to Bond (1997), female travellers tend to be more concerned with issues of physical and psychological security as well as physical comfort, which could have important implications in initiatives to protect tourists against crime. Women, according to Westwood, Pritchard and Morgan (2000), also tend to place a higher value on social interaction during travel and appreciate attention to detail in the provision of goods and services. A satisfied female client is more likely to remain loyal to that product and will more readily spread information about her experiences through word-of-mouth contact with other women. There is also evidence that males and females differ significantly in their use of the internet as a source of travel information (see Technology and tourism: Differences between females and males in online travel information search).

technology and tourism

DIFFERENCES BETWEEN FEMALES AND MALES IN ONLINE TRAVEL INFORMATION SEARCH

Emerging information technologies such as the internet spawn new modes of information search and processing, but appear to perpetuate behavioural differences between females and males in this regard. A survey of 1334 Canadians and Americans, conducted by the Canadian Tourism Commission during 2001 (Kim, Lehto & Morrison 2007), found that females tended to regard as more important 'search features' such as searching by keyword, location and activity, and ease of surfing. They also were more likely to state that planning the entire trip online was important, as was price comparison and saving one's personal profile. Females visit more websites than males when researching travel options, and spend more time on average at each site. However, with respect to the various sections of travel websites, males were likely to make more visits to those focused on accommodation, weather and rental cars, while females made more visits to sections on entertainment, local information, restaurants and maps.

These results corroborate earlier research which identified females as comprehensive information processors who make decisions after taking ample time to assess multiple sources of information. Males, in contrast, are selective processors who make decisions as quickly as possible, selectively consulting a few sources and then relying on their own judgement. The survey results further supported this theory in finding that females were also significantly more likely than males to report traditional media, such as word-of-mouth recommendations, brochures and guidebooks, as important sources consulted when seeking travel information. One implication is that the designers of tourism-related websites cannot assume that males and females will react similarly to a given site. If appeal to females is desired, then designers apparently need to provide user-friendly interactive and search features that facilitate systematic access to a comprehensive selection of information sections and associated external linkages. Colours and designs that minimise eye strain should also be used. Male-focused sites, in contrast, should focus on ready access to a small amount of crucial information that is directly and objectively presented (Kim, Lehto & Morrison 2007).

Gender can also be construed in terms of sexual orientation, and in this sense three stages of development can be identified:

1. For many years, gay and lesbian tourism was either ignored by the tourism industry, or existed only as an informal fringe element. As in the Cayman Islands, a 'don't ask/don't tell' attitude prevailed, and overt gay activity was largely an 'underground' phenomenon.
2. With the liberalisation of sexual attitudes in the late twentieth century, this component of tourism became more visible through the emergence of specialised formal businesses and activities, particularly in the areas of accommodation (e.g. Turtle Cove Resort north of Cairns), tour operators, special events (e.g. the Gay Games) and the cruise ship sector.
3. Since the late 1990s, the mainstream tourism industry has recognised the formidable purchasing power of gays and lesbians and has actively and openly pursued these markets (Clift, Luongo & Callister 2002). Some estimates suggest that the **pink dollar** accounts for 10–15 per cent of all consumer purchasing power. Destinations that are regarded as gay and lesbian 'friendly' include Sydney, San Francisco, London, Cape Town (Visser 2003) and Amsterdam. Sydney in particular

is making a concerted bid to be recognised as a major gay and lesbian tourism destination, with its highly successful annual Gay and Lesbian Mardi Gras, and its hosting of the Gay Games in 2002.

A fourth stage may now be emerging, wherein some gay and lesbian activists who resent the 'invasion' of gay environments by 'mainstream' tourists and businesses are seeking to create their own 'queer' spaces where they can feel more empowered.

Age and family lifecycle

Age and lifecycle considerations are popular criteria used in sociodemographic segmentation, since these can also have a significant bearing on consumer behaviour. Specific consideration is given in the following subsections to older adults, young adults and the traditional family lifecycle.

Older adults

Along with the emergence and growing acceptance of the gay and lesbian community, the rapid ageing of population is one of the dominant trends in contemporary Phase Four societies (see chapter 3). In the year 2010 the first baby boomers turned 65 (see the case study at the end of chapter 3), and this will accelerate interest in the 'older adult' market segment. Traditionally, the 65+ market was assumed to require special services and facilities due to deteriorating physical condition. Their travel patterns, moreover, were believed to be influenced by the dual impact of reduced discretionary income and increased discretionary time caused by retirement. Finally, older adults were commonly perceived to constitute a single uniform market.

All these assumptions, however, are simplistic. In postindustrial Phase Four societies the 65-year age threshold is no longer a strict indicator of a person's retirement status. Many companies facilitate early retirement options, while there is a concurrent trend to remove artificial age-of-retirement ceilings established during the industrial era. As for income, the current cohort of retirees is likely to be better off financially than their predecessors. The assumption of physical deterioration is also false, as the 65-year-old of 2000 is in much better physical condition than their counterpart of 1950, and has a much longer life expectancy. Finally, the assumption of market uniformity is also untenable, as demonstrated by research among Australian older adults that differentiates between such substantial sub-segments as 'enthusiastic connectors', (about 20 per cent), 'discovery and self-enhancers' (26 per cent), 'nostalgic travellers' (29 per cent) and 'reluctant travellers' (25 per cent) (Cleaver Sellick 2004). Another relevant trend with implications for tourism participation is the growing number of grandparents who raise their own grandchildren and/or live with them in multigenerational households (ABS 2003).

Young adults

In contrast to the 65+ cohort, young adults, and especially those in their teens and early 20s, are often associated with higher levels of loutish and high-risk behaviour. This is especially evident in ritual events such as the 'spring break' phenomenon in the United States and Australia's 'Schoolies Week' (the celebration of a student's completion of high school), which destination managers on the Gold Coast are attempting to convert into an orderly festival. Involving up to 100 000 young visitors, Schoolies Week is regarded with ambivalence by local residents, who appreciate the positive economic benefits of the influx and its containment largely within the heavily developed Surfers Paradise neighbourhood. However, there is concurrent concern over the event's association with high levels of alcohol and drug abuse, predatory sexual activity, littering and disorderly conduct (Scott 2006).

Family lifecycle

The **family lifecycle (FLC)** consists of a series of stages through which the majority of people in a Phase Four society are likely to pass during the time from young adulthood to death (see figure 6.3). The FLC stages are associated with particular age brackets, although there are many exceptions to this. All stages are also related to significant changes in family status, such as marriage, the raising of children, and the death of a partner. Retirement (i.e. change in work status) is also identified as an important stage transition.

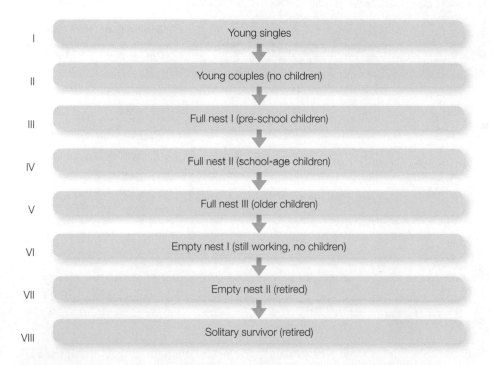

I — Young singles

II — Young couples (no children)

III — Full nest I (pre-school children)

IV — Full nest II (school-age children)

V — Full nest III (older children)

VI — Empty nest I (still working, no children)

VII — Empty nest II (retired)

VIII — Solitary survivor (retired)

FIGURE 6.3 The traditional family lifecycle

Lawson (1991), in a classic study, assigned a sample of inbound visitors in New Zealand to appropriate stages in the FLC and found this variable to be important for predicting the tendency to travel, the amount of expenditure made while touring and the types of activities pursued. Regarding tendency to travel, table 6.2 reveals the overrepresentation of young singles, young couples and empty nest Is as tourism participants (i.e. observed cases in the sample) in relation to the overall population structures of major source countries (i.e. expected cases). Young singles in this study were especially enthusiastic as travellers, being overrepresented by a factor (i.e. difference ratio) of almost six.

In contrast, the constraining effect of young children is evident in the underrepresentation of all full nest categories (and especially full nest Is, who are underrepresented by a factor greater than seven). Solitary survivors also demonstrate a pattern of curtailed travel. Only empty nest IIs are represented at a level comparable to their overall population share. Significant differences are also evident in expenditure patterns. Larger groups, such as full nest IIs and IIIs, not surprisingly, have greater total expenditures, but young singles are the highest spenders on a per capita basis. In terms of activity, young singles and couples are important as markets for rafting, waterskiing, entertainment and spas, while empty nesters place a high priority on museums, tours and Maori-related culture and performances. The continuing robustness of Lawson's findings is indicated by more recent research among consumers in the USA which found similarly high travel proclivities among young couples with no children and working empty nesters (Hong et al 2005).

TABLE 6.2 Tourism participation and expenditure in New Zealand by FLC type

FLC type	Observed cases	Expected cases[1]	Difference ratio[2]	Expenditure (1990 NZ$)	
				Per person	Total
I	312	55	+5.7	913	913
II	392	95	+4.1	851	1702
III	51	375	−7.4	490	1496
IV	192	519	−2.7	468	1831
V	165	227	−1.4	648	2200
VI	587	203	+2.9	832	1666
VII	262	264	1.0	674	1350
VIII	106	329	−3.1	764	764

Notes:
1 Distribution of the observed cases if these were representative of the overall population structure of major source countries
2 Calculated as a ratio of the higher figure in each row relative to the lower figure, for example 312/55 = +5.7, with the plus sign indicating overrepresentation
Source: Lawson (1991)

Empirical evidence from New Zealand and the USA therefore suggests that the FLC is a potentially useful sociodemographic basis for tourist market segmentation. However, one major drawback is that an increasing number of people do not conform to the cycle. In Lawson's 1991 study, 1359 individuals, or 40 per cent of the total sample, did not fit into any of the stages. This is likely to be even higher in the early 2000s. Exceptions include permanently childless couples or those who have children relatively late in life, divorced people, single parents, long-term gay and lesbian couples, multigenerational families, 'permanent singles' and those whose spouses die at an early age. In essence, the FLC reflects the traditional nuclear family of the 1950s and 1960s rather than the present era of familial diversity. In addition, even if individuals do conform to the FLC, this is not necessarily reflected in the composition of travel groups. People in relationships may decide to travel by themselves, or with a group of friends, while married couples may be accompanied by one or more parents, nephews or other married couples. Another confounding factor is pet ownership and the increasing tendency of individuals in all stages of the FLC to regard their animals as household members and desirable travel companions. This has led to responsive products such as specialised pet-friendly hotels (see figure 6.4)

FIGURE 6.4 Pet-friendly hotels

Education, occupation and income

Education, occupation and income tend to be interrelated in terms of travel behaviour, since education generally influences occupation, which in turn influences income level. University education, for example, often leads to higher-paying professional employment. Income and education are often accessed indirectly by targeting neighbourhoods that display consistent characteristics with regard to these criteria. Not surprisingly, high levels of income and education, as well as professional occupations, are associated with increased tourism activity and in particular with a higher incidence of long-haul travel. One important implication is that high-income earners are less concerned with financial considerations when assessing destination options, and less likely to alter their travel plans in the event of an economic recession. Destinations and products such as destination clubs that cater to high-income earners are therefore themselves less susceptible to recession-induced slumps in visitation. Distinctive forms of educational segmentation include international students, schoolies and participants in school excursions.

Race, ethnicity and religion

There is a general reluctance to ascribe distinctive character and behavioural traits on the basis of race, ethnicity or religion, and none of these are, therefore, commonly used for generic segmentation purposes. However, these are commonly used as segmentation criteria for specialised attractions that cater to particular racial, ethnic or religious groups. Examples include the marketing of heritage slavery sites in western Africa to African-Americans, and religious pilgrimages and festivals to applicable religious groups. In the case of Australia and New Zealand, it is likely that Aboriginal and

Maori people constitute a growing portion of their respective domestic and outbound tourism sectors, yet research on 'Aboriginal tourism' and 'Maori tourism' are almost exclusively focused on the product side. It is therefore unclear in what ways and to what extent Aborigines and Maori differ from other tourist segments.

Disability

Persons with disabilities are often neglected or overlooked as a significant tourist segment, even though it is apparent that the number of such individuals is immense and their desire to travel as high as the general population's (Yau, McKercher & Packer 2004; Stumbo & Pegg 2005). According to Australian Bureau of Statistics criteria, 20 per cent of the Australian population (or almost 4 million people) were considered to have a disability in 2003 (ABS 2004b). Three factors that indicate the need for tourism managers to pay greater attention to this segment are the:

- ageing of Phase Four populations (given the higher incidence of disabilities among older adults)
- availability of technology to expedite travel by persons with disabilities
- increasing recognition of the basic human rights, including the right to travel, of such persons.

Nevertheless, it is apparent that many tourism-related products and services still do not adequately address the needs of persons with disabilities (see Contemporary issue: Tourism websites and persons with disabilities).

contemporary issue

TOURISM WEBSITES AND PERSONS WITH DISABILITIES

Ongoing debate is occurring in legal circles as to whether websites are 'public accommodations' requiring their sponsors to provide a reasonable degree of access to persons with disabilities, and those with visual impairments in particular. However this debate unfolds, tourism businesses should consider the market potential of such individuals — it is estimated that, for example, one in every six persons over 65 has a visual impairment — and facilitate access to their websites accordingly. To see whether tourism-related companies were responsive to persons with visual impairments, Mills, Han and Clay (2008) used a research randomiser tool to examine 20 sites from Alexa.com's travel directory. All were found to be deficient in one or more substantive ways. The most prevalent deficiency was failure to provide alternative means for representing colour-conveyed information. Second was the failure to provide equivalent alternatives to images, while third was the use of tables that could not be effectively transformed into usable information. Accessible alternatives to script-based information were also infrequently provided.

The researchers recommend that website managers apply Watchfire.com's Bobby software, which identifies and (where feasible) repairs content that is not compatible with ADA (Americans with Disabilities Act) guidelines for persons with visual impairments. Websites that achieve an exceptional degree of access are likely to gain a competitive advantage in this large and well-networked market, assuming that the products they sell are similarly accessible to visually impaired purchasers. Other advantages include broader positive publicity deriving from this demonstration of the company's social sustainability, and the opportunity during website redesign to improve the effectiveness of the site for all potential users.

Psychographic segmentation

The differentiation of the tourist market on the basis of psychological character-istics is referred to as **psychographic segmentation**. This can include a complex and diverse combination of factors, such as motivation, personality type, attitudes and perceptions, and needs. Psychographic profiles are often difficult to compile due to problems in identifying and measuring such characteristics. Individuals them-selves are usually not aware of where they would fit within such a structure. Whereas most people can readily provide their income, age, country of residence and so on for a questionnaire, their psychological dimension often has to be inferred through their responses to complex surveys, and then interpreted by the researcher. Whether they can then be placed into neat categories, as with age or income, is also highly questionable, as is the degree to which resulting profiles predict actual purchasing behaviour.

Also problematic is how much psychological characteristics can change, depending on circumstances. The factors that motivate a tourist to visit one destination may be entirely absent in the tourist's next trip. Similarly, personality type can change as a result of a person's experiences, but this often occurs imperceptibly and in a way that is difficult to quantify, unlike changes of address or income level. Identification of a person's 'usual' personality can also be misleading to the extent that an 'alternate' per-sonality may emerge during a tourism experience, since this constitutes a change of routine for the traveller. Because of such complexities, psychographic research usually requires more time and money than other types of segmentation, and often yields con-flicting and uncertain results.

Plog's psychographic typology

The personality typology of Stanley Plog (Plog 1991, 1998) is widely cited within tourism studies. According to Plog, a 'normal' (i.e. representative) population, rep-resented as a bell curve, can be divided into several categories based on personality dimensions with intermediate categories provided to recognise the continual rather than discrete nature of these dimensions (see figure 6.5). **Venturers** or 'allocentrics' (as he originally described them) are intellectually curious travellers who enjoy immersing themselves in other cultures and willingly accept a high level of risk. They tend to make their own travel arrangements, travel by themselves or in pairs and are open to spontaneous changes in itinerary. They tend to avoid places that are heavily devel-oped as tourist destinations, seeking out locales in which tourism is non-existent or incipient. Table 6.3 provides a more detailed list of characteristics and tourism behav-iour attributed to allocentrics.

In contrast, **dependables** (or 'psychocentrics') are self-absorbed individuals who seek to minimise risk by visiting familiar, extensively developed destinations where a full array of familiar goods and services are available. Plog estimated that only about 4 per cent of the American population were 'pure' venturers and a similar propor-tion 'pure' dependables, while about 17 per cent were in each of the 'near' categories (Plog 1998). The remaining 60 per cent of the population, as depicted in figure 6.5, are **midcentrics** (or 'centrics') whose personalities compromise between the depend-able and venturer dimensions. Typical midcentric behaviour is an eagerness to attend a local cultural performance and sample the local cuisine, but similar eagerness to have access to comfortable accommodation, hygienically prepared meals and a clean bathroom.

Plog's typology has important implications for the evolution and management of tourism systems. Dependables, for example, tend to visit well-established destinations dominated by large corporations and well-articulated tourism distribution systems, while allocentrics display an opposite tendency. A dependable would prefer to eat at McDonald's, stay overnight at the Sheraton and visit a theme park, all mediated by a package tour, while an allocentric would eat at a local market stall, stay overnight in a small guesthouse situated away from the tourist district and explore the local rainforest.

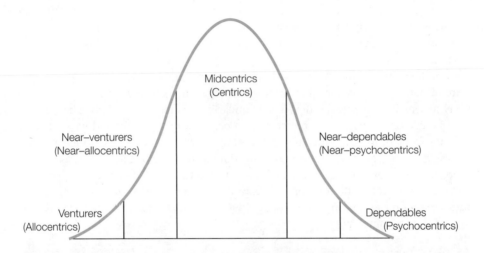

Midcentrics
(Centrics)

Near–venturers
(Near–allocentrics)

Near–dependables
(Near–psychocentrics)

Venturers
(Allocentrics)

Dependables
(Psychocentrics)

FIGURE 6.5 Plog's psychographic typology

Source: Adapted from Plog (1991, 1998, 2004)

The model's conceptual simplicity makes it very popular among tourism students and academics. However, the model should not be accepted without criticism. Litvin (2006) points out the following shortcomings:

- empirical testing to date has been extremely limited
- it does not account for the same individual visiting both allocentric and psychocentric destinations
- financial limitations could force allocentric tourists to visit close-by midcentric destinations
- travel to allocentric destinations may simply force psychocentrics deeper into their shell.

In addition, Plog's methodology for identifying dependable trends has never been publicly revealed due to its commercial sensitivity, and researchers are therefore unable to test the theory using similar methods. Litvin's (2006) own empirical research in Singapore found that actual destination visitation was heavily skewed toward psychocentric destinations, whereas travel desire (where they would like to go) much more closely resembled the normal distribution in figure 6.5. In sum, Plog's model is perhaps best utilised as a useful indicator of personality dimensions and a focal point for empirical psychographic research, but not as a definitive predictor of personality distribution or tourist behaviour.

TABLE 6.3 Personality and travel-related characteristics of allocentrics and psychocentrics

Venturers	Dependables
Intellectually curious	Intellectually restricted
Moderate risk-taking	Low risk-taking
Use disposable income	Withhold income
Try new products	Use well-known brands
Exploring/searching	Territory bound
Feel in control	Sense of powerlessness
Relatively anxiety free	Free-floating anxiety/nervousness
Interested/involved	Non-active lifestyle
Adventurous	Non-adventurous
Self-confident	Lacking in confidence
Prefer non-touristy areas	Prefer the familiar in travel destinations
Enjoy sense of discovery and delight in new experiences, before others have visited the area	Like commonplace activities at travel destinations
Prefer novel and different destinations	Prefer sun'n'fun spots, including considerable relaxation
High activity level	Low activity level
Prefer flying to destinations	Prefer destinations they can drive to
Tour accommodation should include adequate-to-good hotels and food, not necessarily modern or chain-type hotels, and few 'tourist-type' attractions	Prefer heavy tourist development (lots of hotels, family-type restaurants, tourist shops, etc.)
Enjoy meeting and dealing with people from a strange or foreign culture	Prefer familiar atmosphere (hamburger stands, familiar-type entertainment, absence of foreign atmosphere)
Tour arrangements should include basics (transportation and hotels) and allow considerable freedom and flexibility	Complete tour packaging appropriate, with heavy scheduling of activities
Travel more frequently	Travel less
Spend more of income on travel	Spend more of income on material goods and impulse buys
Inquisitive, curious about the world and its peoples	Little interest in events or activities in other countries
Demanding, sophisticated, active travellers	Naïve, non-demanding, passive travellers
Want much spontaneity in trips	Want structured, routinised travel
Will learn languages or foreign phrases before and during travels	Expect foreigners to speak in English
Seek off-the-beaten-path, little-known local hotels, restaurants	Want standard accommodation and conventional (American) meals
Buy native arts/crafts	Buy souvenirs, trinkets, common items
Want different destination for each trip	Prefer returning to same and familiar places
Prefer small numbers of people	Enjoy crowds

Source: Plog (1991, 2004)

Motivation

Travel **motivation** is different from travel purpose (see chapter 2) in that it indicates the intrinsic reasons the individual is embarking on a particular trip. Thus, a person might be travelling for VFR purposes, but the underlying motivation is to resolve a dispute with a parent, or to renew a relationship with a former partner. A stated pleasure or leisure purpose often disguises a deeper need to escape routine. In all these cases, the apparent motivation may itself have some even more fundamental psychological basis, such as the need for emotional satisfaction or spiritual fulfillment. Motivation is implicit in Plog's model, in that allocentrics are more driven by curiosity than psychocentrics, who in turn are more likely to be motivated by hedonism. Top motivations for travellers in the USA are depicted in table 6.4.

There are numerous theories and classification schemes associated with motivation. One of the best known is Maslow's hierarchy of human needs (in Page 2003), which ranges from basic physiological needs (e.g. food, sleep, sex) to the needs for safety and security, love, esteem, self-actualisation, knowledge and understanding, and finally, aesthetics. Maslow has been interpreted within tourism studies to imply that Phase Three and Four societies engage in tourism because their more basic needs have already been met. However, this is misleading. Travel for purposes of health and to access warm weather may be construed by contemporary tourists as meeting basic physical needs, while 'love needs', the third most basic need according to the hierarchy, are potentially met through the comradeship of group travel or the bonding with like-minded individuals in a battle re-enactment.

TABLE 6.4 Reasons for taking a vacation, American Traveler Survey, 2003

Reason	%	Reason	%
Get rid of stress	70	Have time for friends	23
Time with spouse	60	Learn history/culture	23
Enjoy no schedules	59	Important part of life	21
See/do new things	56	Romantic time	21
I feel alive/energetic	33	Like solitude/isolation	16
Gain perspective	31	Enjoy being outdoors	14
Like being waited on	24	Enjoy physical tests	10

Source: Plog (2005)

Behavioural segmentation

The identification of tourist markets on the basis of activities and other actions undertaken during the tourism experience is an exercise in **behavioural segmentation**. In a sense, it employs the *outcomes* of prior destination or product buying decisions as a basis for market segmentation, and therefore omits the non-travelling component of the population (unless non-travel behaviour is included as a category). Basic behavioural criteria include:

- travel occasion
- destination coverage (including length of stay)
- activities
- repeat patronage and loyalty.

Travel occasion

Travel occasion is closely related to purpose. Occasion-based segmentation differentiates consumers according to the specific occasion that prompts them to visit a particular tourism product. The destination wedding and honeymoon markets are examples that are heavily targeted by various destinations within Australia, the South Pacific and South-East Asia. Hawaii, for example, successfully branded itself as a destination wedding venue by capitalising on its longstanding status as a major honeymoon destination (McDonald 2005). Birthdays, anniversaries, funerals and other rites of passage are other examples of individualised travel occasion, while Schoolies Week and sporting spectacles indicate mass variants.

Destination coverage

Destination coverage can be expressed by length of stay, and also by the number of destinations (as opposed to stopovers and other transit experiences) that are visited during a particular trip. Visitors to Australia, for example, can be segmented by how much their visits are focused on a single state (as in the case of Japanese package tours to Queensland) or a multistate itinerary (as in the case of backpackers from Europe). Both single-destination and multi-destination trips usually display a great deal of variety with respect to destination coverage, as modelled by Oppermann (1995) (see figure 6.6). Numerous implications follow from this model, including the extent to which tourists are concentrated or dispersed within a country, the length of time (and thus amount of money) spent in different parts of the country and the types of services that are accessed during the tourism experience. Multi-destination itineraries continue to grow in popularity as countries and regions pursue mutually beneficial bilateral and multilateral destination marketing and development initiatives. Visitors to East Africa, for example, are taking advantage of tours that combine the accessibility and services of Kenya with the undeveloped natural attractions of neighbouring Tanzania.

Activities

Variables that can be segmented under the generic category of 'activities' include accommodation type, mode of transportation, total and per-day expenditure, attractions visited and types of tourist activities undertaken. The latter, in particular, are extremely diverse. Relevant market segments in Australia include ecotourists (see chapter 11), theme park visitors, honeymooners, beach bathers, bush walkers, visitors to Aboriginal sites and performances, backpackers, heritage tourists and wine tourists. Whether these activities are of primary or secondary importance to the relevant segment is also a critical factor. The stakeholders who would most obviously be interested in attraction/activity segmentation are the operators of such businesses, or the destinations that specialise in these attractions or activities.

A relevant issue is whether tourists are mainly interested in specific activities, and therefore choose their destination accordingly, or whether they are primarily interested in a particular destination, within which available activities are then pursued. The second scenario is less common than the first. This mainly involves tourists who are constrained by financial or time limitations to travel within their own state or country or, more rarely, who are motivated by patriotic considerations or a compelling desire to visit a particular destination that they encountered in a book or the media. The Queensland coastal resort community of Hervey Bay illustrates both scenarios. Some of its whale-watching tourists are there because they are primarily interested in that activity. Others are there because they are primarily interested in visiting Hervey Bay, and whale-watching happens to be one of the available activities.

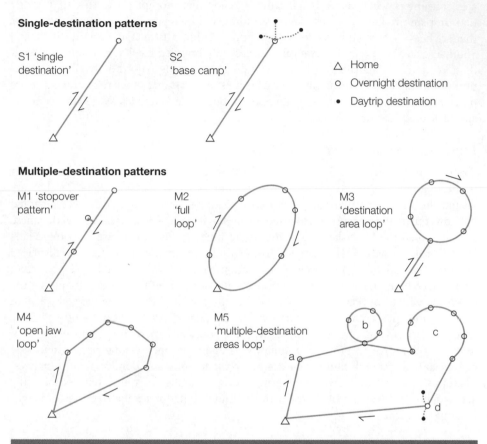

FIGURE 6.6 Model of single-and multiple-destination itineraries

Source: Oppermann (1995b)

It is important for destinations to determine what proportions of their visitors fall into each category in order to better understand both their markets and their competitors. In attracting tourists mainly interested in whale-watching, Hervey Bay is competing with destinations in other parts of the world (e.g. New Zealand, Canada) and potentially in other parts of Australia. In attracting tourists in the second category, Hervey Bay is competing with the Sunshine and Gold Coasts, as well as other destinations that happen to be located within Queensland but do not necessarily offer whale-watching.

Repeat patronage and loyalty

As with any type of product, high levels of repeat visitation (i.e. repeat patronage) are regarded as evidence of a successful destination, hence the critical distinction between first-time and repeat visitors. One practical advantage of repeat visitation is the reduced need to invest resources into marketing campaigns, not only because the repeat visitors are returning anyway, but because these satisfied customers are more likely to provide free publicity through positive word-of-mouth and electronic word-of-mouth (eWOM) contact with other potential visitors. Use frequency is an important segmentation variable that essentially quantifies repeat patronage by indicating the number of times that a product (e.g. a destination or an airline flight) is purchased over a given period of time. Frequent flyer and other repeat-user programs are perhaps the best example of an industry initiative that responds to and encourages high use frequency. Moreover, they provide an excellent database for carrying out relevant marketing and management exercises (see chapter 7).

Repeat patronage and lengthy stays are often equated with product **loyalty**. However, the concept of loyalty goes beyond this single factor to incorporate the psychological attitudes towards the products that compel such behaviour. When both attitudinal and behavioural (repeat purchase) dimensions are taken into account, a four-cell loyalty matrix emerges (see figure 6.7):

- Consumers who demonstrate a pattern of repeat visitation and express a high psychological attachment to a destination (or any other tourism-related product), including a willingness to recommend the product to others, belong in the 'high' loyalty category.
- Conversely, those who have made only a single visit, and indicate negative attitudes about the destination, are assigned to the 'low' loyalty cell.
- 'Spurious' loyalty is a paradox, occurring when a pattern of repeat visitation is exhibited along with a weak psychological attachment. This could result when someone feels compelled to make repeat visits to a destination due to family or peer group pressure, or because of financial limitations that prohibit visits to more desirable destinations.
- 'Latent' loyalty is also paradoxical, describing the opposite scenario where someone regards a destination very highly, but only makes a single visit. The commonest example of this behaviour is a 'once-in-a-lifetime' visit to an exotic but expensive location.

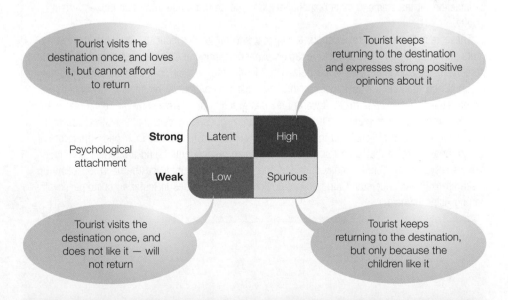

FIGURE 6.7 The loyalty matrix

The loss of the spuriously loyal clientele usually does not indicate any serious problem for a business, since their visits are mainly a matter of habit, convenience or coercion rather than conviction. In contrast, high-loyalty visitors are highly valued by destinations because of their predictability, and because they are more likely to continue their patronage for longer even if the situation in the destination, or in their personal circumstances, begins to deteriorate (i.e. they are more resistant to the erosion of relevant push and pull factors). These tourists, then, constitute an important indicator group, in that the loss of this group's patronage may show that the product is experiencing a very serious level of deterioration or change — as, for example, in association with changing destination lifecycle dynamics (see chapter 10). Failure to foster or retain high loyalty traits in some markets, however, may simply indicate a failure to understand cultural characteristics that give rise to loyalty (see Breakthrough tourism: The influence of face and harmony on loyalty in Chinese customers).

breakthrough tourism

THE INFLUENCE OF FACE AND HARMONY ON LOYALTY IN CHINESE CUSTOMERS

Recent research suggests that face and harmony, core characteristics of Chinese culture, play a role in affecting the loyalty of Chinese restaurant patrons (Hoare & Butcher 2008). 'Face' describes the relationship of reciprocal respect and courtesy with peers, while 'harmony' is the balance that is sought within each individual, within society, and between people and the natural environment. 'Slow eating' is an important aspect of harmony that includes avoidance of overindulgence. Surveying 109 international business students from China, Hong Kong and Taiwan studying at an Australian university, Hoare and Butcher (2008) found that customer loyalty (defined as holding a favourable attitude toward a provider, committing to repatronise that provider, and recommending the provider to others) was significantly and directly affected by customer satisfaction, but not by face or harmony. However, face (but not harmony) was significantly and directly related to satisfaction, at least among male respondents, and therefore had an important indirect effect on loyalty.

These results lead the researchers to suggest several loyalty-inducing strategies for restaurants attracting or hoping to attract the rapidly expanding inbound Chinese tourist market. Service personnel, for example, need to be trained to identify the host of an incoming Chinese dining group. Once identified, it is important that the host be continually recognised and honoured, especially if that person is male. A warm personal greeting and farewell by the restaurant manager is strongly recommended. With regard to *all* male guests, respect and sensitivity are paramount to avoid loss of face, and ignoring or criticising them in front of their peers therefore is inappropriate. Noting that earlier surveys of East Asian respondents found a stronger correlation between loyalty and both harmony and face, the researchers emphasise the need for follow-up research to better understand the role of traditional cultural values in fostering customer loyalty among Asian tourists.

CHAPTER REVIEW

Since the 1950s there has been a shift in the perception of the tourist market as a homogeneous group of consumers, to the identification of increasingly specific or niche market segments. This has occurred in part because of the growing sophistication and size of the market, which has added complexity to the demand for tourism-related products and made it viable for operators to serve ever more specialised groups of consumers. In addition, technologies have emerged to readily identify these specialised segments and facilitate the development and marketing of appropriate niche tourism products. The culmination of this process has been the ability of marketers and managers to regard each customer as an individual segment, or market of one.

All consumers experience a similar decision-making process when selecting destinations and other tourism products. However, the specifics of the process (and subsequent tourism behaviour) vary according to many push and pull forces as well as personal characteristics such as culture, personality and motivations. Many of these forces and characteristics are therefore potentially useful as segmentation variables, though their relevance in any given situation depends on factors such as measurability, size, homogeneity and compatibility.

Four major categories of market segmentation are widely recognised. Geographic segmentation considers spatial criteria such as region or country of origin, subnational origins and the urban–rural distinction. This type of segmentation is the most commonly employed, and is becoming more sophisticated due to the development of GIS technologies. Sociodemographic segmentation includes gender, age, disability and family lifecycle as well as the highly interrelated criteria of education, occupation and income. Gay and lesbian tourists, along with older adults and women, are three market segments that have attracted industry attention due to their growth and purchasing power. Psychographic segmentation is the most difficult to identify. Plog's distinction between allocentrics, psychocentrics and midcentrics is the best-known example, although motivation is also sometimes used. Finally, behavioural segmentation considers such factors as travel occasion, the number of destinations visited during a trip, activities, and repeat patronage and loyalty.

▪ SUMMARY OF KEY TERMS

Behavioural segmentation the identification of tourist markets on the basis of activities and actions undertaken during the actual tourism experience

Dependables 'self-centred' tourists who prefer familiar and risk-averse experiences; originally known as 'psychocentrics'

Family lifecycle (FLC) a sequence of stages through which the traditional nuclear family passes from early adulthood to the death of a spouse; each stage is associated with distinct patterns of tourism-related behaviour associated with changing family and financial circumstances

Gender segmentation the grouping of individuals into male and female categories, or according to sexual orientation

Geographic segmentation market segmentation carried out on the basis of the market's origin region; can be carried out at various scales, including region (e.g. Asia), country (Germany), subnational unit (California, Queensland), or urban/rural

GIS (geographic information systems) sophisticated computer software programs that facilitate the assembly, storage, manipulation, analysis and display of spatially referenced information

Loyalty the extent to which a product, such as a destination, is perceived in a positive way and repeatedly purchased by the consumer

Market segmentation the division of the tourist market into more or less homogenous subgroups, or tourist market segments, based on certain common characteristics and/or behavioural patterns

Market segments portions of the tourist market that are more or less distinct in their characteristics and/or behaviour

Markets of one an extreme form of market segmentation, in which individual consumers are recognised as distinct market segments

Midcentrics 'average' tourists whose personality type is a compromise between venturer and dependable traits; originally known as 'centrics'

Motivation the intrinsic reasons why the individual is embarking on a particular trip

Multilevel segmentation a refinement of simple market segmentation that further differentiates basic level segments

Niche markets highly specialised market segments

Pink dollar the purchasing power of gay and lesbian consumers, recognised to be much higher than the average purchasing power (sometimes used to describe the purchasing power of women)

Psychographic segmentation the differentiation of the tourist market on the basis of psychological and motivational characteristics such as personality, motivations and needs

Simple market segmentation the most basic form of market segmentation, involving the identification of a minimal number of basic market segments such as 'female' and 'male'

Sociodemographic segmentation market segmentation based on social and demographic variables such as gender, age, family lifecycle, education, occupation and income

Tourist market the overall group of consumers that engages in some form of tourism-related travel

Venturers according to Plog's typology, 'other-centred' tourists who enjoy exposing themselves to other cultures and new experiences, and are willing to take risks in this process; originally known as 'allocentrics'

■ QUESTIONS

1. For managers and marketers, what are the advantages and disadvantages, respectively, of treating the tourist market as a single entity or as a collection of markets of one?

2. To what extent do you believe visiting gay and lesbian tourists in the Cayman Islands are obligated to behave in a manner that does not offend conservative local residents?

3. What strengths and weaknesses are associated with 'country of residence' and 'region of residence' as criteria for identifying tourist market segments?

4. Given financial constraints, should females or persons with visual impairments be given priority by a tourism company seeking to make its website more effective?

5. What are the strengths and limitations of employing the traditional family lifecycle as a segmentation variable for the tourist market?

6. (a) What criteria should a destination use in deciding whether to target specific racial or ethnic groups?
   (b) What are the risks in targeting specific racial or ethnic markets?

7. What difficulties are associated with the operationalisation of psychographic segmentation in general, and with Plog's typology in particular?

8. (a) What is the difference between trip purpose and trip motivation?
   (b) What are the strengths and weaknesses of each as segmentation criteria?

9. (a) How can the 14 specific motivations depicted in table 6.4 be combined into three or four more general categories
   (b) What is the relative importance of each of these broader categories, based on the frequencies indicated in table 6.4?

10. How can the loyalty matrix be operationalised to assist in the management and marketing of destinations?

■ EXERCISES

1. Write a 1000-word report in which you:
   (a) describe the differences between the Japanese and Chinese inbound markets to Australia, based on table 6.1 and additional information from Tourism Research Australia's Japanese and Chinese visitor profiles (www.tra.australia.com), and
   (b) suggest strategies, based on the profiles, for marketing Australia in either Japan or China.

2. Assume that you are the manager of a local wildlife park and that you have obtained funding to identify your market through the use of a questionnaire. Because these funds are very limited, you must keep your questionnaire to only two pages, which allows you to obtain no more than 15 customer characteristics.
   (a) List the 15 characteristics of your market base (e.g. gender, age, eye colour, personality) that you believe to be most important to the successful management of your attraction.
   (b) Indicate why you selected these particular characteristics.
   (c) Design the questionnaire.

■ FURTHER READING

Daniels, M. (Ed.) 2005. Special Issue: Travelers with Specialized Needs. *Tourism Review International* **8 (3).** This collection of ten refereed articles is the most thorough compilation of academic research to date on the issue of tourism and disabilities.

Lück, M. Ed. 2008. *The Encyclopedia of Tourism and Recreation in Marine Environments.* **Wallingford: CABI.** Behavioural segmentation distinguishes marine tourism as a widespread and rapidly growing form of tourism activity. This edited compilation is the most thorough source of knowledge available on this topic.

Patterson, I. 2006. *Growing Older: Tourism and Leisure Behaviour of Older Adults.* **Wallingford: CABI.** The author describes the behaviour, attitudes, etc. of older adults, and focuses this information on strategies that will help destinations and businesses to more effectively market and manage this growing market segment.

Plog, S. 2005. 'Targeting Segments: More Important than Ever in the Travel Industry'. In Theobald, W. (Ed.) *Global Tourism.* **Third Edition. Sydney: Elsevier, pp. 271–93.** Plog discusses the importance of market segmentation and describes six tourist segments that emerged from a major annual household survey in the United States.

Waitt, G. & Markwell, K. 2006. *Gay Tourism: Culture and Context*. New York: Haworth. Chapters in this book focus on the emergence of gay tourism, the formation of 'gay spaces', marketing, and the challenges of practicing gay tourism within heterosexual spaces.

case study

IDENTIFYING THE GREEN CONSUMER

There is increasing evidence of growth in the number of consumers who are motivated to behave in an environmentally and socioculturally sensitive way because of concern over contemporary ecological and social problems. Accordingly, it is important for managers of tourism products and businesses to gauge whether these 'green' consumers constitute a market segment that warrants attention with respect to product development and marketing.

Measurability

Green proclivities can be measured in several ways, and it is initially helpful to make a distinction between perceptions and behaviour. Green attitudes and intentions are readily accessible through consumer surveys that regularly solicit opinions about current environmental and social issues, and ask whether a vote for the Green Party or equivalent is likely. More immediately important to managers, however, is actual behaviour. Variables that can be measured and assessed collectively to estimate the size of the green market include the number of subscribers to specialised environmental publications such as *G Magazine*, tendency to purchase organic food products and/or belong to organic food cooperatives, and membership in or a previous first preference vote for the Green Party.

Size and homogeneity

The green market is not homogenous, and 'shades of green' must be taken into account when assessing its size. At one extreme, the great majority of Australian adults apparently feel morally obligated to not litter, not damage trees or shrubs, repair water leaks, wash the car less often, use less water for the lawn, re-use things, and recycle (Dolnicar & Leisch 2008). Poll results, moreover, consistently show about three-quarters of Australian adults to be concerned over environmental issues such as climate change. Smaller numbers behave in a more actively green (i.e. 'deep green') manner (Weaver 2007). For example, the Green Party attracting over 1 million votes in the Australian Senate in 2007, or about 9 per cent of the electorate (AEC 2007), while *G Magazine* currently attracts about 35 000 subscribers.

Based on such empirical evidence, the Australian green segment can be visualised as a series of concentric circles, with about half the population in the outer circle being consistently concerned about the environment, but unwilling to make any resultant changes in their personal behaviour that would cause inconvenience; they do not litter and recycle regularly, but are unlikely to support a carbon tax on petrol or pay more to purchase a hybrid vehicle. In contrast to these 'veneer', 'superficial' or 'light green' consumers, the next circle consists of the 20 per cent or so who are concerned and who make changes that are inconvenient, though not to the extent of a lifestyle transformation. The latter, rather, is characteristic of the inner circle of 5 per cent of 'deep greens' who are fundamentally restructuring their lives by using only bicycle or mass transit, purchasing only organic products, etc. This latter group mirrors research by Dolnicar and Leisch (2008) who identified a small Australian consumer segment of nature loving travellers who express high moral obligation levels. In contrast, the first group is represented by a group of 'budget fun seekers' willing to act in an environmentally friendly only if it is convenient.

Compatibility and actionability

The tourism industry is diverse, and affiliated products are more or less compatible with the various green segments identified above. Casinos, for example, may have difficulty attracting deep greens, who are likely to gravitate to ecotourism and volunteer tourism products that more clearly conform to their moral beliefs and attitudes. Mainstream tourism products not explicitly aligned with environmental or social themes appear to be 'hedging their bets' by introducing high profile and profitable practices, such as recycling and re-use, that appeal to the superficial environmentalist mainstream. Perhaps the most ubiquitous example is the tag found in hotel bathrooms which exhorts guests to 'Save Mother Earth!' by reusing their bath towels. Such superficial practices, however, may not attract deeper green tourists. Conversely, a great onus is placed on ecotourism and volunteer tourism providers to live up to expectations by offering a holistic green experience; failure to fall short of this challenging goal could result in low levels of satisfaction and repeat visitation.

Accessibility

Overt green products, such as *G Magazine*, the Green Party and local organic groceries, are logical and accessible vehicles for accessing the green market. Media and marketing that target females, professionals, persons with graduate degree qualifications, and inner city residency are also more likely to reach green consumers, since all of the former are overrepresented in the green market. Such consumers tend to be active information seekers and avid readers of a diverse array of media, but also highly sceptical and alert to corporate 'greenwashing', where allegedly environmental branding or eco-showcases are used to disguise otherwise unsustainable practices (BSDglobal.com 2008).

Durability

The historical growth in the green market is apparent in the observation that very few Australians would have expressed concern over environmental issues in the 1950s. More recent evidence of growth in actual environmental behaviour is provided by the Green Party, which attracted the Senate first preference vote of one of every 11 Australians in 2007 (see above), compared with 7.7 per cent in 2004, 4.9 per cent in 2001 and 2.7 per cent in 1998. Further growth in this and other deeper green indicators may result from concurrent publicity surrounding climate change and escalating energy costs. These may be helping to bring about a societal transformation that challenges longstanding and fundamental assumptions about growth and the relationship between humans and the natural environment (see chapter 11).

Relevance

There is empirical support for the theory that environmentally responsible behaviour at home does not necessarily translate into an equivalent level of green behaviour while travelling for leisure purposes (Dolcinar & Leisch 2008). This is an extremely important tendency to confirm in determining the relevance of the green trend for the tourism industry. Factors that may help to account for this apparent discrepancy and inform the industry's response include the following:

- Many theorists believe that tourists are motivated by a desire to escape routine; if green behaviour is part of a person's normal lifestyle, then associated practices might be consciously or subconsciously suspended when travelling.
- Tourism-related purchases and experiences may not be frequent enough to foster the sort of green behaviour patterns and knowledge associated with, for example, weekly visits to the organic grocery store.

- Unlike the organic grocery store, green tourism products are neither highly visible nor publicised, nor widely identified by a certification scheme as widespread and visible as the Australian Certified Organic certification scheme.
- As discussed above, advocates for green tourism may be focused on more visibly green products such as ecotourism and volunteer tourism, and therefore disengaged from mass tourism or efforts to make it more sustainable.
- There are no highly visible advocates for tourism greening such as a David Bellamy or Oprah Winfrey who might be able to influence public attitudes (Weaver 2006).

Of the above factors, the emergence of a celebrity advocate and the introduction of a high profile and popularly embraced certification scheme are the two that are most likely to increase the relevance of the green market to the tourism industry as a whole.

QUESTIONS

1. Conduct a survey of your class to identify:
   (a) how many students have experienced a 'green' tourism product such as ecotourism or volunteer tourism during the past two years, and
   (b) whether they behave in a more or less environmentally friendly way when travelling (for whatever tourism purpose) as opposed to their normal day-to-day behaviour
   (c) what these results say about the relationship between tourists and the green movement.

2. (a) Identify green behaviour patterns in New Zealand, Japan and China with regard to membership in green organisations, environmental opinion polls, and the purchase of green products.
   (b) Discuss in class how the patterns evident in these three countries compare with Australia.
   (c) What implications emerge for Australian tourism providers trying to determine whether they need to be 'green' in order to attract inbound tourists from these three sources?

7 TOURISM MARKETING

LEARNING OBJECTIVES

After studying this chapter, you should be able to:

1. appreciate the scope of marketing as an essential component of tourism systems

2. list and describe the key characteristics of services marketing and identify how these are different from goods marketing

3. identify the strategies that can be adopted to address imbalances between supply and demand

4. explain why market failure occurs in tourism marketing

5. describe the role of destination tourism organisations in tourism marketing

6. outline the rationale for and the stages involved in strategic marketing

7. define the basic components of the 8P marketing mix model

8. discuss the importance of database marketing in the tourism industry

9. explain the pricing techniques that tourism businesses can use to set prices

10. identify the costs and benefits associated with the various forms of media that are used in tourism promotion.

■ INTRODUCTION

Chapter 6 examined market segmentation, or the process whereby consumers are divided into relatively uniform groups with respect to their attitudes and behaviour. This is a critical component of tourism product management in that different market segments, distinguished by one or more geographical, sociodemographic, psychographic or behavioural criteria, are likely to have distinct impacts upon the tourism system. They also require different strategies in the area of tourism marketing, which is the subject of the present chapter. Following a discussion of the nature and definition of marketing in the next section, the key characteristics of services marketing, and tourism marketing in particular, are examined. The need to maintain a balance between supply and demand is then discussed, while the phenomenon of market failure is addressed in the section that follows. This section also considers the approaches and strategies that can be used to overcome this problem. Strategic marketing, and in particular the components of a SWOT (strengths, weaknesses, opportunities, threats) analysis, forms the core of the 'Strategic tourism marketing' section. The final section presents an overview of the elements involved in the product-focused marketing mix.

■ THE NATURE OF MARKETING

Marketing is commonly perceived as involving little more than the promotional advertisements that are displayed through television and other forms of media. However, these advertisements are only one form of promotion, and promotion is only one aspect of marketing. Advertising and promotion, and the people who work in these industries, are important, but marketing implicates *everyone* in the tourism and hospitality sector, including tourists, potential tourists and residents of destinations. Thus, marketing is pervasive throughout the tourism system.

Definition of marketing

There are numerous definitions of marketing (see, for example, Kotler & Keller 2005; Morrison 2009). The following definition, which combines elements of the most commonly cited definitions, is used in this book:

> Marketing involves the interaction and interrelationships among consumers and producers of goods and services, through which ideas, products, services and values are created and exchanged for the mutual benefit of both groups.

In place of the popular perception of marketing as a one-way attempt by producers (e.g. the tourism industry and destinations) to sell their products to the market, this definition emphasises the two-way interactions that occur between these producers and the actual as well as potential tourist market. Successful marketing, for example, depends on feedback (e.g. customer satisfaction, proclivity to purchase new products) flowing from the market to the producer. In addition, it recognises the importance of financial and other benefits to both parties, and includes interactions among the 'internal customers' within a company, organisation or destination.

■ SERVICES MARKETING

Services marketing applies to service-sector activities such as tourism and is fundamentally different from the marketing of goods. This holds true even though the tourism sector interfaces with goods such as souvenirs, luggage and duty-free merchandise, and notwithstanding the fact that many important marketing principles are equally applicable to both goods and services. In general, the key marketing characteristics that distinguish services from goods are (a) intangibility, (b) inseparability, (c) variability and (d) perishability (Bowen, Makens & Kotler 2005).

Intangibility

In contrast to physical products and goods, services have **intangibility**. This means that they cannot be directly seen, tasted, felt or heard prior to their purchase and consumption. Furthermore, customers usually have only a receipt, a souvenir or other memorabilia such as photographs as evidence that they actually had that experience. Customers purchase tourism and hospitality services for the first time with little more than knowledge of the price, some pictures of the destination and its facilities, endorsement by some well-known personality, friends or relatives or the sales intermediary (e.g. travel agent) and, in some instances, their own prior experiences. In the service industry, the concept of compensation for an unsatisfactory purchase is also distinctive. As with goods, money can be refunded or compensating products made available free of charge, but the product itself cannot be returned once it has been consumed.

Because of the intangible nature of the service sector, word of mouth is especially important as a source of product information, as this involves access to those who have already experienced a particular destination or hotel, or know of someone who has. Accordingly, word of mouth has a high degree of influence among potential customers as an image formation agent (Morrison 2009). However, word of mouth can also be problematic. Circumstances regarding the product may have changed from the time of the informant's experience, or the information may be third- or fourth-hand (e.g. the informant knows someone who knows someone who travelled to Bali and did not like it). In addition, the psychographic profile and tastes of the informant may be different from the person who is receiving the information (see page 167).

Thus, even with access to word-of-mouth information, the level of perceived risk in purchasing a service, especially for a first-time purchaser, is relatively high compared to goods (although this is not to say that goods purchasing is risk free). To reduce this risk perception, service providers offer tangible clues as to what the customer can expect from the product and the producer, thereby creating confidence in the service. These include articulate and uniformed personnel, a clean and professional office setting, glossy brochures that convey attractive images to the potential buyer, and websites that take advantage of virtual reality technologies. Experiential merchandising is another increasingly popular technique that can help to compensate for service intangibility (see Managing tourism: Intangibility in the hotel sector).

managing tourism

INTANGIBILITY IN THE HOTEL SECTOR

A new feature that can be found increasingly on hotel websites is a section where one can purchase the bedding, furniture, cosmetics and other products found in company guestrooms. Apart from its potential to diversify and increase revenue, this practice can help businesses to cope with the perennial problem of service intangibility by providing customers with a tangible long-term reminder of their presence (Rosenwald 2005). That is, a guest who is impressed enough with a particular type of bedding to purchase it and use it in their home may be constantly (and positively) reminded of the hotel where these products were first experienced, and more inclined to patronise that hotel again when they travel. This creates a more effective service/goods linkage than typical souvenirs, which may be impractical or used/displayed only periodically. An additional consideration is the likelihood that guests staying in the house of the customer will also be exposed to the hotel room products. To encourage purchases, hotels make available high-end designer products at affordable prices, which they can do by ordering such goods in bulk from overseas sources.

The success of the above strategy, however, still depends on convincing consumers to make the initial visit to the hotel chain. Boutique hotels achieve this by fostering a market reputation as reputable designer showrooms featuring the best, most fashionable and most comfortable in contemporary (or traditional) décor. For consumers, spending $300 a night to 'roadtest' such goods, then buying them through the internet, is a more rational strategy than hiring a designer or researching purchase options themselves. Larger hotel chains are imitating the boutiques by moving from practical 'utility' furnishings to a similarly upscale position. Marriott, for example, now provides granite bathroom countertops and 'Heavenly Bedding' sheets and pillows as standard unit features. W Hotel, a well known boutique facility in New York, has now moved one step beyond by opening a retail store where featured goods can be purchased off the shelf. Some hotels use the novel strategy of observing what people try to steal to determine which goods are most likely to sell (Rosenwald 2005).

Inseparability

Tourism services are characterised by **inseparability**, meaning that production and consumption occur simultaneously and in the same place. This is demonstrated by the flight of a passenger aboard an aeroplane (i.e. the flight is being 'produced' at the same time the passenger is 'consuming' it), or by a guest's occupation of a hotel room. Because the consumers and producers of these products are in frequent contact, the nature of these interactions has a major impact on customer satisfaction levels. Customer-oriented staff training and initial staff selection should thus ensure that 'frontline' employees such as airline attendants and front-desk clerks display appropriate **emotional labour** attributes such as empathy, assurance and responsiveness (Anderson, Provis & Chappel 2003).

Tourists also need to respect the applicable protocol and regulations, since misbehaviour on their part can also negatively affect the product. For example, patrons who smoke in a smoke-free restaurant detract from the quality of the experience for non-smoking customers. Tourists who walk into a church wearing shorts and talking loudly may offend local residents or other visitors. While it is assumed that frontline service staff should receive training to be made aware of appropriate standards of service behaviour, the same assumption is seldom if ever applied to tourists, even though these two examples clearly demonstrate the negative ramifications of inappropriate tourist behaviour. At the very least, it is incumbent on the service sector to make any relevant rules and regulations evident to tourists in a diplomatic but unambiguous way.

Variability

Tourism services have a high level of **variability**, meaning that each producer–consumer interaction is a unique experience that is influenced by a large number of often unpredictable factors. These include 'human element' factors such as the mood and expectations of each participant at the particular time during which the service encounter takes place. A tourist in a restaurant, for example, may be completely relaxed, expecting that their every whim will be satisfied, while the attending waiter may have high levels of stress from overwork and expect the customer to be 'more reasonable' in their demands. Such expectation incongruities are extremely common in the tourism sector, given the tourist's perception of this experience as a 'special', out-of-the-ordinary (and expensive) occasion, and the waiter's view that this is just a routine experience associated with the job. The next encounter, however, even if the same waiter is involved, could involve an entirely different set of circumstances with a more positive outcome.

The problem for managers is that these incongruities can lead to unpleasant and unsatisfying encounters, and a consequent reduction in customer satisfaction levels and deteriorating local attitudes towards tourists. Often, just one such experience can sour a tourist's view about a particular destination, offsetting a very large number of entirely satisfactory experiences during the same venture that, because they were expected, do not make the same impression. This is why a tourist returning to the same hotel may have a completely different experience during the second trip — the combination of moods, expectations, experiences and other factors among all participants is likely to be entirely different from the first trip.

This uncertainty element, combined with the simultaneous nature of production and consumption (i.e. it is more difficult to undo any mistakes), makes it extremely difficult to introduce quality control mechanisms in tourism similar in rigour to those that govern the production of tangible goods such as cars and clothing. For tourism destinations and products, it is again a matter of decreasing the likelihood of negative outcomes by ensuring that employees are exposed to high-quality training opportunities, and that tourists are sensitised to standards of appropriate behaviour and reasonable expectations.

Perishability

Tourism services cannot be produced and stored today for consumption in the future. For example, an airline flight that has 100 empty seats on a 400-seat aeroplane cannot compensate for the shortfall by selling 500 seats on the next flight of that aeroplane. The 100 seats are irrevocably lost, along with the revenue that they would normally generate. Because some of this loss is attributable to airline passengers or hotel guests who do not take up their reservations, most businesses 'overbook' their services on the basis of the average number of seats that have not been claimed in the past. This characteristic of **perishability** also helps to explain why airlines and other businesses such as wotif.com offer last-minute sales or stand-by rates at drastically reduced prices. While they will not obtain as much profit from these clients, at least some revenue can be recouped at minimal extra cost. For a tourism manager, one of the greatest challenges in marketing is to compensate for perishability by effectively matching demand with supply. An optimal match contributes to higher profitability, and therefore the supply and demand balance is discussed more thoroughly in the following section.

■ MANAGING SUPPLY AND DEMAND

If possible, the tourism manager will attempt to produce an exact match between the supply and the corresponding demand for a product. This is because, all other things being equal, resources that are not fully used will result in reduced profits. When considering the supply and demand balance, there are two main cost components that must be taken into account:

• **Fixed costs** are entrenched costs that the operation has little flexibility to change over the short term. Examples include taxes, the interest that has to be paid on loans and the heating costs that are incurred in a hotel during the winter season. In the latter case, these must be paid whether the rooms are occupied or not, as otherwise building and contents damage could result.

• **Variable costs** are those costs that can be adjusted in the short term. For example, during the low season hotels can dismiss their casual nonunionised staff and cut back on their advertising, thereby adjusting to low occupancy rates by saving on salaries and promotion. It may also be possible to obtain cheaper and smaller supplies of food if the hotel is not already under an inflexible long-term contract with a specific supplier.

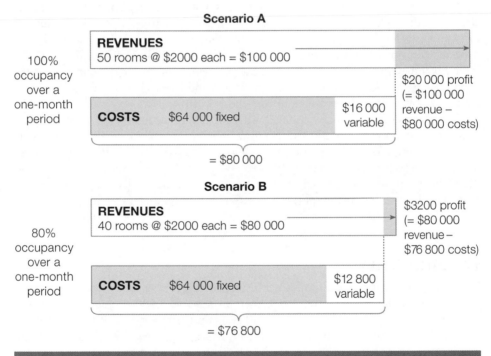

FIGURE 7.1 Effect of a high fixed cost structure on hotel room profits

There is no set boundary between these two categories, and it is helpful to think of costs as falling along a fixed-to-variable spectrum that varies from one operation to another. Tourism businesses tend to have a relatively high proportion of costs concentrated in the fixed segment of the spectrum, implying that large amounts of money have to be budgeted whether a flight or hotel is fully booked or almost empty. As a result, even small shortfalls in occupancy can lead to significant declines in profit. Figure 7.1 demonstrates this problem by showing the contrasting profits that result from two different levels of occupancy in a hypothetical hotel with 50 rooms and monthly fixed costs of $64 000. In scenario A, full occupancy results in a $20 000 monthly profit when costs are subtracted from revenues. However, in scenario B, with just a 20 per cent decline in occupancy, the corresponding profit declines by 84 per cent to $3200. This is because the variable costs fall by 20 per cent (the same as the occupancy rate fall), but the $64 000 fixed costs cannot move at all. Being able to maintain a high occupancy rate is therefore absolutely critical for the hotel. Demand for tourism-related services such as accommodation, however, is usually very difficult to predict, given the complexity of the destination or product decision-making process (chapter 6), and the uncertainty factor (see the case study at the end of chapter 2). To help achieve a better understanding and thus a higher level of control over the demand portion of the supply/demand equation, daily, weekly, seasonal and long-term patterns in demand can be identified.

Daily variations in demand

The level of demand for most tourism services changes on a daily basis. For example, in a hotel reception area, the peak check-out time is in the morning between approximately 7 am and 10 am, and in large hotels queues commonly form during that period if an efficient online check-out procedure has not been implemented. Similarly, late afternoon and early evening is a busy time, as guests arrive to check in. However, for the housekeeping department, the intervening period is usually the busiest time as rooms are cleaned and prepared for the next guests to arrive. Different types of hotels also have different demand patterns. An airport hotel, for example, often faces unpredicted demand surges at any time of the day or night if aeroplanes are delayed or cancelled. In many types of attractions, such as theme parks, a peak often occurs between midday and late afternoon, while country markets usually experience peak visitation in the early morning. When analysed from the perspective of daily demand, salaries are a fixed cost unless there is provision for sending staff home early without compensation.

Weekly variations in demand

Differential demand patterns on a weekly basis are illustrated in the hotel industry by the distinction between the 'four-day' and 'three-day' market. The four-day market is a largely business-oriented clientele that concentrates in the Monday to Thursday period. Hotels that focus on this market tend to experience a downturn on the weekend. Conversely, the three-day or short holiday market peaks on the weekend and during national or state holidays. Exurban tourist shopping villages that draw much of their tourist traffic from nearby large cities, such as Tamborine Mountain and Maleny in Queensland, also tend to experience weekend peak use periods.

Seasonal variations in demand

Variations can also be identified over the one-year cycle, with a distinction being made between the high season, the low season and shoulder periods in many types of destinations and operations. 3S resort communities and facilities often experience 100 per cent occupancy rates during the high season, which is in the summer for high-latitude resorts and in the winter for tropical or subtropical pleasure periphery resorts. This may then be offset by closures during the low season due to very low occupancy rates, with subsequent negative impacts throughout the local community (see chapter 8). In contrast, business-oriented city hotels and urban attractions often experience their seasonal downturn during the summer, when business activity is reduced.

Long-term variations in demand

The most difficult patterns to identify are those that occur over a period of several years or even decades. Long-term business cycles, which have been identified by many economists (Ralf 2000), do not necessarily affect the usual daily, weekly and seasonal fluctuations, but can result in lower-than-normal visitation levels at all of these scales. Some tourism researchers have also theorised that destinations and other tourism-related facilities, irrespective of macro-fluctuations in the overall economy, experience a product lifecycle that is characterised by alternating periods of stable and accelerated demand (Toh, Khan & Koh 2001). This very important concept is discussed more thoroughly in chapter 10.

Supply/demand matching strategies

Most tourism managers operate in an environment that is largely capacity restrained — that is, supply is fixed and cannot be expanded rapidly. They therefore concentrate on optimising the volume of demand, although there is usually some scope for modifying supply as well. There are two broad circumstances in which a manager needs to take action — when supply exceeds demand and when demand exceeds supply — each of which is accompanied by its own set of strategies (see figure 7.2). The strategies that are adopted (see below) depend in large part on whether the imbalances are daily, weekly, seasonal or long term in nature.

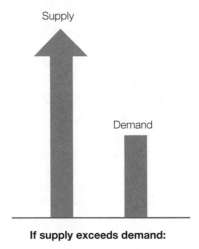

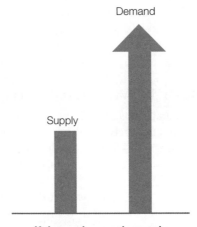

If supply exceeds demand:

- Increase demand
- Reduce supply
- Redistribute supply.

If demand exceeds supply:

- Reduce demand
- Increase supply
- Redistribute demand.

FIGURE 7.2 Supply/demand imbalances and appropriate strategies

If supply exceeds demand: increase demand

The assumptions underlying this strategy are that either the total demand is below capacity or the demand is low only at certain times. Potentially, demand can be increased through a number of strategies.

Product modification or diversification is illustrated by attempts since the mid-1990s to incorporate the rainforests and farms of the Gold Coast's exurban hinterland into that destination's tourism product. To prevent supply from exceeding demand, during the 1990s many casinos in Las Vegas developed 'family-friendly' attractions and ambience to diversify their client base beyond hardcore gamblers, but then returned to an edgier approach with the slogan 'What happens in Vegas stays in Vegas' when growth in the family market slowed. Another strategy is the *alteration or strengthening of distribution channels*, as when a small bed and breakfast operation is linked with a large tour operator through its membership in a bed and breakfast consortium. Attempts since the early 2000s to attract Middle Eastern tourists to the Gold Coast, and to encourage domestic tourism within Australia, indicate the *identification of new or alternative sources of demand*, without necessarily modifying the existing product. *Pricing discounts*, such as those provided by wotif.com (see preceding section), and *redesigned promotional campaigns* that focus more effectively on the existing product and market mix are other options.

Reduce supply

This strategy assumes that it is not possible or desirable to increase demand in any substantial way, and that it is desirable or essential to reduce costs. Supply can be reduced in hotels by closing individual rooms or wings, or by closing the entire hotel in the low season as an extreme measure to reduce fixed and variable costs. This strategy is commonly adopted in the Caribbean at the level of individual operations. Airlines react in a similar fashion by putting certain aircraft out of service, leasing these out to other companies, or cancelling flights.

Redistribute supply

Redistribution or restructuring of supply is necessary when the existing product is no longer suited to the demand it was originally intended to satisfy. In the case of a hotel, rooms can be modified to better reflect contemporary demand. This could involve the conversion of two rooms into an executive suite, the conversion of some rooms into 'courtesy suites' (used only during the day for showers and resting) and the provision of non-smoking rooms. The conversion of hotel rooms into timeshare units is an illustration of a long-term adaptive strategy in the accommodation sector. Theme parks usually introduce new rides or renovate old rides periodically to sustain demand, while the conversion of scheduled flights to charter flights in the airline industry is another example of adaptive supply redistribution.

If demand exceeds supply: reduce demand

Where demand for a product exceeds its capacity, tourism product managers can raise the price of a seat or room, thereby reducing demand while obtaining additional revenue per unit. A similar demand reduction strategy is to increase entrance fees in national parks that are being negatively impacted by excessive visitation levels (see chapter 9). Another option often applied to protected areas and other natural or cultural sites but seldom to countries or municipalities is a formal quota on the number of visitors allowed per day, month, season or year. Some destination managers may also take the controversial move of proactively discouraging visits from some or all tourists on a temporary or permanent basis (see Contemporary issue: Reducing demand by demarketing).

Increase supply

As an alternative to induced demand reduction, managers can accommodate higher demand levels by expanding current capacity. Many 3S resort communities respond effectively to short-term demand fluctuations by making their patrolled beaches available on the basis of daily or weekly patterns of demand. A hotel can build an additional wing, acquire new facilities or utilise external facilities on a temporary basis. To increase bed capacity in a single room, cots and convertible sofas are often provided. Primitive hut-type accommodations, such as the *bures* provided by some Fijian hotels, have the great advantage of being highly attractive to 3S tourists. However, at the same time, they can be erected and disassembled rapidly depending on seasonal fluctuations.

contemporary issue

REDUCING DEMAND BY DEMARKETING

Demarketing in a tourism context is the process of discouraging all or certain tourists from visiting a particular destination (Beeton & Benfield 2002). **General demarketing** occurs when all visitors are temporarily discouraged from visiting a location, usually due to perceived carrying capacity problems. A notable example is Venice, where intensive summer crowding occasionally prompts local authorities to run ads depicting unpleasant scenes of litter, polluted water, dead pigeons and the like. The assumption is that the brand image of Venice is so strong that such imagery will not cause any permanent damage to the tourism industry. Most other destinations, however, do not have such a robust brand and hence are generally reluctant to countermand brand-building efforts with demarketing.

Selective demarketing is a far more prevalent strategy which focuses on permanently discouraging particular market segments perceived to be inherently problematic or incompatible with the destination. South-East Asian countries such as Thailand and Cambodia, for example, use explicit language to dissuade visits from sex tourists, while authorities on the European continent warn British football hooligans that they will be intercepted and deported at the border. More problematic is the city of Fort Lauderdale, Florida, which more politely suggests that students wishing to have a satisfying spring break experience should consider alternative destinations such as Daytona Beach. This accords with Fort Lauderdale's efforts to rebrand itself as an upscale destination catering to older adults. Similarly, Maroochy Shire Council on the Sunshine Coast is trying to discourage the presence of schoolies, who it believes are incompatible with the family friendly image it is trying to convey (*The Sydney Morning Herald* 2007). Selective demarketing can be more subtle, as when promotional emphasis on a certain aspect of the destination, such as its appeal to the wealthy or families, conveys an implicit message that mass tourists or students are unwelcome. This may be employed by destinations hoping to dissuade certain segments without inviting discrimination lawsuits or boycotts. All types of demarketing, therefore, are strategic alternatives within the marketing mix that should be employed only after the utmost consideration of their social and economic consequences.

A similar principle applies to the tent-like structures available commercially from the US-based company Pacific Yurts (yurts.com), which are patterned after the traditional Mongolian nomad tent, the yurt. These inexpensive and lightweight structures can be erected or disassembled in less than a day (as demand permits) and have a minimal environmental impact, yet they provide a roomy and comfortable experience for guests (see figures 7.3 and 7.4) (Grossman 2002). As with bures, they are an effective means of meeting the problem of high fixed costs associated with 'permanent' facilities.

FIGURE 7.3 A Pacific Yurt in a natural setting

Source: © 2009 Pacific Yurts Inc., Cottage Grove, Oregon USA

FIGURE 7.4 An optional interior for a Pacific Yurt

Source: © 2009 Pacific Yurts Inc., Cottage Grove, Oregon USA

Redistribute demand

This strategy works by transferring demand from times of excess use to times of low demand. The differential seasonal price structure in many Caribbean resorts, for example, is an attempt to redistribute demand from the high-demand winter period to the low-demand summer season. At the weekly scale, many attractions attempt to divert traffic from the busy weekend period to the rest of the week by offering weekday discounts on entrance fees and other prices.

■ MARKET FAILURE

Tourism is an industry where **market failure** occurs frequently. Mainstream economic theory suggests that market demand and product supply will attain equilibrium in the long term. Companies that identify a need for promotion to fill their hotel rooms or aeroplane seats, therefore, will spend the necessary funds on that promotion. In return, they will benefit financially from their investment when the anticipated increase in demand materialises. In destination marketing, however, the case is not so straightforward. It is widely recognised that tourists usually decide first on a particular destination, and then select specific tourism products (e.g. accommodation) within that destination. However, specific tourism operators are rarely willing to invest money in destination promotion, since this type of investment will provide benefits to their competitors as well as to themselves. Hence, the situation arises where financial investment is required for destination promotion to achieve demand/supply equilibrium but operators are unwilling to contribute since the returns do not accrue directly to the individual companies. The market therefore does not function as it should in taking action to attain supply and demand equilibrium.

Destination tourism organisations

Destination promotion, as a result, is normally the responsibility of **destination tourism organisations (DTOs)** established as government or quasi-governmental agencies at the national, regional, state or municipal level. This is a role that serves to reinforce the importance of destination governments within the overall tourism system. Historically, such bodies have been funded from general tax revenues, and therefore individual tourism operators receive direct benefits from destination promotion that the wider community (including the tourism businesses) has funded. However, this public funding is usually justified by the tax revenues, jobs and other economic benefits that trickle down from prosperous tourism businesses to the broader community (see chapter 8).

Market failure has implications not only for destination promotion and marketing but also applies to the provision of infrastructure (i.e. the roads and airports that benefit businesses but are also funded through general tax revenues), specific tourism facilities (e.g. convention centres) and tourism research. However, in the present context of tourism marketing it is the area of promotion and those related activities that are particularly relevant. The following subsections will therefore discuss some of the marketing functions that are usually performed by DTOs such as Tourism Australia (www.tourism.australia.com),Tourism Queensland (www.tq.com.au) and Gold Coast Tourism (www.goldcoasttourism.com.au), depending on mandate and level of available funding.

Marketing functions of destination tourism organisations

Historically, the principal marketing role of DTOs has been promotional. However, despite widespread funding reductions, this is changing as the contemporary international tourism industry becomes more competitive and complex, and tourists become increasingly sophisticated in their destination choice behaviour. Progressive elements within the tourism industry, accordingly, recognise the importance of collaboration between the public and private sector in implementing effective marketing strategies (Formica & Littlefield 2000).

The following sections describe the array of activities that ideally are carried out by a well-funded and collaborative destination tourism organisation.

Promotion

Advertising directed at key market segments is a core activity and is often focused on fostering **destination branding**, or efforts to build a positive destination image that represents that destination to certain desired markets (Blain, Levy & Ritchie 2005) (see the case study at the end of this chapter). The extremely successful '100% Pure New Zealand' campaign, for example, employs the common logo and slogan but different activities and images in the key inbound markets of Australia, Japan, the United States, the United Kingdom, Germany and Singapore. To expedite these campaigns, larger DTOs often maintain offices in the major cities of key market countries. Related activities include participation in domestic and international tourism trade shows, the organisation of familiarisation tours for media and industry mediators, handling media inquiries and coordinating press releases. Destination tourism organisations also produce and distribute or coordinate the production and distribution of promotional material and work to promote a favourable destination image in key origin regions. Some organisations engage in joint promotion with other jurisdictions.

Research

Research, or the informed acquisition of strategic knowledge (see chapter 12), is an increasingly important activity pursued by destination tourism organisations. This can focus on visitation trends and forecasting, identification of key market segments and their expenditure and activity patterns, perceptions of visitor satisfaction and effectiveness of prior or current promotional campaigns. If resources are available, these bodies may also try to identify the key threats and opportunities presented by external environments.

Coordination of the tourism industry

Although the tourism industry and its constituent subsectors maintain their own representative bodies, destination tourism organisations often provide support to new and existing tourism businesses, advise on their product development and otherwise assist in educating and encouraging the industry. They may also function as a lobby group to represent the interests of their constituents in relevant political arenas.

Information for tourists

This function is distinct from promotion in its emphasis on providing basic information to tourists who are already in the destination through tourist information centres at key destination sites and gateways. Related functions are usually informed by and directed towards the overriding strategic objectives of the DTO. In the case of Tourism Australia, a national DTO, the latter include:

- influencing tourists to travel to Australia to see sites as well as to attend events
- influencing visitors to travel as widely as possible throughout Australia
- influencing Australians to travel within Australia
- fostering sustainable tourism within Australia, and
- helping to realise economic benefits for Australia from tourism (Tourism Australia 2005).

Such broad objectives are usually shared and/or developed in conjunction with the **destination tourism authority (DTA)**, which is the government agency (usually a department or office within a department, and sometimes the same agency as the DTO) that is responsible for broad tourism policy and planning.

National DTOs are normally mandated to promote the country as a whole, which can generate conflict with states or provinces that perceive an imbalance in coverage with respect to their own jurisdiction. For example, South Australia and Western Australia might complain that Tourism Australia places too much emphasis on iconic attractions such as the Sydney Opera House, the Great Barrier Reef and Uluru, thereby reinforcing the tendency of inbound tourism to concentrate at these locations. While DTOs are sympathetic with such concerns and do try to integrate less frequented locations into their publicity and strategic planning (see the mandate of Tourism Australia above), the presentation of icons serves to reinforce distinctive and positive images that are pivotal for inducing potential tourists to favour Australia over its competitors. One way that DTOs can compromise between the more popular and less-known internal destinations is to portray generic lifestyles and landscapes that do not evoke specific places. Frequently, these images are varied to target particular markets identified by segmentation research.

■ STRATEGIC TOURISM MARKETING

Whether undertaken by an DTO and/or a DTA for a country destination, or by a business just for itself, effective tourism marketing must take into account the basic mission statement of the organisation, and both the internal and external environment of the destination or company (see figure 7.5). The mission statement is usually some very basic directive that influences any further statement of objectives or goals. For example, a DTO's mission statement usually espouses a viable and expanding tourism industry as a means of improving the quality of life for the broad local community. A business, in contrast, may have a mission of offering the highest quality products within a particular sector.

SWOT analysis and objectives

SWOT analysis (strengths, weaknesses, opportunities, threats) is a popular and proven method for facilitating **strategic marketing** and management. The strengths and weaknesses component refers to the internal environment of the destination or business, while opportunities and threats are factors associated with the external environment.

The external environment includes not only elements of the general environment (i.e. the external technological, political, social, cultural and physical environments of tourism systems, as discussed in chapters 2, 3 and 4), but also an analysis of competing destinations or businesses. Key questions when examining the external environment include the following:

- Who are the competitors? (For example, New Zealand is a competitor with Australia.)
- What strategies are being employed by these competitors?

- What are *their* strengths and weaknesses?
- Who are their customers, and why do they purchase their products?
- What are their resources?
- What nontourism external environments are affecting or are going to affect us? How much can we influence these environments?

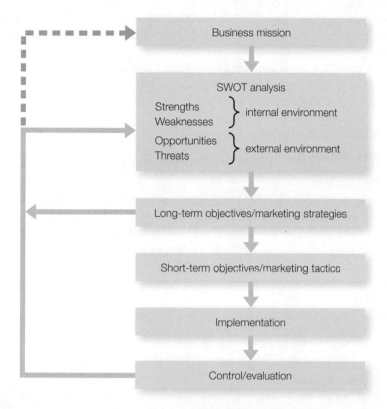

FIGURE 7.5 Strategic tourism marketing

Questions that are pertinent to the internal environment of the destination or company include the following:

- What is the current level of visitation or patronage, and how does this compare with past trends?
- What products are actually and potentially available?
- Who are the customers, and how are they segmented?
- What are the activities and behaviour of the customers?
- How satisfied are customers with the available products?
- What are the reasons for these satisfaction levels?
- How effective are current destination branding efforts?
- What are the available financial and human resources?

Objectives

A SWOT analysis assists in the identification of long-term objectives for the company or destination. Such horizons may extend to the next ten or 15 years, but are usually not less than five years. Given the complex and unpredictable nature of the factors that will influence tourism over that timeframe, it is not sensible to stipulate specific long-term objectives. Rather, the objectives should reflect characteristics that are likely to remain desirable in ten or 15 years whatever else transpires. Relevant long-term objectives for a destination might include:

• increase the average length of stay
• increase average visitor expenditures per day
• increase the proportion of inputs (e.g. food, labour) that are obtained from the local region
• achieve a more dispersed distribution of the tourism sector
• diversify the market base to reduce dependence on the primary markets
• ensure that tourism development occurs in an environmentally and socioculturally sustainable way.

Given a different set of priorities, the long-term objectives for a company are likely to be very different to those identified by destination managers — for example, to be the most highly capitalised company and to capture the largest share of consumer dollar in the sector.

Based on the broad and deliberately vague objectives and goals that are formulated for this extended timeframe, more specific short-term goals and marketing tactics should be established that have a horizon of six months to three years, depending on feasibility. Short-term goals that parallel the long-term objectives noted above might include:

• increase the average length of stay from 2.6 days to 3.2 days within the next two years
• increase average expenditures from $100 to $150 per day over the next two years
• initiate legislation within the next year that requires hotels to obtain at least one-half of their food inputs from local suppliers
• increase the promotional budget for regional tourism attractions by 10 per cent in the next financial year
• open three new tourist offices in large but nontraditional markets over the next three years
• limit the increase in annual arrivals to 5 per cent a year over the next two years.

Control/evaluation

These precise figures and target dates inform the implementation process, and allow for a performance evaluation — have they been achieved or not? The control/evaluation process provides feedback for further SWOT analyses, which reassess the internal and external environmental factors that have helped or hindered the attainment of the objectives. This in turn may lead to a reassessment of the long-term and short-term objectives, as well as associated marketing strategies and tactics.

Strategic marketing recognises that a tourist destination or company does not exist in a vacuum. Such entities are just one component in complex tourism systems that are in turn affected by a myriad of factors generated in environments that are external to those systems. It also recognises that the managers of successful destinations, however success is defined, must have a vision for the future, an awareness of the strategies that are required to achieve success and the will and means to carry out those strategies. Only with long-term thinking will destinations and businesses minimise negative impacts and attain a sustainable tourism sector (as discussed in the next four chapters).

■ MARKETING MIX

The critical components that determine the demand for a business or destination product are collectively known as the **marketing mix**. Several different marketing mix structures have been proposed, a popular one being the **8P model** (Morrison 2009), which includes the following:

- place
- people
- packaging
- promotion
- product
- price
- programming
- partnerships.

All these components need to come together in a mutually reinforcing way to achieve maximum effectiveness. In many respects the marketing mix factors discussed below overlap with the pull factors that were considered in chapter 4. One major difference is that the 8P model reconfigures those factors in a way that facilitates marketing and promotional efforts. That is, they are conceptualised as factors that can be marketed and managed to the greatest possible extent. In addition, the marketing mix is applicable to individual companies as well as destinations.

Place

As indicated in chapter 4, place is essential because tourists must travel to the destination in order to consume the tourist product. Relative location (proximity to actual and potential markets and competitors) is a critical element of place, as is coverage (the other places that are identified or not identified as target markets for marketing and promotional efforts). Australia, for example, maintains a highly visible presence in East Asia, New Zealand, western Europe and North America, but places a low priority on emerging markets in Africa, eastern Europe and Latin America. The Middle Eastern market is moving from the latter to the former category. Accessibility represents the extent to which the markets and destinations are connected, and this too must be taken into account in marketing strategies. Essentially, these three elements encompass the three geographical elements of tourism systems, as discussed in chapter 2 — destination regions, origin regions and transit regions.

An increasingly important concept in the marketing mix is sense of place (see chapter 5), which brands the destination as a unique product offered nowhere else, thereby enhancing its competitive advantage by positioning it at the 'unique' pole of the scarcity continuum. This strategy, moreover, has important implications for a destination's environmental and sociocultural sustainability, because it counteracts the tendency towards uniformity and community alienation that characterises many destinations as they become more developed (see chapters 9 to 11) (Walsh, Jamrozy & Burr 2001).

Product

The product component encompasses the range of available goods and services, their quality and warranty and aftersales service. 'Range' is a measure of diversification, and can be illustrated by a tour operator that offers a broad array of opportunities, as opposed to a niche operator. Similarly, a destination may provide a large number of diverse attractions, or just one specific attraction. The concepts of quality and warranty must be approached differently when comparing a destination with a specific operator. In the case of a specific operator, the manager of the business exercises considerable control in ensuring that the customer receives certain specific services in a satisfactory way, and that some kind of restitution is available if the customer is unsatisfied. In a destination, however, there is relatively little that the manager can do about litter-strewn streets, unfriendly residents and the persistence of rainy weather during a tourist's entire visit. This is because much of the 'product' consists of generic, public goods over which the tourism manager has minimal control and no scope or direct obligation to provide any warranties for unsatisfactory quality. Similarly, the notion of aftersales service is difficult to apply to tourism services or destinations, and is mainly restricted to determining tourists' post-trip attitudes about their tourism experience.

People

People enter the marketing mix equation in at least three ways:
• service personnel
• the tourists themselves
• local residents.

The service personnel issue was considered earlier under the topics of inseparability and variability, which demonstrated the critical role of highly trained employees at the consumer/product interface. The importance of fostering tourist sensitivity and aware-ness was also stressed, since inappropriate tourist behaviour can reduce the quality of the product for all participants. For many destinations, the local residents also fall into the category of product, since tourists may be attracted by the culture and hospitality of the resident population. Again, tourism managers can attempt to control public behaviour towards tourists through education programs, but there is very little that can be done in the way of quality control if some local residents maintain a hostile attitude, unless this is expressed in unlawful activities.

It has been argued that the treatment of residents as a mere element of 'product' that can be manipulated for the benefit of the tourism industry and tourists is an approach that breeds hostility and resentment within the local community. As a result, a community-based approach to tourism management and planning, which gives first priority to the needs and wants of residents and acknowledges their lead role as deci-sion makers, has become more popular (Singh, Timothy & Dowling 2003). High-level input from the community is, moreover, more conducive to the development and presentation of a product that effectively conveys the destination's sense of place.

Database marketing

The incorporation of the 'people' component in the marketing mix (and the tourist component in particular) has been greatly assisted by the emergence of **database marketing**, which can be defined as a comprehensive computer-driven marketing approach that is based on a memory of prior business transactions with customers. It involves the continuous collection, accumulation and analysis of data on customer behaviour and characteristics as a means of informing market segmentation and sub-sequent marketing decisions (Law 2005). As such, it exemplifies the holistic, two-way model of marketing advocated in this chapter.

Database marketing makes feasible the identification and targeting of particularly small niche markets as well as 'markets of one' (see chapter 6). In addition, increas-ingly sophisticated technologies are constantly improving their effectiveness for iden-tifying customers who are most likely to continue patronising the tourism business or destination (i.e. high-loyalty customers), and those who are likely to provide the most business (see Technology and tourism: The case for object-oriented database marketing). This latter point recognises the marketing adage that 20 per cent of a company's customer base accounts for 80 per cent of its business (Alford 1999). In the tourism industry, database marketing is exemplified in loyalty schemes such as airline frequent flyer and hotel frequent user programs, which involve the compilation of sophisticated databases on a large array of consumer variables. The utility of these variables in dealing with the special challenges of services marketing is illustrated by a situation where a hotel's database shows that a customer requested several packages of macadamia nuts during a previous stay, prompting the hotel to provide extra macadamia nuts in the room of that customer prior to their next visit. This is pleasing and personalised service that fosters continued high loyalty.

technology and tourism

THE CASE FOR OBJECT-ORIENTED DATABASE MARKETING

Most databases used in the hotel sector are relational, consisting of multiple files each focused on a specific trait such as room type, customer, or mode of payment. Storage and representation of data in relational databases are not difficult to achieve, but access and retrieval are technical issues that may be problematic when managers attempt to identify patterns amongst the different types of information on file. To overcome these problems, object-oriented database marketing (OODM) is recommended by Law (2005). An OODM schemata consists of Rating and Decision fields for each customer and an 'object' for each of these fields. Objects are packages of data and computational methods that allow those data to be manipulated. For example, in deciding whether a promotional email message about a niche product should be sent to past customer John Smith, the Rating object for John Smith is activated and a rating returned. This rating object contains known data about John Smith's past experiences with the hotel and, perhaps, other hotels if that information is also collected. The Decision object contains a preset threshold related to the niche product, and this is then evoked to see whether the Rating object is higher or lower; if the Rating object is positive (i.e. higher than the Decision object), then it is appropriate to send the email message to John Smith.

The use of encapsulation, or hiding the technical details, allows managers to focus on the problem at hand without having to cope with complex databases and their manipulation. More generally, OODM better allows hotel managers to target the customers who are most likely to respond positively to a particular offer. However, Law (2005) cautions that hotels in East Asia are still rudimentary in their use of relational databases and hence risk losing competitive advantage to hotels in other regions where database marketing, including OODM, is more established.

Price

Price is a critical marketing mix element, since affordability constitutes an important pull factor in drawing tourists to particular destinations. Airlines, attractions and hotels commonly reduce their prices until a desirable level of occupancy is achieved (i.e. a strategy of increasing the demand), given the profit implications of empty seats or rooms for products that have high fixed costs (see figure 7.1). However, the relationship between reduced price and increased patronage is not entirely straightforward, as many consumers perceive price as an indicator of quality — if the price is too low, this might indicate a poor-quality product. For this reason, reduced price may dissuade wealthier travellers who can afford higher prices, and may convey a lasting image of poor quality. Permanent or temporary discounts, nevertheless, are often used to target specific groups who are sensitive to high prices, including older adults, families and students.

Given the importance of price in a high fixed cost environment, it is important for tourism managers to be aware of the pricing techniques that can be employed by businesses. The emphasis here is on companies, since the cost of a destination is based on the cumulative pricing decisions of the businesses and operations, public and private, that function within that destination. Destination managers might possibly influence those prices through tax concessions, grants, regulations and other means, but cannot by themselves determine the pricing structure. The pricing techniques can be separated into four main and largely self-explanatory categories as follows.

Profit-oriented pricing

Pricing techniques that are oriented towards profit include typical approaches such as the maximisation of profits and the attainment of satisfactory profits (however these might be defined) and target return on investment. Such strategies do not place the priority on what the competition is doing.

Sales-oriented pricing

There are many varieties of pricing techniques that focus on consumer sales. These include basing the strategy on the prices that the market, or some target segment thereof, is willing to pay for a product, maximising the volume of sales, increasing market share through (for example) aggressive promotion and reduced prices, gaining market penetration through low initial entry prices, and maintaining high prices as a signal of outstanding quality (prestige pricing).

Competition-oriented pricing

The emphasis here is on competitor behaviour as the major criterion for setting prices. This reactive approach can involve the matching of a competitor's prices, or the maintenance of price differentials at a level above or below the competitor's prices, depending on the type of market that is being targeted.

Cost-oriented pricing

These strategies base pricing structures on the actual cost of providing the goods or services. First, costs are established, and then an appropriate profit margin is added. This margin can be either a fixed sum (e.g. $50 per ticket) or a relative amount (e.g. 10 per cent profit per ticket). It is a common practice in cost-oriented pricing to calculate break-even points — that is, combinations of price and occupancy where revenues and costs are equal (e.g. $100 per room at 84 per cent occupancy, or $120 per room at 70 per cent occupancy). Any incremental increase in occupancy above the break-even point represents a profit margin.

Packaging

Packaging refers to the deliberate grouping together of two or more elements of the tourism experience into a single product. This is best illustrated in the private sector by the provision of set-price package tours that integrate transportation, accommodation, visits to attractions and other complementary tourism components (see chapter 5). For destinations, the packaging element can be more ambiguous and informal, involving attempts by NTOs or subnational tourism organisations to market the destination as an integrated 'package' of attractions, activities, relevant services and other tourism-related opportunities. For Australia's Gold Coast, the 'Green Behind the

Gold' campaign in the 1990s was an explicit attempt to package the rainforest experience with the beach experience.

According to Morrison (2009), packaging is popular because it provides greater convenience and economy for customers, allows them to budget more easily, and eliminates the time required to assemble the constituent items individually. From an operator perspective, packages can stimulate demand in off-season periods (e.g. 'summer special packages'), attract new customers, encourage the establishment of partnerships with operators offering the complementary services and make business planning easier (in part because packages are often paid for well in advance of the experience).

Programming

Programming is closely related to packaging in that it involves the addition of special events, activities or programs to a product to make it more diverse and appealing (Morrison 2009). Examples include the inclusion of scuba diving lessons or academic lectures on a cruise, 'chance' encounters with historical impersonators at a heritage theme park, broadcasting live rugby matches at a sports bar and the periodic announcement of prizewinners at a convention. For the theme park or sports bar (or, potentially, the destination), such program add-ons allow the operator to alter their product package frequently and inexpensively without having to undertake risky and costly actions such as introducing new rides or menus. Moreover, the programs could be altered to draw specific market segments (e.g. broadcasting women's hockey to attract young adult females).

Promotion

As indicated earlier, many people see promotion as being synonymous with marketing. Promotion attempts to increase demand by conveying a positive image of the product to potential customers through appeals to the perceived demands, needs, tastes, values and attitudes of the market or a particular target market segment (see the case study at the end of this chapter).

Promotion consists of:
- presentation
- personal selling
- sales promotion
- publicity
- merchandising
- advertising.

Presentation can include the provision of uniformed and well-groomed staff and an attractive physical environment, which give potential customers a favourable impression of the company. Personal selling entails a direct approach to a particular client, usually a large corporation whose potential patronage justifies the added costs of this individual approach. Sales promotions are short-term strategies that promote a product through temporary discounts (e.g. special discount of 80 per cent off a product for one day only in order to increase exposure to consumers).

Publicity

Publicity can occur through press releases and is one of the least expensive means of promotion, and one that can be readily used by destination managers. Even better is coverage by way of a *National Geographic* magazine article or television special accessed by millions of consumers. However, there is a higher risk in such unsolicited media coverage that the publicity, and resulting product image, will be negative, one example being the media presentation of Thailand following the 2004 Indian Ocean tsunami.

This forces the destination or company to engage in damage control by releasing its own counterbalancing publicity.

Merchandising

Merchandising can be used very effectively as a promotional tool when it involves the sale of products that are readily associated with a particular company or destination (Doyle 2004). This might involve items of clothing on which a resort or tour operator's logo is prominently displayed, or furnishings used in a hotel room (see the Managing tourism feature earlier in this chapter). There are several advantages associated with well-formulated merchandising strategies:
- First, unlike other forms of promotion, merchandising also generates direct income, and all the more so since logo products often sell at a premium.
- Second, since such products are usually purchased as souvenirs, they tend to be prominently displayed as status symbols back in the origin region, thereby maximising exposure to potential customers.
- Third, it is commonly the more frequently worn items of clothing, such as baseball caps and T-shirts, that are merchandised, and therefore the purchasers of these products are likely to spend more time acting as walking billboards for the company or destination.

Hard Rock Café illustrates the effective application of merchandising to the tourism sector. More of the company's revenue is generated from the sale of Hard Rock Café-branded merchandise than from food and beverages. The range of available items has expanded from simple but enormously popular T-shirts to lapel pins, teddy bears and beer glasses. Because of their desirability as collectables, many consumers purchase two items — one for display as a status symbol (e.g. a T-shirt or key chain) and one preserved in mint condition for its future resale value. More ingeniously, names of individual locations (e.g. Surfers Paradise, Las Vegas) are included on certain items of merchandise, making each a discrete collectable and prompting dedicated collectors to accumulate specimens from all Hard Rock Cafés worldwide (see figure 7.6).

FIGURE 7.6 Hard Rock Café souvenirs

Advertising

Advertising is the most common form of promotion, and constitutes a major topic of investigation and management in its own right (see for example Morgan & Pritchard 2000). An important distinction in advertising can be made between a 'shotgun approach' and a 'rifle approach'. In **shotgun marketing**, an advertisement is placed in a mainstream media source that is accessed by a broad cross-section of the tourist market. As with a shotgun, much of the delivery will miss the target audience altogether (unless the market is an inclusive one, as in the case of a Disney theme park), but the high level of saturation will ensure that the target audience will also be reached. For example, an advertisement for a backpacker hotel in *Time* magazine will be ignored by most readers, but will almost certainly reach a large number of backpackers who read this magazine. Shotgun marketing also attracts new recruits to the product, that is, non-backpackers whose interest is aroused by the advertisement. The high costs associated with the mainstream media, however, are a major drawback to this approach.

In contrast, **rifle marketing** occurs when the advertisement is directed specifi- cally to the target market, like a single bullet fired from a rifle. This would occur if the above-mentioned hotel advertisement were placed in a backpackers' magazine or posted on the discussion group site of a specialty organisation. Its major disadvantages are the lack of product exposure to the broader tourist market and competition with the advertisers of similar products. Beyond the shotgun/rifle dichotomy, a major deci- sion in advertising and public relations dissemination is the selection of a media type that will best convey the desired message to the target market. Major media outlets are discussed below, except for travel guides, which were discussed in chapter 5.

Television

The attraction of television as a media outlet is based in part on its ubiquity and frequency of consumer use, even within less affluent societies. Moreover, television is more effective than any other contemporary mainstream media in conveying an animated, realistic image of a product. To be cost-effective (since television adver- tising time is relatively expensive), television-oriented advertisements must capture the viewer's attention quickly (else the viewer may leave to visit the kitchen or toilet) and convey the message within a short period of time (e.g. 30 seconds). Also, they should be timed to optimise exposure to the target audience. For example, it is a wasted effort to target young children during the late evening hours. Similarly, it is critical to match the product with the program. Highly educated viewers, for example, are more likely to watch news programs or documentaries.

Internet

The internet is emerging as a mainstream media outlet that will eventually rival or even exceed television or newspapers and magazines. Its creative use as a promotional tool and distribution channel is illustrated by the rapid development of **webcasting** technologies, which deliver interactive multimedia (video and audio) in real time. Configured effectively, webcasting can help to overcome the intangibility dilemma dis- cussed earlier (see page 183). Another innovative marketing application involves the facilitated provision and delivery of postcards over the internet as **e-postcards**. Given the rapid development of such technological innovations, it is not surprising that the internet is growing in popularity as a means of accessing information about poten- tial destinations and other tourism-related goods and services (see Technology and tourism: Spreading the word digitally through eWOM).

An extremely important characteristic of the internet is its democratising effects. That is, almost anyone can develop and update a website due to their low cost and technical simplicity, which means that even the smallest operator or destination can obtain the same potential exposure as any large corporation. Similarly, internet features such as blogs and chat rooms allow almost anyone to expose their opinions to a potentially large audience. In both senses, the internet is therefore instrumental in leveling the promotional 'playing field' (see Breakthrough tourism: Spreading the word digitally through eWOM).

Radio

As a media outlet, radio has long been overtaken by television, but it is still important in Phase Two and Three societies as a promotional device. In Phase Four societies radio remains important as a source of information during work time, either through advertisements or through the pronunciations of popular talk show hosts. From 9 am to 5 pm radio may reach as many potential customers as television. Although less expensive than television, a major disadvantage of radio is the inability to convey visual information. Effective auditory stimuli, however, can evoke desirable and attractive mental images.

breakthrough tourism

SPREADING THE WORD DIGITALLY THROUGH EWOM

The internet has made possible electronic word-of-mouth communication (eWOM), which can be defined as all informal communication about goods and services directed to potential consumers through the internet and other electronic media (Litvin, Goldsmith & Pan 2008). eWOM is a diverse phenomenon, ranging from 'synchronous' one-to-one instant messaging and email to 'asynchronous' one-to-many websites as well as many-to-many blogs and virtual communities. In contrast to traditional word-of-mouth, blogs in particular allow the exact same message to be received by a potentially large number of people over a short period of time. However, unlike other forms of mass media, almost anyone can participate. For marketers, eWOM has the added quality of continuing to exist in online space, thereby allowing information to be analysed to inform product development and promotional strategies, and to continuously monitor changing perceptions of brand and product reputation. However, because such communication tends to involve those with strongly positive or negative experiences with a product, the resulting information must be treated as indicative rather than representative.

Such knowledge can also influence a business's participation in eWOM, for example to counter the dissemination of malicious or inaccurate content, or to encourage the output of positive feedback from satisfied customers. These practices, however, entail ethical concerns that involve 'stealth marketing', an example being the use of employees to pose as satisfied customers of the company or as unsatisfied customers of a rival company's products. Web technologies make such deception virtually undetectable, and even reputable companies may be tempted to participate if they believe that they are the target of such activity (Litvin, Goldsmith & Pan 2008). Also controversial is the use of email and instant messaging to instantaneously deliver promotional messages to large numbers of recipients at minimal cost, which can lead to a junk mail reputation. Within marketing spheres, website design is a rapidly developing area of interest given the potential of web pages to stimulate positive eWOM among site visitors if designed effectively to provide convenient access to desirable blogs and virtual communities.

Newspapers and magazines

Newspapers and magazines have the advantage of containing messages that can be accessed at any time, and may persist for many years in the form of accumulated or circulating copies. However, this also means that the advertisement becomes obsolete as prices increase and the product is modified. In addition, the images are static and the quality of reproduction can be quite crude in newspapers, even when colour is used. Print media also assumes a literate market, which is a serious impediment in Phase Two and some Phase Three societies. An added complication in highly literate countries is the abundance of newspaper and magazine options, which requires marketers to conduct extensive research in order to identify the most effective target outlets. An estimated 4500 magazine titles are available in Australia alone, and 90 per cent of all such sales occurring through retail outlets rather than subscription makes it difficult to predict the readership of any particular issue (Magazine Publishers of Australia 2005).

Brochures

Tourism brochures are perhaps the most utilised form of promotion across the tourism industry and within destinations, and are an important means through which package tours and products within particular destinations are selected. A characteristic that distinguishes brochures from television or other printed media is their specialised nature — they are not provided as an appendage to a newspaper article or a television program, but concentrate 100 per cent on the promotional effort. Brochures are usually printed in bulk quantities, and made available for distribution through travel agencies, tourism information centres, hotels, attractions and other strategic locations, as well as by mail. Brochures can range in complexity from a simple black-and-white leaflet to a glossy booklet, such as those commonly available from large tour operators.

A way of making brochures more attractive and of minimising their disposal is to include practical information (e.g. safety suggestions, directions) and discount coupons or to treat the brochure itself as a means of gaining discounted entry at qualifying attractions. Nevertheless, research among Swiss consumers indicates that they are preferred by older and less educated consumers rather than the more educated potential visitors sought by many destinations (Laesser 2007).

Partnerships

As illustrated by the formation of airline alliances (see page 137) and credit cards that feature a particular business or organisation (e.g. the Marriott Rewards VISA card), mutual benefits can result when similar or dissimilar businesses embark in cooperative product development and marketing on a temporary or longer-term basis (Fyall & Garrod 2005). These include exposure to new markets, expanded product packages, greater ability to serve customer needs, more efficient use of resources through sharing, image improvement through association with well-regarded brands and access to partners' databases and expertise (Morrison 2009).

Partnerships are especially important for small operations that lack the economies of scale to engage in these efforts efficiently and effectively on their own. For example, vacation farms in certain countries, such as Austria, have formed consortiums of ten or more operators who all benefit from the collective pooling of resources. Another illustration is the UNWTO-sponsored Silk Road marketing campaign in Central Asia, which employs a well-known overriding historical theme to promote tourism in otherwise obscure central Asian countries such as Kyrgyzstan, Turkmenistan, Uzbekistan and Tajikistan (www.unwto.org). Partnerships can also be created between suppliers of products and their customers, as demonstrated by repeat-user programs.

CHAPTER REVIEW

Marketing involves communication and other interactions among the producers and consumers of tourism experiences. The marketing of a service such as tourism differs from goods because of the intangibility, inseparability, variability and perishability of the former. These qualities present challenges to managers and marketers in their attempt to match the supply of tourism products with market demand. For example, intangibility means that the consumer cannot directly experience the product before its consumption, while inseparability implies that production and consumption occur simultaneously, thus limiting the scope for employing quality control mechanisms. Because profit margins in the tourism sector are narrowed by high fixed costs, and because demand varies considerably over a daily, weekly, seasonal and long-term timeframe, managers must be aware of the strategies that can be implemented to foster equilibrium between demand and supply. Depending on the circumstances, these involve the reduction, increase or redistribution of supply or demand.

Conventional macro-economic theory suggests that equilibrium between supply and demand will eventually be achieved, but market failure (i.e. the failure to attain this balance) often occurs in the marketing of 'public goods' such as an entire tourist destination. To compensate for market failure, destination tourism organisations are established (usually by government) to market and promote specific regions, countries, states or municipalities. Whether undertaken by these public authorities or private companies, strategic marketing procedures should be practised in order to achieve optimum outcomes. This includes the use of a SWOT analysis to inform long- and short-term objectives. In strategic marketing, demand can be gauged and manipulated through the use of marketing mix frameworks such as the product-focused 8P model, which takes into account place, product, people, price, packaging, programming, promotion and partnerships.

■ SUMMARY OF KEY TERMS

8P model a product-focused marketing mix model that incorporates place, product, people, price, packaging, programming, promotion and partnerships

Database marketing a comprehensive marketing strategy that is based on a memory of prior business transactions with customers; the use of accumulated customer data to inform marketing decisions

Demarketing the process of discouraging all or certain tourists from visiting a particular destination temporarily or permanently

Destination branding the process of fostering a distinctive and integrated image about a destination that represents that destination to one or more target markets; usually undertaken by a destination tourism organisation

Destination tourism authority (DTA) the government agency responsible for broad tourism policy and planning within a destination entity

Destination tourism organisations (DTOs) publicly funded government agencies that undertake promotion and other forms of marketing; these are distinct from the government departments or bodies, or government tourism authorities, that dictate tourism-related policy

Emotional labour a characteristic of services marketing, involving the expression of the willingness to be of service to customers, as through demonstrations of assurance, responsiveness and empathy

e-postcards virtual postcards that are selected through the internet and sent to recipients by email

Fixed costs costs that the operation has little flexibility to change over the short term, such as interest costs on borrowed funds and basic facility maintenance costs

General demarketing demarketing that is directed towards all tourists, usually temporarily

Inseparability a characteristic of services marketing, where production and consumption of tourist services occur at the same time and place and are thus inseparable

Intangibility a characteristic of services marketing, where the actual tourism service cannot be seen, touched or tried before its purchase and consumption

Market failure the failure of market forces to produce a longer-term equilibrium in supply and demand, such as when individual businesses in the tourism industry are unwilling to provide the funds for destination promotion (to increase demand) because such investment will provide benefits to their competitors as well as to themselves

Marketing mix the critical components that determine the demand for a business or destination product

Marketing the interactions and interrelationships that occur among consumers and producers of goods and services, through which ideas, products, services and values are created and exchanged for the mutual benefit of both groups

Perishability a services marketing characteristic; because production and consumption are simultaneous, services cannot be produced and stored in advance for future consumption (e.g. empty aircraft seats are a permanent loss that cannot be recouped)

Rifle marketing a mode of promotional advertising that is aimed just at the target market

Selective demarketing demarketing that is directed towards a particular tourist segment, usually intended as a permanent measure against groups deemed to be undesirable

Services marketing the marketing of services such as those associated with the tourism industry, as opposed to the marketing of the goods industry

Shotgun marketing a mode of promotional advertising where the message is disseminated to a broad audience on the assumption that this saturation will reach target markets and perhaps attract new recruits

Strategic marketing marketing that takes into consideration an extensive analysis of external and internal environmental factors in identifying strategies that attain specific goals

SWOT analysis an analysis of a company or destination's strengths, weaknesses, opportunities and threats that emerges from an examination of its internal and external environment

Variability a services marketing characteristic, where service encounters, even if they involve a similar kind of experience, are highly variable due to the differences and rapid changes in mood, expectation and other human element factors that affect the participants

Variable costs costs that can be readily reduced in the short term, such as salaries of casual staff

Webcasting the delivery of interactive multimedia to customers through the internet on either an 'on demand' or 'real-time' basis

■ QUESTIONS

1. In what ways does marketing go beyond the simple presentation of advertisements through various forms of media?
2. (a) Why is 'emotional labour' especially important in the tourism industry?
   (b) How can tourism businesses enhance the emotional labour capabilities of front-line employees?
3. Bures and yurts are temporary accommodation types that help to address a hotel's problem of high fixed costs. What are the potential disadvantages associated with their use?
4. (a) What are the risks of using demarketing as a tactic for reducing the demand for a particular destination?
   (b) How can these risks be minimised?
5. How can government and the private sector collaborate to most efficiently and effectively avoid market failure?
6. How should DTOs determine how they proportionally promote locations and products within their jurisdiction?
7. How could a manager prioritise the strengths, weaknesses, opportunities and threats in a SWOT analysis in terms of devising management and marketing strategies?
8. For tourism businesses, what are the opportunities and threats associated with eWOM?
9. What are the relative strengths and weaknesses associated with television and the internet as marketing media?

■ EXERCISES

1. Write a 1000-word report for a DTO of your choice in which you indicate what percentage of its budget should be allocated to promotion, research, coordination and information. Justify these allocations accordingly.
2. (a) Break into four groups with your peers and conduct a SWOT analysis of a particular destination. Each of the four destinations should be located adjacent to one another either at the international scale (e.g. Singapore, Malaysia, Indonesia and Thailand) or at the subnational scale (e.g. Gold Coast, Brisbane, Sunshine Coast and Hervey Bay).
   (b) Show how the other three destinations fit into the SWOT analysis of each destination.
   (c) Indicate ways in which the competition-related threats of these other destinations can be converted into opportunities.
3. List ten critical questions that a destination manager should ask departing tourists in compiling a visitor database that can effectively aid the marketing of that destination.

■ FURTHER READING

Anderson, B., Provis, C. & Chappel, S. 2003. 'The Selection and Training of Workers in the Tourism and Hospitality Industries for the Performance of Emotional Labour'. *Journal of Hospitality and Tourism Management* 10: 1–12. The authors present the concept of emotional labour as a way of compensating for the problem of inseparability in the hospitality industry.

Bowen, J., Makens, J. & Kotler, P. 2005. *Marketing for Hospitality & Tourism*. **Fourth Edition. Upper Saddle River, New Jersey: Prentice Hall.** This is an adaptation of Kotler's classic marketing text for the hospitality and tourism sector. It provides a systematic overview of the issues involved in marketing, although the tourism component is not featured as prominently as the hospitality component.

Fyall, A. & Garrod, B. 2005. 'From Competition to Collaboration in the Tourism Industry'. In Theobald, W. (Ed.) *Global Tourism*. **Third Edition. Sydney: Elsevier, pp. 52–73.** The rationale for collaborative partnerships in the tourism industry, and illustrations of them, are covered in this chapter.

Morgan, N., Pritchard, A. & Pride, R. (Eds) 2004. *Destination Branding: Creating the Unique Destination Proposition*. **Second Edition. Sydney: Elsevier.** Using a mixture of theoretically and practically oriented chapters, this book provides a global perspective on the issue of destination branding, a vital component in the marketing of public tourist places.

Morrison, A. 2009. *Hospitality and Travel Marketing*. **Fourth Edition. Albany, New York: Delmar Publishers.** This is a key textbook in the area of tourism marketing, and one of the few that emphasises a tourism rather than a hospitality perspective. It makes extensive use of systems theory.

Pike, S. 2004. *Destination Marketing Organisations*. **Oxford: Elsevier.** Written by a former destination marketer, this text bridges industry and theory by synthesising a wealth of academic literature of practical value to destination-marketing organisations.

case study

WHAT THE BLOODY HELL IS HAPPENING TO AUSTRALIA'S DESTINATION BRAND?

In February 2006, Tourism Australia, the lead federal tourism marketing body, launched a major new international promotional campaign. The ads began with a series of typical Australians announcing among other things that 'the lights have been turned on' (against a backdrop of the skylighted Sydney Opera House), a spot has been 'saved for you on the beach' (against an idyllic Australian beach scene), and 'we've bought you a cold beer' (against an Outback pub scene). Celebrity Lara Bingle then addresses viewers with the punch line 'so where the bloody hell are you?'

In its launch of the campaign, tourism officials described the preliminary vignettes as compelling scenes of urban and rural Australia that are narrated by friendly Australians, none of whom are professional actors. Viewers are invited in the climatic part of the ad to visit with a uniquely Australian vernacular expression that captures the directness and openness of the national culture, and emphasises the message that viewers want to visit Australia but have been putting if off for too long. Bingle's presence adds the element of celebrity endorsement and recognition to the initiative, which was designated officially as the 'Uniquely Australian Invitation' campaign despite rarely being referred to as such. According to the then-Managing Director of Tourism Australia, the campaign reflected Australia's need to convey an authentic product and to be aggressive and direct if it wants to be heard in the competitive international marketplace. Allegedly, 86 focus groups were conducted to test the ad as part of a research effort involving also segmentation studies, brand tracking, international visitor studies and in-depth interviews costing $6.2 million and involving input from 47 000 international tourist consumers (Tourism Australia 2006a).

Within days of the launch, the campaign attracted controversy when the UK broadcasting authority refused to allow the word 'bloody' to be included in British television ads (Tourism Australia 2006b). The ban was eventually rescinded, and the Managing Director welcomed this as a victory that reinforced earlier publicity generated as a result of the ban. A large number of UK consumers apparently heeded the advice of ads ran in UK newspapers by Tourism Australia to view the uncut version on the wherethebloodyhellareyou.com website. The agency described this as a successful global 'viral campaign' (Tourism Australia 2006c). Encouraged by these initial outcomes, the 'Bloody Hell' campaign was rolled out in full over the next two years in all of Australia's major inbound markets (Tourism Australia 2006d).

While consistently defended by its Tourism Australia sponsors, the 'Bloody Hell' campaign has been condemned by others as unsuccessful. In mid-2008, Tourism Minister Martin Ferguson went as far to describe it as a dismal failure in some markets (Canning 2008), while Prime Minister Kevin Rudd labelled it a 'rolled gold disaster' that failed to benefit the tourism sector (eTurboNews 2008). The fact that the campaign was conducted during the tenure of the federal opposition party must be taken into account when assessing the credibility of such comments. In addition, the relatively poor performance of Australian inbound tourism during the time of the campaign is likely a multifaceted phenomenon that cannot be attributed solely to poor marketing (see the case study at the end of chapter 2).

Yet, critics point out that inbound numbers from the three countries where the ad was especially prominent (UK, Japan and Germany) had all fallen. In the case of the Japanese segment, failure may have resulted in part and ironically from the translation of the key phrase into the insipid question 'so why aren't you coming?' Representatives of church groups in the USA and elsewhere publicly criticised Australia and its use of the 'bloody hell' expression in its promotion as a bad example for children, while some observers were critical of one particular vignette in which an Aboriginal dancer tells viewers that 'we've been rehearsing for 40 000 years', suggesting that Aboriginal culture exists only to please tourists.

Whether the 'Bloody Hell' campaign is seen to merit condemnation or support, it raises questions about Australia's long-term destination branding strategy, which was given an enormous boost in the 1980s by the 'Come and Say G'day' campaign that famously featured celebrity Paul Hogan putting a 'shrimp on the barbie'. Now ensconced in the Smithsonian Museum in Washington DC as an icon of popular American culture, the campaign is credited with positioning and maintaining Australia as the most favourably regarded foreign tourist destination in the USA. Before the campaign, it was rated in the seventy-eighth position (Baker & Bendel 2005). In late 2005, just prior to the release of the 'Bloody Hell' campaign, Australia was similarly rated as the world's number one destination brand in the Anholt GMI Nation Brands Index (nationbrandindex.com).

There is no empirical evidence at the time of writing that the 'Bloody Hell' ads have damaged Australia's international destination brand and hence the desire (if not the ability) of foreign consumers to visit Australia. One outcome of the controversy, however, has been unprecedented critical scrutiny of subsequent promotional campaigns. During 2008 and 2009, Tourism Australia invested heavily in Baz Luhrmann's epic Hollywood movie *Australia* (released in November 2008) as the focal point of major international efforts. Counting on the star-appeal of featured actors Nicole Kidman and Hugh Jackman, the movie supported the $50 million 'See the Movie, See the Country' campaign (Tourism Australia 2008d), although actual movie scenes were not incorporated into federal and state promotional material.

This effort to link movie and destination was perhaps an attempt by Australia to imitate New Zealand's highly successful strategy of linking its destination brand to the hugely popular *Lord of the Rings* trilogy while retaining its iconic '100% Pure' byline (Weaver & Lawton 2006). Critics of the *Australia* strategy were concerned that so much emphasis was being placed on a yet-to-be-released movie which, indeed, did not generate the high levels of popular and critical acclaim that were anticipated. Compounding this lacklustre reception was criticism that the sophisticated and 'artsy' advertisements produced by Luhrmann were not reflective of the 'plain bloke' image so successfully conveyed by the Paul Hogan ads of the 1980s. Tourism Australia has also admitted that it backed the campaign 'site unseen', that is, based on knowledge of the movie's themes rather than the actual script (Canning 2008). Others have questioned the wisdom of using the movie to attract Japanese tourists, given that prominent scenes of the aerial bombing of Darwin by the imperial Japanese air force are included.

QUESTIONS

1. (a) Search online for the Where the Bloody Hell Are you? ad and view it.
   (b) Discuss with your peers any favourable or unfavourable perceptions of the ad, and identify the arguments made for and against it as an effective tool for maintaining Australia's high status tourism brand.
2. (a) Watch the movie *Australia*, and describe how Tourism Australia's current campaign incorporates the film and its contents. (Promotional material can be downloaded from the Tourism Australia website.)
   (b) Do you believe that the campaign is effectively integrated with the film?
   (c) What could Tourism Australia do to more effectively tie the campaign in with the film?

CHAPTER 8

ECONOMIC IMPACTS OF TOURISM

LEARNING OBJECTIVES

After studying this chapter, you should be able to:

1. name the top destination countries in terms of tourism revenue earnings, compare these with the top stayover-receiving countries, and explain any discrepancies

2. outline the main positive and negative economic impacts of tourism and describe how each negative impact acts as a counterpoint to one or more positive impacts

3. explain the concept of the tourism multiplier effect (TME) and describe the circumstances under which a high or low TME is likely to occur

4. describe how tourism can function as a propulsive activity within a growth pole strategy

5. differentiate between the informal and formal sectors and describe their implications for tourism management

6. identify the circumstances under which a destination is more likely to experience negative rather than positive economic impacts from tourism

7. discuss the negative consequences of revenue leakages for a destination and explain where and why they occur

8. explain the fluctuating patterns of demand that characterise tourism and the implications of this for destinations

9. indicate how tourism can maintain a competitive or complementary relationship with agriculture

10. discuss employment-related problems that are associated with tourism.

INTRODUCTION

Marketing, as discussed in chapter 7, is a pervasive process, which includes attempts to attract and retain a client base for individual tourism-related businesses or entire destinations. Once the client–product link is established, however, a range of potential positive and negative impacts is possible and these must be taken into account in the strategic marketing and planning undertaken by destination managers. It is common in the tourism literature to distinguish between economic, sociocultural and environmental impacts. This tendency to use discrete categories, however, should not distract from the fact that impacts are often closely interrelated. For example, negative social reactions to tourism could result from residents' perceptions of accompanying economic and environmental costs. The placement of economic impacts as the first topic of discussion does not imply that these are inherently any more important than the sociocultural or environmental dimension. Rather, this reflects the primary importance that destinations have tended to place on economic benefits as a rationale for pursuing tourism. The structure of this chapter is straightforward, with the following section examining the potential economic benefits of tourism and the final one considering the potential economic costs.

ECONOMIC BENEFITS

When tourism emerged as a significant economic sector in the decades following World War II, most researchers and government administrators assumed its growth to be a positive and desirable process. Conspicuous by its absence through the 1950s and 1960s was any concerted critique of tourism, prompting the description of this period as the era of the advocacy platform (see chapter 1). It is essentially this perspective that is represented below in the discussion of economic benefits.

Direct revenue

The prospect of substantial tourism-derived **direct revenue** has long been the most compelling incentive for destinations to attract and support tourism activity (see Technology and tourism: An Encore performance for festivals and events). Fuelling this incentive is the global tourism revenue reported since 1950. **International tourism receipts** are defined by the UNWTO (WTO 1996) as encompassing all consumption expenditure, or payments for goods and services, made by international tourists (stayovers and excursionists) for their own use or to give away. Due largely to inflationary effects, these receipts have increased at a substantially higher rate than the actual global intake of international stayovers, and exceeded US$850 billion in 2007 (see table 3.1). For that year, 23 countries recorded international tourism receipts that exceeded US$10 billion (see table 8.1).

technology and tourism

AN ENCORE PERFORMANCE FOR FESTIVALS AND EVENTS

The injection of public or private funds into festivals and other tourism-related events is usually justified by evidence of significant financial outcomes resulting from these investments. However, smaller organisations in particular often lack the research capabilities to collect accurate and reliable economic data about their events. This problem has now been addressed through the ongoing development of an economic impact assessment software package — Encore — by the Australian-based Sustainable Tourism Cooperative Research Centre (STCRC) (Jago 2005). Key features of Encore include its user-friendly applications and its diverse and flexible data collection modules, which allow new funds arriving in the region or destination as a result of the event to be calculated. Supporting modules focus on visitor demographics, marketing and visitor satisfaction. These data can be collected simultaneously at multiple on-site locations using personal digital assistants (PDAs), and data can be imported from Excel.

Additional advantages for the small organisation include the relatively low cost of the software (around $450 in 2008) and the minimal training required to collect and analyse data. A potential disadvantage of catering to those who are not formally trained in event evaluation, however, is a higher risk of error from non-representative sampling and incorrect analysis and interpretation of data. Nevertheless, if applied correctly, consistently and widely, Encore will allow organisers to benchmark their festivals against similar events in other locations, and see how their own event performs from year to year. The application of Encore to the 2004 Festival of Darwin identified a mainly local audience and a low level of attendee expenditure in the region. Another identified problem was that only 12 of 28 sponsors could be recalled by at least 10 per cent of the respondents, suggesting problems with sponsor visibility (Tremblay et al. 2006).

TABLE 8.1 World's top tourism earners, 2002 and 2007

Rank		Country	Tourism receipts (US$ billion)		% share of receipts worldwide	
2002	2007		2002	2007	2002	2007
1	1	United States	66.5	96.7	14.0	11.3
2	2	Spain	33.6	57.8	7.1	6.8
3	3	France	32.3	54.2	6.8	6.3
4	4	Italy	26.9	42.7	5.7	5.0
5	5	China	20.4	41.9	4.3	4.9
7	6	United Kingdom	17.6	37.6	3.7	4.4
6	7	Germany	19.2	36.0	4.0	4.2
14	8	Australia	8.1	22.2	1.7	2.6
8	9	Austria	11.2	18.9	2.4	2.2

Rank			Tourism receipts (US$ billion)		% share of receipts worldwide	
2002	2007	Country	2002	2007	2002	2007
12	10	Turkey	9.0	18.5	1.9	2.2
15	11	Thailand	7.9	15.6	1.7	1.8
10	12	Greece	9.7	15.5	2.0	1.8
11	13	Canada	9.7	15.5	2.0	1.8
19	14	Malaysia	6.8	14.0	1.4	1.6
9	15	Hong Kong SAR (China)	10.1	13.8	2.1	1.6
17	16	Netherlands	7.7	13.4	1.6	1.6
13	17	Mexico	8.9	12.9	1.9	1.5
25	18	Sweden	4.5	12.0	0.9	1.4
17	19	Switzerland	7.6	11.8	1.6	1.4
—	20	India	2.9	10.7	0.5	1.3
18	21	Belgium	6.9	10.7	1.5	1.3
24	22	Poland	4.5	10.6	0.9	1.3
20	23	Portugal	5.9	10.1	1.2	1.2
26	24	Macao (China)	4.5	9.8	0.9	1.1
28	25	Russia	4.2	9.6	0.8	1.1
—	26	Japan	3.5	9.3	0.6	1.1
30	27	Egypt	3.8	9.3	0.8	1.1
29	28	Croatia	3.8	9.3	0.8	1.1
23	29	Singapore	4.9	8.7	0.9	1.0
—	30	South Africa	2.7	8.4	0.5	1.0

Source: UNWTO (2008), Weaver & Lawton (2006)

These figures do not reflect all expenses that are incurred by tourists, but only those that accrue to the destination itself. The first component of these accruing expenditures are those paid in advance in the origin region, as through a package tour arrangement, while the other component involves money spent at the actual destination. The latter is usually characterised by a diverse array of expenditure categories. In the Australian inbound context, food, drink, accommodation, transport and shopping are revealed as major areas of expenditure. Education fees are also extremely important with regard to average expenditures, but pertain only to the relatively small cohort of inbound tourists who are international students.

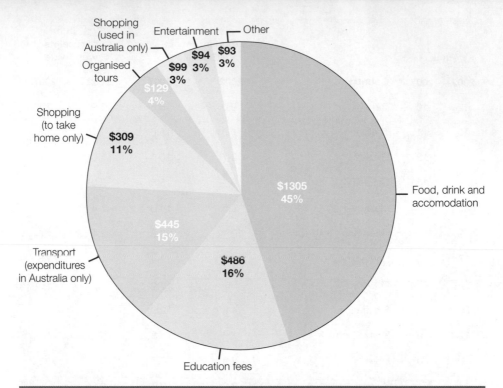

FIGURE 8.1 Average expenditure for all visitors to Australia by expenditure category, 2007

Source: TRA 2008g

Taxation revenue

Subsumed under the umbrella of tourism receipts are levies such as the Australian departure tax, a fee paid by all departing inbound visitors. Governments regard taxes as an attractive form of revenue generation, and one that costs little to collect (see the case study at the end of this chapter). Taxes are often hidden as part of a package arrangement or within the overall cost of a good or service, so that the consumer is unaware of their existence. In addition, taxes can be increased substantially without bringing about a significant negative response from the tourist market. This is because taxes usually comprise only a very small portion of the overall trip expenditure. For example, a 100 per cent increase in a $10 departure tax will not add significant costs to a $3000 trip. Governments, on the other hand, stand to gain a substantial increase in revenue from the cumulative intake of such a doubled levy (e.g. 500 000 inbound tourists paying a departure tax of $20 each instead of $10 equates to added revenue of $5 million).

Common examples of tourism-related taxation include airport departure taxes (like the Australian departure tax), bed (or hotel room) taxes, permits for entry to public attractions such as national parks, entry or transit visas, and gaming licences. Tourists also generate taxation revenue through the purchase of goods and services subject to sales tax (e.g. Australia's GST) and other levies. Bed and sales taxes are examples of *ad valorem* taxes (that is, they are set as a percentage of price), while departure taxes and visas are specific (that is, they are set at a given price). More unusual are taxes directed at the outbound tourist flow, which are usually implemented to reduce the loss of foreign exchange.

Influence of other government departments

One potentially frustrating aspect of taxation from the destination manager or tourism department's perspective is the control exercised by destination government departments not directly related to tourism, which may not always be sympathetic to the interests of the tourism sector. For example, the Department of Immigration and Citizenship (DIAC) is the Australian federal body responsible for issuing and pricing visas and for establishing qualification requirements. A possible decision to ease or tighten these requirements, to greatly increase the visa costs or to take more time in processing applications could thus create a major deterrent to travel that the tourism stakeholders have little power to control. Conversely, the introduction of the Electronic Travel Authority (ETA) in 1996 illustrates how agencies such as DIAC can facilitate tourism by expediting application procedures. The ETA can be obtained by potential visitors from qualifying countries (e.g. major markets such as the United States, Canada, Japan, Singapore, Hong Kong and South Korea) in just a few minutes from the agency website for a small fee. It replaces the visa stamp normally affixed to the traveller's passport, and when the tourist arrives at the airport to board their flight to Australia, check-in staff can quickly confirm electronically whether they are ETA approved. In general, however, more concerns have been expressed within the tourism industry over the increasing tendency of governments to regard tourism as a revenue-generating 'cash cow', with little of the revenue typically re-invested within the tourism industry itself (see the case study at the end of this chapter).

Strategies to increase direct revenue

Tourism receipts (taxes aside), can be expanded by increasing:
• the number of visitors
• their average length of stay
• their average daily expenditure (see figure 8.2).

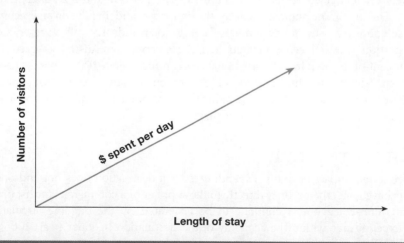

FIGURE 8.2 Factors influencing tourism revenue in a destination

Most basic is the visitor intake, and it is the fluctuation in this statistic that usually attracts the greatest attention. However, it is the average length of stay and the amount spent per day that actually determines the amount of revenue generated by these tourists. The impact of these factors among different market segments is demonstrated by the contrasting length of stay and spending patterns of Japanese and Chinese inbound tourists to Australia. As depicted in table 6.1, Chinese visitors spend less per day, but more overall due to their much longer stay. Accordingly, many destinations devise strategies that encourage longer vacations and high-spending markets. In some cases, a 'quality' over 'quantity' approach is deliberately implemented to reduce the social and environmental impacts of high visitation levels (see chapter 9).

Contribution of tourism to GNP

Tourism receipts, while a crucial indicator of the sector's size, cannot be used on their own to compare tourism's relative importance from one destination to another or within the overall economy of a particular destination. To facilitate such comparisons, the value of international tourism receipts is calculated for a one-year period as a percentage of a country's gross national product (GNP; or sometimes termed gross national income, GNI) (see appendix 3). There is no definitive percentage threshold that differentiates the countries where tourism is a critical component of the economy. However, a 5 per cent figure can be taken to indicate a highly significant contribution in lieu of more sophisticated techniques, such as the Tourism Satellite Account (TSA), that more accurately measure tourism's economic contribution but are just starting to be widely adopted.

Statistics on the contribution of international tourism receipts to GNP are available for 178 countries or dependencies as of 2004, the most recent year for which a near full set of data was available (see appendix 3). Of these, at least 63 (or 35 per cent) met or exceeded the 5 per cent criterion. However, about one-half of these destinations are pleasure periphery SISODs (see chapter 4), some of which display a pattern of 'hyperdependency' on tourism. Extreme cases included Palau (68.3 per cent), Maldives (61.3 per cent), and St Lucia (43.8 per cent). Notably, many destination countries with large absolute tourism receipts, such as the United States and France, had a relatively small GNP contribution from tourism (0.6 per cent and 2.2 per cent, respectively). This apparent anomaly reflects the immense and highly diverse economies of these countries, wherein even a very large tourism industry still represents only a small portion of overall economic output. This also applies to Australia, which derived 2.7 per cent of its GNP from international tourism receipts in 2004. Such statistics are critical in determining the allocation of government resources to the tourism sector, and therefore any recalibrations that reduce the percentage contribution to GNP constitute a serious threat to destination managers.

Indirect revenue

The economic impact of tourist expenditures on a destination does not end once the tourists have given their money directly to the supplier of a commercial tourist product. Rather, **indirect revenues** continue to be generated by the ongoing circulation of these expenditures within the economy of the destination (Cooper et al. 2005). This **multiplier effect** has both an indirect and induced component that come into play once the **direct (or primary) impact**, that is the actual spending of money by the tourist, has taken place (see (a) of figure 8.3). The first-round **indirect impacts**, (b), occurs when the business (e.g. a hotel) uses a portion of these direct expenditures to purchase goods (e.g. food, pool-cleaning equipment) and pay wages to its employees. Second-round indirect impacts, (c), then occur when the suppliers of these goods and services use a portion of revenues received from the hotel to buy goods and services for their own use. This process continues into subsequent rounds, (d), although the revenues involved by this time are substantially diminished and often very difficult to trace.

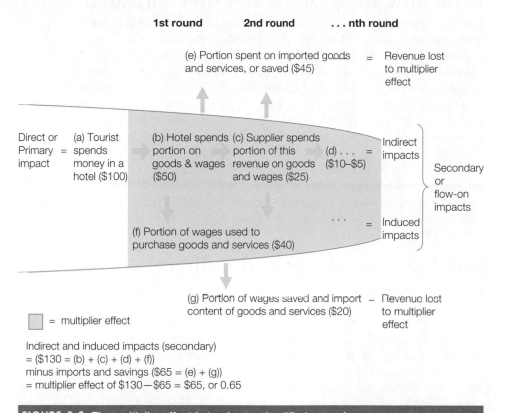

FIGURE 8.3 The multiplier effect in tourism: a simplified example

Through each round of indirect impact, revenues are lost to the destination multiplier effect due to the purchase of imported goods and services, and the allocation of money to savings, (e). If the initial hotel purchases in stage (a) are all allocated to imported goods and services, then essentially no multiplier effect takes place (i.e. there is no circulation of any portion of the revenue within the destination). Also in each indirect impact round, the multiplier effect is increased by **induced impacts** that take place when wages paid by the hotels and their suppliers are used by employees to purchase goods and services such as televisions, food, cars and haircuts, (f). However, as in (e), the multiplier effect of these wages is also eroded by savings, and by the import component of the goods and services they purchase, (g). In simple terms (since its actual calculation is complicated), the multiplier effect is obtained by adding together the sequential rounds of the indirect and induced impacts (i.e. **secondary (or flow-on) impacts**), and subtracting the revenue that is lost through allocations to imports and savings. The $100 initial expenditure shown in figure 8.2 thereby produces an additional multiplier effect of $65, or 0.65.

Higher multiple effects as a general rule are associated with larger and more diverse destination economies, since these have the capacity to provide the array and magnitude of goods and services consumed by tourists, and hence allow for the sustained internal circulation of direct tourism revenue. An analysis of multiplier effect studies by Cooper et al. (2005) revealed a multiplier value range of 2.00–3.40 for medium to large industrialised destinations, but 1.12–1.35 for rural economies.

Economic integration and diversification

The multiplier effect is closely linked to the idea of **backward linkages**, which encompass the goods and services that 'feed into' the tourism industry through the indirect impacts described above. The link occurs when these goods and services are obtained from within the destination rather than through imports. The sectors that typically account for most of the backward linkages in tourism include agriculture and commercial fisheries, transportation, entertainment, construction and manufacturing. The full list of backward linkages in tourism is extensive and complex, attesting to tourism's great potential to stimulate local economic integration and diversification, provided that these goods and services can be supplied from within the destination. For example, the manufacturing component in tourism ranges from the furniture and appliances used in resort hotels, to pool-cleaning equipment, kitchen utensils and bathroom sinks. In Australia, tourism accounts for about 3 per cent of the gross value added in the manufacturing sector, and about 2 per cent of agriculture, forestry and fishing (TTF 2008c).

Employment (direct and indirect)

From the perspective of the destination community, the creation of jobs is an especially relevant reason for a destination to promote its tourism sector. Just how much employment tourism generates, however, is a subject of controversy. The World Travel and Tourism Council (the WTTC), as described in chapter 1, espoused a figure of 231 million jobs worldwide for 2007, but such an impressive figure is only credible if calculated as the full-time equivalent of all tourism employment; that is, by combining the cumulative hours of several part-time and contractual employees to generate one full-time job equivalent and then adding all of these together to the actual full-time jobs. Australia's Department of Resources, Energy and Tourism estimated that tourism accounted directly 483 000 jobs in Australia in 2007 (DRET 2008b). Another 351 000 full-time job equivalents were indirectly associated with tourism, represented, for example, by the hours spent by construction workers building hotels, or by surgeons operating occasionally on tourists (TTF 2008d). Both examples illustrate the multiplier effect that also pertains to employment.

Regional development

Proponents of the advocacy platform, and other stakeholders, emphasise the effectiveness of tourism in initiating and promoting the development of regions where economic options are otherwise constrained. The classic example is 3S (sea, sand, sun) tourism, wherein 'unspoiled' natural sites and regions possessing little value for most conventional economic activities have been redefined as valuable resources for the tourism industry. Environmental consequences aside, the rapid physical development of the European Riviera, the small islands of the Caribbean, Australia's Gold and Sunshine coasts and other parts of the pleasure periphery is fundamentally an outcome of the sustained global demand for 3S tourism. A similar effect is evident in the ecotourism sector, which places a high value on rainforests, national parks and other relatively natural settings as tourism venues (see chapter 11).

Other types of tourism product suited to marginal settings include the farm tourism sector (Ollenburg 2008) and specialised components of agriculture such as wineries (see chapter 5). Skiing and other winter sports have a substantial economic impact on Australia's small alpine region and other peripheral mountain regions. Casinos, as noted in chapter 5, contribute substantially to the economic development of economically underdeveloped locations such as Native American reservations in the United States. In the Australian and New Zealand context, nature-based and cultural tourism are providing a stimulus for the economic development of historically marginalised indigenous communities and other peripheral areas.

Growth pole strategy

In most cases the development of tourism in a peripheral area occurs as a spontaneous, mostly unplanned process. However, there are countries where tourism is deliberately mobilised as a **propulsive activity** in a so-called **growth pole strategy**. Examples are found in the Dominican Republic (Freitag 1994), Mexico (e.g. Cancún) and Indonesia (e.g. Bintan). In essence, this involves the establishment of resorts at a strategically selected location (i.e. the growth pole) as a way of stimulating economic development in the region. A growth pole strategy in tourism entails a sequence of stages along the following lines:

1. An appropriate site (the growth pole) is identified by government, usually in an economically marginal area that is deemed suitable for sustaining some predetermined form of tourism development such as 3S resorts.
2. Through government initiative and incentives, public and private investment is injected into this area, commonly in the form of subsidised facilities and infrastructure. These incentives reduce financial risk for investors.
3. This investment attracts employees, supportive services and other tourism facilities, often induced by continuing government incentives.
4. Economic growth eventually becomes self-sustaining and independent of tourism in a direct sense when a critical mass of residential population is attained (i.e. new investment and settlement is attracted by the large local market rather than by tourism opportunities *per se*). At this point incentives are normally withdrawn. At the same time, the developmental benefits of tourism 'trickle down' from the growth pole into the surrounding region.

The growth pole principle can also be applied at a local or micro-scale, for example by fostering the development of a single attraction to serve as a nucleus to attract additional investment and employment (see Breakthrough tourism: Garden path to rural development in north-eastern England).

breakthrough tourism

GARDEN PATH TO RURAL DEVELOPMENT IN NORTH-EASTERN ENGLAND?

Agricultural decline, rural deprivation, and an aging and declining population are chronic problems in many of England's peripheral regions. Where iconic natural or historical attractions are available in such areas, tourism may serve as an 'organic' stimulant for economic rejuvenation. Where they are not available, a similar role can potentially be filled by flagship attractions innovatively conceived and executed with this goal in mind. Alnwick Garden in Northumberland, north-eastern England, is one such example (Sharpley 2007). Opened in 2001, the garden was expected to draw 67 000 visitors during its first year of operation, but attracted 304 000. The following year, 570 000 visits were recorded, and significant increases in local employment and business income were evident. Among the factors that underlie this success is the strong sense of regional authenticity conveyed by the fourteenth century castle grounds setting. Innovative landscaping and architectural features, in addition, extend the traditional viewing function of gardens to a broader experience of play, conversation, participation and socialising, available 364 days of the year. The constant maturation of the gardens contributes to a long-term diversity of experience, since the visual display changes each year and seasonally. Strong community support was fostered by the creation of the Friends of Alnwick Garden organisation, which was configured as a charitable trust eligible for public funding.

It is often argued that community-based attractions in rural areas should be small-scale to harmonise with their surrounds, but Alnwick Garden from its inception was intended to be a large-scale or 'flagship' attraction big enough to stimulate significant regional development. It appears to be doing so without compromising its authentic presentation of the local sense of place. The main complaint thus far, which is testament to the need for an integrated planning framework to contextualise such developments, is the inadequacy of the local lodging sector and labour force to accommodate the tourist demand created by the Garden (Sharpley 2007).

Formal and informal sectors

Managers and governments within most destinations usually assume that economic benefits are most efficiently achieved through a strong **formal sector** — that is, the component of the economy that is subject to official systems of regulation and remuneration. Because the formal sector includes the largest and most technologically sophisticated businesses, it is seen as the primary generator of wealth and indicator of economic development. Government bias in its favour also owes much to the formal sector that generates substantial tax revenue and subjects itself to a significant degree of government regulation.

In contrast, the **informal sector** is unregulated and external to the formal institutions of society. Participating businesses generally:

• operate beyond the legal system
• are not subject to formal quality control measures
• are not registered or enumerated
• do not provide regular working hours for their employees and
• do not officially pay any regular wages or taxes (Smith & Henderson 2008).

Because the informal sector cannot be measured or regulated easily, and because it does not generate tax revenue for government, public officials often try to suppress, or at best ignore, this element. A large informal sector, in addition, is psychologically perceived as an indicator of economic underdevelopment, and its incorporation into or replacement by the formal sector is therefore generally seen as a prerequisite for attaining Phase Four status as per Burton's model (see page 60).

Within the tourism industry, the informal sector is often criticised by the formal sector and government for its 'harassing' and 'unprofessional' attitude towards tourists, who are thought to be offended by the often aggressive behaviour of souvenir hawkers and other itinerant businesspeople. This argument relates directly to the concept of inseparability, and the consequent importance of service quality control, as discussed in chapter 7. However, the formal sector also opposes the informal sector because it captures a significant portion of tourist expenditures and may be perceived by many tourists as a more authentic form of host/guest encounter. This is a valid argument in many LDCs, where a substantial and highly visible informal sector paralleling the mainstream tourism system is evident in tourism subsectors such as guest houses, services and crafts-related activities, souvenir vending, prostitution, guiding, pedicab driving, markets, beach hawking and food stalls (see figure 8.4).

FIGURE 8.4 Beach hawkers in Bali: authentic or intimidating experience?

Government authorities often harass and discourage such operations, and only in a few isolated instances, such as the Indonesian city of Yogyakarta (Dahles 2001), are they attempting to work out a mutually beneficial strategy of peaceful coexistence or cooperation. In the case of Yogyakarta, the positive attitude was prompted by the realisation that street vendors are a major tourist attraction in their own right, as well as a major employer that forms robust backward linkages with local industry and has great resilience in adapting to changing business conditions. The informal tourism sector also exists within many MDCs, but is less visible and less of a 'problem' because of the dominance of formal sector businesses.

Economic costs

As the size and scope of the global tourism industry continued to increase through the late 1960s and 1970s, evidence accumulated that the economic impacts of the sector were not all positive. It was in response to this evidence that the cautionary platform emerged within the field of tourism studies to argue that the economic, social, cultural and environmental costs of unregulated tourism tend to outweigh its benefits. Destination managers, they argued, should therefore be extremely cautious about pursuing tourism in an uncritical way (see chapter 1). This section considers the major economic costs that are potentially incurred by tourist destinations, and is thus essentially a summary of the cautionary platform's economic critique.

Direct financial costs

Proper assessments of revenue intake from tourism should first of all take into account the **direct financial costs** that are necessarily incurred by the public sector to generate and sustain this intake. To point out these costs is not to be critical, but merely to indicate that tourism, as with any other economic activity, requires financial inputs to realise financial benefits. The situation in Australia illustrates the nature and magnitude of these costs. For the four years from 2004 to 2007, the federal Department of Industry, Tourism and Resources (DITR), the agency responsible for tourism during that period, committed almost $240 million to tourism promotion and development. As depicted in table 8.2, most of the funds were allocated towards international and domestic marketing.

TABLE 8.2 DITR funding allocations to tourism 2004–07	
Funding area	**Amount ($ million)**
International marketing	120.6
Domestic regional marketing and development	45.5
Australian Tourism Development Program (ATDP)	24.0
Enhanced research and statistics capacity	21.5
Niche segment development	14.7
Tourism and conservation programs	4.6
Business Ready Program for Indigenous Tourism	3.8
National Voluntary Tourism Accreditation System	2.3
Administration, implementation and coordination of Tourism White Paper	1.5
World Tourism Organization membership	1.4
Total	239.9

Source: Data derived from DITR (2005b)

To these amounts should be added a similar spectrum of cost allocations incurred at the state and territory level. For example, Tourism Queensland, which is similar to Tourism Australia in its mandate and responsibilities, received more than $51 million in state government funding for 2007, in addition to $13 million in 'cooperative marketing income' obtained from industry partners (Tourism Queensland 2007).

Direct incentives, usually disbursed by nontourism agencies within government, constitute a distinct set of costs in the development of the tourism sector (Wanhill 2005). Potential entrepreneurs are usually willing to commit their own resources into a project in anticipation of strong profits. However, in more uncertain situations, destination governments may have to entice these entrepreneurs with capital grants, labour and training subsidies or the provision of infrastructure at public expense (as demonstrated in growth pole strategies). Incentives are more likely to be necessary when several destinations offer a similar product, such as a generic 3S experience, and therefore must compete with each other for investment. In such a situation, the entrepreneur will usually locate within the destination that offers the most lucrative incentive package, all other things being equal. This was demonstrated in early 1999 when the producers of the popular television series *Baywatch* entered negotiations with both

Hawaii and the Gold Coast of Australia to obtain the best package of incentives in its attempt to select a long-term filming site (Hawaii was selected). Where a destination, in contrast, is in a monopolistic situation of offering iconic attractions (as with Niagara Falls, Uluru, the Sydney Opera House or the Eiffel Tower), the level of anticipated long-term demand is more likely to attract entrepreneurs even without the offer of incentives.

Indirect financial costs

A major thrust of the cautionary platform was its emphasis on the substantial **indirect financial costs** that are incurred by tourism in a destination. The best-known are the costs subsumed under the category of **revenue leakages**. Some or all of the following leakages may curtail the circulation of tourist receipts in the destination economy as depicted in segment (e) of figure 8.2, and thereby erode the multiplier effect:

- imported current goods and services that are required by tourists or the tourist industry (e.g. petrol, food)
- imported capital goods and services required by the tourist industry (e.g. furnishings, taxis, architect's fees)
- factor payments abroad, including repatriated profits, wages and hotel management fees
- imports for government expenditure (airport, road and port equipment)
- induced imports for domestic producers who supply the tourist industry (e.g. fertiliser to grow the food consumed by tourists).

Serious revenue leakages, as suggested earlier, are more likely to occur in small and specialised economies, given their lack of capacity to supply the goods and services required by the local tourism industry. In addition, the relatively small population of these destinations does not normally possess sufficient investment capital to sustain desired levels of tourism development. Severe revenue leakages are associated with **enclave resort** situations, or self-contained facilities where patrons are discouraged from spending their money outside of the operation's confines, and where most of the goods are imported from beyond the local community (Freitag 1994). More broadly, the term **enclave tourism** has been used to describe formal sector tourism industries in particular regions, such as the Okavango Delta of Botswana that are controlled by foreign interests, include enclave resorts, and have weak linkages with the local economy (Mbaiwa 2005). They may also be induced more indirectly by the **demonstration effect** of tourism, where for status or role-model reasons, locals seek to emulate the behaviour of tourists by consuming the imported goods favoured by the tourists (Shaw & Williams 2002).

Problems with revenue leakage

Revenue leakages are regarded as insidious for several reasons, particularly when the leakages accrue to a different country rather than another region within the same country:

1. They siphon away circulation effects (i.e. the multiplier effect) that could benefit the economy of the destination.
2. The cumulative indirect component is less tangible and harder to measure than direct expenses, and therefore more difficult to quantify as a first step towards addressing the problem.
3. Even if they can be measured, their existence usually reflects basic shortcomings in the economic structure of the destination that are extremely difficult to resolve.

4. Imports not only dissuade local entrepreneurs from supplying similar goods, but they may displace existing local (i.e. small-scale) producers who cannot match the quality, price or quantity provided by the exporter.

5. The presence of leakages implies, to a greater or lesser extent, an economic dependency of the destination on the exporter, which constrains the ability of destination stakeholders to manage their own affairs. This is especially problematic when businesses are dominated by expatriate managers.

For all these reasons, integrated and long-term tourism management strategies should try to foster linkages between tourism and the destination economy, so as to reduce the potential for revenue leakage and maximise the multiplier effect.

Indirect incentives

Augmenting the direct incentives outlined in the 'Direct financial costs' section are various indirect incentives. These include preferential or reduced interest rates, the provision of land for sale or lease on favourable terms, depreciation allowances, tariff and quota exemptions on tourism-related imports, and tax holidays. An example of the latter are the ten-year tax-free periods commonly offered to developers who construct hotels of a certain size in the Caribbean. Other indirect incentives include loan guarantees and special depreciation allowances on tourism-related capital goods. Such provisions are often more popular in governments than direct incentives because they do not involve the direct outlay of money. Rather, governments obtain less revenue than they would if the incentives were not offered (e.g. the interest realised at full market rates rather than reduced interest rates).

Fluctuations in intake

A stable and predictable flow of inputs and outputs in many industries contributes to financial stability and facilitates the management process, as enormous investments in time and energy are not required to gauge and prepare for continual changes in the supply/demand equation (see chapter 7). The dairy industry is an example of a sector with low demand uncertainty. Demand in this sector is not significantly influenced by weather or other changeable factors, nor is the market likely to suddenly stop purchasing dairy products. In addition, since consumers consider dairy products to be a basic necessity, consumption patterns will not be seriously affected by a downturn in the economy.

Supply-side factors

Tourism is an example of an activity that is frequently at the opposite end of the spectrum to the dairy industry, being highly vulnerable in some manifestations to changes in weather, fashion and sociopolitical conditions. It is worth re-emphasising that the *in situ* nature of consumption inherent in tourism is one reason for this uncertainty in demand. Tourists must travel to the place of 'production' (i.e. the destination), whereas dairy products exhibit the opposite tendency; they travel from the place of production to the homes of consumers. Supply-side disruptions within the destination, such as political uncertainty or a disruption of infrastructure, thus have a major and sometimes overwhelming bearing on visitor intakes (see chapter 4 and also the chapter 1 case study). Factors that are not specific to particular destinations can also be influential, as indicated by the 12–14 per cent decrease in global travel reservations that followed the terrorism actions of September 2001, and the 26 per cent decrease in the number of inbound tourists to Thailand in January 2005 (i.e. the month following the tsunami) over the same month in 2004 (ILO 2005).

Demand-side factors

Also by way of reiteration, demand-side factors such as the availability of discretionary income have a particularly harsh effect on tourism, given its status as an essentially luxury or discretionary product. Most consumers will direct their first cutbacks towards their tourism activities rather than dairy products should disruptions in the economy reduce their discretionary income or generate feelings of financial insecurity. As noted in chapter 7, tourism suffers an additional liability in that the products cannot be stockpiled — an empty hotel room produces no economic value, but is a fixed cost that still requires maintenance, mortgage repayment etc.

These cautionary comments about the instability of tourism demand and supply do not contradict earlier information in this textbook that claims a positive global outlook for the tourism sector. Rather, problems can arise for managers when the patterns and underlying factors that apply at the global level are assumed to be valid for individual destinations as well. In other words, the steady growth experienced worldwide represents a pattern of cumulative behaviour that does not necessarily indicate the performance of specific destinations. For any individual destination country, a similar analysis of arrival trends since 1950 would likely reveal a great deal of fluctuation. In the wake of the 2001 terrorist attacks, for example, many Muslim-dominated countries experienced a prolonged period of reduced inbound visitation.

Seasonality

The tendency to report destination arrival data for an entire year (as in table 3.1) is misleading, since such statistics usually disguise significant variations in intake that affect the supply/demand equilibrium. These temporal variations are caused partially by demand-side factors such as holiday time availability in the origin markets (e.g. summer holidays, winter break). However, equally, or more, influential are supply-side factors such as changing opportunities in attractions and activities and how much the destination is dependent on these changeable products. Resorts that are dependent on winter sports or 3S-based activities readily come to mind as tourism products that are subject to significant seasonal variations in demand.

Australia is not plagued by seasonality to the same extent as pleasure periphery destinations such as Spain or the Caribbean, partly because of the diversity of major market sources and variations in their peak periods of outbound travel. Substantial variations in climatic conditions within Australia at any given time mean additionally that there is no particular season in which the country can be uniformly characterised as 'hot' or 'cold'. Yet, as depicted in figure 8.5, diverse seasonality effects are still evident within various inbound segments. A further complication is the deviation of specific market segments from this pattern. Holiday travellers, for example, more or less paralleled the overall trend, while business travel peaked in the period from July to November and then dropped sharply in December and January.

Where strong seasonal variations are part of the normal annual tourism cycle of a destination, a large amount of economic and social disruption can occur if appropriate compensating measures are not taken by tourism managers. The problem can be described as one of undercapacity and overcapacity, or to use an analogy from the farming sector, a 'drought-flood' cycle. In the context of the supply/demand matching strategies outlined in chapter 7, the off-season is a period when supply exceeds demand, while the high season is characterised by an excess of demand over supply. During the off-season, low occupancy rates result in reduced business, which subsequently reverberates in a negative way throughout the economy and labour force in a sort of reverse multiplier effect. In contrast, the high season is often characterised by overbookings, stress on infrastructure, overcrowding, and shortages of goods and services (which may in turn give rise to inflation).

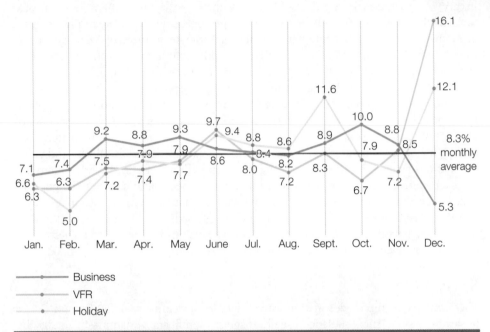

FIGURE 8.5 Seasonality in selected Australian inbound tourist segments in 2007, by month

Source: Data derived from ABS (2008d)

Strategies that individual companies can adopt to address seasonal and other demand fluctuations have been outlined in chapter 7. Destination managers, however, are more constrained in their options, because they can only influence the strategies and tactics of the businesses that dominate the tourism sector, and themselves only control a portion of the sector. One option for destination governments is to stimulate alternative but complementary economic activities such as hi-tech industries, so that the off-season effect in tourism is offset by the continuing output from these other sectors.

Within tourism itself, local governments can withdraw or restrict certain variable cost services, such as beach patrolling and garbage collection. They can also promote their destination to markets that have unconventional or more evenly distributed patterns of seasonal travel (see Managing tourism: Seasonality through VFR tourism). Gold Coast tourism managers, for example, actively market in the United Arab Emirates and other Middle Eastern countries, recognising that their residents are more likely to visit Australia in the winter off-season when temperatures in the Middle East are at their most intense. Other strategies include the development of attractions and activities that will draw visitors during the off-season. An example of off-season adaptation of infrastructure is found at the Australian ski resort of Thredbo, where otherwise unused ski lifts provide scenic rides to summer visitors as well as access to walking tracks in the high meadows around Mt Kosciuszko.

managing tourism

SEASONALITY THROUGH VFR TOURISM

VFR tourists have traditionally been neglected as a target market segment by GTOs (government tourism organisations), which assume that they have low expenditures and are not influenced by marketing efforts (Backer 2007, Bischoff & Koenig-Lewis 2007). A major argument for a more proactive approach toward this segment is evidence that VFR tourists are distributed more evenly throughout the year and hence can help to mitigate the negative effects of chronic tourism seasonality. An especially dramatic effect is evident among international students, who tend to host visitors from their home countries during schooling periods in the tourism off-season (Bischoff & Koenig-Lewis 2007). Contrary to the conventional wisdom about low expenditures, Backer (2007) found in a survey of visitors and residents on the Sunshine Coast of Queensland that once accommodations were removed from the equation (since most VFR tourists stay in the homes of friends and relatives), VFR tourists spent more per trip than non-VFR tourists on all expenditure categories. This was in part because they averaged a 9.5-night stay, compared with 6 nights for other visitors. Extrapolating the survey results, Backer (2007) estimated that 640 000 VFR tourists were hosted in the study area over a one-year period. A notable aspect of this phenomenon was that almost 14 per cent of total average VFR trip expenditures were incurred by these hosts through their purchases of groceries and other goods and services consumed by their hosts.

Pending the corroboration of these findings in other destinations, it appears that efforts by GTOs to stimulate the VFR market are a good investment of resources. On the 'supply side', residents could be better educated about local attractions so that they are more likely to accompany or inform their guests about a larger number of potential places to visit. In addition, 'local tourist' programs (which often offer a reduced entry fee to local residents) could be extended by offering free entry to hosts accompanied by at least one out-of-town guest. VFR tourists could be offered 'honorary resident' passes that provide discounts on local attractions and accommodations, as well as 'special' insights into the local sense of place. Rebates for non-residents on local taxes would provide even more of a stimulus effect. Resentment from non-VFR tourists and abuse arising from false declarations of VFR status are potential problems that would have to be monitored.

Fashion

Much less predictable than the seasonal variations are the effects of fashion. As discussed in chapter 4, this is demonstrated by the shifting perceptions in 'Western' societies towards sunbathing, beaches and water sports, which became popular during the Industrial Revolution but may eventually fall out of general favour due to concerns about skin cancer. This would force 3S destinations to develop and promote alternative tourism products.

Another perspective on fashion is the rise and fall of specific destinations. Places often become fashionable due to novelty and curiosity, but are soon superseded by newer destinations offering a similar (i.e. easily substitutable) product. Thus, St Lucia may have the status of being the 'in' Caribbean destination one particular year, only to be replaced, in turn, by Anguilla, St Martin and Grenada. This effect is experienced in many other industries, but one dilemma for tourism is the tendency in destinations to acquire an accommodation inventory commensurate with the level of the highest demand. When visitor arrivals decline because of the fashion factor (as opposed to the cyclic seasonal effect), the specialised nature of hotels means that they are difficult to convert permanently to other uses when high fixed costs become too much of a burden. The fashion effect is closely associated with the resort cycle concept, which is discussed in chapter 10.

Vulnerability to instability

More uncertain and potentially harmful than the vagaries of fashion are the effects of social and political instability within or in the vicinity of a destination. Especially insidious is the potential for just one random and completely unpredictable act of terrorism or sabotage to cripple a destination's tourism industry, as demonstrated by the terrorist attacks on the United States in September 2001 and the Bali bombings of 2002. Even though little can be done to prevent such occurrences, tourism managers need to be aware of this vulnerability, and of the possibility that very positive growth performance can be reversed in an instant. Accordingly, a strategy of broader economic diversification would help to cushion such impacts, as it would with seasonal variations.

Competition with other sectors

The multiplier effect is attractive because it stimulates a diverse local economy through the generation of significant linkages within the destination. In some cases, however, a competitive rather than a complementary relationship evolves between tourism and other sectors in the local economy. It was noted earlier, for example, that tourism-induced food imports may displace or dissuade local production if the scale economies of the exporter and the bilateral trade environment are such that a cheaper and better quality non-local product can be offered to the hotels.

Further marginalisation of agriculture occurs because of tourism's status as a more competitive bidder for land. A golf course or resort hotel, for instance, represents a far more lucrative use of prime agricultural land than a sugar cane operation. Where farming is already a marginal activity, as the sugar industry was on the Caribbean island of Antigua in the 1960s, tourism serves to accelerate its decline by offering strategically located land owners a viable alternative land use. Finally, the **opportunity cost** of using a resource for tourism over some other activity should be taken into consideration. Money or land allocated to tourism, in effect, is money or land denied to agriculture, which thus represents a forgone opportunity for the destination. This effect has been noted in the wine-producing regions of South Australia, where investment in tourism is seen to divert attention and investment from wine production (Beverland 1999).

Employment problems

It cannot be denied that tourism is an efficient generator of direct and indirect employment, but the nature of this employment may not always be conducive to the comprehensive economic development of the destination. Wages in the tourism sector tend to be low compared with other sectors (although agriculture in many cases is an exception), with 'hospitality workers' in Australia averaging just over $19 per hour in 2006 compared with almost $26 per hour in comparable service sectors (ABS 2006b). Several interrelated factors account for this differential:
- the unskilled nature of most tourism jobs, with relatively few opportunities for upward mobility and few training opportunities
- the tendency of employers to treat jobs requiring higher levels of skill (as in the emotional labour component of customer service) as unskilled
- high labour turnover (i.e. unstable labour force)

- the weakness or absence of unionisation and collective bargaining arrangements
- the tendency of many employers to flout minimum wage regulations, sometimes through the employment of illegal migrants
- where there are few or no alternatives to tourism, local wages may be depressed because of the lack of competition.

Because of the seasonal and cyclical nature of tourism, the sector is also characterised by a high incidence of seasonal, part-time and casual employment, thereby further contributing to the discrepancy between the actual number of people employed and the actual hours and wages achieved. Tourism in Australia and elsewhere has additionally been criticised, like certain other sectors, for fostering a ghetto-like environment that provides women with lower pay (ABS 2006b, Thrane 2008), poorer working conditions, less career mobility, less access to training programs and less effective trade union support. Ironically, the advocacy platform has interpreted many of these alleged shortcomings as advantages, in that low wages mean that more workers can be hired, and unskilled workers can find employment opportunities more readily. Furthermore, part-time and seasonal jobs may be more desirable among certain segments in the workforce, such as single mothers and students (see Contemporary issue: International tourism students and part-time employment).

contemporary issue

INTERNATIONAL TOURISM STUDENTS AND PART-TIME EMPLOYMENT

It is commonly assumed that high levels of part-time employment among students taking degrees in the hospitality and tourism areas are a result of financial pressure and/or a desire to obtain workplace experience. To learn more about this increasingly prevalent reality, Barron (2007) surveyed the practices and attitudes of 487 hospitality and tourism undergraduate students at a major Australian university. It was found that 85 per cent were either currently working at least on a part-time basis or were actively searching for work. On average, those already working were employed for 16 hours per week, and had worked for their current employer either for less than 3 months or 25 months or longer. Unsurprisingly, almost one-half worked in the hospitality sector, while 20 per cent were in the retail sector. Earnings were indeed the main reason for working, while interaction with colleagues slightly outranked experience as the second most important reason. Disturbingly, dealing with customers was the most cited disadvantage, followed by boredom, shift work and problems with supervisors.

Over one-half of the students reported that their employment distracted somewhat from their studies, but not seriously. While not expecting the university to fully accommodate their decision to pursue employment while studying, almost all respondents agreed that the university should become more involved as facilitators. A substantial portion supported greater flexibility in course content and delivery as well as provision for electronic assignment submission. Others suggested that the university should help students to find work that would best complement their program of study, and/or give academic credits for such activity. Barron (2007) concludes by suggesting that universities must recognise the normality and even the essentiality of the study/employment mix and make reasonable accommodations accordingly. In so doing, it is reasonable to expect that the many of the problems associated with tourism and hospitality employment will be alleviated and that outcomes for both the students and their employers will be more mutually beneficial.

CHAPTER REVIEW

This chapter has considered the potential economic costs and benefits of tourism for a destination. The main argument for tourism, as expounded by supporters of the advocacy platform, is the generation of earnings through direct tourist expenditures and related taxation. Another important economic benefit is the generation of indirect local revenue through the multiplier effect, and the concurrent diversification and integration of the local economy through the stimulation of backward linkages with agriculture and other sectors within the destination. Tourism is also an effective stimulant for direct and indirect employment opportunities and a vehicle for regional development. This can occur as a result of spontaneous processes (such as the development of most vacation farms or nature-based operations), or as the consequence of a deliberate growth pole strategy, as with the Mexican resort of Cancún. When considering the economic benefits of tourism, it is generally assumed that a strong formal sector is the best engine for achieving these benefits, rather than the unregulated informal sector.

The cautionary platform, in contrast to the advocacy platform, holds that the positive economic impacts of tourism may be much lower than alleged. First, the direct financial costs involved in maintaining an effective administrative bureaucracy, marketing activities and providing incentives are substantial. Second, revenue leakages, which result from a high import content, profit repatriation and other processes, can drastically reduce the multiplier effect. Tourism, moreover, engenders economic uncertainty because of its vulnerability to fluctuations in intake arising from seasonal variations, the effects of fashion and social or political unrest, in both the destination and source regions. Tourism also has the capacity to foster a competitive rather than a complementary relationship with agriculture and other local sectors, and a tendency to create part-time, low-wage and low-skill employment dominated by females. How much a destination derives net economic benefits or costs from tourism depends on the circumstances that pertain to each particular place. In general, destinations with large and diverse economies are most likely to benefit from tourism, since these can generate the backward linkages that give rise to a strong multiplier effect. In contrast, small destination economies, such as those found in the SISODs, are most likely to incur the economic costs described in this chapter. Essentially, the destinations that are therefore most desperate to obtain economic benefits from tourism are those that are most likely to experience the negative economic impacts of tourism.

■ SUMMARY OF KEY TERMS

Backward linkages sectors of an economy that provide goods and services for the tourism sector; includes agriculture, fisheries and construction

Demonstration effect the tendency of a population, or some portion thereof, to imitate the consumption patterns and other behaviours of another group; this can result in increased importation of goods and services to meet these changing consumer demands

Direct (or primary) impact expenditure or direct revenue obtained from tourists

Direct financial costs direct expenses that are necessarily incurred to sustain the tourism sector; within the public sector, typical areas of outlay include administration and bureaucracy, marketing, research and direct incentives

Direct revenue money that is obtained directly from tourists through advance or immediate expenditures in the destination and associated taxes

Enclave resort a self-contained resort complex; enclave resorts are associated with high revenue leakages because of their propensity to encourage internal spending on imported goods

Enclave tourism a mode of tourism characterised by external domination and weak linkages with the local economy

Formal sector the portion of a society's economy that is subject to official systems of regulation and remuneration; formal sector businesses provide regular wage or salaried employment, and are subject to taxation by various levels of government; the formal sector dominates Phase Four societies

Growth pole strategy a strategy that uses tourism to stimulate economic development in a suitably located area (or growth pole), so that this growth will eventually become self-sustaining

Indirect financial costs costs that do not entail a direct outlay of funds, but indicate lost revenue

Indirect impacts revenues that are used by tourism businesses and their suppliers to purchase goods and services

Indirect revenues revenue obtained through the circulation of direct tourist expenditures within a destination

Induced impacts revenue circulation that results from the use of wages in tourism businesses and their suppliers to purchase goods and services

Informal sector the portion of a society's economy that is external to the official systems of regulation and remuneration; dominant in many parts of the less developed world, informal sector businesses are characterised by small size, the absence of regular working hours or wage payments, family ownership and a lack of any regulating quality control

International tourism receipts all consumption expenditure, or payments for goods and services, made by international tourists (stayovers and excursionists) to use themselves or to give away

Multiplier effect a measure of the subsequent income generated in a destination's economy by direct tourist expenditure

Opportunity cost the idea that the use of a resource for some activity (e.g. tourism) precludes its use for some other activity that may yield a better financial return (e.g. agriculture)

Propulsive activity an economic activity that is suited to a particular area and thus facilitates the growth pole strategy; in the case of Cancún and other subtropical or tropical coastal regions 3S tourism is an effective propulsive activity

Revenue leakages a major category of indirect financial costs, entailing erosion in the multiplier effect due to the importation of goods and services that are required by tourists or the tourist industry, through factor payments abroad such as repatriated profits, and through imports required for government expenditure on tourism-related infrastructure such as airports, road and port equipment

Secondary (or 'flow-on') impacts the indirect and induced stages of money circulation in the multiplier effect that follows the actual tourist expenditure

■ QUESTIONS

1. (a) As per table 8.1, which countries respectively gained or lost share in international tourism receipts between 2002 and 2007?
   (b) What patterns are evident in this analysis?
   (c) What factors might account for these patterns?

2. Under what circumstances is a destination likely to have (i) a low income multiplier effect and (ii) a high income multiplier effect?

3. (a) What factors would limit the implementation of a growth pole strategy in Australia and New Zealand?
   (b) How could these factors be overcome?

4. Are governments in less developed countries such as Indonesia justified in favouring the formal tourism sector over its informal sector counterpart? Explain your reasons.

5. How might a focus on developing a destination's 'sense of place' help to form strong linkages between tourism and the local food sector?

6. (a) What seasonal patterns are evident for the three target segments of Australian inbound tourism depicted in figure 8.5?
   (b) What factors might account for the differences within and between segments?

7. (a) What kind of employment structure tends to be characteristic of the tourism industry?
   (b) What are the positive and negative impacts of this structure?

8. To what extent should universities accommodate tourism and hospitality students who are working part-time during their study semesters?

■ EXERCISES

1. (a) On a base map of the world, colour in red all countries and dependencies in which tourism accounts for at least 5 per cent of GNP and colour in blue all countries and dependencies where tourism accounts for less than 1 per cent of GNP.
   (b) Write a 500-word report in which you describe and account for the spatial patterns that emerge.

2. (a) Assess the economic benefits and costs discussed in this chapter as you would expect them to apply to Australia and Tonga, respectively.
   (b) Gather as much economic information as possible about the tourism sectors in both destinations, and determine whether the actual situation meets your expectations.
   (c) Account for those instances where your expectations are not met.

■ FURTHER READING

Cooper, C., Fletcher, J., Wanhill, S., Gilbert, D. & Fyall, A. 2004. *Tourism Principles and Practice*. Third Edition. London: Prentice Hall. The economic dimension of tourism is thoroughly covered in this general tourism textbook.

Dahles, H. (Ed.) 2001. *Tourism, Heritage and National Culture in Java: Dilemmas of a Local Community*. Richmond, UK: Curzon Press. Dahles provides an insightful discussion of the relationships among the formal and informal tourism sectors, tourists and government in Java, Indonesia.

Ollenburg, C. 2008. 'Regional Signatures and Trends in the Farm Tourism Sector'. *Tourism Recreation Research* 33: 13–23. This is the first academic paper to consider trends and characteristics associated with the farm tourism sector in Australia and elsewhere. Its potential to stimulate regional development is discussed.

Torres, R. 2003. 'Linkages Between Tourism and Agriculture in Mexico'. *Annals of Tourism Research* 30: 546–66. Torres relies on an extensive series of interviews with hoteliers, food wholesalers, tourists and local farmers to investigate the reasons hotels in Cancún do not obtain their food supplies from within the state of Quintana Roo.

Wanhill, S. 2005. 'Role of Government Incentives'. In Theobald, W. (Ed.) *Global Tourism.* **Third Edition. Sydney: Elsevier, pp. 367–90.** A comprehensive outline of government incentives to the tourism industry is provided in this chapter, which includes a short discussion of market failure.

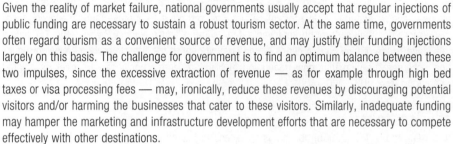 — case study

GOVERNMENT GIVE AND TAKE IN AUSTRALIA

Given the reality of market failure, national governments usually accept that regular injections of public funding are necessary to sustain a robust tourism sector. At the same time, governments often regard tourism as a convenient source of revenue, and may justify their funding injections largely on this basis. The challenge for government is to find an optimum balance between these two impulses, since the excessive extraction of revenue — as for example through high bed taxes or visa processing fees — may, ironically, reduce these revenues by discouraging potential visitors and/or harming the businesses that cater to these visitors. Similarly, inadequate funding may hamper the marketing and infrastructure development efforts that are necessary to compete effectively with other destinations.

Within Australia, the Tourism and Transport Forum (TTF) is the peak national organisation that attends to the interests of these two closely allied sectors. Key among its responsibilities is lobbying of the federal and state governments to:

- maximise government injections of public funding into tourism and transportation
- minimise government extraction of tourism and transportation-related revenue
- ensure that revenues extracted by government are reinvested to best effect in the two sectors.

As of late 2008, the urgency of the lobbying effort, and specific aspects thereof as described below, was underscored by the unprecedented challenges faced by the Australian tourism sector at that time (see the case study at the end of chapter 2).

Net subsidy equivalent

In making its case for additional funding and reduced revenue extraction, the TTF in 2008 emphasised alleged inequities in the way the federal government supports tourism as compared with other government-aided sectors such as agriculture and manufacturing. Whereas tourism is primarily supported by funding the marketing initiatives of Tourism Australia, the latter two sectors benefit from a longstanding array of measures including subsidies, tax concessions, grants for research and development, and tariff protection. The resultant 'net subsidy equivalent' for tourism (that is, direct budget outlays minus these industry-related tax measures) was calculated at $145 million per year, compared with $1.18 billion and $5.4 billion for primary production and manufacturing respectively. Moreover, the $20 million provided by the Commonwealth to assist small tourism businesses following the 2001 terrorist attacks was greatly exceeded by the $500 million provided in drought assistance to agriculture through to June 2004, despite the comparable magnitude of the crises that were faced in each case (TTF 2008a).

Tax averaging

Beyond the emphasis on such inter-sectoral inequalities, the TTF also sought to address specific federal government policies and measures that were perceived as harming or impeding the tourism sector. For example, efforts were made to allow rural and remote tourism businesses to take advantage of 'tax averaging' provisions already available to primary producers since 1920. 'Tax averaging' means that gross income and payable taxes are evened out, usually over a 5-year period, so that excessive taxes are not levied during highly productive years. Tourism, arguably, is similar to the primary producers in being subject to 'boom and bust' cycles of supply and demand that result in heavier tax burdens not faced by those having a regular long-term income stream (TTF 2008a).

Accelerated depreciation

In the aviation sector, the TTF argued that the current policy of allowing Australian airlines to depreciate the value of their aeroplanes over a 10-year period should be replaced with a 5- or 3-year timeline as allowed in Hong Kong and Singapore respectively. With a short write-off period, airlines have an added incentive to replace aging aircraft more frequently, thereby allowing them to be more competitive through improved safety, comfort and efficiency. Wisely, the TTF linked this issue to the federal government's strong commitment at the time to carbon emission reduction schemes, arguing that new generation aircraft are better positioned to meet associated reduction targets (TTF 2008b).

Tourism taxes

According to the TTF (2008b), tourism is an excessively taxed sector, with net taxes representing 17 per cent of tourism's $38.9 billion contribution to the Australian GDP in 2004–05. Attracting criticism was the federal government's decision to raise the Passenger Movement Charge (PMC) from $38 to $47 in the 2008 budget (with little accompanying transparency as to how the extra funds would be spent), and visa application fees from $75 to $100. The TTF noted that a visitor from India or China had to pay $147 in combined visa and PMC payments when visiting Australia, whereas a visit to the European Union required no payments, and to the USA just $15. As with the carbon emission link used to further support the accelerated depreciation of aircraft, the TTF wisely emphasised that tourism taxes were, *de facto*, a tax on the aviation industry since reduced demand for Australian tourism products translates into reduced passenger loads for Australian airlines (TTF 2008b).

Export Market Development Grant Scheme (EMDG)

In part as a result of TTF lobbying, the tourism sector did celebrate one notable victory in 2008 related to the introduction of more generous provisions to the Export Market Development Grant Scheme (EMDG). This is a Commonwealth initiative that reimburses up to 50 per cent of the expenses incurred by exporters in promoting their products in overseas markets (Austrade 2008). It has traditionally been available to tourism businesses and destinations promoting themselves at foreign trade shows and other overseas venues. Effective for export promotion expenditures incurred from 1 July 2008:

- the maximum grant threshold was increased from $150 000 to $200 000
- the maximum eligible annual company turnover was increased from $30 million to $60 million
- the minimum expenditure threshold was reduced from $15 000 to $10 000 (that is, reimbursements can now be claimed on all expenses above $10 000)
- the number of grants that could be applied for in a given year was increased from 7 to 8
- State, Territory and regional economic development and industry bodies can access the Scheme.

QUESTIONS

1. (a) To what extent should the TTF be involved in facilitating the arrival and internal travel of international students ?

   (b) What measures could it support with regard to this ?

2. (a) Under what circumstances is it justifiable for government to allocate tourism-derived revenue to areas that are not directly related to tourism?

   (b) Should government be required to allocate all or a stipulated portion of tourism-related revenues to the tourism sector? Why?

CHAPTER 9

SOCIOCULTURAL AND ENVIRONMENTAL IMPACTS OF TOURISM

LEARNING OBJECTIVES

After studying this chapter, you should be able to:

1. list the potential social and cultural benefits of tourism

2. describe how tourism can promote both traditional culture and the modernisation process

3. explain commodification and its positive and negative consequences, and understand how tourism can contribute to this process

4. differentiate between frontstage and backstage and discuss their implications for the management of tourist destinations

5. explain the linkages that can exist between tourism and crime

6. identify the circumstances that increase or decrease the probability that a destination will experience negative sociocultural impacts from tourism

7. assess the nature of resident attitudes toward tourism

8. describe the potential positive and negative environmental consequences of tourism for destinations

9. cite examples of the environmental impact sequence using an array of stressor activities

10. discuss the utility of ecological footprinting as a means of measuring environmental impact.

INTRODUCTION

The basic aim of tourism management at a destination-wide scale is to maximise the sector's economic, sociocultural and environmental benefits, while minimising its associated costs. To meet this objective, destination managers must understand the potential positive and negative impacts of tourism, and the circumstances under which these are most likely to occur. Chapter 8 considered economic costs and benefits, and concluded that small-scale, developing destinations are most likely to incur high costs as a consequence of tourism development. Chapter 9 extends our understanding of tourism impacts by considering their sociocultural and environmental dimensions. The following section examines the alleged sociocultural benefits of tourism, while the 'Sociocultural costs' section considers its potential sociocultural costs as expressed through the phenomenon of commodification, the demonstration effect and the relationship between tourism and crime. The possible environmental benefits of tourism is then discussed, and this is followed by an examination of its environmental costs, as modelled through the environmental impact sequence. The consideration of the sociocultural dimension before the environmental dimension is not intended to suggest the greater importance of the former, but rather that the cautionary platform (see chapter 1) initially placed more emphasis on social and cultural issues in its critique of the tourism sector. The two dimensions, in reality, are often closely interrelated.

SOCIOCULTURAL BENEFITS

Although supporters of the advocacy platform emphasise the economic benefits that could result from tourism for a destination, they also cite various secondary sociocultural advantages. These include:

- the promotion of cross-cultural understanding
- the incentive value of tourism in preserving local culture and heritage
- the promotion of social stability through positive economic outcomes.

Counter-arguments are made for all of these impacts in the following section, but the intention in this section is to present only the advocacy point of view.

Promotion of cross-cultural understanding

When individuals have had only limited or no contact at all with a particular culture, they commonly hold stereotypical, or broad and usually distorted behavioural generalisations, about that culture and its members. In the absence of direct experience, stereotypes provide a set of guidelines that are used to indicate what can be expected when encountering members of that culture. It can be argued that direct contacts between tourists and residents dispel such stereotypes and allow the members of each group to perceive one another as individuals and, potentially, as friends (Tomljenovic & Faulkner 2000). Tourism is thus seen as a potent force for cross-cultural understanding because huge numbers of people come into contact with members of other cultures both at home and abroad. In Australia, direct contacts with Japanese and other Asian tourists have undoubtedly contributed to the erosion of stereotypes held by some Australians, while the same effect has also occurred in reverse through the exposure of outbound Australians to Asia and other overseas destinations.

A force for world peace

One manifestation of this cross-cultural perspective is the perception of tourism as a vital force for world peace. Aside from spontaneous day-to-day contacts, this considers the role of tourism in facilitating deliberate 'track-two diplomacy', or unofficial face-to-face contacts that augment official or 'track-one' avenues of communication. This phenomenon is illustrated by the way that cricket Test matches in 2004 helped to build rapprochement between India and Pakistan, which have fought three wars since 1947 (Beech et al. 2005). Preceded by confidence-building measures such as an agreement to resume normal diplomatic and civil aviation links, a decision was made in 2003 to hold a Test series between the countries in Pakistan during the following year. The government of Pakistan issued visas for 10 000 Indians, whose warm and hospitable treatment by their Pakistani counterparts during the match was widely reported in the Indian press. More importantly, a regional television audience of 600 million was treated to a remarkable spectacle of incident-free sporting conduct and camaraderie throughout this 'proxy war', which ended in an Indian victory. Beech et al. (2005) speculate that this massive grassroots exposure to a sustained atmosphere of mutual goodwill has done and will do much to build the impetus for further improvement in the bilateral relationship, a consideration that is of no small import given the nuclear-weapon capabilities of both countries. Yet, such initiatives are inherently fragile. In 2008, cricket teams from Australia, England and New Zealand pulled out of Pakistan tours due to security concerns, while the country's sporting reputation was devastated in March 2009 by terrorist attacks against the visiting Sri Lankan team. Within the tourism sector itself, initiatives that explicitly attempt to foster peace and cross-cultural understanding include Oxfam's Community Aid Abroad tours to Guatemala, and Camp Coorong's 'reconciliation tourism' in South Australia (Higgins-Desbiolles 2003).

Incentive to preserve culture and heritage

Tourism may stimulate the preservation or restoration of historical buildings and sites. This can occur directly, through the collection of entrance fees, souvenir sales and donations that are allocated to the site, or indirectly, through the allocation of general tourism or other revenues to preservation or restoration efforts intended to attract or sustain visitation. This is best illustrated at a destinationwide scale by **tourist–historic cities** such as Quebec City (Canada), Bruges (Belgium) and York (UK) where the restoration and revitalisation of entire inner-city districts has been induced and sustained at least in part by tourism (Ashworth & Tunbridge 2004). Australia does not have any urban places that would qualify as a tourist–historic city but has examples of tourism-related historical preservation ranging from relatively large sites such as the Port Arthur convict ruins in Tasmania and the Millers Point district of Sydney, to small sites such as the Springvale Homestead in Katherine, Northern Territory. The Art Deco architectural district of Napier is a good New Zealand example. Destination residents benefit from these actions to the extent that restored sites are more attractive to tourists and therefore generate additional revenues, and because they provide residents with opportunities to appreciate and experience their history that might not otherwise exist.

The same principles apply to culture. Ceremonies and traditions that might otherwise die out due to modernisation may be preserved or revitalised because of tourist demand. As with historical sites, the examples are numerous, and include the revival of the *gol* ceremony in Vanuatu, where boys and young men jump from tall wooden towers in a way that superficially resembles bungee jumping (de Burlo 1996), and the revival of traditional textile and glass crafts in Malta. Other examples are the expansion of Native American arts and crafts in the American Southwest (Turco 1999), and the revitalisation of traditional dances and ceremonies on Bali (Hitchcock 2000). Similar processes are evident in Australia, with tourism serving to stimulate the production and presentation of Aboriginal crafts and dances (see Breakthrough tourism: Celebrating Aboriginal art at Desert Mob).

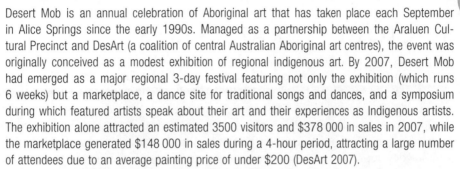

CELEBRATING ABORIGINAL ART AT DESERT MOB

Desert Mob is an annual celebration of Aboriginal art that has taken place each September in Alice Springs since the early 1990s. Managed as a partnership between the Araluen Cultural Precinct and DesArt (a coalition of central Australian Aboriginal art centres), the event was originally conceived as a modest exhibition of regional indigenous art. By 2007, Desert Mob had emerged as a major regional 3-day festival featuring not only the exhibition (which runs 6 weeks) but a marketplace, a dance site for traditional songs and dances, and a symposium during which featured artists speak about their art and their experiences as Indigenous artists. The exhibition alone attracted an estimated 3500 visitors and $378 000 in sales in 2007, while the marketplace generated $148 000 in sales during a 4-hour period, attracting a large number of attendees due to an average painting price of under $200 (DesArt 2007).

A challenge for Desert Mob is ensuring that outcomes of authenticity, revenue generation, and visitor satisfaction are all achieved as the festival becomes an increasingly important tourism product for remote central Australia. The DesArt coalition is a major strength, given its emphasis on cultural authenticity, indigenous control, the return of all profits to Indigenous artists and communities, and maintaining highly professional standards. Since most of the 41 participating Aboriginal art centres are extremely isolated, Desert Mob provides an opportunity for artists to meet in a single venue and to gain exposure to a relatively large number of potential buyers, given Alice Springs' status as a regional gateway and the sophisticated facilities of the festival venue. The egalitarian nature of the event also allows emerging artists to feature their work while encouraging interaction between Indigenous and non-Indigenous attendees (Oster 2006).

FIGURE 9.1 The Indigenous artists of Desert Mob

Source: Courtesy of Araluen Cultural Precinct. Photo by Clair Ashard

Promoting social wellbeing and stability

Through the generation of employment and revenue, tourism promotes a level of economic development conducive to increased social wellbeing and stability. This promotion also occurs when a destination attempts to improve its international competitiveness by offering services and health standards at a level acceptable to visitors from the more developed countries. Although implemented because of tourism, local residents derive an obvious and tangible social benefit from, for example, the elimination of a local malaria hazard or the introduction of electricity, anticrime measures or paved roads to the district where an international-class hotel is located.

■ SOCIOCULTURAL COSTS

Supporters of the cautionary platform have acknowledged that tourism can produce positive sociocultural outcomes under certain conditions, but maintain that unregulated mass tourism development is likely to result in substantial social and cultural costs to destination residents. This is especially true, it is argued, if those destinations are located in less developed countries or peripheral areas within more developed countries. The widespread dissatisfaction of local residents as a result of inappropriate tourism development is an extremely important consideration for destination managers, since this can lead to direct and indirect actions against tourists and tourism that will destabilise a destination and give rise to a negative market image. The maintenance of support among local residents through the prevention and amelioration of negative impacts is, therefore, a prerequisite for the long-term wellbeing of the tourism sector managed from a systems perspective. The following subsections examine the main sociocultural issues that influence the management of tourism destinations.

Commodification

The **commodification** of a destination's culture, or its conversion into a commodity in response to the perceived or actual demands of the tourist market, is commonly perceived as a major negative sociocultural impact associated with tourism (Matheson 2008). To the extent that this confers a tangible monetary value on a product (i.e. the culture) that already exists but otherwise generates no economic return, it may be regarded as a positive impact. The problem, however, occurs when the inherent qualities and meanings of cultural artefacts and performances become less important than the goal of earning revenue from their reproduction and sale. Concurrently, the culture may be modified in accordance with the demands of the tourist market, and its original significance eroded or lost altogether. There are several ways that cultural commodification can occur as a result of tourism, and the following scenario gives one extreme possibility:

- *Phase 1.* Tourists are rarely seen in the community, and when they do appear, are invited as 'honoured guests' to observe or participate in authentic local ceremonies without charge. They may be given genuine artefacts as a sign of the high esteem in which they are held by the local community.
- *Phase 2.* Visiting tourists become more frequent and hence less of a novelty. They are allowed to observe local ceremonies for a small fee, and genuine artefacts may be sold to them at a small charge.
- *Phase 3.* The community is regularly visited by a large number of tourists. Ceremonies are altered to provide more appeal to tourists, and performances are made at regular intervals suitable to the tourist market. Authenticity thus gives way to

attractions of a more contrived nature. Prices are set at the highest possible levels allowed by the market. Large amounts of cheaply produced souvenirs are made available for sale.

- *Phase 4*. The integrity of the original culture is entirely lost due to the combined effects of commodification and modernisation. Commodification extends into the most sacred and profound aspects of the culture, despite measures taken to safeguard it.

While the residents of a destination may obtain significant financial returns from tourism by the fourth stage, the contention is that serious social problems arise in association with the loss of cultural identity and the concomitant disruption of traditional norms and structures that maintained social stability. According to Greenwood (1989, p. 179), 'commoditisation of culture in effect robs people of the very meanings by which they organise their lives'. In addition, conflicts can erupt in the community over the distribution of revenue, appropriate rates of remuneration for performers and producers (who may have formerly volunteered their services) and other market-related issues with which the society may not be equipped to cope. Compounding the issue is the possibility that the progression will occur over a relatively short time period, reducing the opportunity to devise and implement effective adaptive strategies.

Traditional societies that are exposed to intensive and invasive levels of tourism development are especially susceptible to commodification. Classic case studies include Tana Toraja in Indonesia (Crystal 1989), the Basque community of Fuenterrabia in Spain (Greenwood 1989) and Tonga (Urbanowicz 1989). Maori cultural performances in New Zealand carried out in hotels tend to be more commodified and altered than performances given in villages, suggesting that venue can play an important role in the process (Tahana & Oppermann 1998).

Frontstage and backstage

Local residents are not powerless in the face of commodification pressures, and can adopt various measures to minimise their negative impact. One of these strategies, as identified by MacCannell (1976), is the recognition of **frontstage** and **backstage** distinctions within the destination. The frontstage is an area where commercial and possibly modified performances and displays are provided for the bulk of visiting tourists. The backstage, in contrast, is an area set aside for the personal or in-group use of local people and, potentially, selected VFR or business tourists. The backstage accommodates the 'real life' of the community and maintains its 'authentic' culture. As long as the distinctions are maintained and respected by the tourists and local residents, then the community can in theory achieve the dual objectives of income generation from tourism (in the frontstage) and the preservation of the local way of life (in the backstage).

The distinction between frontstage and backstage can be implicit, or some kind of physical barrier may be used to differentiate the two spaces. These range from the crude canvas screens erected by Alaskan Inuit to shield their backyards from the gazing eyes of tourists (as described by Smith 1989), to walls, ditches and 'do not enter' signs that attempt to confine tourists to the frontstage. It is possible that the very same space can be differentiated as frontstage or backstage depending on the time, so that, for example, a beach is tacitly recognised as tourist space on weekdays during daylight hours, and as local space at other times. Such distinctions can also be made on a seasonal basis. In some countries, the frontstage/backstage principle is applied as part of a comprehensive nationwide strategy for regulating contact between local residents and tourists. For example, all of Bhutan is effectively a backstage, given the government's policy of strictly limiting the number of inbound tourists and ensuring that the effects of westernisation are minimised throughout the country (Gurung & Seeland 2008). The government of the Maldives (an Indian Ocean SISOD) confines 3S tourism development to selected uninhabited atolls as a means of curtailing the influence of tourists on the country's traditional way of life (Carlsen 2006).

The frontstage/backstage distinction, however, can have unexpected consequences and dimensions that raise difficult questions about cultural authenticity. In some native Indian communities in North America, the frontstage is occupied by traditional cultural artefacts and performances that have long been abandoned or modified by the community as items of everyday use, but are of great interest to tourists. The backstage, in contrast, is occupied by a cultural landscape that is similar in many respects to that found in nonindigenous communities of a similar size and location, reflecting the evolving and adaptive nature of the living indigenous culture. It is important to note that the frontstage/backstage distinction is by no means confined to traditional communities. Local governments in Australia and other Phase Four countries often use zoning to control the intrusion of tourism-related activities and businesses into residential areas, thus effectively demarcating the latter as backstage territory.

Prostitution

Prostitution can of course thrive in non-tourism settings, but is encouraged by tourism characteristics such as host/guest (i.e. vendor/buyer) proximity, the suspension of normal behaviour by some holidaying tourists, and often large gaps in wealth between tourists and locals. Destination marketing that emphasises cultural and sexual stereotypes is a further facilitating factor. Examples include the use of the suggestive coco de mer fruit by tourism authorities in Seychelles, and an early promotional campaign in the Bahamas that used the phrase 'It's better in the Bahamas'. While successful in attracting some types of tourists, it is less clear whether this form of advertising actually leads tourists to expect sexual promiscuity among local women, or whether such demands, if they exist, are met through increased levels of prostitution. However, there is no doubt that prostitution is well established either formally or informally in many destinations as a result of tourist demand. The male prostitute, or 'beach boy', is a familiar figure on the beaches of the Caribbean and parts of Africa, where competition for female tourists is associated with increased social and economic status for impoverished local males (Herold, Garcia & DeMoya 2001).

The sex industry is a very large and well-established formal component of tourism in European cities such as Amsterdam and Hamburg, in South-East Asian destinations such as Thailand and the Philippines, and within some areas of Australia and New Zealand, such as the Kings Cross district of Sydney. Yet sex tourism is a complex phenomenon that should not automatically be condemned as unequivocally negative. Coercive and child-focused sex tourism clearly are great evils that cannot be justified. However, under other circumstances, sex tourism may be benign, empowering and financially beneficial to sex workers, at least according to some researchers (e.g. Oppermann 1998; Bauer & McKercher 2003).

The demonstration effect revisited

The concept of the demonstration effect as a potential economic cost for destinations was considered in chapter 8. From a sociocultural perspective, problems occur when residents (usually the young) gravitate towards the luxurious goods paraded by the wealthier tourists or the drugs and liberal sexual mores demonstrated by some tourists. As a result, tensions may result between the older and younger community members, as the latter increasingly reject local culture and tradition as inferior, in favour of modern outside influences (Mathieson & Wall 2006).

Case studies as diverse as the Cook Islands (Cowan 1977) and Singapore (Teo 1994) provide evidence for a tourism-related demonstration effect within local societies. However, as with most phenomena associated with tourism, this process is more complex and ambiguous than it first appears. Specifically:

- The overall role of tourism in conveying and promoting outside influences is usually relatively minor compared with the pervasive impact of television and other media, especially since the latter are also effective vehicles for the promotion of consumer goods. Hence, it is not easy to isolate the specific demonstration effect of tourism.
- The effect is not always unidimensional (i.e. tourists influencing locals), but may also involve the adoption of destination culture attributes by the tourists (see chapter 2).
- The demonstration effect can have beneficial outcomes depending on the motivations of the adopter and the elements of the tourist culture that are adopted.
- Exposure to tourists may cause traditional or 'anti-Western' local residents to become even more conservative, indicating the possibility of an 'anti-demonstration' effect.

The relationship between tourism and crime

The growth of tourism often occurs in conjunction with increases in certain types of crime, including illegal prostitution (Brunt, Mawby & Hambly 2000; Clift & Carter 2000). The tourism-intensive Surfers Paradise neighbourhood of the Gold Coast, for example, reports significantly higher levels of criminal activity than adjacent suburbs. It is tempting to conclude from such evidence that the presence and growth in tourism are attracting increased illegal behaviour, but the linkage is more complicated. As with the demonstration effect, the growth of tourism may coincide with a broader process of modernisation and development that could be the primary underlying source of social instability and, hence, criminal behaviour. Yet tourism makes a good scapegoat because of its visibility, ubiquity and emphasis on 'others' as perpetrators. In addition, some tourism-related crimes are highly publicised, resulting in a disproportionate emphasis on tourism as the reason for such activity. Another perspective is that tourism growth is usually accompanied by growth in the resident population, so that the actual number of criminal acts might be increasing without any actual growth in the per capita crime rate.

The link between tourism and crime, with the above qualifications, can be discussed first with respect to tourism in general and then with reference to specific types of tourism that entail or foster a criminal connection. A distinction can also be made between criminal acts directed *towards* tourists (i.e. ultimately a sociocultural impact mainly on the origin region) and those committed *by* tourists (i.e. a sociocultural impact mainly on the destination region).

Crime towards tourists

The general connection in the first scenario largely occurs because tourists are often wealthier than local people, and the two groups come into close contact with one another. As a result, tourists offer a tempting and convenient target for the minority of local residents that is determined to acquire some of this wealth for themselves, or who wish to exploit the tourists in some other way. Tourists can also fall victim to criminal activity associated with broader social trends (see Contemporary issue: Deportation and crime in the Caribbean). Workers within tourism may be perpetrators, as evidenced by sexual assaults on tourists by some guides in Nepal (Brown 1999). At one end of the spectrum where the element of illegality is vague or borderline are residents who engage in deliberate overpricing or begging. Progressing towards the other end of the spectrum are unambiguously criminal activities involving theft, assault and murder, such as those connected with tourism-targeted terrorism. The attractiveness of tourists as targets of crime is increased by several factors, as depicted in figure 9.2.

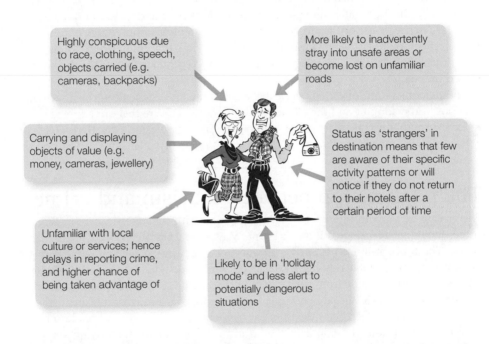

FIGURE 9.2 Factors that make tourists targets of criminal activity

contemporary issue

 DEPORTATION AND CRIME IN THE CARIBBEAN

In the summer of 2008, Catherine and Benjamin Mullany, a honeymooning couple from the United Kingdom, were brutally assaulted in their luxury bungalow in Antigua's boutique Cocos Hotel. Catherine was killed instantly and Benjamin was left in a brain-dead state. This violent crime generated an enormous amount of negative media publicity for Antigua, long regarded as one of the safest Caribbean 3S destinations. Asked to account for the assault and for the overall dramatic increase in the island's violent crime rate, local residents and authorities cited the enforced return of emigrant criminal citizens from certain countries including the United Kingdom, United States and Canada. Almost 300 such individuals were returned to Antigua since 1998, representing about one in every 250 residents (Colvin 2008). Often having no family or cultural links with the island of their birth, deported criminals are commonly ostracised and frequently resort to criminal activity. Wealthy tourists offer a convenient and tempting target. In addition to murders of an increasingly violent and random nature, the deportees are also credited with changing the drug culture in the Caribbean from the smoking of marijuana to the consumption of cocaine and crack, and with encouraging the formation of gang culture among local youths.

While it must be emphasised that the vast majority of crime victims have been local residents, growing violence against tourists is a major concern because of its effect of seriously damaging Antigua's image as a safe and welcoming destination, thereby inducing reduced levels of visitation and associated revenues and employment. Authorities in 2008 felt compelled for the first time to assign armed guards to the annual Race Week sailing regatta, perhaps realising that this highly visible symbol of crime risk could only reinforce the growing harm to Antigua's destination brand. Others accuse the police of being part of the problem, ignoring or failing to pursue criminal activity because of low salaries, being paid off by criminal elements, or both.

Crime by tourists

Criminal acts are also committed by the tourists themselves, either against the locals or other tourists. Where certain forms of tourism either encourage or cause criminal activities, tourists are often the initiator or lead players. Sex-related activity that is defined as illegal by destination authorities or under international law, such as that which involving children or human trafficking (Tepelus 2008), is a high profile example. In other cases, the tourism activity is not inherently illegal, but attracts criminal interest. Casino-related gambling is an example of this indirect relationship, given the involvement of organised crime elements, prostitutes and participants who steal or embezzle to feed their gaming addiction (Stitt, Nichols & Giacopassi 2005). Another involves student holiday events, such as the North American 'spring break' or Australia's 'Schoolies Week', which are associated with high levels of alcohol and drug consumption (Scott 2006). Rivalry situations involving biker gangs or football fans also have a high potential for social unrest, as in the phenomenon of drunken English soccer hooligans travelling to France with the explicit intent of fighting with French fans.

Factors contributing to the increased likelihood of sociocultural costs

For the managers of destinations, it is vital to know the circumstances under which negative sociocultural impacts are most likely to occur. This allows them to assess whether these circumstances are present in the destination, and if so, to implement appropriate demand- or supply- side ameliorative measures. If these actual or potential impacts are ignored, there is a danger that the social or cultural **carrying capacity** of the destination (or the amount of tourism activity that can be accommodated without incurring serious damage) will be exceeded. Each of the factors outlined here should not be looked at in isolation, since it is more probable that negative effects will result from a combination of mutually reinforcing circumstances. Thus, the greater the number of factors present, the greater the probability of negative outcomes. No order of priority is intended in this inventory.

Extensive inequality in wealth between tourists and residents

As mentioned earlier, tourists who are visibly wealthier than the majority of the resident population, as in an LDC destination, are more likely to generate resentment and induce a demonstration effect among some residents that cannot be fulfilled by conventional means (e.g. increased earnings). Hence, there is a greater probability that these individuals will revert to tourist-directed crime to meet these perceived needs. A broader issue of relevance to this factor of wealth disparity is that residents are just as likely to rely on stereotypes as tourists, prompting many to assume that *all* tourists from Australia or the United States are extremely wealthy. A widespread sense of envy and resentment can emerge under such circumstances.

Cultural and behavioural differences between tourists and residents

Large cultural differences can result in the identification of tourists as a group distinct from the 'local' population, hence reinforcing the sense of the 'other' and, as discussed above, making them more vulnerable to crime. Where the gap between the tourist and resident cultures is wide, the probability of culturally based misunderstandings is also increased, even if tourist actions are well-intended. The problem is exacerbated when tourists make little or no attempt to recognise and respect local sensibilities and persist in adhering to their own cultural norms. The same also applies to the attitudes of local residents, although more of an onus is justifiably placed on visitors since the latter cannot reasonably expect that a destination will transform itself just for their convenience. Inappropriate behaviour has been fairly or unfairly associated with psychocentric tourists (see chapter 6), who allegedly become more prevalent as a destination becomes more developed. For such groups, contact with other cultures is likely to reinforce rather than remove existing cultural stereotypes.

Overly intrusive or exclusive contact

Whether differentials in wealth and culture create social problems is also influenced by the nature of contact between tourists and residents. As discussed in chapter 7, this is an extremely complex factor, given the large number of individual face-to-face contacts that occur over the course of a typical visit and the numerous variables that mediate such interactions, which include personality type, group characteristics (e.g. a bus tour group or a young couple), the moods of the individuals involved and how extroverted or introverted the culture or individuals within the culture are.

Some supporters of the advocacy platform argue that direct contact can dissolve stereotypes, but it has been suggested earlier that this can make the situation even worse under certain circumstances, for example when the contacts are overly intrusive and extend into backstage areas. However, problems can also result when tourists are channelled into exclusively tourism-focused spaces such as retail frontstages or enclave resorts (see chapter 8). Accusations may arise in such cases that the tourists are monopolising the most desirable spaces, that they are being deliberately snobbish or that small operators are being denied the opportunity to engage tourists in commercial transactions. Further, the reduction in direct contact that results from these attempts to remove tourists from local areas may indeed reinforce the cultural stereotypes that each group holds about the other. This discussion illustrates the **paradox of resentment** that is faced by tourism managers, wherein tensions can be generated whether destination managers choose to maximise contact between tourists and locals through a strategy of dispersal or to minimise these contacts by pursuing a policy of isolation.

High proportion of tourists relative to the local population

Where the number of tourists is high compared with the resident population, the former may be perceived as a threat that is 'swamping' the destination. Again, the influence of other variables should be considered, as the perceived number of tourists may be inflated by their cultural or racial visibility, or by their concentration within confined boundaries of space or time. An excellent example of this phenomenon occurs in the cruise ship industry when a large number of passengers is discharged into a port of call. These excursionists tend to concentrate within restricted shopping areas in the central business district for a short period of time, and are usually unaware of and unprepared for the actual sociocultural conditions prevailing in the destination.

Hyperdestinations are the extreme expression of the spatial and temporal distortions that emerge in most tourist destinations under free market conditions (see chapters 4 and 8). The situation is especially acute in tourist shopping villages, on small islands and in remote villages, where even a small number of tourists can be overwhelming. For this reason, managers should be extremely careful about placing too much reliance on ratios that measure the number of locals per tourist or visitor-night over an entire country or state. For example, for Australia as a whole, there were about four residents for every inbound tourist in 2007. However, this statistic is rendered almost meaningless because the number would be much lower for an area such as the Gold Coast (and would vary considerably between the coastal and inland suburbs and between summer and winter), and much higher in inland farming areas.

Rapid growth of tourism

If tourism is growing at a rapid pace, the local society, along with its economy and culture, may not have time to effectively adjust to the associated changes. For example, sufficient time may not be available to devise and formalise the necessary backstage/ frontstage distinctions. The result can be a growing sense of anxiety and powerlessness within the local community. As with the tourist/host ratio factor, this issue is closely related to the size of the destination — even a small absolute increase in visitor numbers, or the construction of just one mid-sized hotel, can represent high relative growth that challenges the capacities and capabilities of the small destination.

Dependency

Problems can occur if a destination becomes too dependent on tourism, or if the sector is controlled (or is perceived to be controlled) by outside interests. In the first scenario, sociocultural problems occur indirectly as seasonal or cyclical fluctuations in demand generate widespread unemployment or, alternatively, an influx of outside workers (see chapter 8). High levels of control by outside forces, as per the second scenario, are problematic for several reasons, including resentment over the repatriation of profits and monopolisation of high-status jobs (e.g. hotel managers and owners) by nonlocals. In addition, locals may feel that they are not in control of events that affect their everyday lives. This sense is reinforced by the increased power of large transnational corporations and the uncertainty associated with globalisation (see chapter 5).

Different expectations with respect to authenticity

Cultural differences notwithstanding, tourist–resident tensions arise if there is a misunderstanding about the status of a cultural performance or other tourism products in terms of their perceived 'authenticity', which itself is a contentious and highly subjective concept (see chapters 5 and 9). On one level it can be argued that everything, including fake copies of local art, is 'authentic' or 'genuine' because of the simple fact that it exists and conveys some kind of meaning. However, this view is not helpful, since the concept can then no longer be used to distinguish between different tourism products and experiences. A more conventional view is to consider authentic goods and experiences as those that embody the actual culture (past or present) of the destination community. However, even this is problematic. In the example of the Native American village noted earlier, is the nontraditional culture that is being practised in the backstage, which represents the contemporary reality of that group of people, any less authentic than the tepee displayed in the frontstage?

One way of approaching the issue is to consider perceptions of authenticity. Four generalised scenarios are possible, as depicted in figure 9.3. In the first scenario, (a), the attraction is presented as authentic and is perceived as such by the visiting tourist. This is the ideal option that is likely to characterise the first two stages of the commodification model outlined in earlier. The opposite situation, (b), is also benign in terms of its implications for host–guest relationships. In this scenario, a performance is presented as contrived and is perceived as such by the tourists. While a philosophical argument can be made as to the inherent value or legitimacy of a contrived (or 'inauthentic'?) product, the crucial point is that both parties recognise and accept this contrived status. There is no attempt at deception, and no fundamental misunderstanding among most participants. Disneyworld and Las Vegas are classic examples of venues hosting 'doubly contrived' attractions. In these fantasy worlds, no one believes, or is seriously deceived into believing, that the Magic Kingdom or the Excalibur casino are 'real' — everyone accepts that these are hardcore frontstage fantasy environments designed to attract and entertain tourists.

Residents' presentation of attraction	Tourists' perception of attraction	
	Genuine	Contrived
Genuine	(a) Positive impact (both parties recognise authentic nature)	(d) Negative impact (tourists believe that a genuine production is contrived)
Contrived	(c) Negative impact (tourists misled or confused into mistaking the contrived for the genuine)	(b) Positive impact (both parties recognise inauthentic nature)

FIGURE 9.3 Resident tourist cross-perception of attractions

The remaining two scenarios, (c) and (d), are more problematic and require special attention from managers. In one case, (c), the performance is contrived, but tourists believe, through inadvertent (e.g. frontstage is confused with or misinterpreted as backstage) or deliberate reasons (e.g. frontstage is deliberately purveyed as backstage or the two are mixed), that they are viewing something that is traditional. The limbo performance in a Caribbean hotel, the sale of 'genuine' religious artefacts at Lourdes and the 'greeting' given to visitors by 'native' Hawaiian women, are all examples of this perceptual discord. Tourists may emerge from such experiences feeling cheated, embarrassed or exploited. MacCannell (1976) describes as 'staged authenticity' the deliberate attempt to convey contrived culture as authentic.

The opposite situation, (d), occurs when the performance is genuine, but tourists see it as contrived, in some cases because of scepticism obtained from previous experience with scenario (c). Residents may be offended when tourists react to a sombre local ceremony, for example, in a disrespectful or flippant manner, as sometimes occurs in the religious events that are held during Carnival time in the Caribbean or Latin America.

Resident reactions

Early consideration of resident reactions toward tourism focused on a model of escalating resident irritation proposed by Doxey (1976). This '**irridex**' (see figure 9.4) alleges that residents are 'euphoric' in the initial stages of tourism as a growing number of allocentric-type tourists provide good company and good monetary returns for the local community. As the flow becomes larger, tourists are taken for granted and interactions become more formal and commercial (commodified). This 'apathy' stage gives way to 'irritation' or 'annoyance', and then outright 'antagonism', as the social, cultural and environmental carrying capacities of the destination are approached and then exceeded. An attitude of 'resignation' then sets in once the residents realise that they must adapt to a drastically altered community setting. For some residents, resignation is manifested in a quiet acceptance of the tourism-intensive destination, while others choose to leave the destination altogether, presumably to live in a place that has substantially less tourism intensity.

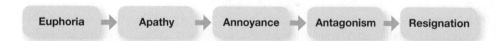

FIGURE 9.4 Stages of the irridex

Source: Doxey (1976)

Empirical research has revealed only partial support for the irridex. A major criticism involves its treatment of the local community as a homogeneous entity evolving along a single perceptual and behavioural trajectory. In reality, any community is likely to display an array of reactions to tourism at any given stage of development, depending on such factors as the residents' proximity to the tourist districts, the amount of time that they have resided in the destination, their socioeconomic status and whether or not they are employed within the tourism industry. A major factor is how much any particular individual derives personal or family benefits from the presence of tourists, whatever the overall effect for the community. Also, if it is possible to undertake a psychographical differentiation of the tourist market, then the same can be said of residents — local allocentrics are likely to react to tourists in a very different manner than local psychocentrics, although this proposition has not yet been empirically tested.

Finally, many residents will harbour mixed views towards tourism — for example, they cite its social costs to the destination but highly value its economic benefits. This is apparent in the Gold Coast hinterland hyperdestination of Tamborine Mountain, where 51 per cent of residents in a survey displayed this ambivalent tendency, while the remainder was about evenly divided between 'supporters' and 'opponents'. Yet even supporters conceded that tourism created high levels of traffic congestion, while opponents admitted that tourism created local employment and attracted desirable services (Weaver & Lawton 2001). In some situations residents may tolerate a significant level of personal inconvenience if they perceive that the benefits of tourism to the community as a whole are substantial. This is evident in the attitudes of Gold Coast residents towards the annual Indy car race during its run from 1991 to 2008 (Fredline & Faulkner 2000).

Early deterministic models such as the irridex can also be criticised for its assumption of a reactive rather than a proactive community response. As the local situation deteriorates, many communities implement official or unofficial measures (e.g. curtailing development, introducing or changing zoning, introducing quotas, introducing education programs, improving infrastructure, limiting non-local ownership) to cope with tourism, pre-empting antagonistic responses. Thus, among the Maasai of Kenya, attitudes toward tourists and tourism became progressively more positive as the efforts of tribal members to gain more control over tourism within their territories became more successful (Irandu 2004). Among indigenous people in general, resistance and adaptation to externally imposed tourism is a common phenomenon that may help to open the way to re-empowerment (see the case study at the end of this chapter).

■ ENVIRONMENTAL BENEFITS

Various environmental benefits have been cited by the advocacy platform as a supplement to the dominant economic benefits:

- Clean, scenic settings are desirable assets for attracting tourists in most places, whatever their specific attractions. Destination managers therefore have an incentive to protect and enhance their peripheral environmental assets.
- In certain kinds of tourism (e.g. ecotourism), an 'unspoiled' environment and its associated wildlife may constitute a focus tourist attraction, providing an added incentive for its preservation. The resultant use of such resources for tourism in this and the previous scenario may be a more economically rational option than potentially less benign activities such as agriculture or logging, provided that the associated generation of revenue is sufficiently compensatory (this idea is discussed more thoroughly in chapter 11).
- Tourists have been credited with exposing environmental abuses in remote areas. For example, they were instrumental in publicising the practice of clear-cutting in the forests of British Columbia and in exposing pollution problems in Antarctica scientific bases (Stonehouse & Crosbie 1995).
- Individuals who personally experience endangered natural sites through tourism may be more willing to support their preservation in the political arena, and to become more sensitive to environmental issues. Eighty-three per cent of a sample of ecolodge guests in Lamington National Park, Queensland, for example, agreed or strongly agreed that participation in ecotourism had made them more environmentally conscientious (Weaver & Lawton 2002).

■ ENVIRONMENTAL COSTS

In the latter half of the twentieth century, the tourism industry demonstrated a remarkable capacity to intrude on, and sometimes overwhelm, certain kinds of physical environment, thereby providing contrary evidence to the earlier argument that tourism protects such environments from less benign forms of use. Of particular concern has been the effect of 3S tourism on coastal areas and inland bodies of water. Because of market demands, the developers of 3S accommodation and other tourism facilities try to locate as close as possible to water-based attractions. However, ironically, these high-demand coastal and shoreline settings are also among the most complex, spatially constrained and vulnerable of the Earth's natural environments. In effect, the greatest concentrations of tourism activity have been established, within an exceptionally short period of time, in the very settings that are least capable of accommodating such levels of development.

The sprawling and ever expanding coastal resort agglomerations of eastern Florida, the Riviera, the insular Caribbean and south-east Queensland all demonstrate this dilemma. On a smaller scale, a similar problem is being experienced in fragile mountain environments such as the European Alps, the Australian Alps, the Himalaya and the Rockies. Small islands are also highly vulnerable because of their limited environmental resource base, and the fact that just one or two major resort developments can impact on a significant proportion of the total environment. A great problem for tourism is that environmental deterioration, like cultural commodification, may progress to a state where visitors are no longer attracted to the destination — and the destination is then faced with the double dilemma of a degraded environment and a degraded tourism sector (see chapter 10).

Environmental impact sequence

In the late 1970s the Organisation for Economic Cooperation and Development (OECD 1980) formulated a simple and still relevant four-stage **environmental impact sequence**, which uses a systems approach to model the environmental effects associated with tourism (see figure 9.5):

- **stressor activities** initiate the environmental impact sequence
- **environmental stresses** associated with these activities alter the environment
- **environmental responses** occur as a result of the stresses; these can be immediate or longer term, and direct or indirect
- **human responses** occur as various stakeholders and participants react to the environmental responses; these can also range from immediate to long term, and from direct to indirect. These responses, notably, may themselves be new stressor activities that trigger new environmental stresses and responses.

Four categories of stressor activity ('permanent' environmental restructuring, generation of waste residuals, tourist activities and indirect and induced activities), as described in the subsections below, account for all such impacts.

'Permanent' environmental restructuring

This category encompasses environmental alterations directly related to tourism that are intended to be permanent. Associated stressor activities include the construction of specialised facilities such as resort hotels and theme parks, as well as tourist-dominated golf courses, marinas and airports. Focusing on the construction of a new resort hotel, the following list indicates just some of the possible associated environmental stresses:

- clearance of existing natural vegetation
- selective introduction of exotic plants
- levelling of terrain
- reclamation of natural wetlands such as mangroves or estuaries

- sand mining on local beaches
- quarrying
- blocking of breezes and sunshine by tall structures
- extraction of groundwater.

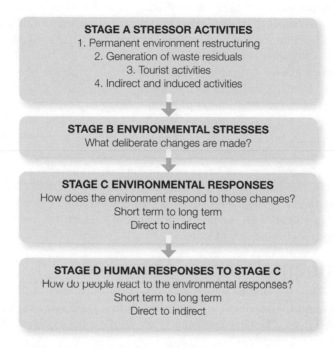

STAGE A STRESSOR ACTIVITIES
1. Permanent environment restructuring
2. Generation of waste residuals
3. Tourist activities
4. Indirect and induced activities

STAGE B ENVIRONMENTAL STRESSES
What deliberate changes are made?

STAGE C ENVIRONMENTAL RESPONSES
How does the environment respond to those changes?
Short term to long term
Direct to indirect

STAGE D HUMAN RESPONSES TO STAGE C
How do people react to the environmental responses?
Short term to long term
Direct to indirect

FIGURE 9.5 Environmental impact sequence in tourism

Source: Adapted from OECD (1980)

The potential environmental responses to clearance include the reduced biodiversity of native flora and fauna and increased numbers of undesirable and opportunistic exotic plants and animals. Levelling is commonly associated in the short term with soil erosion and landslides, and in the longer term, particularly in more distant locations, with flooding problems due to increased run-off and the raising of streambeds by the downstream deposition of sediments. Also note that sand mining and quarrying may be carried out at a considerable distance from the actual development site. It is important to stress that environmental responses also are not restricted to the site where restructuring is occurring, but can be realised in far away locations within the ecosystem. This can be problematic for a destination that is itself well managed, but suffers the effects of poor management within, say, an upstream destination that discharges untreated wastes into the river shared by both destinations.

In coastal areas an adverse environmental impact sequence is frequently associated with such activities as the construction of beach piers for the accommodation of watercraft that interfere with normal geophysical processes. Under normal conditions, the stability of the beachfront is maintained as sand particles removed by lateral offshore currents are replaced by new material eroded from nearby headlands or other beaches and are deposited elsewhere by this same current (see figure 9.6). The effect of constructing a pier (i.e. the environmental stress) is to interrupt this pattern, causing sand to pile up behind the pier in a spit-like formation. Lacking replenishment by this sand, the beach on the other side of the pier is eroded by the modified current. This eventually eliminates portions of the beach, and threatens adjacent resorts and other structures. Possible human responses in the short term include reduced visitor numbers in the eroded beach environment, which would lead to a loss of income in the adjacent resorts. The resort owners could respond by constructing their own small pier to trap sand in front of the resorts. In the longer term, the facilities might have to be abandoned if no countervailing measures are undertaken. Remedial measures relevant to this or other coastal development scenarios include the removal of the pier, the pumping of sand across the pier from the artificial spit to the down-current beach, or the construction of an offshore artificial reef to modify wave action (see Managing tourism: The sand on Australia's Gold Coast).

Normal conditions

Erosion   Deposition

Beach
(bird's eye view)

Resort

Modified by construction of pier

Deposition

Erosion

Resort

FIGURE 9.6 Environmental impact sequence involving construction of a pier

managing tourism

THE SAND ON AUSTRALIA'S GOLD COAST

In 1962, the sea wall at the mouth of the Tweed River in northern New South Wales was lengthened to keep the waterway open to navigation. One outcome was the accumulation of sand at Leticia Spit and resultant sand impoverishment on the iconic beaches of the Gold Coast to the north. To address the problem, the Tweed River Entrance Sand Bypassing Project (TRESBP) was launched in 2001 to replenish the Gold Coast sand supply while keeping the river mouth open to traffic. Some now argue that the project has been too successful, with excessive replenishment 'killing off' the famous Kirra surf break and leaving in its stead desert-like conditions. The problem has been attributed to multiple factors, including an excessive rate of sand replenishment that was intended to make up for almost 40 years of beach erosion, and the absence of major storms that were assumed to occur and which would have removed some of this excess sand. To address the imbalance, which includes high rates of beach erosion in the areas of New South Wales from which the sand is being pumped, additional outlets for the dredged sand are being proposed for locations north of Kirra (Bruce 2008a).

Experts in coastal management contend that equilibrium will be restored eventually as managers learn to 'fine tune' the TRESBP to better emulate natural processes. However, stakeholders in the area are demanding more immediate solutions, pointing to heavy financial losses as surfers relocate to other areas, and reduced quality of the eroding beach experience in New South Wales. Ironically, the embarrassment of sand riches at Kirra is also a cause for concern, with accommodation providers complaining that beachgoers have too far a distance to walk to access the ocean. Pending government approval of the additional outlet option, others are proposing the placement of a geotextile mega sandbag at Kirra which would lengthen the existing groyne at Kirra and in theory restore the break by stabilising the flow of sand from the south (Bruce 2008b).

Generation of waste residuals

Waste residuals in tourism typically include the following:
- blackwater (i.e. sewage) and greywater (e.g. water from showers and kitchens)
- garbage (organic and inorganic)
- atmospheric emissions from aircraft, vehicles, generators and air-conditioners
- noise from aircraft and vehicles
- run-off of fertilisers and pesticides from golf courses and lawns.

Focusing on the first of these stressor activities as an example, blackwater is a significant environmental stress when it is discharged in large quantities directly into a nearby body of water or into a local water table. Environmental responses might include localised water contamination, the harming or killing of marine life and a loss in aesthetic appeal. Initial human responses, which include various health problems, will likely lead to reduced visitation unless steps are taken to deal with the problems (as with the beach erosion scenario).

Climate change

In recent years, the issue of atmospheric emissions has been strongly framed by the phenomenon of **climate change**, which is the gradual increase in global surface temperatures that is widely attributed to the release of so-called 'greenhouse gases' by human activity. By some estimates, the global tourism sector accounts for around 5 per cent of all such emissions, symbolised perhaps most cogently by the airline industry. Tourism-related human responses to climate change have mitigation as well as adaptation components, with the former considered in more detail in chapter 11. With respect to adaptation, pleasure periphery destinations in particular have been implicated as sites of high concern given that coastal and alpine areas are expected to be among the environments most impacted by the effects of climate change. This will occur through rising sea levels and increasingly intensive and more numerous storms in the first case, and through the loss of snow cover in the second (Becken & Hay 2007; Hall & Higham 2005). Adaptation includes the adjustments that are made in response to such perceived threats by industry (e.g., stronger building codes for seaside hotels, alternative activities for longer off-seasons in ski resorts), but also the decisions made by potential tourists. Consumers, for example, may believe media reports that the Great Barrier Reef is dying due to higher water temperatures, and decide instead to visit cooler water reefs in higher latitude locations. In such a case, industry adaptation must then also include public education and/or investment in destinations adjacent to more resilient coral populations or higher altitude snowfields.

Tourist activities

There is a relatively large body of literature on the effects of tourist activity on various natural environments (Buckley 2004; Marion & Farrell 1998; Newsome, Moore & Dowling 2002). Associated stressor activities in tourism include:
- walking on coral reefs
- disturbing aquatic sediments by divers and boaters
- trampling vegetation
- littering
- approaching and observing wildlife
- pedestrian or vehicular traffic congestion
- the use of trail bikes, jet-skis and off-road vehicles
- consuming food and other resources
- elimination of bodily wastes.

While some of the environmental stress results from actions of a deliberately destructive nature (e.g. littering, harassment of wildlife or destroying vegetation with an off-road vehicle), apparently benign acts also cause damage when their cumulative impact exceeds local environmental carrying capacities. Examples include trail erosion and disruption of wildlife resulting from too much hiking or wildlife-viewing activity. Even more insidious is the inadvertent introduction of potentially harmful pathogens into remote areas by hikers, backpackers and other tourists. Buckley, King and Zubrinich (2004), for example, describe how spores of the jarrah dieback pathogen (*Phytophthora cinnamomi*), which can destroy 50–75 per cent of plant species in some Australian plant communities, are readily dispersed by off-road vehicles, trail bikes, mountain bikes, hiking boots and horses. Solutions to contain this spread, such as the quarantine of unaffected areas or the complete sterilisation of all equipment, vehicles and clothing before entering such areas, are widely regarded as prohibitively expensive, excessive or ineffective.

In a coastal context, the negative effects of tourist activity on coral reefs are well documented and widespread (Cater & Cater 2007; Lück 2007b). Notably, serious damage such as coral breakage is attributable mostly to inadvertent and often unavoidable activities such as contact with fins (Harriott, Davis & Banks 1997) and sedimentation caused by fin agitation (Zakai & Chadwick-Furman 2002). Such impacts can only be partially controlled by diver education and skills enhancement, and hence it is likely that increases in coral damage will be commensurate with increases in the amount of diving activity that occurs in a particular site.

Indirect and induced activities

In earlier discussions on tourism revenue and employment (see chapter 8), the concept of ongoing indirect and induced impacts was noted. A similar effect applies to the stressor activities associated with the environmental impact sequence. Road improvements or airport expansions that occur because of tourism are examples of indirect permanent environmental restructuring. Induced effects include the construction of houses for people who have moved into an area to work in the tourist industry, and

amenity migrants who move to an area for lifestyle purposes after experiencing that area as a tourist.

The indirect and induced effects of tourism at a global scale are enormous, given the number of facilities that are at least partly affiliated with tourism, and the number of people who are employed in the tourism industry or are dependent on those who are. It is evident, for example, that most of the inland (and non-tourism oriented) suburbs of Queensland's Gold Coast would have never been developed had it not been for the presence of tourism as a propulsive industry and generator of regional wealth. However, as with revenue and employment, it is difficult to measure the extent of tourism-related effects on such 'external' environments when the interrelationship is not immediate and direct.

Ecological footprinting

Increased concerns over climate change and other environmental impacts of tourism have prompted attempts to calculate the **ecological footprint (EF)** of various types of tourism activity. An EF is the measurement of the resource exploitation that is required and the wastes that are generated to sustain a particular type of tourist or tourism activity, such as an aeroplane trip, festival, or stay in a resort hotel (see Technology and tourism: The real cost of admission) (Hunter & Shaw 2007). An increasingly popular subtype is the carbon footprint, which focuses on the greenhouse gases generated by such activity. The purpose of ecological footprinting is firstly to identify with as much precision as possible the resource and waste implications of the target activity, and then to use this information to devise appropriate mitigation responses (see chapter 11). Given the complexity of tourism systems, it is not surprising that EF is an imperfect science, especially if the sponsoring body intends to take into account the indirect and induced impacts of tourism. Nevertheless, well developed EF indices are effective in confronting consumers and businesses with seemingly convincing evidence of their environmental impacts, and thereby increasing the likelihood of some kind of mitigating action.

technology and tourism

THE REAL COST OF ADMISSION

Organisers of tourism-related events can access the website of Victoria's Environment Protection Authority to obtain free access to a specialised ecological footprint calculator. Transportation of goods and people is a major focus of the calculator, in terms of travel to the venue (i.e., distance, mode) both from the attendees' home and their place of overnight accommodation, if applicable. Consideration is also given to the travel distance and mode of temporary facilities transported to the event venue. Resource information includes energy and water use as well as expenditure on catered items such as 'dairy products' and 'bakery products', and promotional items such as paper and printing. Waste outputs are solicited in categories such as 'paper and cardboard', 'glass' and 'plastic'. The outcome of the calculator is a statistic that measures the event's ecological footprint in total 'global hectares', or the amount of land hypothetically needed to supply the resources consumed and the waste generated. This is then broken down into components such as transportation and accommodations so that areas of relatively high consumption can be targeted for mitigation and/or future amelioration. An overall footprint for Australia is provided for benchmarking purposes.

To obtain the required information, the website provides downloadable questionnaires that can be distributed to attendees, organisers or suppliers, as appropriate. It is clear, nevertheless, that a great amount of effort is necessary to obtain and collate the requested information, even if the data are based on a random sample. An added problem is that some of the information may be difficult to isolate, leading to inaccurate calculator inputs. 'Oil and fats', for example, are products present in all food. The possibility of high error outcomes is compounded by the use of assumptions that may not apply to some of the inputs. All 'tea and coffee', for example, is treated as a single category with regard to their production requirements, even though 'fair trade' products may have lower resource requirements. It is likely that future versions of the calculator will take such factors into consideration, though the outcome may be a more complicated and less user-friendly instrument requiring expert administration.

Management implications of sociocultural and environmental impacts

The discourse on impact, whether environmental or sociocultural, is informed by the following critical observations:

- *All* tourism-related activity causes a certain amount of stress, and this stress is likely to include both positive and negative effects for different stakeholders.
- The critical issue therefore is not whether stress can be avoided altogether, but whether the net effects are acceptable to the destination community or can be reduced to an acceptable level through proactive management strategies. Acceptability, in turn, is influenced by the perception of benefits received — residents normally try to realise optimum benefits, but a high level of environmental or sociocultural stress may be tolerated in exchange for significant job and revenue opportunities for the local community. It may also be reasoned that the negative environmental or sociocultural impacts of tourism are less than those that would result from alternative economic activities such as logging.
- Stress is linked to carrying capacity, which varies from site to site, and is a malleable concept that can be manipulated through site hardening, the formal designation of frontstage/backstage distinctions and other adaptive measures. Ecosystems, as do cultures and societies, have different levels of resilience and adaptability. Thus, a concentration of 500 tourists in a closed-canopy temperate forest would probably have no discernible impact on that biome, but could seriously disrupt an Antarctic site. However, even within the same type of environment (e.g. a tropical rainforest or a coral reef), site-specific carrying capacity will be influenced by variables such as slope, biodiversity, soil type and hydrology. Generalisations about carrying capacity should, therefore, be made with great caution.
- Finally, carrying capacities are often extremely difficult to identify, since stress and its impact are not always dramatic, but rather incremental and long term. A large resort destination such as the Gold Coast may appear to be functioning within local environmental carrying capacities, until a 100-year cyclone event destroys the community because of alterations to the protective dune and estuarine environments that occurred over previous decades. Similarly, a local community may appear to be coexisting peacefully with an adjacent enclave resort, until one particular incident triggers a violent community-wide reaction against that resort. As discussed in more detail in chapter 11, a strong element of uncertainty and ambiguity must always be taken into account when attempting to identify the long-term costs and benefits of tourism in any destination.

CHAPTER REVIEW

This chapter has considered an array of sociocultural and environmental impacts potentially associated with the development of tourism. The major sociocultural benefits focus on tourism's potential to promote cross-cultural understanding, to function as an incentive to preserve a destination's culture and historical heritage and to foster wellbeing and stability within the local society. These advantages were cited by the advocacy platform as secondary benefits to the all-important economic consequences. Sociocultural costs, as emphasised by the cautionary platform, include the gradual commodification of culture and related perspectives on prostitution. Commodification occurs when the local culture becomes more commercialised, and more modified and cheapened, as local residents respond to the opportunities provided by the increased intake of visitors. Other aspects involve the sociocultural consequences of the tourism demonstration effect, and the direct and indirect connections between tourism and crime, wherein tourists and residents can both be victims or perpetrators.

Negative sociocultural impacts that may eventually breach a destination's carrying capacity are more likely to occur in a destination when there is inequality in material wealth between the residents and tourists, strong cultural differentiation and a tendency on the part of tourists to adhere strongly to their own culture. Other factors include tourist–resident contacts that are overly intrusive or exclusive, the extent to which residents are able to differentiate between 'backstage' and 'frontstage' spaces, a high proportion of tourists to residents, an overly rapid pace of tourism growth, a level of dependency on tourism and external control over the same, and differential expectations as to the meaning and authenticity of cultural and historical products. Resident reactions to increasing tourism development, once modeled as a simple linear progression from euphoria to antagonism, are complex, with data indicating that communities and individuals hold diverse and sometimes contradictory perceptions about tourism at all stages of development. Residents also have the capacity to pre-empt or change inappropriate tourism activity.

The main environmental benefit associated with tourism is its provision of an incentive for the protection of natural resources that would probably otherwise be subject to less benign forms of exploitation. However, the environmental impact sequence suggests that tourism development itself may produce negative consequences. This sequence is a four-stage process involving the appearance of stressor activities, environmental stresses that result from these activities, environmental responses to those stresses and human reactions to the responses. The four categories of stressor activities are permanent environmental restructuring, the generation of waste residuals, tourist activities and indirect and induced activities associated with tourism. Empirical evidence for topical phenomena such as climate change suggests that these impacts can often be subtle, indirect, delayed and evident in regions far removed from the location of the original stress, thereby making the calculation of applicable ecological footprints a complicated process.

■ SUMMARY OF KEY TERMS

Amenity migrants people who move to an area because of its recreational and lifestyle amenities, including comfortable weather and beautiful scenery; amenity migrants are usually first exposed to such places through their own tourist experiences

Backstage the opposite of frontstage; areas of the destination where personal or intragroup activities occur, such as noncommercialised cultural performances.

A particular space may be designated as either frontstage or backstage depending on the time of day or year

Carrying capacity the amount of tourism activity (e.g. number of visitors, amount of development) that can be accommodated without incurring serious harm to a destination; distinctions can be made between social, cultural and environmental carrying capacity, all of which can be adjusted with appropriate management

Climate change the gradual increase in global surface temperatures that is usually attributed to the excessive release of heat-trapping greenhouse gases through human activity such as the burning of fossil fuels

Commodification in tourism, the process whereby a destination's culture is gradually converted into a saleable commodity or product in response to the perceived or actual demands of the tourist market

Ecological footprint (EF) the measurement of the resources that are required and wastes generated in sustaining a particular type of tourist or tourism activity

Environmental impact sequence a four-stage model formulated by the OECD to account for the impacts of tourism on the natural environment

Environmental responses the way that the environment reacts to the stresses, both in the short and long term, and both directly and indirectly

Environmental stresses the deliberate changes in the environment that are entailed in the stressor activities

Frontstage explicitly or tacitly recognised spaces within the destination that are mobilised for tourism purposes such as commodified cultural performances

Human responses the reactions of individuals, communities, the tourism industry, tourists, NGOs and governments to the various environmental responses

Irridex a theoretical model proposing that resident attitudes evolve from euphoria to apathy, then irritation (or annoyance), antagonism and finally resignation, as the intensity of tourism development increases within a destination

Paradox of resentment the idea that problems of resentment and tension can result whether tourists are integrated with, or isolated from, the local community

Stressor activities activities that initiate the environmental impact sequence; these can be divided into permanent environmental restructuring, the generation of waste residuals, tourist activities and indirect and induced activities

Tourist-historic city an urban place where the preservation of historical districts helps to sustain and is at least in part sustained by a significant level of tourist activity

■ QUESTIONS

1. What changes could be made to the Desert Mob festival to further promote positive interactions between indigenous and non-indigenous people?
2. (a) How much is commodification a positive or negative impact of tourism for destinations?
   (b) What strategies can a destination adopt to minimise its negative effects while maximising its benefits?
3. (a) Under what circumstances, if any, can sex tourism be regarded as a sociocultural benefit for destinations?
   (b) What role, accordingly, should destination managers play in managing sex tourism?
4. (a) How can the demonstration effect indicate both the weakness and strength of the individual or society in which it is occurring?

(b) How could destination managers mobilise the demonstration effect so that it has positive effects on the society and culture of the destination?

5. (a) In what ways can tourism promote criminal behaviour in a destination?
   (b) How can these effects be minimised?

6. (a) Why is the issue of tourist dispersal versus concentration referred to as a management paradox?
   (b) What can destination managers do about this paradox?

7. What are the opportunities and difficulties of using 'authenticity' as an indicator of tourism's sociocultural impacts within a destination?

8. (a) Why are models such as the irridex no longer considered adequate to describe changing resident reactions toward escalating tourism development?
   (b) What new or revised model better describes these emerging resident attitudes?

9. (a) Why has climate change emerged as such a high profile public issue?
   (b) How much should the developers and managers of a tourism facility be required to take responsibility for the generation of emissions that help to induce climate change?

10. (a) How is ecological footprinting related to the environmental impact sequence?
    (b) What are the strengths and weaknesses of ecological footprinting?

■ EXERCISES

1. Try to recall at least three unpleasant social or cultural incidents that you have personally experienced when travelling to a tourist destination where the dominant culture is different to your own.
   (a) In each case, to what extent was the problem attributable to your own actions or to the actions of a person or persons in that other culture?
   (b) What measures could or should be taken by the managers of that destination to prevent future incidents of that nature?
   (c) What sociocultural impacts might these measures have on the destination?

2. You are the manager of a regional theme park and have been asked by the owners to devise a strategy for offsetting the resources and wastes generated by that facility.
   (a) List the variables that would you include in an ecological footprint calculator designed for this purpose.
   (b) Describe how data for each variable would be quantified and measured.

■ FURTHER READING

Becken, S. & Hay, J. 2007. *Tourism and Climate Change: Risks and Opportunities.* **Clevedon, UK: Channel View.** Climate change is featured in this text from multiple perspectives, including the tourism-climate system, effects on destinations and products, and strategies for adaptation and mitigation.

Buckley, R. (Ed.) 2004. *Environmental Impacts of Tourism.* **Wallingford, UK: CABI Publishing.** The 25 chapters in this book focus mainly on Australia, and encompass an array of outdoor nature-based activities within a variety of physical environments. Several chapters provide comprehensive literature reviews of impacts associated with specific activities.

Clift, S. & Carter, S. (Eds) 2000. *Tourism and Sex: Culture, Commerce and Coercion.* **London: Pinter.** This compendium of 16 chapters examines various sociocultural impacts associated with sex tourism.

Higgins-Desbiolles, F. 2003. 'Reconciliation Tourism: Tourism Healing Divided Societies!' *Tourism Recreation Review* 28: 35–44. The featured site, South Australia's Camp Coorong, is a good and somewhat controversial example of tourism functioning as a force for world peace.

Scott, N. 2006. 'Management of Tourism: Conformation to Whose Standards?' In Prideaux, B., Moscardo, G. & Laws, E. (Eds.). *Managing Tourism and Hospitality Services: Theory and International Applications.* Wallingford, UK: CABI, pp. 54–61. The difficulties of managing an economically lucrative but socially disruptive event such as Schoolies Week is featured in this chapter.

Smith, V. (Ed.) 2001. *Hosts and Guests: The Anthropology of Tourism.* Third Edition. New York: Cognizant Communications. Smith's edited volume of 14 contributions is considered one of the classics in the field of the anthropology of tourism. Most of the case studies are taken from LDCs or peripheral destinations within the MDCs.

case study

PUSHING THE BOUNDARIES OF INDIGENOUS TOURISM

Indigenous people such as the Australian Aborigines, New Zealand Maori and North American Indians have had a longstanding and ambivalent relationship with tourism; the latter variably being regarded as a curse or saviour. Prior to the arrival of European settlers, traditional meeting activities such as the pow-wow, potlatch, and corroboree represented 'pure' forms of indigenous tourism in which native themes and control were total. Early visiting European scientists and artists soon initiated a phase wherein objects of indigenous culture (and often indigenous people themselves) were sent for display in major museums and exhibitions. Indigenous themes remained high if selective in these settings, but indigenous control was non-existent, with the displays serving to emphasise the alleged superiority of European culture. For example, indigenous Canadian displays at the Great Exhibition of 1851 in London were located next to an exhibit of modern manufactured goods to emphasise the virtues of encroaching European 'civilisation' over the 'savagery' of the vanishing and quaint native people (Maurer 2000).

The expansion of road and rail networks into peripheral areas resulted in a new stage wherein tourists from main population centres were able to travel to reservations and other places where remaining indigenous populations could be found. An early example in the American Southwest was the Fred Harvey Corporation, which sold 'Indian Detours' that allowed train passengers to 'discover' native people in their pueblo villages (Evans 1995). Around Rotorua, New Zealand, Maori 'warriors' in traditional costume were a 'must-see' element of the tourist experience since the late 1800s. As with the previous stage, control was almost entirely invested in non-indigenous entrepreneurs and mediators, thereby perpetuating the earlier discourse of European colonialism and cultural appropriation. However, even under such adverse circumstances, strategies of overt and covert resistance are evident. Examples include Indians putting blankets over their heads so that they could not be photographed by tourists (Francis 1992) and erecting barriers to prevent tourists from entering certain areas. Green (1996) describes how indigenous people in the American Southwest deliberately resisted the 'second invasion' of tourists by caricaturising and mocking tourists without their knowledge, and by selling deliberately misrepresented cultural objects to the tourists.

These tactics of resistance, along with the self-reliance and pride in culture fostered by increasing involvement in tourism, indicate a resilience and adaptability that have allowed indigenous people to reassert a high degree of empowerment within their remaining territories during the past three decades. Equally important, however, has been the abetting influence of the broader Human Rights agenda, which culminated in the 1993 International Year of Indigenous Peoples and the accompanying Declaration of Indigenous Peoples Rights (Sinclair 2003). The earlier Treaty of Waitangi Act of 1975 provided legal recognition of Maori tribal sovereignty in New Zealand as well as indigenous control over land ownership and use of natural resources (Zeppel 1998). National governments, concurrently, have been increasingly explicit in their recognition of native jurisdiction over tourism in their home areas, as represented for example by the 1997 National Aboriginal and Torres Strait Islander Tourism Industry Strategy (Higgins-Desbiolles 2003). Such strategies typically allow indigenous people to control the planning and management of tourism within their own territories, interpreting their culture in ways deemed to be most appropriate and determining where and when tourists are allowed to access native space.

According to Weaver (2008), indigenous people continue to become involved in activities such as ecotourism and community-based tourism during this stage to achieve political objectives by: using deep interpretation of longstanding occupancy to debunk Eurocentric notions that indigenous lands were 'empty' land earning widespread public sympathy through this interpretation projecting sovereignty by dictating the terms under which tourists access native space and culture demonstrating self-sufficiency through successful operation of commercial tourism businesses, and maintaining continuous involvement with tourism as evidence of ongoing gainful occupation of their territory.

The 'reconciliation tourism' pursued at the Camp Coorong Race Relations and Cultural Education Centre, South Australia is an example with overt and strong political overtones (Higgins-Desbiolles 2003).

The extension of indigenous empowerment to traditionally occupied lands (that is, all of Australia, New Zealand and North America) is a logical progression stemming from initiatives such as the 2007 United Nations Declaration on the Rights of Indigenous Peoples. Article 26 of this document declares that 'Indigenous peoples have the right to the lands, territories and resources which they have traditionally owned, occupied or otherwise used or acquired'. Until recently, this extended empowerment was evident mainly in national parks and other protected areas where local indigenous people were embraced as 'co-managers' having say in matters of interpretation and access. Recent conflicts between tourists wanting to climb the Uluru monolith in Australia's Northern Territory and local Aborigines opposing the practice symbolise the growing tensions that are inherent in such schemes (James 2007).

More threatening perhaps to some non-indigenous interests has been the reassertion of indigenous prerogatives in areas dominated by non-indigenous people. Indian groups in some US states have acquired exclusive rights to open casinos in urban areas, and are using these monopoly revenues to successfully pursue compensatory land and other claims (McAvoy 2002). In New Zealand, the operation of a successful whale watching enterprise at Kaikoura by local Maori has generated tension and resentment among local non-Maori who perceive themselves as having fewer rights (Orams 2002). Increasingly, indigenous people are asserting their right to have a say in tourism initiatives that have no explicit indigenous theme or occur in areas with no significant contemporary indigenous presence. This 'shadow indigenous tourism' is evident in a 2007 call for bids on the construction of a marina on the Gold Coast Spit. The process requires bidders to:

- assume the risk of resolving attendant native title and cultural heritage issues
- commit to appropriately recognising and protecting the traditional indigenous culture of the area
- include a statement of their approach to resolving native title and cultural heritage requirements

- demonstrate a willingness to negotiate in good faith with relevant Indigenous parties
- adhere to best practice standards in the management of the social, cultural, economic and environmental impacts of the Project in relation to indigenous issues, and
- (for the successful bidder) negotiate an Indigenous Land Use Agreement (ILUA) between the Preferred Proponent and the Indigenous Parties to allow the necessary approvals to be obtained and permit the required tenure arrangements to be implemented. This may include the construction of an Aboriginal Cultural Centre (Queensland Government 2007).

QUESTIONS

1. (a) How were indigenous people able to move from a position of disempowerment to empowerment both within and beyond their currently occupied territories?
   (b) What lessons can be learned from the experience of indigenous people by other communities who feel disempowered by the spread of tourism-related development?
2. (a) How much control should indigenous people have over tourism in areas of Australia, New Zealand and North America where they no longer formally occupy land?
   (b) What can indigenous people do to reduce tensions with non-indigenous people as their empowerment over tourism development extends deeper into their traditionally occupied territories?

10

DESTINATION DEVELOPMENT

LEARNING OBJECTIVES

After studying this chapter, you should be able to:

1. discuss the relevance and implications of the destination cycle concept for tourism managers

2. outline the destination cycle model as presented in the Butler sequence

3. explain how different elements of the tourism experience can be incorporated into the destination cycle model

4. critique the strengths and limitations of the Butler sequence, and of the destination cycle concept in general, as a device to assist destination managers

5. categorise the factors that contribute to changes in the destination cycle process

6. explain how tourism development at a national scale can be described as a combined process of contagious and hierarchical spatial diffusion

7. describe how the destination cycle concept can be accommodated within the pattern of tourism development that occurs at the national scale.

■ INTRODUCTION

The previous two chapters considered the economic, sociocultural and environmental costs and benefits that are potentially associated with tourism, primarily from a destination perspective. All tourism activity induces change within a destination, and this usually involves a combination of both costs and benefits. Whether the net impacts are positive or negative depends on a variety of factors, including the destination's level of economic development and diversity, its sociocultural and physical carrying capacity, and, critically, the amount, rate and type of tourism development relative to these internal factors. This chapter examines the process of destination development in more detail, by integrating the content of earlier chapters on impacts, markets, destinations and the tourism product. The following section considers the concept of the destination cycle, and focuses specifically on the Butler sequence, which is the most frequently cited application. This section also provides a critique of the model, and examines the factors that can contribute to changes in the destination cycle. The dynamics of tourism development at a national scale, which are usually not adequately described by the cycle concept as represented by the Butler sequence, are then considered. The concept of spatial diffusion is presented as an alternative model that more accurately describes the evolution of tourism at a national scale.

■ DESTINATION CYCLE

The idea that destinations can experience a process analagous to birth, growth, maturation, decline, and then perhaps death and rejuvenation is embodied in the concept of the **destination cycle**. This theory, to the extent that it is demonstrated to have widespread relevance to the real world, is of great interest to tourism managers, who would then know where a particular destination is positioned within the cycle at a given point in time and what implications this has if no intervention is undertaken. The destination cycle, this latter clause suggests, should not be regarded as an unavoidable process, but rather one that can be redirected through appropriate management measures to realise the ecologically and socioculturally sustainable outcomes that are desired by destination stakeholders (see chapter 11).

Allusions to the idea of a destination cycle were made in the early tourism literature, as illustrated in the following 1963 quotation by Walter Christaller, a famous geographer:

> The typical course of development has the following pattern. Painters search out untouched unusual places to paint. Step by step the place develops as a so-called artist colony. Soon a cluster of poets follows, kindred to the painters; then cinema people, gourmets, and the jeunesse dorée. The place becomes fashionable and the entrepreneur takes note. The fisherman's cottage, the shelter-huts become converted into boarding houses and hotels come on the scene. Meanwhile the painters have fled and sought out another periphery ... More and more townsmen choose this place, now en vogue and advertised in the newspapers. Subsequently, the gourmets, and all those who seek real recreation, stay away. At last the tourist agencies come with their package rate travelling parties; now, the indulged public avoids such places. At the same time, in other places the same cycle occurs again; more and more places come into fashion, change their type, turn into everybody's tourist haunt (Christaller 1963, p. 103).

During the 1970s, the work of Plog (psychographic segmentation) and Doxey (the irridex) also implied a destination cycle, though their research focused only on specific aspects of that progression rather than the macro-process (see chapter 9). Particularly influential in the tourism evolution literature of that decade was a detailed empirical case study of Atlantic City (New Jersey, United States) by Stansfield (1978). This study described how the famous seaside resort attained prominence, gradually declined through the first half of the twentieth century and then experienced a process of revitalisation following the introduction of casino-based gambling. The title of this article made specific use of the term 'resort cycle', but did not attempt to translate the findings of this specific case into any broader theoretical model.

The Butler sequence

Drawing on this earlier research, in 1980 Butler presented his S-shaped resort cycle model, or **Butler sequence**, which proposes that tourist destinations tend to experience five distinct stages of growth (i.e. exploration, involvement, development, consolidation, stagnation) under free market and sustained demand conditions (Butler 1980). Depending on the response of destination managers to the onset of stagnation, various scenarios are then possible, including continued stagnation, decline and/or rejuvenation (see figure 10.1). Although usually not stated in applications of the model, the Butler sequence assumes a sufficient level of demand to fuel its progression, as per the 'push' factors outlined in chapter 3.

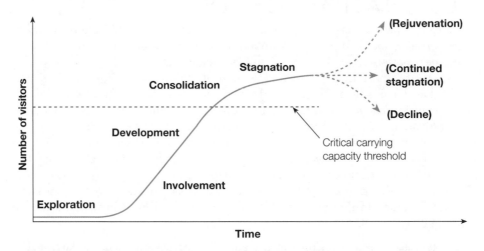

FIGURE 10.1 The Butler sequence

Source: Butler (1980)

Before describing the stages in more detail, it is important to stress that this model quickly attained, and has maintained, its status as one of the most cited and applied models within the field of tourism studies. Its longstanding appeal is based on several factors, some of which merit mention here, and others that will be elaborated on in the critique that follows the presentation of the stages.

The model is structurally simple, being based on a concept — the product life-cycle curve — that has long been used by economists and marketers to describe the behaviour of the market in purchasing consumer goods such as televisions and cars. The reader will also note its superficial similarity to the pattern of population growth depicted in the demographic transition model (see figure 3.5). Its simplicity and prior applications to areas such as marketing and demography make Butler's resort cycle curve accessible and attractive, as well as readily applicable using available data such as visitor arrivals or a surrogate such as accommodation units.

Butler's model has intuitive appeal, in that anyone who has travelled extensively or who has participated in the field of tourism studies will agree that some kind of cyclical dynamic is indeed evident across a broad array of destinations. According to Lundgren (1984, p. 22), 'Butler put into the realistic cyclical context a reality that everyone knew about, and clearly recognised, but had never formulated into an overall theory'.

The Butler sequence is a comprehensive, integrated model that allows for the simultaneous incorporation of all facets of tourism in a destination beyond the visitor numbers that are used to construct the curve. Table 10.1 summarises the more important of these facets in terms of their relationship to the first five stages of the model and forms the basis for the following discussion of the individual stages.

TABLE 10.1 Changing characteristics within the Butler sequence

Variable	Exploration	Involvement	Development	Consolidation/ stagnation
Status of the destination within the tourism system	Peripheral	Early incorporation	Integration	Full integration
Rate of growth in visitation	None (low-level equilibrium)	Slow growth	Rapid growth	None (high-level equilibrium)
Spatial pattern of tourism activity	Dispersed	Nodes of concentration appear	Concentrated	Highly concentrated
Attractions	Cultural/natural, unique to destination	Mainly cultural/ natural	Mainly specialised tourist orientation	Specialised and contrived tourist orientation; generic
Ownership of operations	Local	Local, some nonlocal	Mainly nonlocal	Nonlocal
Accommodation	No specialised accommodation	Small-scale, unobtrusive	Mainly large-scale	Large-scale 'international' style
Market origins	Diverse	Less diverse	Dominant markets emerge	Dominant markets
Psychographics of market	Allocentric	Allocentric– midcentric	Midcentric– psychocentric	Psychocentric
Seasonality	None	Emergent	Seasonal	Highly seasonal
Length of stay	Extended	Relatively long	Relatively short	Brief
Economic status of tourism	Insignificant	Minor, supplementary	Dominant	Overwhelming dependency
Tourism-derived revenue	Insignificant and stable	Small and growing	Large and growing	Large and stable
Multiplier effect	Extremely high	High	Declining	Low
Linkages	Local	Mainly local	Mainly nonlocal	Nonlocal
Leakages	None	Minor	High	Very high

(continued)

TABLE 10.1 *(continued)*

Variable	Exploration	Involvement	Development	Consolidation/stagnation
Commodification of attractions	Noncommercial, 'authentic'	Somewhat commercial, mainly authentic	Commercial, increasingly contrived	Highly commercial, contrived
Irridex	Pre-euphoria	Euphoria	Apathy (early), annoyance (later)	Antagonism, then resignation
Environmental stress	Very low	Low but increasing	High	Very high

It appears to be universally applicable, in that there is nothing inherent in its structure that restricts its relevance to only certain types of destination or environment at least at a localised scale. It is for all of these reasons that the Butler sequence is described in chapter 1 as the culmination of the tourism-critical cautionary platform.

Exploration

According to Butler, the **exploration** stage is characterised by very small numbers of visitors who are dispersed throughout the destination and remain for an extended period of time. The tourism 'industry' as such is nonexistent, as negligible visitor numbers do not merit the establishment of any specialised facilities or services. The tourists themselves are adventurous, allocentric types who are drawn by what they perceive to be authentic and 'unspoiled' cultural and natural attractions. These visitors arrive from a wide variety of sources and are not influenced significantly by seasonality. Although the absolute revenue obtained from the tourists in the exploration stage is very small, linkages with the local economy are extensive because of the desire to consume local products, and hence the multiplier effect is large. For this reason, and because the locals maintain control, the relationship with tourists is extremely cordial, and the tourists tend to be treated either as curiosities or honoured guests. These attitudes may be described as pre-euphoric, in that tourism is not yet making a large enough impact to substantially benefit the economy of the destination.

In essence, exploration can be described as a kind of informal 'pre-tourism' stage where visitors must accommodate themselves to the services and facilities that already exist in the area to serve local residents. For example, tourists would have to shop in the local market and travel by the local bus system. From a systems perspective, the exploration-stage destination is only peripherally and informally connected to any origin or transit regions.

On a worldwide scale, the number of places that can be described as being in the true exploration stage is rapidly diminishing due to the explosive growth of tourism since World War II. The remaining exploration-stage places largely coincide first with wilderness or semiwilderness areas where any kind of formal economic activity is absent, rudimentary or focused on some specialised primary activity such as mining or forestry. Most of the Australian interior and northern coast, aside from urban areas and certain high-profile national parks, is in the exploration stage. A similar logic applies to many locations within northern Canada, the Amazon basin, Siberia and central Asia, Antarctica, Greenland and the Congo River Basin in Africa. Residual exploration-stage locations also include settled areas that lack tourism activity due to conditions of war or civil unrest (e.g. Afghanistan), inaccessibility imposed internally or externally (e.g. North Korea and Iraq before the US invasion, respectively) or a general combined lack of significant pull effects (e.g. large parts of rural China and India).

Involvement

Several developments characterise the **involvement** stage:

- Local entrepreneurs begin to provide a limited amount of specialised services and facilities in response to the appearance of tourists, thereby inaugurating an incipient tourism industry. These services and facilities typically consist of small guesthouses and inns, eating places, the provision of guides, small tour operations and a few small semi-commercial attractions. Often, residents simply make one or two rooms within their houses available for a nominal fee.
- This incipient and still largely informal tourism sector begins to show signs of concentration within local settlements, transportation gateways or near tourist attractions. However, the sector is still small-scale, and has little visual or environmental impact on the landscape.
- The visitor intake begins to increase slowly in response to these local initiatives, ending the low-level equilibrium of visitor arrivals that characterised the exploration stage.

The involvement stage is associated with the 'euphoria' phase of the irridex. This is due to the confluence of two facts: visitor numbers are large enough to generate significant revenues, but tourism is still undeveloped enough that the destination maintains local control, extensive backward linkages with agriculture and other local sectors, a high multiplier effect and a mainly allocentric-oriented visitor intake. However, the growing intake is already mediated to some extent by the formal tourism system, thereby opening the way for nonlocal participation and for greater numbers of midcentric tourists. For example, while some backpackers and academics might still arrive by walking or by four-wheel drive or relatively primitive local transport, others of a less adventurous persuasion begin to arrive by mini-vans provided by tour operators in a nearby city or by small aeroplane. These developments indicate that the area is gradually becoming more integrated into the tourism system, with formal businesses becoming more involved because of the increased tourist demand. Concurrently, residents begin to consciously or subconsciously demarcate backstage and frontstage spaces and times to cope with the growing number of visitors.

Factors that trigger the involvement stage

The factors that trigger the transition from exploration to involvement can be either internal or external. Internal forces are those that arise from within the destination community itself, such as the adventurous entrepreneur who builds and advertises a new kind of attraction as a way of inducing increased visitation levels. External forces originate from outside the destination. These can be small-scale and cumulative, as in word-of-mouth marketing by previous visitors within their origin regions. Each visitor, for example, might relate their adventures in the 'untouched' destination to ten other people, some of whom are subsequently inspired to visit the destination. The contemporary phenomenon of electronic word of mouth (eWOM), considered in chapter 7, accelerates this process further. The result in either case is an increase in tourism numbers.

Conversely, the external factor can be a high-profile event, such as the publication of a *National Geographic* magazine article, a television documentary, the visit of a celebrity or exposure to a popular movie (see Breakthrough tourism: From setting to sightseeing in Iowa, USA). The construction of a major airport or road are other possible triggers. In these instances, specific events serve as catalysts for dramatic and almost immediate increases in visitation. All of the examples given, of course, can also occur at later stages, though in those instances the tourism sector and the lifecycle dynamics are already well established (see the 'Factors that change the destination cycle' section).

The importance of understanding the trigger factors is demonstrated by the effect that these can have on the subsequent dynamics of the destination cycle. Internal forces imply that the destination, or a stakeholder within a destination, is taking a proactive approach towards tourism development, which increases the likelihood that local control will be retained and the community will be better equipped to adjust to increases in visitation, perhaps through a deliberately prolonged involvement stage. In contrast, external forces of the singular, large-scale variety tend to induce rapid change that is directed by outside interests — the community has the immediate disadvantage of being placed on the defensive, having to react to events rather than directing them. Under these circumstances, the involvement stage is likely to be little more than a brief prelude to the development stage.

In Australia the involvement stage characterises many rural Aboriginal communities, which are making tentative attempts to pursue tourism as a means of bringing about effective economic development (see the Breakthrough tourism feature in chapter 9). In such cases, the employment of a proactive approach to the trigger factors is essential given the cultural and economic circumstances of those communities (Altman & Finlayson 2003). The issue is also imperative in non-Aboriginal rural areas and settlements, which, while faced with different circumstances and issues, are also increasingly entering the involvement stage in their own quest for a viable economy.

breakthrough tourism

FROM SETTING TO SIGHTSEEING IN IOWA, USA

A popular film has an enormous potential to stimulate the tourism industry of the place or places in which it is set, even if these locations do not possess outstanding natural or cultural resources (Beeton 2005). Two destinations in the midwestern US state of Iowa illustrate this phenomenon. Dyersville is a small, nondescript farming town which in 1988 was selected as the setting for the highly successful baseball-themed movie *Field of Dreams*, which featured Kevin Costner. The baseball diamond built for the film was maintained by the owners as a tourist attraction after the filming, and attracts substantial numbers of visitors who can wander the site and purchase souvenirs from an adjacent shop. The broader influence of the film on Iowa's tourism industry is indicated by the use of the slogan 'Is this Heaven?' — a quote from the film — on the state license plate. Madison County is a rural municipality featured in the 1994 Robert Redford/Meryl Streep film *Bridges of Madison County*. Unlike *Field of Dreams*, the latter is focused on several existing covered bridges which as a result of the film were transformed from minor into major tourist attractions.

These two cases have several additional facilitating characteristics in common. Both are based on successful novels that may have induced a small amount of prior tourist traffic to the respective settings. Each location, in addition, is the site of minor tourist attractions not related to either film. Dyersville is the home of a major manufacturer of miniature farm toys, while Winterset, the seat of Madison County, is the birthplace of John Wayne, the famous American actor. Finally, the producers of both films were encouraged and assisted in selecting an Iowa site by the state government, which established the Iowa Film Office as a vehicle for this purpose. In 2007, the Iowa Film Promotion Act was passed by the state legislature to provide tax incentives for producers and investors spending at least US$100 000 within Iowa for purposes of film production.

Development

The **development** stage is characterised by rapid tourism growth and dramatic changes over a relatively short period of time in all aspects of the tourism sector. As with all other phases of the model, the change from involvement to development is usually marked by a transition rather than a sharp boundary, although specific events (e.g. construction of the first mega-resort or a celebrity visit) can act as a catalyst for accelerated change. The rate and character of the growth will depend on the pull factors (see chapter 4) that prevail during the stage, and the attempts made in the destination to manage the process. In the Butler sequence, a rapid erosion in the level of local control is assumed to occur as the community is overwhelmed by the scale of tourism development. As the destination is rapidly integrated into the formal tourism system, larger non-local and transnational companies gain control over the process, attracting the midcentric and psychocentric consumers who arrange and facilitate their travel experiences (often through package tours) within these highly organised structures.

Spatially, the development stage is a time of rapid landscape change, as small hotels and guest houses give way to large multi-storey resorts; agricultural land is replaced by golf courses, second-home developments and theme parks; and mangroves are removed to make way for marinas. Large areas of farmland may be abandoned after being purchased by speculators, or because labour and investment has been diverted towards tourism. The 'sense of place' or uniqueness of the destination that was associated with the exploration and involvement stages gives way to a generic, 'international'-style landscape. Concentrated tourism districts form along coastlines, in alpine valleys or in any other area that is close to associated attractions or gateways. At this point environmental stresses are widespread, and negative environmental responses are apparent. The general attitude of residents towards visitors also experiences a rapid transformation. In the early development stage, tourists become a normal part of the local routine, prompting widespread apathy. However, as tourist numbers continue to mount, and as resultant pressures are placed on local carrying capacities, apathy may give way to annoyance within a growing portion of the population.

Australian destinations that appear to be in the development stage include the Sunshine Coast, Cairns, New South Wales coastal resorts such as Port Macquarie, Coffs Harbour and Byron Bay, and the Western Australian resort town of Broome. Non-coastal destinations that also appear to qualify include alpine resorts such as Thredbo, and tourist shopping villages such as Maleny, Mount Tamborine and Hahndorf in the respective hinterlands of the Sunshine Coast, the Gold Coast and Adelaide.

Consolidation

The **consolidation** stage is characterised by a decline in the growth rate of visitor arrivals and other tourism-related activity, although the total amount of activity continues to increase. Visitor numbers over a 12-month period are usually well in excess of the resident population. Of paramount importance in this stage is the breeching of the destination's environmental, social and economic carrying capacities, thereby indicating increased deterioration of the tourism product.

During consolidation, crowded, high-density tourism districts emerge and are dominated by a psychocentric clientele who rely largely on short-stay package tour arrangements affiliated with large tour operators and hotel chains. The destination is wholly integrated into the large-scale, globalised tourism system, and tourism dominates the economy of the area. Attractions are largely specialised recreational sites of a contrived, generic nature (symbolised by theme parks and casinos), which overwhelm or replace authentic natural or cultural attractions that previously formed the basis for the destination's popularity. Seasonality emerges as a major influence on the destination's economy, along with high turnover in hotel and restaurant ownership, and abandonment of facilities and areas due to a lack of interest in redevelopment. Much of this is due to transnational companies that 'abandon' the destination to seek the greener pastures alluded to by Christaller (see page 267).

It is in the consolidation stage that the local social 'breaking' point is likely to be reached, with some residents becoming blatantly antagonistic towards tourists, while others become resigned to the situation and either adjust to the new environment or leave the area altogether. As predicted by Doxey (1976), a large proportion of residents blame tourism for all problems, justifiably or not. As negative encounters with the local residents and local tourism product increase, word-of-mouth exchange of information between tourists and acquaintances contributes to the reduced visitor intakes.

The Surfers Paradise district of the Gold Coast is perhaps the best Australian example of consolidation stage dynamics, while international examples include pleasure periphery resort areas along the French and Spanish Rivieras, in Florida and the Bahamas, and in the Waikiki area of Honolulu (see figure 10.2).

FIGURE 10.2 Strained social and environmental carrying capacities

Stagnation

Peak visitor numbers and levels of associated facilities, such as available accommodation units, are attained during the **stagnation** (or 'saturation') stage. Surplus capacity is a persistent problem, prompting frequent price wars that lead to further product deterioration and bankruptcies, given the high fixed costs involved in the sector. One way that companies respond to this dilemma is to convert hotel-type accommodation into self-catering apartments, timeshare units or even permanent residences for retirees, students or others. The affected destination may have a high profile, but this does not translate into increases in visitation due to the fact that the location is perceived to be 'out of fashion' or otherwise less desirable as a destination. Indicative of stagnation, aside from the stability in the visitor intake curve, is the reliance on repeat visits by psychocentrically oriented visitors — the moribund destination is now less capable of attracting new visitors.

The best examples of the stagnation stage are found in parts of the Riviera, such as Spain's Costa Brava, and in some areas of Florida and the Caribbean (e.g. the Bahamas' New Providence Island). Beyond the global pleasure periphery, it is discernible in the recreational hinterlands that have developed within a one-day drive of large north American cities, including Muskoka (Toronto), the Laurentians (Montreal) and the Catskills (New York City). The rural nature of these regions, however, suggests different structural characteristics than those associated with urban areas.

Decline or rejuvenation

The stagnation stage can theoretically persist for an indefinite period, but it is likely that the destination will eventually experience either an upturn or a downturn in its fortunes.

Decline

The scenario of **decline** will occur as a result of some combination of the following factors:

- Repeat clients are no longer satisfied with the available product, while efforts to recruit new visitors fail.
- No attempts are made by destination stakeholders to revitalise the local tourism product, or these attempts are made but are unsuccessful.
- Resident antagonism progresses to the level of outright and widespread hostility, which contributes to the negative image of the destination.
- New competitors, and particularly intervening opportunities, emerge to divert and capture traditional markets.

As tourist numbers decline, more hotels and other specialised tourism facilities are abandoned or converted into apartments, health care centres or other uses suitable for retirees. Ironically, this may have the effect of allowing locals to re-enter the tourism industry, since outmoded facilities can be obtained at a relatively low price. Similarly, the decline of tourism often reduces that sector's dominance of the destination as other service industries (e.g. health care, call centres, government) are attracted to the area in response to its changing demographics. The decline stage may be accelerated by a 'snowballing' effect, wherein the abandonment of a major hotel or attraction impacts negatively on the viability of other accommodation or attractions, thereby increasing the possibility of their own demise.

The number of destinations that have at some point experienced significant decline-stage dynamics is not large. The Coolangatta district of the Gold Coast is probably the best Australian example (Faulkner & Russell 1998), while one of the most illustrative international cases is Atlantic City from the post–World War I period to the 1970s (Stansfield 1978). Other historical examples include Cape May (New Jersey) whose pre-eminence as a summer seaside resort for Philadelphia ironically was destroyed in the late 1800s by the emergence of Atlantic City. Additional examples can be found within the older established areas of southern Florida (e.g. Miami Beach in the 1970s), the French and Spanish Rivieras and Hawaii.

Rejuvenation

The other alternative is a **rejuvenation** of the destination's tourism industry. While the Butler sequence shows this occurring after the stagnation stage, it is also possible that rejuvenation will take place following a period of decline, with decreasing numbers serving as a catalyst for action. This was the case with Atlantic City's decision to introduce legalised casino-based gambling, breaking the monopoly held by Las Vegas. According to Butler, rejuvenation is almost always accompanied by the introduction of entirely new tourism products, or at least the radical reimaging of the existing product, as a way of recapturing the destination's competitive advantage and sense of uniqueness. Instances of reliance on new products include Atlantic City with its gambling initiative, and Miami Beach, which restructured the existing 3S product in the 1980s to capitalise on the city's remarkable art deco hotel architecture, which had appeal to the nostalgia market. A similar scenario of nostalgia-based reimaging is feasible for Coolangatta and older summer resorts on the Atlantic coast and Great Lakes shoreline of North America. Miami's rejuvenation was assisted in the mid-1990s by a crackdown on crime, which did much to change the city's image as a dangerous destination. Finally, Douglass and Raento (2004) describe how the gambling haven of Las Vegas has been periodically reinvented, shifting from its shady image in the 1980s to a 'family friendly' destination, and then more recently to an edgier product exemplified by the advertising slogan 'What happens in Vegas stays in Vegas'.

The implication of these examples is that rejuvenation seldom occurs as a spontaneous process, but arises from deliberate, proactive strategies adopted by destination managers and entrepreneurs. Success in achieving revitalisation is associated with the ability of the public and private sectors to cooperate in focusing on what each does best. The public sector provides destination marketing, suitable services and the management of public attractions, and the private sector assumes a lead role in industry sectors such as accommodation, food and beverages, tour operations, transportation and some categories of attraction.

Critique of the Butler sequence

The examples used in the preceding discussion illustrate the broad potential applicability and intuitive appeal of the Butler sequence as a model to describe the development of tourist destinations, wherein negative economic, sociocultural and environmental impacts increase and accumulate as the destination moves through the development stage. A major implication of the model is the idea that tourism carries within itself the seeds of its own destruction, and that proactive management strategies are essential if this self-destruction is to be avoided.

Cycle applications

Since its publication in 1980, the Butler sequence has been empirically tested no fewer than 50 times just within the published English-language literature. Most of these applications have identified a general conformity to the broad contours of the model, supporting its potential as an important theoretical as well as practical device for describing and predicting the evolution of destinations. However, most applications have also identified one or more aspects where the sequence does not apply to the targeted case study, and/or where the overall results of the exercise remain ambiguous (see the case study at the end of the chapter). For example, Weaver (1990) and Douglas (1997), in the respective cases of Grand Cayman Island and Melanesia, found that the earliest tourism initiatives in these colonial situations were carried out by external interests associated with the colonial power, and that local, non-elite participation increased as tourism became more developed. Douglas also found evidence of serious resident annoyance and antagonism in the Solomon Islands when this destination was barely into the involvement stage.

In the case of Niagara Falls, there was no evidence for the loss of local control until well into the late development stage, nor was there evidence that the clientele was shifting towards a psychocentric mode. Furthermore, specialised recreational attractions, such as theme parks, have not superseded the iconic waterfall as the destination's primary draw (Getz 1992). Agarwal (1997) found, in the case of the English seaside resort of Torbay, that local control was retained during the development stage and beyond. In addition, visitors did not display any behaviour during these later stages suggestive of psychocentrism. Faulkner and Russell (1997) found that the involvement stage in Coolangatta (on the southern Gold Coast) was effectively bypassed by the rapid onset of mass tourism, and that the dynamics of the consolidation stage were far more complex and multifaceted than proposed by Butler. (Butler himself recognised that the involvement stage could be pre-empted by the 'instant resort' effect created by Cancún-like growth pole strategies.)

Baum (1998) noted that although the Canadian province of Prince Edward Island could be described as experiencing stagnation on the basis of visitation levels, the destination retained a structure of small-scale and local ownership typical of the involvement stage. With regard to seasonality, Digance (1997) points out that Thredbo, the Australian ski resort, evolved from an essentially winter-only resort to a year-round destination. In regard to the Eastern Townships of Quebec (Canada), Lundgren (2005) identifies at least three tourism cycles over a 200-year history, each focused on a different regional tourism product.

General criticisms

Clearly, then, many deviations have been identified when the Butler sequence has been subjected to empirical testing. At a general level, the model can be criticised for its determinism, that is, the implication that a destination's progression through a particular sequence of stages is inevitable. In reality, there is no inherent reason to assume that all exploration- or involvement-stage destinations are fated to pass beyond these initial phases. Such a progression may be highly probable in a small fishing village on a scenic coastline, but much less so in an isolated agricultural settlement in New South Wales or northern China. Tourism planners and managers should therefore make the effort to identify and then focus on those early stage destinations that are *likely* to experience further development, rather than worrying that every such destination *will* face this problem. Determinism is also evident in the assumption that the cyclical dynamics of tourist destinations begin with the exploration stage (see Contemporary issue: Indigenous people and 'pre-exploration dynamics').

contemporary issue

INDIGENOUS PEOPLE AND 'PRE-EXPLORATION DYNAMICS'

The theoretical structure of the Butler sequence and most subsequent empirical descriptions are 'Eurocentric' to the extent that they associate the beginning of the tourism dynamic with the introduction of 'Western' visitors, whether they are explorers in the classical sense or modern backpackers. Left unconsidered are the tourism-type dynamics within the indigenous community that preceded this exploration stage. As mentioned in the chapter 9 case study, activities involving social travel, such as the pow-wow and corroboree, were important elements in the pre-European indigenous cultures of North America and Australia respectively. It is for this reason that Weaver (2005) explicitly associates the beginning of the exploration stage in the Caribbean with the advent of European colonisation in the 1600s. Perhaps the only example of the incorporation of pre-exploration indigenous dynamics into a revised model is Johnston (2005), who suggests that the cycle in the Kona area of Hawaii began with the Hawaiian Royal Capital stage in the period from 1779 to 1844, that is, prior to the arrival of European visitors.

The pre-European dynamic should be recognised in the tourism cycle in order to make it more universal and less Eurocentric, although considerable research would be necessary to determine how this pre-exploration stage (or stages) was structured in Australia and elsewhere with respect to the characteristics featured in figure 10.1. Constructs such as 'commodification', 'multiplier effect' and 'market' for example, might prove irrelevant or may have to be reconceptualised to conform to an indigenous context. Such research would not only yield valuable insights into alternative models of tourism development, but would provide disempowered indigenous people with clues for implementing a more sustainable tourism model less likely to breech the ecological and social carrying capacities of contemporary indigenous communities.

This issue of determinism extends to the proposed carrying capacity thresholds (see figure 10.1). According to the Butler sequence, tourism development escalates until these thresholds are exceeded, but communities can and often do override free market forces and take proactive measures to ensure that tourism does not impact negatively on the destination. As depicted in figure 10.3, there are two basic ways in which this can be achieved.

Supply-driven scenario

In supply-driven scenario (a), the carrying capacities are left as they are, but the level of development is curtailed so that they remain below the relevant thresholds. Essentially, a long involvement stage of slow growth is induced, followed by consolidation at a desired level, with 'development' being avoided altogether. This could be achieved through a number of strategies, alone or in combination, including:

- placing restrictions or quotas on the allowable number of visitors (as in Bhutan)
- imposing development standards
- introducing limitations to the size and number of accommodation facilities
- zoning only certain limited areas for tourism development
- prohibiting the expansion of infrastructure, such as airports, that would facilitate additional tourism development
  - increasing entry fees to the destination (e.g. visa fees) in order to reduce demand.

Many of these strategies relate to the tactics of obtaining supply–demand equilibrium as outlined in chapter 7, although the emphasis there was mainly in the private sector, at a microscale, and related to corporate profitability rather than destination-wide impacts. It should be noted here, however, that such public sector strategies may be resisted by a local tourism industry that sees this as an erosion of its customer base and profitability.

Demand-driven scenario

In demand-driven scenario (b), the conventional sequence of involvement and development takes place, but measures are taken to raise carrying capacity thresholds in concert with the increased visitor intake. This can be achieved on the sociocultural front by demarcating and enforcing frontstage/backstage distinctions (see chapter 9) or by introducing tourist and resident education and awareness programs (see chapter 7). On the environmental front, destinations can make pre-emptive human responses to environmental stresses, including site-hardening initiatives such as the installation of improved sewage and water treatment facilities. Economic adjustments might include the expansion of local industries in order to supply the required backward linkages (see chapter 8). In effect, scenario (b) involves the increase of supply to meet demand, while scenario (a) involves the reduction of demand to fit the existing supply. The issue of proactive responses to the 'classic' Butler sequence in order to achieve more sustainable outcomes is pursued further in chapter 11.

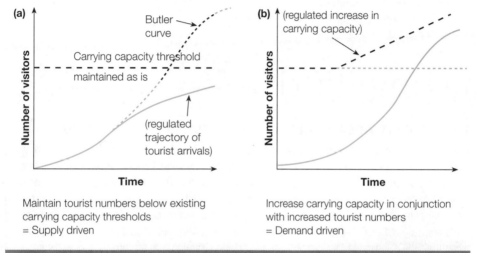

FIGURE 10.3 Alternative responses to the Butler sequence

The question of geographic scale

As discussed in earlier chapters, the term 'destination' can be applied at different scales, ranging from a single small attraction to an entire continent (e.g. Asia or Europe) or macroregion (e.g. the pleasure periphery). This raises the question as to whether certain scales are more suited to the application of the Butler sequence than others (see Managing tourism: The tourist area cycle in a Chinese protected area). Because visitation levels and surrogates such as the number of accommodation units can be graphed at any scale, there has been a tendency in the literature to assume that the Butler sequence can be applied across the geographical spectrum.

The resemblance to Butler's curve, however, is often superficial. This is because the dynamics discussed by Butler cannot be meaningfully applied at the country level, unless the country happens to be a particularly small entity such as a SISOD. The problem can be illustrated by considering Spain, where national visitation levels indicate the later development or very early consolidation stage. However, it is absurd to imagine that all or most of Spain's 40 million residents are now expressing antagonism towards tourists, or that all of its tourist accommodation is now accounted for by large, 'international'-style hotels. Such circumstances may apply to parts of the Spanish Riviera, but not to most parts of inland rural Spain, which is mostly at the involvement or early development stage. Similarly, overall inbound arrival statistics for Australia disguise great disparities between the exploration-stage Outback and poststagnation dynamics that are evident in parts of the Gold Coast. In essence, Butler's cycle, in its classic format, does not apply to such large countries because of the tendency of large-scale tourism to concentrate only in certain areas of these countries (see chapter 4) (Toh, Khan & Koh 2001). More productive, as discussed in the final section, are attempts to model the diffusion of tourism, and hence the differential progression of the resort cycle, within large areas.

The Butler sequence itself is more appropriately applied at the scale of a well-defined individual resort concentration such as the Gold Coast, Byron Bay, Spain's Costa Brava, a small Caribbean island such as Antigua, or an alpine resort such as Thredbo or St Moritz (Switzerland). However, caution must still be exercised since significant internal variations often occur even at this scale. This is illustrated by the Gold Coast, where the apparent stagnation stage of Surfers Paradise contrasts with the appearance of exploration-type dynamics in many parts of the hinterland.

managing tourism

THE TOURIST AREA CYCLE IN A CHINESE PROTECTED AREA

Protected areas have rarely been tested for their conformity to the Butler sequence since they seldom have a resident human population and are closely regulated by relevant government agencies. Nevertheless, Zhong, Deng and Xiang (2008) found that the evolution of China's Zhangjiajie National Forest Park, an extremely popular tourist attraction in northern Hunan Province, generally conformed to the first four stages of the sequence as of the mid-2000s. The exploration period (1978–81) involved a small number of visitors accessing minimal services, while the 1980s indicated 'involvement' through rising visitation and the provision of basic services for tourists. Visitation levels increased dramatically during the 'development' 1990s when a network of roads and services was provided for visitors, many of them from South Korea. Environmental deterioration as a result of excessive visitation, increasing resident populations and the use of coal as fuel, also became evident. Since 2000, slowing growth rates and higher levels of international tourists have indicated consolidation.

Despite this overall conformity, discrepancies with the Butler sequence that reveal management issues possibly unique to the Chinese context are evident. First, tourists outnumbered local residents from the beginning due to the small human population allowed to reside within the park; hence there never was a high degree of 'local' control. Second, these local residents were much more involved in the provision of tourism services during the development and consolidation stages than during exploration or involvement (i.e. 29 per cent in 2004 as opposed to 7 per cent before 1982). This is attributed to a recent local government policy encouraging and supporting family hostels as a means of revenue generation. Third, ecological carrying capacity thresholds breeched during 'development' have now apparently been raised through the introduction by government of environmentally friendly transport, sewage treatment facilities and reduced coal consumption. Fourth, environmental degradation never did act as a deterrent to tourists, who were more interested in seeing the park's iconic rock formations than having a serene experience in an untouched natural setting. Hence, they were less sensitive to environmental problems that would disturb Western tourists, and highly satisfied with intensive facilities and services that were ecologically invasive but made their visits more comfortable.

Cross-sectoral considerations

A related concern is the influence on destination development of sectors external to tourism. Applications of the resort cycle model often give the impression that tourism is the only economic activity carried out in the destination, so that resident reactions and environmental change are influenced only by this one sector. This isolationist approach ignores the external environment that must be taken into consideration in the analysis of tourism systems (see chapter 2). In reality, few (if any) destinations are wholly reliant on the tourism industry. In the case of Las Vegas, the city is also extremely important as a wholesale distribution point, centre for military activity and health care, and a magnet for high-tech industry. The question of tourism growth leading to the breaching of carrying capacity thresholds must therefore take into account the moderating (or exacerbating) influences of these coexisting activities. The problem can also be illustrated by a large nonresort city such as London or Paris. Such centres have a very large tourism industry that appears to be in the consolidation stage, but this sector accounts for only a small portion of the city's total economic output. Hence, it is not rational to assume that the onset of tourism consolidation in Paris or London will result in widespread antagonism, or a complete dependency on tourism.

Tourism dynamics are additionally affected by non-economic external factors such as political unrest and natural disasters, which also need to be taken into account in the management of destination development. The dramatic decline in visitation induced by the 2004 tsunami in Phuket (Thailand) is one notable recent Asian example. Within Australia, the 1998 flood in the Northern Territory town of Katherine had a similar devastating short-term impact on visitation. However, community mobilisation and effective managerial responses to sensationalist media coverage and damaged tourism infrastructure allowed the tourism industry in Katherine to recover rapidly, resulting in only a small anomaly within the visitation curve (Faulkner & Vikulov 2001).

The Butler sequence as an 'ideal type'

The Butler sequence, in summary, best describes destinations that are:
• relatively small
• spatially well defined
• highly focused on tourism
• dominated by free market (or 'laissez-faire') imperatives
• in high demand.

Its applicability to real-life situations, therefore, seems to be limited, and out of all proportion to the considerable attention that it has received in the tourism literature. Yet, the attention paid to the Butler sequence is entirely justified because of the model's utility as an **ideal type** against which real-life situations can be measured and compared. In other words, the Butler model (as with any model) shows what takes places when the distortions of real life are removed — it is, in essence, a deliberately idealised situation that functions as a benchmark.

With this 'pure' structure as a frame of reference, the researcher can see how much a real-life case study situation deviates from that structure, and then try to identify why this deviation occurs. For example, it was noted that local control actually increased with accelerated tourism development on Grand Cayman Island, a situation that can be attributed to the status of this island as a colony where British and Jamaican interests had the capital and inclination to initiate the involvement stage while most locals were focused on working in the fisheries or other maritime industries. In the case of

Niagara Falls, the presence of an overwhelmingly dominant and iconic natural attraction appears to prevent a situation where contrived, specialised recreational attractions become more important than the original primary cultural or natural attractions. The implication, which can be illustrated with many more examples, is that different types of circumstances result in different types of deviations from the model. Continued identification and testing for such deviations may allow distinctive variants of the cycle to be identified, resulting eventually in a constellation of subsets that take these real-life circumstances into account.

FACTORS THAT CHANGE THE DESTINATION CYCLE

The trigger factors that induce a transformation from the exploration stage to the involvement stage have been considered. These and other factors also influence change in later stages of the cycle, whether the latter conforms to the Butler sequence or not. Managers benefit from a better understanding of these ongoing influences, in particular, because the destination in the post-involvement stages can experience not only further growth, but also decline. This understanding includes an awareness of the degree to which various factors can be controlled and manipulated. Clearly, it is desirable that the managers of a destination should retain control or at least influence over as many of these as possible, so that they can shape a desirable evolutionary path for the destination.

The factors that influence the evolution of tourism in destinations can be positioned within a simple eight-cell **matrix model of cycle trigger factors** (see figure 10.4). As with the attraction inventory discussed in chapter 5, the dotted lines indicate that each variable can be measured along a continuum — discrete categories are used as a matter of convenience for discussion purposes, rather than as an indication that all factors neatly fit into eight homogeneous cells.

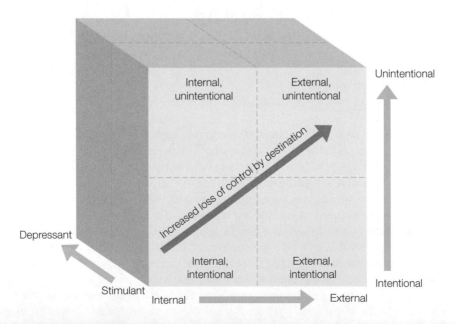

FIGURE 10.4 Matrix model for classifying cycle trigger factors

Internal-intentional actions

From a destination perspective, the 'ideal' situation involves actions that originate deliberately from within the destination, or **internal-intentional actions**. Applicable stimulants that trigger further growth include infrastructure upgrading, effective marketing campaigns directed by the local tourism organisation, innovative investments by local risk-taking entrepreneurs, and the decision by local authorities to pursue a growth pole-type strategy based on tourism. Conversely, internal and intentional depressants, such as entry fees and infrastructure restrictions, can be used deliberately to restrict or reverse the growth of tourism. Not all these factors, however, are instigated or desired by destination managers, as illustrated by home-grown terrorist groups in countries such as Egypt that attempt to sabotage the country's tourism industry.

External-unintentional actions

Trigger factors that originate from beyond the destination, and in an unintentional way, can be described as **external-unintentional actions**. Because they are spatially removed in origin from the destination, and because they are not the deliberate result of certain actions, they tend to be highly unpredictable both in character and in outcome, and mostly uncontrollable by destination managers. They are therefore the least desirable outcome from a destination perspective, and furthermore, indicate how much developments within the destination are vulnerable to uncertain, external forces. Examples of external-unintentional depressants include cyclones that periodically disrupt the tourism industry in northern Queensland or Vanuatu, climate change and its harmful impact on the Great Barrier Reef, and political chaos in Indonesia in so far as it hinders tourism in Bali. Ironically, many of these same factors are external-unintentional tourism stimulants for other destinations. For example, political instability in Indonesia has had the effect of diverting many Australian tourists to destinations within Australia itself or to long-haul regions such as Europe.

Internal-unintentional actions

Internal-unintentional actions, as with external-intentional actions (see below), are intermediate between the first two categories with respect to the control that can be exercised by the destination. Examples of internal-unintentional depressants include a prolonged civil war (though some civil wars can also be intentional) or coral reef destruction caused by a local pollution source. Originating within the jurisdiction of the destination, managers and other authorities are in a better position to deal with these situations in comparison to those associated with outside forces.

External-intentional actions

The opposite situation is described by **external-intentional actions**. Depressants in this category include a country that drastically and dramatically devalues its currency, perhaps in part to become a more affordable and attractive destination competitor relative to an adjacent country. The legalisation of gambling in Atlantic City was a potential depressant for Las Vegas, but in retrospect could be considered a stimulant because of its role in inducing Las Vegas to rejuvenate its product. A clearer example of a stimulating effect is the opening of a new transportation corridor such as a railway within a transit region, to expedite the movement of tourists from an origin to a destination region. Movies and television shows are also potential external-intentional stimulants, as demonstrated by the study of two Iowa communities featured earlier in this chapter.

◼ NATIONAL TOURISM DEVELOPMENT

As argued, the Butler sequence, and the destination cycle concept in general, are not applicable at the scale of entire countries, except for those that are exceptionally small. To gain insight into the process of tourism development at the country scale, it is helpful to revisit the internal spatial patterns described in chapter 4, which involve the concentration of tourism within large urban centres and in built-up areas adjacent to attractions such as beaches and mountains. To understand how these patterns have emerged and are likely to evolve in the future, an understanding of the concept of **spatial diffusion** is essential.

Spatial diffusion

Spatial or geographical diffusion is the process whereby an innovation or idea spreads from a point of origin to other locations (Getis, Getis & Fellman 2004). Spatial diffusion can be either contagious or hierarchical. In **hierarchical diffusion**, the idea or innovation typically originates in the largest urban centre, and gradually spreads through communications and transportation systems to smaller centres within the urban hierarchy. This process is modelled in part (a) of figure 10.5. To illustrate, television stations in the United States first became established in large metropolitan areas such as New York and Chicago in the late 1940s, and soon thereafter started to open in second-order cities such as Boston and Denver. Within five years, they were established in small regional cities of about 100 000 population and in many cities of 50 000 or fewer by 1960. The larger the city, the higher the probability therefore of early adoption. Less frequently, diffusion can occur in the opposite direction, as illustrated by the movement of musical forms such as the blues and country from rural areas of origin to large urban centres.

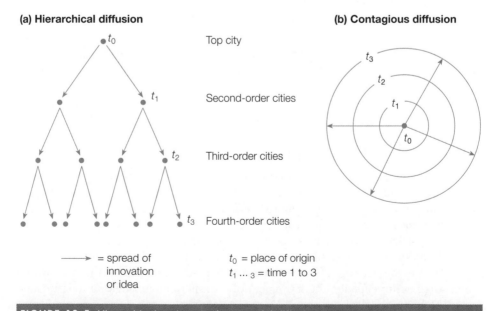

(a) Hierarchical diffusion

t_0 — Top city

t_1 — Second-order cities

t_2 — Third-order cities

t_3 — Fourth-order cities

(b) Contagious diffusion

t_3 t_2 t_1 t_0

⟶ = spread of innovation or idea

t_0 = place of origin
$t_{1 \ldots 3}$ = time 1 to 3

FIGURE 10.5 Hierarchical and contagious spatial diffusion

In **contagious diffusion**, the spread occurs as a function of spatial proximity. This is demonstrated by the likelihood that a contagious disease carried by a student in a classroom will spread first to the students sitting next to the infected student, and lastly to those sitting farthest away. Contagious diffusion is sometimes likened to the ripple effect made when a pebble is thrown into a body of still water. A good example is the expansion of Islam from its origins around the cities of Mecca and Medina to the remainder of the Arabian Peninsula, and then rapidly into the rest of the Middle East and north Africa.

In both modes of diffusion, the ideal depictions in figure 10.5 are distorted by real-life situations, as with the Butler sequence. It is useful in the diffusion discourse, therefore, to identify barriers that delay or accelerate the process, and that channel the process in specific directions. The contagious diffusion of Islam, for example, was halted by effective resistance from Ethiopian Christians and the French. The discussion will now focus on the combined application of these spatial diffusion concepts to national-scale tourism development.

Effects of hierarchical diffusion

The concentration of tourism activity in urban areas is a manifestation of hierarchical diffusion. A country's largest city (e.g. Paris, Sydney, Toronto, New York, Nairobi and Auckland) is likely to function as the primary gateway for inbound tourists. Also, because of its prominence, it will contain sites and events of interest to tourists (e.g. opera house, parliament buildings, museums and so on). The dominant city, then, is often the first location in a country to host international tourism activity on a formal basis. For the same reasons, this centre also acts as a magnet for domestic visitors.

As the urban hierarchy of the country evolves, the same effect occurs on a smaller scale as the smaller cities (e.g. state capitals, regional centres) offer more services and provide more attractions in their own right. Thus, tourism spreads over time into lower levels of the urban system, a process that is assisted by improvements in the transportation networks that integrate the urban hierarchy — in essence, the tourism system expands by 'piggybacking' on the expansion of external systems such as transportation. However, tourism itself may contribute in some measure to this expansion of the urban hierarchy, in so far as it acts as a propulsive activity for spontaneous (e.g. Gold Coast) or planned (e.g. Cancún) urban development in coastal areas or other regions where tourist attractions are available.

Effects of contagious diffusion

The effects of contagious diffusion follow on from the effects of hierarchical diffusion. As cities grow, they emerge as significant domestic tourism markets in their own right as well as increasingly important destinations for inbound tourists. Both markets stimulate the development of recreational hinterlands around these cities, the size of which is usually proportional to the size of the urban area. As the city grows, the recreational hinterland expands accordingly. The tourist shopping villages in the urban–rural fringe of the Gold and Sunshine coasts are examples of this phenomenon at the excursionist level, while Muskoka (in the Canadian province of Ontario) and the Catskills (in the American state of New York) illustrate stayover-oriented recreational hinterlands.

Once a community becomes tourism oriented (i.e. 'adopts' the 'innovation' of tourism, in diffusion terminology), nearby communities become more likely to also experience a similar process within the next few years because of their proximity to centres of growing tourism activity. This observation is also relevant to Christaller's description of early tourists escaping to less-developed destinations when their old haunts become overcrowded (see page 267), and thus links the process of national tourism development with the destination cycle. In other words, the destination cycle will first affect communities on the edge of existing tourism regions, and then gradually incorporate adjacent communities as the recreational hinterland spreads further into the countryside. The same effect can occur in a hierarchical way — as a country develops, funds may be made available to upgrade the airport or road connection to third-order regional cities, which then becomes a trigger factor that initiates the involvement stage.

Barriers to diffusion

This process, however, is not likely to continue indefinitely, in part because demand is not unlimited, but also because of barriers that terminate, slow or redirect the tourism diffusion process. These can take numerous forms, the most common being the lack of attractions capable of carrying the destination beyond the exploration stage. Other barriers include community resistance, political boundaries and climate (e.g. 3S tourism can only develop within a certain latitudinal range). Conversely, factors that can accelerate the diffusion process include an extensive area of tourism potential such as a beach-lined coast or an alpine valley, and upgraded transportation networks (see Technology and tourism: Seeing Norway through the tunnels). It should be noted here that a road network is likely to facilitate contagious diffusion, while an air network will facilitate hierarchical diffusion.

technology and tourism

SEEING NORWAY THROUGH THE TUNNELS

The diffusion of tourism in Norway has long been impeded by the country's severe geography of high mountain ranges and isolated fjords, which fostered an exceptionally high dependency on ferry transportation in many regions. Infusions of oil revenue since the 1970s, however, have allowed the government to construct a sophisticated and expensive network of road tunnels that now numbers more than 900 and extends for 750 kilometres. Most notable among these is the tunnel that connects the towns of Laerdal and Aurland. At 24.5 kilometres, the US$125 million Laerdal Tunnel was opened in 2000 to connect the remote coastal region of Sogn with eastern Norway. The sole previous road access to Sogn was a winding high mountain road open to traffic only during the summer months. Superlative technical features of Laerdal Tunnel include an internal air treatment system that uses an electrostatic filter to remove dust and soot from air drawn in from a separate ventilation tunnel, and then a carbon filter to remove nitrogen dioxide. To relieve driver monotony, three large caverns constructed at equal intervals throughout the tunnel use special lights to create the illusion of daylight, while emergency telephones, turnaround lanes and fire extinguishers are available every 50 meters or so in the case of emergencies.

These engineering features combine with status as the world's longest facility of its kind to position the Laerdal Tunnel as a significant tourist attraction in its own right. More notable, however, are the potential impacts on the Sogn region, which was first opened to tourism in the mid-1800s. Small numbers of hunters and fishers were superseded in the 1900s by sightseers arriving by ferry and cruise ship. With Laerdal Tunnel now accommodating more than 1000 vehicles per day, Sogn is now positioned to become a mass tourism destination in which the accommodation of buses, cars and other recreational vehicles may emerge as a new technical challenge in an area that has little suitable terrain for such facilities.

Model of national tourism development

Figure 10.6 provides a model of national-scale tourism development that takes into account both hierarchical and contagious diffusion in a hypothetical country. The following sequence is depicted, with each interval representing, for the sake of illustration, a ten-year period:

- *Time 0*: in this earliest phase of evolution, there is some inbound and domestic tourism activity, indicative of the involvement stage, in the capital city and main gateway.
- *Time 1*: ten years later, a small recreational hinterland forms around the capital city, while tourism is introduced to a coastal city because of interest from the cruise ship industry and the presence of nearby beaches; this introduction may be spontaneous, or the result of a deliberate growth pole strategy.
- *Time 2*: the recreational hinterland of the dominant city expands outward (= contagious diffusion), while tourism is introduced as a significant activity in several second-order cities (= hierarchical diffusion); concurrently, tourism development takes hold in other coastal communities because of their 3S resources, while the hinterland of the original resort expands further, both inland and along the coast.
- *Time 3*: the pattern identified at Time 2 continues: recreational hinterlands expand and new places experience 'involvement'; in addition, where physical geography permits, fourth-order settlements in the interior become important as alpine tourist resorts.
- *Time 4*: expansion continues, especially along transportation corridors, alpine valleys and the coastline, as well as in other interior fourth-order settlements.

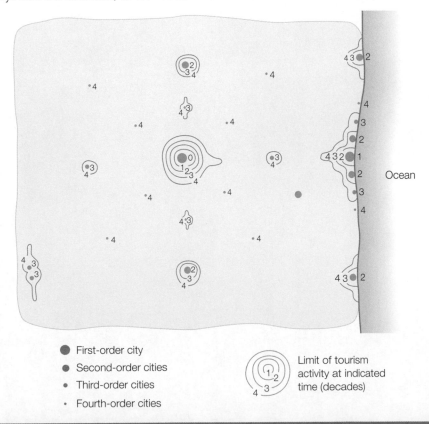

FIGURE 10.6 Tourism development in a hypothetical country

Models such as figure 10.6 are potentially useful for predicting when and whether a particular place within a country is likely to enter the cycle process beyond the exploration stage. It is also valuable to those who are responsible for the management and planning of destination-countries, and in particular those who are seeking to direct this process. Like the Butler sequence, the ideal type depicted in the figure can probably be augmented by a constellation of subtypes that take into consideration different types of countries. These might include landlocked states (such as Zimbabwe and the Czech Republic), alpine states (such as Norway or Switzerland), very large states (such as Australia, Russia, Canada), LDCs (such as Colombia and Papua New Guinea) and 3S-dependent SISODs (such as the Bahamas and Maldives).

CHAPTER REVIEW

Although allusions to the destination cycle were already made in the 1960s, this concept is most closely associated with the S-shaped Butler sequence introduced in 1980. This integrative model proposes that destinations tend to pass through a series of stages: involvement, development, consolidation and stagnation. Depending on circumstances, the destination may then undergo continuing stagnation, decline and/or rejuvenation. One major implication of the model is that tourism appears to contain within itself the seeds of its own destruction, as negative impacts accumulate and finally undermine the local tourism product as the stages progress. Applications of the intuitively appealing and simple Butler sequence to case study situations have revealed a broad adherence to the model, although most of these studies have also uncovered deviations. The results of many such applications remain ambiguous. While criticised as well for being too deterministic and for not taking into account the existence and influence of sectors other than tourism in the destination, the Butler sequence has enormous value as an 'ideal type' against which real-life situations can be measured and benchmarked. It is also clear, however, that the model is applicable only at certain geographic scales, and should in general not be applied at the national scale.

Whether the evolution of a destination is best described by the Butler sequence per se or by some variant, tourism managers should try to gain an understanding of the trigger factors and actions that induce significant change in a destination. These range from internal-intentional factors (the most favourable option) to those that are external-unintentional (the factors over which the destination has the least control, and hence the least favourable option). These factors, furthermore, can be generally classed as tourism stimulants or depressants. In larger countries tourism development is best described as a combined hierarchical and contagious diffusion process that is distorted both positively and negatively by assorted barriers and opportunities. The destination lifecycle concept can be situated conveniently within this context of national tourism development, in that it is possible to anticipate whether, when and how a particular place is likely to move beyond the incipient stages of the cycle.

■ SUMMARY OF KEY TERMS

Butler sequence the most widely cited and applied destination cycle model, which proposes five stages of cyclical evolution described by an S-shaped curve; these might then be followed by three other possible scenarios

Consolidation as local carrying capacities are exceeded, the rate of growth declines; the destination is now almost wholly dominated by tourism

Contagious diffusion spread occurs as a function of spatial proximity; the closer a site is to the place of the innovation's origin, the sooner it is likely to be exposed to that phenomenon

Decline the scenario of declining visitor intake that is likely to ensue if no measures are taken to arrest the process of product deterioration and resident/tourist discontent

Destination cycle the theory that tourism-oriented places experience a repeated sequential process of birth, growth, maturation, and then possibly something similar to death, in their evolution as destinations

Development the accelerated growth of tourism within a relatively short period of time, as this sector becomes a dominant feature of the destination economy and landscape

Exploration the earliest stage in the Butler sequence, characterised by few tourist arrivals and little impact associated with tourism

External-intentional actions deliberate actions that originate from outside the destination

External-unintentional actions actions that affect the destination, but originate from outside that destination, and are not intentional; these present the greatest challenges to destination managers

Hierarchical diffusion spread occurs through an urban or other hierarchy, usually from the largest to the smallest centres, independent of where these centres are located

Ideal type an idealised model of some phenomenon or process against which real-life situations can be measured and compared

Internal-intentional actions deliberate actions that originate from within the destination itself; the best case scenario for destinations in terms of control and management

Internal-unintentional actions actions that originate from within the destination, but are not deliberate

Involvement the second stage in the Butler sequence, where the local community responds to the opportunities created by tourism by offering specialised services; associated with a gradual increase in visitor numbers

Matrix model of lifecycle trigger factors an eight-cell model that classifies the various actions that induce change in the evolution of tourism in a destination. Each of the following categories can be further divided into tourism stimulants and depressants

Rejuvenation the scenario of a renewed development-like growth that occurs if steps are taken to revitalise the tourism product offered by the destination

Spatial diffusion the process whereby some innovation or idea spreads from a point of origin to other locations; this model is more appropriate than the destination lifecycle to describe the development of tourism at the country level

Stagnation the stage in the Butler sequence wherein visitor numbers and tourism growth stagnate due to the deterioration of the product

■ QUESTIONS

1. Is the popularity that the Butler sequence has maintained since the early 1980s justified? Explain your reasons.
2. Why is the Butler sequence referred to as the culmination of the cautionary platform?
3. Why are 'ideal types' such as the Butler sequence extremely useful to managers, even though they seldom if ever describe real-life situations?
4. How can the recognition and understanding of 'pre-exploration' dynamics better position contemporary indigenous communities to avoid tourism development that breeches critical carrying capacity thresholds within their communities?
5. (a) Which of the eight cells that comprise the matrix model for classifying cycle trigger factors (as per figure 10.4) best describes the Laerdal Tunnel (see page 286)?
   (b) What strategies should be adopted by the tourism managers of Sogn to cope with the increasing influx of vehicular visitors from eastern Norway?
6. How does the matrix model (see figure 10.4) complement and overlap with SWOT analysis to better understand and manage the dynamics of destination development?

7. How can the concept of spatial diffusion complement the destination cycle model in helping to explain the process of tourism development at the national level?
8. How does figure 4.7 reveal the effects of hierarchical diffusion on the distribution of inbound tourism in Australia?

■ EXERCISES

1. (a) For any major resort destination (e.g. the Gold Coast, Phuket, Bali, Cairns, the Sunshine Coast), obtain visitor statistics for as many years as possible and plot these on a graph similar to the format of figure 10.1 (i.e. time on the x-axis and quantity on the y-axis).
   (b) According to the resultant curves, where does this destination situate within the Butler sequence?
   (c) Gather as much evidence as you can about the tourism industry within the selected destination, and determine the extent to which Butler's model is both corroborated and contradicted by this material.
   (d) Where the information does not conform to the model, what factors might account for these deviations?
   (e) What factors appear to be influential in triggering the transition from one stage to another?
2. Select any large country (e.g. Australia, New Zealand, Canada, the United States, Germany, France, South Africa) and write a 1000-word report in which you describe how the national pattern of tourism development is accounted for by both diffusion and destination cycle processes, and explain how this pattern affects the management of the country as a whole as well as individual destinations within the country.

■ FURTHER READING

Beeton, S. 2005. *Film-induced Tourism.* **Clevedon, UK: Channel View.** This broad overview of the relationship between films and tourism includes consideration of the extent to which specific films have induced subsequent tourism development in their respective settings. A variety of international and Australian case studies is featured.

Butler, R. W. 1980. 'The Concept of a Tourist Area Cycle of Evolution: Implications for Management of Resources'. *Canadian Geographer* **24: 5–12.** This is the original article that introduced the Butler sequence; it is better for students to read this and other original articles, rather than rely entirely on the interpretations of others.

Butler, R. (Ed.) 2005. *The Tourism Area Life Cycle: Theoretical and Conceptual Implications.* **Clevedon, UK: Channel View.**

Butler, R. (Ed.) 2005. *The Tourism Area Life Cycle: Applications and Modifications.* **Clevedon, UK: Channel View.** These two volumes comprise a major collection of articles that critically explore the origins, theory, applications and modifications of the destination lifecycle in a wide variety of case studies. Butler, the editor of both volumes and originator of the S-curve lifecycle, provides a valuable personal commentary and synthesis of contributions.

Russell, R. & Faulkner, B. 2004. 'Entrepreneurship, Chaos and the Tourism Area Lifecycle'. *Annals of Tourism Research* **31: 556–79.** The authors make a strong case for the role of individual entrepreneurs as agents of change — i.e. chaos makers — within destinations such as the Gold Coast.

case study

BALI ON THE BRINK?

Bali is one of the best known 3S destinations of South-East Asia and is often described as a good example of resilient and culturally sustainable tourism. In recent years, however, continued tourism growth, indicated by an increase in accommodation units from 40 000 to 60 000 between 2005 and 2008 (Forbes 2008), has been associated with problems that have called into question Bali's reputation as a successful destination capable of recovering rapidly from diverse external threats such as terrorism and financial crises. Particular attention recently focused on the relationship between tourism and water consumption. Local environmental activists alleged, for example, that new resorts and their golf courses were unsustainably extracting the island's ground water, forcing villagers within a short distance of these resorts to truck in their drinking water (Vaessen 2008) or obtain it at high cost from nearby suppliers. The loss of water through over-consumption has been exacerbated by excessive logging throughout the island induced by tourism-related construction activity, which has reduced the capacity of Bali's watersheds to retain their surface and ground water (Forbes 2008).

Ironically, the unsustainable exploitation of water, forests and other natural resources is commonly rationalised by the island's dependence on tourism, which requires enormous environmental inputs to maintain the tropical paradise imagery that attracts most international tourists. Yet, this very image is being threatened by the relentless expansion of new and often speculative tourism developments, including an obtrusive multi-storey shopping complex that looms above the formerly iconic Dreamland beach on the Bukit Peninsula. Previously sacrosanct land surrounding Hindu sacred sites such as the Uluwatu Temple are also being exploited in defiance of cultural and environmental regulations, resulting in local protests and calls for stronger laws and their enforcement (Forbes 2008). Surprisingly, Balinese stakeholders also opposed and were recently successful in preventing the designation of a major temple complex as a prestigious UNESCO World Heritage Site, which would have conceded significant management powers to Indonesian authorities already often implicated in tourism-related corruption and environmental distress (Hitchcock & Darma Putra 2007).

More ambiguous is the impact of tourism on traditional Balinese dances such as the *barong*. Regarded as a central component of island culture, dance has undoubtedly experienced change as a direct result of tourism, which has removed some performances from their religious or ceremonial context, modified others to satisfy the preferences of tourists, and spawned tourist-specific innovations such as the *Panyembrama*. Some sociologists and anthropologists bemoan the resultant emergence of a superficial 'touristic culture' that relentlessly sabotages and trivialises 'authentic' Balinese culture, while others admiringly note the ability of the Balinese people to actively and selectively adapt their culture to the contingencies of modernity without compromising its fundamental integrity. As part of this 'intelligent assimilation' (Hitchcock & Darma Putra 2007), the latter further cite the imposition of quality control standards, minimum wage regulations, and a distinction between 'sacred' and 'non-sacred' performances that dictates whether they can be performed in tourism settings or not. Complicating such positive commentary, however, is evidence that performers expressing the strongest support for tourism are also those that receive the most financial return from performing for tourists (Barker, Darma Putra & Wiranatha 2006). Notably, the debate about tourism and its impacts upon Bali's dance traditions has been waging since the 1970s, when Bali had arguably entered the involvement stage, with no consensus apparent yet.

Notable demographic changes are also associated with tourism. One of these concerns the establishment and growth of privileged expatriate and seasonal amenity migrant communities that reflect longstanding patterns of inbound tourism from Europe and northern Asia. Sexual liaisons between Western tourists and Balinese also result in small numbers of new migrants. Of greater demographic import, however, is the role played by tourism in attracting substantial numbers of entrepreneurial migrants from other parts of Indonesia. Surveying in the 1990s, for example, revealed that the overwhelming majority of souvenir vendors in major tourist areas such as Kuta and Sanur were non-Hindus from Java and other parts of Indonesia (Cukier & Wall 1994). Indonesians of Chinese descent are heavily involved as investors, while various small ethnic groups dominate niche areas of the tourism industry. To a greater or lesser extent, members of these non-Balinese ethnic groups are perceived by many Balinese as competitors and as aggressive, clannish and/or dishonest, though even cumulatively they do not yet threaten the ethnic dominance of the latter. Moreover, Balinese entrepreneurs, including an elite known as the 'Kuta billionaires', continue to play a major role in the island's tourism industry, often in collaboration with stakeholders from other ethnic groups (Hitchcock & Darma Putra 2007).

In late 2008, negative media coverage, especially of the water issue, had not yet had a negative impact on the number of visitor arrivals. This is despite newspaper articles such as that which appeared in *The Sydney Morning Herald* in early October featuring the headline 'Island paradise sucked dry' and an uncomplimentary photograph featuring an ugly construction site adjacent to a beach (Forbes 2008). Presumably, enough potential or returning visitors from Australia and elsewhere continue to perceive Bali as a sort of paradise worthy of visiting, although repeated exposure to such negative publicity could eventually to sully the Bali 'brand'.

A relevant issue is the relationship of the latter to the Indonesian destination brand, which is negatively associated with political and ethnic instability, corruption, deforestation and poverty by many potential visitors. Whilst clearly located within Indonesia, Bali is still regarded as a distinct brand because of its insular status, the dominance of the minority Hindu religion, and the availability of direct flights that reduce or eliminate the need for transit through Jakarta or other Indonesian gateways. A repeat of the 2002 Bali bombings, or continued coverage of water and other environmental problems, however, could reduce the disassociation with Indonesia. The stakes for Bali are enormous, given that tourism now accounts for about two-thirds of the island economy, and tourists now have access to a growing array of 3S destinations within the region, many of which utilise Bali-type imagery in their promotion.

QUESTIONS

1. Write a 1000-word report in which you argue the case for and against regarding Bali as a single case study of the destination cycle.
2. In a 1000-word report:
   (a) assess where Bali's tourism sector is situated in relation to the ecological and sociocultural critical carrying capacity thresholds, and
   (b) propose strategies that will prevent this threshold from being breeched.

11
SUSTAINABLE TOURISM

LEARNING OBJECTIVES

After studying this chapter, you should be able to:

1. explain the concept of a 'paradigm shift' and its relevance to contemporary society

2. indicate how mass tourism is related to the dominant Western environmental paradigm

3. define sustainable tourism and show how this is related to the green paradigm and sustainable development

4. identify key indicators that gauge sustainability and describe their strengths and shortcomings

5. list the reasons for the tourism industry's adoption of sustainable tourism, and explain the advantages that larger companies have in its implementation

6. describe the sustainable tourism measures practised by the tourist industry

7. list examples of alternative tourism and discuss their advantages and disadvantages

8. appreciate how ecotourism differs from other nature-based tourism, and describe its characteristics

9. discuss the positive and negative arguments for encouraging tourism within protected areas

10. critique the broad context model of destination development scenarios as a framework for describing the evolutionary possibilities for tourist destinations.

INTRODUCTION

As manifested in the Butler sequence, the destination cycle concept suggests that tourism degrades destinations and ultimately undermines itself if managers implement no remedial or precautionary measures during the growth of the sector, especially as development-stage dynamics come into effect. The desire to avoid these negative impacts and still derive positive economic, sociocultural and environmental impacts from tourism has given rise to the concept of sustainable tourism, or tourism that occurs within the carrying capacities of a particular destination. This chapter on sustainable tourism begins by examining the nature of paradigms and paradigm shifts, and considers the likelihood that the dominant scientific paradigm and its associated environmental perspective are in the process of being replaced or at least modified by a more environmentally sensitive 'green paradigm' that emphasises the concept of 'sustainable development'. This provides a context for understanding the emergence of 'sustainable tourism'. After outlining potential key indicators of sustainable tourism and the shortcomings of indicator monitoring, we examine sustainability in the context of mass tourism. The reasons for the tourism industry's interest in sustainability are considered, along with associated practices and measures. A critique of these developments is also provided. The 'Sustainability and small-scale tourism' section focuses on 'alternative tourism' and its various manifestations, as well as the problems that potentially accompany this small-scale counterpoint to mass tourism. Ecotourism, which can occur as either mass or alternative tourism, is then examined while the final section considers strategies that potentially improve the sustainability of destinations. It concludes with a broad context model of destination development scenarios that integrates these concepts and incorporates the Butler sequence.

A PARADIGM SHIFT

Defined in its broadest sense, a **paradigm** is the entire constellation of beliefs, assumptions and values that underlie the way in which a society interprets reality at a given point in time. A paradigm can therefore also be described as a 'worldview' or 'cosmology'. According to Kuhn (1962), a **paradigm shift** is likely to occur when the prevailing paradigm is faced with contradictions and anomalies in the real world that it cannot explain or accommodate. In response to this crisis, one or more alternative paradigms appear that seemingly account for these contradictions and anomalies, and one of these gradually emerges as the new dominant paradigm for that society. The period from when the contradictions are first apparent to the replacement of the old paradigm with the competing paradigm can last for many decades, or even centuries. It is also important to note that the replacement of one dominant paradigm by another does not usually involve the disappearance of the formerly dominant paradigm. Rather, the latter can persist as a coexistent worldview retained by some groups or individuals. As well, the new dominant paradigm often incorporates compatible (or at least non-contradictory) aspects of the old paradigm, and may even emerge as a synthesis between the old paradigm and other radically opposing worldviews that initially arise.

Dominant Western environmental paradigm

Such a paradigm shift occurred in Europe during the fifteenth and sixteenth centuries. During this time, the Catholic Church was dominant, and its theological worldview held that the world was located in the centre of the universe, and that humans were created spontaneously in the image of God. This theological paradigm, however, was challenged by the discoveries of scientists such as Copernicus and Galileo. Gradually, the theological paradigm was replaced by a **scientific paradigm** that offered coherent and logical explanations for the radical new evidence uncovered by these pioneers. Fundamentally, the scientific paradigm perceives the universe as a 'giant machine', not unlike an automobile, that can be 'disassembled' in order to see how it operates. Once these subcomponents and their functions are perfectly understood, then future events within the universe can be predicted with certainty. Underlying the scientific paradigm is the 'scientific method', which reveals knowledge through a rigorously objective procedure of hypothesis formulation and empirical testing (see chapter 12).

By the nineteenth century, science was established as the dominant paradigm within Europe, and then within the world as a whole through the colonial expansion of England, France, Spain and other major European powers. Accompanying the scientific paradigm was acceptance of the anthropocentric belief (a retention, perhaps, from the theological paradigm) that humans are the centre of all things and are apart from and superior to the natural environment. The latter, in this perspective, is seen as having no intrinsic value, but only extrinsic value in relation to its perceived usefulness for people. Thus, some types of woodland such as conifer plantations came to be valued because of their usefulness as a fuel and source of timber, while wetlands were assigned little or no value to the extent that they are perceived to be economically unproductive.

Related to this is the belief in 'progress', or the idea that the application of science and technology will result in a continuous improvement in the quality of human life. Ideologically, the parallel view that progress can best be attained through a growth-oriented capitalist economic system became widely accepted in certain countries such as the United Kingdom and the United States. This perspective emphasises the role of individual incentive and competitive free market forces that determine the value (defined in terms of contribution to GDP) of various elements of the natural environment, such as oil (high) and wetlands (low). These natural environment-related aspects of the scientific paradigm are described by Knill (1991) as comprising the **dominant Western environmental paradigm**.

Contradictions in the dominant Western environmental paradigm

Since the mid-twentieth century, the dominant Western environmental paradigm has been confronted with a variety of anomalies and contradictions that challenge many of its fundamental assumptions about progress and nature. Ironically, many of these inconsistencies were revealed by science itself. For example, the field of physics demonstrated the apparently random and chaotic behaviour of subatomic particles, and revealed that the very act of observation can change the nature of these particles (Faulkner & Russell 1997). Such findings call into doubt the universal applicability of the objective, mechanistic, deterministic worldview posited by the dominant Western environmental paradigm and science more generally.

At the same time, research in biology, geography and ecology shows that present levels of economic development and growth, deriving from notions of progress and dominance over nature, may be inconsistent with the world's environmental carrying capacity. Processes and events that support this contention include:

- a series of high-profile environmental disasters, including the *Torrey Canyon* oil tanker spill off the coast of the United Kingdom in 1967, the partial meltdown of the Three Mile Island nuclear power plant in the United States in 1979, the gas leak

from the Union Carbide pesticide plant in Bhopal, India, in 1984, the nuclear power plant meltdown at Chernobyl, Ukraine, in 1986, the *Exxon Valdez* oil tanker spill off Alaska in 1989, and Hurricane Katrina's impact on New Orleans in 2005
* escalation in anthropogenic (human-induced) climate change, a phenomenon that was exposed widely to the global public through Al Gore's Oscar-winning film *An Inconvenient Truth*.
* accelerating ozone depletion, especially in polar regions
* increased incidence of dangerous viral and bacterial mutations
* rampant desertification and deforestation.

Some supporters of the dominant Western environmental paradigm, often described as 'technological utopians', argue that technology will solve all these problems as the necessity for solutions become apparent (e.g. scarcity, health concerns). Critics, however, point out that many of the problems are themselves caused by the same modern technologies (such as nuclear power and genetic manipulation) that claim to address other problems (such as depleted fossil fuels and increased population growth). Critics also suggest that the damage to the environment may soon progress to a point of irreversibility, if this is not already the case.

The dominant Western environmental paradigm and tourism

The tourism sector has also been implicated in these developments. The criticisms of contemporary mass tourism raised in chapters 8 and 9, and the cautionary platform that articulated these criticisms, are reactions against a prevalent pattern of large-scale tourism development that is an outcome of the dominant Western environmental paradigm. As encapsulated in the Butler sequence (see chapter 10), this critique holds that the emphasis on unlimited free-market growth produces the contradiction of initially desirable tourist destinations that eventually self-destruct as they become overcrowded, polluted and crime-ridden, and hence increasingly less desirable to both tourists and residents.

Towards a green paradigm

Criticism of the dominant Western environmental paradigm was made long before the present century — for example, in the writings of the American author Henry David Thoreau and the English author and social critic Charles Dickens. However, these were individual and isolated voices that initially did little to challenge the dominant paradigm and its damaging environmental or social impacts, especially since these problems were offset by demonstrable improvements in the physical wellbeing of societies undergoing the Industrial Revolution (see page 000). Since World War II the critique has gained momentum, in part because of the highly publicised environmental problems and disasters outlined above, and in part due to a sequence of high-profile publications that have both reflected and stimulated the post–World War II environmental movement (see figure 11.1). Challenges to the dominant Western environmental paradigm are also evident in allied perspectives such as contemporary feminism and the global reassertion of the rights of indigenous people, as well as through interest in the New Age movement.

The growing crisis in the dominant Western environmental paradigm is, therefore, resulting in the articulation of a competing worldview that can be described as the **green paradigm** (Knill 1991). Both paradigms are depicted as contrasting ideal types in figure 11.2, but it must be reiterated that a full shift to the green paradigm ideal type is unlikely. Rather, the *actual* (as opposed to ideal type) green paradigm of the future is likely to incorporate elements from each paradigm. This is evident in the emergence of **corporate social responsibility** as a business imperative that imbeds the core green principle of 'social responsibility' within the core 'corporate' principle of the dominant Western environmental paradigm. There is, of course, considerable debate as to the compatibility of such combinations.

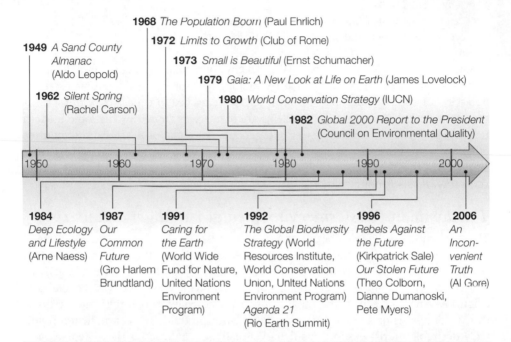

FIGURE 11.1 Milestone publications in the modern environmental movement

Dominant Western environmental paradigm	Green paradigm
Humans are **separate from nature**	Humans are **part of nature**
Humans are **superior to nature**	Humans are **equal with the rest of nature**
Reality is **objective**	Reality is **subjective**
Reality can be **compartmentalised**	Reality is **integrated** and **holistic**
The future is **predictable**	The future is **unpredictable**
The universe has **order**	The universe is **chaotic**
The importance of **rationality** and **reason**	The importance of **intuition**
Hierarchical structures	**Consensus-based** structures
Competitive structures	**Cooperative** structures
Emphasis on the **individual**	Emphasis on the **communal**
Facilitation through **capitalism**	Facilitation through **socialism**
Linear **progress** and **growth**	Maintenance of a **steady state**
Use of **hard technology**	Use of **soft technology**
Patriarchal and **male**	**Matriarchal** and **female**

FIGURE 11.2 The dominant Western environmental paradigm and the green paradigm as ideal types

Sustainable development

A hallmark in the emergence of the green paradigm was the explicit recognition of **sustainable development** as a guiding concept. Although the term was introduced in the early 1980s, it was the release of the Brundtland Report (*Our Common Future*) in 1987 that launched this idea into the forefront of the environmental debate. The Brundtland Report proposed the following definition of sustainable development:

> Sustainable development is development that meets the needs of the present without compromising the ability of future generations to meet their own needs (WCED 1987, p. 43).

This simple and enticing definition has gained widespread support from all sides of the environmental debate, and was employed as a central theme in the Rio Earth Summit of 1992 and its resultant *Agenda 21* manifesto (Miller & Kaae 1993) as well as in the sequel Johannesburg Summit of 2002 ('Rio + 10'). However, a closer scrutiny of the term reveals a number of difficulties. Some critics suggest that the term — like corporate social responsibility — is an oxymoron, or an 'essentially contested concept' (Hall 1998, p. 13) with 'sustainability' (with its steady state implications) and 'development' (with its growth implications) being mutually exclusive. The widespread support that the term enjoys, therefore, may simply reflect the ease with which it can be appropriated by the supporters of various ideologies or platforms to perpetuate and legitimise their own perspective (McKercher 1993). A resultant danger, according to Mowforth and Munt (2003) and others, is that the term can be used for **greenwashing** purposes; that is, to convey an impression of environmental responsibility for a product or business that does not deserve the reputation for it.

Others, however, regard the semantic flexibility of sustainable development as an asset that recognises and is responsive to the complexity and diversity of the real world. Hunter (1997), for example, describes sustainable development as an adaptive paradigm that accommodates both weak and strong manifestations:

- **Weak sustainable development** strategies are essentially anthropocentric and relevant to heavily modified environments (e.g. urban cores, intensively farmed areas), where human quality of life is a more realistic and relevant goal than, say, preserving rare species and their undisturbed habitats.
- **Strong sustainable development** strategies are essentially biocentric and are warranted in relatively undisturbed environments such as Antarctica and most of the Amazon basin.

■ SUSTAINABLE TOURISM

The term **sustainable tourism** became popular following the release of the Brundtland Report. The term at its most basic represents a direct application of the sustainable development concept. Sustainable tourism, in this context, is tourism that meets the needs of present generations without compromising the ability of future generations to meet their own needs. In operational terms, sustainable tourism can be regarded as tourism managed in such a way that:

- it does not exceed the environmental, social, cultural or economic carrying capacity of a given destination, and
- related environmental, sociocultural and economic costs are minimised while related environmental, sociocultural and economic benefits are maximised.

Weaver (2006) adds the caveat that even responsible operators may inadvertently operate on occasion in an unsustainable way, in which case the litmus test for a sustainable tourism operator is the willingness to redress the problem as soon as it is made apparent. Weaver also suggests that the definition should incorporate the need for operators to be *financially* sustainable, since tourism that is not financially viable is not likely to survive for long, no matter how viable it is from an environmental or sociocultural perspective. As with sustainable development, the term 'sustainable tourism' is susceptible to appropriation by those pursuing a particular political agenda, but is also amenable to weak and strong interpretations that adapt to different kinds of destinations.

Indicators

Whether sustainability is perceived from a weak or strong perspective, criteria must be selected and monitored to determine whether sustainable tourism is present in a destination or not. The first step is to identify a set of appropriate **indicators**, or variables that provide information about the status of some phenomenon (in this case, sustainability), so that tourism and affiliated sectors can be managed accordingly. Since the early 1990s, the World Tourism Organization (UNWTO) has played a lead role in identifying and 'road testing' tourism-related indicators. In the latest iteration of this process, the UNWTO proposed 12 baseline issues that are applicable to every destination (Antarctica may be an exception since it has no permanent resident community), and suggested indicators that allow for these issues to be measured (see table 11.1) (WTO 2004). The 2004 guidebook offers more than 500 indicators in total, inviting managers to select an array of indicators that is suitable for the specific circumstances of their own destination. To assist in the selection and implementation process, the guidebook supplements the suggested indicators with information about why the indicator is important, how it can be measured, and what benchmarks should be used. The result is the most comprehensive and flexible guidebook thus far for sustainable tourism, but one that is also hindered by its complexity and size as well as its failure to clearly describe the risks and challenges associated with the use of sustainable tourism indicators (Miller & Twining-Ward 2005).

TABLE 11.1 UNWTO baseline issues and suggested indicators

Baseline issue	Suggested indicators
1. Local satisfaction with tourism	• Local satisfaction level with tourism (questionnaire)
2. Effects of tourism on communities	• Ratio of tourists to locals (average and peak period/days) • Percentage of people who believe that tourism has helped bring new services or infrastructure (questionnaire) • Number and capacity of social services available to the community (percentage of which are attributable to tourism)
3. Sustaining tourist satisfaction	• Level of satisfaction by visitors (questionnaire) • Perception of value for money (questionnaire) • Percentage of return visitors
4. Tourism seasonality	• Tourist arrivals by month or quarter (distribution throughout the year) • Occupancy rates for licensed (official) accommodation by month (peak periods relative to low season and percentage of all occupancy in peak quarter or month) • Percentage of business establishments open all year • Number and percentage of tourist industry jobs which are permanent or full-year (compared to temporary jobs)

Baseline issue	Suggested indicators
5. Economic benefits of tourism	• Number of local people (and ratio of men to women) employed in tourism (also ratio of tourism employment to total employment) • Revenues generated by tourism as percentage of total revenues generated in the community
6. Energy management	• Per capita consumption of energy from all sources (overall, and by tourist sector — per person day) • Percentage of businesses participating in energy conservation programs, or applying energy saving policy and techniques • Percentage of energy consumption from renewable resources (at destinations, establishments)
7. Water availability and conservation	• Water use (total volume consumed and litres per tourist per day) • Water saving (percentage reduced, recaptured or recycled)
8. Drinking water quality	• Percentage of tourism establishments with water treated to international potable standards • Frequency of water-borne diseases (number/percentage of visitors reporting water-borne illnesses during their stay)
9. Sewage treatment (wastewater management)	• Percentage of sewage from site receiving treatment (to primary, secondary, tertiary levels) • Percentage of tourism establishments (or accommodation) on treatment system(s)
10. Solid waste management (garbage)	• Waste volume produced by the destination (tonnes) (by month) • Volume of waste recycled (m^3)/total volume of waste (m^3) (specify by different types) • Quantity of waste strewn in public areas (garbage counts)
11. Development control	• Existence of a land use or development planning process, including tourism • Percentage of area subject to control (density, design etc.)
12. Controlling use intensity	• Total number of tourist arrivals (mean, monthly, peak periods) • Number of tourists per square metre of the site (e.g. at beaches, attractions), per square kilometre of the destination (mean numbers/peak period average)

Source: WTO (2004)

Challenges of indicators

Even if it is assumed that the UNWTO framework provides an indicator selection that adequately reflects the diversity of variables that need to be considered by destination managers, several operational challenges must still be confronted that further attest to the complexity of tourism systems, including:

• obtaining adequate stakeholder participation and agreement, including community input and approval (Miller & Twining-Ward 2005)

• fuzzy boundaries between tourism and other sectors (see chapter 1), which make it difficult to determine which impacts should be attributed to tourism

• difficulties in identifying indirect and especially induced impacts, such as the construction of unsustainable housing for workers attracted to an otherwise sustainable hotel

- discontinuities between cause and effect through both time and space, whereby a negative impact in a destination such as. *E. coli* appearing in the water may be caused by unsustainable tourism activity that occurred one month earlier 50 kilometres upstream
- incompatibility between the long-term timeframe of indicator monitoring and the short-term (and unpredictable) timeframe of the political process that supports monitoring
- nonlinear relationships between cause and effect, so that a given input into a system does not necessarily result in a given output that can be reliably predicted. This is illustrated by the **avalanche effect**, in which a small input that caused no apparent problems in the past (e.g. a snowflake), unpredictably triggers massive change in the system (e.g. an avalanche).
- lack of knowledge about the **benchmark** and **threshold** values that indicate sustainability for a particular destination. A benchmark is a value against which the performance of an indicator can be assessed. The benchmark may be the same as a threshold, which is a critical value or value range beyond which the carrying capacity is being exceeded.
- potential incompatibility between environmental and social or cultural sustainability, as when a local community is displaced in the creation of a strictly protected national park that safeguards an endangered ecosystem.

Because of the uncertainties and complexities associated with indicators, it is not realistic to evaluate with complete certainty whether a destination is sustainable, as Weaver (2006) suggests. More prudent is to assess whether an apparently successful destination *appears* to be sustainable in so far as it conforms to best practice knowledge. In any case, the effort of pursuing and assessing sustainability is clearly worthwhile, since to abandon the effort is to virtually guarantee unsustainable outcomes.

SUSTAINABILITY AND MASS TOURISM

Although much of the early attention to sustainable tourism was focused on small-scale and low-intensity situations (see the following section), its relevance to mass tourism is arguably more important, since the latter accounts for most global tourism activity, and most activity that has been evaluated as being 'unsustainable'. The following discussion considers why the mass tourism industry should be interested in becoming more sustainable, and outlines practices and measures that reflect apparent adherence to sustainable tourism.

Reasons for adoption

Several factors justify the adoption of sustainable practices within the mainstream tourism industry, beyond the implications of the Butler sequence (see chapter 10), and in addition to the availability of a weak approach to sustainability that is relatively unthreatening to businesses (see above). These include:

- ethical considerations
- the growth of the 'green traveller' market
- the profitability of sustainability
- the suitability of larger corporations to adopt sustainable practices.

Ethical considerations

One school of thought is that corporations should pursue sustainability because ethical behaviour is what society expects from entities that exercise great power over the environment and culture, even if such expectations are not enshrined in the law. This is the essence of corporate social responsibility. For some executives and managers, this may be motivated by religious fiat (e.g. the Golden Rule), while for others it may reflect an attitude of enlightened self-interest; that is, a belief that a failure to behave ethically will at some point result in a negative public image or consumer boycotts.

Growth of the green consumer market

As a consequence of the growing environmental movement, there is growing evidence that consumers are becoming more discerning, sophisticated and responsible when it comes to purchasing decisions and behaviour. In Phase Four societies such as Australia, the United States and the United Kingdom, various surveys suggest that approximately one-quarter of consumers can be described as 'true' green consumers, meaning that environmental and social considerations exert a major influence on their purchasing behaviour (see figure 11.3). True green consumers, to a greater or lesser extent, are willing to make inconvenient concessions — of cost or time, for example — for the sake of environmentally responsible behaviour (Weaver 2006). They are, for example, more willing to pay extra for 'environmentally friendly' food and cars, and believe that government should spend more on social and environmental issues.

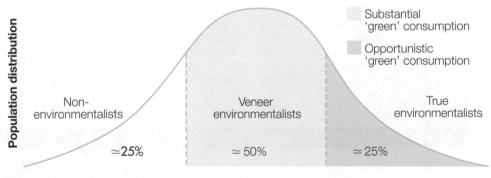

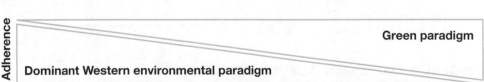

FIGURE 11.3 Environmentalism-related population clusters

A larger group, consisting of about one-half of the population, includes marginal or 'veneer' green consumers, who are concerned about the issues but tend to purchase appropriate goods and services only if convenient, as for example if the latter are priced competitively with comparable 'non-green' goods and services. However, many will behave temporarily or permanently like 'true' green consumers once convinced that an environmental crisis is at hand, or if the adoption of such behaviour becomes less inconvenient. Business ignores this diverse phenomenon of **green consumerism** at its peril, particularly since these attitudes and behaviour within society were virtually indiscernible before the emergence of the environmental movement after World War II, a fact that lends credence to the theory of a contemporary paradigm shift. One financial indication of this shift is the growth in socially responsible investment (SRI) portfolios, whose assets increased in value from about US$40 billion in 1984 to US$2.71 trillion in 2003, or about 11 per cent of all professionally managed funds (Social Investment Forum 2007).

There is growing evidence that true green consumerism is manifest within tourism through the emergence of the **green traveller** segment, the ideal type of which is depicted in figure 11.4. A survey of 489 air travellers in the United States, for example, showed as long ago as the late 1990s that 70 per cent were more likely to patronise a hotel with a good environmental record, while more than 90 per cent agreed that hotels should offer energy-efficient lighting (Webster 2000). Such attitudes have also been uncovered in more recent surveys of the expressed attitudes and behaviours of Phase 4 societies such as Australia (see Contemporary issue: Morally obligated Australian tourists).

The green traveller

Green consumer
Sensitive to local cultures
Conscious of social justice concerns
More independent-minded and discerning
Knowledgeable about environmental issues
Prefers flexible and spontaneous itineraries
Carefully assesses tourism products in advance
Searches for authentic and meaningful experiences
Wishes to have a positive impact on the destination
Motivated by a desire for self-fulfilment and learning
Searches for physically and mentally challenging experiences

FIGURE 11.4 Characteristics of the green traveller

contemporary issue

MORALLY OBLIGATED AUSTRALIAN TOURISTS

During 2006, 1000 randomly selected volunteers from an Australian internet panel with 250 000 members completed a 30-minute online questionnaire which included inquiries about their pro-environmental behaviour at home and when travelling, as well as their holiday preferences (Dolnicar & Leisch 2008). Six distinct 'moral obligation' market segments emerged from this analysis, with the largest group (24.1 per cent of the sample) exhibiting very high levels of moral obligation in their everyday behaviour. Similar groups focused such attitudes on activism (16.6 per cent) and purchasing (13.7 per cent). In contrast, only just over one in four participants displayed either low moral obligation (6.2 per cent), or obligation 'if convenient' (21.3 per cent). Unsurprisingly, relative expressions of obligation coincided with actual declared behaviour, with members of the first-mentioned cluster stating the highest level of corresponding behaviour both at home and whilst on holiday, and those with low moral obligation the least. However, in all cases the level of moral behaviour was lower on holiday, with 92 per cent of respondents stating that they felt more of an obligation to behave responsibly at home as opposed to other locations. The researchers speculate that people have a more vested interest in sustaining the environment of the places where they actually live, but that many destinations also do not provide the facilities and services necessary to enable environmentally responsible behaviour. This latter hypothesis was supported by the fact that the purchaser cluster was more likely to continue making environmentally responsible purchases whilst on holiday, since such behaviour is more easily transferred to non-home locations than actions such as recycling (Dolnicar & Leisch 2008).

The researchers also segmented the participants based on holiday preference, and identified six parallel clusters ranging from 'budget fun-seekers' to 'nature lovers'. Examining the two sets of clusters together, they identified four significant overlaps; that is, luxury tourists with low moral obligation, budget fun seekers with average moral obligation, budget fun seekers acting pro-environmentally if convenient, and nature lovers with high levels of moral obligation. Such information allows destination managers to more readily calculate the ecological footprint of particular types of tourist and to therefore target market those who have a smaller impact, and/or explore strategies to reduce the impact of groups with a large footprint, such as luxury tourists.

Profitability of sustainability

Beyond an enhanced ability to attract green travellers, the inherent profitability of many related activities is a major incentive for conventional businesses to become more involved in sustainability. Reduced energy consumption, for example, is a tangible long-term direct cost saving, as is the recycling of certain kinds of materials. Webster (2000) describes a recycling program of Sheraton Hotels that saved US$7000 per month from the sale of plastic and reduced dumping fees. Indirect profits are realised through the introduction of streamlined, nonhierarchical organisational structures, and through the improved employee morale that often accompanies such 'green' reforms. In addition, the fostering of positive community relations may create a friendly tourist–host rapport that enhances the quality of the vacation experience for tourists, and hence encourages repeat visitation and positive word-of-mouth publicity.

Suitability of larger corporations to adopt sustainable practices

Larger corporations are better positioned in many ways than their small-scale counterparts to implement and profit from sustainable tourism measures (McKercher 2001), as demonstrated by the Sheraton example described above. Economies of scale allow big businesses to allocate resources to fund specialised job positions that address sustainability-related issues (e.g. environmental officer, community relations officer), as well as relevant staff training, public education programs and comprehensive environmental audits. Cost-effective recycling and reduction programs are feasible because of the high levels of resource and energy consumption, while vertical and horizontal integration (see chapter 5) allow a company so structured to coordinate its sustainability efforts across a broad array of backward and forward linkages. Because of the volume of business they generate, these companies can also exert pressure on external suppliers to 'go green', thereby making a significant indirect contribution to sustainability. An example is the UK hotel chain Forte, which saved $75 000 in one year just by negotiating a reduction in the packaging of sugar sachets (Webster 2000).

Practices

In a review of sustainability-related practices within the conventional tourism industry, Weaver (2006) finds that:

- Formal institutional mechanisms have been initiated in most sectors to stimulate and facilitate the collective pursuit of sustainable tourism. These include the Cruise Industry Charitable Foundation (www.cruisefoundation.org), the International Tourism Partnership (www.tourismpartnership.org) (see Breakthrough tourism: A collective approach to corporate sustainability) and the Tour Operators Initiative (TOI) for Sustainable Tourism Development (www.toinitiative.org). Most sectors have also now introduced sustainability-related codes of practice.

- Each sector is led by a small number of high-profile innovative leaders. These include British Airways and American Airlines among air carriers, Marriott, Starwood and Grecotel among accommodation providers, and TUI among outbound tour operators.

- Sustainability measures adopted by these leaders and other companies focus on activities that increase profits and lower costs in the short term (e.g. high-volume recycling of glass and aluminium, energy use reduction, cogeneration), encourage brand visibility (sponsor tourism awards such as the WTTC Tourism for Tomorrow Awards) and are not expensive to implement (e.g. provide informational brochures and signage; linen re-use signs in bathrooms are perhaps the most widely used example of the latter). High-level quality control mechanisms have not yet been widely adopted.

- A high level of unawareness and noninvolvement remains within each sector beyond the high-profile activities of sector leaders.

Weaver (2006) speculates that while significant and demonstrable progress has been achieved in the conventional tourism industry since the early 1990s, this progress is uneven and indicates a 'veneer' pattern of sustainability that responds to and parallels the dominance of veneer green consumerism within society (see figure 11.3). By this logic, the lack of a 'deep' commitment, which could for example be expressed in a voluntary decision by industry to declare a moratorium on tourism development in some destinations, is not evident mainly because there is not yet widespread public agitation for such a radically biocentric policy shift. The institutional and leadership foundation for a deeper level of involvement, however, is being established and this could evolve as conventional fossil fuel price increases and technology advances make a wider range of sustainability practices more profitable and practical, and as concerns about climate change and its implications continues to escalate.

breakthrough tourism

A COLLECTIVE APPROACH TO CORPORATE SUSTAINABILITY

In 2004, the International Tourism Partnership (ITP) was founded as the first cross-sector corporate organisation dedicated to the collective pursuit of sustainable tourism. Three factors that bode well for its success are (1) its previous manifestation as the longstanding and successful International Hotels and Environment Initiative, (2) the support of the Prince of Wales through his International Business Leaders Forum, and (3) the involvement of leading tourism companies. In addition, the mandate of the ITP is a clear one focused on serving as a platform to implement practical and collaborative strategies that reflect the principles of sustainability within all facets of participating corporations.

To date, the ITP is best known for its quarterly *Greenhotelier* magazine, which specialises in the dissemination of practical sustainability advice and information, and two manuals — the 350-page *Environmental Manual for Hotels*, and *Sustainable Hotel Siting, Design and Construction* — that are periodically updated through new editions. Another significant publication, released in 2007, is *Going Green* (available free of charge from www.tourismpartnership.org), which provides a short checklist of minimum sustainability-related standards for the hotel sector. With the intent of inducing all or at least most hotels to embark on this path, *Going Green* offers basic advice under the categories policy and framework, staff training and awareness, environmental management, purchasing, people and communities, and destination protection. In conjunction with the UNWTO, the ITP has also launched the Tourism and Human Rights Initiative, which creates a framework for dealing with human rights issues within the tourism industry. Areas such as job security, illegal migrants, child and bonded labour, and workplace health and safety, are all being addressed by the Initiative, toward the creation of a set of guiding principles for the sector. Despite its accomplishments, a major shortcoming of the ITP is the lack of participation from beyond the hotel sector, with American Express being the only non-hotel member as of late 2008.

Quality control

A critical issue in the pursuit of sustainable tourism is the conveyance of assurance, through **quality control mechanisms (or 'quality assurance mechanisms')**, that a particular hotel, ski resort, tour operator or carrier is as environmentally or socially sustainable as it claims to be. **Codes of practice** and **ecolabels** are two of the main quality control mechanisms that attempt to provide this assurance in the tourism industry.

Codes of practice

The adoption of 'green' codes of practice, conduct or ethics is one of the most widespread and visible sustainability initiatives undertaken by the tourism industry. Among examples are the:

- Code of Ethics and Guidelines for Sustainable Tourism (Tourism Industry Association of Canada)
- Environmental Codes of Conduct for Tourism (United Nations Environment Program)
- Sustainable Tourism Principles (Worldwide Fund for Nature and Tourism Concern)
- APEC/PATA Code for Sustainable Tourism
- Environmental Charter for Ski Areas (National Ski Areas Association).

The APEC/PATA code (see figure 11.5) is representative in terms of content. Members are urged to adopt measures related to environmental and social sustainability, many of which relate to the sustainability indicators provided in table 11.1. While acceptance of the code is supposed to indicate that the member is committed to achieving sustainable outcomes, the voluntary nature of the commitment has been much criticised. These codes of practice have also been criticised because of the vague and general nature of the clauses (which allegedly makes them hard to put into operation and too open to interpretation), the lack of timelines for attaining compliance and almost all of them being based on the principle of self-regulation. As such, they are vulnerable to abuse as greenwashing devices (Mason 2007).

APEC/PATA CODE FOR SUSTAINABLE TOURISM

This code urges PATA Association and Chapter members and APEC Member Economies to:

Conserve the natural environment, ecosystems and biodiversity

- **Contribute** to the conservation of any habitat of flora and fauna, affected by tourism
- **Encourage** relevant authorities to identify areas worthy of conservation and to determine the level of development, if any, which would be compatible in or adjacent to those areas
- **Include** enhancement and corrective actions at tourism sites to conserve wildlife and natural ecosystems.

Respect and support local traditions, cultures and communities

- **Ensure** that community attitudes, local customs and cultural values, and the role of women and children, are understood in the planning and implementation of all our tourism related projects
- **Provide** opportunities for the wider community to take part in discussions on tourism planning issues where these affect the tourism industry and the community
- **Encourage** relevant authorities to identify cultural heritage worthy of conservation and to determine the level of development, if any, which would be compatible in or adjacent to those areas
- **Contribute** to the identity and pride of local communities through providing quality tourism products and services sensitive to those communities.

Maintain environmental management systems

- **Ensure** that environmental assessment is an integral step in planning for a tourism project
- **Encourage** regular environmental audits of practices throughout the tourism industry and to promote desirable changes to those practices
- **Establish** detailed environmental policies and indicators, and/or guidelines for the various sectors of the tourism industry
- **Incorporate** environmentally sensitive design and construction solutions in any building or landscaping for tourism purposes.

Conserve and reduce energy, waste and pollutants

- **Foster** environmentally responsible practices for:
  - reducing pollutants and greenhouse gases
  - conserving water and protecting water quality
  - managing efficiently waste and energy
  - controlling the noise levels and
  - promoting the use of recyclable and biodegradable materials.

Encourage a tourism commitment to environment and cultures

- **Encourage** those involved in tourism to comply with local, regional and national planning policies and to participate in the planning process
- **Foster**, in both management and staff of all tourism projects and activities, an awareness of environmental and cultural values
- **Encourage** all those who provide services to tourism enterprises to participate through environmentally and socially responsible actions
- **Support** environmental and cultural awareness through tourism marketing.

Educate and inform others about local environments and cultures

- **Support** the inclusion of environmental and cultural values in tourism education, training and planning
- **Enhance** the appreciation and understanding by tourists of natural environments and cultural sensitivities through the provision of accurate information and appropriate interpretation
- **Encourage** and support research on the environmental and cultural impacts of tourism.

Cooperate with others to sustain environments and cultures

- **Cooperate** with other individuals and organisations to advance environmental improvements and sustainable development practices, including establishing indicators and monitoring
- **Comply** with all international conventions and national, state and local laws which safeguard natural environments and cultural sensitivities.

FIGURE 11.5 Pacific Asia Tourism Association code for environmentally responsible tourism

Source: PATA

However, there are several arguments in favour of codes:

- The membership of organisations such as PATA (Pacific Asia Travel Association) and APEC (Asia Pacific Economic Cooperation) are too diverse to accommodate detailed objectives and relevant indicators within a single code. The codes provide the generic principles that everyone can agree with, and each type of member can then be referred to relevant best practice parameters as defined by a monitoring or other organisation.
- Codes are therefore a low-cost and low-risk gateway for moving gradually towards higher forms of quality control (Bendell & Font 2004).
- Codes can be a powerful form of moral suasion in that uncomfortable questions and scrutiny may be directed at members who do not consciously pursue sustainability, given that members are assumed to have made such a commitment.
- Reputable organisations such as PATA and APEC risk loss of credibility if members are seen to be code-noncompliant, and thus they have an incentive to encourage and tacitly enforce compliance.
- Private corporations are more likely to cooperate with sustainability initiatives if they are not threatened or forced to accept obligatory objectives and deadlines.
- The self-regulation that is implicit or explicit in these codes is based on the premise that voluntary adherence to good practice within the industry itself will pre-empt governments from increasing their own regulations on the sector. Businesses, as a result, will be able to maintain greater control over their own operations if they show themselves to be good 'corporate citizens' by adhering to the spirit of applicable codes.

Ecolabels

Font (2001, p. 3) defines ecolabels as 'methods [that] standardize the promotion of environmental claims by following compliance to set criteria, generally based on third party, impartial verification, usually by governments or non-profit organizations'. As such, they are considered a stronger quality control mechanism than codes. Ecolabels are focused on the interrelated concepts of **certification** and **accreditation**. The former involves an independent expert third party (i.e. other than the applicant or the governing ecolabel body), which investigates and confirms for an ecolabel body whether an applicant complies with that body's specified sustainability standards or indicators. If so, then the ecolabel will formally certify the applicant. Accreditation, in contrast, is a process in which an overarching organisation evaluates the ecolabel and confers accreditation if it is assessed as being sufficiently rigorous and credible. In essence, the accrediting body certifies the ecolabel (Black & Crabtree 2007). A major challenge for the contemporary tourism industry is the absence of such an overarching accreditation body, although the UNWTO is currently collaborating with major NGOs such as Rainforest Alliance, the United National Environment Programme (UNEP) and the International Ecotourism Society (TIES) to establish a Sustainable Tourism Stewardship Council (STSC) for just this purpose.

Most of the approximately 100 tourism-related ecolabels are focused on a particular product or region (e.g. the Blue Flag ecolabel certifies European beaches). EC3 Global (www.ec3global.com) is an exception because it encompasses all tourism products and all regions, and in doing so is attempting to position itself as the world's primary tourism ecolabel. Central to their Green Globe system is a graded membership structure consisting of 4 stages:

1. Benchmarking (Bronze) — based on presentation of a sustainability policy and completion of a benchmarking exercise that is assessed by EC3 Global

2. Certification (Silver) — requires compliance with relevant regulation and policies, and documentation of appropriate performance outcomes; includes an outside audit with onsite visit

3. Certification (Gold) — awarded to recognise five consecutive years of continuous silver certification

4. Certification (Platinum) — awarded to recognise ten years of continuous certification.

As of late 2008, only about 300 tourism products worldwide were participating in the scheme and only a small proportion of these had attained Certified status. This compares with about 500 participants four years earlier. This performance appears to contradict the pattern of greening within the tourism sector, but one problem for EC3 Global is that companies are reluctant to join until it achieves greater visibility among consumers, but this is unlikely to occur without a higher level of participation from industry in the first place. In general, it does not appear yet as if tourism-related consumer purchasing is significantly influenced by whether such products are certified or not.

■ SUSTAINABILITY AND SMALL-SCALE TOURISM

As suggested, much attention in the sustainable tourism literature has been devoted to small-scale tourism projects and destinations, on the assumption that such tourism is more likely to have positive environmental, economic and sociocultural impacts within a destination. The following discussion shows that the theoretical case for this assumption is sound, and there are indeed many examples of small-scale sustainable tourism. However, it should never be automatically assumed that the outcomes of small-scale tourism are always positive.

Alternative tourism

The cautionary platform identified the problems associated with mass tourism, but did not articulate more appropriate options in response. Alternative options appeared in the early 1980s in association with the adaptancy platform (see chapter 1). This new perspective held that large-scale tourism was inherently problematic, and that small-scale alternatives were therefore more desirable in most cases. The associated options, combined under the umbrella term of **alternative tourism**, were thus primarily conceived as alternatives to large-scale or mass tourism specifically, rather than in relation to other types of tourism.

Figure 11.6 depicts mass tourism and alternative tourism as contrasting ideal types. These came to be widely perceived as models of 'bad' and 'good' tourism, respectively. Where mass tourism attractions are 'contrived', alternative tourism attractions are 'authentic'; where mass tourism fosters externally controlled, high-leakage operations, alternative tourism offers locally controlled, high-linkage opportunities and so on. It may be added that alternative tourism is expected to adhere to a strong (as opposed to weak) interpretation of sustainability, while mass tourism was seen by supporters of the adaptancy platform as following an unacceptably weak version.

Circumstantial and deliberate alternative tourism

In some cases, a destination's affiliation with alternative tourism is superficial, the presence of the associated characteristics being simply a function of the fact that the destination is in the 'exploration' or 'involvement' stage of the Butler sequence (see chapter 10).

This 'unintentional' variation can be referred to as **circumstantial alternative tourism (CAT)** meaning that this status is associated with early circumstances of the resort cycle. In contrast, **deliberate alternative tourism (DAT)** occurs when a regulatory environment is present that 'deliberately' maintains the destination in that involvement-type state (Weaver 2000b). Returning to figure 11.6, the full set of alternative tourism characteristics in a destination is therefore indicative of the deliberate variation. If, however, the characteristics listed under 'regulation' are absent, then this indicates the presence of the circumstantial version. The reader should note the similarities between the latter situation and the exploration/involvement stage characteristics listed in table 10.1.

Characteristics	Unsustainable mass tourism	Deliberate alternative tourism
Markets		
Segment	Psychocentric–midcentric	Allocentric–midcentric
Volume and mode	High; package tours	Low; individual arrangements
Seasonality	Distinct high and low seasons	No distinct seasonality
Origins	A few dominant markets	No dominant markets
Attractions		
Emphasis	Highly commercialised	Moderately commercialised
Character	Generic, 'contrived'	Area specific, 'authentic'
Orientation	Tourists only or mainly	Tourists and locals
Accommodation		
Size	Large scale	Small scale
Spatial pattern	Concentrated in 'tourist areas'	Dispersed throughout area
Density	High density	Low density
Architecture	'International' style; obtrusive, non-sympathetic	Vernacular style, unobtrusive, complementary
Ownership	Nonlocal, large corporations	Local, small businesses
Economic status		
Role of tourism	Dominates local economy	Complements existing activity
Linkages	Mainly external	Mainly internal
Leakages	Extensive	Minimal
Multiplier effect	Low	High
Regulation		
Control	Nonlocal private sector	Local 'community'
Amount	Minimal; to facilitate private sector	Extensive; to minimise local negative impacts
Ideology	Free market forces	Public intervention
Emphasis	Economic growth, profits; sector-specific	Community stability and wellbeing; integrated, holistic
Timeframe	Short term	Long term

FIGURE 11.6 Mass tourism and alternative tourism: ideal types

Source: Weaver 1998 (adapted from Butler (1992) and Weaver (1993))

The distinction between circumstantial and deliberate alternative tourism is critical, since a CAT destination has the potential (assuming that there is demand to visit this place) to evolve along an unsustainable path of development, there being no preventative measures in place. In contrast, DAT reflects the influence of specific policy directives and controls (e.g. indicator thresholds and benchmark objectives that reflect a strong sustainability interpretation) that better ensure the maintenance of a sustainable, low-intensity tourism option.

Manifestations

Since the 1980s, DAT-related products and opportunities have become increasingly diverse, but still account for only a very small proportion of all tourism activity despite ongoing growth in the green traveller market. Manifestations include:

- cultural villages — Tourism for Discovery (Senegal)
- homestays — Meet the People (Jamaica), Friendship Force (International)
- feminist travel — Womantrek (United States)
- indigenous tourism — Wanuskewin (Saskatchewan, Canada), Tiwi Tours, Camp Coorong (Australia)
- older adult tourism — Elderhostel (international)
- vacation farms — Willing Workers on Organic Farms (international)
- social awareness travel — Center for Global Education, Global Exchange, Plowshares Institute (all in the United States)
- youth hostels
- personal awareness tourism — ESALEN Institute (California)
- religious tourism — monastery retreats
- educational tourism — The Humanities Institute (United States)
- volunteer activity — Habitat for Humanity, Global Volunteers (both in the United States)
- guesthouses.

While the above activities mostly occur in rural areas, urban DAT is also possible. One example is the urban cultural heritage tourism that is being developed in the African-American Shaw neighbourhood of Washington, DC (Peckham 2003) and in the Soweto township of Johannesburg, South Africa (Rogerson 2004). Ecotourism, another primarily rural activity, first emerged in the 1980s as a nature-based form of alternative tourism. However, because it is now widely recognised as having mass as well as alternative manifestations, it is discussed separately in this chapter.

Critique of alternative tourism

Although a small-scale level of activity is implicit in alternative tourism, the absence of negative impacts cannot be assumed. Problems that can occur in association with this apparently benign form of tourism are depicted in figure 11.7. In conjunction with earlier comments made about the suitability of large-scale enterprises to implement sustainable practices, the opposite can be said about small operations. Operators of the latter often lack the resources or expertise to implement measures compatible with sustainable tourism. Alternative tourists themselves may cause sociocultural stress by being overly intrusive in their desire to experience 'backstage' lifestyles over a prolonged period of time, thereby increasing the potential for cross-cultural misunderstanding (see chapter 9 and this chapter's Managing tourism: Volunteer tourism). Similarly, they may unintentionally distress wildlife by their presence, or introduce harmful pathogens into sensitive natural locales that have not been site-hardened to accommodate even small numbers of visitors. In both situations, these tourists may function as 'explorers', as per the Butler sequence, who inadvertently open the destination to less benign forms of tourism development. Despite their philosophical discomfort with mass tourism, alternative tourists also use related products, such as air transport, which contribute to unsustainability at a global level.

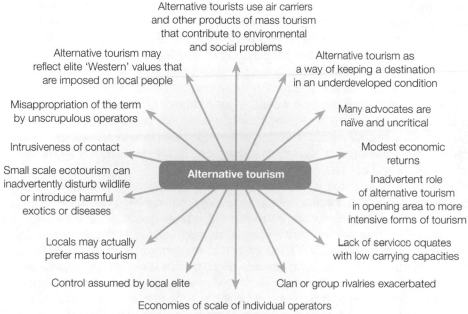

Alternative tourists use air carriers and other products of mass tourism that contribute to environmental and social problems

Alternative tourism may reflect elite 'Western' values that are imposed on local people

Misappropriation of the term by unscrupulous operators

Intrusiveness of contact

Small scale ecotourism can inadvertently disturb wildlife or introduce harmful exotics or diseases

Locals may actually prefer mass tourism

Control assumed by local elite

Economies of scale of individual operators inadequate to implement sustainable practices

Alternative tourism

Alternative tourism as a way of keeping a destination in an underdeveloped condition

Many advocates are naïve and uncritical

Modest economic returns

Inadvertent role of alternative tourism in opening area to more intensive forms of tourism

Lack of services equates with low carrying capacities

Clan or group rivalries exacerbated

FIGURE 11.7 Criticisms of alternative tourism

Source: Adapted from Weaver (1998)

A commonly cited criticism is the association of alternative tourism with elite 'green' value systems that place a high value on principles (such as the nonconsumption of natural resources) that may be incompatible with local hunting traditions or slash-and-burn farming techniques. Great pressure may be placed on locals to adopt the alternative tourism model, even though local residents in some cases might prefer a more intensive and larger-scale form of tourism that generates higher economic returns. Small-scale ecotourism is even seen as a way of keeping an area in an underdeveloped, primitive state for the benefit of a few wealthy ecotourists from the developed countries (Butcher 2006).

Where local residents are actually in control of an alternative tourism enterprise, most of this power may rest in the hands of the local elite, whose economic and social dominance in the community is thereby reinforced. Similarly, clan rivalries may be exacerbated if one group perceives that a rival group is gaining an advantage, as happened during the 1980s with the development of alternative tourism guesthouses in the Tufi region of Papua New Guinea (Ranck 1987). Other problems include the continued naïvety of some advocates, who may be unwilling or unable to see its potential shortcomings, and the possibility that unscrupulous businesses may use the alternative tourism or ecotourism label to legitimise products that do not meet the appropriate criteria.

managing tourism

VOLUNTEER TOURISM

Volunteer tourism, or 'voluntourism', is becoming increasingly popular as a vehicle for combining high quality visitor experiences with the enhancement of a destination's environmental and sociocultural sustainability (Wearing 2001). The assumption that close contacts between volunteer tourists and local residents foster cross-cultural understanding is often made, but may be naïve. To investigate this phenomenon, Raymond and Hall (2008) examined feedback provided by representatives from ten volunteer tourism programs, including one that is Australian-based. They found that such activity can actually reinforce cultural stereotypes about host cultures and people, and that cross-cultural understanding should therefore be regarded not as an inherent outcome of such programs but rather a desirable *goal* that needs to be fostered through appropriate management. One way of achieving this is by ensuring that the skills of the volunteer are matched with appropriate projects so that they are perceived as credible by the local community and can bring into effect useful outcomes. In so doing, it is critical that volunteers do not displace or exercise authority over local workers.

A second recommendation is that organisations encourage volunteers to constantly reflect on their experience through journal-keeping, role playing and discussion groups to identify and assess (and if necessary rectify) both the positive and negative aspects of their cross-cultural contacts. Finally, organisations should encourage maximum exposure to different cultures by building culturally diverse volunteer teams rather than homogenous (i.e. all-Australian) teams that may function and be perceived as cliques. A related difficulty is that volunteer organisations tend to market to residents of a particular country and might therefore need to form partnership with counterparts in other countries. Exposure can also be achieved by encouraging volunteers to mix socially with local residents during off-hours, and to board with local families. Raymond and Hall (2008) conclude that volunteer tourism does have enormous potential to foster cross-cultural understanding, but only through careful design and management.

ECOTOURISM

Ecotourism is distinguished in three main ways from other types of tourism:

- The natural environment, or some component thereof (e.g. noncaptive wildlife), is the focus of attraction, with associated cultural resources being a secondary attraction given that all 'natural' environments are actually modified to a greater or lesser extent by direct and indirect human activity.
- Interactions with nature are motivated by a desire to appreciate or learn about the attraction. This contrasts with nature-based 3S or adventure tourism, where the natural environment serves as a convenient setting to fulfil some other motivation (e.g. sunbathing or thrill-seeking, respectively, in the two cases given here).
- Every attempt must be made to operate in an environmentally, socioculturally and economically sustainable manner. Unlike other types of tourism, the mandate to be sustainable is explicit, prompting Weaver (2006) to describe ecotourism as the 'conscience of sustainable tourism'.

Within these parameters there are many activities that cluster under the ecotourism umbrella and extend this activity to once-inaccessible areas (see Technology and tourism: Above the tree tops and beneath the waves). As depicted in figure 11.8, activities such as bird-watching, whale-watching and stargazing can be positioned entirely within ecotourism, while safaris, trekking and nature photography usually overlap with the nature-based components of adventure tourism. Similarly, scuba diving and snorkelling are affiliated with 3S tourism while tourism involving indigenous cultures is linked to sociocultural alternative tourism.

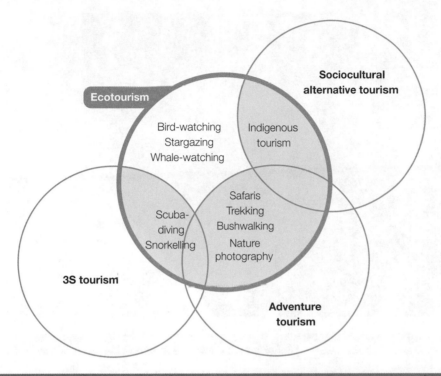

FIGURE 11.8 Major types of ecotourism activity

technology and tourism

ABOVE THE TREE TOPS AND BENEATH THE WAVES

As with all entrepreneurs, the owners and managers of ecotourism attractions should continually strive to attract new visitors and retain existing ones through product innovation. In recent years, technologically sophisticated facilities have been developed that expose visitors to previously inaccessible natural areas. The 420-metre-long Tree Top Walk in Western Australia's Walpole-Nornalup National Park is one example. Situated at its highest point 40 metres above the ground, the Walk has taken more than 2.1 million visitors into the canopy of the high jarrah forests since 1996 (DEC 2008) (see figure 11.9). Whereas many such canopy walkways are unstable suspension bridge-type structures, the Tree Top Walk provides a secure ramp that uses lightweight steel trusses built on top of steel pylons. See-through steel decking reinforces the sensation of high suspension, while the metal is designed to oxidise so that its new 'rusty' colour blends in with the jarrah forest. A different view of the forest is provided by the Skyrail cableway in northern Queensland, which travels above 7.5 kilometres of tropical rainforest canopy as it ferries visitors from a terminal near Cairns to the town of Kuranda.

Technological innovation is especially evident in the construction process, which involved the use of special Russian Kamov helicopters to position the towers that support the cable, and Global Positioning Systems (GPS) to ensure pin-point placement of the towers in the tiny areas cleared to accommodate them.

FIGURE 11.9 Tree Top Walk in Walpole-Nornalup National Park, Western Australia

New opportunities for ecotourism have also been created beneath the ocean's surface. In several South Pacific and Caribbean destinations, Atlantis Adventures operates submarines that can hold either 48 or 64 passengers. The non-polluting battery-powered vessels allow the passengers to view coral reefs and other marine phenomena more than 30 metres below the surface, with ample interpretation made available during the almost-two hour experience. Sophisticated sensors and other onboard technologies ensure that the submarines cause almost no disruption to the marine habitat, which includes artificial reefs specially constructed by the operators to relieve any potential stress on the natural environment. Since the mid-1990s, over 12 million passengers have been accommodated by Atlantis Adventures.

Soft and hard ecotourism

Ecotourism activities can be further classified as hard or soft, although as with mass and alternative tourism, these labels should be seen as two ends of a spectrum rather than as mutually exclusive categories (Weaver 2008). **Hard ecotourism**, as an ideal type, emphasises an intense, personal and prolonged encounter with nature. Associated trips are usually specialised (i.e. undertaken solely for ecotourism purposes) and take place within a wilderness setting or some other mainly undisturbed natural venue where access to services and facilities is virtually nonexistent. Participants are environmentalists who are highly committed to the principles of sustainability. This mode of ecotourism is most clearly aligned with alternative tourism and with a strong interpretation of sustainability.

In contrast, **soft ecotourism** is characterised by short-term, mediated interactions with nature that are often just one component of a multipurpose tourism experience. Participants have some appreciation for the attraction and are open to learning more about sustainability and related issues, but the level of commitment to environmentalism, as a philosophy, is not as strong, indicating a higher incidence of veneer green consumer participation. Soft ecotourism takes place within less natural settings (e.g. park interpretation centre, scenic lookout, signed hiking trail, wildlife park) that provide a high level of services and facilities. This form of ecotourism can potentially exist as a type of mass tourism informed by a weaker interpretation of sustainability. Nevertheless, with appropriate educational opportunities provided through effective product interpretation, there is evidence that both soft as well as hard ecotourism can produce positive environmental impacts (Littlefair 2004).

Magnitude

The magnitude that one attributes to ecotourism depends on how much of the hard–soft spectrum and how many overlapping activities are embraced in the accepted definition. If one restricts ecotourism to the hard ideal type, then this sector is miniscule. A liberal definition that embraces an array of soft ecotourism products and hybrid activities such as scuba diving produces a much higher figure, probably in the 15–20 per cent range. Complicating such calculations is the multipurpose nature of most travel (see page 30), wherein most participation in ecotourism occurs as one component within a multipurpose itinerary. The difficulties that arise in quantifying ecotourism and its relationships with other forms of tourism are illustrated by inbound tourism patterns in Kenya. The great majority of inbound visitors are conventional mass tourists who spend most of their time in the capital city (Nairobi) or in Indian Ocean beach resorts. However, surveys have revealed that 70 per cent of these visitors selected Kenya for their 3S holiday because of the opportunity to participate in a wildlife-watching safari excursion (Akama 1996). The resultant soft ecotourism activity often occurs on a large scale within certain accessible protected areas, confirming ecotourism's dominant status as a form of mass tourism.

Location

Ecotourism destinations are usually associated with 'natural' or 'relatively undisturbed' settings. It is therefore not surprising that most ecotourism activity takes place within protected areas such as national parks, which provide both a relatively undisturbed setting and a DAT-like regulatory environment that restricts potentially harmful activities (Butler & Boyd 2000). Hard ecotourism tends to occur in the more remote regions of countries or individual parks, while soft ecotourism, as noted above, concentrates in the more accessible portions of parks that are located within a few hours drive from major cities or 3S resort areas (Weaver 2008). In the latter situations, it is typical for 90–99 per cent of all tourist activity to occur within just 1–5 per cent of the park area. Given that such protected areas are expected to fulfil two potentially conflicting mandates — the preservation of local biodiversity and the accommodation of increasing visitor numbers — it is not surprising that situations arise and management decisions are taken that call into question the sustainability of ecotourism in such areas.

Protected areas and other relatively undisturbed natural environments clearly do provide a potentially optimal venue for authentic, high-quality encounters with nature, but there is no inherent reason for excluding modified environments such as reservoirs and farmland that may also attract interesting birds or mammals. Weaver (2005) makes the case for urban ecotourism, arguing that extremely site-hardened locations such as bridges and skyscrapers can provide excellent wildlife-viewing opportunities. The Congress Avenue Bridge in Austin, Texas, for example, hosts a colony of 1.5 million Mexican free-tailed bats that annually attracts 100 000 visitors and $10 million in revenue.

Ecotourism activity occurs in all parts of the world, but some regions and countries have attained a reputation as ecotourism destinations. Prominent among these are Australia (see the following), New Zealand and the Central American corridor extending from the Yucatan Peninsula and Belize to Costa Rica. Other important regions are the Amazon Basin, the 'safari corridor' from Kenya to South Africa, the Himalaya, the Pacific Northwest of Canada and the United States, peripheral Europe, and South-East Asian destinations such as Thailand, Borneo and Sumatra (see figure 11.10). Rainforest, savanna, coastal and marine environments are especially well represented as ecotourism venues, while deserts and grasslands have relatively little related activity.

FIGURE 11.10 Prominent world ecotourism destinations

Ecotourism in Australia

An indication of the magnitude of ecotourism in Australia is provided by figure 5.1, which shows that almost one-half of inbound tourists visited a national or state park on their visit to Australia in 2006. The likelihood that many of these visits were related to soft ecotourism is indicated by the fact that 'bushwalking' — an indicator of a more intensive level of ecotourism — is not included in this top ten list of activities. High-profile Australian ecotourism destinations include the Great Barrier Reef, the tropical and temperate rainforests that extend intermittently from Cape York to Tasmania, Fraser Island (Queensland), and Rottnest Island, the Kimberley and Shark Bay (Western Australia). Other venues include Uluru and Kakadu national parks (Northern

Territory), the alpine region extending through New South Wales and Victoria, Phillip Island (Victoria), and Kangaroo Island and the Flinders Ranges (South Australia).

■ DESTINATION SUSTAINABILITY

Although constrained by vested interests associated with other sectors, destination governments and tourism authorities have access to mechanisms that facilitate the pursuit of sustainable tourism. Development standards, or legal restrictions that dictate the physical aspects of development, are one such option (Weaver 2006). Included in this category are:

- density and height restrictions
- setbacks (distances separating the outer edge of a development from another object, such as a footpath, floodplain or beach high water mark)
- building standards (e.g. conformance of new construction to traditional architectural styles, minimum insulation requirements)
- noise regulation
- signage control (e.g. prohibitions on motorway billboards).

In addition, municipalities can pursue social sustainability by requiring resorts to provide reasonable pedestrian access between a public road and a public beach, as is often done in the Caribbean.

Zoning regulations, which demarcate specific areas for defined uses and development standards, are another important tool for destination planning and management, as are districting strategies that designate special urban or rural landscapes for focused management or planning that seeks to preserve the special historical, natural or cultural properties of these places. In the designated Chinatown district of Toronto, bilingual Chinese and English road signs and relaxed standards for the display of food and other commercial goods are both permitted in order to distinguish this neighbourhood as a Chinese–Canadian culture area and tourist attraction. Destination governments also have considerable scope for offering sustainability-related incentives to their constituent private sector tourism operators. One example is the Barbados *Tourism Development Act* (2002), which allows a 150 per cent tax deduction on expenses related to the pursuit of Green Globe hotel certification.

Extending the Butler sequence

Attempts to model the process of tourist destination development in the field of tourism studies have mostly focused on the Butler sequence and its pessimistic outcomes (see chapter 10). However, recent developments in the field of sustainable tourism suggest that a broader framework is necessary in order to encompass the full range of possible developmental scenarios. Such a framework is provided in figure 11.11. This **broad context model of destination development scenarios** consists of four basic tourism ideal types, based on the scale of the sector (small to large) and the amount of sustainability-related regulation that is present (Weaver 2000b).

In this model, small-scale destinations fall into either the CAT (i.e. little or no regulation) or DAT (extensive regulation) category. Similarly, large-scale destinations in theory are either unsustainable (= unsustainable mass tourism, or UMT) or sustainable, depending on the presence or absence of a suitable regulatory environment (= sustainable mass tourism, or SMT). As with other category-based models cited previously in this book (e.g. the attraction inventory in chapter 5 or Plog's psychographic model in chapter 6), the graphed data fall along a continuum rather than into discrete categories. Thus, many different types of CAT destination will emerge, depending on the extent to which CAT-like criteria of scale and regulation are evident.

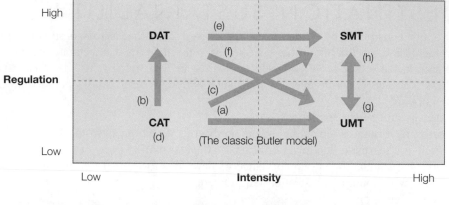

DAT Deliberate alternative tourism   SMT Sustainable mass tourism
CAT Circumstantial alternative tourism   UMT Unsustainable mass tourism

FIGURE 11.11 Broad context model of destination development scenarios

Source: Weaver (2000)

Possible paths of evolution

If only CAT destinations are taken into consideration initially, the broad context model offers four distinct possibilities for future development:

1. The Butler sequence is but one possible scenario, involving the movement of a destination from CAT to UMT (a). The progression in this scenario is from an unregulated 'involvement' stage to an unregulated and unsustainable 'consolidation' stage or beyond.

2. Alternatively, a CAT destination can move to DAT through the implementation of the regulatory environment required to maintain the characteristics of alternative tourism (b). The Caribbean island of Dominica and the South Pacific island state of Samoa appear to illustrate this possibility.

3. A CAT-to-SMT sequence can occur when a mass tourism industry is superimposed over an undeveloped region in a highly regulated way (c).

4. A CAT destination where there is the absence of any evolution at all (d). This scenario assumes that not all CAT destinations will attract sufficient levels of demand to stimulate any further tourism development. For example, most of outback Australia is not likely within any foreseeable timeframe to move beyond exploration- or involvement-stage dynamics, given the absence of push or pull factors that would draw these areas into a more robust tourism system. One implication is the lack of need in such cases to allocate resources towards the establishment of DAT. Instead, resources should be directed to identifying and managing locations where the potential for intensification to occur is higher, such as coastal and alpine destinations.

Moving beyond CAT, other depicted scenarios include the movement from DAT to either SMT (e) or UMT (f). The former situation occurs when the destination is able and wants to increase its carrying capacity thresholds to accommodate higher visitation levels. A DAT destination, however, can also move towards UMT if the appropriate adjustments to carrying capacity are not made, or cannot be made. This is illustrated by national parks such as Amboseli (Kenya), where visitation levels during the 1970s far outpaced the capacity of park managers to cope with the resultant stresses (Weaver 1998).

Finally, SMT can be transformed into UMT as a result of similar dynamics (g), while the opposite is also possible. Calviá, on the Spanish pleasure periphery island of Mallorca, is an example of a previously unsustainable tourism-intensive destination that is making significant progress towards the attainment of sustainability (h).

CHAPTER REVIEW

In response to increasing contradictions and anomalies in the dominant Western environmental paradigm, our society appears to be shifting towards an ecocentric green paradigm. This shift has seen the concept of sustainable development become the focus of contemporary tourism sector management, with weak and strong interpretations possible, depending on whether a particular destination consists mainly of undeveloped natural habitat or heavily modified landscapes, respectively. These developments all suggest the emergence of a synthesis between the dominant Western environmental paradigm and the green paradigm. In any case, the identification and monitoring of indicators at the destination and operations level is essential if sustainable tourism (however defined) is to be achieved, but associated procedures are marred by our basic lack of understanding about the complexities of tourism systems, and other problems. Nevertheless, the concept is still worth pursuing, since not to do so is to virtually ensure unsustainable outcomes. The mass tourism industry, long notorious for following an unsustainable path of development, is now pursuing sustainable tourism more seriously because of the rapid growth in green consumerism, the potential profitability of sustainability-related measures and self-enlightened ethical considerations. It is assisted in this effort by its own economies of scale. Nevertheless, the penetration of sustainability-related practices within the conventional tourism industry does not appear to extend much beyond the establishment of facilitating structures within various sectors and the leadership of a few corporate innovators, suggesting a shallow level of adherence that complements the dominance of 'veneer' environmentalists within society at large. The rudimentary state of specialised quality control mechanisms supports this contention. Codes of practice, for example, are abundant but controversial, while the highest-profile certification-focused global ecolabel, EC3 Global, has attracted only minimal participation to date, and no overarching accreditation body has yet been established to 'police' such tourism-related ecolabels.

Many researchers, therefore, remain sceptical about the motives of the conventional mass tourism industry, and a great amount of attention is still being given to the concept of alternative tourism as a presumably more benign alternative to mass tourism. Even so, alternative tourism itself has been criticised on many grounds, including its intrusiveness into backstage spaces, its limitations of scale, and its potential for opening destinations to less benign forms of tourism. Ecotourism was initially conceived in the 1980s as a nature-based form of alternative tourism but has since been widely acknowledged as having both a hard (mainly alternative tourism) and soft (mainly mass tourism) manifestation. Protected areas remain the most popular ecotourism venue, though more attention is being paid to the suitability of less ecologically vulnerable urban and other highly modified spaces.

Tourist destinations, as opposed to businesses, present distinctive sustainability-related challenges such as the presence of diverse public and private constituencies as well as a usually dominant nontourism sector. Nevertheless, destination governments possess tools such as the establishment of development standards and zoning regulations that aid the pursuit of sustainable tourism. They are assisted in this pursuit by the broad context model of destination development scenarios, which depicts the range of potential tourism options, of which the Butler scenario (CAT-to-UMT) is just one. Deliberate alternative tourism (DAT) and sustainable mass tourism (SMT) are the two desirable scenarios, depending on whether a weak or strong interpretation of sustainability is warranted.

■ SUMMARY OF KEY TERMS

Accreditation the process by which the ecolabel is determined by an overarching organisation to meet specified standards of quality and credibility

Alternative tourism the major contribution of the adaptancy platform, alternative tourism as an ideal type is characterised by its contrast with mass tourism

Avalanche effect the process whereby a small incremental change in a system triggers a disproportionate and usually unexpected response

Benchmark an indicator value, often based on some past desirable state, against which subsequent change in that indicator can be gauged

Broad context model of destination development scenarios a framework for modelling the evolution of tourist destinations, which takes into account scale and sustainability-related regulations; various transformations are possible among four ideal tourism types CAT, DAT, UMT (unsustainable mass tourism) and SMT (sustainable mass tourism)

Certification the outcome of a process in which an independent third party verifies that a product or company meets specified standards, allowing it to be certified by the ecolabel

Circumstantial alternative tourism (CAT) alternative tourism that results by default from the fact that the destination is currently situated within the early, low-intensity stages of the resort cycle

Codes of practice commonly developed and espoused by tourism corporations and industry associations, these are intended to provide general guidelines for achieving sustainability-related outcomes

Corporate social responsibility the concept that corporations have a moral duty to operate in a socially and environmentally responsible way; it is increasingly recognised as a business imperative that combines elements of the green (i.e. 'social responsibility') and dominant Western environmental ('corporate') paradigms.

Deliberate alternative tourism (DAT) alternative tourism that is deliberately maintained as such through the implementation of an enabling regulatory environment

Dominant Western environmental paradigm the scientific paradigm as applied to environmental and related issues, holding the anthropocentric view that humankind is at the centre of all things, and constitutes the primary focus of reference in all relationships with the natural environment; humans are seen as being superior to nature, which exists only for their benefit

Ecolabels mechanisms that certify products or companies that meet specified standards of practice

Ecotourism a form of alternative tourism (and potentially mass tourism) that places primary emphasis on a sustainable, learning-based interaction with the natural environment or some constituent element

Green consumerism the proclivity to purchase goods and services that are deemed to be environmentally and socially sustainable; situates along a spectrum from 'true' green to 'veneer' green attitudes and behaviour

Green paradigm an emerging ecocentric worldview that is challenging the basic assumptions of the dominant Western environmental paradigm and accounting for its related anomalies and contradictions

Green traveller an emerging market niche that is highly discerning and critical in ensuring that its travel behaviour does not negatively affect destinations; similar to Plog's allocentric tourist

Greenwashing the process of conveying an impression of environmental responsibility that is not actually deserved; often associated with the misuse of terms such as 'sustainable tourism' and 'ecotourism'

Hard ecotourism a form of ecotourism that stresses an intensive, specialised and prolonged interaction with nature in a relatively undisturbed natural environment with few available amenities; a form of alternative tourism

Indicators variables or parameters that provide information about some phenomenon in order to facilitate its management in a desirable way

Paradigm shift the replacement of one paradigm with another when the formerly dominant paradigm can no longer adequately account for various contradictions and anomalies

Paradigm the entire constellation of beliefs, assumptions and values that underlie the way that a society interprets the nature of reality

Quality control mechanisms (quality assurance mechanisms) mechanisms that provide some degree of assurance to consumers, government or others that a particular operation, product or destination follows standards associated with sustainable tourism

Scientific paradigm the currently dominant paradigm, which holds that reality is reducible and deterministic and can be understood through the application of the 'scientific method'

Soft ecotourism a form of ecotourism that emphasises a short-term interaction with nature as part of a multipurpose trip with ample provision for services and facilities; can exist as a form of mass tourism

Strong sustainable development an approach to sustainable development that assumes relatively rigorous environmental expectations in recognition of areas, such as wilderness, that are relatively undisturbed and have a low carrying capacity

Sustainable development in principle, development that meets the needs of present generations while ensuring that future generations are able to meet their own needs

Sustainable tourism tourism that is developed in such a way so as to meet the needs of the present without compromising the ability of future generations to meet their own needs

Threshold a critical value of indicator sustainability; when the threshold is exceeded, this indicates an unsustainable situation

Weak sustainable development an approach to sustainable development that assumes relatively relaxed environmental expectations in recognition of areas, such as intensively developed beach resorts, that are already extensively modified and have high carrying capacities

■ QUESTIONS

1. (a) What is meant when it is said that a clash between competing paradigms is likely to result in a synthesis of the two paradigms?
   (b) How is this synthesis evident in contemporary society?
2. Under what circumstances is a weak or strong interpretation of sustainable development warranted in tourism?
3. What are some of the major challenges associated with the collection and use of sustainable tourism indicators?
4. (a) How much has the conventional mass tourism industry actually embraced the practice of sustainable tourism?

(b) What accounts for this?

(c) How could a higher level of engagement by the industry be achieved?

5. (a) What is the difference between certification and accreditation?

(b) Why are these two processes important to the pursuit of sustainable tourism?

6. What is the difference between deliberate and circumstantial alternative tourism, and why is this distinction important to tourism managers?

7. What cross-cultural conflicts could potentially emerge if organisations were to implement the strategies recommended by Raymond and Hall (2008) to increase cross-cultural understanding (see page 314)?

8. What are the managerial implications of Weaver's (2006) statement that eco-tourism is the 'conscience of sustainable tourism'?

9. Are the canopy walks, cableways and submarines described on pages 315–6 an appropriate form of ecotourism? Explain your reasons.

10. How is the broad context model of destination development scenarios potentially useful to the managers of tourist destinations?

■ EXERCISES

1. Assume that budgetary constraints allow you, as a destination manager, to collect only eight of the 29 UNWTO suggested sustainable tourism indicators listed in table 11.1. List your destination and choice of eight indicators, and write a 500-word report in which you justify your selection.

2. (a) Identify a region or locale in your country that has the appearance of circum-stantial alternative tourism (CAT).

(b) Discuss the likelihood that this destination will experience each of the four sce-narios that can affect such a destination, according to the broad context model of destination development.

(c) As a class, compare and contrast the findings from the various destinations.

■ FURTHER READING

Black, R. & Crabtree, A. Eds. 2007. *Quality Assurance and Certification in Ecot-ourism*. **Wallingford, UK: CABI.** Twenty-four chapters consider the practice and evolution of certification within the ecotourism sector, which has provided leader-ship for tourism as a whole. Australia is featured, as is the community perspective and the role of awards and codes of conduct.

Butler, R. W. 1990. 'Alternative Tourism: Pious Hope or Trojan Horse?' *Journal of Travel Research* 28: 40–5. Butler offers one of the most insightful and articulate critiques of alternative tourism, still relevant after two decades, pointing out the problems associated with different aspects of this subsector.

Fennell, D. & Dowling, R. (Eds) 2003. *Ecotourism Policy and Planning*. **Walling-ford, UK: CABI Publishing.** Leading ecotourism researchers contribute case study chapters that include indigenous territories, World Heritage sites and Australian protected areas.

Hunter, C. J. 1997. 'Sustainable Tourism as an Adaptive Paradigm'. *Annals of Tourism Research* 24: 850–67. Hunter suggests that the concept of sustainable tourism acquires a different meaning depending on the context of each destination. Sustainability in a large urban resort, for example, means something very different to sustainability in a sensitive natural area.

Miller, G. & Twining-Ward, L. 2005. *Monitoring for a Sustainable Tourism Transition: The Challenge of Developing and Using Indicators*. Wallingford, UK: CABI. Following a detailed introduction to sustainable development and sustainable tourism, the authors examine relevant motivations for measuring indicators, as well as issues related to indicator selection, monitoring and implementation. International case studies accompany the analysis.

Weaver, D. 2006. *Sustainable Tourism: Theory and Practice*. London: Elsevier. Weaver provides a comprehensive overview of sustainable tourism practices and theories in the context of alternative tourism, mass tourism and destinations, using global case studies.

Weaver, D. 2008. *Ecotourism*. **Second Edition. Brisbane: John Wiley & Sons.** This thorough analysis of the ecotourism sector elaborates issues such as the role of external environments and the emergence of new concepts such as mass, urban and comprehensive ecotourism.

case study

TOWARDS QUALITY TOURISM IN NEW ZEALAND

One outcome of New Zealand's highly successful and ongoing '100% Pure New Zealand' marketing campaign (see Weaver & Lawton 2006, pp. 235–37) is that international visitors expect to experience a pristine environment as well as tourism products that reflect and perpetuate this quality setting. To meet this expectation, a Responsible Tourism Operations component (also known as Qualmark Green) was added to the country's well established Qualmark certification scheme in 2008. Qualmark is a program that seeks to foster consumer and brand confidence in New Zealand tourism businesses through a formal annual assessment of selected product characteristics (e.g. quality of service, cleanliness, facilities etc.) that cumulatively indicate its 'quality' according to category and sector-specific criteria. Assessed accommodations and other venues are star-rated (where 1 star = 'acceptable', 2 stars = 'good', 3 stars = 'very good', 4 stars = 'excellent', and 5 stars = 'exceptional'), while other tourism products, such as those related to transport or tour operators, receive 'Endorsed' status if they score above 60% in the assessment process. As of late 2008, 2166 participating businesses were rated under this certification scheme (Qualmark 2008).

The inclusion of the Responsible Tourism Operations (RTO) component was also reflected in the 2007 release of the New Zealand Tourism Strategy 2015 (Ministry of Tourism 2008). The vision of this document is to position tourism as the leading contributor to a sustainable New Zealand economy in 2015, based on the underlying principles of *manaakitanga (*hospitality and sharing based on mutual respect) and *kaitiakitanga (*guardianship and sustainable management of natural and cultural resources for the benefit of future generations). Four expected outcomes by 2015 are:

• the provision of a world class visitor experience
• a prosperous tourism industry that attracts investment
• a lead role for tourism in protecting and enhancing the environment
• a tourism sector that works effectively with communities to their mutual benefit.

These outcomes, according to the relevant authorities, indicate a 'balanced approach toward economic, environmental and social priorities' (Ministry of Tourism 2008).

In late 2008, most of the details of the RTO component were contained in a toolkit available only in a passport-protected website (www.responsibletourism.co.nz). Hard copies (printed on sustainably sourced paper) were also sent to licence holders, along with a checklist for them to use. For any level of certification (i.e. a star rating or endorsement), six basic 'minimum criteria' must be met before the actual quality scoring process is undertaken:

- any past environmental or social problems have been effectively overcome
- all required statutory licenses, consents or permits have been obtained and are current
- operations comply with existing regional and local management plans, especially as they pertain to national parks and other protected areas
- facilities are in place where customers can do their own recycling
- applicants have completed a responsible tourism checklist, which provides a portrait of where the business is currently situated and what needs to be done
- all environmental claims in promotional and informational material can be substantiated.

Subsequent scoring considers a variety of criteria and activities pertaining to energy efficiency, waste management, water conservation, conservation, and community. For each of these five criteria, the toolkit provides links to relevant organisations and numerous suggestions of activities that can be implemented. This is illustrated by waste management, which is linked to entities such as Zero Waste (www.zerowaste.co.nz), Hazmobile (www.hazmobile.govt.nz), and Waste Exchange (www.nothrow.co.nz). Related 'tips and actions' include the reduction or elimination of disposable items, donation of used or surplus equipment to local schools or charities, use of rechargeable batteries, and the substitution of websites for brochures and other printed material.

The RTO component in late 2008 accounted for 5 per cent of the total Qualmark® score for accommodations and venues, and 8 per cent for visitor activities, transport and services. The RTO assessment procedure that occurs on site once each year as part of the broader assessment exercise involves 12 boxes, each of which is checked or not. As depicted in figure 11.12, products can be awarded from 1 to 5 stars, based on the number of boxes checked and their distribution among three columns which provide increasingly more intensive levels of adherence to the relevant criteria. Three stars earn the right to apply for the Qualmark® Enviro-Bronze logo (designed to be used next to the regular Qualmark® logo), while 4 and 5 stars respectively mean operators can apply for Enviro-Silver and Enviro-Gold status (see figure 11.13).

In determining whether certain actions are being practiced, the assessment exercise relies more on 'evidence' rather than specific measurements which can vary dramatically depending on the size and type of operation being assessed. In this way, the criteria and assessment are not prescriptive. This takes into account both an evaluation of the size and scope of the action as well as progress made in relation to prior assessment exercises. Scoring takes into consideration whether the operator is monitoring their resource use and whether they provide a Responsible Tourism Statement (or similar — it may have a different name) that indicates how the business is reducing its environmental impact and contributing to the community, and promotes staff awareness training and the involvement of customers in efforts ranging from linen re-use to community volunteering. New operators of a business do not inherit the Qualmark® rating of the previous owner, but must apply anew.

The first operator to be certified under the RTO was awarded the Enviro-Silver logo in August 2008. Its owner stated that the effort involved the integration of environmental measures throughout the business as well as the surrounding community and environment, and demonstrated that good business practices were consistent with good environmental practice. While the effort was described as 'costly', continuing collaboration and maintenance of a 'whole life' philosophy about sustainability contributed to successful outcomes. Many other operators who are performing strongly in the criteria are saying that improving their ways has not necessarily been a costly exercise where new investment was required — rather it was about behaviour change that relied on management commitment and staff buy-in (personal communication with Qualmark staff).

0	1	2	3	4	5

Column 1

☐ Where applicable, effective air, water, noise and/or light pollution management is in place.

☐ Evidence that a checklist has been used to create a Responsible Tourism plan of action* which is regularly reviewed, and is included in staff induction and training.

☐ Evidence of effort made to reduce waste, energy and water consumption (1 action in each aspect or 3 actions in total.)**

Column 2/3

☐ Evidence from the Responsible Tourism plan of action that you are monitoring at least 1 aspect with evidence of improving efficiency e.g. in water, waste, gas, electricity, fuel or reduction of carbon emissions.***

☐ Staff follow the Responsible Tourism plan of action and can communicate it.

☐ Evidence of effort made to reduce waste, energy or water consumption (3 in each aspect or 9 actions in total, including at least 1 in each aspect).**

☐ Evidence of contributing towards at least 1 community or conservation activity.**

Column 4/5

☐ Evidence from the Responsible Tourism plan of action that you are monitoring at least 2 aspects with evidence of improving efficiencies e.g. in water, waste, gas, electricity, fuel or reduction of carbon emissions.***

☐ Evidence that a Responsible Tourism statement/policy is publicly displayed, so guests/customers can offer feedback.

☐ Evidence of effort made to reduce waste, energy or water consumption (5 in each aspect or 25 actions across all aspects, including at least 2 in each aspect).*

☐ Evidence of contributing towards at least 1 community and 1 conservation activity.**

☐ An individual or team within the business has formal responsibility for implementation of the plan and possible improvements.

Scoring criteria

Ticks	Score	Logo eligibilty	Footnotes
At least 2 ticks in column 1	One	N/A	* Use the responsible Tourism Guide for examples and ideas. The Responsible Tourism Checklist can help form your plan and what you might target for improvement.
All ticks in column 1 and 2 ticks in column 2	Two	N/A	
All ticks in column 2	Three	Qualmark® Enviro-Bronze	** Use the Responsible Tourism Guide for explanation and examples.
All ticks in column 2 and three ticks in column 3	Four	Qualmark® Enviro-Silver	
All ticks in column 1, 2 and 3	Five	Qualmark® Enviro-Gold	*** Qualmark expects monitoring to have been in place for at least 6 to 12 months to show improvements.

FIGURE 11.12 Quality scores

FIGURE 11.13 Qualmark Enviro logos

QUESTIONS

1. Write a 1000-word report in which you describe the advantages and disadvantages for a small nature-based tourism business operator of seeking certification from:
   (a) an integrated certification scheme with a sustainability component such as Qualmark only
   (b) a sustainability-specific certification scheme such as EcoCertification only
   (c) both (a) and (b).

2. Write a 500-word report in which you argue the case for and against raising the RTO component of the Qualmark scheme for accommodation providers from 5 per cent to a higher percentage of your selection.

CHAPTER 12

TOURISM RESEARCH

LEARNING OBJECTIVES

After studying this chapter, you should be able to:

1. appreciate the critical role of research within the field of tourism management

2. describe the main types of research that are relevant to the field of tourism studies and outline the circumstances under which each is best applied

3. differentiate between induction and deduction, and describe how these two approaches are complementary

4. classify specific research initiatives as per their adherence to the main types of research

5. list the major types of techniques associated with primary and secondary research

6. discuss the basic stages of the research process

7. describe the four main levels of investigation and explain how they complement each other within a comprehensive research project.

■ INTRODUCTION

The previous chapters of this book demonstrate that tourism is an increasingly diverse and complex phenomenon that requires sophisticated management and planning if it is to be practiced in a sustainable as well as competitive manner by destinations and businesses. Whether the primary motivation is to maximise the positive impacts and minimise the negative impacts of tourism (as with most destinations), or to maximise profits (as with most businesses), stakeholder objectives can only be achieved if decisions are informed by a sound knowledge base. This is derived through the pursuit of properly conceived and executed **research**, or the systematic search for knowledge. It is therefore critical for students of tourism management to be familiar with the research process and related issues. The purpose of this chapter is to provide an introduction to research as it relates to the field of tourism studies. The following section examines the various types of research and illustrates their applicability to tourism. The broader research process, including problem recognition and formulation, identification of appropriate methodologies or methods, data collection, data analysis and interpretation, and data presentation, is described in the final section in the context of the tourism sector.

■ TYPES OF RESEARCH

There are several standard ways of classifying research in the field of tourism studies and elsewhere, and four of the most important are discussed below:

- basic versus applied
- cross-sectional versus longitudinal
- qualitative versus quantitative
- primary versus secondary.

Allowing for a certain amount of overlap within each pairing (e.g. a particular research design may combine elements of the qualitative and quantitative approach), any research initiative can be described simultaneously in terms of all four approaches. For example, a long-term research project examining changing consumer preferences may be applied, longitudinal, quantitative and primary all at the same time. Each of these research types in turn is associated with a particular **research methodology**, or set of assumptions, procedures and methods that is used to carry out the research process. Methodological issues, because they are pervasive, are raised in the following section as well as in the discussion of the research process in the final section.

Basic research

The distinction between **basic research** (sometimes referred to as pure research) and **applied research** focuses on the intended end result of the investigation. Basic research reveals knowledge that will increase the understanding of tourism-related phenomena per se, and is not intended to address specific short-term problems or to achieve specific short-term outcomes (Jennings 2001). However, the knowledge gained from basic research may prove relevant in the subsequent context of more specific issues, especially if the knowledge is expressed in the form of general laws, theories or models. This is illustrated by the Butler sequence, which is an outcome of basic research that has proven to be highly relevant to the field of applied tourism. The same can be said for Doxey's irridex (see chapter 9) and the broad context model of destination development scenarios (see chapter 11).

Basic research is commonly associated with universities, given their core mandate to engage in the unfettered search for knowledge. Corporations, and smaller ones in particular, are less inclined to carry out this type of investigation, since the ensuing applications are not usually apparent right away, and therefore cannot be readily justi-fied on financial grounds. Jones and Phillips (2003) go as far as describing the research cultures of universities and corporations as fundamentally different. One intriguing type of basic research is sometimes referred to as the 'fishing expedition'. This occurs when the researcher applies many different techniques and experiments to some data-base or subject matter without knowing what will result, but in the hope that some major 'big catch' revelation will emerge.

Induction and deduction

Basic research can be carried out through methodologies of **induction** or **deduction**. In induction, the repeated observation and analysis of data lead to the formulation of theories or models that link these observations in a meaningful way. Deduction, in contrast, begins with an existing theory or model, and applies this to a particular situ-ation to see whether it is valid in that case. In other words, induction progresses from the specific (i.e. the evidence) to the general (i.e. the theory), while deduction moves from the general to the specific (Sarantakos 2004). Gilbert (1993) alludes to the close association between the two approaches by pointing out that theories are generated through induction and then applied through deduction. The case study on indigenous tourism that concludes chapter 9 illustrates how inductive models can be formulated (see Contemporary issue: An inductive model of indigenous tourism development).

contemporary issue

AN INDUCTIVE MODEL OF INDIGENOUS TOURISM DEVELOPMENT

As described in the chapter 9 case study, indigenous people in Australia, Canada, New Zealand and the USA have had a longstanding and ambivalent association with tourism. The contours of this association, with its six apparent stages, emerged after examining over 200 academic articles, chapters and books on the topic of indigenous tourism (Weaver 2010). To put structure to these contours, it is necessary to situate the six stages within a relevant framework and to designate a suitably descriptive label for each. The framework is derived from Butler and Hinch (2007) who propose that several types of indigenous tourism emerge depending on the degree to which indigenous *control* is low or high, and whether an indigenous *theme* is absent or high. Figure 12.1 results when the six stages are superimposed over this matrix:

- *In situ (on site) control* describes the pre-European situation when indigenous people prac-ticed and fully controlled their own tourism-like activity
- *In situ exposure* is when the first European scientists, artists and others make contact as indigenous control gives way to European colonisation
- *Ex situ (off site) exhibitionism and exploitation* occurs when indigenous themes were displayed in museums, world fairs etc.
- *In situ exhibitionism and exploitation* appears when tourists from core areas started to visit the indigenous people on their remnant reservations
- *In situ quasi-empowerment* is when indigenous control over tourism in these remnant territo-ries is reasserted, though to a lesser extent than during the first stage
- *Ex situ quasi-empowerment* represents the extension of indigenous control into areas tradi-tionally occupied.

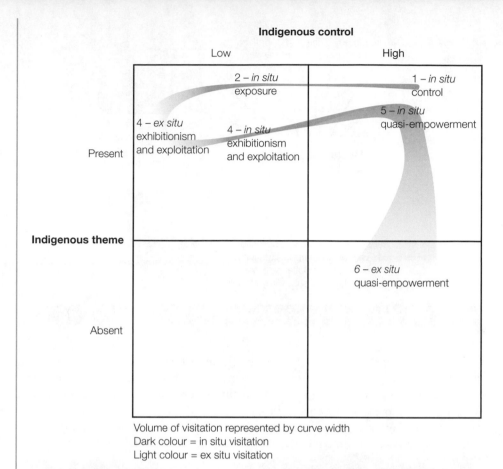

Indigenous control

Low   High

2 – *in situ*
exposure

1 – *in situ*
control

4 – *ex situ*
exhibitionism
and exploitation

4 – *in situ*
exhibitionism
and exploitation

5 – *in situ*
quasi-empowerment

Present

Indigenous theme

6 – *ex situ*
quasi-empowerment

Absent

Volume of visitation represented by curve width
Dark colour = in situ visitation
Light colour = ex situ visitation

FIGURE 12.1 Proposed stages of indigenous tourism

Figure 12.1 also accommodates the generalised volume of tourist flows by varying the width of the connecting line and by shifting between black and white colour to depict the 'in situ' and 'ex situ' venues respectively. Structured in this way, this ideal type provides a basis for subsequent empirical testing through deductive research. Specific indigenous communities within the four target countries provide one logical basis for testing the model, as do similar communities within less developed countries such as Guatemala, Papua New Guinea, Thailand and China.

Figure 12.2 illustrates this relationship with respect to the Butler sequence, wherein many different observations and unconnected studies led to the formulation of the resort cycle concept through a process of inductive generalisation. These observations pointed towards a common process of accelerated growth culminating in the breaching of a destination's carrying capacities (see chapter 10). Subsequently, many other researchers have applied Butler's general model in a deductive way to specific destinations, leading to varying conclusions about its applicability as well as refinements and extensions that take into account these new investigations. These notions of refinement and extension are very important to basic research, since they imply an evolution in our knowledge of tourism-related phenomena.

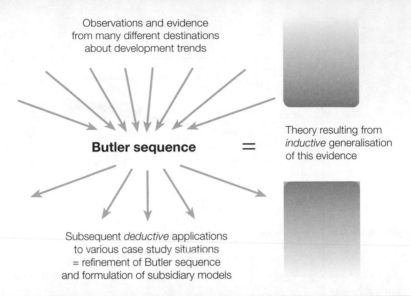

Observations and evidence
from many different destinations
about development trends

Butler sequence   =   Theory resulting from
inductive generalisation
of this evidence

Subsequent *deductive* applications
to various case study situations
= refinement of Butler sequence
and formulation of subsidiary models

FIGURE 12.2 The place of induction and deduction in the Butler sequence

Often, the testing of a model through the inductive or deductive approach is informed by the formulation of one or more **hypotheses**, which are informed tentative statements or conjecture about the nature of certain relationships that can be subsequently proved or disproved through systematic hypothesis testing and other investigation. For example, a researcher testing the Butler sequence (i.e. a deductive approach) may establish the following hypothesis to address one particular aspect of the model:

'The control of the tourism sector tends to pass from the local community to external interests as the level of tourism development increases.'

Such a statement then provides a focal point for research into the applicability of the model. As long as investigations continue to verify the hypothesis, then there is no need to alter the model. However, once the hypothesis is rejected, then the model itself needs to be reconsidered. In some cases, the rejection may be a 'one-off' occurrence resulting from unusual local circumstances. However, as with paradigm shifts, a pattern of repeated rejection means that a fundamental modification of the original model may be required.

Applied research

As implied in the term, the orientation in applied research is directed towards specific practical problems and outcomes. These may be associated with product development, the identification of target market segments, community reactions towards specific planning scenarios, and the relationship between tourism and climate change (see the case study at the end of this chapter). Applied research is commonly associated with private corporations or government agencies charged with the task of addressing specific issues within certain time and resource constraints. If industry-based, the research results may be kept confidential so that competitors cannot use this same information for their own purposes. However, like basic research, applied research can also lead to theoretical breakthroughs and the advancement of knowledge if the results are made available to the public. Plog's psychographic segmentation is one example (see chapter 6). Government tourism organisations such as Tourism Australia are also often mandated to produce and disseminate applied research. Through the specialised agency Tourism Research Australia, 'superior research information' is provided that facilitates 'improved decision making, marketing and tourism industry performance for the Australian community' (TRA 2008h).

Cross-sectional research

The difference between **cross-sectional research** (sometimes referred to as latitudinal research) and **longitudinal research** is based on the time period that is represented by the resulting data. Cross-sectional research entails a 'snapshot' approach that describes a situation essentially at one point in time (although the data may be collected over several weeks or months) (Ryan 1995). In its simplest form, cross-sectional research is undertaken at a single site (scenario (a) of figure 12.3). A more complex variation involves the collection of information at multiple sites scenario (b). Scenario (a) might involve the administration of a one-time survey over a two-week period in 2008 to determine the attitude of international visitors to the quality of the main Olympic stadium in Beijing. Scenario (b) might involve a similar one-off survey that is carried out at all Olympic venues in and near Beijing. The advantage of the second scenario is the opportunity that is provided to make comparisons and perhaps identify common trends, but it has the disadvantage of being more expensive. In addition, careful planning must be exercised in order to ensure that all the surveys are carried out at about the same time and in a similar manner.

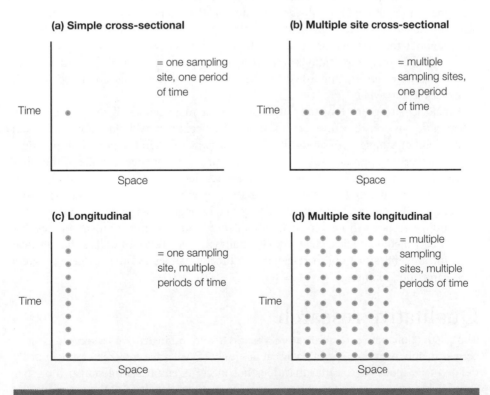

FIGURE 12.3 Basic cross-sectional and longitudinal surveying options

Longitudinal research

Longitudinal or 'trend' research examines changes in the target phenomenon over a period of time. Forward longitudinal research commences at some present or future time and continues for a usually defined period into the future. Backward longitudinal research involves the reconstruction of the phenomenon during some stipulated period in the past. In both scenarios, a sequence of snapshots is produced and analysed. An example of scenario (c) of figure 12.3 (i.e. single-site forward longitudinal research) is the monitoring of visitor attitudes toward main stadium facilities over the course of five summer Olympic Games. The most comprehensive (and most expensive) form of forward longitudinal research entails the examination of many sites over multiple time periods (scenario (d) of figure 12.3). This scenario would occur if visitors were interviewed at all sporting venues for each of the five consecutive summer Olympic Games. The International and National Visitor Surveys, conducted by Tourism Research Australia, are good illustrations of this approach. As a result of such ambitious investigations, considerable insight is gained into spatial as well as temporal patterns, and on this basis we are more likely to generate useful models and theories. Continuing problems, however, include the possible necessity of extending the time period of the inquiry if no clear trends emerge within a given timeframe, and logistical challenges in doing so.

A variation in forward longitudinal research carried out by survey is the continued solicitation of the same respondents from one time period to the next. The advantage of this approach is the ability to monitor the changing behaviour of a given sample. However, such an approach may not be practical due to the attrition of respondents due to death, migration or respondent fatigue. This is a more realistic option where the time period of the research is more limited. For example, consumers who have already booked a trip to a particular location may be asked to express their expectations about that destination. Upon their return several weeks later, they could be asked whether their expectations were met. Note that this form of forward longitudinal research is also distinguished by the different questions that are asked in each phase of the surveying.

A major challenge for longitudinal research is the maintenance of consistency in the research design over the entire period. If, for instance, the survey questions, definition of 'resident' or sample size is radically altered halfway through the period of investigation (whether the approach is forward or backward), or a change is made in the cities where residents are surveyed, the subsequent results will no longer be neatly comparable to data collected prior to the changes. Any apparent trends that emerge from the study will therefore be misleading. In general, longitudinal research, and forward longitudinal research in particular, is infrequently undertaken in tourism studies due to the many methodological challenges it entails (Ritchie 2005), as well as the practical need for academics to publish research in a timely manner in order to best progress their career development.

Qualitative research

The distinction between **qualitative research** and **quantitative research** is concerned mainly with the type of data that is sought. Qualitative research can be initially defined as a mode of research that does not place its emphasis on statistics or statistical analysis; that is, on the objective measurement and analysis of the data collected (Goodson & Phillimore 2004). In terms of subject matter, it usually involves a small number of respondents or observations, but considers these in depth. It is for this reason that qualitative research methods are sometimes referred to as 'data enhancers' that allow crucial elements of a problem or phenomenon to be seen more clearly (Ragin 1994). Qualitative research is suited for situations where little is known about the subject matter, since the associated methodology is intended to gain insight into the phenomenon in question. Socially or psychologically complex research issues are also amenable to qualitative analysis, which is well suited to capture or clarify nuances of meaning, associated external factors etc.

An example of qualitative research would be a situation where the researcher non-randomly selects a group of ten Gold Coast residents and conducts an in-depth two-hour interview with each to see what they think about the future of the tourism sector in their community. Many researchers criticise such qualitative research for lacking the objective rigour and validity of a statistical approach, and for not necessarily being representative of any group larger than that which was actually interviewed or observed. This criticism, however, is best directed towards the careless execution of qualitative methods, and not to qualitative methodology itself, which can be extremely rigorous and challenging in its assumptions and applications.

Quantitative research

Quantitative research relies on the collection of statistics that are then analysed through a variety of statistical techniques. Numerous quantitative research methods are used in the field of tourism studies, and it is beyond the scope of this introductory tourism management text to describe these methods. It can be said, however, that quantitative research techniques typically are 'data condensers' that yield a relatively small amount of information about a large number of respondents or observations (Ragin 1994). Table 12.1 depicts some of the contrasting characteristics associated with quantitative and qualitative research techniques and in so doing illustrates the very different assumptions and philosophies that inform each approach.

TABLE 12.1 Quantitative and qualitative research styles

Quantitative style	Qualitative style
Measure objective facts	Construct social reality, cultural meaning
Focus on variables	Focus on interactive processes, events
Reliability is the key	Authenticity is the key
Value free	Values are present and explicit
Independent of context	Situationally constrained
Many cases or subjects	Few cases or subjects
Statistical analysis	Thematic analysis
Researcher is detached from subject	Researcher is involved in subject

Source: Neuman (1997, p. 14)

Because it often involves a rigorous process of hypothesis formulation, detached observation, data collection, data analysis and acceptance or rejection of the hypotheses, quantitative research is regarded as the core of the scientific method. This paradigm has always been at the heart of the natural sciences, but has only recently become more prevalent in tourism studies. It claims to 'reliably' reflect the 'real world' through its rigorous procedures and the ability to extrapolate its results to a wider population. Many of its exponents, accordingly and unfairly, adopt a dismissive attitude towards 'soft' and subjective qualitative research approaches.

This perception is unfortunate, since the two research approaches are not uncomplementary. For example, much inductive research is qualitative and intuitive, but can generate models and hypotheses that may be tested using quantitative (or qualitative) techniques. Similarly, we may accept or reject a hypothesis based on some test of statistical significance, but find that we subsequently have to conduct in-depth qualitative interviews to interpret or account for these outcomes. Another link is the possibility of analysing qualitative data, such as newspaper letters to the editor, using quantitative methods such as content analysis.

The student, therefore, should be aware of the circumstances under which a qualitative or quantitative approach is warranted, but should further realise that a particular research agenda can usefully combine both. This potential for synergy is illustrated by questionnaires that provide for quantitative response patterns (e.g. 'How old are you?' or 'On a scale of 1 to 5, how would you rate Uluru as a tourist attraction?') as well as qualitative insights through open-ended questions (e.g. 'Why did you rate Uluru in this way?') and follow-up focus groups and one-on-one interviews.

Primary research

The distinction between **primary research** and **secondary research** depends on the source of the data that are being used by the researcher. In primary research, the data are collected directly by the researcher, and did not exist prior to their collection. This is necessary when the data required to address some issue or problem that is of concern to the researcher are absent. Hence, a major advantage of primary research is the ability of the investigator to design a tailored research framework relevant to the specific topic and questions of interest. As with longitudinal and multiple site cross-sectional data, a widespread problem is high cost in time and money. There are numerous techniques associated with primary research methodology, some of the most important of which are described in the following.

Surveys

The survey is undoubtedly the most common method for conducting primary research in tourism studies, as well as in the social sciences more generally. Accordingly, much useful generic information is available for students wishing to undertake this type of investigation (e.g. Alreck & Settle 1995). The design and administration of any specific survey (and whether a survey is even the right way to proceed), however, ultimately depends on the goals of the researcher and the resources that are available to conduct the survey. Depending on the responses to those concerns, the researcher can select from three basic types of surveys:

- face-to-face interviewing (conducted at households, in the field, or at some other agreed-upon location)
- telephone interviewing
- distributed (self-completed) surveys (with field, postal, fax, iPod/mobile phone, internet and email variations) (see Managing tourism: Web-based survey responses).

Table 12.2 provides an overview of the key characteristics associated with each of these surveying techniques, with the postal option used to illustrate distributed surveys. If the researcher has a limited budget and no access to trained interviewers, then a distributed survey is usually the best way to proceed, even though there is evidence that response rates to postal surveys have declined substantially since the early 1970s (Connelly, Brown & Decker 2003). A face-to-face procedure is warranted where the researcher is interested mainly in in-depth, qualitative responses with a small number of respondents.

managing tourism

WEB-BASED SURVEY RESPONSES

The use of web-based distributed surveys in tourism research has increased exponentially since the late 1990s, in concert with dramatic growth in the possession of personal computers, and technological progress that has made their employment inexpensive, interactive and efficient (Cole, S.T. 2005). Internet protocols, for example, now allow respondents to complete online questionnaires rapidly, and the data to be instantaneously entered into a database and concurrently analysed. Nevertheless, the strong temptation to use such survey instruments should be tempered by due consideration of their numerous shortcomings. Extremely low response rates to unsolicited web-based questionnaires are a persistent problem, with capture rates below 10 per cent not uncommon.

Low response rates are partly attributable to survey fatigue and disinterest issues that characterise all survey-based data collection, but additional factors implicate the internet itself. Email databases, for example, are likely to contain far more defunct, incorrect or repetitive addresses than telephone directories. For valid addresses, very high levels of erosion result from computer filters that register the incoming survey as spam and delete them accordingly, while most of those that survive automatic filtering are identified as spam and deleted by end users who are conditioned to delete incoming mail from unfamiliar sources (Sax, Gilmartin & Bryant 2003). Potential respondents may be further dissuaded by the impersonal nature of web-based questionnaires, concerns about virus infiltration, and frustration with the use of 'forced answer' formats (which may then produce unreliable responses). Finally, it is not unreasonable to assume that individuals with personal computers differ from those without in ways (e.g. income, comfort with technology) that could produce non-response bias if only web-based instruments are used. Similarly, individuals receiving high volumes of incoming email may differ from those receiving low volumes, and may be less likely to open unfamiliar email messages. In light of such limitations, S.T. Cole (2005) recommends the distribution of questionnaires through multiple channels whenever possible.

Focus groups

Focus groups involve face-to-face group discussions conducted with a small number of people usually pre-selected because of their relevance to a particular research problem (Bloor 2001). A researcher who is concerned about resident reactions to a proposed resort hotel, for example, may gather together ten community leaders who are judged to be informed, concerned and representative of a broader cross-section of the local community. Focus groups rely a great deal on the interactions and synergies that take place among the participants, and are an excellent means of obtaining in-depth, qualitative data (Weeden 2005). They are often used in the initial phases of research to identify problems and issues, and as a prelude to quantitative inquiry. Yau, McKercher and Packer (2004) used focus groups along with in-depth interviews to explore the tourism experiences of people with disabilities in Hong Kong.

TABLE 12.2 Characteristics of three survey ideal types

Characteristic	Face-to-face surveys	Telephone surveys	Postal surveys
Cost	High	Medium	Low
Response time	Medium	Fast	Slow
Response rate	High	Medium	Low
Interviewer bias	High	Medium	Low
Need for trained interviewers	Very high	High	None
Accommodation of sensitive questions	Difficult	Good	Good
Accommodation of multiple item scales and ranking questions	Reasonable	Difficult	Good
Accommodation of qualitative questions	Very good	Good	Difficult
Survey length	Medium	Short	Long
Sample size	Small	Medium	Large

Relevant questions that must be asked when considering focus groups as a research method include how large a group to form (optimum group size may be affected by cultural and political factors), who to include and whether to offer some kind of incentive to participants. A more detailed analysis of the advantages and disadvantages of this approach, including the possibilities of virtual focus groups, is provided by Krueger and Casey (2000), Bloor (2001) and Weedon (2005).

The Delphi technique

The Delphi technique involves a panel of experts, ranging in size from ten or less to as many as one thousand (but typically around 40–50), who are asked to respond to several rounds (usually three or four) of questioning about a particular research issue (Garrod & Fyall 2005). In each subsequent round, all participants (who remain anonymous) are made aware of the results of the previous round of questioning, so that the opinions expressed in that new round are influenced by those earlier outcomes. Knowledge and opinion are thus systemically focused as feedback to arrive at an eventual consensus about the issue. The Delphi technique is often applied as a forecasting tool to obtain a general picture of the future, rather than as a means of achieving highly accurate predictions (which are almost always impossible to attain). Its fundamental principle is that useful speculations will emerge from the repeated and focused questioning of a group of individuals who are highly qualified and informed about a particular issue. Among the problems associated with this technique are:
• identifying the appropriate pool of experts who represent the desired balance of opinions, philosophies, experience etc.
• soliciting expert participation
• obtaining panel feedback in a timely fashion
• the assumption that participants are willing to have their judgements changed by exposure to judgements of other participants

- panel attrition (tight time commitments are a common reason for this and the previous two problems)
- misinterpretation of responses, e.g. 'specious consensus' caused by experts who conform in order to be left alone or because of participation fatigue
- an inability to obtain consensus or the temptation to 'fit' responses into a pattern of consensus (Garrod & Fyall 2005).

From a student perspective, few if any experts are likely to participate in a study that is not being sponsored and coordinated by a well-known professor or university. Despite these pitfalls, the results can still be prophetic. One Delphi study undertaken in 1974 (Shafer & Moeller 1974) predicted that wildlife resources would be used mainly for nonconsumptive recreational uses such as photography by the year 2000, a forecast which has largely been realised through the growth of ecotourism (see chapter 11). More recently, the Delphi technique was used by Garrod (2003) to define 'ecotourism'. This approach revealed consensus as to its core criteria, but exposed divisions as to the importance of local ownership, and the status of ecotourism as a process rather than just a type of tourism. Participating experts also tended to favour medium-length definitions that compromised between simplicity and comprehensiveness.

Observation

The collection of information through observation is relevant to many tourism-related research problems. Applications include:
- noting the changing number and condition of hotels in a particular resort strip over a given period of time
- recording the average length of time that visitors to a theme park have to wait in a queue before gaining entry, and noting their body language during the wait
- counting the number of people who attend a large festival (Raybould et al. 2000)
- observing where a hotel disposes of its garbage over a certain time period
- recording the reaction of tourists towards souvenir hawkers at the entrance to a scenic site
- following a tour group or individual tourists to observe the behaviour and spatial distribution of tourists.

In anthropological research, observation usually assumes that the humans being investigated are aware of and interact closely with the researcher who is trying to understand the subjects' perspective (Cole, S. 2005). However, some efforts to observe the 'unselfconscious' behaviour of human subjects may involve attempts to remain undetected. Serious ethical questions are raised if this involves 'stalking' or the use of deception so that subjects are unaware that they are the subject of an investigation. The latter can occur in certain types of 'participant observation' research, as when the researcher temporarily assumes a certain false identity in order to gain access to the unselfconscious views and behaviour of the target group (Bowen 2002). For example, a researcher might work for several months among a group of lifeguards who assume that the researcher is 'one of them'. In reality, the real intention of the researcher is to gain the confidence of the group so that the authentic behaviour and perceptions of the lifesaving subculture can be observed as part of a research project. New technologies such as webcams and GPS enhance the possibilities for observation-based research, but generate additional ethical and practical concerns (see Technology and tourism: Using GPS to track tourists in Germany).

Most universities maintain special committees that assess the ethical dimensions of such research and outline the conditions under which the projects are allowed to proceed. Because of the ethical questions raised and the amount of time involved, observation is not widely practised as a research technique within tourism studies despite its potential to yield knowledge that cannot be obtained through survey or questionnaire-based methods.

technology and tourism

USING GPS TO TRACK TOURISTS IN GERMANY

Having reliable knowledge about the movement of tourists within a destination allows revealed issues of overcrowding or under-utilisation to be addressed and provides an understanding as to whether tourism information is being distributed effectively. Affected businesses are also better able to amend their marketing strategies accordingly. During the summer of 2005, researchers in Germany equipped 65 volunteering tourists in the city of Görlitz with mobile GPS devices which allowed their movements in the downtown area to be tracked (Modsching et al 2008). The devices continuously recorded the location of each bearer and delivered this information to a database that could then be statistically analysed to identify spatial patterns of tourist activity. The results showed that most tourist time was spent in the medieval city centre (which was therefore designated a 'hot area') while almost no one visited a nearby major church or an architecturally significant neighbourhood on the periphery of the centre ('cold areas'). In total, the average tourist visited only 3.5 local attractions (and only briefly in each case), compared with 13 in a typical guided tour of the city. It was also found that most of the time within the centre was occupied in restaurants rather than visiting attractions.

The results indicate that information about high quality local attractions is probably not reaching individual tourists, who gravitate to hot spots where other tourists are already congregated. However, before using these findings to modify existing marketing and management practices, short-comings in the research methodology need to be recognised. One issue is the awareness of the volunteers that they are carrying the GPS devices, which may influence their mobility behaviour. Those tourists willing to wear the device, in addition, may not be representative of tourists in Görlitz as a whole. Another problem is that a recorded stop in a particular location may involve a request for directions or a brief conversation with a friend rather than an interaction with an attraction. In general, the GPS data provide no details about any of these interactions. Finally, there is a risk of technology failure caused by faulty devices or bearer behaviour (e.g. not wearing the device properly, or dropping it) that interferes with data transmission. Cost is less of an issue given the rapidly declining prices of the mobile GPS devices.

Content analysis

Content analysis (CA) describes a variety of techniques that are used to systematically examine and measure the meaning of communicated material by classifying and evaluating selected words, themes or images (Hall & Valentin 2005). Three examples illustrate the varied use of CA within the contemporary tourism literature. First, Garrod (2008) had resident and tourist volunteers in a Welsh seaside resort take photographs of sites that were meaningful to them. The photographs were then content analysed and compared, revealing a high level of commonality in the meanings held by both groups. Second, Buckley (2008) analysed recent editions of the popular Lonely Planet guidebook series to assess whether the content was congruent with relevant academic theory, and found that the publication tended to reflect current social sustainability thinking more than the environmental ones. Finally, Govers, Go and Kumar (2007) analysed destination images by applying artificial neural network software to narratives solicited from a web-based survey.

Secondary research

In secondary research, the investigator relies on material and research that has been compiled previously by other researchers. This substantially reduces the time and money required to obtain the desired information, especially given the availability of comprehensive and easily searched databases (such as www.leisuretourism.com) that contain a large number of secondary sources. However, a disadvantage is that users of this information cannot be entirely sure about its validity or reliability, since they were not involved in its original collection or compilation. Information sources that are important in secondary research are discussed below.

Academic journals

The ongoing proliferation of refereed journals within the field of tourism studies was discussed in chapter 1. Articles in academic journals, as described in that chapter, have the advantage of having undergone a double-blind reviewing process, which in theory increases the quality and objectivity of the published results. However, the time involved in undertaking the review process and then queuing for publication means that the results are often outdated by the time the article is released to the public. In addition, refereed journals often tolerate tedious and difficult writing styles that are not readily accessible to students, the tourism industry or even other academics. Proliferation itself is an emerging problem in the tourism field to the extent that there may not be enough quality manuscripts being submitted to sustain the many titles, forcing the editors of many of the newer journals in particular to accept mediocre manuscripts which would otherwise be rejected. Nevertheless, academic journals are a core source of secondary data for students and other researchers wishing to access research outcomes in all aspects of tourism.

Academic books

Academic books have also proliferated since the early 1990s. Although books usually undergo a less rigorous process of peer review, they are also generally subject to much less stringent page limitations, allowing for more in-depth analyses of particular issues. Increasingly, academic tourism books are edited compilations covering specific themes, in which individual authors or author teams prepare one or more chapters. The following are just a few of the edited academic books useful to researchers wishing to investigate the indicated and often highly specialised themes:
- *Tourism and the Consumption of Wildlife* (Lovelock 2008)
- *Philosophical Issues in Tourism* (Tribe 2009)
- *River Tourism* (Prideaux & Cooper 2009)
- *Asian Tourism: Growth and Change* (Cochrane 2007)
- *Backpacker Tourism: Concepts and Profiles* (Hannam 2007)
- *Journeys of Discovery in Volunteer Tourism: International Case Study Perspectives* (Lyons & Wearing 2008)
- *Tea and Tourism: Tourists, Traditions and Transformations* (Jolliffe 2007)
- *Tourism and Climate Change Mitigation: Methods, Greenhouse Gas Reductions and Policies* (Peeters 2007).

Statistical compilations

Tourism statistics are compiled by various government departments and nongovernmental organisations. Within Australia, Tourism Research Australia publishes a number of important compilations, including the *International Visitor Survey* and the *National Visitor Survey* (see chapter 2). The Australian Bureau of Statistics (ABS) publishes *Overseas Arrivals and Departures*, which details the origins of inbound tourists and the destinations of outbound Australians. The ABS also publishes the *Survey of Tourist Accommodation (STA)*, which is a quarterly Australia-wide survey of supply and demand for hotels containing at least 15 rooms. New Zealand is similarly comprehensive with regard to the regular serials that describe the development of its tourism sector, and is additionally innovative in making a large proportion of its tourism-related data publically accessible (see Breakthrough tourism: Accessing tourism data in New Zealand).

breakthrough tourism

ACCESSING TOURISM DATA IN NEW ZEALAND

New Zealand's Ministry of Tourism (2008b) releases numerous serials which describe the ongoing performance of the country's inbound, outbound and domestic tourism sectors. Publications such as the *International Visitor Survey (IVS)* and *Regional Visitor Monitor (RVM)* are not only available cost-free from the internet, but are based on data sets which are also available through free downloadable reader software. For most applications, an 'intermediate' level of database management knowledge is recommended, and online tutorials are provided. The IVS, which is based on an annual sample of 5000 departing inbound tourists, illustrates the research opportunities for New Zealand tourism stakeholders. The tutorial that accompanies the IVS uses the example of an operator wishing to compare the number of inbound visits and visitors in the Rotorua and Queenstown regions. This specific information is not explicitly available from Ministry publications, but manipulation of the database allows an operator to find out that each region has an equal share of visitors but Queenstown has a higher share of total visits. Inbound tourists therefore are more likely to make more than one trip to Queenstown during their visit to New Zealand, indicating a different type of itinerary for visitors to that region. Database users have a variety of options to display such information in graphic form, and to track these trends over a stipulated time period.

For users with a more advanced level of statistical knowledge, the Ministry provides a Power User function that contains a greater array of options for manipulating tourism databases. This function is only available by application, and approval is granted on a case-by-case basis. With 'accessibility' described as the new mantra of the Ministry's research program (Ministry of Tourism 2008b), initiatives are underway to make an even more comprehensive array of tourism data available in the public arena, and to clearly provide potential users with a clear explanation of the strengths and shortcomings of each database.

Trade publications

Trade publications include paper magazines, electronic magazines ('ezines') and newsletters published by various industry organisations as well as government. As a source of data, they have the disadvantage of being 'unscientific' and journalistic in orientation. There is no equivalent of a double-blind review process, and the content often mirrors the vested interests and biases of the organisation producing the material. However, they are extremely useful for providing news of events that may have happened within the previous few weeks and indications of industry trends and perspectives. A prominent Australian trade publications relating to the tourism sector is www.TravelWeekly.com.au.

Newspapers and magazines

Newspapers and nonspecialised magazines such as *Time* and *Newsweek* (now usually available in abbreviated and/or augmented form on the internet) are subject to the same advantages and disadvantages as outlined for trade publications. Students should therefore use these mainly as a source of current news, and also as a basis for content analysis exercises (i.e. a secondary source used to conduct primary analysis).

The internet

In addition to its increasingly important role as a medium for conducting primary research, the internet is now also a very popular source of secondary research information, especially as many of the above-mentioned publications are being made available online as a more accessible alternative to hard copy. While much reliable data can be obtained through the internet, quality and reputability are major issues that must be considered when using this source. The internet is an extremely attractive source of information for students as well as professional academics due to the convenience of being able to access an enormous amount of material on even the most obscure topics at a single computer terminal. An internet search, moreover, requires far less time to undertake than an exploration of conventional research sources. However, there are no standards or controls that regulate material appearing on the internet, and the result is an enormous oversupply of useless, unreliable and misleading information that overwhelms the reputable material.

■ THE RESEARCH PROCESS

In order to produce substantive and useful outcomes, research must be carried out in a deliberate and systematic manner. The steps that are required to carry out a research project from its origins to its conclusions comprise the **research process** (see figure 12.4). The specific way in which each of these stages and their attendant sub-stages is operationalised will vary from project to project, and the process is seldom one that is strictly sequential. For example, the results that emerge from an analysis of data may prompt a rethinking of the original research questions. Alternatively, the research methods may have to be reconsidered once the researcher has begun to collect the data and discovers that in-depth interviewing would be more effective than a mail-out survey in eliciting information from a particular group. More fundamentally, the methodological biases of the researcher often dictate, in the first instance, the problems that are identified and the questions that are posed.

Problem recognition

The first step in any research process is **problem recognition**, or the identification of the broad issues or problems that interest the investigator. For a tourism-based corporation, core issues that require research include declining market share, high employee turnover, and high levels of customer dissatisfaction. From a destination perspective, additional concerns may be harboured about negative community reactions to tourism or declining environmental conditions that both affect and are affected by tourism (see the case study at the end of this chapter). Existing theories, such as the Butler sequence, may provide a useful framework for clarifying or contextualising the broad problem, which often emerges as a consequence of subjective perceptions, personal experiences or other qualitative input. As suggested above, methodological bias might dictate the problems that are identified. For example, a scientist trained in 'hard' quantitative techniques might not perceive a relatively subjective issue such as cultural commodification (see chapter 9) as being amenable to or worthy of scientific analysis, and hence would not recognise it as a problem that fits into their research agenda.

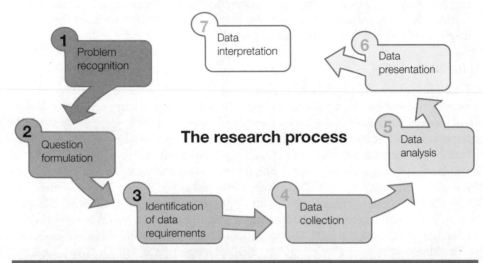

FIGURE 12.4 The research process

Question formulation

Once these broad problems or issues are identified, the research questions must be focused, at least in applied research, so that time and resources are not wasted on tangential or distracting avenues of investigation. As a basis for **question formulation** (which may be expressed as hypotheses or propositions), it is helpful to clarify the level of investigation that is warranted by the problem and the resources of the company or destination that are available. Four levels of investigation (description, explanation, prediction and prescription) are possible, each of which builds on the previous level.

Description

Description is the most basic level of inquiry. Imagine that the managers of a destination are concerned that local residents appear to be behaving in an increasingly hostile way towards tourists. The logical first step in addressing this issue is to describe and clarify the actual situation. The following questions might be posed:

- What are the attitudes of local residents towards visiting tourists?
- How have these attitudes changed in comparison with past attitudes?
- How much do these attitudes vary within the local population?
- Are there particular times of the day or the year in which the antitourist sentiment is more noticeable?
- Are there particular locations within the destination where the antitourist sentiment is more noticeable?
- Are there particular groups of tourists at which this hostility is directed?

Explanation

The decision whether to proceed to the next level of investigation, which is to explain the resultant patterns, is often constrained by the availability of resources. However, the decision should be based on whether one or more serious problems have been revealed after the research process has been completed at the descriptive level. If it is found, for example, that the perceived hostility of residents involves only a few isolated incidents instigated by known troublemakers, then there is probably no compelling reason to proceed any further with the investigation. If, however, the suspicions of a broader hostility within the population have been confirmed, then explanation is a necessary stage towards its resolution. In the hypothetical situation described above, the following explanation-based questions may emerge:

- Why is a growing proportion of young adults in the community expressing unfriendly behaviour toward Australian tourists in particular?
- Why is most of the antitourist behaviour evident in the main tourist shopping area, and during evening hours in particular?

The subsequent research process might reveal a high level of unemployment among young adults and resentment that 'their' jobs are being taken by outsiders. The evening may be a period of peak alcohol consumption and the main shopping area is a place where the intermingling of large numbers of tourists and locals creates numerous opportunities for conflict.

Prediction

Once plausible explanations for the problems are identified, the next level of investigation is to predict the consequences of the problem if no remedial measures are taken. As with any prediction involving humans, this stage of inquiry is speculative and often begins with a process of extrapolation wherein past patterns are assumed to continue into the future. However, extrapolation must be qualified by intelligent and well-considered speculation that takes into account all available information, including the experience of similar destinations. Following on from the above example, the following predictive questions can be posed:

- At what point and in what location is a serious confrontation (e.g. murder, riot) involving tourists and locals likely to occur?
- What will happen to the local tourism industry if no steps are taken to address the hostility of young adults towards tourism?
- What will subsequently happen to the local community in terms of economic and social impacts?

Prescription

Prescription is the culmination of the research process, involving the informed consideration of various solutions to minimise the problem. If the predictive phase reveals that the above situation is highly volatile, and that the community will endure great suffering if nothing is done, then the prescriptive phase will be essential. The following questions may emerge:

- What immediate steps can the community take to ensure that the situation does not escalate out of control?
- What medium- and long-term steps can be taken to defuse the situation and to instil a more positive attitude to tourism among young adults in the community?

For the first question, the 'research process' may have to be accelerated or abandoned altogether given the immediacy of the crisis (e.g. a very high risk of a riot within the next two months). Possible responses include increased policing of the main shopping area during evening hours, and reduced operating hours of a particularly notorious bar). The second question, however, is more amenable to the rigour that is normally associated with the research process, though it may have to be reformulated depending on the outcome of the immediate measures that are adopted.

The question of intervention, or the actions that should be taken to ensure optimum outcomes for the company or destination, is a core component of the management process, and a very important arena for applied research. However, appropriate solutions or prescriptions will only emerge as a result of the knowledge that is obtained through good preliminary research at the levels of description, explanation and prediction. Furthermore, if the research questions raised at those levels are engaged effectively, it is more likely that problem areas will be intercepted and addressed before they evolve into major crises. Hence, it is difficult to see how good management can be undertaken in the absence of good research.

Identification of research methodology or methods

The next stage usually involves the identification of the specific **research methods** that will best allow the questions to be addressed. This is usually informed by a search of secondary literature sources to see how other researchers have approached similar problems. In the descriptive phase of the example used, the investigator may initially focus on observing tourist–local interactions at a variety of locations and times. This can be augmented by quantitative surveying among residents and tourists to provide a statistical basis for determining whether certain groups are more hostile towards tourism than others. Depending on resources and time, observation and community focus groups may augment observation and surveying.

Cultural and social context must be considered in selecting an appropriate research methodology. For example, Likert-scaled survey questions (e.g. agreement with a statement on a 1 to 5 scale) are a reasonably effective means of eliciting accurate information from adults in mainstream, 'Western' societies such as those that predominate in Australia. However, there is evidence that East Asians for cultural reasons tend to avoid extreme responses on such instruments (i.e. they avoid 'strongly' agree or 'strongly' disagree options), even if this is the way they really feel about the situation. For research issues involving indigenous people, a standard quantitative methodology based on the scientific paradigm is often grossly inappropriate given the importance in those cultures of building trust through face-to-face contact over a long period (Schuler, Aberdeen & Dyer 1999). When interviewing local residents, it might be appropriate to employ trained locals rather than 'outsiders' who may be viewed with suspicion.

At the explanatory level, the researcher, in virtually any cultural context, should consider engaging in qualitative, in-depth interviews (e.g. with a sample of young adults) to identify the reasons for revealed attitudes and behaviour. For prediction, the interviewer has a number of options that can be pursued in conjunction with each other to see whether the different methods yield the same results, or whether the outcomes can be combined to arrive at a probable scenario. These include:

- an interview or survey question that asks the young adults what they are likely to do next if the situation does not change
- a modified Delphi technique to see what experts believe will occur
- a literature review to identify the outcomes of similar situations in other destinations

- extrapolation of past trends (e.g. if the number of hostile encounters has been increasing by 2 per cent a year over the past five years, then it could be assumed that this trend will continue to increase by a similar percentage in subsequent years).

To use all of the above techniques in the same research process (whether at the explanatory or some other level of investigation) is to engage in methodological **triangulation**, or the use of several methods to gather information about and gain insight into the research issue (Belhassen & Santos 2006). If all of the above four methods reveal similar outcomes, then the researcher has a high degree of confidence that the real situation has been identified. Moreover, it is likely that each method will yield its own unique insights into this situation, thereby strengthening the knowledge base that is obtained from the research. Constraints of time, expertise and money, however, often rule out the use of triangulation.

At the prescriptive level, many approaches are also possible, including continued Delphi inquiries as to appropriate solutions, as well as solicitation of the community to see what local residents (and young adults in particular) are willing to accommodate or suggest. Interviews with tourism managers in other destinations may also provide insight.

Data collection

Once the most appropriate methods have been identified, the **data collection** phase of the research process can proceed. In most cases, the researcher cannot access the entire population that is being investigated, or observe every event associated with a particular process. It is therefore expedient in such circumstances to select a sample from the target population. Sampling can be carried out on a probability or nonprobability basis. In the former case, a sample is randomly drawn from the population so that each member of that population has an equal or known probability of being selected. This can be done by simply drawing names out of a hat (in a small population), by using random number tables or selecting every nth name from a telephone directory or other source list.

However attained, it is important to select a large enough sample so that inferences can be made about the entire population. If carried out properly, a sample of 2000 households (or about 0.02 per cent) can accurately reflect all Australian households within a very small margin of error. However, for a population of around 1000, it is necessary to sample at least 30 per cent of the population to achieve the same effect, while a population of 100 would require a sample of around 80 per cent (Neuman 1997). Nonprobability or convenience sampling is commonly practised in qualitative research, and involves the deliberate selection of certain cases to build the sample. This type of sampling is not recommended for quantitative research except under certain circumstances.

Once the sample size and selection procedure have been decided, the actual collection of data can begin. Factors that must be considered at this stage include the timing of interviews or observations, consistency in the application of the research method or methods, and the collection of all results in as short a time period as possible. Specific issues may have to be considered depending on the research method and the conditions that are encountered in the 'field'. For example, telephone surveys carried out around dinner time are likely to yield a high response rate (i.e. people are likely to be at home), but a lower participation rate (i.e. because they do not wish to be bothered at that time).

Data analysis

The **data analysis** stage attempts to answer the relevant research questions by examining and assessing the collected information to identify patterns and meanings. Examination usually involves the filtering and organising of the database to eliminate invalid responses. This is then followed (at least in quantitative research) by the coding and entering of the data into a computer software system such as SPSS (Statistical Package for the Social Sciences), which facilitates further classification and analysis. Once the data are 'cleaned' to eliminate errors in the coding procedure, the actual analysis can be undertaken.

The most basic analysis in quantitative research is the recording of simple descriptive statistics such as frequencies, means and standard deviations (i.e. how much the data clusters around the mean). These are sufficient to answer many types of questions. At a more sophisticated level, tests of significance can be used to see whether the responses of one particular group are significantly different than those of the overall population or other specified subsections of that population. The relationships between many different variables and groups can be examined simultaneously using multivariate techniques such as factor analysis, cluster analysis and structural equation modeling (SEM). The level of sophistication that is appropriate depends on the nature of the research questions, the competency of the researcher and the characteristics of the data that are collected.

In qualitative research, analysis can involve the sorting, comparing, classifying and synthesis of the collected information, usually with a much higher level of subjective or personal judgement than occurs in quantitative analysis. Because of this subjectivity, qualitative researchers are more likely to practise triangulation.

Data presentation

In the **data presentation** stage, the results of the analysis should be communicated in a way that can be easily interpreted by the target audience. Tables and graphs are the most common devices for presenting data, but great care should always be taken to avoid complexity and clutter, particularly if the intended audience is not academic. Confusion often results when researchers wrongly assume that the audience is familiar with specific techniques and jargon. In general, the reader should be able to read a table or figure on its own, so that the accompanying text can focus on analysis rather than description.

Maps are underused as a means of data presentation, even though they are an extremely efficient means of presenting spatial information if constructed properly. Imagine, for example, that the researcher wishes to examine global patterns of visa-free travel privileges. To identify these, figure 12.5 uses a technique known as choropleth mapping which uses darker shades or colours to depict the degree to which countries are accessible visa-free. Almost instantaneously, the observer can appreciate the high level of accessibility afforded to the residents of North America, Europe, Australia and New Zealand, and the relative absence of accessibility for residents of African and Asian (except for Japan and South Korea) countries. Latin America occupies an intermediate position.

Data interpretation

The final stage, and in many ways the most difficult, is the extraction of meaning from the research results through **data interpretation**. This is where the significance and implications of the results are considered from a theoretical or practical perspective or both. The researcher may consider higher levels of investigation at this stage (e.g. move from description to explanation), or may revisit previous stages. As with earlier stages in the research process, interpretation will be influenced by the methodological and other biases of the researcher. In quantitative research, the acceptance or rejection of a hypothesis at the previous stage is a more objective form of interpretation, since this is determined by the outcome of a particular statistical application. In such instances, the term 'significance' has a specific meaning — that is, the result of the technique tells us, for example, whether the difference between two populations is statistically significant within some specified margin of error. Interpretation may or may not in this case lead to broader and more subjective speculations about less tangible matters, such as the implications of these results for the community or company.

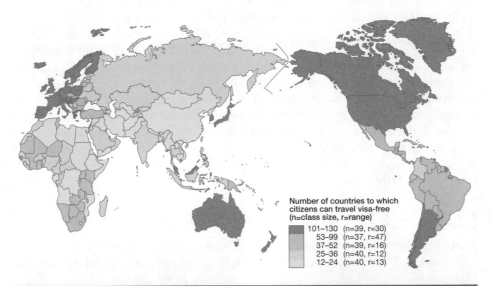

FIGURE 12.5 Effective cartography: Number of other countries to which citizens of each country can travel visa-free, 2006

Notes:
n = number of countries
r = value range
Source: Whyte (2008)

While it is possible for two researchers to produce almost identical results up to the point of hypothesis acceptance or rejection, it is likely that their interpretations of the results will differ greatly at this broader level. Interpretation, in essence, can be as much an art as a science, and the effective interpreter is an individual who is well versed and experienced in the broader topic area and knowledgeable about the external environments that affect tourism. The importance of effective interpretation at the specific or broad level cannot be overstated, since this leads to the translation of research results into policy decisions and other outcomes that are important to the target audience.

CHAPTER REVIEW

The essential role of research is to provide a sound knowledge base that allows the managers of destinations and businesses to make the best possible management decisions. Research can be categorised into several dichotomies. Basic research uses an inductive or deductive approach to broaden our understanding of tourism, while applied research is directed towards addressing a particular problem or issue. Cross-sectional research is undertaken during a single time period, while longitudinal research considers trends over two or more time periods in the past or future. Qualitative research tends to examine a small number of cases in great detail, while quantitative research usually considers a large number of cases in less depth. Finally, primary research occurs when the investigator gathers their own data, while secondary research involves the use of data that has already been gathered by other researchers.

The process through which research is undertaken comprises seven stages, although there is usually considerable flexibility in the sequence of steps that are actually followed in a research project. The process begins with problem recognition, and proceeds to the formulation of questions or hypotheses that provide a specific focus for investigation. At this point, the researcher also needs to consider the level of investigation that is of interest — description, explanation, prediction or prescription. Subsequently, a methodology (if not predetermined) and methods must be selected that address the research questions, and data collected that can then be analysed using those techniques. Once the data have been presented, the research process culminates in the interpretation of the results, which allows these to be translated into usable outcomes by the target audience.

■ SUMMARY OF KEY TERMS

Applied research research that addresses some particular problem or attempts to achieve a particular set of outcomes; it is usually constrained by set time schedules

Basic research research that is broadly focused on the revelation of new knowledge, and is not directed towards specific outcomes or problems

Cross-sectional research a 'snapshot' approach to research that considers one or more sites at one particular point in time

Data analysis the process by which the collected information is examined and assessed to identify patterns that address the research questions

Data collection the gathering of relevant information by way of the techniques identified in the research methodology stage

Data interpretation the stage during which meaning is extracted from the data

Data presentation the stage during which the results of the analysis are communicated to the target audience

Deduction an approach in basic research that begins with a basic theory that is applied to a set of data to see whether the theory is applicable or not

Hypotheses tentative informed statements about the nature of reality that can be subsequently verified or rejected through systematic deductive research

Induction an approach in basic research whereby the observation and analysis of data leads to the formulation of theories or models that link these observations in a meaningful way

Longitudinal research a trends-oriented approach to research, which examines one or more sites at two or more points in time or, more rarely, on a continuous basis

Primary research research that involves the collection of original data by the researcher

Problem recognition the first stage of the research process, which is the identification of a broad problem arena that requires investigation

Qualitative research research that does not place its emphasis on the collection and analysis of statistical data, and usually tends to obtain in-depth insight into a relatively small number of respondents or observations

Quantitative research research that is based mainly on the collection and analysis of statistical data, and hence tends to obtain a limited amount of information on a large number of respondents or observations; these results are then extrapolated to the wider population of the subject matter

Question formulation the posing of specific questions or hypotheses that serve to focus the research agenda arising from problem recognition; these questions can be descriptive, explanatory, predictive or prescriptive in nature

Research a systematic search for knowledge

Research methodology a set of assumptions, procedures and methods that are used to carry out a search for knowledge within a particular type of research

Research methods the techniques that will be used to answer the questions or prove or disprove the hypotheses

Research process the sequence of stages that are followed to carry out a research project from its origins to its conclusions

Secondary research research in which the investigator uses previously collected data

Triangulation the use of multiple methods, data sources, investigators or theories in a single research process

■ QUESTIONS

1. From a corporate perspective, what are the advantages and disadvantages of pursuing basic (as opposed to applied) research?
2. (a) What is the difference between induction and deduction?
   (b) How do the two approaches work together in long-term research projects?
3. What are the main advantages and disadvantages of:
   (a) cross-sectional research, and
   (b) longitudinal research?
4. (a) What are the relative strengths and weaknesses of:
       (i) qualitative research, and
       (ii) quantitative research?
   (b) In what ways can qualitative and quantitative research display a complementary relationship?
5. Why should the researcher be cautious when considering GPS-based observation (see page 342) as a means of gathering primary tourism-related data?
6. (a) Why has the internet become so popular as a source of information for tourism researchers?
   (b) What measures could be taken to assure that the secondary material accessed from the internet is appropriate for research purposes?
7. When interviewing local residents, what are the advantages and disadvantages respectively of having other local residents or outside academics conduct the interviews?
8. What are the strengths and weaknesses of methodological triangulation?

9. Why is a sampling rate of 80 per cent appropriate to represent a population of 100 individuals, but just 0.02 per cent for a population of 20 million individuals (e.g. the entire Australian population)?
10. (a) Why can interpretation be considered an art as much as a science?
    (b) How important is interpretation to the research process?

▉ EXERCISES

1. Write a 1000 word report that:
   (a) empirically tests the inductive model of indigenous tourism development (see pages 332–3) in the context of either southern China, the Amazon Basin, or the Lapland region of Scandinavia, and
   (b) assesses the applicability of this model to the selected case study.
2. (a) Using any recent article from *Annals of Tourism Research, Tourism Management* or the *Journal of Travel Research*, identify the type of research that is represented and the type of primary and/or secondary research methods and sources that are employed.
   (b) Describe how these types of research and methods are related to the problem recognition, question formulation and identification of data requirements (i.e. first three stages of the research process in the final section of this chapter) used in the article.

▉ FURTHER READING

Ritchie, B., Burns, P. & Palmer, C. Eds. 2005. *Tourism Research Methods: Integrating Theory with Practice.* **Wallingford, UK: CABI.** The 17 chapters in this collection encompass a comprehensive array of research issues and methods, including longitudinal research, participant observation, qualitative research, and content analysis.

Garrod, B. 2003. 'Defining Marine Ecotourism: A Delphi Study'. In Garrod, B. & Wilson, J. (Eds) *Marine Ecotourism: Issues and Experiences.* **Clevedon, UK: Channel View Publications, pp. 17–36.** Garrod's exploration of the definition of 'ecotourism' provides an effective demonstration of the utility of the Delphi technique in tourism research.

Goodson, L. & Phillimore, J. (Eds) 2004. *Qualitative Research in Tourism: Ontologies, Epistemologies and Methodologies.* **London: Routledge.** This book provides a comprehensive exposure to and analysis of qualitative research methods as they pertain to the tourism sector.

Jennings, G. 2001. *Tourism Research.* **Brisbane: John Wiley & Sons.** Jennings discusses all essential aspects of research from a tourism studies perspective, including data sources, ethical considerations, qualitative and quantative methods, and the preparation of research proposals.

Raybould, M., Mules, T., Fredline, E. & Tomljenovic, R. 2000. 'Counting the Herd. Using Aerial Photography to Estimate Attendance at Open Events'. *Event Management* 6: 25–32. This intriguing article demonstrates the challenges and creative thinking involved in researching unusual situations, such as crowd size at non-secured events. The 1998 Wintersun Festival, on the Gold Coast, is the case study.

Sarantakos, S. 2004. *Social Research.* **Third Edition. Melbourne: Palgrave Macmillan.** This is an excellent introduction to a wide range of methods and issues associated with research in the social sciences and related fields, such as tourism.

case study

PURSUING RESEARCH ON CLIMATE CHANGE AND TOURISM IN AUSTRALIA

Prioritisation of research into the relationship between tourism and climate change is a recent development in Australia. For example, the Tourism White Paper, released by the Howard government in the early 2000s (Commonwealth of Australia 2003), made no reference to climate change in the brief section on sustainability. Instead, research issues associated with tourism's contribution to the Australian economy were emphasised, including small tourism enterprises, regional tourism, developing niche markets, identifying infrastructure and access problems, and attracting major events. A more conducive policy environment for climate change research became evident in 2008, when the new tourism portfolio (Department of Resources, Energy and Tourism, or DRET) was restructured by the Rudd government to foster 'an industry that promotes the principles of environmental responsibility and sustainable development', while retaining the commitment to maximise the net contribution of tourism to the Australian economy (DRET 2008c). In addition, the new portfolio's discussion paper for its National Long-Term Tourism Strategy identified climate change as one of eight major supply-side tourism issues that required attention, along with investment, labour training and retention, productivity, attracting business events, improving inbound access, improving research capabilities, and enhancing domestic tourism (DRET 2008d).

The climate change component of the Strategy has in turn been strongly influenced by a policy initiative commenced under the previous Commonwealth government. In 2007, the Council of Australian Governments (COAG) tasked the Tourism Ministers' Council (TMC) with developing the Tourism Action Plan on Climate Change. The framework for this Plan, released in mid-2008 by a specialised taskforce, emphasised the delivery of four outcomes (DRET 2008e) that entail associated research initiatives and directives.

Understanding the vulnerability of tourism to climate change

Industry requires the best possible information about the physical impacts of climate change so that Australian tourism operations can make the necessary adaptations. A key research project has been conducted by the Sustainable Tourism Cooperative Research Centre (STCRC 2008) to identify the likely impacts of climate change on five important tourism regions, i.e. the Victorian Alps, Cairns, Kakadu, the Blue Mountains, and the Barossa Valley, over the next 10, 40 and 60 years. The adaptive capacities of each region are assessed in this research, and appropriate strategies identified.

Preparation of the tourism industry for a 'carbon constrained' future

DRET has also been collaborating with the STCRC to identify the carbon footprint of the Australian tourism industry, so that appropriate mitigation strategies can be implemented. Modified Tourism Satellite Account methodology has tentatively revealed a tourism contribution of 7.2 per cent to Australia's greenhouse gas emissions, and the research indicates that significant improvements in fuel efficiency are being offset by increased demand for air travel. Research has further revealed that tourism businesses are uninformed and confused as to the available array of carbon offset tools and benefits (DRET 2008e). The taskforce has recommended in addition to the continuing emissions research that emission management tool factsheets be distributed to the industry, that best practice guidelines for the industry be identified, that the evolving national accreditation system for tourism takes greenhouse gas emissions into consideration, and that the impacts of future carbon prices on the tourism industry be modelled.

Marketing strategies repositioned to take into account climate change effects

There is concern that consumers in major market regions are rethinking their long-haul travel plans in light of climate change concerns and environmental group lobbying. To assess the legitimacy of this concern, DRET hired consultants to examine the extent to which travellers in the UK and Germany have altered their travel intentions to take into account climate change (Donnelly 2008). This qualitative research (small group discussions including participants with differing opinions) revealed that German travellers are more sensitive to the issue than their UK counterparts, and that while overall concern about the environment was high, there was also a desire to continue engaging in long-haul travel, and to blame other parties for climate change-related problems. The researchers also found a high level of 'buy in' to carbon offset schemes that yielded visible results to travellers. To provide more information of this nature, supplementary questions on the purchase of voluntary carbon travel offsets were added to the National and International Visitor Surveys in 2008. It is hoped that such information will inform the repositioning of tourism marketing campaigns to take into account climate change perceptions.

Effective and consistent industry outreach and communication

There is awareness of the need to ensure that research outcomes are communicated to the tourism industry in the most effective and efficient manner. To this effect, the taskforce has recommended that all relevant knowledge is made available through ongoing factsheets and a specialised Tourism Australia website. Workshops also provide an opportunity to obtain industry feedback that can further inform the research and communication agendas.

A major source of industry input into the Tourism Action Plan on Climate Change was a submission from the Tourism and Transport Forum (TTF 2007), which strongly supported increased research to address 'critical knowledge gaps'. It was the TTF that recommended in its submission the establishment of a tourism greenhouse gas emissions satellite account, but also pushed for a targeted analysis of aviation emissions which indicated that the latter constituted only a small portion of tourism-related emissions. The TTF was also influential in encouraging research on consumer travel attitudes related to climate change, so that revealed misperceptions could be addressed in future overseas promotion. Other research recommendations in the TTF submission focused on evaluating the impacts of climate change policy on the tourism industry, the vulnerability of the latter to climate change, and appropriate adaptation and mitigation strategies.

QUESTIONS

1. Design a 4-page questionnaire for distribution in the US that examines:
   (a) level of climate change awareness
   (b) effects of this awareness on past travel behaviour and future travel intentions
   (c) effects of this awareness on intentions to travel to Australia and New Zealand
   (d) effects that a variety of carbon offset programs might have on intentions to travel to Australia and New Zealand.
   (e) relevant respondent characteristics.
2. Write a 1000-word report in which you describe how the data from this survey will be analysed in order to provide the Australian and New Zealand tourism industries with timely knowledge that will help them to best respond to emerging consumer perceptions about climate change and tourism.

APPENDIX 1

Tourism organisation	Original date established	Purpose	Headquarters
Australian Bureau of Statistics (ABS) www.abs.gov.au	1976	Australia's official statistical organisation	Belconnen, ACT
Australian Tourism Export Council (ATEC) (predecessor Australian Incoming Tour Operators Association) www.atec.net.au	1972	Peak industry association representing Australia's inbound tourism industry	Sydney, NSW
Tourism Australia (predecessor Australian Tourist Commission) www.tourism.australia.com	1967	The Australian government statutory authority established to promote Australia as an international tourist destination	Canberra, ACT
Tourism Research Australia (predecessor Bureau of Tourism Research) www.tra.australia.com	1987	A branch of Tourism Australia that collects, analyses and disseminates information regarding the Australian tourism industry to government, industry and the general public	Canberra, ACT
Sustainable Tourism CRC www.crctourism.com.au	1996	An Australian partnership (cooperative research centre) between universities, government and industry to promote sustainable tourism through the timely delivery of strategic knowledge; the continued funding of the STCRC after mid-2010 was uncertain as of mid-2009	Gold Coast, QLD
Ecotourism Australia (predecessor Ecotourism Association of Australia) www.ecotourism.org.au	1991	Promotes an understanding of ecotourism and environmental issues in Australia, and aims to develop ethics and standards for the industry, and facilitate interaction between ecotourism stakeholders	Brisbane, QLD
EC3 Global (predecessor Green Globe) www.ec3global.com	1992	A private intercorporate company that promotes certified environmental sustainability among its member tourism companies	Turner, ACT

(continued)

SELECTED INTERNATIONAL AND AUSTRALIAN TOURISM ORGANISATIONS *(continued)*

Tourism organisation	Original date established	Purpose	Headquarters
Pacific Asia Travel Association (PATA) **www.pata.org**	1951	A nonprofit travel industry association that promotes travel and tourism destinations in the Asia–Pacific region through networking, marketing, promotion and sales, destination promotion and trade shows; consists of approximately 2100 organisations, including governments, travel organisations and companies	San Francisco, United States (administrative headquarters)
Department of Resources, Energy and Tourism (DRET) **www.ret.gov.au**	1996	Provides advice and policy support to relevant sectors to increase Australia's international competitiveness; operates under the principles of environmental and social responsibility	Canberra, ACT
Tourism and Transport Forum (TTF) (predecessor Tourism Task Force) **www.ttf.org.au**	1989	Australia's peak national body promoting the interests and perspectives of the tourism and transport industries	Sydney, NSW
The World Tourism Organization (UNWTO) (predecessor IUOTO — International Union of Official Travel Organisations) **www.world-tourism.org**	1975	A United Nations agency that provides a forum to discuss global tourism policy and issues, and has a mission to promote and develop tourism as a way of encouraging world peace, and as an agent of economic development; includes 133 countries and territories, and more than 300 affiliate members	Madrid, Spain
World Travel and Tourism Council (WTTC) **www.wttc.org**	n/a	The main forum for global tourism chief executive officers, including accommodation, catering, cruises, entertainment, recreation, transportation and travel-related services; central goal is to work with governments to fulfil the full economic potential of tourism	London, United Kingdom

APPENDIX 2

Journal title	Date of first issue	Country of editor(s)
Journal of Travel Research (formerly *Travel Research Bulletin*) **http://jtr.sagepub.com**	1962	United States
Annals of Tourism Research **www.sciencedirect.com**	1973	United Kingdom
Tourism Recreation Research **www.trrworld.org**	1976	India
Journal of Hospitality & Tourism Research **http://jht.sagepub.com**	1976	United States
Tourism Management **www.elsevier.com**	1980	New Zealand
Journal of Hospitality and Tourism Education **www.chrie.org**	1989	United States
Anatolia **www.anatoliajournal.com**	1990	Turkey
Journal of Travel & Tourism Marketing **www.haworthpress.com**	1992	Hong Kong SAR (China)
Event Management (formerly *Festival and Event Management*) **www.cognizantcommunication.com**	1993	United States
Journal of Hospitality and Tourism Management (formerly *Australian Journal of Hospitality Management*) **www.australianacademicpress.com.au**	1993	Australia
Journal of Sustainable Tourism **www.tandf.co.uk**	1993	United Kingdom
Journal of Vacation Marketing **http://jvm.sagepub.com**	1994	Australia
International Journal of Tourism Research (formerly *Progress in Tourism and Hospitality Research*) **www3.interscience.wiley.com**	1995	United Kingdom

(continued)

REFEREED ENGLISH LANGUAGE TOURISM JOURNALS (2009) *(continued)*		
Journal title	**Date of first issue**	**Country of editor(s)**
Tourism Economics **www.ippublishing.com**	1995	United Kingdom
Asia Pacific Journal of Tourism Research **www.tandf.co.uk**	1996	Hong Kong SAR (China)
Journal of Sport Tourism **www.tandf.co.uk**	1996	United Kingdom
Tourism (formerly *Turizam*) **www.iztzg.hr**	1996	Croatia
Tourism Analysis **www.cognizantcommunication.com**	1996	United States
International Journal of Hospitality and Tourism Administration (formerly *Journal of International Hospitality, Leisure and Tourism Management*) **www.haworthpress.com**	1997	United States
Studies in Travel Writing **www.erica.demon.co.uk**	1997	United Kingdom
Tourism Review International (formerly *Pacific Tourism Review*) **www.cognizantcommunication.com**	1997	United States
Current Issues in Tourism **www.multilingual-matters.net**	1998	New Zealand
Information Technology and Tourism **www.cognizantcommunication.com**	1998	United States
Journal of Convention & Event Tourism (formerly *Journal of Convention & Exhibition Management*) **www.haworthpress.com**	1998	United States
Tourism Culture and Communication **www.cognizantcommunication.com**	1998	Australia
Tourism Geographies **www.geog.nau.edu**	1999	United States
Journal of Tourism: An International Research Journal **www.usm.edu**	2000	India
Journal of Quality Assurance in Hospitality & Tourism **www.haworthpress.com**	2000	United States

Journal title	Date of first issue	Country of editor(s)
Journal of Hospitality, Tourism and Leisure Science **http://hotel.unlv.edu**	2001	United States
Journal of Teaching in Travel & Tourism **www.haworthpress.com**	2001	Hong Kong SAR (China)
Journal of Travel and Tourism Research **http://stad.adu.edu.tr**	2001	Turkey
Scandinavian Journal of Hospitality and Tourism **www.tandf.co.uk**	2001	Norway
Tourism & Hospitality Research **www.palgrave-journals.com**	2001	United Kingdom
Tourist Studies **http://tou.sagepub.com**	2001	Australia/ United Kingdom
Journal of Ecotourism **www.informaworld.com**	2002	Canada
Journal of Hospitality, Leisure, Sport & Tourism Education **www.heacademy.ac.uk**	2002	United Kingdom
eReview of Tourism Research (ejournal) **http://ertr.tamu.edu**	2003	United States/ Canada
Journal of Tourism and Cultural Change **www.tandf.co.uk**	2003	United Kingdom
Tourism and Hospitality Planning & Development **www.tandf.co.uk**	2004	United Kingdom
Tourism in Marine Environments **http://cognizantcommunication.com**	2004	New Zealand
Journal of China Tourism Research **www.haworthpress.com**	2005	Hong Kong SAR (China)
Journal of Heritage Tourism **www.tandf.co.uk**	2006	United States
Tourismos: An International Multidisciplinary Journal of Tourism **www.chios.aegean.gr**	2006	Greece

(continued)

REFEREED ENGLISH LANGUAGE TOURISM JOURNALS (2009) *(continued)*		
Journal title	**Date of first issue**	**Country of editor(s)**
International Journal of Culture, Tourism and Hospitality Research **http://info.emeraldinsight.com**	2007	United States
International Journal of Tourism Policy **http://www.inderscience.com**	2007	Greece and United Kingdom
Journal of Tourism Consumption and Practice	2008	United Kingdom
European Journal of Tourism Research	2009	Bulgaria
ARA Journal of Tourism Research **www.tourism-futures.org**	2009	Dominican Republic
International Journal of Hospitality Knowledge Management **www.inderscience.com**	2009	United Kingdom
Journal of Tourism History **www.tandf.co.uk**	2009	United Kingdom
Journal of International Volunteer Tourism and Social Development **www.tandf.co.uk**	2009	Australia

■ APPENDIX 3

INBOUND TOURISM DATA						
Entity	Region	Population (000s) 2007	GDP per capita (2007) (US$)	Inbound (000s) 2002	Inbound (000s) 2007	International tourism receipts 2004 (US$m)	Tourism as percentage of GNP (2004)
Albania	SEur	3 582	5 800	n/a	57	735	11.3
Algeria	NAfr	32 930	6 700	998	1 743	178	0.2
Andorra	SEur	71	38 800[2]	3 388	2 189	n/a	n/a
Angola	MAfr	12 127	7 800	91	194	66	0.1
Anguilla	Car	13	8 800	44	78	69	n/a
Antigua & Barbuda	Car	69	18 300	n/a	273[1]	338	39.5
Argentina	SA	39 922	13 100	2 820	4 562	2 235	1.6
Armenia	CEEur	2 976	5 800	n/a	450	86	2.5
Australia	AusSP	20 264	37 300	4 841	5 064[1]	15 191	2.7
Austria	WEur	8 193	39 300	18 611	20 766	15 334	5.8
Bahamas	Car	304	28 000	n/a	1 528	1 884	n/a
Bahrain	ME	699	33 900	3 167	4 519[1]	864	8.4
Bangladesh	SAsia	147 365	1 400	207	289	67	0.1
Barbados	Car	280	18 900	498	575	764	n/a
Belarus	CEEur	10 293	10 600	n/a	105	270	1.3
Belgium	WEur	10 379	36 200	6 724	7 045	9 233	2.8
Belize	CA	288	7 900	200	252	133	13.4
Bermuda	Car	66	69 900[2]	284	306	354	n/a
Bhutan	SAsia	2 280	5 200	6	21	12	1.7
Bolivia	SA	8 989	4 400	n/a	556	192	2.2
Bosnia & Herzegovina	SEur	4 499	6 100	160	306	519	5.8
Botswana	SAfr	1 640	14 300	1 037	1 675[2]	549	7.1
Brazil	SA	188 078	9 500	3 783	5 026	3 222	0.6

(continued)

Entity	Region	Population (000s) 2007	GDP per capita (2007) (US$)	Inbound (000s) 2002	Inbound (000s) 2007	International tourism receipts 2004 (US$m)	Tourism as percentage of GNP (2004)
British Virgin Is.	Car	23	38 500	285	358	391	n/a
Brunei	SEAsia	379	51 000	n/a	179	n/a	n/a
Bulgaria	CEEur	7 385	11 800	3 433	5 151	2 221	10.1
Cambodia	SEAsia	13 881	1 900	787	1 873	603	11.6
Canada	NA	33 099	38 600	20 057	17 931	12 871	1.4
Cape Verde	WAfr	421	3 200	126	267	98	11.7
Cayman Islands	Car	45	43 800[2]	303	292	519	n/a
Chad	MAfr	9 944	1 500	n/a	25	14[3]	0.4[3]
Chile	SA	16 134	14 300	1 412	2 507	1 150	1.4
China	NEAsia	1 313 974	5 400	36 803	54 720	25 739	1.3
Colombia	SA	43 593	7 400	541	1 193	1 058	1.2
Cook Islands	AusSP	21	9 100	73	97	72	n/a
Costa Rica	CA	4 075	11 100	1 113	1 973	1 358	7.2
Croatia	SEur	4 495	15 500	6 944	9 307	6 848	22.0
Cuba	Car	11 383	11 000	1 656	2 119	1 915	n/a
Cyprus	EMed	784	27 100	2 418	2 416	2 253	16.5
Czech Republic	CEEur	10 235	24 500	4 579	6 680	4 172	4.4
Denmark	NEur	5 451	37 200	2 010	4 716[1]	5 670	2.5
Dominican Rep.	Car	9 184	6 600	2 811	3 980	3 152	17.6
Ecuador	SA	13 548	7 200	654	953	462	1.5
Egypt	ME	78 887	5 000	4 906	10 610	6 125	6.7
El Salvador	CA	6 822	6 000	951	1 339	441	2.8
Estonia	CEEur	1 324	21 800	1 360	1 900	891	9.3
Ethiopia	EAfr	74 778	700	156	303	173	1.9
Fiji	AusSP	906	3 900	398	539	420	17.7
Finland	NEur	5 231	36 000	2 875	3 519	2 076	1.2

INBOUND TOURISM DATA (continued)

Entity	Region	Population (000s) 2007	GDP per capita (2007) (US$)	Inbound (000s) 2002	Inbound (000s) 2007	International tourism receipts 2004 (US$m)	Tourism as percentage of GNP (2004)
France	WEur	62 752	32 600	77 012	81 900	40 841	2.2
French Polynesia	AusSP	275	17 500[4]	189	218	553	n/a
Gambia	WAfr	1 642	1 200	n/a	143	28[5]	6.9[5]
Germany	WEur	82 422	34 100	17 969	24 420	27 668	1.1
Ghana	WAfr	22 410	1 400	483	497[1]	466	5.7
Greece	SEur	10 688	30 600	14 180	16 039[1]	12 872	6.9
Grenada	Car	90	10 500	132	129	83	20.3
Guam	AusSP	171	15 000	1 059	1 225	n/a	n/a
Guatemala	CA	12 294	5 100	881	1 448	776	2.9
Guyana	SA	767	3 700	104	131	28	4.0
Honduras	CA	7 326	4 300	550	831	439	6.0
Hong Kong SAR	NEAsia	6 940	42 000	16 566	17 154	8 999	4.8
Hungary	CEEur	9 981	19 300	15 870	8 638	4 061	4.8
Iceland	NEur	299	40 400	278	1 054	372	3.2
India	SAsia	1 095 352	2 600	2 370	4 977	6 121	0.9
Indonesia	SEAsia	245 453	3 600	5 033	5 506	4 798	1.9
Ireland	NEur	4 062	46 600	6 476	8 001[1]	4 398	3.1
Israel	EMed	6 352	26 600	862	2 268	2 380	2.0
Italy	SEur	58 134	30 900	39 799	43 654	35 656	2.3
Jamaica	Car	2 758	7 400	1 266	1 704	1 438	16.5
Japan	NEAsia	127 464	33 500	5 239	8 347	11 269	0.2
Jordan	ME	5 907	4 700	1 622	3 431	1 330	11.1
Kenya	EAfr	34 708	1 700	838	1 644[1]	486	3.1
Kiribati	AusSP	105	3 600	5	5	3[3]	2.5[3]
Korea, South	NEAsia	48 847	25 000	5 347	6 448	6 069	0.9
Kuwait	ME	2 418	55 900	n/a	292	180	0.3
Latvia	CEEur	2 275	17 700	848	1 653	267	2.1

(continued)

INBOUND TOURISM DATA *(continued)*

Entity	Region	Population (000s) 2007	GDP per capita (2007) (US$)	Inbound (000s) 2002	Inbound (000s) 2007	International tourism receipts 2004 (US$m)	Tourism as percentage of GNP (2004)
Lebanon	ME	3 874	10 300	956	1 017	5 411	25.0
Lesotho	SAfr	2 022	1 400	n/a	300	34	2.6
Liechtenstein	WEur	34	25 000	49	60	n/a	n/a
Lithuania	CEEur	3 586	16 800	1 433	2 180[1]	776	3.9
Luxembourg	WEur	474	79 400	876	917	3 659	13.9
Macau (China)	NFAsia	453	28 400[1]	6 565	12 945	7 479	n/a
Macedonia	SEur	2 051	8 400	123	230	72	1.5
Madagascar	EAfr	18 595	900	n/a	344	105	2.0
Malawi	EAfr	13 014	800	285	714	24	1.2
Malaysia	SEAsia	24 386	14 500	13 292	20 973	8 198	7.3
Maldives	SAsia	359	4 600	485	676	471	61.3
Mali	WAfr	11 717	1 100	96	164	130	3.0
Malta	SEur	400	23 400	1 134	1 244	790	16.3
Marshall Islands	AusSP	60	2 900[2]	6	7	4[3]	2.33
Mauritius	EAfr	1 241	11 300	682	907	853	14.8
Mexico	NA	107 450	12 400	19 667	21 424	10 796	1.5
Moldova	CEEur	4 467	2 300	18	13	113	4.3
Monaco	WEur	33	30 000	263	328	n/a	n/a
Montenegro	SEur	631	3 800[2]	n/a	984	n/a	n/a
Montserrat	Car	9	3 400[3]	10	8	9	n/a
Morocco	NAfr	33 241	3 700	4 193	7 408	3 924	8.4
Myanmar	SEAsia	47 383	1 900	217	248	84	n/a
Namibia	SAfr	2 044	5 200	n/a	833[1]	403	8.4
Nepal	SAsia	28 287	1 000	n/a	384[1]	230	3.5
Netherlands	WEur	16 491	39 000	9 595	11 008	10 333	1.8
New Caledonia	AusSP	219	15 000[4]	104	103	241	n/a

Entity	Region	Population (000s) 2007	GDP per capita (2007) (US$)	Inbound (000s) 2002	Inbound (000s) 2007	International tourism receipts 2004 (US$m)	Tourism as percentage of GNP (2004)
New Zealand	AusSP	4 076	27 200	2 045	2 466	4 790	6.0
Nicaragua	CA	5 570	2 800	472	800	192	4.3
Niue	AusSP	2	5 800[4]	2	4	n/a	n/a
Northern Marianas	AusSP	82	12 500	466	429[1]	n/a	n/a
Norway	NEur	4 611	53 300	3 107	3 945[1]	3 087	1.3
Pakistan	SAsia	165 804	2 400	498	840	178	0.2
Palau	AusSP	21	7 600[2]	59	86[1]	97	68.3
Panama	CA	3 191	10 700	534	1 103	651	4.8
Papua New Guinea	AusSP	5 671	2 100	54	104	18	n/a
Paraguay	SA	6 506	4 000	250	416	70	1.3
Peru	SA	28 303	7 600	846	1 812	1 142	1.7
Philippines	SEAsia	89 469	3 200	1 933	3 092	2 017	2.0
Poland	CEEur	38 537	16 200	13 980	14 975	5 833	2.5
Portugal	SEur	10 606	21 800	11 666	12 321	7 846	4.9
Puerto Rico	Car	3 927	18 400	3 087	3 687	3 024	n/a
Romania	CEEur	22 304	11 100	3 204	1 551	505	0.8
Russia	CEEur	142 894	14 800	7 943	20 199[1]	5 225	1.1
St. Kitts & Nevis	Car	39	13 900	68	117	103	27.9
St. Lucia	Car	168	10 700	253	287	326	43.8
St. Maarten	Car	14	n/a	381	469	613	n/a
St. Vincent	Car	118	9 800	78	101	96	23.5
Samoa	AusSP	177	5 400	89	122	70	21.3
Saudi Arabia	ME	27 020	19 800	7 511	11 531	6 486	2.7
Serbia	SEur	9 396	10 400	448	696	n/a	n/a
Seychelles	EAfr	81	16 600	132	161	172	25.5
Singapore	SEAsia	4 492	49 900	6 996	7 957	5 219	4.9
Slovakia	CEEur	5 439	20 200	1 399	1 685	901	2.6

(continued)

INBOUND TOURISM DATA *(continued)*

Entity	Region	Population (000s) 2007	GDP per capita (2007) (US$)	Inbound (000s) 2002	Inbound (000s) 2007	International tourism receipts 2004 (US$m)	Tourism as percentage of GNP (2004)
Slovenia	SEur	2 010	28 000	1 302	1 751	1 630	5.5
Solomon Islands	AusSP	552	1 900	n/a	14	4	1.5
South Africa	SAfr	44 188	9 700	6 550	9 090	6 282	3.8
Spain	SEur	40 398	33 600	51 748	59 193	45 248	4.9
Sri Lanka	SAsia	20 222	4 000	393	494	513	2.6
Sudan	NAfr	41 236	1 900	52	328[1]	21	0.1
Suriname	SA	439	8 700	n/a	163	17	1.7
Swaziland	SAfr	1 136	4 700	332	870	95	5.0
Sweden	NEur	9 017	37 500	7 459	5 224	6 196	1.9
Switzerland	WEur	7 524	40 100	10 000	8 448	10 556	2.9
Syria	ME	18 881	4 700	2 809	4 566	2 057	8.6
Taiwan	NEAsia	23 036	30 100	2 726	3 716	4 054	n/a
Tanzania	EAfr	37 445	1 300	550	692	746	6.4
Thailand	SEAsia	64 632	8 000	10 873	14 464	10 034	6.3
Togo	WAfr	5 549	900	n/a	86	15[4]	0.8[4]
Tonga	AusSP	115	5 100	37	46	15	8.4
Tunisia	NAfr	10 175	7 400	5 064	6 762	1 970	7.5
Turkey	EMed	70 414	12 000	12 782	22 248	15 888	5.9
Uganda	EAfr	28 196	1 000	254	642	266	3.9
Ukraine	CEEur	46 711	7 000	6 326	23 122	2 560	4.3
United Arab Emirates	ME	2 563	37 000	5 445	7 126[2]	1 593	1.5
United Kingdom	NEur	60 609	35 000	24 180	30 677	28 221	1.4
United States	NA	298 444	45 800	41 892	55 986	74 547	0.6
US Virgin Islands	Car	109	4 500	553	510	1 356	n/a
Uruguay	SA	3 432	10 800	1 258	1 752	494	3.7

Entity	Region	Population (000s) 2007	GDP per capita (2007) (US$)	Inbound (000s) 2002	Inbound (000s) 2007	International tourism receipts 2004 (US$m)	Tourism as percentage of GNP (2004)
Vanuatu	AusSP	209	3 900	49	81	52	17.9
Venezuela	SA	25 730	12 800	432	771	481	0.5
Vietnam	SEAsia	84 403	2 600	n/a	4 172	n/a	n/a
Yemen	ME	21 456	2 500	89	379	214	2.0
Zambia	EAfr	11 502	1 400	565	897	161	3.5
Zimbabwe	EAfr	12 237	200	n/a	2 287[1]	194	2.6

Notes:

1   2006

2   2005

3   2002

4   2003

5   2001

AusSP = Australia South Pacific

Car = Caribbean

CEEur = Central Eastern Europe

EAfr = East Africa

EMed = Eastern Mediterranean

MAfr = Middle Africa

ME = Middle East

NA = North America

NAfr = North Africa

NEAsia = North-East Asia

NEur = Northern Europe

SA = South America

SAfr = South Africa

SAsia = South Asia

CA = Central America

SEAsia = South-East Asia

SEur = Southern Europe

WAfr = West Africa

WEur = Western Europe

GDP per capita figures are estimates based on purchasing power parity — that is, adjusting for relative cost of living expenses

Source: CIA 2008, NationMaster.com 2008, UNWTO 2008

■ REFERENCES

Abdullah, A., Ebrahim, S., Fielding, R. & Morisky, D. 2004. 'Sexually Transmitted Diseases in Travelers: Implications for Prevention and Control'. *Clinical Infectious Diseases* 39: 533–38.

ABS 1998a. *1998 Year Book Australia*. ABS Catalogue No. 1301.0. Canberra: Australian Bureau of Statistics.

ABS 1998b. *Overseas Arrivals and Departures*. ABS Catalogue No. 3204.0. Canberra: Australian Bureau of Statistics.

ABS 1999. *1999 Yearbook Australia*. ABS Catalogue No. 1301.1. Canberra: Australian Bureau of Statistics.

ABS 2000. 'Tourism Feature Article: Australian Tourism Satellite Account'. *Australian Economic Indicators*. ABS Catalogue No. 1350.0. Canberra: Australian Bureau of Statistics.

ABS 2001. *2001 Year Book Australia*. Canberra: Australian Bureau of Statistics.

ABS 2003. *Family Characteristics, Australia*. Catalogue No. 4442.0. www.abs.gov.au.

ABS 2004. *Australian Historical Population Statistics*. Catalogue No. 3105.0.65.001. www.abs.gov.au. Canberra: Australian Bureau of Statistics.

ABS 2005. *Overseas Arrivals and Departures*. Catalogue No. 3401.0. www.abs.gov.au. Canberra: Australian Bureau of Statistics.

ABS 2006a. *Australian and New Zealand Standard Industrial Classification (ANZSIC), 1993*. Catalogue No. 1292.0. www.abs.gov.au. Canberra: Australian Bureau of Statistics.

ABS 2006b. *Employee Earnings and Hours, Australia, May 2006*. Catalogue No. 6306.0. www.abs.gov.au. Canberra: Australian Bureau of Statistics.

ABS 2007. 'Attendance at Selected Cultural Venues and Events 2005–06'. www.ausstats.abs.gov.au. Canberra: Australian Bureau of Statistics.

ABS 2008a. 'Year Book Australia 2008: Households and Families'. www.abs.gov.au. Canberra: Australian Bureau of Statistics.

ABS 2008b. 'Year Book Australia 2008: Population Size and Growth'. www.abs.gov.au. Canberra: Australian Bureau of Statistics.

ABS 2008c. *Overseas Arrivals and Departures*. Catalogue No. 3401.0. www.abs.gov.au. Canberra: Australian Bureau of Statistics.

ABS 2008d. *Overseas Arrivals and Departures*. Catalogue No. 3401.0. www.abs.gov.au. Canberra: Australian Bureau of Statistics.

AEC 2007. 'Senate First Preferences by Group'. http://results.aec.gov.au. Canberra: Australian Electoral Commission.

Agarwal, S. 1997. 'The Resort Cycle and Seaside Tourism: An Assessment of its Applicability and Validity'. *Tourism Management* 18: 65–73.

Akama, J. 1996. 'Western Environmental Values and Nature-based Tourism in Kenya'. *Tourism Management* 17: 567–74.

Alford, P. 1999. 'Database Marketing in Travel and Tourism'. *Travel & Tourism Analyst* 1: 87–104.

Alpine Pearls 2008. 'Alpine Pearls — The Facts'. Alpine Pearls. http://alpine-pearls.com.

Alreck, P. L. & Settle, R. B. 1995. *The Survey Research Handbook*. Second Edition. London: Irwin.

Altinay, L., Var, T., Hines, S. & Hussain, K. 2007. 'Barriers to Sustainable Tourism Development in Jamaica'. *Tourism Analysis* 12: 1–13.

Altman, J. & Finlayson, J. 2003. 'Aborigines, Tourism and Sustainable Development'. *Journal of Tourism Studies* 14: 78–91.

Anderson, B., Provis, C. & Chappel, S. 2003. 'The Selection and Training of Workers in the Tourism and Hospitality Industries for the Performance of Emotional Labour'. *Journal of Hospitality and Tourism Management* 10: 1–12.

Ashworth, G. J. & Tunbridge, J. 2004. 'Whose Tourist-Historic City? Localizing the Global and Globalizing the Local'. In Lew, A., Hall, C. & Williams, A. (Eds.). *A Companion to Tourism*. Oxford: Blackwell, pp. 210–22.

ATC 1997. *Australia 96/7: Annual Report*. Canberra: Australian Tourist Commission.

ATC 2000. *Financial Reports*. Canberra: Australian Tourist Commission.

ATEC 2005. 'ATEC Slams Productivity Commission Report'. Australian Tourism Export Council. www.atec.net.au.

ATEC 2008. 'Tourists Slugged by Budget: ATEC'. May 13. Australian Tourism Export Council. www.atec.net.au.

Atherton, T. & Atherton, T. 2003. 'Current Issues in Travel and Tourism Law'. In Wilks, J. & Page, S. (Eds.). *Managing Tourist Health and Safety in the New Millennium*. London: Pergamon, pp. 101–15.

Austrade 2008. 'Export Market Development Grants (EMDG)'. www.austrade.gov.au.

Backer, E. 2007. 'VFR Travel: An Examination of the Expenditures of VFR Travellers and their Hosts'. *Current Issues in Tourism* 10: 366–76.

Bailey, M. 1995. *China. International Tourism Reports*. Number 1. London: Economist Intelligence Unit, pp. 19–37.

Baker, B. & Bendel, P. 2005. '"Come and Say G'Day!"' www.atme.org.

Baloglu, S. & Brinberg, D. 1997. 'Affective Images of Tourism Destinations'. *Journal of Travel Research* 35 (4): 11–15.

Barisic, S. 2008. 'New Program at Colonial Williamsburg'. YAHOO! News. http://news.yahoo.com.

Barker, T., Darma Putra, I. & Wiranatha, A. 2006. 'Authenticity and Commodification of Balinese Dance Performances' In Smith, M. & Robinson, M. (Eds) *Cultural Tourism in a Changing World: Politics, Participation and (Re)presentation*. Clevedon, UK: Channel View, pp. 215–24.

Barron, P. 2007. 'Hospitality and Tourism Students' Part-time Employment: Patterns, Benefits and Recognition'. *Journal of Hospitality, Leisure, Sport & Tourism Education* 6 (4): 40–54.

Bauer, J. & Herr, A. 2004. 'Hunting and Fishing Tourism'. In Higginbottom, K. (Ed.) *Wildlife Tourism: Impacts, Management and Planning*. Altona, Vic.: Common Ground Publishing, pp. 57–77.

Bauer, T. & McKercher, B. (Eds.). 2003. *Sex and Tourism: Journeys of Romance, Love and Lust*. Binghampton, USA: Haworth Hospitality Press.

Baum, T. 1998. 'Tourism Marketing and the Small Island Environment: Cases from the Periphery'. In Laws, E., Faulkner, B. & Moscardo, G. (Eds) *Embracing and Managing Change in Tourism: International Case Studies*. London: Routledge, pp. 116–37.

Becken, S. & Hay, J. 2007. *Tourism and Climate Change: Risks and Opportunities*. Clevedon, UK: Channel View.

Beech, J., Rigby, A., Talbot, I. & Thandi, S. 2005. 'Sport Tourism as a Means of Reconciliation? The Case of India–Pakistan Cricket'. *Tourism Recreation Research* 30: 83–91.

Beedie, P. & Hudson, S. 2003. 'Emergence of Mountain-based Adventure Tourism'. *Annals of Tourism Research* 30: 625–43.

Beeton, S. 2005. *Film-induced Tourism*. Clevedon, UK: Channel View.

Beeton, S. & Benfield, R. 2002. 'Demand Control: The Case for Demarketing as a Visitor and Environmental Management Tool'. *Journal of Sustainable Tourism* 10: 497–513.

Belhassen, Y. & Santos, C. 2006. 'An American Evangelical Pilgrimage to Israel: A Case Study on Politics and Triangulation'. *Journal of Travel Research* 44: 431–41.

Bendell, J. & Font, X. 2004. 'Which Tourism Rules? Green Standards and GATS'. *Annals of Tourism Research* 31: 139–56.

Beverland, M. 1999. 'Wine Tourists: A Missed Opportunity or a Misplaced Priority?' *Pacific Tourism Review* 3: 119–31.

Binder, J. 2004. 'The Whole Point of Backpacking: Anthropological Perspectives on the Characteristics of Backpacking'. In Hannam, K. & Ateljevic, I. (Eds). *Backpacker Tourism: Concepts and Profiles*. Clevedon, UK: Channel View, pp. 92–108.

Bischoff, E. & Koenig-Lewis, N. 2007. 'VFR Tourism: The Importance of University Students as Hosts'. *International Journal of Tourism Research* 9: 465–84.

Black, R. & Crabtree, A. Eds. 2007. *Quality Assurance and Certification in Ecotourism*. Wallingford, UK: CABI.

Blain, C., Levy, T. & Ritchie, J. 2005. 'Destination Branding: Insights and Practices from Destination Management Organizations'. *Journal of Travel Research* 43: 328–38.

Bloor, M. 2001. *Focal Groups in Social Research*. London: Sage.

Bond, M. 1997. 'Women Travellers: A New Growth Market?' *PATA Occasional Papers Series, Paper No. 20*. Singapore: Pacific Asia Travel Association.

Boniface, B. & Cooper, C. 2005. *Worldwide Destinations: The Geography of Travel and Tourism*. Fourth Edition. Sydney: Elsevier.

Boo, E. 1990. *Ecotourism: The Potentials and Pitfalls*. Volume 1. Washington, DC: World Wildlife Fund.

Bowen, D. 2002. 'Research through Participant Observation in Tourism: A Creative Solution to the Measurement of Consumer Satisfaction/Dissatisfaction (CS/D) among Tourists'. *Journal of Travel Research* 41: 4–14.

Bowen, J., Makens, J. & Kotler, P. 2005. *Marketing for Hospitality and Tourism*. Fourth Edition. Upper Saddle River, NJ, USA: Prentice Hall.

Brewer, K., Poffley, J. & Pederson, E. 1995. 'Travel Interests Among Seniors: Continuing Care Retirement Community Residents'. *Journal of Travel and Tourism Marketing* 4 (2): 93–8.

Brown, D. O. 1999. 'Debt-funded Environmental Swaps in Africa: Vehicles for Tourism Development?' *Journal of Sustainable Tourism* 6 (1): 69–79.

Bruce, M. 2008a. 'How Dredging Changed Our Beaches'. www.goldcoast.com.au.

Bruce, M. 2008b. 'Heyday Became Mayday at Kirra'. www.goldcoast.com.au.

Brunt, P., Mawby, R. & Hambly, Z. 2000. 'Tourist Victimisation and the Fear of Crime on Holiday'. *Tourism Management* 21: 417–24.

BSDglobal.com 2008. 'Who are the Green Consumers?' www.bsdglobal.com.

Buckley, R. (Ed.) 2004. *Environmental Impacts of Tourism*. Wallingford, UK: CABI Publishing.

Buckley, R. 2008. 'Testing Take-up of Academic Concepts in an Influential Commercial Tourism Publication'. *Tourism Management* 29: 721–29.

Buckley, R., King, N. & Zubrinich, T. 2004. 'The Role of Tourism in Spreading Dieback Disease in Australian Vegetation'. In Buckley, R. (Ed.) *Environmental Impacts of Tourism*. Wallingford, UK: CABI Publishing, pp. 317–24.

Budiani-Saberi, D. & Delmonico, F. 2008. 'Organ Trafficking and Transplant Tourism: A Commentary on the Global Realities'. *American Journal of Transplantation* 8: 925–29.

Burkart, A. J. & Medlik, S. (Eds) 1981. *Tourism: Past, Present and Future*. Second Edition. Oxford: Heinemann.

Burnett, J. 2006. 'Long- and Short-haul Travel by Air: Issues for People with Diabetes on Insulin'. *Journal of Travel Medicine* 13: 255–60.

Burns, D. & Murphy, L. 1998. 'An Analysis of the Promotion of Marine Tourism in Far North Queensland, Australia'. In Laws, E., Faulkner, B. and Moscardo, G. (Eds) *Embracing and Managing Change in Tourism: International Case Studies*. London: Routledge, pp. 415–30.

Burton, R. 1997. *Travel Geography*. Second Edition. London: Longman.

Bushell, R., Faulkner, B. & Jafari, J. (Eds) 1996. *Tourism Research in Australia: A Strategy for Mobilising National Research Capabilities*. Position paper emerging from the Collaborative ARC Tourism Research Strategic Planning Workshop, University of Western Sydney, Hawkesbury, 24–25 November.

Business Events Australia 2008. 'Conference/Convention Arrivals to Australia — May 2008'. www.businessevents.australia.com.

Butcher, J. 2006. 'The United Nations International Year of Ecotourism: A Critical Analysis of Development Implications'. *Progress in Development Studies* 6: 146–56.

Butler, R. W. (Ed.) 2005a. *The Tourism Area Life Cycle: Theoretical and Conceptual Implications*. Clevedon, UK: Channel View.

Butler, R. W. (Ed.) 2005b. *The Tourism Area Life Cycle: Applications and Modifications*. Clevedon, UK: Channel View.

Butler, R. W. 1980. 'The Concept of a Tourist Area Cycle of Evolution: Implications for Management of Resources'. *Canadian Geographer* 24: 5–12.

Butler, R. W. 1992. 'Alternative Tourism: The Thin Edge of the Wedge'. In Smith, V. L. & Eadington, W. R. (Eds) *Tourism Alternatives: Potentials and Problems in the Development of Tourism*. Philadelphia: University of Pennsylvania Press, pp. 31–46.

Butler, R. W. & Boyd, S. (Eds) 2000. *Tourism and National Parks: Issues and Implications*. Chichester, UK: John Wiley.

Butler, R. W. & Hinch, T. (Eds) 2007 *Tourism and Indigenous Peoples: Issues and Implications*. Oxford: Butterworth-Heinemann.

Butler, R. W., Hall, C. M. & Jenkins, J. (Eds) 1998. *Tourism and Recreation in Rural Areas*. Chichester, UK: John Wiley.

Canning, S. 2008. '"Bloody Hell" Campaign a Failure: Ferguson'. www.theaustralian.news.com.au.

Carlsen, J. 2006. 'Post-tsunami Tourism Strategies for the Maldives'. *Tourism Review International* 10: 69–79.

Carter, B. 1996. 'Private Sector Involvement in Recreation and Nature Conservation in Australia'. In Charters, T., Gabriel, M. & Prasser, S. (Eds) *National Parks: Private Sector's Role*. Toowoomba, QLD: SQU Press.

Casson, L. 1994. *Travel in the Ancient World*. Baltimore: Johns Hopkins University Press.

Cater, C. & Cater, E. 2007. *Marine Ecotourism: Between the Devil and the Deep Blue Sea*. Wallingford, UK: CABI.

Chadwick, R. 1994. 'Concepts, Definitions, and Measures Used in Travel and Tourism Research'. In Ritchie, J. R. B. & Goeldner, C. R. (Eds) *Travel, Tourism, and Hospitality Research: A Handbook for Managers and Researchers*. Second Edition. Chichester, UK: John Wiley, pp. 65–80.

Chambers, D. & McIntosh, B. 2008. 'Using Authenticity to Achieve Competitive Advantage in Medical Tourism in the English-speaking Caribbean'. *Third World Quarterly* 29: 919–37.

China 1998. *The Outline of China Tourism Statistics*. Beijing: National Tourism Administration of the People's Republic of China.

Chinadaily.com 2008. 'Outbound Tourism Sector to Open Wider'. http://chinadaily. com.cn.

Chinatour.com 2008. 'China Tourism Statistics'. www.chinatour.com.

Christaller, W. 1963. 'Some Considerations of Tourism Location in Europe'. *Papers and Proceedings of the Regional Science Association* 12: 95–105.

CIA 2008. 'The World Factbook'. www.cia.gov.

Cleaver Sellick, M. 2004. 'Discovery, Connection, Nostalgia: Key Travel Motives Within the Senior Market'. *Journal of Travel & Tourism Marketing* 17: 55–71.

CLIA 2008. '2008 CLIA Cruise Market Overview'. Cruise Lines International Association. www.cruising.org.

Clifford, H. 2002. *Downhill Slide: Why the Corporate Ski Industry is Bad for Skiing, Ski Towns and the Environment*. San Francisco: Sierra Club Books.

Clift, S. & Carter, S. (Eds) 2000. *Tourism and Sex: Culture, Commerce and Coercion*. London: Pinter.

Clift, S., Luongo, M & Callister, C. (Eds) 2002. *Gay Tourism: Culture, Identity and Sex*. London: Continuum.

CNTA 2003. *China Statistical Yearbook 2003*. Beijing: China National Tourism Administration.

CNTA n.d. 'International Tourists by Locality 2000'. www.cnta.com/lyen/2fact/6–2. htm (visited 9 March 2005).

Cochrane, J. Ed. 2007. *Asian Tourism: Growth and Change*. London: Elsevier.

Cohen, E. 2004. 'Backpacking: Diversity and Change'. In Richards, G. & Wilson, J. (Eds.). *The Global Nomad: Backpacker Travel in Theory and Practice*. Clevedon, UK: Channel View, pp. 43–59.

Cole, S. 2005. 'Action Ethnography: Using Participant Observation'. In Ritchie, B., Burns, P. & Palmer, C. (Eds) *Tourism Research Methods: Integrating Theory with Practice*. Wallingford, UK: CABI, pp. 63–72.

Cole, S. T. 2005. 'Comparing Mail and Web-based Survey Distribution Methods: Results of Surveys to Leisure Travel Retailers'. *Journal of Travel Research* 43: 422–30.

Collins, J. & Wallace J. 1995. 'The Use of Census Data for Target Marketing — The Way Forward for the Tourism Industry'. *Journal of Vacation Marketing* 1: 273–80.

Colonial Williamsburg 2008. 'Annual Report 2007'. www.history.org.

Colvin, M. 2008. 'Deportees Fuel Violent Crime Wave Across Caribbean'. *The Australian*, 4 August, p. 15.

Commonwealth of Australia 2003. 'Tourism White Paper: A Medium to Long Term Strategy for Tourism'. www.tourism.australia.com.

Connelly, N., Brown, T. & Decker, D. 2003. 'Factors Affecting Response Rates to Natural Resource-focused Mail Surveys: Empirical Evidence of Declining Rates over Time'. *Society and Natural Resources* 16: 541–49.

Cooper, C., Fletcher, J., Fyall, A., Gilbert, D. & Wanhill, S. 2005. *Tourism Principles and Practice*. Third Edition. London: Prentice Hall.

Cowan, G. 1977. 'Cultural Impact of Tourism with Particular Reference to the Cook Islands'. In Finney, B & Watson, K. (Eds) *A New Kind of Sugar: Tourism in the Pacific*. Honolulu: East–West Center, pp. 79–85.

Craig-Smith, S. & Dryden, G. 2008. 'Australia as a Safari Hunting Destination for Exotic Animals'. In Lovelock, B. (Ed.). *Tourism and the Consumption of Wildlife: Hunting, Shooting and Sport Fishing*. London: Routledge, pp. 268–80.

Crompton, J. L. 1992. 'Structure of Vacation Destination Choice Sets'. *Annals of Tourism Research* 19: 420–34.

Crompton, J. L. 1979. 'An Assessment of the Image of Mexico as a Vacation Destination and the Influence of Geographical Location on that Image'. *Journal of Travel Research* 17 (1): 18–23.

Cukier, J. & Wall, G. 1994. 'Informal Tourism Employment: Vendors in Bali, Indonesia'. *Tourism Management* 15: 464–67.

Crystal, E. 1989. 'Tourism in Toraja (Sulawesi, Indonesia)'. In Smith, V. L. (Ed.) *Hosts and Guests: The Anthropology of Tourism*. Second Edition. Philadelphia: University of Pennsylvania Press, pp. 139–68.

CSIRO 2008. 'Fuel for Thought: The Future of Transport Fuels: Challenges and Opportunities'. Commonwealth Scientific and Industrial Research Organisation. www.csiro.au.

Dahles, H. (Ed.) 2001. *Tourism, Heritage and National Culture in Java: Dilemmas of a Local Community*. Richmond, UK: Curzon Press.

Davidson, T. 2005. 'What Are Travel and Tourism: Are They Really an Industry?' In Theobald, W. (Ed.) *Global Tourism*. Third Edition. Sydney: Elsevier, pp. 25–31.

de Burlo, C. 1996. 'Cultural Resistance and Ethnic Tourism on South Pentecost, Vanuatu'. In Butler, R. and Hinch, T. (Eds) *Tourism and Indigenous Peoples*. London, International Thomson Business Press, pp. 255–76.

DEC 2008. 'Valley of the Giants: Fact File'. Department of Environment and Conservation [Western Australia]. www.dec.wa.gov.au.

DesArt 2007. 'DesArt News'. www.desart.com.au.

Desmarest, F. & Monroe, D. 2008. 'A New Concept in the Luxury Tourism Market: The Destination Club'. *Espaces, Tourisme & Loisirs*, No. 255: 14–18.

Digance, J. 2003. 'Pilgrimage at Contested Sites'. *Annals of Tourism Research* 30: 143–59.

DITR 2004. 'Economic Impact of the Rugby World Cup 2003 on the Australian Economy — Post Analysis'. Department of Industry, Tourism and Resources. www.industry.gov.au.

DITR 2005a. 'Regional Australia'. Department of Industry, Tourism and Resources. www.industry.gov.au.

DITR 2005b. 'Tourism White Paper Initiatives'. Department of Industry, Tourism and Resources. www.industry.gov.au.

Dolnicar, S. & Leisch, F. 2008. 'An Investigation of Tourists' Patterns of Obligation to Protect the Environment'. *Journal of Travel Research* 46: 381–91.

Donnelly, D. 2008. 'Propensity for UK and German Travelers to Adapt Travel Intentions Due to Rising Awareness of Climate Change Issues'. Department of Resources, Energy and Tourism. www.ret.gov.au.

Douglas, N. 1997. 'Applying the Life Cycle Model to Melanesia'. *Annals of Tourism Research* 24: 1–22.

Douglass, W. & Raento, P. 2004. 'The Tradition of Invention — Conceiving Las Vegas'. *Annals of Tourism Research* 31: 7–23.

Dowling, R. (Ed.) 2006. *Cruise Ship Tourism*. Wallingford, UK: CABI.

Doxey, G. 1976. 'When Enough's Enough: The Natives are Restless in Old Niagara'. *Heritage Canada* 2 (2): 26–27.

DRET 2008a. 'China Approved Destination Status (ADS) Scheme'. Department of Resources, Energy and Tourism. www.ret.gov.au.

DRET 2008b. 'Tourism Industry Facts and Figures at a Glance, June 2008'. Department of Resources, Energy and Tourism. www.ret.gov.au.

DRET 2008c. 'Tourism Policy'. Department of Resources, Energy and Tourism. www.ret.gov.au.

DRET 2008d. 'National Long-term Tourism Strategy: Discussion Paper'. Department of Resources, Energy and Tourism. www.ret.gov.au.

DRET 2008e. 'Tourism and Climate Change — A Framework for Action'. Department of Resources, Energy and Tourism. www.ret.gov.au.

Duval, D. 2007. *Tourism and Transport: Modes, Networks and Flows*. Clevedon, UK: Channel View.

Elliott, J., O'Brien, D., Leder, K., Kitchener, S., Schwartz, E., Weld, L., Brown, G., Kain, K. & Torresi, J. 2004. 'Imported *Plasmodium Vivax* Malaria: Demographic and Clinical Features in Nonimmune Travelers'. *Journal of Travel Medicine* 11: 213–19.

English, E. P. 1986. *The Great Escape? An Examination of North–South Tourism*. Ottawa, Canada: North–South Institute.

eTurboNews 2008. 'MP Defends "Bloody Hell" Tourism Ad'. www.eturbonews.com.

Eurofound 2008. 'EurLIFE: Car Ownership'. www.eurofound.europa.eu.

Evans, G. 1995. 'Tourism and Indigenous Cultural Heritage in New and Old Mexico'. In Burns, P. (Ed.). *Tourism and Minorities' Heritage: Impacts and Prospects*. London: University of North London Press, pp. 18–40.

Evans-Pritchard, A. 2008. 'Australia Faces Worse Crisis than America'. www.telegraph.co.uk.

EventPlan 2003. 'Gettysburg Re-enactment 1998' www.eventplan.co.uk.

Faulkner, B. 1998. 'Some Parameters for Exploring Progress in Tourism and Hospitality Research'. In Faulkner, B., Tidesswell, C. and Weaver, D. B. (Eds) *Progress in Tourism and Hospitality Research*. Proceedings of the Eighth Australian Tourism and Hospitality Research Conference. Canberra: Bureau of Tourism Research, pp. 4–8.

Faulkner, B. & Russell, R. 1997. 'Chaos and Complexity in Tourism: In Search of a New Perspective'. *Pacific Tourism Review* 1: 93–102.

Faulkner, B. & Tidesswell, C. 1997. 'A Framework for Monitoring Community Impacts of Tourism'. *Journal of Sustainable Tourism* 5: 3–28.

Faulkner, B. & Vikulov, L. 2001. 'Katherine, Washed Out One Day, Back on Track the Next: A Post-mortem of a Tourism Disaster'. *Tourism Management* 22: 331–44.

Faulkner, B. & Walmsley, D. J. 1998. 'Globalisation and the Pattern of Inbound Tourism in Australia'. *Australian Geographer* 29 (1): 91–106.

Feng, R. & Morrison, A. 2002. 'GIS Applications in Tourism and Hospitality Marketing: a Case in Brown County, Indiana'. *Anatolia* 13: 127–43.

Fennell, D. & Dowling, R. (Eds) 2003. *Ecotourism Policy and Planning*. Wallingford, UK: CABI Publishing.

Finney, B. & Watson, K. (Eds) 1975. *A New Kind of Sugar: Tourism in the Pacific*. Honolulu: East–West Center.

Fletcher, K., Wheeler, C. & Wright, J. 1994. 'Strategic Implementation of Database Marketing: Problems and Pitfalls'. *Long Range Planning* 27: 133–41.

Foley, M. & McPherson, G. 2000. 'Museums as Leisure'. *International Journal of Heritage Studies* 6: 161–74.

Font, X. 2001. 'Regulating the Green Message: The Players in Ecolabelling'. In Font, X. & Buckley, R. (Eds.). *Tourism Ecolabelling: Certification and Promotion of Sustainable Management*. CABI Publishing, pp. 1–17.

Forbes, M. 2008. 'Island Paradise Sucked Dry'. *Sydney Morning Herald*. 4–5 October, p. 21.

Formica, S. & Littlefield, J. 2000. 'National Tourism Organizations: A Promotional Plans Framework'. *Journal of Hospitality & Leisure Marketing* 7: 103–19.

Francis, D. 1992. *The Imaginary Indian: The Image of the Indian in Canadian Culture*. Vancouver: Arsenal Pulp Press.

Frank, R. 2005. 'Resort Clubs Raise the Price of Admission'. *Wall Street Journal*, August 24, pp. D1 & D3.

Fredline, E. & Faulkner, B. 2000. 'Host Community Reactions: A Cluster Analysis'. *Annals of Tourism Research* 27: 763–84.

Freitag, T. G. 1994. 'Enclave Tourism Development: For Whom the Benefit Rolls?' *Annals of Tourism Research* 21: 538–54.

Fyall, A. & Garrod, B. 2005. 'From Competition to Collaboration in the Tourism Industry' In Theobald, W. (Ed.) *Global Tourism*. Third Edition. Sydney: Elsevier, pp. 52–73.

Gammon, S. 2004. 'Secular Pilgrimage and Sport Tourism'. In Ritchie, B. and Adair, D. (Eds) *Sport Tourism: Interrelationships, Impacts and Issues*. Clevedon, UK: Channel View, pp. 30–45.

Garrod, B. 2003. 'Defining Marine Ecotourism: A Delphi Study'. In Garrod, B. & Wilson, J. (Eds.). *Marine Ecotourism: Issues and Experiences*. Clevedon, UK: Channel View Publications, pp. 17–36.

Garrod, B. 2008. 'Exploring Place Perception: A Photo-based Analysis'. *Annals of Tourism Research* 35: 381–401.

Garrod, B. & Fyall, A. 2005. 'Revisiting Delphi: The Delphi Technique in Tourism Research'. In Ritchie, B., Burns, P. & Palmer, C. (Eds) *Tourism Research Methods: Integrating Theory with Practice*. Wallingford, UK: CABI, pp. 85–98.

Getz, D. 1992. 'Tourism Planning and Destination Life Cycle'. *Annals of Tourism Research* 19: 752–70.

Getz, D. 2000. *Explore Wine Tourism: Management, Development & Destinations*. Elmsford, USA: Cognizant Communication.

Gilbert, E. W. 1949. 'The Growth of Brighton'. *Geographical Journal*, 114 (1): 30–52.

Gilbert, N. 1993. 'Research, Theory and Method'. In Gilbert, N. (Ed.) *Researching Social Life*. London: Sage, pp. 18–31.

Glaesser, D. 2003. *Crisis Management in the Tourism Industry*. Sydney: Butterworth–Heinemann.

Goeldner, C. & Ritchie, J. 2006. *Tourism: Principles, Practices, Philosophies*. Tenth Edition. Hoboken, New Jersey, USA: John Wiley.

Goodall, B. 1991. 'Understanding Holiday Choice'. In Cooper, C. (Ed.) *Progress in Tourism, Recreation and Hospitality Management. Volume 3*. London: Belhaven, pp. 58–77.

Goodson, L. & Phillimore, J. (Eds) 2004. *Qualitative Research in Tourism: Ontologies, Epistemologies and Methodologies*. London: Routledge.

Gössling, S. 2003. 'The Political Ecology of Tourism in Zanzibar'. In Gössling, S. (Ed.) *Tourism and Development in Tropical Islands: Political Ecology Perspectives*. Cheltenham, UK: Edward Elgar, pp. 178–202.

Govers, R., Go, F. & Kumar, K. 2007. 'Virtual Destination Image: A New Measurement Approach'. *Annals of Tourism Research* 34: 977–97.

Green, R. 1996. 'We Never Saw these Things Before: Southwest Indian Laughter and Resistance to the Invasion of the Tse va ho'. In Weigle, M. & Babcock, B. (Eds.). *The Great Southwest of the Fred Harvey Company and the Santa Fe Railway*, pp. 201–6.

Greenwood, D. 1989. 'Culture by the Pound: An Anthropological Perspective on Tourism as Cultural Commoditization'. In Smith, V. L. (Ed.) *Hosts and Guests: The Anthropology of Tourism*. Second Edition. Philadelphia: University of Pennsylvania Press, pp. 171–85.

Grossman, L. 2002. 'Home is Where the Yurt Is'. Pacific Yurts. http://yurts.com.

Gunn, C. 1994a. 'A Perspective on the Purpose and Nature of Tourism Research Methods'. In Ritchie, J. R. Brent & Goeldner, C. R. (Eds) *Travel, Tourism, and Hospitality Research: A Handbook for Managers and Researchers*. Second Edition. Chichester, UK: John Wiley, pp. 3–11.

Gunn, C. 2004. *Tourism Planning: Basics, Concepts, Cases*. Third Edition. London: Taylor & Francis.

Gurung, D. & Seeland, K. 2008. 'Ecotourism in Bhutan: Extending Its Benefits to Rural Communities'. *Annals of Tourism Research* 35: 489–508.

Haig, B. & Anderssen, J. 2007. 'Australian Consumption Expenditure and Real Income: 1900 to 2003–2004'. *The Economic Record* 83: 416–31.

Hall, C.M. 1998. 'Historical Antecedents of Sustainable Development and Ecotourism: New Labels on Old Bottles?' In Hall, C.M. & Lew, A. (Eds) *Sustainable Tourism: A Geographical Perspective*. Harlow, Essex, UK: Longman, pp. 13–24.

Hall, C.M. 2002. 'ANZAC Day and Secular Pilgrimage'. *Tourism Recreation Research* 27: 83–87.

Hall, C.M. & Higham, J. (Eds) 2005. *Tourism, Recreation and Climate Change*. Clevedon, UK: Channel View Publications.

Hall, C. M. & Valentin, A. 2005. 'Content Analysis'. In Ritchie, B., Burns, P. & Palmer, C. (Eds) *Tourism Research Methods: Integrating Theory with Practice*. Wallingford, UK: CABI, pp. 191–209.

Hall, C. M., Jenkins, J. & Kearsley, G. 1997. 'Tourism Planning and Policy in Urban Areas: Introductory Comments'. In Hall, C. M., Jenkins, J. & Kearsley, G. (Eds) *Tourism Planning and Policy in Australia and New Zealand: Cases, Issues and Practice*. Sydney: McGraw-Hill/Irwin, pp. 198–208.

Hall, C.M., Sharples, L., Mitchell, R., Macionis, N. & Cambourne, B. (Eds) 2003. *Food Tourism Around the World: Development, Management and Markets*. Sydney: Butterworth–Heinemann.

Hall, D., Marciszweska, B. & Smith, M. 2006. *Tourism in the New Europe: The Challenges and Opportunities of EU Enlargement*. Wallingford: CABI.

Hamilton, C. & Attwater, R. 1997. 'Measuring the Environment: The Availability and Use of Environmental Statistics in Australia'. *Australian Journal of Environmental Management* 4 (2): 72–87.

Hannam, K. & Ateljevic, I. Eds 2008. *Backpacker Tourism: Concepts and Profiles*. Clevedon, UK: Channel View.

Harriott, V., Davis, D. & Banks, S. 1997. 'Recreational Diving and Its Impacts in Marine Protected Areas in Eastern Australia'. *Ambio* 26: 173–9.

Hart, E. 1983. *The Selling of Canada: The CPR and the Beginnings of Canadian Tourism*. Banff, Canada: Altitude Publishing.

Hatch, D. 2008. 'Qantas Boss Predicts "New World Order" in Aviation'. www.travelmole.com.

Healey, J. 2000. 'USA Today Auto Track: Automakers Prepare Onslaught of New SUVs'. www.usatoday.com.

Henderson, J. 2003. 'Terrorism and Tourism: Managing the Consequences of the Bali Bombings'. *Journal of Travel & Tourism Marketing* 15: 41–58.

Henderson, J. 2004. 'Food as a Tourism Resource: A View from Singapore'. *Tourism Recreation Research* 29 (3): 69–74.

Henderson, J. 2006. 'Tourism in Dubai: Overcoming Barriers to Destination Development'. *International Journal of Tourism Research* 8: 87–99.

Henderson, J. 2007. 'Corporate Social Responsibility and Tourism: Hotel Companies in Phuket, Thailand, after the Indian Ocean Tsunami'. *Hospitality Management* 26: 228–39.

Herold, E., Garcia, R. & DeMoya, T. 2001. 'Female Tourists and Beach Boys: Romance or Sex Tourism?' *Annals of Tourism Research* 28: 978–97.

Heung, V. & Cheng, E. 2000. 'Assessing Tourists' Satisfaction with Shopping in the Hong Kong Special Administrative Region of China'. *Journal of Travel Research* 38: 396–404.

Higgins-Desbiolles, F. 2003. 'Reconciliation Tourism: Tourism Healing Divided Societies!' *Tourism Recreation Research* 28: 35–44.

Higham, J. (Ed.) 2005. *Sport Tourism Destinations: Issues, Opportunities and Analysis*. Sydney: Elsevier.

Hitchcock, M. & Darma Putra, I. 2007. *Tourism, Development and Terrorism in Bali*. Aldershot, UK: Ashgate.

Hoare, R. & Butcher, K. 2008. 'Do Chinese Cultural Values Affect Customer Satisfaction/Loyalty?' *International Journal of Contemporary Hospitality Management* 20: 156–71.

Hoffman, B. 2008. 'Tourism Struggling through 'Desperate' Times'. June 10. www.thedaily.com.au.

Holden, P. (Ed.) 1984. *Alternative Tourism With a Focus on Asia*. Bangkok: Ecumenical Council on Third World Tourism.

Holden, A. (Ed.) 2005. *Tourism Studies and the Social Sciences*. Abingdon, UK: Routledge.

Homeland Security 2008. 'Homeland Security and State Departments Announce WHTI Land and Sea Final Rule'. www.dhs.gov.

Hong, G-S., Fan, J., Palmer, L. & Bhargava, V. 2005. 'Leisure Travel Expenditure Patterns by Family Life Cycle Stages'. *Journal of Travel & Tourism Marketing* 18(2): 15–30.

Hsu, C. (Ed.) 2006. *Casino Industry in Asia Pacific: Development, Operation, Impact*. Binghampton, USA: Haworth Press.

Huck, P. 2007. 'America's War on Tourists'. www.nzherald.co.nz.

Hudson, B. 2004. 'Australian Waterfalls as Tourism Attractions'. *Tourism Review International* 7: 81–94.

Hunter, C. 1997. 'Sustainable Tourism as an Adaptive Paradigm'. *Annals of Tourism Research* 24: 850–67.

Hunter, C. & Shaw, J. 2007. 'The Ecological Footprint as a Key Indicator of Sustainable Tourism'. *Tourism Management* 28: 46–57.

ILO 2005. 'After the Tsunami: In Thailand, the Tourist Industry Fights Back'. International Labour Organization. www.ilo.org.

Irandu, E. 2004. 'The Role of Tourism in the Conservation of Cultural Heritage in Kenya'. *Asia Pacific Journal of Tourism Research* 9: 133–50.

Israeli, A. & Reichel, A. 2003. 'Hospitality Crisis Management Practices: The Israeli Case'. *International Journal of Hospitality Management* 22: 353–72.

Issa, I. & Altinay, L. 2006. 'Impacts of Political Instability on Tourism Planning and Development: The Case of Lebanon'. *Tourism Economics* 12: 361–81.

Jafari, J. 2001. 'The Scientification of Tourism'. In Smith, V. L. and Brent, M. (Eds) *Hosts and Guests Revisited: Tourism Issues of the 21st Century*. New York: Cognizant, 28–41.

Jago, L. 2005. *Encore Festival and Event Evaluation Kit: A Guide to Using the Encore Festival and Event Evaluation Kit*. Gold Coast, Australia: Sustainable Tourism CRC.

Jamal, T., Smith, B. & Watson, E. 2008. 'Ranking, Rating and Scoring of Tourism Journals: Interdisciplinary Challenges and Innovations'. *Tourism Management* 29: 66–78.

James, S. 2007. 'Constructing the Climb: Visitor Decision-making at Uluru'. *Geographical Research* 45: 398–407.

Jansen-Verbeke, M. 1999. 'Industrial Heritage: A Nexus for Sustainable Tourism Development'. *Tourism Geographies* 1: 70–85.

Jenkins, J. 1993. 'Fossickers and Rockhounds in Northern New South Wales'. In Weiler B. and Hall, C. M. (Eds) *Special Interest Tourism*. London: Belhaven Press, pp. 129–40.

Jennings, G. 2001. *Tourism Research*. Brisbane: John Wiley.

Jolliffe, L. (Ed.) 2007. *Tea and Tourism: Tourists, Traditions and Transformations*. Clevedon, UK: Channel View.

Johnston, C. 2005. 'Shoring the Foundations of the TALC in Tropical Island Destinations: Kona, Hawai'i'. In Butler, R. (Ed). *The Tourism Area Life Cycle: Theoretical and Conceptual Implications*. Clevedon, UK: Channel View, pp. 198–221.

Jones, P. & Phillips, D. 2003. 'What Use Is Research Anyway? Industry and Academe's Differing Views'. *International Journal of Contemporary Hospitality Management* 15: 290–3.

Jutla, R. 2000. 'Visual Image of the City: Tourists' Versus Residents' Perception of Simla, a Hill Station in Northern India'. *Tourism Geographies* 2: 404–20.

Ketchell, M. 2008. 'Australian Tourist Numbers Down'. February 7. www.news.com.au.

Kim, D., Lehto, X. & Morrison, A. 2007. 'Gender Differences in Online Travel Information Search: Implications for Marketing Communications on the Internet'. *Tourism Management* 28: 423–33.

Knill, G. 1991. 'Towards the Green Paradigm'. *South African Geographical Journal* 73: 52–9.

Kotler, P. & Keller, K. 2005. *Marketing Management*. Twelfth Edition. Sydney: Pearson.

Krueger, R. & Casey, M. A. 2000. *Focus Groups: A Practical Guide for Applied Research*. Third Edition. London: Sage.

Kuhn, T. 1962. *The Structure of Scientific Revolutions*. Chicago: University of Chicago Press.

Kurtzman, J. & Zauhar, J. 2003. 'Virtual Sport Tourism'. In Hudson, S. (Ed.) *Sport and Adventure Tourism*. Binghamton, USA: Haworth Hospitality Press, pp. 293–309.

Laesser, C. 2007. 'There is a Market for Destination Information Brochures — But is There a Future?' *Tourism Review* 62(3/4): 27–31.

Lattimore, R. & Pobke, C. 2008. 'Recent Trends in Australian Fertility'. Australian Government Productivity Commission. www.pc.gov.au.

Law, R. 2005. 'Hotel Database Marketing in Asia: Towards an Object-Oriented Approach'. *Journal of Travel & Tourism Marketing* 18(1): 59–66.

Laws, E. & Scott, N. 2003. 'Developing New Tourism Services: Dinosaurs, a New Drive Tourism Resource for Remote Regions?'. *Journal of Vacation Marketing* 9: 368–80.

Lawson, R. 1991. 'Patterns of Tourist Expenditure and Types of Vacation Across the Family Life Cycle'. *Journal of Travel Research* 30 (2): 12–18.

Lawton, L. & Weaver, D. 2009. 'Travel Agency Threats and Opportunities: The Perspective of Successful Owner'. *Journal of Hospitality and Tourism Administration* 10 (1), 68–92.

Leiper, N. 2000. 'An Emerging Discipline'. *Annals of Tourism Research* 27: 805–9.

Leiper, N. 2004. *Tourism Management*. Third Edition. Sydney: Pearson Education Australia.

Lennon, J. & Foley, M. 2000. *Dark Tourism: The Attraction of Death and Disaster*. London: Continuum.

Leung, P. & Lam, T. 2004. 'Crisis Management during the SARS Threat: A Case Study of the Metropole Hotel in Hong Kong'. *Journal of Human Resources in Hospitality and Tourism* 3: 47–57.

Littlefair, C. 2004. 'Reducing Impacts Through Interpretation, Lamington National Park'. In Buckley, R. (Ed.) *Environmental Impacts of Tourism*. Wallingford, UK: CABI Publishing, pp. 297–307.

Litvin, S. 2006. 'Revisiting Plog's Model of Allocentricity and Psychocentricity... One More Time'. *Cornell Hotel and Restaurant Administration Quarterly* 47: 245–53.

Litvin, S., Goldsmith, R. & Pan, B. 2008. Electronic Word-of-mouth in Hospitality and Tourism Management. *Tourism Management* 29: 458–68.

Lo, A. & Lam, T. 2004. 'Long-haul and Short-haul Outbound All-inclusive Package Tours'. *Asia Pacific Journal of Tourism Research* 9: 161–76.

Lockwood, A. & Medlik, S. 2001. *Tourism and Hospitality in the 21st Century*. Oxford: Butterworth–Heinemann.

Lovelock, B. (Ed.) 2008. *Tourism and the Consumption of Wildlife: Hunting, Shooting and Sport Fishing*. London: Routledge.

Lück, M. (Ed.) 2007a. *Nautical Tourism Development: Opportunities and Threats*. Elmsford, USA: Cognizant.

Lück, M. 2007b. 'The Cruise Ship Industry: Curse or Blessing?' In Lück, M. (Ed.) *Nautical Tourism: Concepts and Issues*. Elmsford, USA: Cognizant, pp. 75–82.

Lück, M. (Ed.) 2008. *The Encyclopedia of Tourism and Recreation in Marine Environments*. Wallingford: CABI.

Lundgren, J. 1984. 'Geographic Concepts and the Development of Tourism Research in Canada'. *GeoJournal* 9: 17–25.

Lundgren, J. 2005. 'An Empirical Interpretation of the TALC: Tourist Product Life Cycles in the Eastern Townships of Quebec'. In Butler, R. (Ed) *The Tourism Area Life Cycle: Theoretical and Conceptual Implications*. Clevedon, UK: Channel View, pp. 91–106.

Lynch, R. & Veal, A. 2006. *Australian Leisure*. Third Edition. Sydney: Longman.

Lyons, K. & Wearing, S. (Eds) 2008. *Journeys of Discovery in Volunteer Tourism: International Case Study Perspectives*. Wallingford, UK: CABI.

MacCannell, D. 1976. *The Tourist: A New Theory of the Leisure Class*. New York: Schocken Books.

Magazine Publishers of Australia 2005. 'Key Circulation Facts'. www.magazines.org.au.

Main, M. & Dearden, P. 2007. 'Tsunami Impacts on Phuket's Diving Industry: Geographical Implications for Marine Conservation'. *Coastal Management* 35: 467–81.

Mandelbaum, R. & Lerner, G. 2008. 'Hotel Operators Massage More Profits from Their Spa Operations'. *Cornell Hospitality Quarterly* 49 (2): 99–104.

Maoz, D. 2008. 'The Backpacking Journey of Israeli Women in Mid-life'. In Hannam, K. & Ateljevic, I. (Eds.). *Backpacker Tourism: Concepts and Profiles*. Clevedon, UK: Channel View, pp.188–98.

Marion, J. & Farrell, T. 1998. 'Managing Ecotourism Visitation in Protected Areas'. In Lindberg, K., Epler Wood, M. & Engeldrum, D. (Eds) *Ecotourism: A Guide for Planners and Managers. Volume 2*. North Bennington, VT, USA: The Ecotourism Society, pp. 155–81.

Market Economics Ltd. 2003. 'Summary of the Economic Impact of the 2003 America's Cup Defence'. Ministry of Tourism. www.tourism.govt.nz.

MarketWatch 2008. 'U.S., Australia Sign Open Skies Agreement'. www.marketwatch.com

Maslow, A. 1954. *Motivation and Personality*. New York: Harper & Row.

Mason, P. 2007. "No Better than a Band-aid for a Bullet Wound!': The Effectiveness of Tourism Codes of Conduct', In Black, R. & Crabtree, A. (Eds). *Quality Assurance and Certification in Ecotourism*. Wallingford, UK: CABI, pp. 46–64.

Matheson, C. 2008. 'Music, Emotion and Authenticity: A Study of Celtic Music Festival Consumers'. *Journal of Tourism and Cultural Change* 6: 57–74.

Mathieson, A. & Wall, G. 2006. *Tourism: Change, Impacts and Opportunities*. Harlow: Pearson Prentice Hall.

Maurer, E. 2000. 'Presenting the American Indian: From Europe to America'. In Kawasaki, A. (Ed.). *The Changing Presentation of the American Indian: Museums and Native Cultures*. Washington: Smithsonian Institution, pp. 15–28.

Mazur, N. 2001. *After the Ark? Environmental Policy-making and the Zoo*. Carlton South, Victoria: Melbourne University Press.

Mbaiwa, J. 2005. 'Enclave Tourism and its Socio-economic Impacts in the Okavango Delta, Botswana'. *Tourism Management* 26: 157–72.

McAvoy, L. 2002. 'American Indians, Place Meanings and the Old/New West'. *Journal of Leisure Research* 34: 383–96.

McDonald, M. 2005. 'Tourist Weddings in Hawai'i'. In Cartier, C. & Lew, A. (Eds) *Seductions of Place: Geographical Perspectives on Globalization and Touristed Landscapes*. London: Routledge, pp. 171–92.

McKercher, B. 1993. 'The Unrecognised Threat to Tourism: Can Tourism Survive "Sustainability"?' *Tourism Management* 14: 131–6.

McKercher, B. 2001. 'The Business of Ecotourism'. In Weaver, D. B. (Ed.) *The Encyclopedia of Ecotourism*. Wallingford, UK: CABI Publishing, pp. 565–77.

McKercher, B. 2003. 'SIP (SARS Induced Panic): A Greater Threat to Tourism Than SARS (Severe Acute Respiratory Syndrome)'. *e–Review of Tourism Research* 1 (1). http://ertr.tamu.edu.

McKercher, B. & Lew, A. 2003. 'Distance Decay and the Impact of Effective Tourism Exclusion Zones on International Travel Flows'. *Journal of Travel Research* 42: 159–65.

McKercher, B. & Tang, E. 2004. 'The Challenges of Developing Transit Tourism'. *Asia Pacific Journal of Tourism Research* 9: 151–60.

McNichol, D. 2005. *The Roads that Built America: The Incredible Story of the U.S. Interstate System*. New York: Sterling.

Meyer-Arendt, K. & Justice, C. 2002. 'Tourism as the Subject of North American Doctoral Dissertations, 1987–2000'. *Annals of Tourism Research* 29: 1171–4.

Miller, G. & Twining-Ward, L. 2005. *Monitoring for a Sustainable Tourism Transition: The Challenge of Developing and Using Indicators*. Wallingford, UK: CABI.

Miller, M. L. & Kaae, B. 1993. 'Coastal and Marine Ecotourism: A Formula for Sustainable Development?' *Trends* 30 (2): 35–41.

Mills, J., Han, J-H., & Clay, J. 2008. 'Accessibility of Hospitality and Tourism Websites'. *Cornell Hospitality Quarterly* 49: 28–41.

Ministry of Tourism 2008a. New Zealand Tourism Strategy 2015. www.nztourismstrategy.com.

Ministry of Tourism 2008b. Accessing New Zealand's Official Tourism Data. www.tourismresearch.govt.nz.

Modsching, M., Kramer, R., Ten Hagen, K. & Gretzel, U. 2008. 'Using Location-based Tracking Data to Analyze the Movements of City Tourists'. *Information Technology & Tourism* 10: 31–42.

Moeller, G. & Shafer, E. 1994. 'The Delphi Technique: A Tool for Long-Range Travel and Tourism Planning'. In Ritchie, J. R. Brent & Goeldner, C. R. (Eds) *Travel, Tourism, and Hospitality Research: A Handbook for Managers and Researchers*. Second Edition. Chichester, UK: John Wiley, pp. 473–80.

Morgan, N. & Pritchard, A. 2000. *Advertising in Tourism and Leisure*. Oxford: Butterworth–Heinemann.

Morgan, N., Pritchard, A. & Piggott, R. 2002. 'New Zealand, 100% Pure. The Creation of a Powerful Niche Destination Brand'. *Brand Management* 4: 335–54.

Morgan, N., Pritchard, A. & Pride, R. (Eds) 2004. *Destination Branding: Creating the Unique Destination Proposition*. Second Edition. Sydney: Elsevier.

Morrison, A. 2009. *Hospitality and Travel Marketing*. Fourth Edition. Albany, New York, US: Delmar Thomson Learning.

Morrision, J. 2004. 'Give Me Liberty or Give Me a Massage?' *American Way*. www.americanwaymag.com.

Mowforth, M. & Munt, I. 2003. *Tourism and Sustainability: Development and New Tourism in the Third World*. Second Edition. London: Routledge.

Nanda, D., Hu, C. & Bai, B. 2006. 'Exploring Family Roles in Purchasing Decisions During Vacation Planning: Review and Discussions for Future Research'. *Journal of Travel & Tourism Marketing* 20: 107–25.

National Visitor Safety Program 2008. 'National Visitor Safety Handbook'. Tourism Australia. www.tourism.australia.com.

NationMaster.com 2008. 'Economy Statistics'. www.nationmaster.com.

Neuman, W. L. 1997. *Social Research Methods: Qualitative and Quantitative Approaches*. Third Edition. London: Allyn and Bacon.

Newsome, D., Moore, S. & Dowling, R. 2002. *Natural Area Tourism: Ecology, Impacts and Management*. Clevedon, UK: Channel View Publications.

Nielsen, C. 2001. *Tourism and the Media*. Melbourne: Hospitality Press.

OECD 1980. *The Impact of Tourism on Development*. Paris: Organisation for Economic Cooperation and Development.

Ollenburg, C. 2008. 'Regional Signatures and Trends in the Farm Tourism Sector'. *Tourism Recreation Research* 33: 13–23.

ONT 1998. *A Monthly Facts Sheet on the Economic Impact of Tourism & The Latest Visitor Arrival Trends*. Canberra: Office of National Tourism. August.

Oppermann, M. 1995. 'Models of Tourist Flow Destinations'. *Journal of Travel Research* 33 (4): 57–61.

Oppermann, M. 1998. 'Service Attributes of Travel Agencies: A Comparative Perspective of Users and Providers'. *Journal of Vacation Marketing* 4: 265–81.

Orams, M. 2002. 'Marine Ecotourism as a Potential Agent for Sustainable Development in Kaikoura, New Zealand'. *International Journal of Sustainable Development* 5: 338–52.

Ospina, G. 2006. 'War and Ecotourism in the National Parks of Colombia: Some Reflections on the Public Risk and Adventure'. *International Journal of Tourism Research* 8: 241–46.

Oster, J. 2006. 'Aboriginal Community Art as Sustainable Business'. desART. www.desart.com.au.

Parsons, C. 1996. 'Tourism, Whale Watching and the Federal Government'. In Colgan, K., Prasser, S. & Jeffery, A. (Eds) *Encounters with Whales. 1995 Proceedings*. Canberra: Australian Nature Conservation Agency, pp. 87–92.

Patterson, I. 2006. *Growing Older: Tourism and Leisure Behaviour of Older Adults*. Wallingford: CABI.

PATA n.d. *Code for Environmentally Responsible Tourism*. San Francisco: PATA.

Peckham, V. 2003. *BEST Community Profile: The Shaw Heritage Tours*. The Conference Board and WTTC.

Peeters, P. (Ed.) 2007. *Tourism and Climate Change: Methods, Greenhouse Gas Reductions and Policies*. Breda, The Netherlands: Stichting NHTV.

Phillips, M. 2001. 'Working Longer, Working Harder? You're Not Alone'. *Weekend Bulletin* (Gold Coast), 17–18 February, p. 30.

Plog, S. 1991. *Leisure Travel: Making it a Growth Market — Again!* Chichester, UK: John Wiley.

Plog, S. 1998. 'Why Destination Preservation Makes Economic Sense'. In Theobald, W. (Ed.) *Global Tourism*. Second Edition. Oxford: Butterworth–Heinemann, pp. 251–66.

Plog, S. 2004. *Leisure Travel: A Marketing Handbook*. Upper Saddle River, NJ, USA: Pearson Prentice Hall, p. 51.

Plog, S. 2005. 'Targeting Segments: More Important than Ever in the Travel Industry'. In Theobald, W. (Ed.) *Global Tourism*. Third Edition. Sydney: Elsevier, pp. 271–93.

Pocock, E. 2008. 'World's Largest Shopping Malls'. www.easternct.edu.

Prideaux, B. 2003. 'International Tourists and Transport Safety'. In Wilks, J. & Page, S. (Eds). *Managing Tourist Health and Safety in the New Millennium*. London: Pergamon, pp. 143–54.

Prideaux, B. & Cooper, M. (Eds) 2009. *River Tourism*. Wallingford, UK: CABI.

Qualmark® 2008. New Zealand's Official Quality Tourism Website. www.qualmark.co.nz.

Queensland Government 2007. 'Gold Coast Marine Development Project: Northern Development Area'. www.infrastructure.qld.gov.au.

Ragin, C. 1994. *Constructing Social Research*. Thousand Oaks, CA, USA: Pine Forge Press.

Raj, R. & Morpeth, N. (Eds) 2007. *Religious Tourism and Pilgrimage Festivals Management*. Wallingford, UK: CABI.

Ralf, K. 2000. *Business Cycles: Market Structure and Market Interaction*. Heidelberg, Germany: Physica–Verlag.

Ranck, S. 1987. 'An Attempt at Autonomous Development: The Case of the Tufi Guest Houses, Papua New Guinea'. In Britton, S. & Clarke, W. (Eds) *Ambiguous Alternative: Tourism in Small Developing Countries*. Suva, Fiji: University of the South Pacific, pp. 154–66.

Raybould, M., Mules, T., Fredline, E. & Tomljenovic, R. 2000. 'Counting the Herd. Using Aerial Photography to Estimate Attendance at Open Events'. *Event Management* 6: 25–32.

Raymond, E. & Hall, C. 2008. 'The Development of Cross-cultural (Mis)understanding through Volunteer Tourism'. *Journal of Sustainable Tourism* 16: 530–43.

Richards, G. & Wilson, J. (Eds) 2004. *The Global Nomad: Backpacker Travel in Theory and Practice*. Clevedon, UK: Channel View.

Richardson, J. & Fluker, M. 2008. Understanding and Managing Tourism. Second edition. Frenchs Forest, NSW: Pearson Australia.

Rigby, M. 2001. 'Graceland: A Sacred Place in a Secular World?' In Cusack, C. and Oldmeadow, P. (Eds) *The End of Religions? Religion in an Age of Globalization*. Sydney: University of Sydney, pp. 155–68.

Ritchie, B. 2005. 'Longitudinal research methods'. In Ritchie, B., Burns, P. & Palmer, C. (Eds) *Tourism Research Methods: Integrating Theory with Practice*. Wallingford, UK: CABI, pp. 131–48.

Rogerson, C. 2004. 'Urban Tourism and Small Tourism Enterprise Development in Johannesburg: The Case of Township Tourism'. *GeoJournal* 60: 249–57.

Rojek, C. 1993. *Ways of Escape: Modern Transformations in Leisure and Travel*. Basingstoke, UK: Macmillan.

Rosenwald, M. 2005. 'At Chic Hotels, You Can Take It With You'. *Washington Post*, 5 December, p. A01.

Ross, K. 2000. 'Booming Marketplace: 13 Truths About Baby Boomer Travel'. Association of Travel Marketing Executives. www.atme.org.

Russell, R. & Faulkner, B. 1998. 'Reliving the Destination Life Cycle in Coolangatta'. In Laws, E., Faulkner, B. & Moscardo, G. (Eds) *Embracing and Managing Change in Tourism: International Case Studies*. London: Routledge, pp. 95–115.

Russell, R. & Faulkner, B. 2004. 'Entrepreneurship, Chaos and the Tourism Area Lifecycle'. *Annals of Tourism Research* 31: 556–79.

Ryan, C. 1995. *Researching Tourist Satisfaction*. London: Routledge.

Sarantakos, S. 2004. *Social Research*. Third Edition. Melbourne: Macmillan Education.

Sax, L., Gilmartin, S., & Bryant, A. 2003. 'Assessing Response Rates and Nonresponse Bias in Web and Paper Surveys'. *Research in Higher Education,* 44: 409–32.

Scott, N. 2006. 'Management of Tourism: Conformation to Whose Standards?' In Prideaux, B., Moscardo, G. & Laws, E. (Eds). *Managing Tourism and Hospitality Services: Theory and International Applications*. Wallingford, UK: CABI, pp. 54–61.

Semuels, A. 2008. 'Baz Luhrmann's 'Australia' to be Part of Epic Tourism Campaign'. *The Huffington Post*, July 29. www.huffingtonpost.com.

Sengupta, A. & Nundy, S. 2005. 'The Private Health Sector in India is Burgeoning, but at the Cost of Public Health Care'. *British Medical Journal* 331: 1157–58.

Shafer, E. & Moeller, G. 1974. 'Through the Looking Glass in Environmental Management'. *Parks and Recreation* 9 (2): 20–3, 48–9.

Sharpley, R. 2007. 'Flagship Attractions and Sustainable Rural Tourism Development: The Case of the Alnwick Garden, England'. *Journal of Sustainable Tourism* 15: 125–43.

Shaw, G. & Williams, A. 2002. *Critical Issues in Tourism: A Geographical Perspective*. Second Edition. London: Blackwell.

Sinclair, D. 2003. 'Developing Indigenous Tourism: Challenges for the Guianas'. *International Journal of Contemporary Hospitality Management* 15: 140–6.

Singh, S. 2004. 'Religion, Heritage and Travel: Case References From the Indian Himalayas'. *Current Issues in Tourism* 7: 44–65.

Singh, S., Timothy, D. & Dowling, R. (Eds) 2003. *Tourism in Destination Communities*. Wallingford, UK: CABI Publishing.

The Sydney Morning Herald 2007. 'Sunshine Coast Council Scraps Schoolies'. www.smh.com.au.

Smith, C. & Jenner, P. 2000. 'Health Tourism in Europe'. *Travel & Tourism Analyst*, No. 1, pp. 41–59.

Smith, R. & Henderson, J. 2008. 'Integrated Beach Resorts, Informal Tourism Commerce and the 2004 Tsunami: Laguna Phuket in Thailand'. *International Journal of Tourism Research* 10: 271–82.

Smith, V. L. 1989. *Hosts and Guests: The Anthropology of Tourism*. Second Edition. Philadelphia: University of Pennsylvania Press.

Smith, V. L. 2004. 'Tourism and Terrorism: The "New War"'. In Aramberri, J. and Butler, R. (Eds) *Tourism Development: Issues for a Vulnerable Industry*. Clevedon, UK: Channel View, pp. 275–90.

Social Investment Forum 2007. Social Investment Forum. www.socialinvest.org.

Spiegel Online 2007. 'US Plans New Travel Restrictions for Europeans'. www.spiegel.de.

STCRC 2008. 'Climate Change Project'. Sustainable Tourism Cooperative Research Centre. www.crctourism.com.au.

Stewart, J., Bramble, L. & Ziraldo, D. 2008. 'Key Challenges in Wine and Culinary Tourism with Practical Recommendations'. *International Journal of Contemporary Hospitality Management* 20: 303–12.

Stitt, B., Nichols, M. & Giacopassi, D. 2005. 'Perceptions of Casinos as Disruptive Influences in USA Communities'. *International Journal of Tourism Research* 7: 187–200.

Stonehouse, B. & Crosbie, K. 1995. 'Tourist Impacts and Management in the Antarctic Peninsula Area'. In Hall, C. M. and Johnston, M. (Eds) *Polar Tourism: Tourism in the Arctic and Antarctic Regions*. Chichester, UK: John Wiley, pp. 217–33.

Stumbo, N. & Pegg, S. 2005. 'Travelers and Tourists With Disabilities: A Matter of Priorities and Loyalties'. *Tourism Review International* 8: 195–209.

Svenson, S. 2004. 'The Cottage and the City: An Interpretation of the Canadian Second Home Experience'. In Hall, C.M. and Müller, D. (Eds). *Tourism, Mobility and Second Homes: Between Elite Landscape and Common Ground*. Clevedon, UK: Channel View, pp. 55–74.

Tahana, N. & Oppermann, M. 1998. 'Maori Cultural Performances and Tourism'. *Tourism Recreation Research* 23 (1): 23–30.

Teo, P. 1994. 'Assessing Socio-Cultural Impacts: The Case of Singapore.' *Tourism Management* 15 (2): 126–36.

Tepelus, C. 2008. 'Social Responsibility and Innovation on Trafficking and Child Sex Tourism: Morphing of Practice into Sustainable Tourism Policies?' *Tourism and Hospitality Research* 8: 98–115.

Thompson, E. P. 1967. 'Time, Work Discipline and Industrial Capitalism'. *Past and Present* 38: 56–97.

Thrane, C. 2008. 'Earnings Differentiation in the Tourism Industry: Gender, Human Capital and Socio-demographic Effects'. *Tourism Management* 29: 514–24.

Timothy, D. & Tosun, C. 2003. 'Tourists' Perceptions of the Canada–USA Border as a Barrier to Tourism at the International Peace Garden'. *Tourism Management* 24: 411–21.

Toh, R., Khan, H. & Koh, A. 2001. 'A Travel Balance Approach for Examining Tourism Area Life Cycles: The Case of Singapore'. *Journal of Travel Research* 29: 426–32.

Tomljenovic, R. & Faulkner, B. 2000. 'Tourism and World Peace: A Conundrum for the Twenty–first Century.' In Faulkner, B., Moscardo, G. & Laws, E. (Eds). *Tourism in the 21st Century: Lessons from Experience*. London: Continuum, pp. 18–33.

Toohey, K. & Veal, A. 2007. 'The Ancient Olympics and Their Relevance to the Modern Games.' In Toohey, K. & Veal, A. (Eds). *The Olympic Games: A Social Science Perspective*. Wallingford, UK: CABI, pp. 9–25.

Torres, R. 2003. 'Linkages Between Tourism and Agriculture in Mexico'. *Annals of Tourism Research* 30: 546–66.

Tourism Australia 2003. 'China: ADS Visitor Experience Study 2003'. www.tourism.australia.com.

Tourism Australia 2004. 'Top Ten: Activities (Market Insights Tourism Facts)'. www.tourism.australia.com.

Tourism Australia 2005. 'About Tourism Australia'. www.tourism. australia.com.

Tourism Australia 2006a. 'So Where the Bloody Hell are You? Tourism Australia Invites the World to Australia'. www.tourism.australia.com.

Tourism Australia 2006b. 'Thanks a 'Bloody' Lot!' www.tourism.australia.com.

Tourism Australia 2006c. '60 000 Brits Can't Be Wrong — UK Lifts Tourism Ad Ban'. www.tourism.australia.com.

Tourism Australia 2006d. "So Where the Bloody Hell Are You?' Campaign Moving Forward'. www.tourism.australia.com.

Tourism Australia 2007. 'International Market Tourism Facts: December 2006 — Top Ten Activities'. www.tourism.australia.com.

Tourism Australia. 2008a. 'China'. www.tourism.australia.com.

Tourism Australia. 2008b. 'China Aviation Profile: Understanding How Chinese Tourists Travel to Australia'. www.tourism.australia.com.

Tourism Australia 2008c. 'China: Country Overview'. www.tourism.australia.com.

Tourism Australia 2008d. 'Baz Luhrmann's "Australia" Huge Promotion Opportunity for Australia'. www.tourism.australia.com.

Tourism Queensland 2007. 'Tourism Queensland Annual Report 2006–2007'. www.tq.com.au.

Towner, J. 1996. *An Historical Geography of Recreation and Tourism in the Western World 1540–1940*. Chichester, UK: John Wiley.

Towner, J. 2002. 'Literature, Tourism and the Grand Tour'. In Robinson, M. & Andersen, H. (Eds). *Literature and Tourism: Reading and Writing Tourism Texts*. London: Continuum, pp. 226–38.

TRA 2007a. 'Forecast 2007 Issue 2'. www.tourism.australia.com.

TRA 2007b. 'Travel by Australians, December 2007: Quarterly Results of the National Visitation Survey'. www.tra.australia.com.

TRA 2007c. 'Outbound Trips: Domestic Market Tourism Facts, Year Ending March 2007'. www.tra.australia.com.

TRA 2008a. 'Travel by Australians, March 2008: Quarterly Results of the National Visitation Survey'. www.tra.australia.com.

TRA 2008b. 'International Visitors in Australia, March 2008: Quarterly Results of the International Visitation Survey'. www.tra.australia.com.

TRA 2008c. 'Snapshot: Backpackers in Australia 2007.' www.tra.australia.com.

TRA 2008d. 'Domestic Tourism Facts, Year Ended December 2007: Activities'. www.tra.australia.com.

TRA 2008e. 'Japan Visitor Profile 2007'. www.tra.australia.com.

TRA 2008f. 'China Visitor Profile 2007'. www.tra.australia.com.

TRA 2008g. 'International Visitors in Australia, December 2007: Quarterly Results of the International Visitor Survey'. www.tra.australia.com.

TRA 2008h. 'Tourism Research Australia'. www.tra.australia.com.

Tremblay, P. 2001. 'Wildlife Tourism Consumption: Consumptive or Non-consumptive?' *International Journal of Tourism Research* 3: 81–6.

Tremblay, P., Boyle, A., Rigby, H. & Haydon, J. 2006. *Assessing the Value and Contribution of the Darwin Festival 2004*. Gold Coast, Australia: Sustainable Tourism CRC.

Tribe, A. 2004. 'Zoo Tourism'. In Higginbottom, K. (Ed.) *Wildlife Tourism: Impacts, Management and Planning*. Altona, Vic.: Common Ground Publishing, pp. 35–56.

Tribe, J. (Ed.) 2009. *Philosophical Issues in Tourism*. Clevedon, UK: Channel View.

Tse, A. 2003. 'Disintermediation of Travel Agents in the Hotel Industry'. *International Journal of Hospitality Management* 22: 453–60.

TTF 2007. *Submission on the Tourism Action Plan on Climate Change*. Sydney: Tourism & Transport Forum.

TTF 2008a. *Driving Tourism Demand: Laying the Foundations for a Profitable Future*. Sydney: Tourism & Transport Forum.

TTF 2008b. *National Aviation Policy: Aviation and the National Interest*. Sydney: Tourism & Transport Forum.

TTF 2008c. *National Tourism Infrastructure Priorities*. Sydney: Tourism & Transport Forum.

TTF 2008d. *National Tourism Employment Atlas '08*. Sydney: Tourism & Transport Forum.

Turco, D. 1999. 'Ya' 'At 'Eeh: A Profile of Tourists to Navajo Nation'. *Journal of Tourism Studies* 10(2): 57–68.

Turner, L. & Ash, J. 1975. *The Golden Hordes: International Tourism and the Pleasure Periphery*. London: Constable.

Turpie, J. & Joubert, A. 2004. 'The Value of Flower Tourism on the Bokkeveld Plateau — a Botanical Hotspot'. *Development Southern Africa* 21: 645–62.

Um, S. & Crompton, J. 1990. 'Attitude Determinants in Tourism Destination Choice'. *Annals of Tourism Research* 24: 432–48.

UNWTO. 2008. *UNWTO World Tourism Barometer*. Volume 6, Number 2, June. Madrid: World Tourism Organization.

Urbanowicz, C. F. 1989. 'Tourism in Tonga Revisited: Continued Troubled Times?' In Smith, V. L. (Ed.) *Hosts and Guests: The Anthropology of Tourism*. Second Edition. Philadelphia: University of Pennsylvania Press, pp. 105–17.

US Bureau of the Census. 1999. *World Population Profile: 1998*. WP/98. Washington, DC: US Government Printing Office.

Vaessen, S. 2008. 'Tourism Leaves Bali's Poor Facing Drought'. http://english.aljazeera.net.

Valentine, P. & Birtles, A. 2004. 'Wildlife Watching'. In Higginbottom, K. (Ed.) *Wildlife Tourism: Impacts, Management and Planning*. Altona, Vic.: Common Ground Publishing, pp. 15–34.

Van Doren, C., Koh, Y. K. & McCahill, A. 1994. 'Tourism Research: A State-Of-The-Art Citation Analysis (1971–1990)'. In Seaton, A. V. et al. (Eds) *Tourism: The State of the Art*. New York: John Wiley, pp. 308–15.

Vidal, J. 2005. 'Scorched Earth'. www.guardian.co.uk.

Visser, G. 2003. 'Gay Men, Tourism and Urban Space: Reflections on Africa's "Gay Capital"'. *Tourism Geographies* 5: 168–89.

Vlahakis, V., Ioannidis, N., Karigiannis, J., Tsotros, M., Gounaris, M., Stricker, D., Gleue, T., Döhne, P. & Almeida, L. 2002. 'Archeoguide: An Augmented Reality Guide for Archaeological Sites'. *IEEE Computer Graphics and Applications* 22 (5): 52–60.

Waitt, G. 2004. 'A Critical Examination of Sydney's 2000 Olympic Games'. In Yeoman, I., Robertson, M., Ali-Knight, J., Drummond, S. & McMahon-Beattie, U. (Eds). *Festival and Events Management: An International Arts and Culture Perspective*. Sydney: Elsevier, pp. 391–408.

Waitt, G. & McGuirk, P. 1996. 'Marking Time: Tourism and Heritage Representation at Millers Point, Sydney'. *Australian Geographer* 27: 11–29.

Waitt, G. & Markwell, K. 2006. *Gay Tourism: Culture and Context*. New York: Haworth.

Walmsley, D. J. & Jenkins, J. M. 1993. 'Appraisive Images of Tourist Areas: Application of Personal Constructs'. *Australian Geographer* 24 (2): 1–13.

Walsh, J., Jamrozy, U. & Burr, S. 2001. 'Sense of Place as a Component of Sustainable Tourism Marketing'. In McCool, S. & Moisey, R. (Eds) *Tourism, Recreation and Sustainability*. Wallingford, UK: CABI Publishing, pp. 195–216.

Wang, K.-C., Hsieh, A.-T., Yeh, Y.-C. & Tsai, C.-W. 2004. 'Who is the Decision-Maker: The Parents or the Child in Group Package Tours?' *Tourism Management* 25: 183–94.

Wang, Y. & Sheldon, P. 1995. 'The Sleeping Dragon Awakes: The Outbound Chinese Travel Market'. *Journal of Travel & Tourism Marketing* 4 (4): 41–54.

Wang, Y. & Wall, G. 2007. 'Administrative Arrangements and Displacement Compensation in Top-down Tourism Planning — A Case from Hainan Province, China'. *Tourism Management* 28: 70–82.

Wanhill, S. 2005. 'Role of Government Incentives' In Theobald, W. (Ed.) *Global Tourism*. Third Edition. Sydney: Elsevier, pp. 367–90.

WCED (World Commission on Environment and Development). 1987. *Our Common Future*. Oxford: Oxford University Press.

Wearing, S. 2001. *Volunteer Tourism: Experiences that Make a Difference*. Wallingford, UK: CABI Publishing.

Weaver, D. 1988. 'The Evolution of a 'Plantation' Tourism Landscape on the Caribbean Island of Antigua'. *Tijdschrift voor Economische en Sociale Geografie* 70: 319–31.

Weaver, D. 1990. 'Grand Cayman Island and the Resort Cycle Concept'. *Journal of Travel Research* 29 (2): 9–15.

Weaver, D. 1993. 'Ecotourism in the Small Island Caribbean'. *GeoJournal* 31: 457–65.

Weaver, D. 1998. *Ecotourism in the Less Developed World*. Wallingford, UK: CAB International.

Weaver, D. 2000a. 'The Exploratory War-distorted Destination Life Cycle'. *International Journal of Tourism Research* 2: 151–61.

Weaver, D. 2000b. 'A Broad Context Model of Destination Development Scenarios'. *Tourism Management* 21: 217–24.

Weaver, D. 2004. 'The Contribution of International Students to Tourism Beyond the Core Educational Experience: Evidence from Australia'. *Tourism Review International* 7: 95–105.

Weaver, D. 2005. 'The 'Plantation' Variant of the TALC in the Small-island Caribbean'. In Butler, R. (Ed.) *The Tourism Area Life Cycle: Theoretical and Conceptual Implications*. Clevedon, UK: Channel View, pp. 185–97.

Weaver, D. 2006. *Sustainable Tourism: Theory and Practice*. London: Elsevier.

Weaver, D. 2007. 'Toward Sustainable Mass Tourism: Paradigm Shift or Paradigm Nudge?' *Tourism Recreation Research* 32(3): 65–69.

Weaver, D. 2008. *Ecotourism*. Second Edition. Brisbane: Wiley Australia.

Weaver, D. 2010, 'Indigenous tourism stages and their implications for sustainability', *Journal of Sustainable Tourism* (forthcoming).

Weaver, D. & Lawton, L. J. 2001. 'Resident Perceptions in the Urban-Rural Fringe'. *Annals of Tourism Research* 28: 439–58.

Weaver, D. & Lawton, L. J. 2002. 'Overnight Ecotourist Market Segmentation in the Gold Coast Hinterland of Australia'. *Journal of Travel Research* 40: 270–80.

Weaver, D. & Lawton, L. 2007. '"Just Because It's Gone Doesn't Mean It Isn't There Anymore': Planning for Attraction Residuality'. *Tourism Management* 28: 108–17.

Weaver, D. & Lawton, L. 2008. 'Not Just Surviving, but Thriving: Perceived Strengths of Successful US-based Travel Agencies'. *International Journal of Tourism Research* 10: 41–53.

Weber, K. & Ladkin, A. 2003. 'The Convention Industry in Australia and the United Kingdom: Key Issues and Competitive Forces'. *Journal of Travel Research* 42: 125–32.

Webster, K. 2000. *Environmental Management in the Hospitality Industry: A Guide for Students and Managers*. London: Cassell.

Weedon, C. 2005. 'A Qualitative Approach to the Ethical Consumer: The Use of Focus Groups for Cognitive Consumer Research in Tourism'. In Ritchie, B., Burns, P. & Palmer, C. (Eds) *Tourism Research Methods: Integrating Theory with Practice*. Wallingford, UK: CABI, pp. 179–90.

Westwood, S., Pritchard, A. & Morgan, N. 2000. 'Gender-blind Marketing: Businesswomen's Perceptions of Airline Services'. *Tourism Management* 21: 353–62.

Whetton, P., Haylock, M. & Galloway, R. 1996. 'Climate Change and Snow–cover Duration in the Australian Alps'. *Climate Change* 32: 447–79.

Whyte, B. 2008. 'Visa-free Travel Privileges: An Exploratory Geographical Analysis'. *Tourism Geographies* 10: 127–49.

Wilks, J. & Page, S. (Eds) 2003. *Managing Tourist Health and Safety in the New Millennium*. London: Pergamon.

Wilson, J. & Richards, G. 2008. 'Suspending Reality: An Exploration of Enclaves and the Backpacker Experience'. In Hannam, K. & Ateljevic, I. (Eds.). *Backpacker Tourism: Concepts and Profiles*. Clevedon, UK: Channel View, pp. 9–25.

Winter, C. 2007. 'Tourism, Nation and Power: A Foucauldian Perspective of 'Australia's' Ghan Train'. In Church, A. & Coles, T. (Eds). *Tourism, Power and Space*. London: Routledge, pp. 101–21.

Wiseman, J. 2008. 'Murray Diversion Would Kill $1bn Worth of Crops'. *The Australian*, 3 September, pp. 1, 6.

Withey, L. 1997. *Grand Tours and Cook's Tours: A History of Leisure Travel 1750 to 1915*. London: Autum Press.

WTO 1996a. *Compendium of Tourism Statistics*. Seventeenth Edition. Madrid: World Tourism Organization.

WTO 1996b. *What Tourism Managers Need to Know: A Practical Guide to the Development and Use of Indicators of Sustainable Tourism*. Madrid: World Tourism Organization.

WTO 1998. *Yearbook of Tourism Statistics. Volume One*. Fiftieth Edition. Madrid: World Tourism Organization.

WTO 2004. *Indicators of Sustainable Development for Tourism Destinations: A Guidebook*. Madrid: World Tourism Organization.

Yau, K., McKercher, B., & Packer, T. 2004. 'Traveling with a Disability — More Than an Access Issue'. *Annals of Tourism Research* 31: 946–60.

Zakai, D. & Chadwick-Furman, N. 2002. 'Impacts of Intensive Recreational Diving on Reef Corals at Eilat, Northern Red Sea'. *Biological Conservation* 105: 179–87.

Zeppel, H. 1998. 'Land and Culture: Sustainable Tourism and Indigenous Peoples'. In Hall, C. & Lew, A. (Eds). *Sustainable Tourism: A Geographical Perspective*. Harlow, Longman, pp. 60–74.

Zhang, G., Pine, R. & Zhang, H. 2000. 'China's International Tourism Development: Present and Future'. *International Journal of Contemporary Hospitality Management* 12: 282–90.

Zhong, L., Deng, J. & Xiang, B. 2008. 'Tourism Development and the Tourism Area Life-cycle Model: A Case Study of Zhangjiajie National Forest Park, China'. *Tourism Management* 29: 841–56.

■ GLOSSARY

3S tourism a tourism product based on the provision of sea, sand and sun; that is, focusing on beach resorts. (p. 82)

8P model a product-focused marketing mix model that incorporates place, product, people, price, packaging, programming, promotion and partnerships. (p. 197)

Academic discipline a systematic field of study that is informed by a particular set of theories and methodologies in its attempt to reveal and expand relevant knowledge; e.g. psychology examines individual behaviour, while geography examines spatial patterns and relationships. (p. 6)

Accommodation within the context of the tourism industry, commercial facilities primarily intended to host stayover tourists for overnight stays. (p. 140)

Accreditation the process by which the ecolabel is determined by an overarching organisation to meet specified standards of quality and credibility. (p. 309)

Adaptancy platform a follow-up on the cautionary platform that argues for alternative forms of tourism deemed to be better adapted to local communities than mass tourism. (p. 11)

Advocacy platform the view that tourism is an inherent benefit to communities that should be developed under free market principles. (p. 10)

Alternative tourism the major contribution of the adaptancy platform, alternative tourism as an ideal type is characterised by its contrast with mass tourism. (p. 310)

Amenity migrants people who move to an area because of its recreational and lifestyle amenities, including comfortable weather and beautiful scenery; amenity migrants are usually first exposed to such places through their own tourist experiences. (p. 258)

Applied research research that addresses some particular problem or attempts to achieve a particular set of outcomes; it is usually constrained by set time schedules. (p. 331)

Attraction attributes characteristics of an attraction that are relevant to the management of an area as a tourist destination and thus should be periodically measured and monitored; includes ownership, orientation, spatial configuration, authenticity, scarcity, status, carrying capacity, accessibility, market and image. (p. 132)

Attraction inventory a systematic list of the tourist attractions found in a particular destination. (p. 115)

Avalanche effect the process whereby a small incremental change in a system triggers a disproportionate and usually unexpected response. (p. 302)

Baby boomers people born during the post–World War II period of high TFRs (roughly 1946 to 1964), who constitute a noticeable bulge within the population pyramid of Australia and other Phase Four countries. (p. 66)

Backstage the opposite of frontstage; areas of the destination where personal or intragroup activities occur, such as noncommercialised cultural performances. A particular space may be designated as either frontstage or backstage depending on the time of day or year. (p. 243)

Backward linkages sectors of an economy that provide goods and services for the tourism sector; includes agriculture, fisheries and construction. (p. 220)

Basic research research that is broadly focused on the revelation of new knowledge, and is not directed towards specific outcomes or problems. (p. 331)

Basic whole tourism system an application of a systems approach to tourism, wherein tourism is seen as consisting of three geographical components (origin, transit and destination regions), tourists and a tourism industry, embedded within a modifying external environment that includes parallel political, social, physical and other systems. (p. 20)

Behavioural segmentation the identification of tourist markets on the basis of activities and actions undertaken during the actual tourism experience. (p. 170)

Benchmark an indicator value, often based on some past desirable state, against which subsequent change in that indicator can be gauged. (p. 302)

BRIC countries Brazil, Russia, India and China, which had a collective population of about 2.7 billion in 2008 and are expected to achieve Burton's Phase Four status within two decades. (p. 60)

Broad context model of destination development scenarios a framework for modelling the evolution of tourist destinations, which takes into account scale and sustainability-related regulations; various transformations are possible among four ideal tourism types CAT, DAT, UMT (unsustainable mass tourism) and SMT (sustainable mass tourism). (p. 319)

Butler sequence the most widely cited and applied destination cycle model, which proposes five stages of cyclical evolution described by an S-shaped curve; these might then be followed by three other possible scenarios. (p. 268)

Carrying capacity the amount of tourism activity (e.g. number of visitors, amount of development) that can be accommodated without incurring serious harm to a destination; distinctions can be made between social, cultural and environmental carrying capacity, all of which can be adjusted with appropriate management. (p. 247)

Cautionary platform a reaction to the advocacy platform that stresses the negative impacts of tourism and the consequent need for strict regulation. (p. 11)

Certification the outcome of a process in which an independent third party verifies that a product or company meets specified standards, allowing it to be certified by the ecolabel. (p. 309)

Circumstantial alternative tourism (CAT) alternative tourism that results by default from the fact that the destination is currently situated within the early, low-intensity stages of the resort cycle. (p. 311)

Climate change the gradual increase in global surface temperatures that is usually attributed to the excessive release of heat-trapping greenhouse gases through human activity such as the burning of fossil fuels. (p. 256)

Codes of practice commonly developed and espoused by tourism corporations and industry associations, these are intended to provide general guidelines for achieving sustainability-related outcomes. (p. 307)

Commodification in tourism, the process whereby a destination's culture is gradually converted into a saleable commodity or product in response to the perceived or actual demands of the tourist market. (p. 242)

Condensed development sequence the process whereby societies undergo the transition to a Phase Four state within an increasingly reduced period of time. (p. 72)

Consolidation as local carrying capacities are exceeded, the rate of growth declines; the destination is now almost wholly dominated by tourism. (p. 273)

Contagious diffusion spread occurs as a function of spatial proximity; the closer a site is to the place of the innovation's origin, the sooner it is likely to be exposed to that phenomenon. (p. 285)

Corporate social responsibility the concept that corporations have a moral duty to operate in a socially and environmentally responsible way; it is increasingly recognised as a business imperative that combines elements of the green (i.e. 'social responsibility') and dominant Western environmental ('corporate') paradigms. (p. 298)

Cross-sectional research a 'snapshot' approach to research that considers one or more sites at one particular point in time. (p. 335)

Crusades a series of campaigns to 'liberate' Jerusalem and the Holy Land from Muslim control. While not a form of tourism as such, the Crusades helped to re-open Europe to the outside world and spawn an incipient travel industry. (p. 51)

Culinary tourism tourism that involves the consumption of usually locally produced food and drink. (p. 127)

Cultural events attractions that occur over a fixed period of time in one or more locations, and are more constructed than natural; these include historical commemorations and re creations, world fairs, sporting events and festivals. (p. 130)

Cultural sites geographically fixed attractions that are more constructed than natural; these can be classified into prehistorical, historical, contemporary, economic, specialised recreational and retail subcategories. (p. 123)

Dark Ages the period from about AD 500 to 1100, characterised by a serious deterioration in social, economic and political conditions within Europe. (p. 51)

Dark tourism tourism involving sites or events associated with death or suffering, including battlefields and sites of mass killings or assassinations. (p. 124)

Data analysis the process by which the collected information is examined and assessed to identify patterns that address the research questions. (p. 350)

Data collection the gathering of relevant information by way of the techniques identified in the research methodology stage. (p. 349)

Data interpretation the stage during which meaning is extracted from the data. (p. 350)

Data presentation the stage during which the results of the analysis are communicated to the target audience. (p. 350)

Database marketing a comprehensive marketing strategy that is based on a memory of prior business transactions with customers; the use of accumulated customer data to inform marketing decisions. (p. 198)

Decline the scenario of declining visitor intake that is likely to ensue if no measures are taken to arrest the process of product deterioration and resident/tourist discontent. (p. 275)

Decommissioning the process whereby vendors of travel products (e.g. airlines, cruise lines) no longer provide a monetary or other commission to an intermediary such as a travel agency in exchange for the sale of their products to consumers. (p. 136)

Deduction an approach in basic research that begins with a basic theory that is applied to a set of data to see whether the theory is applicable or not. (p. 332)

Deliberate alternative tourism (DAT) alternative tourism that is deliberately maintained as such through the implementation of an enabling regulatory environment. (p. 311)

Demarketing the process of discouraging all or certain tourists from visiting a particular destination temporarily or permanently. (p. 190)

Demographic transition model (DTM) an idealised depiction of the process whereby societies evolve from a high fertility/high mortality structure to a low fertility/low mortality structure. This evolution usually parallels the development of a society from a Phase One to a Phase Four profile, as occurred during the Industrial Revolution. A fifth stage may now be emerging, characterised by extremely low birth rates and resultant net population loss. (p. 65)

Demonstration effect the tendency of a population, or some portion thereof, to imitate the consumption patterns and other behaviours of another group; this can result in increased importation of goods and services to meet these changing consumer demands. (p. 225)

Dependables 'self-centred' tourists who prefer familiar and risk-averse experiences; originally known as 'psychocentrics'. (p. 167)

Destination branding the process of fostering a distinctive and integrated image about a destination that represents that destination to one or more target markets; usually undertaken by a destination tourism organisation. (p. 193)

Destination clubs an accommodation option that offers exclusive access to luxury facilities, usually for two weeks, in exchange for a membership fee and annual dues. (p. 140)

Destination community the residents of the destination region. (p. 39)

Destination cycle the theory that tourism-oriented places experience a repeated sequential process of birth, growth, maturation, and then possibly something similar to death, in their evolution as destinations. (p. 267)

Destination government the government of the destination region. (p. 39)

Destination region the places to which the tourist is travelling. (p. 38)

Destination tourism authority (DTA) the government agency responsible for broad tourism policy and planning within a destination entity. (p. 194)

Destination tourism organisations (DTOs) publicly funded government agencies that undertake promotion and other forms of marketing; these are distinct from the government departments or bodies, or government tourism authorities, that dictate tourism-related policy. (p. 192)

Development the accelerated growth of tourism within a relatively short period of time, as this sector becomes a dominant feature of the destination economy and landscape. (p. 273)

Direct (or primary) impact expenditure or direct revenue obtained from tourists. (p. 218)

Direct financial costs direct expenses that are necessarily incurred to sustain the tourism sector; within the public sector, typical areas of outlay include administration and bureaucracy, marketing, research and direct incentives. (p. 224)

Direct revenue money that is obtained directly from tourists through advance or immediate expenditures in the destination and associated taxes. (p. 213)

Discretionary income the amount of income that remains after household necessities such as food, housing, clothing, education and transportation have been purchased. (p. 49)

Discretionary time normally defined as time not spent at work, or in normal rest and bodily maintenance. (p. 49)

Disintermediation the removal of intermediaries such as travel agents from the product/consumer connection. (p. 136)

Distance–decay in tourism, the tendency of inbound flows to decline as origin regions become more distant from the destination. (p. 87)

Domestic excursionists tourists who stay within their own country for less than one night. (p. 30)

Domestic stayovers tourists who stay within their own country for at least one night. (p. 30)

Domestic tourist a tourist whose itinerary is confined to their usual country of residence. (p. 23)

Dominant Western environmental paradigm the scientific paradigm as applied to environmental and related issues, holding the anthropocentric view that humankind is at the centre of all things, and constitutes the primary focus of reference in all relationships with the natural environment; humans are seen as being superior to nature, which exists only for their benefit. (p. 296)

Double-blind peer review a procedure that attempts to maintain objectivity in the manuscript refereeing process by ensuring that the author and reviewers do not know each other's identity. (p. 9)

Early modern tourism the transitional era between premodern tourism (about AD 1500) and modern mass tourism (since 1950). (p. 52)

Earned time a time management option in which an individual is no longer obligated to work once a particular quota is attained over a defined period of time (often monthly or annual). (p. 63)

Ecolabels mechanisms that certify products or companies that meet specified standards of practice. (p. 307)

Ecological footprint (EF) the measurement of the resources that are required and wastes generated in sustaining a particular type of tourist or tourism activity. (p. 258)

Ecotourism a form of alternative tourism (and potentially mass tourism) that places primary emphasis on a sustainable, learning-based interaction with the natural environment or some constituent element. (p. 314)

Emotional labour a characteristic of services marketing, involving the expression of the willingness to be of service to customers, as through demonstrations of assurance, responsiveness and empathy. (p. 184)

Enclave resort a self-contained resort complex; enclave resorts are associated with high revenue leakages because of their propensity to encourage internal spending on imported goods. (p. 225)

Enclave tourism a mode of tourism characterised by external domination and weak linkages with the local economy. (p. 225)

Environmental impact sequence a four-stage model formulated by the OECD to account for the impacts of tourism on the natural environment. (p. 253)

Environmental responses the way that the environment reacts to the stresses, both in the short and long term, and both directly and indirectly. (p. 253)

Environmental stresses the deliberate changes in the environment that are entailed in the stressor activities. (p. 253)

Ephemeral attraction an attraction, such as a wildflower display or rarely filled lakebed, that occurs over a brief period of time or on rare occasions only. (p. 123)

e-postcards virtual postcards that are selected through the internet and sent to recipients by email. (p. 203)

Excursionist a tourist who spends less than one night in a destination region. (p. 25)

Exploration the earliest stage in the Butler sequence, characterised by few tourist arrivals and little impact associated with tourism. (p. 270)

External-intentional actions deliberate actions that originate from outside the destination. (p. 283)

External-unintentional actions actions that affect the destination, but originate from outside that destination, and are not intentional; these present the greatest challenges to destination managers. (p. 283)

Family lifecycle (FLC) a sequence of stages through which the traditional nuclear family passes from early adulthood to the death of a spouse; each stage is associated with distinct patterns of tourism-related behaviour associated with changing family and financial circumstances. (p. 163)

Fixed costs costs that the operation has little flexibility to change over the short term, such as interest costs on borrowed funds and basic facility maintenance costs. (p. 186)

Flexitime a time management option in which workers have some flexibility in distributing a required number of working hours (usually weekly) in a manner that suits the lifestyle and productivity of the individual worker. (p. 62)

Formal sector the portion of a society's economy that is subject to official systems of regulation and remuneration; formal sector businesses provide regular wage or salaried employment, and are subject to taxation by various levels of government; the formal sector dominates Phase Four societies. (p. 222)

Four major types of tourist an inclusive group of tourist categories that combines the spatial and temporal components, and assumes adherence to the qualifying purposes of travel. (p. 30)

Freedoms of the air eight privileges, put in place through bilateral agreements, that govern the global airline industry. (p. 137)

Frontstage explicitly or tacitly recognised spaces within the destination that are mobilised for tourism purposes such as commodified cultural performances. (p. 243)

Functional adaptation the use of a structure for a purpose other than its original intent, represented in tourism by canals used by pleasure boaters and old homes converted into bed and breakfasts. (p. 128)

Gender segmentation the grouping of individuals into male and female categories, or according to sexual orientation. (p. 160)

General demarketing demarketing that is directed towards all tourists, usually temporarily. (p. 190)

Geographic segmentation market segmentation carried out on the basis of the market's origin region; can be carried out at various scales, including region (e.g. Asia), country (Germany), subnational unit (California, Queensland), or urban/rural. (p. 158)

GIS (geographic information systems) sophisticated computer software programs that facilitate the assembly, storage, manipulation, analysis and display of spatially referenced information. (p. 158)

Global inequality in tourism a fundamental distinction pertaining to the relative spatial distribution of tourism at a global level. (p. 81)

Globalisation the process whereby the operation of businesses and the movement of capital is increasingly less impeded by national boundaries, and is reflected in a general trend towards industry consolidation, deregulation and privatisation. (p. 145)

Golfscapes cultural landscapes that are dominated by golf courses and affiliated developments. (p. 129)

Grand Tour a form of early modern tourism that involved a lengthy trip to the major cities of France and Italy by young adults of the leisure class, for purposes of education and culture. (p. 52)

Green consumerism the proclivity to purchase goods and services that are deemed to be environmentally and socially sustainable; situates along a spectrum from 'true' green to 'veneer' green attitudes and behaviour. (p. 303)

Green paradigm an emerging ecocentric worldview that is challenging the basic assumptions of the dominant Western environmental paradigm and accounting for its related anomalies and contradictions. (p. 297)

Green traveller an emerging market niche that is highly discerning and critical in ensuring that its travel behaviour does not negatively affect destinations; similar to Plog's allocentric tourist. (p. 304)

Greenwashing the process of conveying an impression of environmental responsibility that is not actually deserved; often associated with the misuse of terms such as 'sustainable tourism' and 'ecotourism'. (p. 299)

Growth pole strategy a strategy that uses tourism to stimulate economic development in a suitably located area (or growth pole), so that this growth will eventually become self-sustaining. (p. 221)

Hard ecotourism a form of ecotourism that stresses an intensive, specialised and prolonged interaction with nature in a relatively undisturbed natural environment with few available amenities; a form of alternative tourism. (p. 316)

Hierarchical diffusion spread occurs through an urban or other hierarchy, usually from the largest to the smallest centres, independent of where these centres are located. (p. 284)

Horizontal integration occurs when firms attain a higher level of consolidation or control within their own sector. (p. 143)

Hotels the most conventional type of tourist accommodation; can be subcategorised into city, convention, airport, resort and apartment hotels, and motels. (p. 140)

Human responses the reactions of individuals, communities, the tourism industry, tourists, NGOs and governments to the various environmental responses. (p. 253)

Hyperdestinations destinations where the annual intake of visitors dramatically outnumbers the permanent resident population; often characteristic of tourist shopping villages. (p. 106)

Hypotheses tentative informed statements about the nature of reality that can be subsequently verified or rejected through systematic deductive research. (p. 334)

Iconic attraction an attraction that is well-known and closely associated with a - particular destination, such as Mt Fuji (Japan) or the Statue of Liberty (United States). (p. 134)

Ideal type an idealised model of some phenomenon or process against which real-life situations can be measured and compared. (p. 281)

Image in tourism, the sum of the beliefs, attitudes and impressions that individuals or groups hold towards tourist destinations or aspects of destinations. Destination image is a critical factor in attracting or repelling visitors. (p. 93)

Inbound tour operators tour operators that coordinate and manage the component of the package tour within the destination, in cooperation with a partner outbound tour operator. (p. 142)

Inbound tourists international tourists arriving from another country. (p. 24)

Incremental access a policy, practised most notably in China, whereby new destinations within a country are gradually opened up to international (and possibly domestic) tourists. (p. 98)

Indicators variables or parameters that provide information about some phenomenon in order to facilitate its management in a desirable way. (p. 300)

Indigenous theories theories that arise out of a particular field of study or discipline. (p. 6)

Indirect financial costs costs that do not entail a direct outlay of funds, but indicate lost revenue. (p. 225)

Indirect impacts revenues that are used by tourism businesses and their suppliers to purchase goods and services. (p. 218)

Indirect revenues revenue obtained through the circulation of direct tourist expenditures within a destination. (p. 218)

Induced impacts revenue circulation that results from the use of wages in tourism businesses and their suppliers to purchase goods and services. (p. 219)

Induction an approach in basic research whereby the observation and analysis of data leads to the formulation of theories or models that link these observations in a meaningful way. (p. 332)

Industrial Revolution a process that occurred in England from the mid-1700s to the mid-1900s (and spread outwards to other countries), in which society was transformed from an agrarian to an industrial base, thereby spawning conditions that were conducive to the growth of tourism-related activity. (p. 54)

Informal sector the portion of a society's economy that is external to the official systems of regulation and remuneration; dominant in many parts of the less developed world, informal sector businesses are characterised by small size, the absence of regular working hours or wage payments, family ownership and a lack of any regulating quality control. (p. 222)

Infrastructural accessibility the extent to which a destination is physically accessible to markets by air routes, highways, ferry links, etc., and through entry/exit facilities such as seaports and airports. (p. 88)

Inseparability a characteristic of services marketing, where production and - consumption of tourist services occur at the same time and place and are thus inseparable. (p. 184)

Intangibility a characteristic of services marketing, where the actual tourism service cannot be seen, touched or tried before its purchase and consumption. (p. 183)

Interdisciplinary approach involves the input of a variety of disciplines, with fusion and synthesis occurring among these different perspectives. (p. 7)

Internal-intentional actions deliberate actions that originate from within the destination itself; the best case scenario for destinations in terms of control and management. (p. 283)

Internal-unintentional actions actions that originate from within the destination, but are not deliberate. (p. 283)

International excursionists tourists who stay less than one night in another country. (p. 30)

International stayovers tourists who stay at least one night in another country. (p. 30)

International tourism receipts all consumption expenditure, or payments for goods and services, made by international tourists (stayovers and excursionists) to use themselves or to give away. (p. 213)

International tourist a tourist who travels beyond their usual country of residence. (p. 23)

Intervening opportunities places, often within transit regions, that develop as tourist destinations in their own right and subsequently have the potential to divert tourists from previously patronised destinations. (p. 37)

Involvement the second stage in the Butler sequence, where the local community responds to the opportunities created by tourism by offering specialised services; associated with a gradual increase in visitor numbers. (p. 271)

Irridex a theoretical model proposing that resident attitudes evolve from euphoria to apathy, then irritation (or annoyance), antagonism and finally resignation, as the intensity of tourism development increases within a destination. (p. 251)

Knowledge-based platform the most recent dominant perspective in tourism studies, arising from the sustainability discourse and emphasising ideological neutrality and the application of rigorous scientific methods to generate knowledge so that communities can decide whether large- or small-scale tourism is most appropriate. (p. 12)

Leisure class in premodern tourism, that small portion of the population that had sufficient discretionary time and income to engage in leisure pursuits such as tourism. (p. 49)

Less developed countries (LDCs) countries characterised by a relatively low level of economic development. Until recently, the less developed world has not been very important as a recipient or generator of global tourist flows. (p. 81)

Long-haul tourists variably defined as tourists taking trips outside of the world region where they reside, or beyond a given number of flying time hours. (p. 24)

Longitudinal research a trends-oriented approach to research, which examines one or more sites at two or more points in time or, more rarely, on a continuous basis. (p. 335)

Loyalty the extent to which a product, such as a destination, is perceived in a positive way and repeatedly purchased by the consumer. (p. 173)

Market failure the failure of market forces to produce a longer-term equilibrium in supply and demand, such as when individual businesses in the tourism industry are unwilling to provide the funds for destination promotion (to increase demand) because such investment will provide benefits to their competitors as well as to themselves. (p. 192)

Market segmentation the division of the tourist market into more or less homogenous subgroups, or tourist market segments, based on certain common characteristics and/or behavioural patterns. (p. 153)

Market segments portions of the tourist market that are more or less distinct in their characteristics and/or behaviour. (p. 153)

Marketing mix the critical components that determine the demand for a business or destination product. (p. 197)

Marketing the interactions and interrelationships that occur among consumers and producers of goods and services, through which ideas, products, services and values are created and exchanged for the mutual benefit of both groups. (p. 182)

Markets of one an extreme form of market segmentation, in which individual consumers are recognised as distinct market segments. (p. 154)

Matrix model of lifecycle trigger factors an eight-cell model that classifies the various actions that induce change in the evolution of tourism in a destination. Each of the following categories can be further divided into tourism stimulants and depressants. (p. 282)

Medical tourism travel for the purpose of obtaining medical treatment that is unavailable or too expensive in the participant's region of origin. (p. 28)

Merchandise goods purchased as part of the anticipated or actual tourism experience; includes tour guidebooks and luggage in the origin region, and souvenirs and duty-free goods in the destination region. (p. 143)

Mesopotamia the region approximately occupied by present-day Iraq, where the earliest impulses of civilisation first emerged, presumably along with the first tourism activity. (p. 48)

MICE an acronym combining meetings, incentives, conventions and exhibitions; a form of tourism largely associated with business purposes. (p. 27)

Midcentrics 'average' tourists whose personality type is a compromise between venturer and dependable traits; originally known as 'centrics'. (p. 167)

Middle Ages the period from about AD 1100 to the Renaissance (about AD 1500), characterised by an improvement in the social, economic and political situation, in comparison with the Dark Ages. (p. 51)

Modern mass tourism (Contemporary tourism) the period from 1950 to the present day, characterised by the rapid expansion of international and domestic tourism. (p. 57)

More developed countries (MDCs) countries characterised by a relatively high level of economic development. Collectively, the more developed world remains dominant as a recipient and generator of global tourist flows. (p. 81)

Motivation the intrinsic reasons why the individual is embarking on a particular trip. (p. 170)

Multidisciplinary approach involves the input of a variety of disciplines, but without any significant interaction or synthesis of these different perspectives. (p. 7)

Multilevel segmentation a refinement of simple market segmentation that further differentiates basic level segments. (p. 153)

Multiplier effect a measure of the subsequent income generated in a destination's economy by direct tourist expenditure. (p. 218)

Multipurpose travel travel undertaken for more than a single purpose. (p. 30)

Natural events attractions that occur over a fixed period of time in one or more locations, and are more natural than constructed. (p. 122)

Natural sites geographically fixed attractions that are more natural than constructed; these can be subdivided into topography (physical features), climate, hydrology (water resources), wildlife, vegetation and location. (p. 115)

Niche markets highly specialised market segments. (p. 154)

North-south flow a common term used to describe the dominant pattern of international tourist traffic from the MDCs (located mainly in the northern latitudes, except for Australia and New Zealand) to the LDCs (located mainly to the south of the MDCs). (p. 84)

Olympic Games the most important of the ancient Greek art and athletics festivals, held every four years at Olympia. The ancient Olympic Games are one of the most important examples of premodern tourism. (p. 49)

Opportunity cost the idea that the use of a resource for some activity (e.g. tourism) precludes its use for some other activity that may yield a better financial return (e.g. agriculture). (p. 230)

Origin community the residents of the origin region. (p. 34)

Origin government the government of the origin region. (p. 34)

Origin region the region (e.g. country, state, city) from which the tourist originates, also referred to as the market or generating region. (p. 33)

Outbound tour operators tour operators based in origin regions that organise and market volume-driven package tours that include transportation, accommodation, visits to attractions and other items of interest to tourists. (p. 141)

Outbound tourists international tourists departing from their usual country of residence. (p. 24)

Package tour a pre-paid travel package that usually includes transportation, accommodation, food and other services. (p. 57)

Paradigm shift the replacement of one paradigm with another when the formerly dominant paradigm can no longer adequately account for various contradictions and anomalies. (p. 295)

Paradigm the entire constellation of beliefs, assumptions and values that underlie the way that a society interprets the nature of reality. (p. 295)

Paradox of resentment the idea that problems of resentment and tension can result whether tourists are integrated with, or isolated from, the local community. (p. 248)

Perishability a services marketing characteristic; because production and consumption are simultaneous, services cannot be produced and stored in advance for future consumption (e.g. empty aircraft seats are a permanent loss that cannot be recouped). (p. 185)

Phase One: pre-industrial, mainly agricultural and subsistence-based economies where tourism participation is restricted to a small leisure class. (p. 75)

Phase Two: the generation of wealth increases and tends to spread to a wider segment of the population as a consequence of industrialisation and related processes such as urbanisation. This leads to increases in the demand for domestic tourism among the middle classes. (p. 75)

Phase Three: the bulk of the population becomes increasingly affluent, leading to the emergence of mass domestic travel, as well as extensive international tourism to nearby countries. The elite, meanwhile, engage in greater long-haul travel. (p. 75)

Phase Four: represents a fully developed country with almost universal affluence, and a subsequent pattern of mass international tourism to an increasingly diverse array of short- and long-haul destinations. Almost all residents engage in a comprehensive variety of domestic tourism experiences. (p. 75)

Pilgrimage generic term for travel undertaken for religious purpose. Pilgrimages have declined in importance during the modern era compared with recreational, business and social tourism. (p. 51)

Pink dollar the purchasing power of gay and lesbian consumers, recognised to be much higher than the average purchasing power (sometimes used to describe the purchasing power of women). (p. 161)

'Play in order to work' philosophy an industrial-era ethic, which holds that leisure time and activities are necessary in order to make workers more productive, thereby reinforcing the work-focused nature of society. (p. 62)

Pleasure periphery those less economically developed regions of the globe that are being increasingly mobilised to provide 3S and alpine tourism products. (p. 83)

Political accessibility the extent to which visitors are allowed entry into a destination by a governing authority. (p. 88)

Post-Cook period the time from about 1880 to 1950, characterised by the rapid growth of domestic tourism within the wealthier countries, but less rapid expansion in international tourism. (p. 57)

Postindustrial era a later Phase Four stage in which hi-tech services and information replace manufacturing and lower-order services as the mainstay of an economy. (p. 62)

Premodern tourism describes the era of tourism activity from the beginning of civilisation to the end of the Middle Ages. (p. 48)

Primary research research that involves the collection of original data by the researcher. (p. 338)

Problem recognition the first stage of the research process, which is the identification of a broad problem arena that requires investigation. (p. 345)

Propulsive activity an economic activity that is suited to a particular area and thus facilitates the growth pole strategy; in the case of Cancún and other subtropical or tropical coastal regions 3S tourism is an effective propulsive activity. (p. 22)

Psychographic segmentation the differentiation of the tourist market on the basis of psychological and motivational characteristics such as personality, motivations and needs. (p. 167)

Pull factors forces that help to stimulate a tourism product by 'pulling' consumers towards particular destinations. (p. 81)

Push factors economic, social, demographic, technological and political forces that stimulate a demand for tourism activity by 'pushing' consumers away from their usual place of residence. (p. 59)

Qualitative research research that does not place its emphasis on the collection and analysis of statistical data, and usually tends to obtain in-depth insight into a relatively small number of respondents or observations. (p. 336)

Quality control mechanisms (quality assurance mechanisms) mechanisms that provide some degree of assurance to consumers, government or others that a particular operation, product or destination follows standards associated with sustainable tourism. (p. 307)

Quantitative research research that is based mainly on the collection and analysis of statistical data, and hence tends to obtain a limited amount of information on a large number of respondents or observations; these results are then extrapolated to the wider population of the subject matter. (p. 336)

Question formulation the posing of specific questions or hypotheses that serve to focus the research agenda arising from problem recognition; these questions can be descriptive, explanatory, predictive or prescriptive in nature. (p. 346)

Refereed academic journals publications that are considered to showcase a discipline by merit of the fact that they are subject to a rigorous process of double-blind peer review. (p. 9)

Rejuvenation the scenario of a renewed development-like growth that occurs if steps are taken to revitalise the tourism product offered by the destination. (p. 276)

Renaissance the 'rebirth' of Europe following the Dark Ages, commencing in Italy during the mid-1400s and spreading to Germany and the 'low countries' by the early 1600s. (p. 52)

Research a systematic search for knowledge. (p. 331)

Research methodology a set of assumptions, procedures and methods that are used to carry out a search for knowledge within a particular type of research. (p. 331)

Research methods the techniques that will be used to answer the questions or prove or disprove the hypotheses. (p. 348)

Research process the sequence of stages that are followed to carry out a research project from its origins to its conclusions. (p. 345)

Resorts facilities or urban areas that are specialised in the provision of recreational tourism opportunities. (p. 49)

Revenue leakages a major category of indirect financial costs, entailing erosion in the multiplier effect due to the importation of goods and services that are required by tourists or the tourist industry, through factor payments abroad such as repatriated profits, and through imports required for government expenditure on tourism-related infrastructure such as airports, road and port equipment. (p. 225)

Rifle marketing a mode of promotional advertising that is aimed just at the target market. (p. 203)

Scientific paradigm the currently dominant paradigm, which holds that reality is reducible and deterministic and can be understood through the application of the 'scientific method'. (p. 296)

Seaside resorts a type of resort located on coastlines to take advantage of sea bathing for health and, later, recreational purposes; many of these were established during the Industrial Revolution for both the leisure and working classes. (p. 55)

Secondary (or 'flow-on') impacts the indirect and induced stages of money circulation in the multiplier effect that follows the actual tourist expenditure. (p. 219)

Secondary research research in which the investigator uses previously collected data. (p. 338)

Secular pilgrimage travel for spiritual purposes that are not linked to conventional religions. (p. 28)

Selective demarketing demarketing that is directed towards a particular tourist segment, usually intended as a permanent measure against groups deemed to be undesirable. (p. 190)

Sense of place the combination of natural and cultural characteristics that makes a destination unique in comparison to any other destination, and thus potentially provides it with a competitive advantage. (p. 134)

Services marketing the marketing of services such as those associated with the tourism industry, as opposed to the marketing of the goods industry. (p. 182)

Short-haul tourists variably defined as tourists taking trips within the world region where they reside, or within a given number of flying time hours. (p. 24)

Shotgun marketing a mode of promotional advertising where the message is disseminated to a broad audience on the assumption that this saturation will reach target markets and perhaps attract new recruits. (p. 202)

Simple market segmentation the most basic form of market segmentation, involving the identification of a minimal number of basic market segments such as 'female' and 'male'. (p. 153)

Site hardening increasing the visitor carrying capacity of a site through structural and other changes that allow more visitors to be accommodated. (p. 135)

Small island states or dependencies (SISODs) geopolitical entities with a population of less than three million permanent residents and a land mass of less than 28 000 km^2. SISODs are overrepresented as tourist destinations because of their ample 3S tourism resources. (p. 84)

Sociodemographic segmentation market segmentation based on social and demographic variables such as gender, age, family lifecycle, education, occupation and income. (p. 160)

Soft ecotourism a form of ecotourism that emphasises a short-term interaction with nature as part of a multipurpose trip with ample provision for services and facilities; can exist as a form of mass tourism. (p. 317)

Space tourism an emerging form of tourism that involves travel by and confinement within aircraft or spacecraft to high altitude locations where sub-orbital effects such as zero-gravity or earth curvature viewing can be experienced. (p. 38)

Spas a type of resort centred on the use of geothermal waters for health purposes. (p. 54)

Spatial diffusion the process whereby some innovation or idea spreads from a point of origin to other locations; this model is more appropriate than the destination lifecycle to describe the development of tourism at the country level. (p. 284)

Stagnation the stage in the Butler sequence wherein visitor numbers and tourism growth stagnate due to the deterioration of the product. (p. 274)

Standard Industrial Classification (SIC) a system that uses standard alphanumeric codes to classify all types of economic activity. Tourism-related activities are distributed among at least 15 codes. (p. 5)

Stayover a tourist who spends at least one night in a destination region. (p. 25)

Stopovers travellers who stop in a location in transit to another destination; they normally do not clear customs and are not considered tourists from the transit location's perspective. (p. 31)

Strategic marketing marketing that takes into consideration an extensive analysis of external and internal environmental factors in identifying strategies that attain specific goals. (p. 194)

Stressor activities activities that initiate the environmental impact sequence; these can be divided into permanent environmental restructuring, the generation of waste residuals, tourist activities and indirect and induced activities. (p. 253)

Strong sustainable development an approach to sustainable development that assumes relatively rigorous environmental expectations in recognition of areas, such as wilderness, that are relatively undisturbed and have a low carrying capacity. (p. 299)

Subnational inequality the tendency of tourism within countries, states and individual cities to be spatially concentrated. (p. 104)

Sunbelt the name frequently applied to the 3S-oriented American portion of the pleasure periphery. Well-known destinations within the sunbelt include Hawaii, southern California, Las Vegas (Nevada), Arizona, Texas and Florida. (p. 82)

Sustainable development in principle, development that meets the needs of present generations while ensuring that future generations are able to meet their own needs. (p. 299)

Sustainable tourism tourism that is developed in such a way so as to meet the needs of the present without compromising the ability of future generations to meet their own needs. (p. 299)

SWOT analysis an analysis of a company or destination's strengths, weaknesses, opportunities and threats that emerges from an examination of its internal and external environment. (p. 194)

System a group of interrelated, interdependent and interacting elements that together form a single functional structure. (p. 20)

Theory a model or statement that describes, explains or predicts some phenomenon. (p. 6)

Thomas Cook the entrepreneur whose company Thomas Cook & Son applied the principles of the Industrial Revolution to the tourism sector through such innovations as the package tour. (p. 55)

Threshold a critical value of indicator sustainability; when the threshold is exceeded, this indicates an unsustainable situation. (p. 302)

Timesharing an accommodation option in which a user purchases one or more intervals (or weeks) per year in a resort, usually over a long period of time. (p. 140)

Tour operators businesses providing a package of tourism-related services for the consumer, including some combination of accommodation, transportation, restaurants and attraction visits. (p. 141)

Tourism industry the businesses providing goods and services wholly or mainly for tourist consumption. (p. 136)

Tourism industry the sum of the industrial and commercial activities that produce goods and services wholly or mainly for tourist consumption. (p. 40)

Tourism participation sequence according to Burton, the tendency for a society to participate in tourism increases through a set of four phases that relate to the concurrent process of increased economic development. (p. 59)

Tourism platforms perspectives that have dominated the emerging field of tourism studies at various stages of its evolution. (p. 10)

Tourism product consists of tourist attractions and the tourism industry. (p. 115)

Tourism resources features of a destination that are valued as attractions by tourists at some particular point in time; a feature that was a tourism resource 100 years ago may not be perceived as such now. (p. 45)

Tourism the sum of the processes, activities, and outcomes arising from the relationships and the interactions among tourists, tourism suppliers, host governments, host communities, and surrounding environments that are involved in the attracting, transporting, hosting and management of tourists and other visitors. (p. 2)

Tourist attractions specific and generic features of a destination that attract tourists; some, but not all, attractions are part of the tourism industry. (p. 115)

Tourist market the overall group of consumers that engages in some form of tourism-related travel. (p. 153)

Tourist shopping villages small towns where the downtown is dominated by tourism-related businesses such as boutiques, antique shops and cafés. (p. 106)

Tourist a person who travels temporarily outside of his or her usual environment (usually defined by some distance threshold) for certain qualifying purposes. (p. 2)

Tourist–historic city an urban place where the preservation of historical districts helps to sustain and is at least in part sustained by a significant level of tourist activity. (p. 240)

Transit region the places and regions that tourists pass through as they travel from origin to destination region. (p. 36)

Transportation businesses involved in conveying tourists by air, road, rail or water. (p. 37)

Travel agencies businesses providing retail travel services to customers for commission on behalf of other tourism industry sectors. (p. 136)

Travel purpose the reason why people travel; in tourism, these involve recreation and leisure, visits to friends and relatives (VFR), business, and less dominant purposes such as study, sport, religion and health. (p. 26)

Triangulation the use of multiple methods, data sources, investigators or theories in a single research process. (p. 349)

Urban–rural fringe (or 'exurbs') a transitional zone surrounding larger urban areas that combines urban and rural characteristics and benefits from proximity to each. (p. 106)

Variability a services marketing characteristic, where service encounters, even if they involve a similar kind of experience, are highly variable due to the differences and rapid changes in mood, expectation and other human element factors that affect the participants. (p. 184)

Variable costs costs that can be readily reduced in the short term, such as salaries of casual staff. (p. 186)

Venturers according to Plog's typology, 'other-centred' tourists who enjoy exposing themselves to other cultures and new experiences, and are willing to take risks in this process; originally known as 'allocentrics'. (p. 167)

Vertical integration occurs when a corporation obtains greater control over elements of the product chain outside its own sector. (p. 144)

Virtual reality (VR) the wide-field presentation of computer-generated, multi-sensory information that allows the user to experience a virtual world. (p. 70)

War dividend the long-term benefits for tourism that derive from large conflicts, including war-related attractions, image creation, and the emergence of new travel markets. (p. 69)

Weak sustainable development an approach to sustainable development that assumes relatively relaxed environmental expectations in recognition of areas, such as intensively developed beach resorts, that are already extensively modified and have high carrying capacities. (p. 299)

Webcasting the delivery of interactive multimedia to customers through the internet on either an 'on demand' or 'real-time' basis. (p. 203)

Winescapes a cultural landscape significantly influenced by the presence of vineyards, wineries and other features associated with viticulture and wine production; an essential element of wine-focused culinary tourism. (p. 127)

'Work in order to play' philosophy a postindustrial ethic derived from ancient Greek philosophy that holds that leisure and leisure-time activities such as tourism are important in their own right and that we work to be able to afford to engage in leisure pursuits. (p. 63)

INDEX

1988 World Fair   131
2000 Sydney Olympic Games   27, 102, 131
2008 Beijing Olympic Games   131
3S tourism   39, 82–4, 108
  destinations   82
  expansion   84
  potential threats   90
  regional development   220–1
  seasonal variability   187, 189–90
8P marketing model   197–205, 206

Aboriginal art festival   241
academic books as secondary research   343
accessibility as pull factor   135, 197
accommodation industry   140–1
accreditation   309–10
adaptancy platform   11, 16, 38, 310
ad valorem taxes   216 See also bed tax; sales tax
advertising as promotion   202–3
advocacy platform   10–11, 16, 220, 231, 232, 239, 248
  destination-based tourism   38–9
affordability as pull factor   91, 135, 199–200
Africa See also East Africa; Middle Africa; South Africa; West Africa
  impact of negative image   102
  multi-destination segmentation   171
  soft ecotourism   317
Air New Zealand   137
air travel
  deregulation   137–9
  perishability   185
  privatisation   138
  security concerns   138–9
  supply and demand strategies   189
  sustainability-related practices   306
aircraft industry   37–8, 68
airline alliances   137
airline capacity improvements   112
airport hotels   140, 187
Albania   81
allocentrics   167, 168, 251, 271
  personality and travel-related characteristics   169
  travel motivation   170
Alnwick Garden   221–2
Alpine Pearls   69–70, 139
alpine tourism   228

alternative tourism   11, 310–14
  criticisms   312–13
  ideal model   311
  sociocultural   315
  types of   311
amenity migrants   258
American Airways   306
ancient Greek tourism   49–50
ancient Roman tourism   50
ancient spa attractions   53–4
Antigua   100, 117, 230, 280
apartment hotels   140
APEC See Asia Pacific Economic Cooperation
APEC/PATA Code for Sustainable Tourism   307–8
applied research   331, 334–5, 348, 352
approved destination status (ADS) countries   70
Argentina   100
Asia Pacific Economic Cooperation (APEC)   309
Asia–Pacific destinations   98–9
Atlantic City   275, 276
Atlantis Adventures   316
Audissey Guides   127
Austrailpass   139
Australia   60, 81
  Aboriginal tourism development   272
  approved destination status (ADS)   70, 111
  Chinese and Japanese tourist characteristics   159, 218
  Chinese tourist marketing case study   111–12
  climate change impacts case study   355–6
  cultural events attendance 2005–6   132
  declining fertility   63–4
  demographic trends 1901–2008   64
  developmental stage destinations   273
  domestic tourism   23
  domestic tourism distribution   106–7
  ecotourism destinations   318–19
  environmentally obligated tourists   304–5
  green consumer market   178, 303
  heritage preservation sites   240
  inbound crisis case study   45–6
  inbound international students   29
  inbound tourism   102–4, 160
  inbound tourist travel purposes   27

Australia (continued)
    international promotional
        campaigns   45, 46
    international stayovers 1965–2007   103
    international visitors' leisure
        activities   116
    labour work hours   62
    major categories of tourist
        expenditure   215–6
    market regions and countries 1995–2007
        103–4
    market segmentation   171–2
    outbound resident departures
        1965–2006   71
    outbound tourist destinations 2007   87
    per capita consumption expenditure   61
    population pyramid 1901 & 2006   67
    regional tourist attractions   90
    seasonality in inbound tourism
        2007   228
    smartraveller initiative   35–6
    Standard Industrial Classification (SIC)
        system   6
    statistical compilations   344
    top 16 destination regions   107
    topographical sites   117
    tourism funding priorities case
        study   235–6
    tourism gross national product
        contribution   218, 220
    universities with domestic tourism
        programs   8–9
    visitor safety programs   92–3
    wildlife tourism   84
    Where the Bloody Hell Are You?
        campaign case study   209–11
Australian Bureau of Statistics
    publications   344
authenticity of products   134
    expectations   249–50
    staged   251
automotive industry   68
availability of services as pull factor   91
avalanche effect   302

baby boomers   66
    case study   77–8
backpacking phenomenon   53
backstage   243–4, 260
backward linkages   220, 232, 271
backward longitudinal research   336
Bahamas   100, 117, 288
    sex tourism   244
Bali's destination lifecycle case study   292–3

Banff National Park   122
Barbados   319
Barossa Vintage Festival   132
basic research   331–4, 352
    methodologies   332–3
basic whole tourism system   20–1, 42
battlefields as tourist attraction   124
bazaar attractions   130
beach attractions   117–18
bed tax   216
behavioural segmentation   170–4, 175
Belgium   57
benchmarking sustainability   302, 309–10
Bhutan   39–40, 244
Big Banana   90
Big Pineapple   90
Big Prawn   90
bilateral tourist flows   99–100
blackwater   256 See also waste residuals
        management
Blue Flag ecolabel   309
Bobby software   166 See also website
        software for visually impaired
Bond University   9
Botswana   225
boutique hotels   184
Brazil   60, 100
BRIC countries   60–1
British Airways   306
broad context model of destination
        development scenarios   319–21,
        322, 331
brochures as promotion   205
Bruges   240
Brundtland Report   299
Bulgaria   81
Burton's phases of tourism participation   60,
        65 See also tourism participation
        sequence
business tourism   27
Butler's destination lifecycle model   11
Butler's sequence   268–78, 320, 331
    alternatives to   276–9, 319–21
    changing characteristics   269–70
    deduction methodology   333, 334
    ideal model   281–2, 289
    induction methodology   334
    methodological bias   346
    supply and demand alternatives   279

Cambodia   98, 190
Camp Coorong   240, 264
Canada   60, 81, 288
    bilateral tourist flows   99–100

Chinatown   319
   government pro-tourism policies   95
   international students   29
   natural events tourism   122–3
   nature-based tourism   119
   North America Industry Classification
      System (NAICS)   5
Caribbean   98–9
   criminal elements   246–7
   cruise ship tourism   25, 100
   indirect incentives   226
   sex tourism   34
   supply and demand strategies   189, 192
carrying capacity of tourist sites   135,
      247, 259
casinos   129, 179
   criminal elements   247
   economic impact assessment
      software   221
   product modification   188–9
CATI *See* Computer Assisted Telephone
      Interviewing system (CATI)
cautionary platform   11, 16, 38, 223, 225,
      242, 270, 310
Cayman Islands   158
Central America, impact of negative
      image   100
central locations as tourist resource   122
Central Queensland University   8
centrics   167
certification   309–10
   New Zealand case study   326–8
   scoring criteria and quality scores   328
Charles Darwin University   8
Charles Sturt University   8
Chile   100
China   73
   3S tourism   83–4
   approved destination status (ADS)   34,
     70
   Australian tourism program   111–12
   incremental access   98
   tourism participation phase   59–60
   tourist area cycles   280
choropleth mapping   350
circular sites   134
circumstantial alternative tourism
      (CAT)   311, 312, 319, 320
climate change   256–7
   Australian case study   355–6
coastal tourism environmental
      impact   254–5
codes of practice   307, 322
Colombia   288

Colonial Williamsburg Museum   125–6
commodification of culture   242–4,
      260, 292
community-based attractions   222
competition-oriented pricing   200
Computer Assisted Telephone Interviewing
      system (CATI)   33
condensed development sequence for
      domestic trips 1998–2007, 72
Congress Avenue Bridge   318
consolidation stage   273–4, 277
consumptive wildlife tourism   121
contagious spatial diffusion   284, 285–6
contemporary tourism   48, 57–8
content analysis   342–3
convenience sampling   349
convention hotels   140
Cook, Thomas   55–7, 73
Cook Islands   99, 245
Coolangatta   276, 277
corporate social responsibility   298, 303,
      306–7
Costa Rica   84, 123
cost-oriented pricing   200
cross-border shoppers   25, 31 *See also*
      excursionists
cross-cultural understanding   239–40, 314
cross-sectional research   335, 338, 352
Cruise Industry Charitable Foundation   306
cruise ship tourism
   disadvantages   26, 249
   excursionists   25, 31
   regional   139–40
   sustainability-related practices   306
Crusades, the   51
Cuba   34, 100
   medical tourism   28
   transit region   37
culinary tourism   127
cultural and heritage preservation   240–1
cultural events categories   130–1
cultural link as pull factor   90
cultural sites as tourism resource   123–5
cultural tourism   221
Curtin University of Technology   7, 9
Czech Republic   97, 288

dark ages period   50–1
dark tourism   124
data analysis   350
data collection agencies   33
data collection methods   33, 349
data condensers   338
data enhancers   337

data intepretation   350–2
    effective cartography to relay
        information   351
data presentation   350
database marketing   198–9
data-related problems in domestic
        tourism   32–3
decline in family sizes   63–4
declining stage destinations   275
decommissioning   136–7
deduction methodology   332–3
deliberate alternative tourism (DAT)   311,
        319, 320–1, 322
    related products   312
Delphi technique   340–1, 349
demand reduction strategies   189
demarketing in tourism   190
demographic transition model (DTM)   65–6
demonstration effect of tourism   225, 244–5
Denmark   88
Department of Immigration and Citizenship
        (DIAC)   217
Department of Industry, Tourism and
        Resources (DITR)
    tourism funding allocations 2004–7   224
dependables   167, 168 See also
        psychocentrics
description process   346
Desert Mob   241
destination branding campaigns   93–4, 193
    Australian case study   209–11
destination clubs   140, 142, 165
destination communities   39
destination countries
    gay-friendly   161–2
    top 25 spot 2007   97
destination cycle model   267
    Bali case study   292–3
    matrix model for trigger factors   282–3
destination governments   39–40, 192
destination promotion   192
destination regions   38–9
    product lifecycles   188
destination selection process   155–6
    decision makers   156
destination tourism authority (DTA)   194
destination tourism organisations
        (DTOs)   192–4, 206
    functions   193–4
destination-based tourism   38–9
development stage   273
diabetic travellers   24
DIAC See Department of Immigration and
        Citizenship (DIAC)

direct financial costs   224–5
direct revenues   213, 217–18
disability market segmentation   166
discretionary income   49
discretionary time   49
disintermediation of travel industry
        136–7
Disney World   90, 129, 250
distance-decay effect   87
distributed (self-completed) surveys   338
DITR See Department of Industry, Tourism
        and Resources (DITR)
domestic excursionists   30
domestic stayovers   30
domestic tourism   3, 5, 23
    data-related problems   32–3
    tertiary educational programs   8–9
    United Kingdom 19th century   57
Domestic Tourism Monitor   33 See also
        National Visitor Survey (NVS)
dominant Western environmental
        paradigm   295–8, 303, 322
    ideal model   298
Dominican Republic   221
double-blind peer reviews   9–10, 343
doubly contrived attractions   250
Doxey's irritation index   267, 274, 331 See
        also irridex
Dreamworld   129, 134
drought, impact on tourism   120
DTA See destination tourism authority (DTA)
DTOs See destination tourism organisations
        (DTOs)
Dubai   101–2
duty-free shopping   143
Dyersville   272

early modern tourism   48, 52–7
early seaside resorts   54–5
    diffusion in England and Wales
        1750–1911, 56
earned time   63
East Africa   171
EC3 Global   309, 310, 322
ecolabels   307, 309–10, 322, 327
    Blue Flag   309
ecological footprint calculator   258–9, 305
ecological footprints (EF)   258–9
economic impact assessment software   214
ecotourism   11, 121, 220, 312, 314–19
    carrying capacity   259
    hard   316, 317, 322
    major types of categories   315
    prominent destinations   318–19

small-scale   313
soft   317, 322
urban   318
Edith Cowan University   8
educational market segmentation   165
Egypt   49, 100, 283
Electronic Travel Authority (ETA)   217
electronic word-of-mouth (eWOM)   173,
     204, 271
emotional labour   184
employment   220, 231
employment inequities   230–1
enclave resorts   225
enclave tourism   225
Encore software   214
Environment Protection Authority   258
environmental benefits of tourism   252
environmental costs of tourism   252–3
environmental disasters   296–7
environmental impact sequence
     253, 254
environmental movement milestone
     publications   298
environmental responses   253
environmental stresses   253, 259, 280
environmentalism-related population
     clusters   303
ephemeral attractions   123
e-postcards   203
ethics in observation-based research   341–2
ethnic neighbourhoods as tourist
     attraction   126
Eurodisney   129
Europe   81
     border liberalisation   88
     destination pull factors   96–8
     Eastern bloc market   97–8
     labour work hours   62
     spas   120
excursion-based tourism   25
excursionists   30, 106
     cruise ship   25, 249
Expedia   136
experiential merchandising   183–4
explanation process   347
exploration stage destinations   270–1
Export Market Development Grant Scheme
     (EMDG)   236
extended stay hotels   140
external-intentional actions   283
external-unintentional actions   283
extreme locations as tourist resource   122
extreme market segmentations   154–5
exurban tourism   106, 188

face-to-face interviewing   338, 339
family lifecycle (FLC)   163–4
farm tourism   220
fashion effect in tourism   229–30
female tourists   160–1
festival attractions   132, 214
Fiji   84, 98, 190
films and tourism   210–1, 272, 283
fixed costs   186
flexitime   62, 63
Flinders University   9
flow-on impact in tourism   219
focus groups   339–40
food and drink as tourist attraction
     126–7
forecasting tools   340–1
formal sectors   222–3, 225, 273
Forte hotel chain   305
forward longitudinal research   336
four-week holiday standard   62
France   57, 88
     tourism gross national product
          contribution   218
Freedom Air   137
freedoms of the air   137–8
freshwater-based tourism   119
frontstage   243–4, 260
frontstage and backstage boundaries
     250–1
functional adaptation   128

Gatton Agricultural College of the University
     of Queensland   7
gay tourism   158, 161–2, 175
gender segmentation   160–1
general demarketing   190
geographic information systems (GIS)
     158, 175
geographic proximity as pull factor   197
geographic segmentation   158–60, 175
     types of   159–60
geographical diffusion See spatial
     diffusion
geographical proximity in tourism
     87–8, 99
geothermal waters   120 See also spas as
     tourist attractions
Germany   66
global positioning systems (GPS)   69,
     315–16
     observation-based research   341, 342
global tourism   4
global tourism system   21
globalisation   145

Gold Coast   280
    consolidation stage   274
    environmental impact   255–6
    golfscapes   129
    Green Behind the Gold campaign   200–1
    medical tourism   28
    product modification   188
    seasonality marketing strategies   228
    VeryGC campaign   93–4
Gold Coast Tourism   192
golf courses   128–9
golfscapes   128–9
governments *See also* origin governments;
        destination governments
    applied research   334
    growth pole strategies   221, 232
    public funded pro-tourism programs   95,
        235–6
    revenue generation   133
    sustainability legislation   319, 322
    tourism-related taxation   216–20
Grand Canyon   122
Grand Cayman Islands   276, 281
Grand Tour   52–3, 73
Grecotel   306
green consumer market   178–80, 303–4,
        322
    veneer   303, 306, 317
Green Globe System   309, 319
green paradigms   297–9, 303, 322
    ideal model   298
green tourism
    case study   178–80
    codes of practice   307
green traveller segment   304
green washing   299
Griffith University   7
growth pole strategy   221–2, 232
Guatemala   240

Haiti   100
Hard Rock Café   202
Hawaii   171
heritage districts as tourist attraction   124–5
Hervey Bay   171–2
hierarchical spatial diffusion   284, 285
historical attractions   123–5
historical re-enactments attractions   131
honeymoon market   171
Hong Kong   81, 98
horizontal integration structures   143–4
hotel accommodation   140–1, 144
    25 largest worldwide chains   141
    chains   143–4

experiential merchandising   183–4
high fixed costs structures   186
occupancy rates   186–7
recycling programs   305
staff training   184
supply and demand strategies   189–90
sustainability-related practices   306
variability levels   187–8
Hungary   97
hyperdestinations   106, 218, 249, 251
hypotheses   334
    interpretation   351

iconic attractions   134, 194, 225
identification of alternative sources of
        demand   189
Iguacu Falls   119
image of destination as pull factor   93–4
image of destination as push factor   94
inbound tour operators   142
income market segmentation   165
incremental access policy   98
India   73, 99
    3S tourism   83
    medical tourism   29
indigenous communities
    adaptation to tourism case study   263–5
    authenticity perceptions   250
    culture commodification   243, 263–4
    economic development   221
    empowerment   252
    frontstage and backstage
        boundaries   243–4
    involvement stage   272
    land rights   264–5
    pre-exploration stage   277–8
    research methodologies   348
    sociocultural alternative tourism   315
indigenous theories in tourism   6
indigenous tourism development   332–3
indirect financial costs   225–6
indirect impact in tourism   218–19
indirect incentives   226
indirect revenues   218–20
Indonesia   98, 104, 221
    cultural commodification   243
    informal sectors   223
induced impact in tourism   219
induction methodology   332–3, 338
    indigenous tourism   332–3
Industrial Revolution's impact on
        tourism   54–5, 57
informal sectors   222–3
informal–formal sector alliances   223

information technology's impact on
    tourism   70
infrastructural accessibility of
    destinations   88, 102
inseparability   222
internal-intentional actions   283
internal-unintentional actions   283
International Ecotourism Society
    (TIES)   309
international excursionists   30
international stayovers   30, 32
    1950–2007 figures   58
    arrivals by region and subregions
        2007, 96
international students   29, 215
    part-time employment   231
international tourism   23
    first   56
    growth   57
    inbound   24
    outbound   24
    receipts   213
    stages of tourist flows   85–6
International Tourism Partnership   306 7
internet as promotion   203
internet as research   345
intervening opportunities in transit
    regions   37
investigation process   346–8, 352
involvement stage   271–2
irridex   251–2, 267, 271
    stages of   251
Israel   91–2

Jamaica   100
James Cook University   8, 10
Japan   60, 72, 81

Kakadu National Park   122, 318
Kenya   84, 317, 252, 321
knowledge-based platform   11–12, 13, 16
Kuranda   315–16
Kuwait   81

La Trobe University   7, 9
Laerdal Tunnel   286
Lake Eyre basin   123
Lamington National Park   132
Laos   98
Las Vegas   90, 129, 189, 250, 276
    cross-sectoral development   281
latent loyalty   173
latitudinal research   335 See also
    cross-sectional research

LDC See less developed countries (LDC)
Lebanon   92
Leiper's basic whole tourism system,
    20–21, 42
leisure and recreation tourism   26, 42
    activities   116
less developed countries (LDC)   81, 288
    affordability as pull factor   91
    inbound tourism   84–6, 108
    inbound tourism rates   1950–2005, 82
    induction methodology   333
    wealth inequality   247–8
Libya   81, 100
Likert-scaled survey questions   348
linear recreational attractions   129
living economic acitivity as tourist
    attraction   128
living museums   125–6
lobby groups   45–6, 193, 235–6
Lonely Planet series   143, 342
long-haul flights
    environmental stresses   356
    health-related problems   24
    milestones in   68
    routes   37–38
longitudinal research   335, 338
    types of   336
loyalty schemes   198–9
loyalty to destination   172–4
    Chinese customers   174
    four-cell matrix   173

Macquarie University   9
Madison County   272
Malaysia   98
Maldives   218, 244, 288
Malta   240
Maori tourism
    culture commodification   243, 263–4
    market segmentation   165–6
market attractions   130
market failure   192
market segmentation
    factors   157
    green consumer case study   178–80
    types of   153–5, 171
marketing in tourism
    8P marketing model   197–205, 206
    definitions   182
    destination   192
    long-term objectives   195–6
    partnerships   205
    promotional strategies   201–5
    redesigned promotional campaigns   189

marketing in tourism (*continued*)
   services 182–5
   short term objectives 196
   strategic marketing 195
   SWOT analysis 194–6, 206
marketing mix 197–205
markets of one 154–5
Marriott hotels 306
Maslow's hierarchy of human needs 170
mass public transit travel 69–70
mass tourism 153
   alternatives to 310–14
   ideal model 311
   modern 57–8, 73
   stereotypical destinations 117
   sustainable tourism 302, 319,
     321, 322
   unsustainable 319, 321
matrix model for trigger factors 282–3
MDC *See* more developed countries (MDC)
medical tourism 28–9
   India 29
Mediterranean 83
   cruise ship tourism 25
mega mall attractions 130
Melanesia 276
merchandising as promotion 202
Mesopotamia 48–9
Mexico 221
   bilateral tourist flows 99
   North America Industry Classification
     System (NAICS) 5
Miami Beach 276
MICE tourism 27, 140
midcentrics 167, 273 *See also* centrics
Middle Africa 102
Middle Ages 73
Middle Ages period 51
Middle East 100–2
   impact of negative image 94
   terrorism impact on tourism 227
military-related tourist sites 124
Millers Point district 240
mini-packages 142–3
model of escalating resident irritation 251–2
     See also irridex,
modern mass tourism 57–8, 73
Monash University 8
Monte Carlo 129
monuments as tourist attraction 124
more developed countries (MDC)
     81, 108
   international stayovers 81
   international stayovers 1950–2007 82

motels 140
motivation to travel 170
mountain attractions 117
Mt Tamborine 106, 130, 251
multi-destination travel 171
   model of itineraries 172
multilevel market segmentation 153–4
multiple destination events 130
multiplier effect in tourism 218, 219, 230,
     232, 271
multivariate techniques 350
Murdoch University 9
museums as tourist attraction 125
multipurpose tourism 30

Napier 240
national tourism development model 287–8
National Visitor Safety Program 92–3
National Visitor Survey (NVS) 33, 336, 356
natural events as tourist resource 122–3
natural sites attractions 115–16
nature-based tourism 119, 221
New Caledonia 99
New Zealand
   100% Pure New Zealand campaign 193,
     210, 326
   approved destination status (ADS) 70
   certification case study 326–8
   inbound expenditure and participation by
     family lifecycle (FLC) 163–4
   indigenous land rights 264
   international students 29
   Maori culture commodification 243,
     263–4
   Maori market segmentation 165–6
   sport-related tourism 28
   Standard Industrial Classification (SIC)
     system 6
   tourism data access 344
   tourist-historic sites 240
news media as promotion 204–5
news media as research 345
Niagara Falls 119, 277, 282
niche market segmentation 154–5
niche travel products 78
nongovernmental organisations
     (NGOs) 2–3, 22, 309
nonconsumptive wildlife tourism 121–2
nonprobability sampling 349
North America Industry Classification System
     (NAICS) 5
North Korea 34, 39–40, 88
North–south travel flow 84
Norway 286, 288

object-oriented database marketing (OODM)   199
observation-based research ethics   341–2
occasion-based segmentation   171
occupation market segmentation   165
Oceania   98, 99
OECD *See* Organisation for Economic Cooperation and Development (OECD)
Okavango Delta   225
older adults market segment   162
Olympic Games   27, 102, 131
Oman   102
opportunity costs   230
Organisation for Economic Cooperation and Development (OECD)   253
origin communities   33–4
origin governments   2–3, 34–5
origin region merchandises   143
origin regions   33
outbound tour operators   141–2
overcapacity problems   227–8
ownership of attractions   132–4
    public   132–133
Oxfam's Community Aid Abroad tours   240

Pacific Asia Tourism Association (PATA) codes   308–9
Pacific Yurts   190–1
package tours   56–7
    diversification   142–3
    integrated   200–1
    programming   201
    set-price   200
Palau   218
Papua New Guinea   99, 288, 313
paradigm shifts   295–9
paradox of resentment   248
participant observation research   341
partnerships in marketing   205
permanent environmental restructuring   253–5
    indirect   257–8
    induced effects   257–8
personal safety as pull factor   92, 102
pet-friendly hotels   164–5
Phase Four countries   60, 62, 66, 68, 81
    frontstage and backstage boundaries   244
    niche travel products   154
Phase Four in tourism participation   60
Phase Four societies   65, 72, 203–4
    green consumer market   303
    travel motivation   170

Phase One in tourism participation   61
Phase One societies   65
Phase Three in tourism participation   60
Phase Three societies   81, 203
    travel motivation   170
    travel patterns   84–5
Phase Two countries   81
Phase Two in tourism participation   59, 61–2
Phase Two societies   203
pink dollar accounts   161
play in order to work philosophy   62
pleasure periphery destinations   83
    climate change impacts   256–7
    expansion into remote   92, 116
    international arrivals   85
    uneven tourism development patterns   104–5
pleasure tourism, ancient   49
Plog, Stanley   167
    psychographic typology   167–9, 175
PodGuides.net   127
Poland   97
political accessibility of destinations   88
population impact on tourism   63–7
    ageing population   66
Port Arthur   240
post-Cook period tourism   57, 73
post-Industrial period   62–3
prediction process   347
prehistorical attractions   123
premodern tourism   48–51, 73
    transit processes   49
prescription process   347–8
pricing discounts   189
pricing techniques   199–200
primary attractions   134 *See also* iconic attractions
primary impact in tourism   218
primary research   338, 352
Prince Edward Island   277
privatisation in air travel   138
product diversification   188–9 *See also* product modification
product lifecycles   188
product loyalty   172–4
product modification   188–9
professional travel shows   112
programming in package tours   201
promotion in marketing   201–5
propulsive activity   221
prostitution   244, 245
protected natural areas as tourist attraction   122

psychocentrics   167, 248, 251, 273
    personality and travel-related
        characteristics   169
    travel motivation   170
psychographic segmentation   167–70, 175,
    267
public ownership of attractions   132–3
publicity as promotion   201–2
pull factors for destinations   86–92, 108,
    135, 156, 197, 199–200
pure research   331 See also basic research
push factors for destinations   86, 92, 99,
    100, 102, 156

Qantas   137
qualitative research   336–7, 348, 352, 356
    analysis techniques   350
    quantitative research combination   338
quality assurance mechanisms   307 See also
        quality control mechanisms
quality control mechanisms   307–10
Qualmark Green certification scheme
    326–7
quantitative research   336, 337–8, 348,
    351, 352
    analysis techniques   350
    qualitative research combination   338
Quebec City   240
Queensland University of Technology
    (QUT)   8
question formulation   346–8

radio as promotion   203–4
rail transportation   139
Railtours Austria   70
railways as tourist attraction   128 See also
        train tours
Rainforest Alliance   309
reconciliation tourism   240, 264
recreational canals as tourist attraction   128
redistribution of supply   189, 192
refereed academic journals   9–10, 343
    disadvantages   10
regional development   220–2
rejuvenation stage destinations   276
religious pilgrimages   28, 90, 100
    premodern   51
Renaissance period   52
repeat patronage   172–4
Republic of Trinidad   100
research classifications   331
research methodologies   348–9
    cultural and social considerations   348
    triangulation   349

research process   345–51
    biases   346, 351
    problem recognition   345–6, 352
residents' perception of attractions   250
residents' reactions to tourism   251 See also
        irridex
residual attractions   135
resort cycle model   229, 268, 281, 333
resort hotels   140
Responsible Tourism Operations   326 See
        also Qualmark Green certification
        scheme
retail shopping as tourist attraction   130
revenue leakages   225–6, 232
rifle marketing   203
RMIT University   7, 8
road transportation   139
rural origin segmentation   160
Russia   81, 97–8, 288

Saint Lucia   100, 218, 229
sales-oriented pricing   200
sales tax   216
sampling methods   349
Saudi Arabia   28, 81, 100
Scandinavia   66
scarcity of attractions   134
Schoolies Week   162–3, 171
scientific paradigms   296
sea, sand, sun tourism See 3S tourism
seaside resorts   54–5
Sea World   129
seasonal climate attractions   118–19
secondary attractions   134
secondary impact in tourism   219
secondary research   338, 343–5, 352
secular pilgrimages   28
selective demarketing   190
sense of place   134, 197, 273
services marketing   182–5
    inseparability   184
    intangibility of   183–4
    perishability   185
    supply and demand   185–92
    variability levels   184–5, 187–8
sex tourism   34, 247
    demarketing   190
    prostitution   244
Seychelles   84
    sex tourism   244
Sheraton hotels   305
shotgun marketing   202–3
Silk Air   137
simple market segmentation   153

Singapore   60, 81, 98, 245
    culinary tourism   127
        transit passengers revenue   32
        transit tourism   35
Singapore Airlines   137
single destination events   130
single destination travel   171–2
    model of itineraries   172
SISODs See small island states of dependence
        (SISODs)
site hardening   135, 279
ski resorts   129–30
small island states of dependence
        (SISODs)   84, 100
smartraveller initiative   35–6
sociocultural costs   242–52, 260, 313
sociodemographic segmentation   160–6,
        175
soft mobility holidays   70
software systems
    economic impact assessment   214
    geographic information systems
        (GIS)   158, 175
    data analysis   350
    visually impaired   166
Sogn   286
Solomon Islands   277
South Africa   102
South America, impact of negative
        image   100
South Asia   99
South East Asia   98
South Korea   60, 72, 81, 104
South Pacific   98
    3S tourism   83
    cruise excursionists   25–6
Southern Cross University   8
space tourism   38
Spain   120, 243, 279
spas as tourist attractions   54, 120
spatial configuration of attractions
        133–4
spatial diffusion   284–6
    barriers   286
spatial technology software   158 See also
        geographic information systems (GIS)
specialised recreational attractions
        (SRAs)   128–30
    linear   129, 133–4
sport-related tourism   28, 131
Springvale Homestead (Northern
        Territory)   240
SPSS See Statistical Package for the Social
        Sciences (SPSS)

spurious loyalty   173, 174
square sites   134
S-shaped resort cycle model   268 See also
        Butler sequence
stagnation stage   274–5
    destinations   275, 277
stakeholders in tourism industry   2–3, 5,
        21–2, 39, 253
Standard Industrial Classification (SIC)
        5, 41
Starwood hotels   306
statistical compilations   344
Statistical Package for the Social Sciences
        (SPSS)   350
stayovers   25, 30, 32, 58, 96
stopover traffic hubs   31–2
stressor activities   253–5, 260
    associated   253, 257
strong sustainable development   299
structural equation modelling (SEM)   350
study tourism   29
subnational inequality in tourism
        destinations   104–5
subnational segmentation   159–60
Sunshine Rail Pass   139
supply and demand strategies   185–92
    demand-side factors   227, 278–9
    distribution channels   189
    seasonality   227–9
    supply-driven   278
    supply-side disruptions   226–7
Surfers Paradise   245, 274, 280
survey techniques   338–9
    characteristics of ideal types   340
    technology   343
sustainable development   299
sustainable mass tourism (SMT)   319,
        321, 322
sustainable tourism   299–314
    benchmarking   302
    challenges   301–2
    quality control   307–10
    related practices   306–7
    small scale   310–4
    threshold indicators   302
    UNWTO indicators guidelines
        300–1
Sustainable Tourism Cooperative Research
        Centre (STCRC)   214, 355
Sustainable Tourism Stewardship Council
        (STSC)   309
Swinbourne University of Technology   9
Switzerland   57, 288
SWOT analysis   194–6, 206

TAFE
  impact on tourism   5, 12
  Taiwan   24, 60, 81
Tanzania   104–5
taxation revenue   216–20, 235–6
technology
  aircraft industry   37–8
  impact on tourism   93, 127, 315–16
telephone interviewing   338, 349
television-oriented advertisements   203
terrorism
  impact on tourism   57, 100, 226
  tourist-targeted   92, 246, 283
tertiary educational institutions   2–3
  impact on tourism   4, 12–13
  stakeholders in tourism industry
    5, 22
Thailand   84, 98, 190, 201–2, 281
The International College of Tourism and
    Hotel Management   9
theme parks   129, 189
Thredbo   277, 280
tidal action as tourist resource   122
TIES See International Ecotourism Society
    (TIES)
timesharing facilities   140, 142
Tobago   100
Tonga   243
tour operators   141–3
  inbound   142
  outbound   141–2
Tour Operators Initiative (TOI)   306
tourism See also alternative tourism,
    ecotourism, mass tourism
  accreditation   309–10, 355
  basic human rights   63
  climate change impacts case
    study   355–6
  community-based approaches   198
  contextual considerations   135–6
  definitions   2–3
  demarketing   190
  development obstacles   4
  economic factors   59–61
  employment creation   220
  employment inequities   230–1
  factors influencing revenue   217–8
  film tie-ins   210–1, 272
  financial funding   224–5
  general demarketing   190
  global inequality   81
  gross national product (GNP)   218
  historical timelines   48
  intersectoral competition   230, 232

marketing approaches   135
national development model   287–8
platforms   10–12
product diversification   142–3
statistical databases   344
supply and demand   185–92
supply and demand strategies   188–9
sustainability-related practices   306
sustainable   299–314
systems based approaches   20–2
terrorism impact   226
top 30 earning destinations 2002 & 2007
    214–5
war impact on   92
Tourism and Transport Forum (TTF)   235,
    356
Tourism Australia   33, 111, 192, 194, 335
  funding   235
  international marketing campaign
    209–11
tourism economists   6
tourism geographers   6
tourism industry   136–45
  major sectors status   40–1
  structures   143–5
tourism participation sequence
  phases in   59–61
  social factors   61–3
Tourism Queensland   40, 192, 224
Tourism Research Australia   33, 40, 335, 336
  publications   344
tourism resources   115, 116, 120–8
Tourism Satellite Account (TSA)   218, 355
tourism studies as academic discipline   6–9
  domestic tourism programs   8–9
  expansion   7–9
  interdisciplinary approaches   7, 14
  multidisciplinary approaches   6–7, 13
  research cultures   332
tourism systems   20–1, 23
tourism-dependent countries   100
tourism-intensive countries   97, 98–9, 108
tourism-related industrial classification
    codes   5
tourism-related merchandises   143
tourism-related promotional events   112
tourist attractions as pull factor   89–90,
    134–5
  attraction attributes   133
  attraction inventory   115, 116, 132–6
  specialised recreational attractions
    (SRAs)   128–30
tourist market   153
  trends since World War II   154

tourist resources   122, 123–5
tourist shopping villages   106, 187, 249, 285
tourist-historic sites   240
tourists
    crimes against   245–6
    crimes by   247
    definitions   22–3
    disabled   166
    domestic   23
    female   160–1
    incentive   27
    international   23
    length of stays   24–5
    long-haul   24
    major types   30–1
    perception of attractions   250
    short-haul   24
trade publications   344–5
train tours   139
transit passengers   32 See also stopovers
transit regions   35–6
    impact on destination regions   55
transit tourism   35–6, 37
trans-Pacific travel routes evolution   38
transportation in tourism   137–40
travel agencies   136–7
    e-agencies   136
    innovative strategies case study   149–51
travel agents   136
travel guidebooks   143, 342
travel purposes   26–30
Travelocity   136, 150
Tree Top Walk   315

Ukraine   81, 97
Uluru   117, 122, 318
undercapacity problems   227–8
United Airlines   137
United Kingdom   72
    flexitime   63
    green consumer market   303
    international students   29
    post-Cook period   57
    private car ownership impact   68
    public walk trails ownership   133–4
    regional development   221–2
    seaside resorts   54–5
United National Environment Programme
        (UNEP)   309
United States
    bilateral tourist flows   99–100
    green consumer market   303
    hotel sector   140–1
    international students   29

North America Industry Classification
        System (NAICS)   5
political accessibility   88–9
spatial diffusion   285
sunbelt periphery   82, 99
tourism gross national product
        contribution   218
travel agencies case study   149–51
travel motivation   170
urban cultural heritage tourism   312
University of Canberra   8
University of New England   8
University of New South Wales   8
University of Newcastle   8
University of South Australia   9
University of Southern Queensland   9
University of Tasmania   9
University of Technology   8
University of the Sunshine Coast   9
University of Western Sydney   8
University of Ballarat   8
unsustainable mass tourism (UMT)   319,
        321
UNWTO See World Tourism Organization
        (UNWTO)
urban cultural heritage tourism   312
urban ecotourism   318
urban origin segmentation   160
urban–rural fringe   106
Uruguay   100

V Australia   137
Vanuatu   99, 240
variable costs   186
veneer green consumers   303, 306, 317
venturers   167 See also allocentrics
vertical integration   144–5
VFR tourism See visiting friends and relatives
        (VFR) tourism
Victoria Falls   119
Victoria University   8
virtual reality technology   70
visiting friends and relatives (VFR)
        tourism   26–7
    seasonality marketing strategies   229
    visually-impaired tourists   166
volunteer tourism   314
voluntourism   314 See also volunteer
        tourism

Walpole Nornalup National Park   315
war dividend   68
war-related tourist sites   124 See also dark
        tourism

Warner Bros. Movie World   129
waste residuals management   256, 327
waterfall-based tourism   119
weak sustainable development   299, 302
web technology
    gender usage differences   160–1
    impact on marketing   204
    impact on survey techniques   339, 343
    impact on tourism   35–6
    impact on travel agencies   136, 151
    impact on visually-impaired   166
webcasting technology   203, 341
website software for visually impaired   166
wedding destination market   171
West Africa   102
Western Hemisphere Travel Initiative
    (WHTI)   89
wildlife tourism   120–1
    classifications   120
wine tourism   127–8, 220–1
winescapes   127–8
winter sports as tourism resource   119, 221
Woodford Folk Festival   132
word-of-mouth publicity   173, 183
work in order to play philosophy   63, 73
World Fair attractions   131

World Tourism Organization (UNWTO)   4,
    22, 26, 213
    marketing partnerships   205
    sustainability indicator guidelines   300–1
    tourism terminology   31–2
World Travel and Tourism Council
    (WTTC)   3, 59, 220
WTO Global Code of Ethics for Tourism   63
WTTC See World Travel and Tourism
    Council (WTTC)
Wyndham Worldwide   144

Yalong Bay   84
Yellowstone National Park   122
Yemen   100
York   240
Yosemite National Park   122
young adults market segment   162–3
Yugoslavia   81

Zanzibar   104, 106
    hotel accommodation supply
        2003, 105
Zhangjiajie National Forest Park   280
Zimbabwe   288